T0366634

BEFORE CENTRAL PARK

BEFORE CENTRAL PARK

SARA CEDAR MILLER

COLUMBIA UNIVERSITY PRESS

New York

Columbia University Press
Publishers Since 1893
New York   Chichester, West Sussex
cup.columbia.edu

Library of Congress Cataloging-in-Publication Data
Names: Miller, Sara Cedar, author.
Title: Before Central Park / Sara Cedar Miller.
Description: New York : Columbia University Press, 2022. | Includes bibliographical
references and index.
Identifiers: LCCN 2021027671 (print) | LCCN 2021027672 (ebook) | ISBN
9780231181945 (hardback) | ISBN 9780231543903 (ebook)
Subjects: LCSH: Central Park (New York, N.Y.)—History. | New York (N.Y.) —
History—1775-1865. | New York (N.Y.)—History—Colonial period, ca. 1600-1775.
Classification: LCC F128.65.C3 M54 2022 (print) | LCC F128.65.C3 (ebook) |
DDC 974.7/1—dc23
LC record available at https://lccn.loc.gov/2021027671
LC ebook record available at https://lccn.loc.gov/2021027672

Columbia University Press books are printed on permanent and
durable acid-free paper.
Printed in the United States of America

Cover design: Julia Kushnirsky, Sara Cedar Miller, Roxanne Panero
Cover image: photo: Sara Cedar Miller, *Bow Bridge*, Courtesy of the Central Park
Conservancy; map: J.H. Colton & Co, and S. Stiles & Co. *Topographical map of the city
and county of New-York, and the adjacent country: with views in the border of the principal
buildings, and interesting scenery of the island.* New-York: Published by J.H. Colton &
Co., No. 4 Spruce St, 1836. Map. https://www.loc.gov
/item/2007627512/.

Contents

Preface   vii

Introduction   3

PART I: TOPOGRAPHY

1   The First Settlers, 1625–1664   19

2   Along the Kingsbridge Road, 1683–1845   44

3   The Enslaved Bensons, 1754–1846   62

4   The War at McGowan's Pass, 1776–1784   72

5   Valentine Nutter, 1760–1814   91

6   The War of 1812, 1805–1814   103

PART II: REAL ESTATE

7   Dividing Bloomingdale, 1667–1790s   131

8   Dividing Bloomingdale, 1790–1824   149

9   Dividing Bloomingdale, Seneca Village: The Residents, 1825–1857   170

10   Dividing Bloomingdale, Seneca Village: The Black Leaders, 1825–1857   208

11   Dividing Harlem, 1825–1843   234

12   Dividing Yorkville, 1785–1835   244

13   The Receiving Reservoir, 1835–1842   275

14   A Changing Land, 1845–1853   289

PART III: THE IDEA OF A PARK

15   The Battle of the Parks, 1844–1852   323

16   Becoming Central Park, 1853–1856   340

17   The First Commission, 1855–1857   365

18   Designing Central Park, 1857–1858   386

19   Extending the Park, 1859–1863   420

Epilogue: America's Park   437

Afterword by Elizabeth W. Smith, President and CEO of the Central Park Conservancy   445

Acknowledgments   451

Notes   457

Selected Bibliography   575

Index   593

Preface

As photographer and historian for the Central Park Conservancy since 1989, I have given hundreds of tours to visitors. The question I hear most often is, "So, what was here before it became a park?" When I started, we knew some basics—the road, the taverns, the fortifications—but I did not know how to *see* the prepark. In the summer of 1990, I began to fill in the blanks.

That August I had the good fortune to document the work of consulting archeologists Richard Hunter and Lynn Rakos as they conducted a preliminary study of the northern end of Central Park.[1] Trained as an art historian, I appreciated the park as Frederick Law Olmsted and Calvert Vaux's masterpiece of American art, but I had no exposure to prepark fieldwork until Richard and Lynn slowly revealed it to me over those sweltering summer days. Unremarkable soil mounds were, I soon learned, eroded breastworks from the War of 1812, four-foot-high protective walls of earth and sod. An average-looking heap of boulders had actually been the foundation of a long-forgotten military outpost.

The most defining moment for me came when we were gathered near the North Meadow handball courts looking at a contemporary map overlaid with a map of prepark dwellings. Richard noted that we were a few steps away from where the kitchen of German immigrant Christian Gent would have stood, and he explained that nineteenth-century residents, with no concept of trash collection, customarily tossed their broken dishes into their adjacent yard. Without taking a single step, he stooped down and picked up a two-inch piece of blue and white crockery embedded in the grass literally at our feet. Holding that shard in my hand, I marveled at the tangible connection between past and the present. It beckoned to me, inviting me to unravel the mysteries of a place I thought I knew so well. Gradually, with the help of archival material, phantom farms, gardens, orchards, houses, shanties, stables, and barns appeared throughout the park, and the lives of strangers from the distant past unfolded with them. *Before Central Park* is the result of that journey.

My research process for this book has been both magical and maddening. The resources and archives in New York for the prepark from the earliest settlers in the seventeenth century until the mid-1800s are a historian's dream come true. From well-known repositories like the New York City Municipal Archives, the New-York Historical Society, and the New York State Archives in Albany to the more obscure, like New York County Court's Division of Old Records and the General Society of Mechanics and Tradesmen, untold riches are there for the asking, and the buildings they are housed in are some of the most palatial or the most unusual sites in New York City. In the stately library of the New-York Historical Society—my home away from home—my heart almost stopped when I unfolded the puckered and scallop-edged parchment with official red wax seals and black ribbons, the 1802 deed from landowner Samuel Stilwell to Gulian Ludlow for a parcel of land that would later become a section of Seneca Village, the Black community on the west side of today's Central Park.

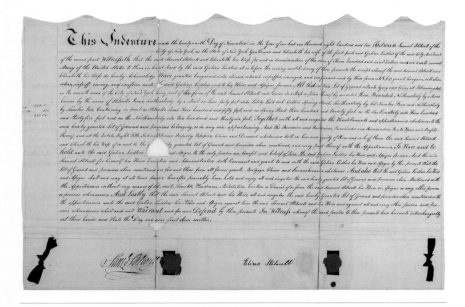

P.1 The land conveyed in 1802 from Samuel Stilwell to Gulian Ludlow would become in 1825 a part of Seneca Village, the former Black community on the west side of Central Park.

Source: Samuel Stillwell survey and indenture, November 29, 1802, mixed materials. Manuscript Collection, MS 2958.915, New-York Historical Society.

31 Chambers Street, the home of the Municipal Archives of the City of New York, is the former Surrogates Court House, a massive block-long building and one of the most elaborate Beaux Arts jewels of New York City. Its exterior features massive allegorical sculptures and figures of New York history. Its three-story-high variegated marble lobby was designed to resemble the villa entrance halls of titans like Morgan, Vanderbilt, and Rockefeller. The Division of Old Records on the seventh floor is equally jaw-dropping, but in a different way. Bound volumes—some bigger than coffee tables—and folders bursting with documents fill every inch of the bookshelves that extend for miles and reach from the floor to the towering ceiling. So many are covered in dust and made of paper so old that tiny fragments of confetti fall in your lap no matter how gingerly you turn the brittle pages. There's a small sink in the corner to rinse off the years of history that coat your hands. It was there that I experienced many a thrilling moment, like when I untied the faded red ribbon enclosing a rolled-up and yellowing transcript of the 1868 court case of *Sylvester Cahill et. al agst. Courtlandt Palmer and others*, untouched for a century and a half until I unfurled it in 2018.

With the exception of George Washington, most of the people you will meet in these pages are not familiar names to us today, though many were quite well known in their own time. Much of this story is of the founding Dutch families of Harlem, the leaders of New York society, and leaders of the Black community who resided downtown. We know about them because they were mentioned in the press or contemporary literature, kept personal records and diaries, wrote letters, had deeds, and appeared in church or government records. I was thrilled to discover several portraits of elite landowners and civic or religious leaders. At last, there were faces, bodies, and possessions to put to the names.

But such a trove does not exist for those who moved onto prepark land from roughly 1825 to 1857. The very poorest squatters remained nameless and uncounted. The immigrant farmers, artisans, and Black or white working class were rarely mentioned in newspapers, and they left us with few letters, diaries, and documents. They often show up in the state or federal censuses, and on immigration lists. If they owned land, we have the deeds, but their wills, when available, are often the best or only source for information about who and what they held dear.

The madness of my research came in the contradictions and inconsistencies in the source material. I felt uncertain when, for example, the testimony from that court case mentioned above did not match the information on an actual map, and the map did not agree with the handwritten tax records. I constantly debated when and whether to trust the written or visual record.

And this study is just a beginning. Many valuable documents were discovered in storage while I was doing my research. As more is found, digitized, and made available to scholars, many of the questions raised by this book will be answered, and help us to clarify, interpret, and add to the Central Park story. My ongoing research will continue on www.beforecentralpark.com. Research on all aspects of Central Park history can be found on the Central Park Conservancy website, www.centralparknyc.org.

BEFORE CENTRAL PARK

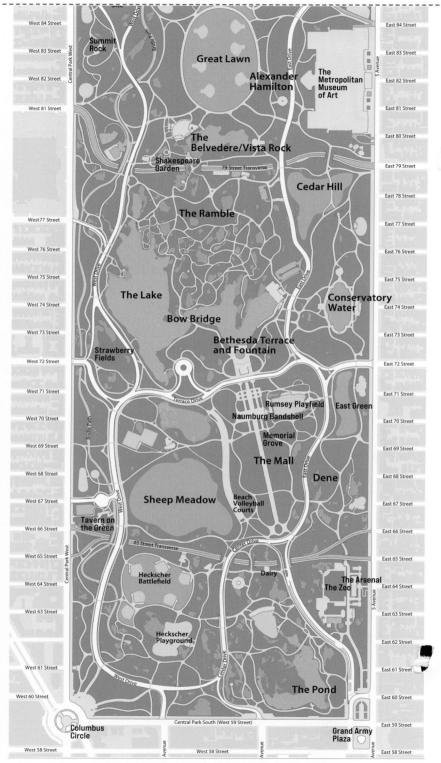

Map of Central Park in 2021, with the landscapes and structures referenced in the book labeled.
Source: Central Park Conservancy, 2021

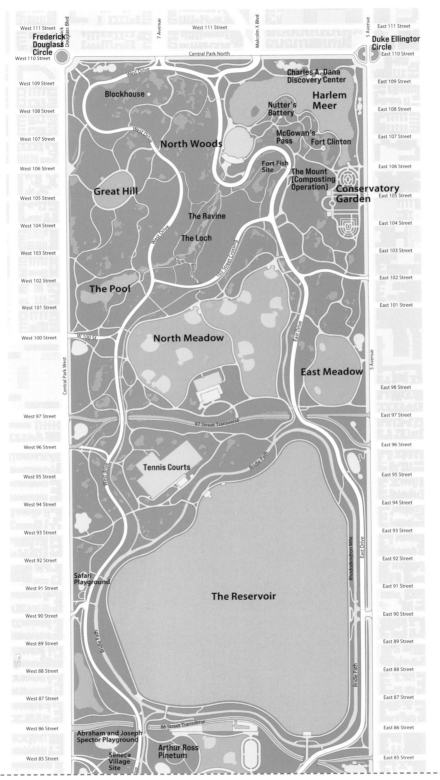

N

Frederick Douglass Circle
Duke Ellington Circle

West 111 Street
West 110 Street
West 109 Street
West 108 Street
West 107 Street
West 106 Street
West 105 Street
West 104 Street
West 103 Street
West 102 Street
West 101 Street
West 100 Street
West 97 Street
West 96 Street
West 95 Street
West 94 Street
West 93 Street
West 92 Street
West 91 Street
West 90 Street
West 89 Street
West 88 Street
West 87 Street
West 86 Street
West 85 Street

West 111 Street
Central Park North
East 111 Street
East 110 Street
East 109 Street
East 108 Street
East 107 Street
East 106 Street
East 105 Street
East 104 Street
East 103 Street
East 102 Street
East 101 Street
East 98 Street
East 97 Street
East 96 Street
East 95 Street
East 94 Street
East 93 Street
East 92 Street
East 91 Street
East 90 Street
East 89 Street
East 88 Street
East 87 Street
East 86 Street
East 85 Street

Douglass Blvd
7 Avenue
Malcolm X Blvd
5 Avenue
Central Park West

West Drive
West Drive
West Drive
West Drive

Blockhouse
North Woods
Great Hill
The Ravine
The Loch
The Pool
North Meadow
W 100 St.
Tennis Courts
97 Street Transverse
Safari Playground
The Reservoir
Bridle Path
86 Street Transverse
Abraham and Joseph Spector Playground
Seneca Village Site
Arthur Ross Pinetum

Charles A. Dana Discovery Center
Harlem Meer
Nutter's Battery
McGowan's Pass
Fort Clinton
Fort Fish Site
The Mount [Composting Operation]
Conservatory Garden

East Meadow
East Drive
East Drive
Rhododendron Mile
Bridle Path
5 Avenue
102 Street Crossing

▲ 85 Street

Introduction

We need only poke below the subsoil of its surface to discover an obstinately rich loam of memory. . . . The sum of our pasts, generation laid over generation, like the slow mold of the seasons, forms the compost of our future. We live off it.

—Simon Schama, *Landscape and Memory*

Central Park was designed in 1858 by the landscape architects Frederick Law Olmsted and Calvert Vaux. Their celebrated design is the most recent layer of the land. The park is a palimpsest of the natural occurrences and the human events that shaped the land in the centuries that preceded it. Evidence is written on its surface, evidence that can still be seen today, yet much of that history is buried beneath. Many landmarks have completely disappeared, and events have faded out of memory. This book explores this layered terrain and its evolution, to show why this slice of Manhattan is both wholly unique and a microcosm of more than two centuries of America's early history.

The story of the land that would become Central Park is the story of three forces, all jockeying for position: topography, real estate, and the idea of a park.

Topography is destiny. The shape, configuration, and proximity of the landscape's natural features—hills and valleys, rock and soil, marshes and meadows, woods and water—determined much of human interaction with it, and the prepark period is no exception. These characteristics influenced the social, political, and military history of the land for over two centuries, and ultimately they determined its future as parkland.

But topography is only part of the story. Much of the rest is real estate. Dating from the first European arrival in the 1620s, Manhattan's greatest obsession became the buying and selling of itself. Profit has always been a driving force of New York's development, and this is true in the history of the prepark as well. Before the arrival of the Dutch, the indigenous peoples had no concept of owning property. When the Dutch came and wanted their land, the local Lenape assumed that their mutual agreements gave the newcomers a use of the land, a sharing. Exclusive ownership was inconceivable to them. Beginning in the 1630s a few European families moved onto the northern end of the prepark to use it as farmland. There were seemingly no objections from the local tribe at the time, but a decade later a cruel and brutal war would herald the beginning of the end for Native habitation on the island.

The southern end of Manhattan grew rapidly, and real estate became an active business. The distance of the prepark from the city's center downtown, the land's challenging topography, and most of its early ownership in Harlem by insulated Dutch and English families sheltered much of the area from settlers until the last years of the eighteenth century.

The growth of American cities after the Revolution also changed the prepark land. In the 1790s, New York City was desperate for money and began to sell off its Commons, the acres of swampy and rocky terrain in the middle of the island held in trust by the city government. The strip of west side prepark land between Seventh and Eighth Avenues was the small eastern edge of the large and exclusive Hudson River estates, which had attracted New York's elite since the 1660s. By the 1790s, much loyalist property was confiscated and eventually sold off to the ascendant merchant class, who valued it as much for investment as for its charm as a summer residence. After 1825, real estate began to trump topography as the definitive shaper of the land's future. The city grew beyond its downtown boundaries and began a relentless march north, increasing the demand for the land that would become Central Park, regardless of its challenging terrain.

Human greed created the villains and victims of land speculation. While the need for a large metropolitan park was debated in New York's social, political, and business circles—often one and the same—the frenzy around buying and selling prepark lots persisted. From 1852, when 779 acres of a "central" site was first being considered for a park, until 1856, when the ink dried on the releases legally transferring the land to the city, real estate remained the central force. And it was real estate again that drove the commissioners' financial assessments and the ensuing petitions and lawsuits.

On the land where Central Park is today there were once businesses, churches, farms, burial grounds, the island's first major post road to the mainland, residents of the Motherhouse and school of the Sisters of Charity of Mount St. Vincent, and approximately 200 households. All these properties were officially condemned to make way for the first major landscaped public park in America. The taking of private property by eminent domain has a long history within American public works projects, and Central Park is no exception. The two largest real estate dislocation projects in New York City, precedents for the park, were the Croton Aqueduct system that brought fresh water to New York City and the street grid that laid out Manhattan.

Taken together, the story of the prepark is a microcosm of the extraordinary history of New York City and even of America, much of it very disturbing. Our shameful national conflicts of racism, sexism, nativism, classism, environmental harm, political corruption, and personal and collective greed all played out on parkland. The 843-acre plot hosted the war between the Native Americans and the Dutch, the beginnings of slavery by the Dutch and its expansion under the English. The gradual struggle from slavery to emancipation in New York State was only legislated in 1799, and several Black landowners participated in the Underground Railroad as a weapon against the Fugitive Slave Act of 1850. America's first major wave of Irish and German immigrants in the 1840s began the virulent xenophobia that would be applied subsequently to every entering group of "aliens," as they were called. The encampment of British and Hessian soldiers during the Revolutionary War, the confiscation of loyalist property by American patriots, and the economic causes that led to the building of fortifications during the War of 1812 also took place. Major social and economic changes also occurred on the land: the rise of the merchant and artisan classes, often the first generation of prepark landowners; the effects of industrialization on urban growth; the city's first modern infrastructure project; the changing criteria for voting rights and women's property rights; the clash between a public park and real estate development; and the love and loss of land.

But this is ultimately a story about the American people and their place in the American class system. Land was first owned by a select group at the top. The elite Dutch of Harlem in the seventeenth century owned the land and kept it in the family through intermarriage and inheritance. They remained elite even after the English takeover in 1664, though they were joined by the English ruling class, who owned lavish country estates along the Hudson River. Empowered by the Revolution and the growing emphasis on individual rights, Americans confiscated the loyalist British land, much of which was acquired and populated by a rising middle class of artisans, merchants, and investors in the nineteenth century. By the 1820s, a small group of free African Americans began to own land and form a community. It was only in the decade directly before the inauguration of Central Park that first- and second-generation Irish and German immigrants formed rental communities and some of the poorest immigrants squatted on the land.

Just like the geological strata of history beneath our feet, the ground of Central Park evidences the many layers of individual lives embedded in it. Today we walk, run, bike, and picnic over the homes, farms, and roads of ghosts. What is now the Lake was once a beaver habitat where the local Lenape would have hunted to sell the pelts to Dutch traders. The Mall was once James Amory's fields, where he grew wheat, corn, and potatoes. Andrew McGowan's tavern and orchard are now the park's composting operation. The mansion and grounds of patrician Grizzel Shaw are now Safari Playground. The asparagus beds of the grocer and merchant David Wagstaff are now on Cedar Hill. The Jewish cemetery of Congregation Shaaray Tefila is now a portion of Conservatory Garden's lawn. The house and barn of Catherine Thompson, the teacher in Colored School No. 3 in Seneca Village, is now the park entrance at West Sixty-Third Street.

Featured here are such stories as that of Hendrick and Isaac de Forest, the first European farmers, whose homestead was likely built in 1637 on the edge of their tobacco farm, and Fredrick Reulein, a German immigrant who tended his vegetable beds over two centuries later on that very same tract, which would later become a part of the Harlem Meer landscape. We will learn about the participants and their contemporaries who waged three wars in the prepark: Kieft's War, the American Revolution, and the War of 1812. At a time when women had few rights, especially if they were married, the lives of several remarkable and indomitable women made their mark on the land: the formerly enslaved Lanaw Benson; Dutch innkeepers Metjie Cornelis and Catherine McGowan; Black entrepreneurs Elizabeth Gloucester, Elizabeth Marshall, and her daughter Mary Joseph

Lyons; real estate tycoon Mary G. Pinkney; and religious leader Mother Superior Elizabeth Boyle and her Sisters of Charity of Mount St. Vincent.

This eclectic group of hunters and capitalists, merchants and sisters, freedmen and farmers, con men and soldiers intersected over two and a half centuries through their shared connection to a parcel of land. Together, their stories recount the diversity and the commonality that foreshadows the great democratic mission of Central Park.

PART I

Topography

View of Haarlem and the Haarlemmermeer by Jan van Goyen hangs in the Dutch painting galleries of the Metropolitan Museum of Art, barely a mile from the actual waters of Central Park's Harlem Meer. The Haarlemmermeer was a inland body of fresh water at the confluence of the Spaarne River. In the painting, the artist looks down from the church bell tower of St. Bavo of Haarlem.[1] In the same way, Central Park's first European residents, the de Forest-Montagne family, scanned the flats of what would become New Harlem and the waters of the Harlem Creek, and the Harlem and East Rivers, from the towering cliffs that still loom above the Meer today. And like the rural farmers, who chose to live at a distance from the city of Haarlem, so too the first settlers of the future park forewent the safety and security of the port of New Amsterdam for a landscape to the north with a combination of favorable topographic elements found nowhere else on Manhattan Island.[2] These features in the northern part of Central Park and today's Harlem and East Harlem shaped its human history, from centuries of Native use to European colonialism to the first decades of the American republic.

At only five feet above sea level, the Harlem Meer, the manmade lake in the northeast corner of Central Park, is the park's lowest point.[3] This low-lying terrain and its adjacent farmland to the north in many ways resembled the Netherlandish homeland of the early Dutch settlers. The circumstances that created this landscape are invisible to the eye, unless we look as much as five hundred feet below the surface. Whereas most of Manhattan is undergirded by a hard bedrock of schist, underneath much of Harlem lies a bed of softer marble.[4]

1.1 Dutch artist Jan van Goyen painted *View of Haarlem and the Haarlemmermeer* in 1646. It depicts a flat and watery terrain, features similar to those that attracted the first prepark family to settle in the similar Harlem landscape.

Source: Jan van Goyen, *View of Haarlem and the Haarlemmermeer.* Metropolitan Museum of Art, Purchase, 1871, accession number 71.62, https://images.metmuseum.org/CRDImages/ep/original/DP146495.jpg.

Marble began as hard-shelled sea creatures from the ocean floor, which after undergoing enormous heat and pressure over millions of years, metamorphosed first into limestone and then into marble, a rock of interlocking calcite crystals. And because the bedrock in this area of Manhattan was composed of this softer stone, it eventually eroded, which allowed the incoming sea to flow inland and form the briny waters of the East River and Harlem River.

The marble bedrock is also responsible for the vast flatlands of today's central Harlem, from the Harlem Meer all the way to West 124th Street. Called Muscoota or "flat land" by the local Lenape tribe, it would later be called Montagne's Flats after a member of the first European family to farm it. This grassy plain had once been a woodland, but the Lenape transformed it. They routinely controlled their environment by felling forests and burning the remaining understory to create trails, plant crops, and hunt game. Burning the woodland, even if only once a decade, added "a pulse of nitrogen" and other nutrients to the soil. It also created

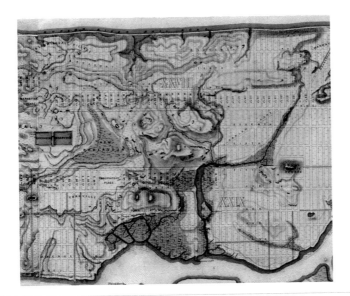

1.2 Egbert Viele's 1865 *Topographical Map of the City of New York* depicts Manhattan's original watercourses. This detail from Seventy-Seventh Street north to 124th Street and from the Hudson River to the East River depicts the vertical Harlem Creek at 108th Street as it entered the marshland that is today the Harlem Meer.

Source: Egbert L. Viele and Ferd. Mayer & Co., *Topographical map of the City of New York: showing original water courses and made land* [New York: Ferd. Mayer & Co., 1865]. Geography and Map Division, Library of Congress, digital image, https://www.loc.gov/item/2006629795/.

a clearing in the canopy so they could grow crops like the three sisters—corn, beans, and squash—and grasses that attracted deer.[5]

The Muscoota was a vast savannah rich with grasses and groves of berry bushes, prized farmland for Natives and the incoming Dutch. In his 1628 letter to Dutch West India Company Director Samuel Blommaert, company agent Isaac de Rasieres described the "large level field, from seventy to eighty morgens [about one hundred and sixty acres] through which runs a very fresh stream, so that land can be plowed without much clearing."[6] In 1858, more than two hundred years later, Central Park's designers, Frederick Law Olmsted and Calvert Vaux, also praised the "dark, fertile soil of the Harlem flats, which here extend into the park."[7]

The Harlem flats was home to a cornucopia of edible plants—nuts, Jerusalem artichokes, wild onions, leeks, juniper berries, currants, wild grapes, mulberries, blueberries, strawberries, prickly pear, gooseberries, wild cherries, persimmons, and plums—enough to provide year-round nourishment for the local tribes and the newly arrived Dutch settlers. In his discussion of "Food Products of the Country," Dutch patroon David De Vries also listed maize (which the Dutch called "Turkish wheat"), mulberry trees, pumpkins, melons, watermelons, chestnuts, wild grapes, and hazelnuts. The Dutch learned from the native tribes how to make linen and hemp from the local flax and weave it into sacks called *notassen*.[8]

The mountain lion, American black bear, and gray wolf were scarce there, unlikely to threaten human habitation. Hunters would have abundant prey: deer, squirrel, muskrat, duck, geese, frogs, snakes, turtles, partridge, pigeons, and wild turkeys, weighing from thirty to forty pounds.[9] Taming and farming this watery topography were familiar practices to the Dutch, who farmed where the marshland met the sea.[10]

The region also enjoyed inland waterways unique to the island. A tongue of underground marble running along a fault line created the circumstances for the Harlem Creek, a twenty-foot-deep, one-hundred-foot-wide watery trench that flowed between what is now East 107th Street and East 108th Street. The creek began at the East River and emptied into the swampland that is now the Harlem Meer landscape. Even though it was shallower toward Fifth Avenue, the inland course to the East River would have been an essential and strategic body of water for the Lenape and the Dutch settlers to reach the riches of Manhattan's coastal waters, with fish, oysters and other shellfish, eel and otter, and salt hay for the cattle.

The waters on Manhattan Island flow west from the highlands to the eastern lowlands into the Harlem River and East River. Two different freshwater streams or "runs" that began in the west merged into the waters of the Harlem Creek. The northern stream originated in the highlands of Manhattanville at West 124th Street and flowed southeast through the central flatlands, irrigating the animal habitats and eventual farms.[11]

The second freshwater run originated at the highlands of today's West Ninety-Fourth Street and Tenth Avenue and snaked northeast through today's Ravine, merging with the wetlands that became the Harlem Meer.[12] Today the original waterway is still there, and flows underground where it mixes with New York City drinking water to form the Pool, the Loch, and the Harlem Meer water bodies.[13]

The metamorphic rock that made most of Manhattan was formed more than 450 million years ago by the collision of tectonic plates called the Taconic

I.3 Since the creation of the park in the nineteenth century, the Loch that meanders
through the steep woodland Ravine has mainly been composed of city drinking water that
comes from pipes hidden in the landscape and is merged with the freshwater "run" or stream,
the natural water body that entered the prepark at Eighth Avenue and 100th Street and
flowed northeast into the marshlands that became today's Harlem Meer.

Source: Sara Cedar Miller, *Loch, Ravine.* Courtesy of the Central Park Conservancy.

Orogeny. The silts and shales were lifted and metamorphosed by heat and pressure into the much-harder schist and gneiss. A huge mountain range erupted underground, of which the rock outcrops in Manhattan are remnants. Most of what was lifted has long eroded away.

An extensive wall of schist bordered the Muscoota plains on its western side, today's Morningside Heights and the rocky spine of Harlem that includes Morningside Park.

On its southern side, the rock barricade crossed the prepark at 106th and 107th Streets. It was through a narrow chink in this wall, later called McGowan's Pass, that the local Wickquasgeck tribe forged their fourteen-mile trail from

I.4 Some of the most significant rock configurations within the prepark were the lofty cliffs that ran along the southern edge of the Muscoota flats. From these bluffs, one could have seen both rivers and the surrounding countryside, providing warning of encroaching enemies. Today those outcrops still loom over the Harlem Meer and meander across Central Park close to its northern terminus.

Source: Sara Cedar Miller, *Fort Clinton, Harlem Meer*. Courtesy of the Central Park Conservancy.

their known campsites in the Bronx and the northern end of Manhattan Island to the seasonally rich hunting and fishing grounds of the southern end.[14] From this gap in the rock, the trail meandered south and east and exited at the prepark around Ninety-Second Street and Fifth Avenue in order to avoid the impassable hills and swampy terrain to the south. British colonists would expand on this Native footpath and name it the Kingsbridge Road after the monarch who ruled New York. In his 1642 journal describing New Amsterdam, David De Vries first mentioned the trail as the "Wickquasgeck road over which the Indians pass daily."[15]

Aside from the Muscoota planting fields and the Wickquasgeck trail, Native peoples seemed to bypass the land of central Manhattan. They neither settled nor farmed there, preferring the more favorable ecologies near the rivers. The two closest settlements were a campsite at the Harlem River and 120th Street and

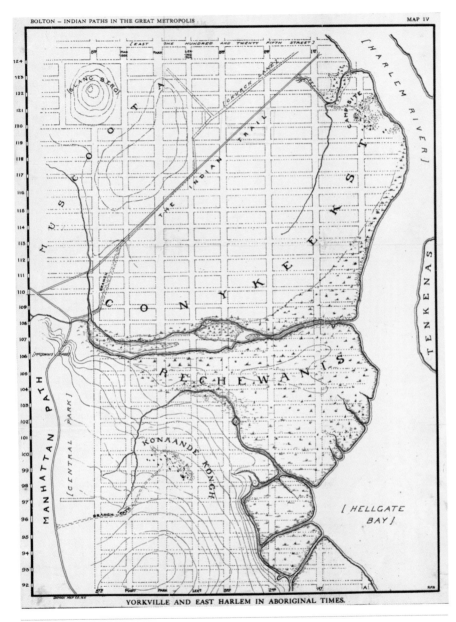

YORKVILLE AND EAST HARLEM IN ABORIGINAL TIMES.

1.5 The map by New York archeologist Reginald Pelham Bolton, "Yorkville and East Harlem in Aboriginal Times," shows the path of the two Native trails that intersected within the prepark. Bolton also placed Konaande Kongh, a Native settlement near the heights of Park or Lexington Avenues at about Ninety-Ninth Street. Rechewanis and Conykeekst are today's East Harlem, and Muscoota is today's central Harlem and the Harlem Meer landscape.

Source: [Reginald Pelham Bolton], "Yorkville and East Harlem in aboriginal times." Lionel Pincus and Princess Firyal Map Division, The New York Public Library, New York Public Library Digital Collections, https://digitalcollections.nypl.org/items/f7162d60-d044-0138-647e-016d95d47a82.

Konaande Kongh, located at the pinnacle of what became known as Carnegie Hill. According to well-respected amateur archeologist Reginald Pelham Bolton's map, another footpath would have entered the park at about East Ninety-Fifth Street and headed north.[16]

Natives took advantage of the richer, more promising land farther south. The local Lenape farmed tobacco, which they smoke ceremoniously. A large plantation was located in what is now the West Village, then known as *Sapokanikan* or "tobacco fields."[17] The land farther south, on the site of today's Center Street courthouses and the African Burial Ground, was inhabited by the Manahate. Their settlement centered around the natural sixty-foot-deep water body known by the Dutch as the *Kalch Hoek*, meaning "a small body of water." In 1922, Bolton identified it as the most significant habitation site in lower Manhattan.[18] By the 1720s, its once-crystalline waters, called by the English "the Collect," were polluted beyond use. Ninety years later, the largest inland water body on Manhattan was filled in.

THE LAND BELOW NINETY-SIXTH STREET

Narratives of Central Park tend to ignore the topography north of Ninety-Sixth Street that attracted early Dutch and English settlements and to focus on the less fertile lands—the southern, central, and western portions of the prepark—that were not settled. The rocky and swampy terrain below Ninety-Sixth Street has always been described as "waste" or "barren," echoing the Dutch who first used the terms. This land, stretching between Fifty-Ninth Street and Ninety-Sixth Street, was part of a larger section of Manhattan Island that was first "purchased" from the indigenous peoples to the Dutch West India Company and then to the colony of New Amsterdam by the Dutch Assembly. In 1686, when the city had fallen under English control, Thomas Dongan, the royal governor of New York, granted the vast and largely undesirable tract that now comprises midtown and much of Central Park to the Corporation of the City of New York, and it became known as the "common lands." Similarly, the royal governor gave Harlem, a separate colony until 1712, the "barren" Harlem Commons.

But it was not all wasteland. The Dutch and the English considered the west side of Manhattan, an area still known today as Bloomingdale, as a place that favored investment, habitation, and cultivation. Its main attraction was its proximity to the Hudson River. Bloomingdale stretched from Fifty-Ninth Street to 107th Street and from the shoreline east to Seventh Avenue, where it butted up against the inhospitable terrain of the city's common lands. This strip comprised a small section of more than ten one-hundred-acre parcels offered to investors in 1667 by the royal governor Richard Nicholl. The prepark land remained uncultivated or uninhabited until the eighteenth century and will therefore be discussed later in this study.

The earliest colonial settlements in the land that would become Central Park, however, were in Harlem. This unique topography north of Ninety-Sixth Street attracted the first farmers and settlers, and it was again this topography that dictated the cultivation, social history, and military events to which we now turn.

chapter 1

The First Settlers, 1625–1664

I n 1621, a consortium of wealthy and ambitious Dutch merchants and investors formed the Dutch West India Company to establish a colonial and economic foothold west of the Netherlands in Africa, the West Indies, and North and South America. Their ultimate goal was to turn a profit for those who invested in their business ventures and to block the control of these lands by their long-standing enemy, Spain. A similar organization, the Dutch East India Company, had been established almost two decades earlier to explore and trade with India and other Asian lands east of the Netherlands.

Between 1623 and 1624, the Dutch West India Company's first few settlers arrived on Manhattan.[1] They named their outpost New Amsterdam, never dreaming that their little community would rival the great Dutch metropolis. The arrival of the Europeans caused the displacement of the local tribe, the Lenape, from their ancestral land, a fate similar to that of other Native peoples throughout American history.

THE BEAVERS

The Dutch West India Company was created because of Henry Hudson, the Netherlands's English-born favored son, an explorer hired by the Dutch East India Company. Hudson was among the seventeenth-century explorers seeking that most elusive prize: a faster passage to the Far East. In 1609, he sailed across the Atlantic and up the North River, which today is called the Hudson River. Although he only got as far north as today's Albany, he reported ample rewards for his efforts. The flora and fauna of the New World—the fur-bearing animals,

1.1 The Harlem Meer area at the northeast corner of Central Park was the site of the first settlement in the prepark. The entrance drive and its adjacent triangular lawn at the top left were possibly the site of the 1637 homestead of the de Forest-Montagne family. Half a century later, it was the site of the prepark's first tavern, the Half-Way House.

Source: Sara Cedar Miller, *Aerial View of Harlem Meer*. Courtesy of the Central Park Conservancy.

and the beaver in particular—were as prized as the silks, spices, and gold he and his employers were seeking in Asia.[2]

In 1614, only five years after Hudson's voyage, the Dutch East India Company set up a fur-trading post on the upper North River. Hearing of the phenomenal abundance of these animals in the New World, the Dutch government created the Dutch West India Company and gave them a monopoly on beaver pelts and permission to establish a trading post, Fort Amsterdam (later New Amsterdam), at the river's southern outlet and at Fort Orange, today's Albany.[3]

Beaver fur and felt were all the rage in seventeenth-century Europe. In the portraiture of Rembrandt and Vermeer, we see well-to-do Dutch burghers wearing beaver hats. The Dutch were drawn to the fur for its warmth, softness, suppleness, and strength, and to castoreum, the oil from the animal's glands, which was thought to cure ailments from rheumatism to tinnitus. Beaver testicles, "either

1.2 Beavers were prodigious in the New World. When the French discovered them in Canada and began to export them to Europe, the Dutch were inspired to establish their own trading outpost in New Amsterdam. The beavers are, depicted in a detail of *A New and Exact Map of the Dominions of the King of Great Britain on ye Continent of North America*, ca. 1711.

Source: Herman Moll, Thomas Bowles, and John Bowles, *A New and Exact Map of the Dominions of the King of Great Britain on ye Continent of North America. Containing Newfoundland, New Scotland, New England, New York, New Jersey, Pensilvania, Maryland, Virginia and Carolina*, ca. 1711 (detail). [London, Printed and sold by T. Bowles, J. Bowles, and I. King, 1.e 1731, 1731] [Map]. https://loc.gov/item/gm71005441/.

rubbed on the forehead or dried and dissolved in water," were considered cures for both drowsiness and idiocy. And the tail was consumed as a delicacy.[4] The European demand for the animals caused their near extinction back home, and even the Russian source was drying up by the 1580s. Then French explorers in Canada discovered beavers everywhere.[5]

Throughout the many histories of Central Park, the rocky and swampy terrain of its central and southern portion has always been described as "waste," a

1.3 Beavers and barrels of milled flour (depicted between blades of the windmill) were the two most valuable exports to Europe from New Netherland and New York. They have appeared on the official seal of the City of New York since 1686. This version, designed by artist Paul Manship, was created in 1915.

Source: Paul Manship, *Seal of the City of New York*, 1915. New York City Municipal Archives.

no-man's-land for any sort of Native settlement, hunting, or gathering. But the Lenape would not have considered it so.[6] In Eric Sanderson's study of beaver habitat, he estimates that central Manhattan would have been full of beavers. The profusion of streams and waterways were a magnet for the animals and for the hunters who had always relied on their fur and meat. Once the Europeans arrived, the Lenapes' livelihood was increasingly dependent on trapping the animals, though they would not have established a settlement there due to the poor topography.[7]

A CLASH OF CULTURES

In 1625, Johannes De Laet, an officer of the Dutch West India Company, published *The New World: Or a Description of the West Indies*. De Laet evoked for readers a Garden of Eden, claiming that Manhattan Island even rivaled the motherland.[8] But while praising the natural riches of the New World, he also alerted his readers to conflicts with the Native peoples that had already caused Hudson and other European explorers much anxiety. He repeated earlier reports that described the Indians as "crafty and wicked," having read accounts of the murder of several white men. He referred to the Manahate tribe as "a fierce nation . . .

suspicious, timid, revengeful and fickle."[9] De Laet voiced the collective hopes—
and illusions—of his countrymen when he suggested that Christian missionaries
would transform the Natives into civilized beings. Yet most colonists dismissed
their language as "made-up, childish," and saw them as hopeless and unworthy,
useful only as fur trappers.[10]

Because most of the Dutch viewed the Lenape through the narrow lens of their
own culture, they neither appreciated nor cared to understand the indigenous culture. As one example, because the women did the bulk of agricultural work, child
care, and domestic chores while the men relaxed after they hunted and fished, the
Dutch saw the men as weak and lazy.[11] That view completely refuted their depen-
dence on the men as hunters and to teach Dutch settlers the lay of the land.

1.4   The illustration *Nieu Amsterdam, al. New Yorck*, by Carel Allard in 1700, depicts the beaver
trade between New Yorkers and the local indigenous hunters. A seated hunter clutches a
beaver in one hand while offering another to the standing European woman, shown holding a
basket of fruit and tending a goat. The contrast between hunting and the symbols of domesti-
cation were intended to indicate European culture was superior to that of the Native peoples.

Source: "Nieu Amsterdam at. New York." The Miriam and Ira D. Wallach Division of Art, Prints and
Photographs: Print Collection, The New York Public Library, New York Public Library Digital Collections,
https://digitalcollections.nypl.org/items/510d47d9-7aae-a3d9-e040-e00a18064a99.

The Lenape believed they and all humans were an integral part of the sky, the stars, the sea, and all living beings, interconnected with them, not superior to them. This belief negated the core of Western civilization's emphasis on individual possession and class domination. They did not crave personal wealth, and the European practice of buying and selling land was incomprehensible to them.[12] Even the agricultural land that sustained them was not owned but simply used. Home too had no real meaning outside of the natural environment itself. Their dwellings and location changed with the seasons that dictated their livelihood. They were considered "wilden" or savages because they lived communally and collectively rather than as individuals divided into superior and inferior social and economic classes. The Dutch saw how they didn't appear to take personal advantage of these natural God-given riches, and therefore, as historian Edwin Burrows wrote, "It was only a short step to the conclusion that they didn't deserve to be there at all."[13]

The company's single-minded stockholders had one agenda: to fill their fur-lined pockets. On November 27, 1626, a few years after the first arrival of settlers, Pieter Janszoon Schagen, the manager of tradable goods, dazzled his employers in his report on his first cargo shipment: "7,246 beaver pelts, 853½ otter pelts, 81 mink pelts, 36 cat-lynx pelts, and 34 small rats, not to mention wheat, rye, barley, oats, buckwheat, canary seed, beans and flax . . . and a considerable quantity of oak timber and nut-wood." And the best news of all: "[We] have bought the Island of Manhattes from the Indians for sixty guilders."[14]

THE FIRST FAMILY

It was an auspicious welcome. On March 1, 1637, "some ten or twenty whales, swimming for at least two hours," escorted Central Park's first European family into New York Harbor. Among the hopeful passengers on the Dutch yacht *Rensselaerswyck* were Hendrick de Forest, his recent bride Geertruyt Bornstra, and his younger brother, Isaac, from Leiden in the Netherlands. Several months later their sister, Rachel, joined them with her husband, Dr. Johannes de la Montagne, and their four children, including five-week-old Marie, who was born as their ship sailed past the coast of Madeira.[15]

Leiden was a major Dutch mercantile center and the seat of a respected university. It had also become a haven for refugees seeking religious asylum, especially

Protestant groups fleeing persecution in neighboring Catholic countries. In 1609, the Pilgrims had found asylum in Leiden ahead of their journey to Plymouth, Massachusetts, in 1620. The de Forests were Walloons from Avesnes in the province of Wallonia, today's Belgium, and they spoke Waalsch, a Romance language related to French.[16]

It was in Leiden that Jessé de Forest, the father of Hendrick, Isaac, and Rachel, took in a boarder, a young medical student from the university named Johannes de la Montagne. Montagne was a Huguenot refugee fleeing religious persecution in the French region of Saintonge, near La Rochelle. Listed in the university records as "Johannes Monerius Montanus Xanto M[edicine]," he was studying with the renowned physician Otto Heurnius.[17] While boarding with the de Forests, the thirty-one-year-old Montagne met seventeen-year-old Rachel, and they were married in the Walloon Church on December 12, 1626. [18]

By the 1620s, the town of Leiden was overcrowded with refugees, and Jessé de Forest, a wool dyer by trade, longed for a place where the Walloons could establish a settlement of their own. So, as early as 1621, de Forest went to The Hague to petition the English ambassador, Sir Dudley Carleton, to permit Walloon and French families to form a separate community in the English colony of Virginia. De Forest presented a joint petition by fifty-six men, who promised "fealty and obedience to their King and Sovereign Lord" if the English governor met their conditions.[19] Most likely, de Forest had heard of Virginia's rich tobacco plantations and wished to develop a similar enterprise for the colony.

When the Virginia Company rejected their proposal to form a separate community, de Forest then petitioned the newly established Dutch West India Company, asking to form a settlement in Guiana, in the northeastern part of South America. The company granted his wish, and in 1624 de Forest, Montagne, and several other Walloon and French refugees sailed to Guiana. But de Forest contracted a fever and passed away on the journey. Montagne returned to Leiden, but in 1629, restless and intrepid, he and his young wife, Rachel, braved another overseas trek to the Caribbean island of Tobago. For four years they made a home there, eventually returning to Leiden, where Montagne pursued "professional improvement" in medical school while they planned for their next move.[20]

They had read De Laet's praise for Manhattan, a land "excellent and beautiful to the eye, full of noble forest trees and grape-vines; and wanting nothing but the labor and industry of man to render it one of the finest and most fruitful regions in that part of the world." De Laet's lush descriptions and news of the small colony's success seduced the de Forest-Montagne family, and in 1637 they uprooted themselves and sailed to the land they hoped would finally answer their prayers.

The Walloons and Huguenot refugees sought a permanent settlement in the New World, but the company, always mindful of the bottom line, considered them a drain on the economy. They were too expensive, and it was too diffi-cult to support them and protect them from the Natives. But the daring and optimistic de Forests went anyway. They sailed under the auspices of a wealthy patroon—a Dutch landholder with manorial rights to vast tracts of land—named Kilian van Rensselaer. Van Rensselaer had been the business partner of their uncle, Gerardus de Forest, and was the most prominent promoter of settlements in New Netherland.[21]

Hendrick had begun his employment six years earlier when a consortium of patroons, van Rensselaer included, tried to establish a whaling settlement in Swanendael, on the South (Delaware) River. Hendrick was appointed to vari-ous positions on the ship. After only ten months and no compensation for his work, he switched his employment to the Dutch West India Company. His uncle Gerardus sued the Swanendael investors for his back pay. After a hiatus of four years, Hendrick was working on the sailing vessel owned by van Rensselaer that brought him, his new wife, and his brother, Isaac, to New Amsterdam. [22]

With van Rensselaer's influence and access to "insider" information on the best land on the island, he must have advised Hendrick to request the Muscoota flatlands that today include the northeastern tip of Central Park from approxi-mately 106th Street to 110th Street, Fifth Avenue to Malcolm X Boulevard. Hen-drick petitioned the council of New Netherland to establish a *bouwerie* or farm on that two-hundred-acre parcel, subject only to the approval of the directors of the Dutch West India Company. It was granted.[23] Although a written "permis-sion" to inhabit and farm the land was a frequent agreement between the com-pany and the Native tribes, in this instance Director Wouter Van Twiller gave de Forest his grant with "no impediment to its immediate occupation.[24]

At the time of their arrival in 1637, the New Amsterdam colony was below Wall Street. But the intrepid de Forests, loaded with guns, tools, and livestock, headed north to their new homestead. They brought with them two indentured servants, a middle-aged wool washer and a teenage orphan, who had both con-tracted with the de Forests for three years in return for transportation and opportunity in New Netherland.[25]

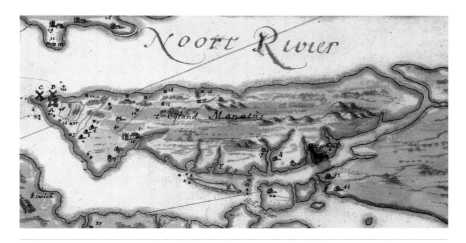

1.5 A detail of the 1639 Manatus map is the first map that indicates the plantations and bouweries of the Dutch settlers. The de Forest-Montagne homestead and their two-hundred-acre tobacco farm lay between the two forks of the Y-shaped creek on land known to the Lenape as Muscoota. The hills that begin at Morningside Park and form the spine of Harlem are depicted in the distance.

Source: Joan Vinckboons, *Manatvs gelegen op de Noot sic Riuier.* 1670. Geography and Map Division, Library of Congress, digital image, https://www.loc.gov/item/97683586/.

The de Forests' presence in the New World is depicted as number 19 on the 1639 Manatus map of Manhattan Island that named its inhabitants and located their *bouweries.*[26] The de Forest farm can be seen at the left hand (southern) branch of the Y-shaped Harlem Creek and stream. The two hundred acres of the Muscoota flats are represented as the land between the two branches of the Y that began at 107th Street, and lay just beyond the northern boundary of the prepark. By 1639, the de Forests were among the very few European inhabitants of the upper island. There were two other families near them and three other Dutch families across the Harlem River in the Bronx.

From a deed issued to the property in 1647, we know that the de Forests' *bouwerie* was "lying between the hills and kill and at a point named Rechawanes stretching betwixt two kills." Although the landmarks are imprecise, the "hills" were the cliffs that today overlook the Harlem Meer at 106th Street and Fifth Avenue and ran across the prepark near its northern terminus. The western bluffs began at today's Morningside Park and headed north through Harlem overlooking the Muscoota flats. The "kills" or streams included the East River

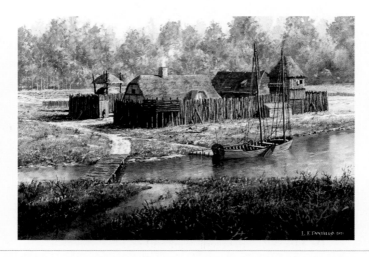

1.6 Len Tantillo, a historian and contemporary painter of New Amsterdam architecture and scenes, has envisioned the de Forest-Montagne homestead and surrounding farm on the edge of the Muscoota flats.

Source: Len Tantillo, *De Forest/Montagne Homestead and Farm.* Courtesy of the artist.

tributaries, bounded by Ninety-Third Street and Second Avenue and narrowed to the Harlem Creek, which began at the river and headed west on 107th Street and Fifth Avenue, then headed north to 116th Street. From there it crossed the flats diagonally to approximately West 124th Street and Tenth Avenue.[27]

We know that the de Forests created a high palisade for protection, an indication that they were most likely in an open and vulnerable area.[28] The nearby Wickquasgeck trail would have afforded good transportation on land, but the Walloons would more likely have traveled by boat. Like the Native tribes, they used canoes to travel up and down the navigable Harlem Creek to the shoreline and adjacent marshland for the salt hay, fodder for their cattle. A farm compound closer to the creek would also have facilitated an easier route in their larger yawl—*jol* in Dutch—for transporting their crops on the East River seven miles to the ports and markets of New Amsterdam.

The first dry land close to the creek, the two-hundred-acre tobacco fields, and the confluence of two Native trails were located inside today's park at 109th Street and Malcolm X Boulevard. We know for certain that a Dutch tavern was erected at that location in 1684. Though no record of the exact site exists, it is possible that the de Forest homestead would have been on the same site nearly half a decade earlier.

Inspired by Virginia's lucrative tobacco farms, the de Forests sought out the rich soil of the Muscoota flats that had been used by Native peoples for growing food and tobacco. For over a century, the rolled-up leaf, or *si-kar*, had been all the rage in Europe, prized for its medicinal benefits and "recreational" pleasures.

But no sooner had Hendrick planted his first tobacco crop and begun to build his house and barn than he was summoned by the company to fulfill his duties as supercargo aboard the *Rensselaerswyck* to Virginia. On his return home, he contracted malaria and died. He was thirty-one. His widow and his brother, twenty-one-year-old Isaac, were the legal heirs to the property, but the family decided Isaac was too immature to take on such responsibilities. Instead, management of the farm went to Dr. Montagne, the competent and mature brother-in-law who lived downtown near the fort. His medical training was valuable to the community, and when medicine did not pay the bills, he made candles.[29] So Montagne moved his young family from the comforts of town to the wild forested cliffs and flats.

As part of his agreement with the company, Hendrick de Forest had agreed to be a *werkbaas*, an overseer of the company's African enslaved, who routinely did most of the physically challenging work for the colony. Given Hendrick's overseer position and the size and complexity of the structure, it is most likely that the company's enslaved people would have done so for their overseer's bouwerie.[30] If so, it is likely that this was the first instance of slavery in the land that became Central Park. After Hendrick's death, Montagne became the supervisor of his indentured servants as they completed construction of the family's house and barns. The company's enslaved people would also have labored in the family's tobacco fields.[31]

The company imported its first eleven enslaved males in 1626. Two years later, the company brought in three enslaved females from Angola to breed children and ensure the future of the institution. In 1637, after the Dutch captured the Portuguese ship on which they were imprisoned, additional men were enslaved, and by 1639, quarters for them were established on the East River across from today's Roosevelt Island. Due to a shortage of white laborers, the company depended on the hard labor of enslaved people to guarantee the physical and economic success of the colony. Enslaved people cleared the land and cut timber and firewood, removed street garbage, maintained the town's protective barricades, built the roads, grew and harvested the crops, and assisted individual settlers like the de Forest-Montagnes in the construction of their homes. The Dutch gave the first enslaved people some privileges, such as the right to own property, to get married (provided the ceremony was in the Dutch Reformed Church), to testify in court cases, and to fight for the company against its enemies. Despite these permissions, the moral issue of slavery was, for some, a nagging problem. Nonetheless, the institution continued to grow.[32]

Forbidden by the company to learn a skilled trade after 1628, the Africans were retained only to provide the labor that whites and their indentured servants were unwilling to do.[33] Enslaved people would have cleared the land, cut the wood, and constructed the house, barn, and protective palisades, though white artisans did the jobs that required training. A chimney of three thousand bricks, sufficient for heating the interior three rooms, took a mason ten days to build. Montagne hired an English carpenter to create a separate tobacco-drying barn, but its construction was flimsy and it soon blew down and damaged his crop.[34]

The first fall harvest on the Muscoota flatlands—which eventually became known as Montagne's Flats—yielded two hundred pounds of tobacco. Montagne sold it for 135 fl. (guilders), but a large portion of his profit went to the company, which also issued strict guidelines, rules, and punishments to guarantee that New Amsterdam tobacco was of the highest quality.[35]

After the company's cut and the cost of maintaining a farm and a large family, and considering that he received only 35 fl. ($14) a month for his service as a counselor and perhaps a bit more for his medical services, it seems Montagne may have lived above his means. In November 1838 he took out a large loan from the deacons of the Reformed Protestant Dutch Church of New Amsterdam. His debt to the company would plague him all his life.[36]

On the whole, Montagne appears in the historical record as a controlled and cautious man. But an incident in August 1638 belies this picture. A man named Claes Cornelison Swits sued Montagne, complaining that Montagne had struck his wife. In the court records, "the defendant acknowledges the fact, and is ordered to settle with the Attorney General." Montagne then countersued Swits for slander. The record offers no further information, but a month later, Montagne was "condemned to pay to the poor 1/6 and satisfy the Attorney General."[37] Swits had leased the neighboring farm a few months earlier, so the slanderous dispute between Montagne and Madam Swits may have involved their adjacent properties.[38] Montagne would also have a dispute about the future of the de Forest farm.

Hendrick's wife, Geertruyt Bornstra, found herself a rich and propertied widow, but not for long. New Amsterdam surveyor Andries Hudde "won the heart and hand" of the widow, and they were betrothed. Hudde was a prominent member of the New Amsterdam community, a counselor and surveyor-general for the company. He applied for a patent to Geertruyt's property and was issued a "groundbrief" or deed on July 20, 1638. Hudde therefore has the distinction of being the first private landowner within the land that became Central Park and the first private landowner on Manhattan Island.[39]

The Huddes sailed to the Netherlands later that same year.[40] Before leaving, Hudde contracted with a Norwegian manager, Hans Hansen, to receive the six or eight workers and tools that he would send over, to provide them with food, shelter, and wages, and to have them construct tobacco houses, an indication that he planned to live on and oversee his new bride's estate.[41]

Hudde also appointed a supervisor for the de Forest farm, a man named Domine Everardus Bogardus, the reverend of the Dutch Reformed Church. That year, Montagne requested that Bogardus reimburse him over one thousand guilders that he had laid out for improvements and expenses on the Huddes's property. Bogardus declined, preferring to reimburse the doctor only upon its sale. The court agreed and ordered an auction to benefit Hendrick's widow and reimburse Montagne. But Montagne was the highest bidder, purchasing not only the farm but also the livestock, tools, tobacco and grain crops, and a boat for a mere 1,800 guilders—a steal.[42] The loss of their homestead must have stunned the Huddeses when they returned from Europe, but the parties managed to work out an amicable financial settlement, "releasing and acquitting each other from all further claims and demands. All in good faith, without any exception whatsoever."[43]

The items for which Montagne sought reimbursement offer a window through which we can glimpse what daily life must have been like for well-to-do New Amsterdam residents. Montagne's purchases from his fellow colonists indicate that his family had a healthy and plentiful diet: bread, rye, maize, peas, wheat, meal, pepper, pumpkins, fish, pork, salted eels, smoked beef, cheese, butter, goats, beef, and venison. They were able to buy or barter for whale oil, train oil (also from whales and used in lamps, soap, and margarine), ropes, nails, candles, spades, and scythes.

For services rendered—either paid for or bartered—Montagne hired farmhands for mowing and haying, bundling reeds (probably for the thatched roof), and tending a calf until he could establish his *bouwerie*. He purchased guns, gunpowder, and shot: the Dutch were hunters and also anticipated that they would have to protect themselves from the Lenape, who had been introduced to fire-arms by the Europeans.[44]

After a lifetime of traveling the globe, from Saintonge to Leiden to Guiana to Tobago, back to Leiden, to New Amsterdam and the wilds of the Muscoota flats, Montagne finally found the freedom and safe haven of which he dreamed. He named his newly acquired property Vredendal, "peaceful valley." At some undetermined date, the spring that still exists near Huddlestone Arch in Central Park became known as Montagne's *fonteyn*, the old Dutch word for both spring and stream.[45]

With the abundance of arable soil, nearby fresh water, tools, and a successful crop, the Montagnes and their neighbors enjoyed peace and plenty for the next two years. Jochem Pieter Kuyter, a neighbor living on a nearby four-hundred-acre plantation named Zegendael (or "vale of blessings"), wrote of their utopia in the New World: "The farmers pursue their outdoor labor without interruption, in the woods as well as in the field and dwell safely, with their wives and children, in their houses, free from any fear of Indians."[46] Relationships between the Dutch and the Natives seemed mostly friendly. Once when Hendrick de Forest had lost his yawl, Montagne noted that he paid a Native ten guilders for retrieving it.[47]

KIEFT'S WAR

The settlers, Montagne included, understood the importance of good relations with the Lenape. They took pains to learn their languages and exchange agricultural techniques. They traded in beavers or Native currency of wampum or seawant, strings or belts of beads created through the difficult process of boring the shells of whelk or quahog clams. Any conflicts were mostly bloodless arguments over land use or misunderstandings over trade agreements. But occasionally there was violence. In 1626, in the fledgling colony, a group of Europeans murdered a Wickquasgeck tribe member in front of his young nephew.[48] Though it took many years, the nephew exacted his revenge. But such brutality was rare in the first two decades of the Dutch colony. The Dutch were dependent on the Lenape to trap the furs they sought, and therefore most problems were swiftly resolved. The Dutch rewarded the Natives with European-made tools and devices, alcohol, and firearms. Ironically, the Lenape, who were accustomed to wearing beaver in winter and summer, chose to trade the animals' pelts for Dutch-made "duffels-cloth," a thick red or blue woolen material that they prized for its ability to repel rain even better than fur.[49] This new trading arrangement distorted the Lenape economy. They were pushed to overhunt beavers, which caused imbalance in the ecosystem. The new trade agreements also disrupted their traditional self-reliance. As their old ways of life began to fade away, an ill wind blew over this fragile arrangement. Almost overnight, a new company director transformed a struggling colony into a theater of war.

On March 28, 1638, the company recalled Director Wouter Van Twiller and replaced him with Willem Kieft.[50] History has not been kind to Kieft—for good reason—but information about his personality only comes down to us from records written by a failed and bitter rival for the company's directorship.[51]

1.7 Dutch West India Company Director Wilhelm (or Willem) Kieft was the most despised man in New Amsterdam history for his genocidal war on the local indigenous tribes.

Source: *Wilhelm Kieft, bust portrait, facing right.* Photograph. Library of Congress, www.loc.gov /item/2005691470/.

Nonetheless, Kieft proved to be an autocrat and the most despised man in the history of New Netherland.[52]

Kieft's first official decision was to organize a council over which he had total control. Less than two weeks after his arrival, Kieft appointed Montagne, one of the most educated men in the colony, to be his sole council advisor. Though over time, Montagne became the voice of reason to Kieft's irrational and violent behavior, their relationship was not one of equals—Kieft retained two votes to Montagne's one.[53] The director may also have deliberately chosen Montagne for his financial vulnerability. Montagne owed the company a great deal of money, several thousand guilders by the end of his life. Activist Adrien van der Donck summed up Kieft's iron control over his subordinates and especially Montagne, who "must always conform to the humor of the Director, and say nothing else but yes; otherwise, the purse is closed, all favor missed."[54]

Kieft made progress within the settlement. He repaired the crumbling infrastructure and the fort. The company's finances were in shambles because rules to protect its control of the fur trade were ignored, and profits that should have been the company's had fallen into the hands of private merchants.[55] The population was dwindling, and the social fabric was fraying "from the fighting; from adulterous intercourse with heathens, Blacks, or other persons; from mutiny, theft, false testimony, slanderous language and other irregularities," and the daily mischief was "occasioned by immoderate drinking." To stop the rampant drunkenness, Kieft issued unpopular policies that regulated the sale of alcohol "at a fair price and where it will be issued in moderate quantities."[56]

But it was not Kieft's economic or social edicts that brought the colony to its knees. Rather it was his monomaniacal attempt to control the Native tribes. The entire success of New Netherland relied on the fragile friendship with the Natives, who captured and traded beaver pelts and other prized natural resources for the company in return for European-made tools, weapons, and alcohol. In exchange for the *use* of the tribal natives' land, the company agreed to protect them with their troops against the enemy Mohawk tribe, but Kieft viewed this costly arrangement as an opportunity to extract tribute from the Natives in the form of furs, corn, and wampum. Montagne strongly advised Kieft against such punitive measures, but his mind was fixed. He would bend the Natives' will to his own. According to historian Russell Shorto, Kieft was "more or less set on a strategy of eventual extermination."[57]

When Kieft's demand for tribute in 1639 was summarily dismissed by the *sachems*, or local chiefs, it would take only one incident for the director to retaliate.

Pigs had been stolen from the Staten Island farm of David de Vries, and though the thieves were later determined to be some Dutch soldiers, Kieft suspected the Natives. He ordered fifty of his soldiers and twenty sailors to attack the neighboring Raritan settlement in what is now New Jersey. De Vries tried to end the violence, but the incident turned into a bloodbath.[58] In retribution, the Raritans murdered four of De Vries's farmhands and burned down his house.

An unsettled peace somehow descended after the Raritan incident, but a year later, another single act of random violence triggered Kieft's reign of terror. Claes Cornelison Swits, the Swiss neighbor whose wife had been struck years earlier by Montagne, was decapitated in his Turtle Bay home in middle Manhattan by a Wickquasgeck man: the nephew of the man murdered fifteen years earlier by a group of Europeans. In the intervening years, as historian E. B. O'Callaghan imagined it,

> His uncle's spirit was still unappeased—his murder still unavenged. His voice was heard in the roaring of the storm—in the rustle of the leaves—in the sighing of the winds; and full of the conviction that the spirit could not find rest until vengeance should be had, the young Wiechquaeseck sought for a victim to offer to the manes of the dead.

The nephew, who had only a passing acquaintance with the elderly Swits, entered his home on the pretense of buying some cloth and decapitated the wheelwright with an axe. Enraged, Kieft demanded immediate "satisfaction" from the sachem, who maintained that the vengeance was entirely justified.[59]

Swits's murder shook the Dutch community to its core, and it set Kieft on the warpath. Most citizens were strongly against immediate retaliation, and Montagne and other advisors cautioned Kieft to deliberate matters more carefully, count their stores of ammunition, wait for the arrival of more men from Europe, and ensure that residents in distant communities, such as Montagne's own family in Harlem, could be protected.

To appear conciliatory, Kieft invited the most prominent families to choose a council to advise him on the Native situation.[60] By January 1642, the Twelve Men, as they came to be called, had come around to the idea of retaliation. Knowing Kieft was a famous coward, they suggested that he lead the soldiers. He declined. So they requested a series of governmental reforms, including a check on the "unlimited power of the executive." They demanded that Kieft form a council made up of popularly chosen representatives to address the Native matter and more administrative and legislative concerns. Kieft found this preposterous. They were there solely to give advice about the response to Swits's murder. Nothing more.[61]

Months of indecision passed, but with few checks on his aggression and the full support of his more bloodthirsty followers, Kieft finally ordered a surprise night raid on the Wickquasgeck tribe in Pavonia, which is today's Hoboken and Jersey City. In desperation, David de Vries, chair of the Twelve Men, pleaded with Kieft to be patient and trust the nature of the Lenape, who, "though cunning enough, would do no harm unless harm was done to them." Montagne also cautioned the director that he was "about to build a bridge over which war would stalk, ere long through the whole country." But Kieft ignored them.[62]

In the dead of a cold winter's night, February 24, 1643, soldiers of the Dutch West India Company annihilated two Native enclaves. The reported atrocities were as savage and inhumane as any in the long history of genocide of indigenous peoples. Only a mile from the fort, on Corlear's Hook (today's Lower East Side), de Vries could hear "the great shrieking" as Kieft's soldiers slew a camp of forty friendly Natives whom the company had agreed to protect from their Mohawk enemies. The larger massacre occurred in Pavonia, across the Hudson River, where the soldiers hoped to rout out Swits's Wickquasgeck assassin. We know the details from de Vries's personal account:

Sucklings were torn from their mother's breasts, butchered before their parents' eyes and their mangled limbs thrown quivering into the river or the flames. Babes were hacked to pieces while "fastened to little boards"—their primitive cradles! —others were thrown alive into the river, and when their parents impelled by nature rushed in to save them, the soldiers prevented their landing, and thus the parents and offspring sunk into one watery grave. Children of half a dozen years, decrepit men of three score and ten, shared the same fate. Those who escaped and begged for shelter next morning were killed in cold blood or thrown into the river. Some came running to us from the country, having their hands cut off, some lost both arms and legs, some were supporting their entrails with their hands, while others were mangled in other horrid ways, too horrid to be conceived. . . . Flushed with victory the respective parties returned to Fort Amsterdam, bringing with them thirty prisoners and the heads of several of the enemy.

As if these details were not macabre enough, the trophy heads were kicked about by the mother-in-law of the massacre's leader, Cornelis Van Tienhoven.[63] The horrors of that night convinced the intrepid de Vries to return to the Netherlands in 1644 and leave the "many perils of savage heathens behind him."[64]

For the next two years, Kieft's War raged on. Over seventeen hundred Native Americans and Dutch men, women, and children were killed. The new Dutch violence encouraged eleven local tribes to postpone their intertribal squabbles and band together, over one thousand strong, to execute frequent counterattacks. Many uptown and outlying settlements were razed to the ground. Farms were burned, crops destroyed, homesteaders and their livestock slaughtered. Families abandoned their once-peaceful valley to seek protection in "hastily constructed straw huts behind the walls of the fort" at the southernmost tip of Manhattan.[65] Montagne was said to have been driven off his land and lost "all he could not carry away."[66] But the counterattacks seemed only to fuel Kieft's thirst for blood—he would retaliate until the "savages" were wiped out.

The conflict soon spread to New Jersey, Long Island, and the Bronx. It was there that a small colony of Puritan freethinkers were murdered, including religious leader Anne Hutchinson, six of her children, and nine of her followers. The Dutch had granted them religious freedom after they were driven out of New England, but in September 1843, the Natives slaughtered them in their Bronx settlement, later memorialized as the Hutchinson River and Parkway. Jonas Bronk, living in the borough that would be named for him, in today's neighborhood of Mott Haven, was also murdered, along with several neighbors.[67]

Montagne's wife, Rachel, died during the war years. He was left a widower with five young children. Although the Wickquasgeck trail ran close to his farm, it had miraculously escaped destruction after the Pavonia retaliation. During a temporary détente in the summer of 1643, Montagne felt confident enough to plant crops again, twenty-six acres of rye, barley, and peas. He rented out his farm in anticipation of the harvest, but within three months, violence erupted once more, and residents abandoned the uptown farms to shelter in the fort.[68] On March 6, 1644, Montagne's neighbor Jochem Pieter Kuyter's "Vale of Blessings" farm was destroyed.[69]

Now the peace-loving Montagne was resigned to the conflict. Kieft ordered him personally to command troops against tribes in Staten Island; Greenwich, Connecticut; and on Long Island in Schout's Bay (today's Manhasset Bay) and Heemsteed (now called Hempsted). The Canarsee, a band of Lenape, lived there on the western points of Long Island, and against them Montagne waged what his biographer called "one of the most ruthless operations of the war."[70] As commander of the troops, Montagne was first responsible for the slaughter of eighty Natives in what is now Maspeth, Queens. He then personally oversaw the slaughter of more than 120 Canarsee, a fact difficult to reconcile with his rational and passive personality. Yet the Canarsee massacre was one of the most ruthless and horrifying operations of the war. Among other unthinkable atrocities, Montagne and Kieft reportedly watched with enjoyment as a soldier brought them "strips" from the live body of a prisoner, castrated him, and then "struck [his genitals] . . . into this mouth while he was still alive and after that [they] placed him on a millstone and beat his head off."[71]

By 1644, the people of New Amsterdam knew they must rid themselves of the West India Company and its director. Secret alliances were forming to petition the States-General in The Hague. Montagne and Cornelis van Tienhoven, Kieft's henchman and leader of the Pavonia raid, were among those leaders singled out for questioning. Van Tienhoven confirmed that Kieft and Montagne were present during the incident with the Canarsee.[72]

But even though most blamed Kieft for the destruction wrought against the Dutch colony, he and Montagne remained in their posts. At one point, Kieft tried to lay the blame for the entire war at the feet of Maryn Adriaensen, a soldier who had taken an active part in the massacre. Adriaensen stormed into Kieft's house and pointed a gun at his chest. But luckily for Kieft, his loyal toady Montagne acted swiftly and covered the pan of the pistol with his hand, "and thus the weapon fortunately missed fire."[73]

By August 1645, Montagne had helped negotiate a peace with the local tribes, and a truce was declared.[74] Kieft remained in New Amsterdam for another two years until he was recalled by the company to answer for his war in the New World. But Kieft never met with justice, for his ship was wrecked off the coast of Wales, and he drowned before reaching Amsterdam. The war he caused destroyed much of the property of New Amsterdam and the surrounding areas, and during this time many fearful colonists returned home to the Netherlands.

On May 9, 1647, two days before Kieft departed, he secured for Montagne a legal patent to Hendrick de Forest's original property in the prepark and on the flats, and also included the extension of Rechewanis, renamed Montagne's Point, today much of East Harlem.[75]

1.8 Inspired by a likeness done during Peter Stuyvesant's lifetime, artist John Trumbull captured the formidable autocrat in his 1808 portrait.

Source: John Trumbull, *Peter Stuyvesant*, 1808. Photograph by Glenn Castellano. Collection of the Public Design Commission of the City of New York.

PETER STUYVESANT

In 1647, Peter Stuyvesant sailed in as the new director general of New Netherland. Stuyvesant had been the governor of the three colonies of Aruba, Bonaire, and Curacao in the West Indies, where he lost in right leg in combat with either the Portuguese or the Spanish. Although he was described as "brave, honest, capable and energetic," he was, like Kieft, "proud, headstrong and tyrannical." His subjects soon learned that he did not take kindly to critics or his predecessor's opponents.[76] Stuyvesant also chose Montagne as his counselor.[77]

Life was better under Stuyvesant's leadership. Trade flourished, and he laid out a plan to rebuild the crumbling infrastructure and add public buildings. To accomplish these goals, he would need financing. Montagne advised him to elect a board of advisors—the Council of Nine Men—to implement his plans.[78] But despite this new board, Stuyvesant's despotic style of ruling was his downfall.

Early in Stuyvesant's regime, a jurist named Adrien van der Donck challenged his leadership. Van der Donck was secretly investigating the true causes of Kieft's War and the general corruption and tyranny of the Dutch West India Company's directors, keeping accounts that he would eventually present to the Dutch States-General. Van der Donck loved his newly adopted country and envisioned New Amsterdam as a prosperous and official part of the Netherlands rather than as a company town. He traveled to The Hague to offer the States-General his vision for a popular government in a document entitled *Remonstrance of New Netherland, and the Occurrences There, addressed to the High and Mighty Lords States General of the United Netherlands*.

While in The Hague, Van der Donck wrote a secret letter to Montagne. "The winds of favor have changed direction," he wrote, strongly suggesting to Montagne that it would be wise to separate himself from the West India Company and join with what he was certain would be the upcoming new governing body. He did not mince words: "The authors of the war are not punished as they should have been," while the actions of the war "are damned here by the whole world."[79] In his report, Van der Donck noted that Montagne later admitted regret for taking part in the massacre and "helped to excuse it to the best of his ability."[80]

In April 1652, after two and a half years in the Netherlands, Adrien Van der Donck finally won his case against Stuyvesant and the Dutch West India Company. The States-General gave its assurance that Stuyvesant would be recalled and a new government established in New Netherland. But Van der Donck's plans were foiled when a trading war arose between the Netherlands and England. An immediate challenge to the successful Dutch trading monopoly, Manhattan included, revived the moribund Dutch West India Company, and consequently Van der Donck and his dream of a more popular government for New Netherland became the greater threat.[81]

In 1655, violence came again, in attacks by a group of tribes led by the Susquehannocks from New Sweden (Delaware). More than three hundred Dutch were killed and their property and crops destroyed. Stuyvesant, who was away from New Amsterdam during the massacre, blamed other officials, Montagne among them. Stuyvesant wrote to the company directors in Amsterdam that Montagne was "a bad instrument—a snake harbored in the bosom of the colony."[82]

Stuyvesant determined that the isolation of rural communities was impracticable and called for an end to uptown development. Vredendal and neighboring farms returned to their presettlement state, unoccupied and unplanted for several years, "except as cattle and goats browsed in its deserted clearings and woodlands."[83]

Eventually Stuyvesant reversed his decision. He realized that a strong uptown presence was vital to the security and growth of New Amsterdam, so in 1658 he established the settlement of Nieuw Haarlem, or New Harlem. It has been suggested that the settlement was named after Haarlem in the Netherlands because that city's resistance to the Spanish in the Eighty Years War was a parallel to the fight against the Lenape.[84] The company reclaimed titles to the devalued farms on the flats, Vredendal included. Stuyvesant parceled out the land by lottery to any freeholder willing to move uptown to New Harlem, which was centered around what is now Third Avenue and 124th Street. He offered such homesteaders a fifteen-year tax break. Thus began the uptown real estate divisions and transactions among members of the insular and interrelated Dutch community, which continued unabated for the next century and a half.

As would-be developers, Montagne's sons and son-in-law petitioned the village of New Harlem to create a community for "six, eight, or ten families" on the old Vredendal property on the flats, the area that today ranges from 109th Street to 124th Street. But the Harlem council rejected the idea on the grounds that the development would interfere with Harlem's use of the flats for its future agricultural needs.

The company then claimed most of the Montagne property as partial repayment of his debt but agreed to a sort of compromise, allowing Willem, Montagne's younger son and the New Harlem schoolmaster, to draw lots in the division lottery. Willem won thirty-two acres from his father's subdivided land. Montagne's oldest son, Jan (or John), was permitted to keep Montagne's Point along Harlem Creek (now East Harlem), but was specifically forbidden to live on or develop it without permission of the town.[85]

Montagne, who had remarried, moved to Fort Orange—today's Albany—where he took a position in 1656 as commissary and vice-director. In 1664, the year Dutch New Amsterdam capitulated to England, Montagne still wallowed in debt. He told Stuyvesant that a mistake had been made in the computation of his accounts and leaned on the director to bail him out. "Never in the sixty-eight years that I have lived, so great distress I have felt," he wrote to Stuyvesant.

"Destitute of all means to provide for my daily bread . . . but my hope rests in those who until now have always helped me."[86]

Stuyvesant heard his pleas and increased Montagne's salary. But money could not solve all his problems. He was embroiled in troubling relationships with tribes in upstate New York, and Esopus Natives abducted his daughter Rachel Van Imbroch. She was eventually released by the friendly Mohawks, but soon after, her house in Wiltyck, today's Kingston, was burned and she and her husband, Gysbert, were killed by a rival tribe.[87]

Little is known of Montagne in the following years. Records from 1665 mention him in a suit against a fellow colonist over payment for some beaver pelts, but by 1670, his son Jan de la Montagne had dropped the "Jr." from his name, suggesting that his father was dead. Montagne took the oath of allegiance to the English colony but probably traveled to the Netherlands in 1670, where he must have died. Where he went and where he is buried are not certain. Today Montagne, the flats, and the point that bore his name are long forgotten, but one of his projects has survived as one of New York's most famous landmarks. In 1653, Montagne was a member of the three-person committee that created the protective palisade or wall on the northern boundary of the city. This fortification would eventually become Wall Street.[88]

THE ENGLISH TAKEOVER

In the summer of 1664, the British were contemplating the takeover of Manhattan Island but were uncertain about the strength of the Dutch military. Unbeknownst to them, the cost-conscious Dutch West India Company had reduced the standing force to a mere 150 soldiers. In August, a British ship off the coast of Long Island captured a Dutch sailor, and to him the English exaggerated the strength of the British force as eight hundred soldiers. When the sailor was released, he went straight to the Dutch authorities with the news that they would soon be attacked and vastly outnumbered.[89] Stuyvesant stood his ground and refused to capitulate, but the community, fearful and exhausted from years of war with the indigenous peoples, pressured him.[90]

On September 8, 1664, New Amsterdam became New York without a single shot fired.

Isaac de Forest was one of the ninety-three Dutch citizens who signed the official surrender to the English and took an oath of allegiance to King Charles II and his brother, the Duke of York, who, according to the terms of capitulation, would receive an annual payment of forty beaver skins from the new English colony.[91] To many Dutch citizens, the English takeover finally put an end to the oppressive yoke of Kieft, Stuyvesant, and the Dutch West India Company. The English allowed the Dutch families to retain their culture, their religion, and their property. The Montagne descendants intermarried with other Dutch families and became leaders in the Harlem community, which retained its separate ways for the following century and a half.

The indigenous tribes had already declined in number by the 1680s. The beavers had been hunted almost to extinction on the island, so the Natives followed them north, upstate and into Canada. European diseases, the encroaching Dutch settlements, and a series of wars had eviscerated the population until the presence of indigenous peoples on the island of Manhattan was in name only.

chapter 2

Along the Kingsbridge Road, 1683–1845

The northern end of what became Central Park is home to a unique combination of topographic features—proximity to the vast agricultural Muscoota plains, access to waterways rich with wildlife, and most importantly, a break in the wall of rock that allowed for a section of the Kingsbridge Road to pass through. From the middle of the seventeenth century into the first quarter of the nineteenth century, a select few families—the Kortrights, the Bensons, and the McGowans—dominate the story of the northern end of the prepark that lay along the Kingsbridge Road. Through their intermarriage and their wills, these families managed their power, properties, and finances, surviving through the English takeover and the American Revolution and well into the nineteenth century.

THE KINGSBRIDGE ROAD

The installation of a new drainage system in Central Park is a fairly routine procedure during restoration projects by the Central Park Conservancy. But whenever such projects occur above Ninety-Seventh Street, where there is well-documented prepark history, the New York City Landmarks Preservation Commission requires a preliminary archeological investigation before construction can begin.

In 2013 during the restoration of the Fort landscape at the northern end of Central Park, archeology consultants uncovered a part of what was once the Kingsbridge Road, the Wickquasgeck trail renamed after the British took over New Amsterdam. Until this rediscovery, it was assumed that Manhattan's

2.1 Evidence of the original Kingsbridge Road was unearthed during routine park operations at McGowan's Pass. The smaller stones are embedded in the roadbed and the larger ones are the base of a barrier gate fortification from the War of 1812.

Source: James Lee, Kingsbridge Road_13025 Do2-194.jpg. Courtesy Hunter Research Inc.

original highway had been completely obliterated.[1] They determined that the roadbed lay anywhere from eighteen inches to three feet below the present surface of the park, was roughly six inches thick, and "comprised a densely packed layer of pebbles and cobbles set in a silty sand with a highly compacted 'metalled' surface." They noted that the two-hundred-year-old road was still so hard that the bucket of the park's backhoe "bounced right off of it!"[2]

The Kingsbridge Road once ran nearly the entire length of Manhattan. In the seventeenth and eighteenth centuries, to create and maintain a road made of billions of small inlaid stones over such a steep incline was an expensive, daunting, seemingly impossible task. Until 1764, when colonial governors raised taxes and hired city laborers, all New Yorkers were required to help maintain the road or pay a large contribution toward its upkeep.[3]

We can trace the route of the old Kingsbridge Road from the Battery at the southernmost point of the island to the Flatiron Building at Fifth Avenue and Twenty-Third Street because it has been paved over and renamed Broadway. From there, the road diverged and headed east, meandering north through the Upper East Side to Eighty-Second Street and Third Avenue, where it veered northwest

2.2 McGowan's Pass—the narrow opening for the Kingsbridge Road situated in a wall of rock outcrops that cross the park at 107th Street—is one of the most historically important spots on Manhattan Island.

Source: Sara Cedar Miller, *McGowan's Pass*. Courtesy of the Central Park Conservancy.

to avoid tidal inlets, the steep slopes of Carnegie Hill, and the former Native settlement of Konaande Kongh farther east to the flatter, drier land of today's bridle path at Fifth Avenue and Ninety-Second Street, parallel to the Reservoir.

From there, the road continued back across the dry land, today's East Meadow, and followed the East Drive until it veered into a steep incline known as McGowan's Pass after a family who lived nearby.[4] The pass was the one narrow gap in a steep wall of rock outcrops that crossed the land from Fifth to Eighth Avenues at 107th Street. Today the former road is a lovely but fairly unremarkable and unnamed path. But looks can be deceiving. McGowan's Pass is one of the most historically significant landmarks on Manhattan Island. For over two centuries, much of New York's social and military history took place where the road met the rock.[5]

THE HALF-WAY HOUSE

Beyond the pass, the road crossed the swamp by a series of low-lying planks and branched into two thoroughfares: the Kingsbridge Road (also known as Harlem Lane) and the Old Harlem Road, which headed east to the village of Harlem. Today that junction is in the middle of the Harlem Meer. In real estate parlance, location is everything, and it was just northwest of this key intersection—located inside the park at 109th Street and across from Malcolm X Boulevard—that weary and hungry travelers were welcomed by the Jansen-Kortright family to the first tavern in the prepark.[6]

In 1603, Flemish-born Walloon Bastian Van Kortryk emigrated with his family to Leerdam, Holland. Like the de Forest Walloons before them, Bastiaen and his sons Jan and Michael Bastiaensen moved from Kortryk—what is today Flanders, Belgium—to evade religious persecution from Catholics.[7] In Holland, they adopted the name Kortright (or Kortreght). By 1663, the family had crossed the Atlantic and settled in Harlem, where they ran a profitable ferry that connected Manhattan to the Bronx. In 1684, Jan's son Cornelis Jansen and his wife (and cousin), Metje opened a tavern at the junction of the two roads close to the island's midpoint.[8] Manhattan is fourteen miles long, and the Jansens' tavern was near the mid-point; hence it was "commonly called the Half-Way House." We know the tavern was situated within the prepark at 109th Street and Sixth Avenue and might possibly have been sited on or near the former de Forest-Montagne homestead.

Kortright family tree

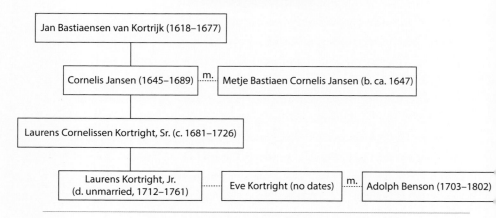

2.3 The Kortright Family Tree.

Source: James Riker, *Revised History of Harlem* (*City of New York*), *Its Origin and Early Annals.*

With a source of fresh water adjacent to the property and a freshwater pond at 111th Street and Seventh Avenue, the location was ideal for a tavern. Cornelis Jansen commissioned a house of about eight hundred square feet, for which he agreed to pay eight hundred guilders "in fat cattle, wheat, and rye."[9]

Taverns, or "ordinaries," especially those along the main roads, were the center of colonial culture in America. They refreshed tired travelers, but they were also places to gossip and spread news, to conduct business, to form and voice political ideas, and to gather in times of joy and times of trouble. According to historian Harrison Bayles, they possessed "an influence second only to the church."[10] In most roadside inns, the food was scarcely edible and accommodations ranged from somewhat comfortable to barely tolerable. One bed might accommodate five or six strangers or might be situated in the corner of a public room, where noisy and drunken customers tarried late into the night. Lice, bedbugs, and fleas were common.

In New Amsterdam, alcohol served in taverns was strictly controlled, particularly to prevent "unseasonable Night reveling and immoderate Drinking on the Sabbath." Sunday laws prohibited the sale of beer or strong liquors before two o'clock in the afternoon—the time by which no sermon was still being preached in church. If there was a long sermon, congregants had to wait until four o'clock to drink. Only travelers, daily boarders, and tavern keepers' own families could partake in the private consumption of alcohol after the ringing of the nine o'clock curfew bell, when the city gates were closed for the night. Drunken hostilities were so common that the city passed a law imposing heavy fines "for every hour after the wound or hurt has been inflicted and is concealed by the Tapster or Tavern keeper." Tavern keepers were forbidden to manufacture beer, and conversely brewers were forbidden to sell their product retail. Both laws were frequently ignored. The tavern keeper license had to be renewed with payment every quarter of the year "on pain of suspension of his business for notorious and obstinate neglect."[11]

Taverns were hubs of information for the community. The idea to establish a postal service is attributed to King Charles II, who understood how exchanging the latest news could strengthen ties between colonies. Taverns received weekly deliveries of local and out-of-town newspapers, letters, and direct news from the post rider himself, who had traveled far and wide. Once mail delivery began in the New England colonies in 1672, the Kingsbridge Road became known as the Eastern Post Road or Albany/Boston Post Road. A monthly mail delivery began from lower New Amsterdam to Saybrook, Connecticut, where riders exchanged mailbags with post riders from Boston. The arrival of mail created "great excitement in the little village of Harlem, when the first postman drew up at the tavern door on the route to refresh himself, his port mantles crammed with letters and small portable goods."[12]

In 1769 the Common Council ordered fourteen milestones placed along the mail route in Manhattan to standardize the cost of posting a letter. The seventh milestone, the halfway mark, was placed on the Kingsbridge Road between Ninety-Seventh and Ninety-Eighth Streets in today's East Meadow, though the Jansens' Half-Way House was a half mile farther north.[13]

When Cornelis Jansen died in 1689, his wife, Metje, oversaw what had become a prosperous establishment. A decade later, in 1699, the tavern still stood, and enjoyed a reputation for once "Entertaining his Excellency the Governour in his Return from Connecticut."[14]

But by 1704, the tavern's accommodations seemed to be hardly in as good repair. In the diary of Sarah Kemble Knight, an intrepid woman who traveled alone by stagecoach from Boston to New York City at the turn of the eighteenth century, she wrote of it only: "left with little regret."[15]

Running an inn was not necessarily Cornelis's first priority. Rather, it was the expansion of the Jansen-Kortright estate. James Riker, the nineteenth-century Harlem historian, noted that Metje or members of her family amassed another two hundred acres of common lands, formerly Montagne's Flats, part of which included much of the prepark land from 106th to 110th Streets.

Eventually 169 acres of the estate fell from her son Lawrence Kortright Sr. to her unmarried grandson Lawrence Kortright Jr., and as we shall see, that would become a problem for the Kortright heirs.[16]

THE BENSONS OF HARLEM

The second tavern, the Black Horse Tavern, and its surrounding property shows how interwoven marriage, business, and property were among the old Harlem families.[17] It was not uncommon for a cousin to marry a cousin, and tracing a person's lineage or property ownership in old Harlem often produces more of a web than a flow chart. In the northern end of the prepark, the Benson-McGowans and Jansen-Kortrights were among the close-knit Harlem families that frequently intermarried. The Kortrights and Bensons first joined together when Metje's son, Lawrence Kortright Sr., married Helena Benson in 1703. In the following generation, Lawrence and Helena's daughter, Eve Kortright, married Helena's nephew, Adolph Benson, thus making Lawrence Kortright both Adolph's uncle and his father-in-law.

The use of the same given name down through multiple generations, another common practice, complicates matters further. The Benson-McGowan family (often spelled McGown or Maggown) is a perfect example. Johannes Benson fathered the first Samson Benson, whose offspring had a Johannes and a Samson. At least three other Benson children were named Samson, sometimes noted as either Sampson or Samuel. A Samson Adolphus Benson may be the same person as Adolphus Samson Benson, while a Samson Benson McGowan may also be S. Benson McGown or Benson McGown, and there were at least five different Andrew McGowans.[18]

Through intermarriage, the Dutch and Danish families living in the newly English colony could retain their religion, language, culture, and property, often buying, selling, dividing, inheriting, reselling, and repurchasing the same tract of land over and over to improve their financial status and increase their real estate holdings. Often they did so again and again because of frequent spousal deaths and remarriages. Families exchanged their land as commonly as they swapped their cattle and crops.[19]

The Half-Way House went out of business sometime after Metje Cornelis's tenure as owner, but by 1748, intermarriage between the Benson and Dyckman

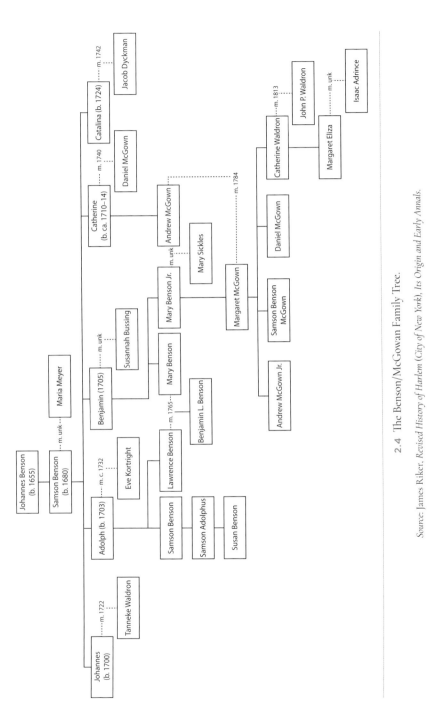

2.4 The Benson/McGowan Family Tree.

Source: James Riker, *Revised History of Harlem (City of New York), Its Origin and Early Annals.*

families had established the Black Horse Tavern on the site of what is today the hill above the East Drive at 105th Street.

——◆——

The Benson family has a typical American story. They were not Dutch, but like many other political refugees, they first emigrated to the Netherlands before coming to America. Danish-born Dirck Bensingh first spent time in Groningen before moving to New Amsterdam and then on to Fort Orange (today's Albany) before settling in Harlem in 1701. He acquired so much land that by the time of his death in 1740, his family were among the largest property owners in Harlem, a position they held for the next century and a half.[20] His grandson Samson Benson married Maria Meyer, who was from another large Dutch landowning family in Harlem. Together they had nine children, and four of them—Adolph, Benjamin, Catherine, and Catalina—inherited, swapped, or married into much of the prepark land above Ninety-Third Street. Even when the Benson women married outside their family, as Catherine Benson McGowan, proprietor of the Black Horse/McGowan tavern, did, they and their children and grandchildren derived their wealth, property, and elite status in the Harlem and New York City communities as members of the Benson family.

Within the Dutch American culture, property was divided equally among the heirs, but after a few generations of splitting up the land, individual plots had shrunk so much that the land was considerably less valuable. As a solution, one sibling, often the eldest, would buy out the shares of the others. When Samson Benson died in 1740, eight of his children sold their shares to their brother Benjamin, who later transferred much of the land to his older brother Adolph, thus keeping the large family property—and investment—intact.[21] In this way, much of the Harlem land that would become Central Park was held throughout the eighteenth century by Samson Benson and handed down through the generations to his son Adolph Benson, his grandson Lawrence Benson, and ultimately to his great grandson Benjamin L. Benson, who sold the land in 1825.[22]

Around 1742, Adolph Benson's sister Catalina married Jacob Dyckman, who partnered with Adolph to expand the Benson family's already vast real estate holdings.[23] One of their business ventures was the 1748 purchase of twenty acres in the prepark. On his ten acres along the Kingsbridge Road, Jacob Dyckman built a stone house in which he established the area's second tavern, the Black

Horse, on what is today's composting operation. Dyckman's sister-in-law, Eve Kortright Benson, was the granddaughter of innkeeper Metje Cornelis—so keeping a roadside inn was already a family affair.[24] To add to the confusion, after the closure of Metje's tavern, people often referred to the Black Horse as the Half-Way House and later Leggett's Halfway tavern.[25]

   Dyckman's Black Horse was the most prominent building in the area. In 1756 *The New York Mercury* described it as a "commodious brick house, with the sign of a black horse." It had "three rooms on a floor with a fireplace in each, a good cellar, and a milk house" on nine acres of land. Jacob Dyckman also planted a young orchard of 120 grafted trees to grow apples and pears, the fruits of which he most likely turned into hard cider and brandies.[26] The Black Horse was near a four-acre garden that grew hops, the main ingredient of beer and ale. While we don't know exactly where the garden was, we know it was east of the tavern, likely on or near what is now Central Park's Conservatory Garden or the Museum of the City of New York, or else farther toward Third Avenue.[27]

2.5 Today's composting operation in Central Park along the East Drive at 105th Street is part of the nine-acre site that originally included Jacob Dyckman's Black Horse Tavern. It was bought by his brother-in-law Daniel McGowan in 1756 and remained in the McGowan family until it was sold in 1846.

Source: Sara Cedar Miller, *Composting Operation*. Courtesy of the Central Park Conservancy.

The tavern was large enough to hold thirty-three members of the Colonial Assembly for their session in 1752, when the politicians met for a month during a smallpox outbreak in the city and while the English City Hall was under repair. Ironically, the assembly passed two relevant acts on the control and taxation of alcohol during these sessions.[28] Each night after the evening session, assembly members from out of town were put up at a nearby farmhouse on 106th Street and Third Avenue, owned by Dyckman's brother-in-law, Benjamin Benson.

Having succeeded with the Black Horse, Jacob Dyckman hatched an even grander scheme. He planned to construct a bridge so the Kingsbridge Road could cross the Spuyten Duyvil creek to the Bronx, and he would open a second tavern on his family's property near the bridge. Dyckman resented the current bridge, called the King's Bridge. To cross it required paying a toll, the money from which lined the pockets of its owner, Frederick Philipse, a wealthy and loyal subject of the king. But even if Dyckman's actions were not politically motivated, he knew travelers would welcome a free bridge.[29] (The King's Bridge was paved and renamed Kingsbridge Avenue in the Bronx in 1916. Dyckman's Bridge, on the line of today's 225th Street, was buried beneath the railroad tracks just west of the present span in 1911–12.[30])

With his neighbors, Benjamin Palmer and John Vermilye Jr., Dyckman built a toll-free crossing to divert customers from Philipse's unpopular and costly bridge. Dyckman and Vermilye, the landowners on either end of the future span, put up the capital, which would be repaid by voluntary subscriptions. Just three years later, on January 2, 1759, the Free Bridge opened with great fanfare: "A fine fat ox roasted on the Green, and thousands from the city and the country . . . rejoiced greatly."[31]

To finance this venture, Dyckman put the Black Horse up for sale in March 1756. He suggested in his ad that it would be a perfect place for a "gentleman's seat," which is what they called a country estate. Eight days later the property was purchased by Benson family member Daniel McGowan. McGowan had married the widowed Catherine Benson Shourd, the sister of Adolph and Catalina.[32]

Daniel McGowan's heritage has been identified variously as either Scottish or Irish.[33] He was a successful "peddler" in New York, owned property downtown, and moved to Harlem around 1749, where records reveal he became an active member of the community.[34] But there the trail ends. He is still mentioned in the records in 1761, but at some date after that he was said to be lost at sea, and his wife, Catherine, and their son, Andrew, a teenager at the time, ran the tavern.

Female innkeepers were often widows who had inherited the business from their deceased husbands and needed the income to keep their families afloat. Like Metje Cornelis, Catherine came from a tight-knit and propertied family, and the tavern's income was merely one revenue source among others, which included profits from properties downtown, Harlem real estate, and revenue from the Benson family's mill on Harlem Creek at Third Avenue.

One story has an irate Catherine ranting, "The curse of the widow and orphans will follow you to your grave!"—a long-feared prophecy from the Old Testament directed at Jacob Dyckman, whom she claimed had deceived her about an encumbrance on her property. But according to her grandson, Samson Benson McGowan, the real target was the unrelated George Dyckman, who had cheated her family out of the *amount* of land, not the purchase price or an existing mortgage. Nonetheless, the site of Jacob's death may have also contributed to the conflation of two unrelated events: the issue of the property and Jacob's accident. We know from the obituary in the *Rivington Gazette* that "Jacob Dyckman fell from his horse at the bottom of a hill below Mrs. McGown's and fractured his skull in such a manner that his life is despaired of."[35]

Jacob Dyckman's death was caused by the steep, dangerous, and unlit Kingsbridge Road leading from the tavern down to McGowan's Pass. This spot was still dangerous almost a century and a half later, when "several fatal accidents occurred there and almost innumerable severe ones."[36] Today it remains a steep and winding descent from the composting operation at 105th Street into McGowan's Pass at 107th Street, though the original road was even more precarious.

In more ways than one, Jacob Dyckman died a broken man. The Free Bridge was an immediate success, but the hoped-for subscriptions from members of the community never came. Despite pleas to the legislature to raise the money, Dyckman and his partners were £500 in debt, and two years before his death, Jacob Dyckman was described as an "insolvent debtor."[37]

After the Revolutionary War, Daniel McGowan's son Andrew was thirty-nine years old, and he married his eighteen-year-old cousin Margaret, the only child of his uncle, Samson Benson Jr.[38] Their first meeting illustrates the importance of family intermarriage to the Dutch colonists. It was so important that it could bridge vast age differences. When Andrew was twenty-one, visiting his uncle's home in Harlem, he first met his cousin and future wife Margaret, at the time an infant crying "lustily" in her cradle. His aunt Mary Sickles Benson—the same age as Andrew—instructed him to rock the baby "and you shall have her for your wife."[39]

2.6 An 1814 detail of the McGowans' home is shown with its enlarged two wings, added in 1790, most likely to accommodate the growing family of Andrew and Margaret McGowan.

Source: John J. Holland (detail), *Fort Fish from Nutter's Battery*, New York City, 1814. Drawing: watercolor, black ink, and graphite with touches of gouache and scratching out on paper laid on heavier paper (together with 1889.14), overall: 10 x 23 1/2 in. (25.4 x 59.7 cm), accession number, 1889.15. New-York Historical Society.

Infant betrothals were popular among the higher classes of Dutch society, and some of these bonds were formed even "while the babies were lying in the cradle."[40]

In 1790, Andrew and Margaret McGowan tore down the old brick tavern and erected a larger frame house.[41] The family needed more space for their four children: Andrew Jr. and Samson Benson, who lived to old age, and Daniel and Catherine Maria, who died as young adults. Catherine Maria had married John P. Waldron in 1812 and died soon after.

Tensions existed between McGowan and Waldron, his son-in-law. In the New York Supreme Court case In re Waldron, 1816, we learn that Waldron had been unable to support his pregnant wife, who returned to the comfort of her prosperous and loving family. When she gave birth to Margaret Eliza Waldron in 1813, the infant's father did not visit his daughter at the McGowans' home, yet he attempted to gain custody of her three years later by motion for a writ of habeas corpus, or "illegal confinement." Lacking resources of his own, he testified that his mother would support them both. Judge Smith Thompson, however, decided that the child would remain in the custody of her maternal grandparents temporarily. Ultimately, the court decided, "in the best interests of the child," to let Waldron see his daughter at appropriate occasions, "taking it for granted that he will not attempt to take her away from the care and custody of her grandparents, except by the aid of some judicial proceeding."[42]

Wills, as much as marriages, reveal the insularity of Dutch colonial families, and Andrew's last will and testament of 1820 was the result of the Benson-McGowans's solidarity behind Margaret Eliza's future. In his will Andrew stipulated that his granddaughter Margaret Eliza would be supported by his estate and educated in the best manner, provided that she always be under the protection of his wife, Margaret, or, in the event of Margaret's death, in the custody of her three uncles. Otherwise she was to receive no financial assistance until Margaret and her three sons had died. McGowan also bought all of his deceased daughter's possessions from Waldron, which according to the law belonged to her husband.[43]

Andrew McGowan was not the only one concerned about Margaret Eliza's future. In her own will in 1830, Mary Sickles Benson passed over her own daughter, Margaret, and bequeathed everything to Margaret Eliza. Her will coincided with the marriage of the seventeen-year-old Margaret Eliza to thirty-six-year-old Isaac Adriance, a wealthy Harlem attorney.[44]

But Mary would make sure the Benson property went only to those with pure Benson blood. In this way, the Dutch families of New Amsterdam preserved their culture and their power. In the event that Margaret Eliza died before maturity, Mary ensured that the Benson property would pass instead to her McGowan grandsons—true Bensons—or, in the case of *their* demise, "the children who came from their bodies."[45] Mary appointed her daughter Margaret as an executrix of her estate but stipulated that the furniture and silver were to be divided between Margaret Eliza and her grandsons, or their genetic offspring. The only possession Mary left her own daughter was "an easy chair."

In the surviving portraits of the Benson-McGowans, we see something of their personalities. There is gravity and restraint in the bearing of these two women. The walls are bare, and the red fabric on Margaret's chair is the only color in either painting. Although the women seem elderly, particularly Margaret, their

2.7 Mary Sickles's marriage to Samson Benson Jr., intertwined two prosperous Harlem landowning families. Mary is the mother of Margaret Benson McGowan (right).

Source: Unidentified artist, *Mrs. Samson Benson, Jr. (1745–1835)* ca. 1825 (1918.14), oil on canvas, Overall: 30 × 25 in. (76.2 × 63.5 cm), New-York Historical Society.

2.8 John Megarey's humble 1837 portrait of Margaret McGowan belies her status as one of the largest and wealthiest landowners in Harlem.

Source: John Megarey, *Mrs. Andrew McGowan I (Margaret Ann Benson, 1766–1851)*, 1837 (1918.15), oil on canvas, overall 30 1/4 in. × 25 in. (76.8 × 63.5 cm), New-York Historical Society.

brown hair suggests that they may have been depicted closer to middle age. Their dress is plain, and their bonnets are the only elements that display attention to personal detail. Margaret's bonnet is frilly, likely made of silk or satin, the only sign she has any interest in personal possessions. Each woman carries a Bible, as if the painter caught them in a momentary break from their pious study. But their gestures and facial expressions speak volumes. Margaret is a closed book, while Mary is as open as her Bible, and her finger points to the specific verse she has just been reading. Margaret does not engage, she gazes somewhere off in the distance, while Mary gazes directly, and somewhat sternly, at the viewer. Mary seems in command. She too doesn't smile, but her face shows more expression. She looks right through us, the viewer.

While Mary left no property to her daughter, Margaret's father, Samson Benson Jr.—known as "Crying Sam" due to "a weakness of the eyes"—left Margaret a very rich woman.[46] She inherited land in Harlem village and the family homestead at Third Avenue and 106th Street and the surrounding area, everything in today's East Harlem from the East River to Madison Avenue. After Andrew's death in 1820, Margaret also inherited the McGowans' homestead in the prepark.[47]

The granddaughter Margaret Eliza lived a long life and carried on the Benson genes. Until her death in 1851, Margaret McGowan cared for her granddaughter and great grandchildren, as her husband had willed.[48]

Margaret's sons, Andrew and Samson, moved into the Benson family estate on 106th and Third Avenue. In April 1844, they advertised their old home for sale:

> That beautiful and healthy situation belonging to the estate of Andrew McGown, deceased, known as McGown's Pass, between Fifth and Sixth avenues and 103d and 107th streets, containing about nine acres of land well stocked with fruit and other trees. On the premises is a respectable dwelling house, two stories high, 4 rooms on a floor with suitable outbuildings. The view from the premises embraces Hurlgate, East and Harlem Rivers, and the islands in the same, and part of Long Island in the foreground. If not sold before the 29th day of May next, it will be offered for sale by public auction.[49]

The next year, in 1845, the house and land were sold for six thousand dollars to a possible relation named Thomas B. Odell. Two years later, Odell sold them for the same price to Sister Elizabeth Boyle, who transformed the property into the Motherhouse and school of the Roman Catholic Sisters of Charity of Mount St. Vincent. The sisters found the McGowan property in quite dilapidated condition, suggesting that it had been vacant or untended for quite some time.[50]

Thirty years later, Andrew Jr. sat for his portrait. It reveals a well-dressed and confident gentleman with a pleasant face. He clutches a walking stick topped with a richly carved silver knob, most often a symbol of wealth. In Mary Sickles Benson's will of 1830 she left her great grandson Andrew, the son of Samson B. McGowan, an inheritance as well as two hundred additional dollars "in consideration of his lameness." A half century later, an 1881 *New York Times* article mistakenly reported that Andrew Sr. was a "cripple."[51] The portrait calls to mind Renaissance paintings in which saints were depicted with the items of their martyrdom: Saint Catherine with her wheel, Saint Sebastian with arrows, and Saint Anthony wandering in the desert with his walking stick.

◆

The McGowans may have changed the name of their tavern from the Black Horse to McGowan's to reflect their new ownership in 1756, or the name may have evolved through popular use.[52] The family probably gave up their tavern business toward the start of the revolution, but a second tavern, named the Black Horse, was already established by the time of the British invasion of New York in September 1776. General Clinton confirmed the presence of "McGown's" and the "Black-Horse" in his description of the invasion. James Riker referred to the Black Horse Tavern "of Revolutionary notoriety." The "notoriety" probably referred to its role as the headquarters of British General Cornwallis during the Battle of Harlem Heights on September 16, 1776.[53]

2.9 James H. Wright's portrait of Andrew McGowan Jr., ca. 1840–1845, son of Andrew and Margaret, depicts a well-to-do gentleman whose silver-tipped walking stick may be a symbol of his wealth and elite status or the hint of a disability.

Source: James H. Wright, *Andrew McGowan II (1785–1870)*, ca. 1840–1845 (1918.16), oil on canvas, Overall: 30 × 25 in. (76.2 × 63.5 cm), New-York Historical Society.

After the war, other taverns sprang up in the area, as the fourteen-mile road still needed points of refreshment. Like ferries, rental property, carting licenses, and wharfage taxes, they were a rich source of income for the city. After the war, the number of taverns climbed annually. As Harlem grew, roads were laid, and at most crossroads, a tavern would open, most often in the proprietor's home.

In 1789 alone, more than three hundred tavern licenses were issued. Among the licensees was a man named John Leggett. Leggett probably took over the Black Horse and changed the name to reflect his ownership. It was located at an important intersection of a cross road, the Apthorp or Jauncey Lane, that connected the west side at Ninety-Third Street with the east side Kingsbridge Road near today's East Meadow at Ninety-Sixth Street. It was probably the Leggett tavern that burned down in 1809.[54]

Although some of the stricter New Amsterdam Sunday laws had been relaxed after the Dutch era, John Leggett's license still forbade gambling at any time, including "any Cock-fighting, Gaming or playing with Cards or Dice, or keep any Billiard-Table, or other Gaming-Table, or Shuffle-Board" within the building or on the surrounding property.

John C. Kimmel took advantage of the intersection of the Kingsbridge Road and Harlem Lane and opened a tavern in his home at about 107th to 108th Streets, today's Harlem Meer. Kimmel rented his house from Lawrence Benson, who had inherited much of the prepark land from his father Adolph. By 1802 it was referred to as the Benson-Kimmel Tavern.[55] Taverns were often the place to conduct official governmental or judicial business, and we know from a signed document that John Kimmel was witness to one of the most historically significant real estate transfers in the history of Central Park.

chapter 3
The Enslaved Bensons, 1754–1846

The Bensons and McGowans also enslaved people. In 1722, Captain Johannes Benson sold his Harlem village lots to his son, Samson Sr. The property included "a negro with a plough."[1] Samson's great grandson, Andrew McGowan, was listed in the U.S. Census as the enslaver of four people in 1790, none in 1800, and one in 1810.[2] Records show that in February 1805, McGowan's enslaved servant Jane gave birth to a daughter named Betty, and in January 1810, to a second daughter named Eliza.

Although Andrew McGowan owned property elsewhere, Jane most likely lived with the family working in their tavern and as a domestic in their home. She was therefore the only known enslaved person to have lived and worked in the prepark. Jane was manumitted by McGowan on June 14, 1814. Her daughters are not mentioned in the decree.[3]

On March 29, 1799, the New York State legislature passed the Gradual Manumission Act for the abolition of slavery in New York State. According to the act, any child born to an enslaved woman after July 4, 1799, was born free, but must serve their mother's enslaver until the age of twenty-eight if male or twenty-five if female. All enslaved person born before that date would not be freed until July 4, 1827.[4] According to historian Shane White, once the act passed, enslaved people could negotiate their freedom outright, either buy their freedom or, if they did not have the funds, agree to serve their former enslaver "without trouble for a fixed number of years," essentially as indentured servants.[5] From 1800 to 1810, the Dutch agricultural communities surrounding Manhattan retained their enslaved servants, though by 1820, less than 5 percent of the total Black population was still enslaved.[6] A few of the Harlem Bensons would hold out until the bitter end.

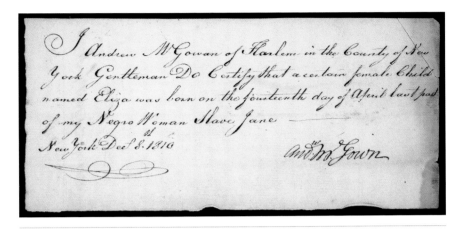

3.1 The birth certificate of Eliza, born April 14, 1810, the daughter of Jane, the enslaved servant of Andrew McGowan.

Source: Andrew McGowan, *Birth certificate of a certain female child named Eliza.* Slavery Collection, 1709–1864. Series VII, Legal Documents, Subseries 1, Birth Certificates, 1800–1818. nyhs_sc_b-05_f-19_078. New-York Historical Society.

Most Benson family members had more than one enslaved person. Margaret's father, Samson Benson Jr., enslaved six. When one of them, Tom, ran away, Benson published this announcement: "Runaway from Subscriber living in Harlem, on Sunday the 24th of September, a negro man named TOM, about 26 years of age, 5 feet 8 or 9 inches high, thin visage, very thick lips, and remarkably black: had on when he went away, a blue cloth jacket and breeches, homespun shirt and trowsers, and a half worn felt hat . . . thirty shillings reward. Samson Benson, jun."[7] Tom was found and returned to Benson. But a year later he ran away again. Thirty years later, in 1812, when many New Yorkers had freed their slaves, a second Tom, possibly the first Tom's son, also ran away. Benson again published a notice, which described him as about twenty years old and five foot nine. He also mentioned "nails in the soals of his shoes" and "small holes through his ears." "It is probable he will pretend that he is free," Benson wrote.[8]

The 1825 will of Adolph Benson's grandson, Samson Adolphus Benson, exemplified the complex relationship between enslavers and the enslaved. Benson gave instructions to free Sarah Combs after his death, and he provided her a "life estate," a house and three lots along the Old Harlem Road.[9] He did not, however, free another enslaved girl or woman, Charlotte, but bequeathed her to his daughter Susan, who, like many widows, was deemed incapable of managing a home without an enslaved person.[10]

LANAW BENSON

The wooded property that Susan Benson inherited from her father was connected to a four-acre triangular parcel, the western edge of which touched lightly on the prepark perimeter from 109th Street to 110th Street and Fifth Avenue. The majority of the tract stretched east to what is now Madison Avenue and north to 113th Street. In 1897, a portion of that prepark parcel became a traffic circle, and in 1995 it was named Duke Ellington Circle.[11] That tract may have been small—about the size of the nearby Conservatory Garden's north and central gardens combined—but its significance to the history of Central Park and New York City is immense.

On June 6, 1793, Harlem landowner David Waldron sold the triangular parcel for £18 to Lanaw Benson, a Black woman, making her the first African American

3.2 The perimeter of Central Park between 109th and 110th Street and Duke Ellington Circle was once the property of the formerly enslaved Lanaw Benson.

Source: Sara Cedar Miller, *Perimeter, 109th to 110th Street and Duke Ellington Circle.* Courtesy of the Central Park Conservancy.

3.3 Duke Ellington Circle was once the property of Lanaw Benson, the formerly enslaved by the Benson and Waldron families.

Source: Sara Cedar Miller, *Duke Ellington Circle.* Courtesy of the Central Park Conservancy.

to own land in the prepark.[12] The name Lanaw was likely a reference to her African homeland in the Shai Hills region of greater Accra, today the capital of Ghana.[13] Her former property now encompasses the African Center, a cultural hub for African exhibits and programs that faces Central Park on Fifth Avenue at 109th Street.[14]

What is more mysterious, however, is Lanaw's last name—Benson—and how she acquired it in the eighteenth century. In Harlem, according to existing documents, there was only one very large Benson family, and not one of them was Black or would have married a Black person or adopted a Black child. Most likely, she was a former enslaved servant whose enslavers gave her their name as a way to claim their property. At some point, she was probably sold or bequeathed to David Waldron, who set her free and sold her the small tract of land. As historian Eric Foner has noted, "Former slaves' ideas of freedom, like those of rural people throughout the world, were directly related to land ownership."[15]

Jill Lepore's "The Tightening Vise" discusses the "Act for preventing, Suppressing and punishing the Conspiracy and Insurrection of Negroes and Other

Slaves." The law, passed by New York State in 1712, was a reaction to a violent revolt by enslaved people in New York City; among other restrictions, it forbade free Blacks from owning or inheriting houses or land. The punitive restriction was only lifted in 1809, sixteen years after Lanaw had purchased her property from David Waldron.[16] How could that be?

A rereading of the 1793 official deed from David Waldron to Lanaw Benson confirms that Lanaw was "the sole and lawful Owner and proprietor of the said Tract or Parcel of Land and premises."[17] The deed was not filed with the city until 1799, when, with tavern keeper John Leggett as a witness, Lanaw divided her four-acre lot and sold most of it, including the prepark sliver along the creek, to John Rankin for £221, more than eleven times what she had paid for it.[18] Why would Rankin pay so much for such a small, remote, and unimproved piece of ground?

John Rankin, a well-to-do Scottish grocer, died only ten months after he purchased Lanaw's property. He left his real estate holdings to his childless widow, Elizabeth. Four years later she bequeathed this piece to her niece Margaret Rankin, the daughter of her husband's wealthy brother Henry. Margaret Rankin Gosman held on to the land for the next three decades, until it wound up, like much of the area, in the hands of speculator Archibald Watt.[19] But the question still remains: Why would John Rankin have purchased Lanaw's property in the first place?

Again, the answer can be found in Lepore's article. The 1712 law further mandated a stiff £200 payment to the government in order to manumit, or set an enslaved person free, and an additional £20 annuity to the freed individual to ensure that he or she would not be a burden on the government.[20] As Lepore notes, "Such a sizeable financial penalty made manumission effectively impossible."[21] But not for Lanaw Benson.

John Rankin had paid £221 to Lanaw to meet the necessary obligations for her manumission. Most likely, Lanaw bought her freedom by turning the £200 over to the government. In the deal with Rankin, Lanaw also gained a £20 annuity and retained the three-quarter-acre house and lot that she now owned clear and free.[22]

In 1785, the state legislature had passed an act negating the exorbitant manumission fee, as long as a manumitted person passed an examination and proved he or she had "sufficient ability" to provide for themselves. But this new ruling applied *only* to young and middle-aged Individuals between the ages of twenty-one and fifty. When an enslaved person was older, the stiff fines were still in place to ensure no burdensome cost to the city.[23] Given Lanaw's long history of bondage, she would have been over fifty years old and therefore unable to attain her freedom without paying.

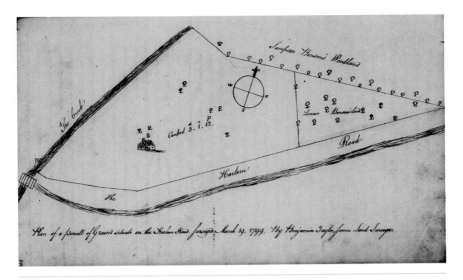

3.4 This diagram appears in the deed from formerly enslaved Lanaw Benson to grocer John Rankin in 1799. The transfer of property financed her manumission. She cleverly divided the property into two sections. The larger one, which included a part of the future Central Park, was sold to Rankin. She retained the smaller triangular tract for herself and moved the house depicted in the deed to her wooded property.

Source: "Plan of a Parcel of Ground Situate on the Harlem Road. Surveyed March 19, 1799, by Benjamin Taylor, Land Surveyor." Liber 56 Page 366.

The last pieces of the puzzle are the motivations behind the real estate and manumission transactions among David Waldron, John Rankin, and Lanaw Benson. In both the 1790 and 1800 U.S. Censuses, David Waldron enslaved five people. We know John Rankin was an enslaver from his wife's will.[24]

No record has come to light of a relationship between David Waldron and John Rankin, but there is a possible explanation for both the conveyance and the manumission. Perhaps Waldron was either unable or unwilling to pay the stiff manumission fee and annuity, making it impossible for Lanaw to either gain her freedom or own property. But Lanaw was probably not a victim passively waiting to have freedom bestowed on her by either her enslaver or legislation. Instead, she took charge of her fate and became the mastermind behind the scheme. White notes that many advertisements for slave sales were at "the instigation of the slaves themselves." It was not uncommon for an enslaver in New York to give their enslaved servant a travel pass to find him or herself a new enslaver, who would agree to buy them and set them free.

Often this third party advanced the enslaver the money, in this case, the £200 from Rankin to Lanaw to Waldron to buy her freedom and the additional £20 for the required annuity.[25] At the same time, the freed Lanaw repaid Rankin not by years of indentured servitude but by selling him most of her property, while retaining a permanent home for herself.[26] For Lanaw, the manumission, annual support provision, and real estate transaction all became one, her means to acquire a home, land, and the money to purchase her freedom.[27]

Perhaps we will never know for certain, but we do know that not only was Lanaw Benson the first Black person to own property in the prepark, but the land that she sold to John Rankin remains the only known property in the future park, possibly all of New York City, that was purchased to set an enslaved person free.

Lanaw Benson would live on her remaining tract—three quarters of an acre lying midway between Fifth and Madison Avenues at 111th to 113th Streets. The property itself offers a glimpse into the world of bonded and freed Blacks, their white enslavers, and their rights.

Though John Rankin was identified as the person responsible for payment of the 1799 property tax assessment, Lanaw's small triangular parcel was billed to "Free Sam" and John Combs, who were named as the parties to be taxed.[28] Further research led from John Combs to the 1814 last will and testament of Ellenor Waldron, which explained both the history of Lanaw's land and the emotional bonds that existed between husbands and wives and parents and children despite the chokehold of slavery that kept them physically apart.

The logical assumption was a family relationship between Ellenor Waldron and David Waldron, but in her will, Ellenor described herself as "formerly the property of Jannike Benson of the Town of Harlem" and the wife of Sam Waldron, "now or late the property of Lewis Morris" of Morrisania.[29]

Jannike was not a common Dutch woman's name, but Tanneke, Jannetie, and Jannetje were popular names, all of which translate to "Janet" in English. There was no Jannike Benson in the records, but Tanneke Waldron was married to Johannes Benson, the oldest brother of Adolph, Benjamin, Catherine, and Catalina.[30]

Adolph Benson's first will was written in 1754, forty-eight years before his death, and was not his final recorded will of 1802. In this first will, Adolph "assigns" to his deceased brother's widow Tanneke "one Negroe Wench Named Len and her Child." Nineteen years later, Tanneke's will bequeathed "my Negro Woman Lane and Children" to her sister-in-law Elizabeth Waldron. "But," Tanneke stipulated, "in case my Negro Woman Lane chuses not to stay with her then I give her liberty to sell her or to buy herself free if they can so agree for a reasonable Sum."[31] It seems almost certain that Lanaw, Len, and Lane were the same person, and that she and her children were first enslaved by Adolph Benson, then Tanneke Benson, and lastly Elizabeth Waldron. Lanaw was probably next bequeathed to Elizabeth's daughter Cornelia, who married her cousin David Waldron, the one who granted the land to Lanaw in 1793.[32]

Knowing she was most likely enslaved by David Waldron, it raises the question of why she was singled out from the others. Perhaps Lanaw was a beloved servant who became especially close to the families she served. Tanneke's will seems to lean in that direction. But given the history of relations between female slaves and their male enslavers, it is also possible that Lanaw was forced into a sexual relationship with one of her former enslavers, possibly Adolph Benson. We may never know the answers.

Family members often transferred land to each other without a deed, and although no conveyance from Lanaw Benson to Ellenor Waldron has been recorded, we can conclude that Ellenor, "formerly the property of Jannike Benson," was Lanaw's daughter. By stating in her will that she had been Jannike's property,

Lanaw Benson family tree

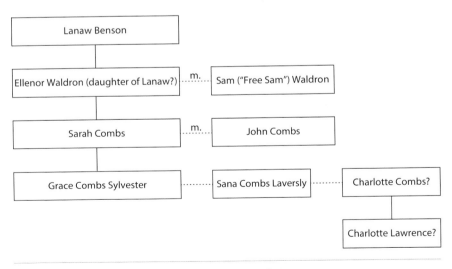

3.5 Lanaw Benson Family Tree.

Author based on information from the "Last Will and Testament of Ellenor Waldron," *Probate*, L52, P185, 1815; conveyance from Sarah Combs to Charlotte Lawrence, L480, P134, 1846.

she implied that Tanneke Benson had been her last and final enslaver. It is possible that Lanaw, before Tanneke's death in 1780, struck a deal to manumit her daughter rather than herself. She herself would not be free for twenty-six more years.

In her will, Ellenor left Sam the use of her property with instructions to sell it after his death, with the proceeds to be divided between their son-in-law, John Combs, and their two married granddaughters. John Combs and his daughter,

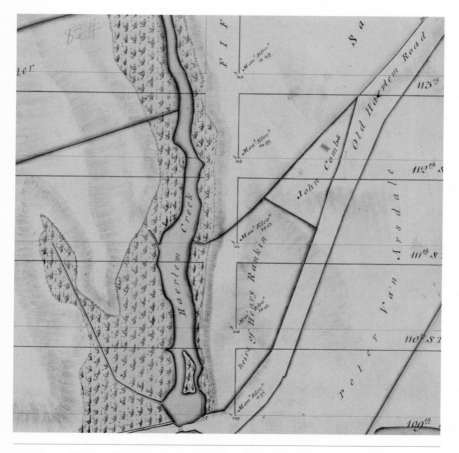

3.6 Lanaw Benson's former property that lay on the eastern edge of the future Central Park was depicted in a map by surveyor John Randel ca. 1820. At the time, her former triangular three quarters of an acre tract belonged to John Combs, the husband of Sarah Combs, Lanaw's purported granddaughter, who became the owner only after the death of her enslaver, Sampson Adolphus Benson in 1825.

Source: The property of John Combs and Heirs of Henry Rankin (detail), Randel Farm Map No. 58, Office of the Manhattan Borough President, Topographical Division.

Grace Sylvester, lived with Ellenor and Sam as "Tenants in Common" until the Waldrons' deaths in 1815. That year Grace Sylvester sold her share of her grandmother's property to her father, John Combs, for $50.[33]

John Combs was the husband of Sarah Combs, enslaved by Samson Adolphus Benson freed only after Benson's death in 1825. When Ellenor made her will in 1814, her daughter Sarah would be in bondage for another eleven years. She therefore could not inherit her mother's property.

After John Combs's death, Sarah Combs, now free, kept the property until 1846, when she sold it to Charlotte Lawrence for two hundred dollars. Charlotte must have been a relation, as the deed was given "in consideration of love and affection." It is conceivable that Charlotte was either formerly enslaved servant of Susan Benson or possibly either Charlotte's daughter or the Combs's third daughter. In an 1851 city directory Charlotte Lawrence is listed as a Black laundress living on Mercer Street, but in 1846 she may have been living in the Combs's house.[34]

The question still remains: Why did Lanaw transfer her property to Sam Waldron and John Combs immediately after legally acquiring it from Rankin? The answer is found in the 1777 New York State Constitution, which allowed any man, Black or white, to vote in assembly elections so long as they paid taxes and owned a certain amount of land. The requisite amount of land must be valued at £20.[35] The Constitution, written during the early years of the Revolutionary War, championed political rights as the essence of the struggle for independence. All stable and responsible Black or white citizens—defined at the time as those owning or leasing expensive property—were rewarded with a vote (though historian Graham Hodges surmises that the Black vote was "granted inadvertently").[36] Two years before Combs officially acquired his property with a recorded deed, the legislature began to restrict and complicate registration and voting procedures. Nonetheless, with the deed to Benson's property, John Combs would have been able to vote in assembly elections, a right not afforded to Lanaw Benson, Ellenor Waldron, Sarah Combs, or Susan Benson.[37]

It would be more than two decades before a group of African Americans owned a much more substantial amount of property in the prepark, known as Seneca Village. But Lanaw's modest sliver holds a significant and unique place in Central Park's history as the first Black-owned land in the prepark.

chapter 4

The War at McGowan's Pass, 1776–1784

To flee or not to flee? That was the question on George Washington's mind during the first week of September 1776. He and fourteen thousand troops were all but trapped on Manhattan Island, and the British were definitely coming.

It had been a harrowing year and a half since the battles of Lexington and Concord had begun the American colonial revolt against the British. The minutemen and New England troops had proven their strength and cunning against the redcoats, but when the professional British army and navy sailed into New York, the Americans were wildly outsmarted. The American officers, including Washington, had never fought in such a complex theater of battle. In the last days of August, the rebel army suffered an embarrassing defeat at the Battle of Long Island. The British had outwitted the inexperienced officers, cornering their troops near Brooklyn Heights and backing them up against the East River.

In desperation and with little to lose, Washington hatched a tactically brilliant scheme. Under cover of darkness on the night of August 29, he and his officers oversaw the secret and silent retreat of more than nine thousand soldiers in hundreds of small boats and watercraft.

Silence was critical. The men were ordered not to cough, and they wrapped their oars in cloth to muffle the sound of rowing. It was raining heavily, and turbulent currents made the one-mile journey from Brooklyn to the shore of Manhattan feel like an ocean crossing. But at sunrise, with the cover of a "providential fog," the last of the troops landed on Manhattan Island.

It was a miraculous maneuver. But now these exhausted rebels were trapped on an even smaller, more vulnerable island, surrounded by the greatest naval force in the world.[1] The price of freedom seemed impossibly high, and many soldiers were

4.1 Charles Willson Peale painted his portrait of General Washington after the Battle of Trenton in 1780, four years after he and his generals decided to evacuate New York City during the council of war meeting held at McGowan's tavern.

Source: Charles Willson Peale, *George Washington*, ca. 1779–81. Metropolitan Museum of Art, Gift of Collis P. Huntington, 1897, accession number 97.33.

prepared to desert, resigned to remain the subjects of a monarchy they despised if it saved their lives.

Both the British and the Americans had their eyes on New York. Both believed it was the key to the war's outcome. Dominion over it meant control of the Hudson River corridor, which stretched from the Atlantic Ocean to Canada. Manhattan was the strategic lynchpin of the thirteen rebellious colonies; if the British captured it, they would sever the continuous flow of communication, troops, and supplies from New England to Georgia. It would spell certain victory. The Marquis de Lafayette called New York the "pivot" of operations.[2]

In their attempt to intimidate the inexperienced Americans, the British overwhelmed New York with 427 ships, 34,000 seamen and soldiers—including thousands of Hessian mercenaries—1,200 cannons, and an armada transporting arms, horses, and provisions.[3] On September 2, an indecisive Washington wrote to John Hancock, president of the Continental Congress in Philadelphia, asking whether to abandon New York, and, if so, whether to leave the city intact or burn it to the ground, depriving the British of comfortable winter quarters.[4]

The next day, Washington received resolutions from Congress advising him to leave the city intact, even if it meant losing their most important stronghold. The officers in trenches knew that New York City was indefensible, but miles away in Philadelphia, Congress's self-styled experts debated the issues on plush couches and assumed that even if the city was evacuated, they had "no doubt of being able to recover the same, tho the Enemy should for a time obtain Possession of it."[5]

Washington was driven by eighteenth-century codes of honor, "a reputation with a moral dimension and an elite cast . . . that encompassed qualities like bravery, self-command, and integrity" as the core requirements for leadership. In this difficult situation, he was bound by an ethical and psychological commitment to persevere—even die—rather than bear the dishonor of retreat.[6]

His most trusted commanders, especially Brigadier-General Nathanael Greene, begged him to abandon the city and lead the army to more defensible ground. Greene was ill, near death, and his absence on Long Island had probably cost the rebels a victory. But his convalescence gave him time to reflect. On September 5, he wrote to Washington, strongly urging "a General and Speedy Retreat." He wanted to torch the city and suburbs to deprive the British of "sufficient place to barracks all their troops." He pleaded that Washington "call a General Council upon that question and take every General Officers opinion upon it."[7]

On September 7, Washington took Greene's advice and convened a council of war meeting at his headquarters at the Mortier mansion, which would have been located at the current intersection of Varick and Charlton Streets in the West Village. Although these proceedings were confidential, Washington's letter to Hancock the following day summarized them: abandoning New York was "considered & debated with great Solemnity & Attention," and most agreed that evacuation would "dispirit the troops and enfeeble our cause." Washington's council interpreted Congress's message to mean that they should stay and fight for New York.[8]

To hold New York, the officers decided to divide troops and position them at three locations: nine thousand stationed under General William Heath at King's Bridge at the northern tip of Manhattan, where the British were thought most likely to attack; five thousand under General Israel Putnam in southern Manhattan; and the newest recruits along the East River, including five hundred at Kip's Bay in today's midtown, which they considered an unlikely target.

On September 11, the British made a last-ditch effort at civilized negotiations. They arranged for an intimate peace conference in the mansion of the loyalist Billopp family on Staten Island, the war headquarters of British Admiral Lord Richard Howe. An America delegation joined him: Benjamin Franklin, John Adams, and Edward Rutledge.

Today the Billopp mansion is known as the Conference House, a national and New York City historic landmark. It is of interest to our story mainly because thirty years after the conference, the loyalists Sarah Billopp Seaman and her husband, Henry Seaman, bought land at three prepark locations that would become Manhattan's Grand Army Plaza at Fifth Avenue and Fifty-Ninth Street, the Ramble shoreline, and a portion of Sheep Meadow and the nearby beach volleyball courts.[9]

Despite his military authority, Howe could only receive his guests as private citizens. British policy dictated that Congress be treated as an illegal body. Rebels against the king were not recognized as a legitimate government.[10]

The conference lasted three hours. Their hosts invited them to a meal of "good claret, good bread, cold ham, tongues and mutton." But despite the pleasantries, both sides stood firm on the subject of independence. The British would not concede to America's demands for self-government, and the three delegates were instructed by Congress to leave if the British would not recognize their absolute autonomy.[11] As they sailed from Staten Island, it was clear to all that blood would soon be shed.

THE SECOND COUNCIL OF WAR

While the four gentlemen were dining at the Billopp estate, seven of Washington's generals were lobbying him for a second council of war. They implored him to reconsider the decision to stay and defend the island despite the "bad policy" and "breach of common forms" of military protocol that would set a precedent to alter an earlier position. They added,

> What we have to offer to Your Excellency in general Council proceeds not from Fear of personal Danger nor the Expectation of deriving to ourselves any Honor & Reputation from a Change of Measures—it proceeds from a Love of our Country and a determined Resolution to urge the best & wisest Measures: & finally to execute if possible even erroneous Ones which on cool dispassionate Reconsideration cannot be avoided.[12]

Washington agreed to meet, and on September 12, 1776, the second war council convened. Washington's account places the second council at General Alexander McDougall's headquarters, a site that was only revealed in a footnote by the editors of *The Papers of George Washington*, though they gave no source for the information: "After the Battle of Long Island, Alexander McDougall's brigade headquarters apparently was at Mrs. Catharine Benson McGown's house or tavern, located a short distance south of the village of Harlem on the post road that ran between King's Bridge and New York City."[13]

In his biography of Alexander McDougall, historian Roger J. Champagne also mentions Mrs. McGowan's tavern when discussing the council of war, though he too cites no source. The answer was only revealed by jumping ahead six years. In 1782, McDougall was stationed near West Point. In what he would later describe as "a social hour," he let slip to a group of fellow officers that the council had taken place at Mrs. McGowan's and described to them the details of this highly confidential meeting.[14]

Washington and thirteen of his generals were present to debate the evacuation of the island. Ten of them voted to evacuate, leaving eight thousand men "for the Defence of Mount Washington & its Dependencies."[15] Only three generals—William Heath, George Clinton, and Joseph Spenser—held fast to their original decision to stay and defend the city. In his memoirs, Heath was elusive on this point, writing only that a "former decision to defend the city was rescinded with three dissentients."[16]

4.2 Major General Alexander McDougall despised his superior officer General William Heath for his pomposity and his unwillingness to support the evacuation of New York during the September 12 council of war meeting.

Source: John Ramage, *General Alexander McDougall* (1732–1786), c. 1785. Miniature on ivory, 1 5/8 x 1 1/4 inches, 1962.49, New-York Historical Society.

4.3 Major General William Heath was McDougall's superior officer while they were both stationed at West Point in 1782. Heath issued a court-martial to McDougall charging him revealing confidential military secrets during the council of war at McGowan's tavern.

Source: "Hon. William Heath." The Miriam and Ira D. Wallach Division of Art, Prints and Photographs: Print Collection, The New York Public Library, New York Public Library Digital Collections, https://digitalcollections.nypl.org/items/510d47da-2eb3-a3d9-e040-e00a18064a99.

It is worth pausing here to note that McDougall despised Heath. While they were stationed at West Point in 1782, Heath was McDougall's superior officer, and they were in constant dispute over military protocol and administrative issues. In a letter to Washington, McDougall complained about Heath's "unmilitary Neglects, Inhumanity and Tyranny," which only exacerbated his contempt for Heath's opposition during the council of war vote.[17]

Then on January 7, 1782, at a gathering of fellow field officers—possibly with the aid of strong drink—McDougall revealed the confidential votes cast on the question of evacuating Manhattan during the council of war meeting. "None were opposed to it," he revealed, "but a fool, a knave, and an obstinate honest man, and that General Heath was the knave."[18] McDougall hated Heath's hypocrisy and pompous formality. To McDougall, Heath was a hypocrite who "carried two faces," knowing that the city was indefensible and yet voting to defend it on the grounds that that would be more favorable to New Yorkers who wanted to be protected from a British attack. The enraged McDougall claimed that Heath's behavior toward him was openly wicked. "In short, he has treated me like a Bastard."[19]

Two days later Heath discharged McDougall from his command, placed him under arrest—though with freedom to come and go—and charged him with seven counts of misconduct "unbecoming an officer" and revealing publicly the confidential details of the council of war.

Washington agreed with Heath about the offense and wrote to McDougall: "It would be a matter of great concern to me that a practice should prevail of publishing to the world the opinions which are given in Councils of War, as I have always considered the transactions on such occasions to be under the inviolable sanction of secrecy and honor."[20] Washington did not receive this breach of conduct well. "I am made extremely unhappy," he continued, "by finding that the difference between General Heath and yourself has proceeded to so disagreeable a height." But despite his anger and frustration *and* preoccupation with fighting a war, Washington still displayed dispassion and fairness: "Had I had any previous notice of this disagreeable affair, I should, as the common Friend of both and for the reputation of the service, have offered my private interposition: But matters, when the thing came to my knowledge, had gone too far to be determined in any other line than that in which they now are."[21]

It took six months after the initial blow-up for the trial to convene, but not before the volatile McDougall had made another enemy in Major General William Alexander, also known as Lord Sterling, whom he opposed as the president of his court-martial at Fishkill. In the end Lord Sterling was dismissed, though not before "rumours" of a duel spread in military circles.[22] McDougall was acquitted of six of the seven charges. Of the seventh, revealing confidential military secrets at McGowan's tavern, he was found guilty, given a reprimand—basically a slap on the wrist—and allowed to stay at West Point and recuperate from the strain of it all.

But McDougall could not let it go. In a long letter with supporting documents to Washington, he attempted to exonerate himself by explaining how and why the publicizing of secret military information was unworthy of a court-martial. He also announced that he was bringing countercharges against Heath.[23] A week later McDougall, still obsessing about the affair, notified the commander-in-chief that he would not be following through on the charges due *only* to external forces. The French army was joining the war effort, and McDougall was mindful that the "altercation" would "lessen us in their opinion." Nonetheless, he grabbed the final word, declaring that he held the "Honor to be with great truth."[24]

There are, to date, no known military works by the Americans built in preparation for a possible land attack near McGowan's Pass, but Washington had had troops stationed there since the spring. On at least one occasion, May 21, Andrew McGowan supplied food to the American troops, and New York State charged the fledgling U.S. government a little more than five pounds to be repaid to McGowan "for subsistence furnished to the American army."[25] Although certain of a shoreline attack, nonetheless, Washington was wise enough to take precautions to protect the inland road, especially at its most strategic point, and holding the second council of war there on September 12 was a reasonable choice.[26]

ATTACK

On September 14, two days after the council of war, Washington moved his headquarters far up the island to the Morris House, at today's Broadway and 160th Street, and informed the Continental Congress, "I fear we shall not effect the whole [retreat] before we meet with some Interruption. I fully expected that an Attack somewhere, would have been made last night. In that I was disappointed, and happy shall I be if my apprehensions of one to-night or in a day or two are not confirmed by the event."[27]

The "interruption" that Washington feared occurred the next morning at Kip's Bay, at today's Thirty-Fourth Street and the East River, where Washington had stationed Captain William Douglas's Connecticut militia, fewer than nine hundred of the least experienced and worst equipped of the American soldiers. It was the least fortified and least anticipated target. At eleven o'clock in the morning, there began an hour-long barrage, which rebel forces for miles around could hear. Five British warships had sailed up the East River and anchored about two hundred yards offshore. They trained more than eighty cannons directly at the few hundred ill-prepared "American hayseeds" huddled in shoreline ditches, poor substitutes for defensive structures. There weren't enough muskets, so many of the novice militiamen were issued only spears to defend themselves. From the warships, more than four thousand British and Hessian sharpshooters were rowing toward the island in smaller boats. Most of the rebels fled; those who were too petrified to move were killed even as they tried to surrender.[28]

Washington heard the cannons from his uptown headquarters, and he raced down the Kingsbridge Road, through the pass, and past the McGowans' house to his troops. He got as far as Murray Hill, where he found himself surrounded by a swarm of deserters, chaos and disorder everywhere. According to eyewitness Colonel Smallwood of Maryland, "the Connecticut troops—wretches who however strange it may appear, from the Brigadier-General to the private sentinel, were caned and whipped by the Generals Washington, Putnam, and Mifflin, but even this indignity had no weight, they could not be brought to stand one shot." From other reports, Washington, known to be somewhat cool and reserved even under pressure, "struck several officers [with his riding crop] in their flight, and throwing his hat to the ground, exclaimed 'Are these the men with which I am to defend America?' or by another account, 'Good God, have I got such Troops as these?'"[29]

While rounding up his soldiers, the general came within fifty yards of the British infantry, and only his aide Joseph Reed saved him from possible death by grabbing the reins of his horse and leading him out of harm's way, Washington "cursing all the way."[30]

Washington funneled his traumatized men westward across the fields and woods of the Forty-Second Street cross road to the Bloomingdale Road—now Times Square—and headed north to the security of Harlem Heights above 125th Street. After the attack and a brief interlude at Incklenberg (now Murray Hill), the British marched north up the Kingsbridge Road. But they were unaware the enemy were marching north too, parallel to them across a divide that now constitutes much of Central Park.[31] Between three and four thousand Americans marched up the Bloomingdale Road. One colonel recalled it like this:

Our soldiers, excessively fatigued by the sultry march of the day, their clothes wet by a severe shower of rain that succeeded towards the evening, their blood chilled by the cold wind that produced a sudden change in the temperature of the air, and their hearts sunk within them by the loss of their baggage, artillery, and works, in which they had been taught to put great confidence, lay upon their arms, covered only by the clouds of an uncomfortable sky.[32]

A few days before the attack, the generals had deemed a water invasion the greater threat, and McDougall's brigade was reassigned to the fortifications below at Hellgate, on the East River at 106th Street. But immediately after the attack, Washington knew that troops were still needed near the pass. He ordered Colonel William Smallwood and his Maryland regiment "to cover the retreat and to defend the baggage" by taking "possession of an advantageous eminence near the enemy, upon the main road." Smallwood and his troops guarded the intersection of the three roads: the Kingsbridge Road, the Harlem Road, and the New Bloomingdale Cross Road, also known as Apthorp's Lane, between today's East Ninety-Second and East Ninety-Sixth Streets and Fifth Avenue, to ensure the safe passage of the Americans less than a mile away. Smallwood later wrote, "We remained under arms the best part of the day," until one of the enemy's columns "endeavored to flank and surround us."[33] When ordered to retreat, the Marylanders were the last American soldiers to walk freely through the pass. Only weeks later, more than two thousand would return to the city as British prisoners after the capitulation at Fort Washington in northern Manhattan.[34]

After Smallwood's retreat, the British took the Kingsbridge Road near the Black Horse tavern at Ninety-Sixth Street, where, it is believed, General William Howe "took post for the night with his right at McGowan's house, or Pass, about 7½ miles from New York."[35]

British fusilier Frederick Mackenzie described McGowan's Pass as the place "where a few troops might stop an army." And that is just what happened. British troops created a north-facing defensive wall stretching from east to west across the island, from today's Eighty-Ninth Street and the East River to Ninety-Sixth Street and the Hudson River. They stayed there for the next seven years. During the longest continuous occupation of the entire war, New York would become the second largest British city in the world, surpassed only by London.

AT MCGOWAN'S PASS

In the following weeks, the British soldiers and Hessian mercenaries erected a line of fortifications from McGowan's Pass westward to the Hudson River. Close inspection of a drawing made in October 1777 by British artist Archibald Robertson proves that British fortifications were built on the high bluffs that overlook the Harlem plains.[36]

4.4 British artist Archibald Robertson sketched the only known image of the upper park and environs during the Revolutionary War. In a detail of his *View of Morisinia, Haarlem, Montressor's & Buchannan's Island, with part of the sound, taken from our lines near McGowan's House. 10 Octr. 1777*, the artist shows a view near today's Great Hill that reveals the presence of British fortifications on the high points of the prepark that overlooked the flat Harlem Plains. The two structures on the left were advanced posts, situated on the north side of today's Harlem Meer. We can also see a small plank bridge crossing the swamp and the walled promontories on what were repurposed as Nutter's Battery, center, and Fort Clinton, right, in the War of 1812.

Source: "View of Morisinia, Haarlem, Montressor's & Buchannan's Islands, with part of the sound, taken from our lines near McGowan's House. 10 Octr. 1777." Spencer Collection, The New York Public Library, New York Public Library Digital Collections, https://digitalcollections.nypl.org/items/beof6d75-d1d4-1529-e040-e00a18065909.

On September 21, the British planned for a working party of four hundred men to march to McGowan's house, most likely to begin the construction of the fortifications that became known to us in the War of 1812 as Nutter's Battery and Fort Clinton. By September 25, that number was reduced to one hundred men, who were stationed there until further orders.[37] Throughout the war the area was occupied mainly by Hessians. The heaviest occupation came in 1782, when nearly ten thousand troops were encamped in the area in September and October, under threat of an invasion from the Continental Army, and more than a thousand troops continued to stay there into the following year.[38]

We know the location of a prepark cantonment—a military garrison made of huts—because much of it was unearthed during the construction of the Great Hill in 1864. High on the crest of the hill at West 106th Street, on the northern slope, park construction workers discovered sixteen distinct traces of a military camp eight feet below ground. Each was "about eight feet square of compactly trodden earth," with "rude fireplaces and bits of strap iron fashioned into pot-hooks, and shot and bayonets."[39]

Like other cantonments in the New York area, the huts on the Great Hill were built into a slope, so that earth on three sides could protect the structure from the harsh winter elements. But whereas most of the other sites, in Brooklyn, Queens, and the Dyckman farm in upper Manhattan's Inwood Hill, faced south to take advantage of the sun's warmth, the prepark encampment faced north, making the huts damper, darker, and colder for the soldiers.

4.5 Based on archeological findings by his contemporaries Reginald Pelham Bolton and William Calver, artist John Ward Dunsmore created the 1915 painting of the British Winter Cantonment on Inwood Hill in upper Manhattan, a similar encampment to the one that would have been on the Great Hill, where relics from the war were discovered during construction of the park.

Source: John Ward Dunsmore, *Hut Camp of the 17th Regiment of Foot, Inwood Hill, New York City* (Dyckman Farm, 1915, oil on academy board, 16 x 24 inches); negative 2377 (broken glass), 1889.28, New-York Historical Society.

4.6 Nineteenth-century visitors to the Ravine in the park used a communal ladle to refresh themselves with a draught of fresh water from the spring or "run" known to the Dutch as a *fonteyn*, an old Dutch word meaning "spring" or "brook." These local waters would have sustained the Hessian and British soldiers during their seven-year encampment in the area.

Source: James Reuel Smith, *Unidentified girl drinking at Montaigne's Spring, McGowan's Pass, Central Park, New York City, July 23, 1898*. Photograph. 5 x 7 in. (nyhs_PR062_b-01_f-02_011_H-100), New-York Historical Society.

The north slope of today's Great Hill may have been chosen because it offered clear views of advancing enemy troops coming down the Kingsbridge Road to the pass or advancing on the East and Hudson Rivers. Early twentieth-century archeologist Reginald Bolton noted that available water was critical to these campsites, and we know that several natural springs, Montagne's *fonteyn* and rivulet, and another spring near Eighth Avenue and 109th Street were readily available on the north and south sides of the Great Hill.[40]

Throughout the takeover of Manhattan, rebel forces were constantly sneaking onto Manhattan Island and attacking British forces. British commander

Frederick Mackenzie kept a diary in which he reported one such guerilla attack on October 16, 1776:

> Lieutenant Bristow of the 16th Dragoons, going forward yesterday evening to the advanced post in front of McGowan's to satisfy his curiosity, was fired [on] by some lurking Rebels and wounded in the leg by a Musket ball. One of the Sentries was wounded in the leg also by a BuckShot . . . Lord Percy, [the commanding British general, living in the McGowan homestead] immediately ordered . . . 2 Howitzer shells to be fired at their Guard.

He later reported that a deserter informed them that they had killed one man by a shell.[41]

John Charles Philipp von Krafft, one of the Hessians frequently stationed at the pass, kept a journal from 1776 to 1784. He chronicled the war's brutality and daily hardships but also his boredom, petty frustrations, and the occasional stolen pleasures. One of these brutalities was the punishment for desertion. As von Krafft reported, no sooner had his unit set up camp at a meadow—probably today's North Meadow—on June 22, 1778, near the second Black Horse tavern, when an English deserter was caught by the English Royalists. He was "hanged on a tree by the road which caused a dreadful uproar because the hanged man had many still bleeding wounds."[42]

Von Krafft witnessed human violence during the course of the war, but he was also a victim of a series of environmental disasters that plagued both sides. The severe weather in the winters from 1779 to 1781 froze the rivers and kept a steady snowfall from mid-November until nearly April. To keep the fires going during the constant blizzards, Thomas Jones, a contemporary New Yorker, wrote, "all the wood upon New York Island was cut down. The forest trees planted in gardens, courtyards, in avenues, along lanes, and about the houses of gentlemen by way of ornament, shared the same fate. . . . These woods were, in the course of the war, all cut down by order of the barrack-masters, carried to New York, and applied as fuel for the use of the army."[43] Manhattan was once covered in thickets of verdant woodlands, groves, and plantations. Then, almost overnight, the land was stripped bare to fuel the fires of soldiers. Although the 1782 British Headquarters Map depicts many agricultural fields or orchards still intact, vast stretches show a stubbled landscape. In 1782, observing from a high point in New Jersey, George

Washington wrote, "the Island is totally stripped of Trees & wood of every kind; but low bushes (apparently as high as a man's waist) appear in places which were covered with Wood in the year 1776." Ecologists Eric Sanderson and Marianne Brown have estimated that the areas of degraded forest and shrub covered 73 percent of the island in 1782.[44]

Brutal winters were followed by harsh dry summers. The loss of the tree canopy made the devastating drought during the summer of 1782 that much more unbearable. Shade was nowhere to be found. In September, Yale president Ezra Stiles wrote in his diary: "a severe Drought the cornfields look deplorably—the Indian Corn half cut-off—no feed for the Cattle . . . The Drought is extensive from Boston to Hudsons [sic] River and beyond. The good Lord prepare us for what is before us."[45] According to the environmental historian William Cronon, the deforestation made "temperatures more erratic, soils drier, and drainage patterns less constant." Without trees, "smaller streams and springs no longer flowed year-round," and this brought drought.[46]

Phillip von Krafft felt the effects of the drought at McGowan's Pass. On September 2, he was ordered to the pass ahead of the foragers and sharpshooters who were expected the following morning. Their orders were to find fresh water "on account of the great heat of this year which had dried up everything." The drought had become a serious impediment to an island surrounded by briny water, and Manhattan's abundant springs and brooks had all run dry. The following day, men were sent out to dig wells thirty or forty feet deep. But even they could not find fresh underground spring water. The nearby swamps of the Harlem Meer and the Harlem Creek channel as well as the fresh water of Montagne's Rivulet were dust bowls. By September 5, the parched troops could not camp at the pass "on account of the dearth of water." And after a terrible fever and a sickness that would last for months, on September 27, von Krafft reported "a general complaint that all the men would die soon for the want of water."[47]

Eventually the rains came, but they did not lift the profound desperation. An entry from July 1 the next year found a depressed Krafft on "a walk to Macgown's pass in great melancholy which had been following me for a long time now." He closed his entry with a plea: "Oh merciful Father, protect me from all Evil!"[48]

In the course of his duties von Krafft often marched up and down the Kingsbridge Road, but he also took personal solitary walks that were of a more amorous nature. He frequently called on Miss Cornelia de la Metre, who lived past the fifth milestone on the road. In 1783 Krafft and de la Metre were secretly married;

then they were married again in a public ceremony once the war ended. De Krafft (he changed his name after the war) stayed in New York and became a surveyor and draughtsman for the new U.S. government against which he had fought with seemingly little conviction.

What became of the Bensons and the McGowans during the war? According to an account by Andrew McGowan's son, Samson B. McGowan, who was born fourteen years after the war, his father, "being quite a youth during the Revolutionary war, remained in charge of his aged mother, Catherine Benson McGowan, on the family homestead. The British also occupied it, but permitted them to be co-inhabitants."[49] An 1881 *New York Times* article, which also described Andrew as a "cripple," reported that he and his mother lived in the McGowan homestead, and "though frequently disturbed by the conflict raging about them, managed to get on without serious difficulty with either contending party."[50]

Samson was wrong about his father's age. Andrew was thirty-one, not a "youth," in 1776. It seems odd that Andrew and his mother, who only days earlier had hosted George Washington and his generals at the historic council of war, would remain in a house occupied by the enemy, but documents suggest that Samson and Lawrence Benson as well as Andrew McGowan remained in New York, though not necessarily in his house.[51] Proof of Andrew's patriotism came in November 1931, when his great grandson, Henry Daily McGown, applied to join the Empire State Society of the Sons of the American Revolution, based on his great grandfather's participation in the war. In his application, Henry cited the 1898 book *New York in the Revolution*, which collected information from original manuscripts related to the war and listed those who served, including Andrew McGown. His Benson relatives, Benjamin and Sampson, were there too. Another item claimed Benjamin Benson contributed the lead from his window weights— many New Yorkers did, and in total it amounted to one hundred tons of lead—to be melted down for ammunition.[52]

Many Dutch families were loyalists, though most Harlem families supported the country's independence. The younger New Netherlanders, whose ancestors had been the generation taken over by the 1664 English invasion, still harbored anti-British sentiment a century later. Since the British armada sailed into New York Harbor months earlier, patriotic families had evacuated the city in huge numbers. After the September 15 attack on Manhattan, eleven thousand refugees fled to surrounding areas. Margaret, her mother, Mary, and her brother "retreated within the American lines," while her father, Samson Benson Jr., joined the rebel army. In an interview with historian Henry P. Johnston, Mrs. Benson McGowan, who was ten years old during the invasion, recalled fleeing with her family to Fishkill in the Hudson Valley. They would later spend the remaining war years in Salisbury, Connecticut, a state so hard-pressed to care for the hordes of exiled New Yorkers that it eventually forced them to return to New York State.[53]

The British seized the Bensons' properties on Third Avenue and 106th Street. The homestead was transformed into a British army hospital. Years later, Samson B. McGowan recalled the "blood-stained floors" of his grandfather's home. The family's gristmill was said to be "too patriotic in its work to stand," and the British burned it down.[54]

As to the McGowan-Benson family's allegiance to the revolutionary cause, it is probably no coincidence that Andrew and Margaret celebrated their love for each other and love of the new nation by marrying on November 21, 1784, the one-year anniversary of the British and Hessian evacuation from McGowan's Pass and the homecoming of the McGowan family after a seven-year exile.

By the late nineteenth century, Andrew McGowan, dead for seventy years, became an unlikely hero to the schoolchildren of New York City. John Flavel Mines embellished the family's reputation in his 1893 guide, *A Tour Around Manhattan and My Summer Acre*, by propagating a myth of Andrew's patriotic role during the British attack on Manhattan. In his wildly fictionalized account, Mines reported that twelve-year-old Andrew was "pressed into service" by a Hessian brigade to lead them to the retreating American troops. According to Mines, the cunning boy lead the enemy on "a merry dance over hill and marsh and meadow down to the North River," while the American army removed themselves from harm's way. Mines proudly declared, "A boy that day was the salvation of his country."[55]

It's a great story, but it is fiction. In 1776, Andrew was a thirty-one-year-old man, not an adolescent boy, and *if* he had led the Hessians toward the Hudson River, they would have encountered and captured the escaping Americans.

The patriotic tale inspired schoolchildren throughout the city to adopt little Andrew as their patron saint for decades. Andrew McGowan City History Clubs abounded. Children were charged a penny a lesson, and some 30,000 pennies were donated. The clubs voted unanimously to use the money to

4.7 The unveiling of the cannons on Fort Clinton by Andrew McGowan's great grandchildren Miss Dorothy Joyce McGowan and Master Henry Daily McGowan in 1906.

Source: Unveiling of the tablet presented by the children of the City History Club. City History Club of New York,,Brochure, F128 HS2725.C52 A3 1907, New-York Historical Society.

memorialize Andrew's valor with a plaque in Central Park. It read, "Through this Pass on September 15, 1776, Andrew McGown, a young lad, guided the British troops, purposely misleading them and by this delay aided the escape of the American force."

Up until about the mid nineteenth century, on November 25 of each year, Americans celebrated Evacuation Day to mark the exit of British troops from the island of Manhattan. On Evacuation Day 1906, a more accurate plaque was unveiled on Fort Clinton by Andrew's great grandchildren Miss Dorothy Joyce McGown and Master Henry Daily McGown. This plaque too was paid for by the collection, and reports mention legions of flag-waving members of the Andrew McGowan History Club proudly looking on. Perhaps this event inspired Henry McGown to join the Empire State Society of the Sons of the American Revolution twenty-five year later.[56]

4.8 The cannon and the smaller carronade from the 1780 sinking of the British ship HMS *Hussar* were recovered in 1856 from Hellgate in the Harlem River and donated anonymously to Central Park in 1865. The two guns are a reminder of the seven-year occupation of British troops in the upper park during the Revolutionary War.

Source: Sara Cedar Miller, Cannon, Carronade and Plaque, Fort Clinton. Courtesy of the Central Park Conservancy.

The plaque read, "This Eminence, Commanding McGowan's Pass, Was Occupied by British Troops Sept. 15, 1776, and Evacuated November 21, 1783. Here Beginning August 18, 1814, the Citizens of New York Built Fort Clinton to Protect the City in the Second War with Great Britain. This Tablet is Erected by the Children of the City History Club of New York. A.D. 1906."

The plaque, missing for at least four decades, was replicated by the Central Park Conservancy and installed in 2014. The two cannons, also remounted that same year, were for years considered American relics of the War of 1812, but, as we shall later see, that's about as accurate as young Andrew's heroic deed.

chapter 5
Valentine Nutter, 1760–1814

The land that had been owned in the seventeenth century by the de Forests and the Montagnes had by half a century later fallen into the hands of the Kortright family, in large part due to the entrepreneurial Half-Way House proprietor Metje Cornelis Jansen. By 1760 most of the prepark land above Ninety-Sixth Street was owned by the McGowans, the Bensons, or the Kortright relations. That year, the unmarried Lawrence Kortright Jr., Metje's grandson and the heir to the Kortright estate, made a huge legal blunder that lost him the land, which went instead to a forty-eight-year-old New York bookseller named Valentine Nutter in the 1790s.

According to the only copy of the April 1760 deed that has come down to us, Kortright sold his property to Valentine's mother, "Sarah Nutter, otherwise Gillmore, the wife of William Nutter."

Most of Kortright's deed reads like the average dry legal document of the day, except for an unusual clause in which he declared his "natural love and affection, which he beareth to the said Sarah Nutter," wording used exclusively for family members, and even more remarkable for employing the intimate phrase toward a married woman. The nature of their relationship is anyone's guess: beloved servant, trusted friend and neighbor, secret lover, possibly all of the above. But Kortright bequeathed his family's vast ancestral lands to Sarah in return for a token ten shillings.[1]

Even more shocking, seven months later Kortright utterly denied this in a second will, in which he revokes "a pretended last Will and Testament said to

---

5.1 (*overleaf*) Valentine Nutter's property, wrested from the heirs of Lawrence Kortright in the 1790s, encompassed today's Harlem Meer and much of the North Woods seen in the distance.

Source: Sara Cedar Miller, *Harlem Meer and North Woods*. Courtesy Central Park Conservancy.

have been made by me in favor of Sarah Nutter which last Will and Testament, (if any such there be) and also certain Deeds of Lease and Release for my Real Estate (if any such there be) pretended to have been made and executed by me to her I do hereby on the faith of a Christian Declare to have been obtained from me by fraud and Circumvention, and without any Valuable Consideration received by me for the same." In this later document, Kortright willed his land to his heirs—including his sister Eve Kortright, wife of Adolph Benson—who laid claim to the family's property.[2] But here is where Kortright or his lawyer made their mistake. The first will was not legally a will at all. It was a deed, in which Kortright conveyed his family's property to Sarah Nutter for a token sum. A deed cannot be revoked, and it always trumps a will. The second document—the will that legally renounced Sarah Nutter's rights to his property—came too late. Hence Valentine Nutter, not the Kortright heirs, claimed legal possession to the land.[3] Kortright, his family, or his lawyer, believing that his second will nullified the first document, had the second document, the proper will, probated, and the family assumed that Sarah Nutter or her heirs were out of the picture.[4]

THE LOYALISTS

William Nutter (born ca. 1730), a Portsmouth, New Hampshire, carpenter, married Sarah Gilmore in New Hampshire. By November 1755, the couple had established themselves in New York. There, he was listed as a carpenter and awarded a freemanship that gave him voting privileges.[5] In 1757, William received a tavern license from the mayor's office. The only record of his death in 1760 cites no sources, but by that year his wife had formed some kind of relationship with Lawrence Kortright, the owner of the property that encompassed much of the prepark above 105th Street to 113th Street along the Kingsbridge Road.[6]

In 1771, a decade after the deaths of Sarah and Lawrence, thirty-year-old Valentine declared his "rightful" ownership to the Kortright lands, but the heirs rejected his claim.[7] Nutter was a bookbinder, recently betrothed to a young woman named Catharine Gordon, and he wanted to start his married life on what he understood to be his mother's legal property. The Nutters were married in the Presbyterian Church, fittingly enough, on Valentine's Day, 1772.[8]

In 1774, after his apprenticeship ended, Nutter opened his own bookshop across from the Coffee-House on Water Street and before long was a successful bookseller, binder, printer, and stationer.[9] He took out advertisements in the

New York Journal or General Advertiser for everything from the latest best-sellers to the jests of Shakespeare, Stackhouse's six-volume *History of the new testament*, and *Fordyce's sermons to young women*, suggesting that he had a wide clientele.[10]

When the British captured New York in the fall of 1776, the rebels were forced to flee, lest they risk incarceration, death, or some other severe punishment. Public tarring and feathering was popular. Their homes and businesses were burned, looted, or repossessed by British soldiers and sailors, Hessian mercenaries, and the remaining New York loyalists who had pledged themselves to King George III. Nutter was among them. He, like many New Yorkers, was a loyalist. As such, he remained in business and anticipated even greater profits now that his rebel bookselling rivals had fled.[11] In the same month that the redcoats moved into town, Nutter, always the savvy opportunist, advertised for sale: "Paper, quills, ink powder, sealing wax, account and orderly books for the Army and Navy."[12]

As a paper and book merchant, Nutter depended on goods from England, but British importation ships were constantly targeted by rebel privateers. To counter them, loyalist merchants became privateers in turn. Valentine Nutter was among those who owned one or more armed vessels and were sanctioned by the Royal Navy to prey on commercial vessels owned by rebel merchants.[13]

But by 1782, the end of the war was near, victory within sight, and the new Americans were hotly debating what to do about the remaining loyalists. The more vengeful patriots considered people like the Nutters traitors to the new nation. The state of New York offered them no protection, security, or tolerance. Their lands and property were confiscated, and they were made pariahs. So, like thousands of others loyalists, the Nutters pulled up roots to start a new life on British soil. They sailed for Nova Scotia.

Valentine and Catherine, along with their two daughters, Sarah and Ann, and their enslaved servants, twenty-two-year-old Sam and thirty-year-old Silvia, arrived in May 1783.[14] Nutter's third enslaved person, Jack, did not sail with them—he ran away. Before embarking, Nutter placed an advertisement in the *New-York Gazette and the Weekly Mercury* offering a five-guinea reward for "a negro man named Jack," approximately twenty-three years old, with "a scar on his left arm and a scar on his nose," a stutter, and speaking "very little English to be understood."[15] Jack was probably born in Africa and had only been enslaved for a short time. No record exists of his capture.

Many loyalists fled America for Nova Scotia. The Port Roseway Association—a membership group of five thousand loyalist refugees—were promised free land from the governor if they would agree to tame the four-hundred-thousand-acre wilderness of primal forest and unyielding granite into a commercial success for British Canada. Port Roseway, a site they would eventually call Shelburne, possessed a deep, nine-mile harbor on the St. John River and the Bay of Fundy, access to superb fishing, vast timberland, and an excellent shipping venue to Europe.[16] The Nutters were among the association members, and Valentine Nutter became the keeper of the subscribers' roll. On board the *Abundance*, he was appointed co-captain of the 17th Dragoons.[17]

The first loyalists arrived in 1783. The population quickly swelled to ten thousand, with everyone from high officials and aristocrats to former soldiers and middle-class merchants and artisans, many of whom arrived with their enslaved servants. There were also free Black citizens and escaped enslaved persons. And for a brief time, Shelburne became the fourth largest city in North America after New York, Philadelphia, and Charleston.[18]

The emigres were shocked to find life in Nova Scotia as harsh as the pilgrims had found Plymouth two hundred years earlier. They arrived just before winter set in, and many families were forced to live in tents pitched directly on the granite outcrops, with little food or warmth to sustain them. The regional British government was remiss in honoring their promise for immediate supplies, shelter, and land grants. Many settlers took off for St. John, New Brunswick, Canada, and the promise of more tillable land. Some returned to New York to face the consequences of their politics. Of those who decided to stay and tough it out in Shelburne, many died that first harsh Canadian winter.

The Nutters had an easier transition. As a successful New York businessman, Valentine arrived with substantial savings. In Shelburne, he opened a general store in which he sold many items that catered to a well-heeled population: "ladies' gloves and purses, watch chains, ivory and tortoiseshell combs, pocket looking glasses, and backgammon tables and cribbage boards."[19]

As a leader in the fledgling community, Nutter was appointed to the committee that would assist the provisional government to assign property to the frustrated and homeless families. The head of the committee was Isaac Wilkins, a leading voice of opposition to independence who had been a Westchester (what is today the Bronx) representative of the New York General Assembly before the war. He had married into the wealthy and exclusive Morris family of Morrisania. His wife, Isabella Morris, was the sister of Lewis Morris, signer to the Declaration of Independence and a member of the Continental Congress. Wilkins had been trained as a lawyer in King's College (now Columbia University), but unlike most of his wife's patriotic family, he remained loyal to Britain. In Shelburne he became a judge and was probably the one who appointed Valentine Nutter justice of the peace.[20] On November 12, 1786, Isaac Wilkins's son Martin married Valentine's daughter Sarah, which elevated the Nutter family to an elite social class unavailable to them in New York.[21]

The British Parliament was aware of the tremendous sacrifice these former colonists had made. Nutter himself claimed to have lost £2,000, but as historian Robert Ernst reported, "Britain eventually reimbursed only a fortunate few for a fraction of their claims."[22]

5.2 *Judgement Day for Tories*, ca. 1770s, depicted a Tory hoisted up on a liberty pole just before his tarring and feathering by a group of angry rebels. After the war, returning loyalists like Valentine Nutter could fear the same punishment unless they pledged an oath of allegiance to the new U.S. government.

Source: Elkanah Tisdale, Engraver, *The Tory's day of judgment / E. Tisdale, del et sculpt*. United States New England, 1795. Photograph, Library of Congress, https://www.loc.gov/item/2006691561/.

The Nutters stayed in Shelburne for seven years. He ventured into the real estate business. Between 1784 and 1791, he held mortgages for twenty-three Shelburne properties.[23] One of them, the Ryer-Davis House, still stands at Shelburne Harbour and is listed on the Canadian Register of Historic Places.[24]

When Valentine Nutter returned to New York in about 1789, it had become the new country's first capital and, after much turmoil and opposition, loyalists were slowly incorporated back into the new body politic. As historian Aaron Coleman suggested, "many of the loyalists viewed their silence as the price of their reintegration, the pound of flesh they had to sacrifice for being left alone."[25] Like so many returning loyalists, Nutter must have taken an oath of allegiance to the new government, or he could not have been allowed to revive his old business at 21 Water Street.[26]

THE NUTTER FARM

Having become an expert in Canadian real estate, Nutter, back in New York, again laid claim to the Kortright property. Records from that year show he was in contact with the Kortright heirs—including Sampson Benson—who finally relented and relinquished their property to Nutter for £40 "after divers differences, controversies, and disputes about said lands."[27] There is nothing in the historical record about the relationship between Sarah and Lawrence or how the parties arrived at a settlement.

The legal issue was laid to rest in 1868 during the Supreme Court *Cahill v. Palmer* trial which, in part, involved the Nutter land. The attorneys for plaintiffs found "not a particle of evidence" to the validity of Nutter's title to his property, but they ultimately lost their lawsuit for valid reasons. Despite any question of the validity of the Kortright/Nutter documents, the defendants' attorneys noted that Nutter and his heirs had proper ownership through the principle of adverse possession under which a person who does not have a legal title to the property can acquire it based on their uninterrupted occupation of it. Under this ruling Valentine Nutter's ownership is incontestable, yet it is also undeniable that Lawrence Kortright's dying wishes never intended to leave his future Central Park property to either Sarah Nutter or her son Valentine.[28]

We do know that Nutter had possession of the Harlem Lane property by October 1795 because of an ad he placed at the time, when a stranger's two stray cows moved onto the entrance to his property. He was still advertising for their owner two months later, but they went unclaimed, as later he advertised the sale of "best prime" beef.[29]

In November 1795, Nutter put up for sale "about 10 or 12 Acres of Land" across from "Mr. McGowan's new House." Surveyor Isaac Doughty, who knew Nutter as early as 1807, described the land: "on the hill or side of the hill" and "very rough and rocky, covered with woods," today's Ravine that encompassed the "run of water that never fails," today's Loch.[30] Nutter also owned that formidable hill known to runners and bikers as the dreaded "Harlem Hill," today adjacent to the North Woods. In October 1797, Nutter put his book business up for sale "for immediate possession."[31] He had decided to become a yeoman farmer, in the fashion of the late Lawrence Kortright.

Nutter tore down Metje's century-old Half-Way House and erected a new home on the same site. Before it was moved in 1852, his house would have stood in the middle of 109th Street and Sixth Avenue, at the entrance drive to the park and along the grassy slopes leading to the shoreline of the Harlem Meer. His property would encompass the 110th Street Playground, the Dana Center, the Harlem Meer, McGowan's Pass west of the Kingsbridge Road, the North Woods and a part of the Ravine.

The New York Supreme Court case called on many to give firsthand accounts of the Nutter farm. Many remembered Valentine Nutter as "the old gentleman." One of them, seventy-year-old Samson Benson McGowan, Andrew's son, had known Nutter since his boyhood. McGowan described Nutter's land as "a very fine farm, what we called meadow land—level land." Most of it was fenced in and cultivated in the "ordinary way." He used the flat lands and the hillsides as pasture for his animals.[32]

Over a century and a half earlier, much of Nutter's land had been a part of the Vredendal farm of Johannes de la Montagne. After 1684, much of it eventually wound up in the possession of the Kortrights through the wheeling and dealing of Metje Cornelis Jansen, Lawrence Kortright's grandmother. Nutter's new land stretched from 105th Street to 113th Street, west from Sixth Avenue to the present Morningside Park. The southern point of the property ran across the high outcrops that, as we shall see in the next chapter, became fortification sites during the War of 1812, including the North Woods, in which the old "powder house" or Blockhouse still stands.

In his testimony, Nutter's grandson, Gouverneur Wilkins, confirmed that his grandfather's woodlands were similar those he saw in the Central Park landscape. He also added detailed information on how his grandfather used the land.

> There was a thick woods on that side of the farm where the tower [Blockhouse] stood, it extended to the limit of the farm and came along the Burrow [Borrowe] land [the Great Hill], and this ravine that now constitutes a part of the Central Park, was well grown in wood. All this land on top of the hill was woodland, and used for wood purposes; it was where an old Hessian camp was on the west side near Borrowe's land. There was an opening and a good piece of pasture, and there was [sic] such patches of pasture around that was on the top of the hill.[33]

The 1800 census confirmed that Valentine and Catherine Nutter had moved to Harlem with their two daughters and enslaved five people, who probably performed both domestic and agricultural work.[34] After all he had done to take possession of his mother's property, it is surprising that he put his new farmhouse and highly cultivated estate up for sale in February 1804, two years after Catherine's death.

> A valuable Farm, situate in the center of the island of New-York, and nearly the center of the 9th ward of the city, equally distant from North to East rivers, to both landings, a good road, and about 7 miles from the city, the post road running through the farm, one hour's pleasant riding, and fine roads.
>
> It contains 130 acres of all good land as any on the island, ninety acres of which may be put into meadow or garden grounds There is a very fine piece of salt meadow that produces 12 to 14 hands of salt hay; about 40 acres of very thrifty young woods, and of the best kinds of woods on which may be got a large quantity of best building stone. Through this farm run two fine streams of water supplied from a number of springs which come out of the high grounds in the rear of the farm, and might be appropriated to many valuable purposes. On the high ground is a very fine view of the East river and surrounding country. On this farm there are four handsome building sites, which would accommodate four families very well; there are three young orchards of very fine fruit.

The dwelling house is a well-built house, a story and a half, four good rooms on the first floor, three in the garret, a good cellar kitchen, dairy, and root cellar under the house; it has a handsome piazza ten feet wide, the whole front of the house, which is 45-feet-long and 30-feet deep with several small necessary buildings near the house; also a well of the finest water on the island.[35]

The property never sold. It remained in Nutter's possession until 1828, when he invested a great deal of it for a risky real estate venture. Ultimately, he lived in the house until 1831, when his grandson sold it against his wishes. According to Wilkins, his mother, Nutter's daughter Sarah, "was anxious" to have her eighty-nine-year-old father live with her, and admitted that selling the "dilapidated" house was the only way to get him to move out.[36]

Valentine Nutter lived out his last five years with his devoted daughter Sarah and grandson on the Wilkins estate of Castle Hill in the Bronx, on a scenic promontory overlooking today's Castle Hill Park. Only a short distance from the Wilkins mansion, Nutter would have had an opportunity to visit his in-laws'

5.3 The seating area overlooking the Harlem Meer, named Nutter's Battery in the War of 1812, was also a fortification during the British occupation. It stood on the site of the property that the Nutters acquired after the Revolution.

Source: Sara Cedar Miller, *Nutter's Battery*. Courtesy Central Park Conservancy.

ancient wooden farmhouse, with its immense fireplace. During the Revolutionary War—and before the Wilkins family were exiled to Nova Scotia—the recesses of that fireplace "gave shelter to three loyalist clergymen: the Rev Messers. Chandler, Cooper and Samuel Seabury, when they were being sought far and wide by the Americans." The Wilkins family would lower them food and drink through a hidden trap door to the "mysterious secret chamber." Nutter's daughter Ann Livingston also reminded her father of his old traditions when, long after the war in an 1829 letter, she sent him warm regards from a Mr. Jenkins, a former loyalist friend, who had fond memories "upon drinking to the King's health with you."[37]

Despite his former loyalties to the Crown, Valentine Nutter became active in Harlem and New York City politics fighting for American rights leading up to the War of 1812. In 1807, he was the chairman of the Ninth Ward Federal Republicans.[38] His participation in the war was memorialized by an 1814 fortification, Nutter's Battery, that stood on his property. Today it is the site of a circular seating area overlooking the Harlem Meer that was part of a line of defensive structures to protect New York from an attack that never happened, in a war that is almost never remembered.

chapter 6

The War of 1812, 1805–1814

After the devastation of the Revolutionary War, the young Americans were anxious about another clash with their former colonial power. This anxiety manifested in great fortification efforts in the first decade of the nineteenth century. The military took advantage of the unique topography in the upper prepark for its operations: stationing troops, constructing fortifications, and housing munitions. We can still see the etchings of these military uses today in the landscape.

When Hurricane Sandy tore through Central Park in October 2012, it felled or injured more than six hundred and fifty trees. The loss of any one of the park's twenty thousand trees is a tragedy, but when the storm uprooted a particular English elm near the site of McGowan's Pass, it unearthed a treasure that had been buried there for two centuries.[1] The Central Park Conservancy immediately contacted archeology consultants Richard Hunter and James Lee to investigate. After clearing away the debris, they discovered a section of the base of the ramparts (also known as earthworks or breastworks) built in 1814 in preparation for a second war with the British.[2]

The original ramparts were four-foot-high protective walls of soil and rubble that connected four of the five fortifications that ran west to east from 106th to 109th Streets: Fort Fish, Nutter's Battery, McGowan's Pass Gatehouse, and Fort Clinton. Only Blockhouse No. 1, the fifth fortification, was placed alone on a distant hilltop, disconnected from the rest. We know from maps and from Archibald Robertson's 1777 sketch of the area that Fort Fish and Fort Clinton were constructed upon walled fortifications that were built during the Revolutionary War by British and Hessian soldiers, though the ramparts connecting them were only constructed in 1814 (see figure 4.4).

6.1 This aerial rendering of the northern end of the land that became Central Park depicts the 1814 fortifications on Harlem Heights: clockwise, Fort Fish, Nutter's Battery, the barrier gate at McGowan's Pass that intersects with the Kingsbridge Road, Fort Clinton and the ramparts abutting the Harlem Creek. The map also depicts the road that connects the woodlands and the Blockhouse through the estate and orchard of Dr. Samuel Borrowe, now the Great Hill. The watercolor is also the clearest visual description of the relationship of prepark landmarks: the northern edge of the Harlem Creek and adjacent marshland, now the Harlem Meer; the meandering rivulet through the woodlands, now the Loch and the Ravine; the edge of the cultivated Muscoota/Harlem Plains, now Harlem above 110th Street; the Kortright/Nutter land, now the Harlem Meer landscape; and the Benson-McGowan house and orchard, east of the Kingsbridge Road, now the Park's composting operation, and Lanaw Benson's original triangular land and house.

Source: *Military Map of Haerlem Heights*, by William James Proctor & Joseph Holland; watercolor, ink on paper, 24 3/4 × 32 1/2 inches, 57700, New-York Historical Society.

6.2 In 2012, a fallen tree from Hurricane Sandy exposed the foundation of the Gatehouse and its attached ramparts in McGowan's Pass.

Source: James Lee, "Ramparts, Gatehouse, McGowan's Pass," Ramparts_13008 D3-014-1. Hunter Research, Inc.

6.3 The two earthen mounds that run down the eastern slope of Fort Clinton to the shore of the Harlem Meer are the remains of the eroded ramparts constructed in 1814.

Source: Sara Cedar Miller, *Eroded Ramparts, Harlem Meer*. Courtesy of the Central Park Conservancy

In in his preliminary study of Fort Clinton in 1990, Richard Hunter had identified the eroded remains of the two parallel breastworks, now two scalloped
berms, that led from the fort to the shoreline of the Harlem Creek at Fifth
Avenue. Then, a year after Hurricane Sandy, Hunter and his team returned to
the site to assess the pass and its historic environs in preparation for the grading and infrastructure improvements to the surrounding landscape. At the time,
their seventy-foot-long excavation trench uncovered a section of the Kingsbridge
Road and the adjacent foundation of the McGowan's Pass Gatehouse. They also
identified features hidden in plain sight from the thousands of park visitors who
strolled through the pass without realizing it.

The vertical cylindrical drill scars on both inner-facing outcrops were evidence of the hurried quarrying to build the gatehouse foundation. After only
two weeks of work, "as many Rock blowers as [Major Horn] should judge necessary" were called for to blast the outcrops with gunpowder to obtain building
stone.[3] The archeologists interpreted a line of four visible drill holes atop the
western outcrop as possible anchors for iron rods that held the ramparts to the
gatehouse. On a line directly northwest of the holes sat a row of five boulders
that Hunter and Lee surmised were also part of the ramparts from the gatehouse
to Nutter's Battery.[4]

THE WAR

In France, Napoleon rose to power amid the chaos that followed in the wake of
the unresolved French Revolution. A series of European coalitions, often led by
the British, opposed Napoleon, and the continent was embroiled in war for most
of the first two decades of the nineteenth century. The wars were felt even across
the Atlantic, in America and especially New York, a hub of world commerce. By
1814, the war would even change the land that would become Central Park.

The British Royal Navy suffered a shortage of men. Death and desertion had
thinned their ranks considerably. Many British sailors left for the more lucrative
wages and better working conditions of the American merchant marine. Desperate to increase their forces by at least ten thousand new sailors each year, and without a surplus of voluntary recruits, the British often captured British or British
American sailors and pressed them into naval service. These seizures of American
ships often took place on the high seas, and they often resulted in casualties.

In April 1806, one such incident shook New York. The British ship *Leander*, on a mission to capture British deserters, shot at the American schooner *Richard* a quarter mile off Sandy Hook, New Jersey. The shots to the ship beheaded John Pearce, the brother of the shipmaster. The murder of Pearce brought an immediate condemnation from the city's merchants, who called for the government to take "prompt and vigorous measures to prevent a repetition of such wanton and inhuman conduct, and so flagrant a violation of our national sovereignty."[5]

New Yorkers banded together to protect deserting British sailors. In September 1807, six sailors from the British frigate *Jason* ran away from their commanding officer while traveling with him through the city. When the lieutenant took out his pistols and threatened to shoot them if they did not return to the ship, a furious mob assembled, "protected the men, abused the Lieutenant, and handled him very roughly."[6] Similar confrontations were common all over the city.

Press gangs kidnapped sailors, literally hauling them out of taverns or docked ships, casting them as deserters and disregarding their official papers. This practice enraged New Yorkers. Other times, British aggressors boarded American merchant vessels and captured innocent sailors. The shared culture and language among British subjects, naturalized Americans, and American-born citizens made it nearly impossible to differentiate between them. Historians estimate ten thousand men fell victim to British impressment.[7]

When the British defeated the French and Spanish fleet at the Battle of Trafalgar in 1805, Britain gained commercial control of the seas. (In fact, after Trafalgar, the Royal Navy would stand as the dominant naval force until the Second World War.) According to nineteenth-century international law, a neutral nation was permitted to trade with all countries, a policy that protected the prosperity that America was enjoying. From 1801 to 1805, New York was the hub of American commerce, collecting nearly $13 million in import duties, 29 percent of the national total.[8]

Much of this prosperity was gained from importing tropical products—sugar, molasses, and coffee—that arrived from the Caribbean and were sent on to Europe. Britain, who had been America's largest trading partner, attacked American ships as they sailed to neutral ports or to France with supplies, sometimes for Napoleon's army.

Just before the *Leander* incident, Congress had passed the Non-Importation Act of 1806, which prohibited the import of a select group of British manufactured goods made chiefly from silver, leather, brass, glass, and paper; hats; woolen clothing over a certain price; and cloth of silk, flax, and hemp, among others. Though the weak law did not prohibit more vital products such as iron, steel, coal, and salt, nonetheless New York's economy suffered.

President Thomas Jefferson wished to avoid a second war with Britain. He had foreseen the prospect and in 1807 ordered a second system of fortification as a preventative measure. Under this system, four forts had been built at New York Harbor.[9] That same year, he used commerce again as a diplomatic tool, imposing a trade embargo forbidding the export of any American produce or manufactured materials to Britain. Shipping was a cornerstone of New York's economy, and the embargo crippled the prosperous growth the city had enjoyed for the last decade. New York businessmen and shipping magnates watched helplessly as British and French merchant ships took advantage of the trade block and seized commercial routes and venues that had been invaluable to American shipping.

In 1809, after fifteen months, the embargo was lifted. But New York found it difficult to recover. In 1812, Napoleon's invasion of Russia ended with his army and reputation greatly weakened. The British, again seizing the upper hand, sent more troops and ships to America. British blockades prevented any ships from leaving the harbors of New York and New England and formed a blockade of Long Island Sound. While the trade war paralyzed the Northeast, conflicts broke out in the Midwest and on the Canadian border. It was obvious that armed conflict was inevitable. And in June 1812, Congress declared war on Britain for the second time.

In April 1814, Napoleon capitulated to Austria, Prussia, and Russia, ending his reign as emperor and sending him into exile on Elba. With Napoleon gone, Britain could turn its full attention to the new war in America. The events of that summer rallied all New Yorkers—regardless of political party, social class, nationality, or race—to the cause with an anti-British passion not seen since the Revolution.[10]

New York felt the enemy closing in on all sides. In early July, a British flotilla occupied part of the Maine coast, threatening New England and New York. That same month at present-day Niagara Falls, Ontario, Americans suffered enormous casualties in one of the bloodiest battles of the war. Though it was considered a stalemate, Americans lost an attempt to take a strategic advantage on the Canadian border, and a strike at Lake Champlain on the New York-Vermont border seemed imminent. South of New York City, six thousand British troops arrived in Chesapeake Bay on August 3; New Yorkers were alerted to this maneuver within the week. Closer to home, British warships under the command of Rear

Admiral Sir George Cockburn had sailed off the coast of Sandy Hook at the entrance to New York Harbor in July. Cockburn was said to have "sent word" to a female friend or relation living in Manhattan that he would soon be dining with her at her home, "as he expected to be in command of the city of New York."[11] He did not linger in New York but headed south and on August 24 led the joint naval and military forces that burned the Capitol, the President's House, and other important government landmarks in Washington.

But the closest attack came from the east. On the evening of August 9, three British ships armed with more than sixty guns fired dangerously close to home

6.4 Rear Admiral Sir George Cockburn is shown on the far left instructing the British troops to torch the brick building in the foreground, having already burned the Capitol, seen in flames in the background on August 24, 1814. The painting by Allyn Cox is on the walls of the House Wing in the Capitol.

Source: Allyn Cox, *British Burn the Capitol*. United States Capitol, Courtesy Architect of the Capitol.

at Stonington, Connecticut, on Long Island Sound, the waters that flowed into the East River. Despite the enemy's powerful advantage, Stonington with only three guns fought back valiantly, and by August 13 the ships left the harbor. With their vulnerability in mind, New Yorkers fortified the East River, building Fort Stevens on today's Astoria, Queens, waterfront and Mill Rock, an island in the middle of the East River, both visible from the new fortifications on Harlem Heights.

THE VOLUNTEERS

New Yorkers have always banded together in a crisis. Headlines in local newspapers implored them, "Arise from your Slumbers! . . . This is no time to talk!"[12] Citizens and soldiers rallied to build defensive fortifications across the city and its islands. On July 7, the Common Council met to consider fortifying the heights of Brooklyn and Harlem.[13] On August 6, General Joseph G. Swift, Chief of Engineers and Superintendent of Land Fortifications, ordered two redoubts built at McGowan's Pass and considered it and the Harlem Commons as "eligible positions" for troop encampments.[14] By August 9, the Stonington attack—only one hundred and forty miles away from the city—had galvanized New Yorkers.

Two days later, a Committee of Defence was formed, chaired by Alderman Nicholas Fish and including a member from every ward. The next day, thousands of citizens assembled downtown, and after rousing speeches, they summoned the resistance of forty years earlier, when their fathers and grandfathers had fought the same enemy. The Committee of Defence put notices in local gazettes inviting volunteers to help build the fortifications.[15] Over five thousand New Yorkers heeded the call, and donations poured in.[16]

At eight o'clock on the morning of August 18, Chairman Fish and his committee, members of the Common Council, General Joseph G. Swift, and Commodore Stephen Decatur broke ground for the "work northeast of Mr. McGowan's House," which would be named Fort Clinton in honor of the city's current mayor, Dewitt Clinton. A salute was fired for the occasion and then members of the state militia and volunteers went to work.[17]

The most endearing and detailed firsthand account of the volunteer builders comes down to us from an interview with Daniel Burtnett, who was at the time a butcher's apprentice.[18] Whereas the master butchers had voted to work on the fortifications at Brooklyn Heights, their apprentices, "filled with spunky national feeling," were assigned by Major Joseph Horn to the work by McGowan's Pass.

No sooner had the boys been given their task then their teenage thoughts turned to their stomachs. They commandeered a horse and a "tasty wagon," which they filled with the tools of their trade—"hams, tongues, roast beef, etc"— and took to the road at 6:00 a.m. with "a fine band of music, colors flying, hearts beating." Passionate and competitive, the boys felt a tremendous pride when they arrived via the Post Road at Harlem Heights a full hour and a half before the first other volunteers arrived by boat. They carried a flag with a white ground and black letters, bearing the inscription

Free trade and Butchers' rights
    From Brooklyn's Fields to Harlem Heights.

Immediately upon arriving in Harlem the boys adjourned to a nearby field, partook of a hearty breakfast, and then went to work. They assisted the militiamen who had come to the city from the upper counties of New York State, and by sundown they had "thrown up a breastwork of about one hundred feet in length, twenty in breadth, and four feet in height, sodded complete; the materials which were carried in hand-barrows from the foot of the hill and adjacent grounds."

6.5 The ramparts or earthen walls connecting the Gatehouse at McGowan's Pass to Fort Clinton (right) were constructed in one day by a group of militiamen with assistance from young volunteers, most of them butcher's apprentices.

Source: John J. Holland, (detail), "Works at McGowan's Pass," New York City, 1814. Drawing: watercolor, black ink, and graphite with touches of gouache and scratching out on paper laid on heavier paper (together with 1889.15), overall: 9 3/4 x 24 in. (24.84 x 61cm), 1889.14. New-York Historical Society.

At the end of the day, they stuck their flag into the adjoining breastwork, and when its folds wafted to the breeze, it was hailed with nine hearty cheers. These ramparts by McGowan's Pass, built that day by the apprentice butchers, were exactly the section exposed by Hurricane Sandy.[19]

With little time to prepare and not enough government funds, the local residents of the Ninth Ward took up collections to feed and shelter the Harlem volunteers. Among the first donors were Valentine Nutter, James Beekman, and Andrew McGowan, all owners of land that would one day be Central Park. The *Evening Post* acknowledged "their friendly attentions to the officers and men by franking the use of their dwellings and barns during the unsettled state of the camp."[20] Lemuel Wells, who owned the land that became Strawberry Fields, arrived with twenty men and five yoke of oxen. The grocer and farmer David Wagstaff lent his home near Fifth Avenue and Seventy-Ninth Street, at the base of today's Cedar Hill, for use as an infirmary and officers club. He also donated ten bushels each of potatoes and corn. Andrew McGowan allowed the military to use his house above the pass for storage. The druggist company Bradhurst & Field, owners of land that would become part of the present Great Lawn and Conservatory Water, contributed in total 480 bushels of potatoes. A "number of patriotic ladies" collected $347 for the purchase of vegetables and other necessaries for the troops. The wealthy and prominent New Yorker James Fairlie, an officer in the current war and former Revolutionary War hero, donated $1,600 toward the construction of the fortifications. Dr. Samuel Borrowe, who owned the house on today's Great Hill that once housed British and Hessian troops during the Revolutionary War, paid nearly $4,000 to buy 100 "common tents" and 50 "fly tents" to house the militiamen, probably on his pastures and meadows.[21]

One of the greatest personal contributions came from formerly enslaved Cato Alexander, who became the celebrated tavern keeper of Cato's Road House, near the Post Road at Fifty-Fourth Street and Second Avenue. Concerned that the volunteers and militia on Harlem Heights "had difficulty obtaining meals," Cato advertised in the *Mercantile Advertiser* on September 3 that he was opening a branch of his establishment that week on the Harlem Road with "dinner on the table every day from half past twelve o'clock till 2pm."[22]

The Committee of Defence published assignments in the local newspapers. The list of volunteer artisans and professionals, charities, associations, and ethnic groups ran the gamut of the New York population. On August 20, for example, the committee advertised need of "Cabinet Makers, Fancy & Windsor Chair Makers" for work in Harlem. Peter A. Schenck, a customs surveyor, showed up with ten of his employees, as did several sawyers from the lumber and saw yards. They were told to assemble at the ferries to Harlem, paid for by the committee to the New York and Jersey Steam Boat Company, whose crew members were occasionally reported as "intoxicated."[23] Artisans from all over the city volunteered: firemen and hook and ladder companies, bookbinders, the United Benevolent Society of Tailors, the Society of Tallow Chandlers, the Neptune Corps of Seafencibles, the Patriotic Sons of Erin, and hundreds came from the downtown Sixth Ward and from out of town: Eastchester as well as Bergen, New Jersey. Mr. Blackwell and eleven of his "rock blowers" were also deployed to blast the many rock outcrops in the area.[24]

Other advertisements called upon "people of colour" to assist in construction of the Harlem fortifications. These efforts were led by educator John Teasman, an activist and the former principal of the African Free School, who had been fired by the white trustees of the Manumission Society in 1809 for his involvement in public parades. He was subsequently hired to run the schools of the New York African Society for Mutual Relief and later became the founder of the Walker Street Academy. In this independent school Teasman held a public meeting he called the "Test of Patriotism," through which he assembled Black volunteers for construction of the fort. He placed a newspaper ad requesting "gentlemen having servants in their employ [to] please spare them on that day." Slavery was still legal in New York, and whites were wary of Blacks assembling in large groups for any reason, which makes it all the more remarkable that Teasman's call to duty successfully summoned fifty men. On August 25, six hundred people of color reported for work in Harlem.[25] Perhaps this was the inspiration that led General Swift, director of the Harlem Heights fortifications, to manumit his enslaved servant Nancy only two days after the last of Teasman's volunteers completed their work on the fortifications.[26] The enslavers who had volunteered their enslaved men for the war effort were entitled to their $25 bounty, but if an enslaved recruit received an honorable discharge, he was rewarded with his freedom.[27]

Much of our knowledge of the fortifications and the surrounding Harlem Heights landscape comes from a group of twenty exquisite watercolor sketches, now in the collection of the New-York Historical Society. According to General Swift, the drawings were done by artist John Joseph Holland, who wanted to serve his country but "to avoid duty in the line of troops."[28] The "View from Fort Fish" shows the watery marsh of the Harlem Creek, today's Harlem Meer, and a strip of the Kingsbridge Road. The two structures beyond it would have been the Valentine Nutter farm.

THE SOLDIERS

On September 12, after only twenty-five days of construction, "the Heights of Harlaem from East River to Hudson River were literally lined with fortifications, occupied by swarms of soldiers." Those soldiers had come to the city mainly from the counties of the mid-Hudson Valley.[29] Governor Daniel Tomkins, Commander of the Third U.S. Military District, had mobilized thousands of state militiamen to work and guard the pass under Brigadiers General Martin Heermance, Peter Curtenius, and Jonas Mapes. By October 24, *The Evening Post* reported that Mapes's men had performed "an elegant and patriotic spectacle," proof, at least to the reporter, that Mapes had transformed his civilians into a sharp military corps, qualified "to enter a contest in the pre-eminence in the field of exercises and maneuvers."[30]

Despite the impressive public display, the troops were not without problems. They were volunteer militia, not a standing army, and they were on the whole ill-trained and unprepared. They were not paid, and the poor accommodations and food, boredom, and abusive officers provoked bad behavior and, in turn, serious disciplinary actions and desertions.[31] By October 19, after a month of work, some of Colonel Ward's laborers at Harlem were reportedly "remiss."

6.6 In his *View of Fort Fish at McGowan's Pass looking at Harlem (and Nutter's Battery)*, John J. Holland depicted aspects of camp life. The militiamen at Fort Fish are seen as social, relaxed, bored and, in one instance—the soldier near the head of the cannon—taking a nap. Only the two soldiers at the left seem to be engaged in their patrol duties. Nutter's Battery is to the left and Fort Clinton to the right.

Source: John Joseph Holland, "View from Fort Fish, McGown's Pass," New York City, 1814. Watercolor, black ink, and graphite with touches of white gouache on paper laid on heavier paper (together with 1889.12) Overall: 10 x 25 in. (25.4 x 63.5 cm), 1889.13. The New-York Historical Society.

To placate them, the committee agreed to provide "an extra gill [five ounces] of rum per diem" for each man.[32]

The abuse of alcohol was common. On or about November 18, twenty-three-year-old Private James Kain entered the tent of his superior officer, Ensign Benjamin Van Deusen, to ask for some "grog," a ration of rum. When the officer denied him, Kain "took a pitcher of water and struck him several times and made his escape in the bushes back of Camp." Van Deusen captured him, and on the way to the guardhouse, Kain again struck him. At the trial where the private was ultimately discharged from service, Van Deusen attested to Kain being "considerably groggy" when he entered his tent looking for a drink.[33]

Gambling was a serious offense, but it was also a popular way to stave off the boredom and discomfort of primitive camp conditions. Lieutenant Barzillai I. Worth, a paymaster from Columbia County, was court-martialed for his defrauding, by "means of cards, dice or some other unwarrantable and illegal means," Private Alva Gregory of Pine Bush, New York, of a pocket handkerchief. Three days later, he cheated another soldier of three dollars. Worth was discharged and instructed to refund the money and the handkerchief and forfeit his pay.[34]

Even officers engaged in criminal behavior, and none more so than General Heermance's Brigade Quartermaster, William Macomb, who was charged with conduct unbecoming of an officer and gentleman on December 1, 1814. Macomb had a long list of verbal offenses, criminal acts, and violence. The quartermaster was the officer in charge of providing the living quarters, blankets, food, and knapsacks, though not clothing, eating utensils, or canteens. The temptation to gamble or extort was too much for devious minds.[35] When Macomb somehow commandeered a rare supply of canteens, he propositioned Lieutenant Colonel Anthony Delameter to offer them for sale to his men for twelve shillings each and pocket one shilling for himself, a proposal "indignantly spurned" by the colonel. Another time, the quartermaster was caught cheating a Mr. Ryder out of fifteen dollars for hiring his wagon and forging a counterfeit receipt for less money.[36]

The greatest of Macomb's offenses was treason. In an angry outburst, he announced to fellow officers that he wished "the British had succeeded and blown Baltimore all to Hell." Macomb came from a pro-Tory Detroit family of wealthy fur traders and purveyors of military provisions, and although he was a U.S. citizen, he must have secretly harbored pro-British sentiments. For these and other offenses, he was given a dishonorable discharge.[37]

THE POWDER MAGAZINES AND BLOCKHOUSE NO. 1

The militias stored their weapons in arsenals along Manhattan Island. These also housed gunpowder, inside what were called powder magazines.[38] The Arsenal that stands today at Fifth Avenue and Sixty-Fourth Street was built between 1847 and 1851. But it was actually the second military storage facility built on that site, preceded by a state-owned powder magazine, located on the spot of today's Central Park Zoo.

In 1807, during the great fortification buildup, the Common Council worried that the state's gunpowder facility on the crowded shores of Collect Pond, near the site of today's City Hall, was unsafe. They instead proposed keeping such dangerous supplies "in retired and unfrequented places."[39] After a few aborted attempts elsewhere, New York State chose a place for the powder magazine, a half-acre of available common lands owned by the Corporation of the City of New York on the Middle Road (today's Fifth Avenue) and Sixty-Fourth Street.[40] These common lands, which today include the central and eastern portion of the prepark, were often let to citizens. This specific lot had been leased to a man named Adam Fink in 1799 and 1803. The state needed only a small portion of Fink's property. They offered him $700 for it, but he held out for "an extravagant consideration." After negotiations, the state agreed to pay $2,500 for two lots, one owned by Fink and the other owned by the city. Governor Tompkins assured the legislature that the liberal increase from the original purchase price was a wise and profitable decision for the state, given the increasing land values in New York City.[41]

The powder house was a square structure with a masonry wall ten feet high, a dwelling for the keeper, "a well of excellent water, and a convenient stone and gravel road from the public street."[42] It was still standing in 1862.

In 1814, with troops stationed only two miles from the magazine, Governor Tompkins was shocked to learn that huge amounts of gunpowder belonging to the state and federal governments and stored close to the Harlem Heights encampment were unguarded. On August 23, on the governor's orders, Major General Lewis commanded a company from the Harlaem Heights troops to guard the facility.[43]

The placement of the powder magazine appears on drainage maps in 1855, and it was still used as active storage as late as May 1858, when Central Park commissioners preparing for construction ordered the State's Commissary General to remove all ammunition and gunpowder except what was "necessary for an emergency."[44]

THE BLOCKHOUSE

The powder magazine and guardhouse were demolished, so the only surviving War of 1812 structure in the park is Blockhouse No. 1.[45]

Located on the brow of a rocky bluff in the North Woods, the thirty-four-foot-high Blockhouse overlooks 109th Street and Seventh Avenue. Except in the winter months, the leafage of the surrounding North Woods trees hides it from view. A blockhouse is a type of fortification built from the eighteenth century to the mid-nineteenth century. It was used as a safe retreat for a small number of soldiers to make a stand against a greater number of enemy troops.

According to West Point military expert D. H. Mahan, the purpose of a blockhouse was to inspire soldiers "with confidence to hold out to the last moment."[46] Most blockhouses had two stories, but the Harlem Heights structure had one, as well as "loopholes for musketry" and "timber breastworks" on the inside that supported heavy cannon.[47] The Blockhouse was constructed when anxiety over an imminent British attack was high. We can see the hurried work in the slapdash placement of the stones in its lower walls.

On August 27, General Swift informed the Committee of Defense that he could not acquire the stone necessary to build the McGowan's Pass gatehouse and was, therefore, forced to construct it out of "trees and earth."[48] Because there was no time to clear the surrounding woodland or to quarry the schist or gneiss bedrock for building blocks, the Blockhouse boulders must have been imported from nearby. The top course of the fortification was clearly constructed under calmer circumstances, after the danger of imminent attack had passed. The three carefully laid rows of red sandstone blocks stand in sharp contrast to the irregular placement of boulders below.

Blockhouse No. 1 is the only surviving structure, once accompanied by Blockhouses Nos. 2, 3, and 4 on Morningside Heights, "within supporting distance of each other, and near enough for the interchange of grape shot; all of them to mount heavy cannon on their terrace," with musketry loopholes for troops stationed inside.[49]

In November 1814, while troops were still in the process of building the structures on Harlem Heights, diplomats in Ghent, Belgium, were already working on peace negotiations that would be signed on December 24. The war never came to the park.

After the peace, the Harlem structures were dismantled gradually. The gatehouse existed until 1824, and the earthworks were visible long after the

6.7 Blockhouse No. 1 in Central Park is the remaining fortification from the War of 1812. The uneven and random placement of the lower course of stonework indicates the urgency with which it was constructed.

Source: Sara Cedar Miller, *Blockhouse*. Courtesy of the Central Park Conservancy.

construction of the park. They can still be seen today. In 1864, the park commissioners noted that the "breastworks of earth," although greatly eroded, were still about three feet high.[50]

The cannon and the smaller carronade, mounted on their granite base atop Fort Clinton, were thought for almost a century to be remnants from the War of 1812. But they are not. They were an anonymous gift to the new park in 1865, said to have been retrieved from the British ship *Hussar*, sunk at Hellgate in the East River in November 1780. The ship was said to be carrying one million dollars in gold to pay the British troops, and for that reason dives for the purported buried treasure have been taking place since 1824 and as recently as 1962. In 1856, a dive by the Worcester Diving Company brought up the guns, which were donated anonymously to Central Park and eventually placed on Fort Clinton. They were the same cannons mounted and unveiled on Evacuation Day in November 1906 by two McGowan descendants. The guns are the only visible reminders in the park of the seven-year British occupation of New York City.[51]

After the war, the Blockhouse property still belonged to Valentine Nutter, and records indicate that he complained to the Committee of Defence that a number of his trees were cut down during the building of the fortifications. This was likely for the construction of the abatis, a thick barricade of felled trees whose sharpened branches point toward the enemy. A map indicates that the militia constructed the abatis "flanked by Fort Fish to obstruct the Ravine between the said Fort and Block House."[52] Nutter was awarded $15,000 for his significantly denuded slopes.[53]

After the war, most of the forts were demolished, though the gatehouse remained at the pass until 1824, when General Scott was informed that residents had complained about the "great obstruction to the passing of carriages on the Road," and it was removed.[54]

The area of the Blockhouse and the fortifications were still in the possession of Nutter and his family, but after a series of sales became the property of a speculator named Mary G. Pinkney. In 1852, she rented the old structure to the Hazard Powder Company, one of the largest gunpowder manufacturers in the country. By 1860, she had sold it to merchant and real estate tycoon Henry H. Elliott. Photographs show a pointed roof on the Blockhouse, a door on its western facade, and a landscape devoid of surrounding trees. The high opening on its most accessible facade was probably created by the Hazard company for the horse-drawn wagons that would pull up and load or unload the casks of gunpowder. The existing stairs were probably added in 1906 when the Blockhouse was recognized as an important historic structure and honored by the Women's Auxiliary of the American Scenic and Historic Preservation Society.[55]

The structure was continuously occupied by the Hazard Company until the land was taken for the park in 1863, although the commissioners allowed them to retain possession of the property for "sometime after they took the ground." The Hazard Company manufactured explosives in Enfield and Hazardville, Connecticut, and was such a major supplier that their stock accounted for 40 percent of all the gunpowder used by the Union Army during the Civil War. The company president, Augustus Hazard, had an office on 86 Wall Street. With the gunpowder made in a neighboring state, New York would have been the biggest and best port for shipping it to the Union troops. With few places in the city for the storage of such highly explosive material, it would have been practical to keep it far from the crowded port.

6.8 In the 1850s, the Hazard Powder Company used the Blockhouse to protect the gunpowder that was stored inside, much of it to blast the rock outcrops during the early years of the park's construction.

Source: Large stone building Central Park, New York. [The Miriam and Ira D. Wallach Division of Art, Prints and Photographs: Photography Collection, The New York Public Library. "Large stone building Central Park, New York City." New York Public Library Digital Collections. https://digitalcollections.nypl.org/items/510d47e2-5732-a3d9-e040-e00a18064a99

The Board of Commissioners of the Central Park also found it convenient to allow the Hazard Company to store its gunpowder in the park, since they so often needed to blast the rock outcrops in the decade before Alfred Nobel invented dynamite in 1867.[56] To impress visitors, tour guides often claim that more gunpowder was used in the construction of Central Park than in the Battle of Gettysburg. This may be an unfair comparison, as Gettysburg lasted three days while blasting the rock for Central Park took sixteen years.[57] Nonetheless, what the two sites may have had in common was the *use* of the Hazard Company's gunpowder, stored in Central Park and fired on the fields of Gettysburg.

In 1847 just before the talk of a large park began, the state began erecting an arsenal on a ten-acre parcel on Fifth Avenue at Sixty-Fourth Street, completed in 1851. In 1859 the Board of Commissioners expressed their displeasure at the "inconvenience" caused by the munitions still in storage in the new arsenal.

6.9 The Arsenal in Central Park was built in 1847 on land that was bought by New York State in 1808 for the storage of gunpowder. The site was chosen for its remote location.

Source: Sara Cedar Miller, *Arsenal*. Courtesy of the Central Park Conservancy.

The state had promised to remove the arms, but the frustrated commissioners realized this was now a remote expectation. Under the circumstances, they suggested to the Common Council that it would be fair for the state to pay rent to the city for the storage, especially since the city had to pay the state $275,000 for the Arsenal, the Powder Magazine, and the ten acres of the city's common lands that New York State had purchased in 1807 from Adam Fink and the city for $2,500.

The Arsenal still stands in Central Park today, although its destruction was contemplated several times. Diarist George Templeton Strong called the building hideous and hoped it would be destroyed by "accidental fire."[58] In 1869, it served as the first U.S. Weather Station for New York City, and thereafter until 1920. In 1877, it was the first home of the American Museum of Natural History, the proposed New-York Historical Society in 1865, and the American Museum of Safety in 1920. It has been the official headquarters of the New York City Department of Parks and Recreation since 1934 and of the Wildlife Conservation Society's Central Park Zoo since 1988.

PART II

Real Estate

The Grid

Houston Street divides New Yorkers from out-of-towners in two ways: first, by how the street is pronounced—"house-ton" to the natives, not "hew-stun" like the city in Texas. And second and more important, by how it divides the jumble of lower Manhattan's named streets—familiar only to locals—from the logical and intuitive numeric grid uptown.[1] Just north of Houston Street is First Street, starting the numbering that marches sequentially north to 155th Street. The avenues, from east to west, start at First Avenue and run to Twelfth Avenue adjacent to the Hudson River. There are a few named avenues between them, most of which have been added or renamed over time, and the tangled streets in Greenwich Village are another outlier. Broadway too mocks the ruler, following a curving indigenous footpath, a reminder of topography's former dominance before it gave way to the formative power of real estate. But besides those anomalies, Manhattan is laid out upon a single, logical grid.

Like Broadway, nature dictated how people below Houston Street developed the land. Even in the more built-up portions of New Amsterdam and later New York, the streets cleaved to the contour of the terrain. The curvilinear Maiden Lane and Minetta Lane traced the footprints of a meandering stream. Pearl Street, named for its contiguous oyster beds, mirrored the island's natural shoreline before the advent of landfill. As we saw in the first chapter, the Wickquasgeck trail was the path of least resistance walking north and south up the island, avoiding the hills and swamps. Until the late eighteenth century, the city expanded haphazardly, creeping slowly north, but with no overarching plan for the its future layout.

After the Revolution, New York's population exploded. At the end of the war in 1783, the city's population had plummeted to 12,000 people. By 1810, it had risen to 100,000.[2] The crooked and narrow thoroughfares and outdated infrastructure could not keep up with the needs for housing and commerce. Floods, fire, inadequate sanitation, tainted water, and overcrowding were blamed on the "evil of confused streets" that incubated public health crises like the cholera epidemic of 1832.[3] While land values went through the roof, vermin, human waste, and polluted water festered in the cellars below.

When the oldest lanes around Wall Street were widened and infrastructure improved for the city's new commercial and financial capital, the residents, both rich and poor, were forced to relocate. They found few places to go. There were no real neighborhoods or even plans to develop them. No one was in charge of the problem, and there was no money to solve it anyway. The chaos overwhelmed the civic leaders, who cried out desperately for a master plan.[4]

To rectify this turmoil, in 1807, the state appointed three distinguished and prominent citizens to be the Commissioners for Laying Out Streets and Highways: the statesman Gouverneur Morris, the businessman John Rutherford, and the state surveyor Simeon DeWitt. Their mandate was "to unite regularity and order with the Public convenience and benefit, and in particular to promote health of the city" and allow for "the free and abundant circulation of air."[5] After three years of study, the commissioners concluded that the most efficient plan for Manhattan Island was a grid of twelve 100-foot-wide avenues running roughly north to south, crossed by 155 60-foot-wide streets running east to west above Houston Street. The grid, as it was called, would divide Manhattan into roughly 125,000 lots.

The commissioners explained their checkerboard design in terms of economics and practicality. They reasoned that "strait-sided and right-angled houses are the most cheap to build and the most convenient to live in." The east-west streets were the most efficient way for the business community to move goods from the Hudson and East River piers, and lots for homes or businesses would be similar in size and equal in value to every other lot, though corner and avenue lots would be priced slightly higher. Before the grid, the development of the island (or lack of it) was determined by the ups and downs of its topography. But the rigidity and predictability of a flat "life-sized" Cartesian grid transformed the island into real estate: more than two thousand blocks, most with sixty-four lots of equal size and relative value, and a logical system for finding one's way among them.[6]

Contemporary New Yorkers mourned the loss of nature. The poet Walt Whitman decried the monotony as "the last things in the world consistent with the beauty of situation." Henry James called it a "primal topographic curse."[7] But no one alive today can remember Whitman's New York, and instead most celebrate the grid plan as a forward-thinking vision and a milestone in the development of one of the world's great cities.[8]

When the streets were opened, the city and its landowners had much to be pleased about. New homes and new neighborhoods arose, followed by services and amenities like the night watch, fire protection, and gas lanterns. These improvements increased property values far beyond what they had been worth as agricultural or preindustrial lots. As land values soared, the city, which had not taxed owners much in the eighteenth century, began to reap a portion of the profits. Land assessments became the price of modernization.[9] With the grid, land speculation as we know it became a preoccupation *and* an occupation for many New Yorkers. Before, land had been the source of sustenance and heritage; now it became a commodity, as easily bought and sold as a jewel.

Not everyone was pleased. One of the earliest, loudest, and most oft-cited protests came in 1818 from landowner Clement Clarke Moore, the future author of "A Visit from St. Nicholas," also commonly known as *'Twas the Night Before Christmas*. Moore was forced to cede a small slice of his estate to create Ninth Avenue and West Nineteenth and Twentieth Streets. He protested, likening the street commissioner to Moses at the Red Sea, "commanding all within the reach of his eye to be overwhelmed." Moore, like every other property owner, had no choice, given the municipality's right of eminent domain. Defeated, he transformed himself from disgruntled member of the landed gentry into a resigned but vastly wealthier participant in Manhattan's second-oldest profession: real estate development. His estate—which Moore's grandfather had named Chelsea after the district in London—was chunked into saleable lots that were sold and resold more than nine hundred times in his lifetime.[10]

Based on the Fifth Amendment to the U.S. Constitution, a state or federal government has the right to take private property for public use provided that the owners receive "just compensation," determined in the courts as the "fair market value" of the property. It's a general misunderstanding that the taking of the land for Central Park was New York City's most extensive and unprecedented employ of eminent domain. By far, that title belongs to the enactment of the grid.[11] In his study, geographer Reuben Rose-Redwood counted the buildings north of Houston Street (excluding Greenwich Village) and discovered that, of the nearly two thousand preexisting buildings on Manhattan Island below 155th Street, nearly 40 percent were in the middle of a street. That means that laying the grid required that two out of every five buildings be either moved at the owner's expense or destroyed.[12]

There were decades of protest from those who had to cede their homes, farms, and businesses to the relentless march of progress. Owners and renters alike mourned the loss of community, the erasure of family land, the annihilation of memory. The grid uprooted and paved over personal histories and replaced them with smoothly graded streets, curbed sidewalks, sewers, and conduits for gas and water. One New Yorker called it "the degrading process of street openings."[13] Nineteenth-century historian Martha Lamb recalled the protests of enraged victims trying to protect their homes and their livelihood:

> Numerous farmers and mechanics of small means had purchased plots of land in various places, laid out and cultivated gardens, and erected comfortable dwellings. When they discovered that the city was about to run streets wherever it pleased, regardless of individual proprietorship, and that their houses and lots were in danger of being invaded and cut in two, or swept off the face of the earth altogether, they esteemed themselves wronged and outraged. At the approach of engineers, with their measuring instruments, maps, and chain-bearers, dogs were brought into service, and whole families sometimes united in driving them out of their lots, as if they were common vagrants. On one occasion, while drawing the line of an avenue directly thorough the kitchen of an estimable old woman, who had sold vegetables for a living upwards of twenty years, they were pelted with cabbages and artichokes until they were compelled to retreat in the exact reverse of good order.[14]

These same protests to the rule of eminent domain would resurface with the building of the Croton Aqueduct system and, on a much smaller scale, the creation of Central Park.

Land division did not start with the 1811 grid. Only three years after capitulation to the English in 1664, the British Royal Governor Richard Nicolls began to divide some of Manhattan's terrain into large tracts of land for investment purposes. The highly desirable Bloomingdale section of Manhattan included the land from the Hudson River east to what became Seventh Avenue. The block-wide strip of west side land from Seventh to Eighth Avenue was included in several of the ten hundred-acre lots. Those parcels would be divided, sold, and resold many times over until the city took the land for Central Park in 1856.

Dividing land into individual gridded lots first occurred in New York in 1762. The Episcopalian Trinity Church—the second largest landowner in Manhattan after the Crown—divided their vast church farm property from Wall Street to Christopher Street into over one thousand rectilinear lots for rental income.[15] Just the same, James Delancey Jr., divided his father's three-hundred-acre property on either side of Delancey Street from Division Street to Houston Street, today's Lower East Side, into blocks and offered leases on them for anywhere from twenty to ninety-nine years. This new system enabled tenants to sublet their property and share in the profits that might be gleaned from the new system of land use. According to historian Elizabeth Blackmar, "Having long regarded their land as storing and transferring family wealth and securing credit, elite proprietors saw real estate as a means of accumulating more wealth."[16]

But some land was not arable or good for any other obvious use. Acres and acres of Manhattan have an underlying foundation of impenetrable hardpan. These less-desirable lands, the common lands, ran from Seventh Avenue southeast, roughly from West Ninety-Third Street to East Twenty-Third Street and down to Second Avenue. The Crown saw that the land was not attractive to investors or potential residents and so decreed it a part of the city's property, granting it to the Corporation of the City of New York by royal charter in 1686.

After the Revolution, the city looked to the sale of its vast undesirable property, much of it a part of Yorkville, as the only way to refill their empty treasury. In 1796, they divided the commons into a grid of more than 160 five-acre lots. Beginning at Forty-Second Street and heading north, the city also designed three new thoroughfares—East Avenue, Middle Avenue, and West Avenue—that traversed the newly divided property. These are today's Park Avenue, Fifth Avenue, and Sixth Avenue. The city's division and sale of its common lands became the precursor to its comprehensive grid plan that swept topography aside and finally conquered Manhattan Island. With that division, middle-class people could buy

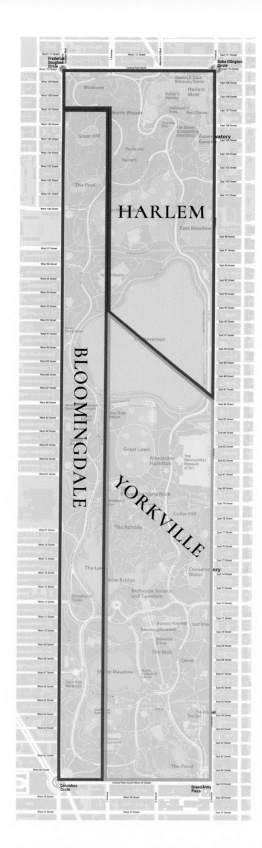

a few lots of land for a home or an investment that only a few years earlier had been out of their reach.

In 1825, the Harlem Freeholders, landowners who governed the Harlem community, joined in the new process of land division. They divided their long-held property, much of it in Central Park north of the Great Lawn, and sold it to hundreds of investors, big and small. It was the end of an era for the old Dutch Harlem families, who had before only divided, sold, and resold their estates through birth, death, and intermarriage within their close-knit community. Benjamin L. Benson, scion of the landowning Bensons, began to sell out to speculators in 1825. His buyers were people like Archibald Watt and his stepdaughter Mary G. Pinkney and business partners Francis Price and Enoch Wiswall, who amassed great Harlem property empires to develop.

Thus began the era when real estate overtook topography as the driving force behind land use in New York City. In the following chapters, we will meet these landowners and follow the divisions of the three "neighborhoods" that comprised the prepark—Bloomingdale, Harlem, and Yorkville—until 1856. That was the year the three merged, and their summary 141 blocks between Fifty-Ninth Street and 106th Street became Central Park.

11.1 The land that became Central Park was on the edge of three Manhattan districts: Bloomingdale, Harlem, and Yorkville.

Source: Randel Farm Maps, Common Lands Map, *Farm Histories*, Municipal Archives.

chapter 7

Dividing Bloomingdale, 1667–1790s

Bloomingdale was a country escape, where New York elite built status-symbol estates above the majestic views and cooling breezes of the Hudson River. The families were wealthy merchants and, like the Delanceys, were also the most powerful political clans in the city. Like the Dutch, these elite merchants and politicians often intermarried to expand their wealth and their property. During the Revolutionary War they stayed loyal to the Crown and kept their elegant lifestyle and their vast properties in the city and upstate. When the war ended the Delanceys fled to England and Canada, much of their vast estates having been confiscated. Others, like Charles Ward Apthorp, were tried for treason but managed to hold on to their property. By the end of the seventeenth century the old elite classes had died out and the new generation of landowners was interested in the land as both investment and for the country pleasures. The rise and fall of Bloomingdale is a microcosm of the rise and fall of the elite European merchant class in the transition from European colony to American city.

The Manhattan street grid was laid out in 1811, but the division of land in New York for real estate investment started nearly two centuries before that. Soon after the English conquest in 1664, the western section of the prepark, an area the Dutch called Bloemendael, later changed by the English to Bloomingdale, was a small slice of larger one-hundred-acre tracts that were divided and sold by the royal governor as investment properties. Bloomingdale ran along the North River (now the Hudson River) from roughly Thirty-Fourth Street to 120th Street. Unlike Harlem, this strip of land, later delineated as the area between Seventh Avenue and Eighth Avenue, remained mostly uninhabited and uncultivated until the 1790s.

7.1 Every spring, Shakespeare Garden in Central Park features a range of colorful tulips that memorializes Bloemendael, a tulip-growing region in Holland for which the neighborhood of Bloomingdale, which included the site of the park's garden, was named.

Source: Sara Cedar Miller, *Shakespeare Garden*. Courtesy of the Central Park Conservancy.

Bloemendael got its name for its swathes of west side wildflowers, which reminded the Dutch of a town of the same name in the tulip-growing country of northern Holland. As late as 1907, a resident of the west side remembered it in earlier days as "a natural wild-flower garden." The land was also prized for its views of the river, cooling summer breezes, and accessibility, since it was right beside the river and also near the Native footpath that was called the Blooming-dale Road and later renamed Broadway.[1] Like all waterfront properties in cities, Bloomingdale attracted New York's elite families, who built country homes and estates along the river.

In 1667, Royal Governor Richard Nicoll granted lots 4 and 5, which stretched from Fifty-Ninth to Sixty-Ninth Street, to a syndicate of five private investors: Jan Vigne, Egbert Wouterse (or Wooters), Jacob Leenderts (or Leendersen), Johannes Van Brugh, and Thomas Hall.[2] The lots were purchased with the assumption that they would eventually be developed.

Of the five investors, Thomas Hall stands out. He was the only Englishman among them, and he had come to the New World as an indentured servant and arrived in New York as a prisoner. Yet he rose to be one of the wealthiest and most esteemed citizens in New Amsterdam.

Hall was born in Gloucestershire in 1614, and he came to America as an indentured servant in the home of Virginian George Holmes. In 1635, Hall and Holmes were among a group of seventeen who, without permission, attempted to establish an English colony within the Dutch New Netherland settlement along the Delaware River. They were captured and brought to a New Amsterdam jail. There Hall learned the Dutch language, customs, and culture. By 1639, all was forgiven, and Hall and Holmes were granted east side land at Turtle Bay for a tobacco bouwerie near the site of today's United Nations. The enterprise was a success, but Hall bored easily and sold his share to Holmes the following year, keeping for himself only "a boat, gun, and dog." Hall moved back to town and began dealing in Manhattan real estate.[3]

Hall rose in importance in the colonial government, and in 1669 he was commissioned by the governor to sit on the committee to lay out the wagon road to Harlem, which would become the Kingsbridge Road.[4] Willem Kieft appointed him to the Council of Eight Men, and later Peter Stuyvesant appointed him as one of the Council of Nine Men. He partook in a failed attempt of the administration to form an effective role in the colony's government. He was one of the signers of the *Remonstrance of the Eight Men of Manatas* that petitioned the Dutch West India Company and the parliament in Amsterdam to establish a representative government. And along with fellow investors Vigne and Van Brugh, Hall was among the ninety-three New Amsterdam citizens who signed the surrender to the English in 1664—an irony, since England was his native land.

THEUNIS IDENS VAN HUYSE

In 1667, the same year the governor granted Bloomingdale lots to Hall and his fellow investors, the governor also granted another royal patent to Isaac Bedlow, a Dutch merchant, ship owner, and alderman. for "a Certaine Tract or Parcell at prsent lyes unmanured and unplanted Now to the End some good Improvem't may be made thereupon."[5] Today the neighborhood that included Bedlow's property lies on the Upper West Side from Eighty-Sixth to 107th Street between the Hudson River and Seventh Avenue, a neighborhood still called Bloomingdale today. Bedlow also owned an island in New York Harbor that bore his name until it was renamed Liberty Island in 1956, more fitting for the home of the Statue of Liberty. Bedlow died about 1673, pursued by creditors. His widow sold the Bloomingdale property. After a hiatus of fifteen years, it was purchased by Theunis Idens (or Eidesse) Van Huyse, a farmer from Saponicken, now Greenwich Village.[6] In the prepark history, Idens may be the first landowner who did not acquire his property through being a member of the elite class.

We know a great deal about Theunis Idens's early life through the journal of missionary Jasper Danckaerts. The diary, written in the decade from 1679 to 1689, must be viewed through the biased eyes of Danckaerts's Labadist (or Dutch Pietist) beliefs, but it remains an invaluable account of the enormous mental, physical, and economic cost paid by the early settlers as they tamed the wilderness of the fledgling colonies.

In 1679, Danckaerts and fellow Labadist Peter Sluyter were traveling from Friesland in the Netherlands through New York to find a place to found a religious community in the New World. The Labadists had defected from the Dutch Reformed Church and belonged to the Christian "vein of mysticism" whose mission was to achieve devoutness of spirit by "enjoining austerities of life, abnegation of the flesh, and renunciation of the world." Danckaerts and Sluyter lodged at the Saponicken farm with Theunis Idens and his wife, children, and aged parents and siblings. Idens, we are told by Danckaerts, "led a godless life, and had been wild and reckless, extraordinarily covetous, addicted to cursing and swearing, and despising all religious things . . . his evil and wickedness were more in the spirit than in the flesh."

Idens's home life was stressful. His "ill-tempered" wife accused him of laziness, despite his hard work. As if his family's abuse wasn't enough, he suffered a series of unfortunate incidents. He and his brother-in-law made a bad investment. A storm dashed his canoe to pieces. His enslaved servant died. His fourteen-year-old daughter was "badly ruptured," with no possibility of ever bearing a child. His cows got sick. His hand was crushed while he was felling a tree. And his horses had become agitated and bewildered. A broken man, Idens sought a rope to hang himself.[7]

Enter the Labadists onto this desperate scene. According to the journal, Danckaerts and Sluyter spoke to the distraught farmer about the power of God over the devil, and almost instantly Idens calmed down. The Labadists told him to return to his chores and admonished his wife, instructing her how to behave toward him. By the very next day, we are told, Idens had miraculously given himself over to the Labadists' philosophy and declared his mundane work unimportant. He "promised he would avoid the world as much as he could," and wished he could join their colony and live in the woods, "away from wicked men." Idens joined the church in June 1680, two months after Danckaerts and Sluyter supposedly healed this humble and grateful convert.[8]

Yet contrary to his Labadist philosophy, Idens committed himself to the worldly affairs of New York real estate. He sold his Greenwich Village farm and moved to Bloomingdale in 1688, where he bought Bedlow's patent and also the northern lots of Van Brugh and Hall. By the time Idens acquired these properties, historian James Riker noted that the process had already begun for new lands "to be brought under the plough . . . on the North River side, settlement pushing out from the city, beyond Saponicken or Greenwich to the region already called Bloemendael."[9]

Idens turned Bedlow's unmanured and unplanted property into a 460-acre farm that stretched from Eighty-Sixth to 107th Street and from the Hudson River to the Harlem Commons at Seventh Avenue. Part of it would eventually become the rolling west side spine of the park landscape, including parts of the West Meadow, the Reservoir, the North Meadow, the tennis courts, the Pool, and the Great Hill. Although Idens probably cultivated his land closer to the river, much of his prepark land had many flat pastures and meadows and the clear spring waters that would have been easily improved. Idens transformed the untamed terrain into a successful farm, and he lived there in peace and contentment for the next thirty years.[10]

In 1720, Idens divided his farm into parcels of roughly sixty acres each, about twenty-six city blocks, and conveyed them to his six children. Four of them inherited land in the prepark and traded properties with one another and other Harlem and Bloomingdale landowners like Cornelius Harsen, Charles Ward Apthorp, Stephen Delancey, and Lawrence Kortright, Sr.[11]

7.2 (overleaf) North Meadow, the largest meadow in Central Park, was once a part of the seventeenth-century farmland of Theunis Idens that reached west to the Hudson River.

Source: Sara Cedar Miller, North Meadow. Courtesy of the Central Park Conservancy.

THE DELANCEYS

By the beginning of the eighteenth century, land on the west side was changing hands frequently. Through a series of consolidations, a large portion of these lots from Fifty-Ninth to Sixty-Ninth Street—originally given to Hall and the Dutch investors and dubbed "Little Bloomingdale"—was purchased in 1729 by a wealthy landowner named Stephen Delancey.[12]

Stephen Delancey also acquired his larger three-hundred-acre Bloomingdale estate from the heirs of Theunis Idens.[13] He eventually sold the one-hundred-and-fifty-acre Little Bloomingdale portion to his eldest son, James. At Stephen's death, his son Oliver bought out his four siblings and built a mansion, farm, gardens, and extensive orchards. The easternmost portion of his property, much of it woodland, lay within the boundaries of the prepark. In 1825, the section of his property spanning Eighty-Third to Eighty-Eighth Streets would become much of Seneca Village, an African American community discussed later in this book. Today Delancey's former property includes Summit Rock, the West Meadow, Delacorte Theater, the Arthur Ross Pinetum, the Shakespeare Garden, a western portion of the Reservoir, the West Drive, and the Eighty-Sixth Street Transverse Road.[14]

Stephen Delancey was born Étienne de Lancey in 1683; he was a French Huguenot from Caen. In 1685, the Edict of Nantes was revoked, automatically declaring all French Protestants to be Catholics and forcing many Protestants, like the Huguenots, to flee. Emigration was forbidden, but Delancey managed to escape first to Rotterdam, then to England, and finally to New York in 1686. There he anglicized his name, though many in his family often retained the French *de Lancey* spelling. He was already a wealthy merchant, in part from cashing in the family heirloom jewels, but when he married Anne Van Cortlandt in 1700, he gained entrée into one of New York's most elite families. As a wedding gift, his father-in-law gave them a valuable corner lot on Pearl Street. There, in 1719, they built the mansion and headquarters of the Delancey family trading business. In 1762 they sold it to Samuel Fraunces, who opened the Queen's Head Tavern, now known as the landmark Fraunces Tavern. It was there, on December 4, 1783, that General Washington bid farewell to his officers after defeating the British. Two years later, the same building once owned by the loyalist Delanceys was leased by Congress for offices of the Treasury and the War Department.[15]

Stephen's eldest son, James, was a prominent colonial leader, the formidable head of one of the two dominant New York political factions, the opposition to Governor George Clinton. James Delancey rose to chief justice of New York, then lieutenant governor, and later acting governor. When he died in 1760, his brother Oliver and his son James Delancey Jr. sustained his legacy by dominating the New York political scene.[16]

James Delancey Sr.'s vast east side property encompassed much of today's Lower East Side, from Division Street north to Houston Street and west to Oliver and James Streets, so named to demarcate the boundary of the Delancey farm. Delancey Street traverses the entire length of the farm. A century and a half later the Delanceys' former property would become the largest enclave of Jewish immigrants from eastern Europe, which is ironic since Oliver Delancey was a known anti-Semite.

OLIVER DELANCEY

Oliver Delancey was a notorious ruffian, who "goes on in his riotous manner, bidding defiance to everybody."[17] On one occasion, he and his friends attacked the home of a recently arrived Jewish merchant, smashed the doors and windows, and destroyed the house. Delancey and his cronies threatened to rape the man's wife because she looked strikingly similar to the wife of Governor Clinton, the leader of their rival political faction: "If he could not have her, he would have her likeness."[18] This behavior is perplexing, as Delancey was married to Phila Franks, the daughter of one of America's wealthiest Jewish families. Phila converted to Episcopalianism, her husband's faith.

In eighteenth-century New York, prosperous Jews frequently conducted business and socialized with elite Christians. Nonetheless, the mixed marriages of Phila and her younger son David and their conversion to Christianity were devastating to Phila's mother, Abigail Levy Franks. Phila and Oliver married on September 8, 1742, and kept that secret for six months, until she finally fled to her husband's country house, never to speak to her mother again. Abigail was distraught, especially since Phila had professed that nothing would ever cause her to disobey her parents.[19]

Even so, Abigail described Oliver as a "man of worth and Charactor [sic]."[20] Whatever virtues he had demonstrated to his future mother-in-law, he did not show them to the rest of the world. Oliver's marriage to Phila did not change his behavior toward Jews. In February 1749, he assaulted one of Abigail's relatives, Judah Mears, the brother of Abigail's stepmother.

Fear and intimidation were the favorite tactics of Delancey's campaign against Governor Clinton's faction. The leading attorneys of the city advised the victims of Oliver's abuse to "make it up," as no lawyer would go against the younger brother of the chief justice. In a letter, Governor Clinton claimed that after Oliver Delancey stabbed Dr. Alexander Colhoun in a tavern, no lawyer dared take the case.[21]

When the Revolution came, the entire Delancey family remained loyal to the Crown. With his own funds, Oliver organized three battalions of 1,500 men from New York, Long Island, and Westchester and Fairfield Counties to fight for the king. He called them De Lancey's Brigade and appointed himself brigadier general. These troops acted as a police force during the British occupation.

Loyalist homes were looted frequently by the American rebels during the war, and the social, political, and military position Oliver Delancey occupied made him a special target for their vengeance.[22] After midnight on November 26, 1777, American rebels rowed across the Hudson to sack his riverside mansion.

Delancey's sixteen-year-old daughter, Charlotte, and her friend Elizabeth Floyd were asleep in the same bed in the Delanceys' Bloomingdale mansion on today's Eighty-Ninth Street overlooking the Hudson River, when they were awakened by loud voices. When they opened the windows, they were told, "Put in your heads, you bitches," and instantly the house was broken into, front and rear. "Get out quick," the rebels told them, as the house was to be burned. One of the "wretches" threw a flaming curtain on Elizabeth. The girls were struck several times with muskets. Then one of the kinder men bid the ladies, "Be off, as fast as you can." Elizabeth and Charlotte were dressed in only flimsy night clothes. They "fled into the woods and swamps, in what is now Central Park, and passed the night in the thickest bushes they could find, sitting upon their feet to keep a little warmth in them, until they were found and taken to Mr. Apthorpe's [now at Ninety-First Street and Columbus Avenue; see figure 7.3] in the morning." Charlotte said the two could not walk for three weeks afterward, for the bruises on their bare feet and legs.

Phila Delancey was too elderly to run fast enough, so she hid in the stone "dog-kennel under the stoop."[23] The attack traumatized her. On the anniversary of that night, exiled in Yorkshire, England, Phila wrote a poem recalling it. She ended with a "fervent prayer" to "dwell contented in our native home."[24] She never returned to America and died in England in 1811. Oliver had died in England in 1785.

In 1777, in the midst of the war, the Continental Congress proposed the confiscation of loyalist property, and all thirteen colonies passed some legislation to that effect, called *forfeiture laws*.[25] In October 1779, New York State passed "An Act for the Forfeiture and Sale of the Estates of Persons who have adhered to the Enemies of this State." It was called the Confiscation Act, and it declared that disloyal New Yorkers forfeited their right to own property and their right even to live in the state. The Commissioner of Forfeiture seized all loyalist property, including the vast empire of Oliver and his nephew James, which included almost the entire Lower East Side Delancey farm and "Little Bloomingdale" in the prepark.[26] Six years later, the Little Bloomingdale tract was purchased for £2,500 by John Somarindyck, whose descendants and their spouses, particularly Sarah Somarindyck and her husband, John Talman, held on to their property until the land was taken to develop Central Park.[27]

But Oliver had seen forfeiture coming and shrewdly conveyed his Bloomingdale property to his daughter Charlotte, who immediately put it up for sale in March 1779: "The Farm so delightfully situated at Bloomingdale . . . containing one hundred and eighty-three and one-half acres, having two large kitchen gardens, well fenced and in good order, sundry orchards, a farm house and two barns thereon, one with sheds and other buildings, forty acres of extraordinary fine wood land in one parcel, four acres in another and several small pieces." [28] The deed to the property is unrecorded, but baker Joseph Orchard, possibly a Quaker, built a home on the site of the destroyed mansion, and received a mortgage from Quakers Daniel Cock and Daniel Underhill.[29]

CHARLES WARD APTHORP

The Apthorp Apartments, a historic full-block apartment building between Broadway and West End Avenue at Seventy-Ninth Street, was built in 1907 for William Waldorf Astor. The Apthorp takes its name from one of the former landowners, Boston-born Charles Ward Apthorp. Charles was the eldest son of Charles Apthorp Sr. of England and Grizzel Eastwick of Jamaica. Apthorp Sr. became the richest merchant in Boston, dealing in European goods and the importation and sale of enslaved Africans. His son Charles was a partner in the business and continued as a slaver after moving to New York in 1755.

Charles had just married into the McEvers family, who happened also to be in-laws of the Delanceys, and he moved in the elite society of New York. In 1763, after a few years of success in the city, Apthorp desired a country home in Bloomingdale, as befit a member of New York high society. He purchased much of Theunis Idens's former property and transformed it into a 263-acre estate, a portion of which lay along the western spine of the prepark. Oliver Delancey also sold him 153 acres of his west side estate, which included the site of the Apthorp Apartments and the woodlands that stretched into the prepark in the area from approximately Seventy-Ninth Street to Eighty-Third Street.[30]

In 1764, Apthorp built one of the most celebrated mansions in New York on a hilltop between today's Columbus and Amsterdam Avenues at Ninety-First Street. He called it "Elmwood" for the American elms that circled the villa. Orchards and parterre gardens surrounded the house, on soil that was enriched by the labor of Theunis Idens.[31]

Along his extensive property, Apthorp built a forty-foot-wide road, which he named Apthorp's Lane. Later it was known as Jauncey's Lane, named for William Jauncey, who purchased Apthorp's estate in 1799.[32] The lane began at the Bloomingdale Road at what would later become Ninety-Third Street and meandered east through the prepark, where it connected to the Kingsbridge Road at Ninety-Sixth Street.[33]

Like Oliver Delancey, Apthorp was a staunch loyalist and was arrested and tried for treason after the war, but he pledged loyalty to the new country and was permitted to keep his New York real estate. His vast properties in Massachusetts and Maine, however, were confiscated. Of all the prepark landowners, Apthorp topped the list of enslavers. An inventory of his property at his death in 1797 listed—along with the furniture, household goods, and livestock—his "servants": "York, a young negro man, aged about 37 worth £125; Jenny, a sickly wench, and her 3 children: a boy age 9½, a girl 5, and a boy 10 months . . . worth £225; John, who was to serve, 4 years, 1 mo., 15 days from Jan 12 worth £132; Molly to be made free at the particular Desine [design] of her late Master; and Maria and Hagar—two infirm old women, aged 75 to 90 years."[34] He is buried in the Apthorp family vault on the grounds of Trinity Church.

7.3 The Apthorp mansion, built in 1764 by wealthy slaver and British loyalist Charles Ward Apthorp, stood on the heights of today's Columbus Avenue and Ninety-First Street. He owned over 300 acres of West Side property, including prepark land from Seventy-Seventh to Ninety-Seventh Street and the site of the landmark building on Broadway and Seventy-Ninth Street that bears his name.

Source: "The Apthorp mansion, residence of Charles Ward Apthorp, merchant and member of Governor's Council in New York, 1763-1783." The Miriam and Ira D. Wallach Division of Art, Prints and Photographs: Print Collection, The New York Public Library, New York Public Library Digital Collections, https:// digitalcollections.nypl.org/items/510d47d9-7aa6-a3d9-e040-e00a18064a99.

THE APTHORP HEIRS

The Apthorps had ten children. Charles's land was bequeathed to his daughters: Rebecca Apthorp, Charlotte Vanden Heuvel, Grizzel Shaw, and Maria Williamson.[35] They and their husbands sold some of their west side land and kept a small portion for themselves, including land in the prepark.

Apthorp's youngest daughter, Rebecca, inherited a fifty-acre parcel of woodland that was formerly owned by Oliver Delancey and lay mainly in the prepark. In 1806, she conveyed the tract to David Wagstaff for about $5,500.[36] Wagstaff owned or leased a great deal of city-owned land on the east side.

Rebecca's sister Grizzel inherited the land above Eighty-Eighth Street to Ninety-Third Street on the western side of the prepark. When Grizzel married John Shaw, the land became his, and when they separated, Shaw was forced to build a home and provide income for his estranged wife. After the death of his first wife, Shaw, who had five grown daughters, married Grizzel, but as often happens in a second marriage, the children did not accept their father's new wife. We know that Grizzel was not welcomed into the family, as she referred to the Shaw women as "the enemies." The situation marked her as a social pariah, and the embarrassment of it all caused her to write bitterly that the rejection "compelled me to relinquish society and that rank in life as a Gentlewoman and a wife I was entitled to."[37]

In an 1805 agreement, John Shaw arranged for Grizzel to receive rents from his properties, £750 annually during her lifetime, or, if she preferred, a lump sum instead. The meager allowance must have seemed insulting and humiliating to a woman who had been raised in patrician luxury. Grizzel's shame and self-effacing

7.4 Gilbert Stuart painted this portrait of John Shaw, a staunch loyalist and a rather disagreeable man who was the estranged husband of Grizzel Apthorp.

Source: Gilbert Stuart, *John Shaw.* Metropolitan Museum of Art, Gift of Mr. and Mrs. Alfred Grima Johnson, 2005, accession number 2005.462.1

rage were expressed when in her will she bequeathed her clothes to one of her wealthier nieces, "if the rigid economy I am obliged to observe in dress should not render them unworthy of her acceptance."

In her will, Grizzel also firmly instructed her executors to make absolutely certain that Shaw's children, "for reasons that must be obvious," never be put in possession of her house, on what is now the site of Safari Playground and surrounding landscape. It was her desire to sell the property after her death.

Shaw knew that Grizzel's will forbade the transfer of her property to his daughters. Yet even before his death in 1817, Francis Barretto, one of Shaw's grandchildren, purchased the property. He lived there with his father and two sisters for several years, a devastating affront to Grizzel's wishes.[38]

Shaw had been a loyalist during the Revolution, and he kept ties to Britain through his business afterward. He was a wealthy partner in the firm Corp, Ellis, and Shaw, one of the most successful importers and exporters of British and

7.5 Grizzel Apthorp was the only member of her family to live in the prepark. Her estate on a promontory overlooking her family's mansion on today's Columbus Avenue between Ninetieth and Ninety-First Streets was on the site of today's Safari Playground and its surrounding landscape.

Source: Sara Cedar Miller, *Safari Playground.* Courtesy of the Central Park Conservancy.

American goods.[39] He did not hide his loyalist views even after the war, provoking contempt from his contemporaries. When news of George Washington's death arrived in New York, a contemporary diarist wrote that Shaw made insensitive and inappropriate comments to a group of gentlemen, saying "it was a pity General Washington had not died five and twenty years ago." Shaw repeated this line that evening in front of Colonel Mansfield, "who, having served under Washington, could scarce restrain from drubbing him at the time, but considering himself as only a visitor in the room, & unwilling to make any disturbance."

But word of what Shaw had said traveled quickly, and he was denounced for his remarks. The following day the two men met on the street and Shaw confronted Mansfield, calling him a liar. The words had scarcely left Shaw's mouth when Mansfield "had his arm up, and the great, the mighty Mr. John Shaw fell."

Shaw sported "a pretty black eye." On December 30, he apologized for the fight, excusing himself for being "in liquor," on which the diarist who recorded the incident wryly commented, "a very good come off to be sure—drunk at twelve o'clock at noon."[40]

Grizzel's sister Charlotte enjoyed a happy marriage to her neighbor John Cornelius Vanden Heuvel, the former governor of Demerara, a Dutch colony that today is British Guiana. He was also a rich plantation owner and merchant. In 1790, fleeing the yellow fever epidemic, he moved his family temporarily to New York, where he continued to import Caribbean goods like rum, Demerara sugar, coffee, and "elephant's teeth," or ivory, though that probably came from Africa.[41] Vanden Heuvel, his wife, Justina, and their three children were immediately absorbed into the elite society of New York. When Justina died, Vanden Heuvel married Charlotte Augusta Apthorp. As part of Charlotte's dowry, her father gave the newlyweds much of his property on the Upper West Side, including the mansion built in 1792 on which stands the Apthorp Apartments.[42] They also inherited land that today is the west side landscape of the park from Ninety-Third Street to Ninety-Fifth Street and was described as "deeply forested" and encircled with a stone wall.[43]After their parents' deaths, the Apthorp children decided to keep the estate intact rather than divide it. In 1827, they sold the larger portion of their property to Francis Price, an early real estate speculator and developer.[44] Price ignored their wishes to maintain the status quo and divided it into saleable lots. Though the sisters and their husbands traded their inherited property among themselves, two of the Vanden Heuvel daughters, Maria Hamilton and Susan Annette Gibbes, retained their land until it was purchased by the city in 1856 for Central Park.

7.6 In 1880, the memorial to founding father Alexander Hamilton was unveiled in Central Park by his son and biographer John Church Hamilton, who was married to Maria Vanden Heuvel, the granddaughter of Charles Ward Apthorp and an heir to his Central Park property.

Source: Carl H. Conrads, *Alexander Hamilton*, photograph, Sara Cedar Miller. Courtesy of the Central Park Conservancy.

Maria married John Church Hamilton, the fourth son of Alexander Hamilton. According to Hamilton's biographer, Ron Chernow, John Church "belatedly disgorged" a seven-volume "hagiographic treatment" of his father's life commissioned by his mother, Eliza Schuyler Hamilton. The son's account tidied up many of the more inappropriate aspects of the father's life or omitted them entirely, in particular his scandalous affair with Maria Reynolds, a married woman. Eliza never saw the completion of the project; she died before the volumes were published.[45]

On November 22, 1880, John Church Hamilton unveiled the granite statue of his father that he had commissioned from American sculptor Carl Conrads. It stands on a lawn facing the Metropolitan Museum of Art, with its back to the former lower reservoir, now the Great Lawn. Mayor Edward Cooper, who accepted the statue on behalf of the city, paid tribute to the "filial piety" that drove the project to completion. In the Great Fire of 1835, another son of Hamilton, Colonel James Hamilton, had rushed to rescue the marble statue of his father that once stood in the Merchants Exchange building on Wall Street. But he could not save it, and its loss—echoing Hamilton's violent demise—must have added to the family's sorrow.[46] Sitting on the dais on that inclement November day, perhaps John Church was musing on the nearly $11,000 award he had received twenty-four years earlier for his wife's west side slice of Central Park.[47]

When it came time to build Central Park, the Susan Vanden Heuvel's husband, Thomas S. Gibbes Jr. of South Carolina was totally against it. By 1856, Gibbes owned the largest share of the former Apthorp property. Like many other wealthy investors, he wanted to hold on to his land indefinitely. He let the commissioners know that he did "sincerely hope for my interest that the entire project for a Park may yet be abandoned."[48] Was he disappointed when the property owned by the Apthorp heirs netted them nearly $68,000—over $2 million in today's currency—of which he alone received about 60 percent?[49]

The Vanden Heuvel children and grandchildren were the last of Bloomingdale's elite. The area was still too distant from the city to be considered a suburb, but its many charms and the rise of real estate speculation attracted a new class of artisans and merchants to its borders.

chapter 8
Dividing Bloomingdale, 1790–1824

The prosperity of the decades following the Revolutionary War led to demographic changes in the landowners within American cities. Bloomingdale was an example of the shift from the landed gentry to the emerging middle class. The estates of the aristocratic families like the Delanceys and their loyalist neighbors were confiscated or sold to an enterprising group of merchants and artisans, who appreciated the alluring charms and investment opportunities of the Manhattan countryside. As the population of the dense urban downtown grew, the city marched northward up the island. When a series of deadly yellow fever epidemics plagued the city for several years, Bloomingdale offered New Yorkers of means a new, healthful retreat. Uptown property prices soared, and new development turned the once-bucolic countryside into a thriving suburb. Even free Black Americans found a corner of uptown to call their own.

MOUNT PROSPECT AND THE GREAT HILL

In 1796, in a succession of real estate transfers beginning with the heirs of Theunis Idens, the northernmost section of his property, now the Great Hill from 103rd Street to 107th Street, was sold to Dr. Samuel Borrowe.[1] Borrowe had graduated from Columbia College of Physicians and Surgeons, and he served as a surgeon at New York Hospital for twenty-two years, from 1795 to 1817. He had established a successful practice and published several articles, including one on *cynanche trachealis*, the nineteenth-century term for the inflammation of the glottis, larynx, or upper trachea that killed George Washington.[2]

8.1 The 1857 *View from Summit Rock* in Central Park shows the popularity of homes along the shoreline of the Hudson River from the West 70s to the West 90s in Bloomingdale.

Source: Aug. Ribstein, *View From Summit Rock [Central Park] looking West, The Hudson River and Palisades,* engraving, Fred Mayer, in the *First Annual Report,* 1857. Courtesy of the Central Park Conservancy.

When the park was under construction in 1865, it was on Borrowe's property that workers unearthed evidence of a British and Hessian Revolutionary War encampment. On the southern brow of the hill between 103rd Street and 104th Street, Borrowe erected an elegant mansion with sweeping views to the Hudson River.[3]

Borrowe's home was most likely the first residence on that site. It passed to several owners, who were attracted to the elegant house, the capacious pasture land, the views of the Hudson and East Rivers, and its proximity to the Kingsbridge and Bloomingdale Roads.[4]

From 1827 to 1836, the property was rented to James G. Russell for a private elite boarding school with about thirty students. In his advertisements for the Elmwood Hill Boarding School, he stressed the "salubrity of air, beauty and extent of play-grounds," and far from the corruption of children "of very different ages, or of improper and confirmed habits," Russell's students would thrive in the protected bubble of a "well-regulated and Christian family." They should be boys ages six to ten "who may have been but little, if at all, at any school, from under the immediate care of their parents or guardians, and raised within the secluded confines of the moneyed classes."[5]

In December 1832, New York City was in the midst of a deadly cholera epidemic, and Russell stressed the continued health of the twenty-six students who remained at the school, where "not a single instance of indisposition" occurred. The epidemic was borne by tainted water, and Elmwood Hill was located near the fresh spring water of Montagne's *fonteyn* and brook. Russell survived both the epidemic and the financial panic of 1837, but the last advertisement appeared in April, 1839.[6]

By 1843, when the aftereffects of a nationwide financial depression, the Panic of 1837, had abated, a hardware manufacturer named Whitney North Seymour purchased the property.[7] He was the first in a succession of wealthy owners. The land changed hands in the 1850s from Seymour to other wealthy merchants until it housed the park's designer, Frederick Law Olmsted, and his new family after the property was taken by the city for the park.[8]

BEFORE SENECA VILLAGE

Samuel Stilwell was a typical New Yorker. He moved from Long Island to the city in the 1780s. He owned a prosperous grocery business and became a leader in the John Street Methodist Church. Yet deep down, a part of him yearned to leave the crush of urban chaos for the simple pleasures of rural life. In 1791, when the New York economy was booming, Stilwell purchased nearly a hundred and fifty acres of Delancey's former west side farm, seeing a chance to return to nature while also becoming part of Bloomingdale's "agreeable society" of country gentlemen.[9]

We know a great deal about Stilwell from his biography written by his adoring grandson Samuel Doughty, son of the Stilwells' adopted daughter, Eliza. Doughty believed that Stilwell, "an intimate of Hamilton," would have enjoyed an official station in the new federal government "were it not for the infamous duel, which became a turning point in Stilwell's life."[10]

Bloomingdale's fertile soil allowed Stilwell to indulge his interest in gardening. He had a particular passion for fruit trees. His green thumb raised "the finest apricots, plums, cherries and peaches. Apricots, especially, grew large and fair, and ripened unstung by insects." Despite his remarkable produce, Stilwell's financial success as a farmer was limited. But he shrewdly recognized the subsequent rise in the value of the land, which made up for his farm's shortcomings.[11]

After five years, the joys of rural life were fading for Mrs. Stilwell, who felt "the time spent at Bloomingdale was lost." She preferred the energy of urban life, and Mr. Stilwell considered his Sunday commute to the John Street Methodist Church far too tedious.

In 1796, he hired Polish surveyor Casimir Goerck to divide his farm into forty saleable plots. The Stilwell property extended from the Bloomingdale Road eastward to the city common lands at Seventh Avenue. Doughty confirmed that his grandfather's former farm "is now almost all within the bounds of Central Park," encompassing everything from the western edge of the Great Lawn to Central Park West, stretching from Seventy-Ninth Street north to Eighty-Ninth Street.[12]

In June 1799, Stilwell advertised for an "exchange for property in this city, a House and 26 acres of Land well-stocked with fruit" six miles from the city, and forty acres in separate lots.[13] The west side had several agricultural lots and fenced property even before Stilwell purchased Delancey's former land, but he instructed Goerck to divide his lots into much smaller parcels for larger profits. Stilwell purchased a modest house on respectable Bowery Lane but kept some choice lots for himself within the prepark.

While many New Yorkers fled to Bloomingdale in 1803 to avoid the yellow fever epidemic, the Stilwells moved even farther north, to Danbury, Connecticut. There Stilwell was mentored in the art of surveying, and from then on he mapped his own property. With his new expertise, he was appointed a city surveyor in 1803, and in 1810 he was promoted to street commissioner. This was the year before the official adoption of the Manhattan street grid, in which the city laid down an orderly grid of twelve avenues and 155 streets to tame the chaotic urban sprawl and plan for uptown development. Surveying for this was a monumental feat, so the commissioners hired a young surveyor named John Randel, an acquaintance of Stilwell. Stilwell greatly admired Randel's methodical, exacting, and inventive genius. Stilwell's grandson, Samuel Doughty, himself a well-respected city surveyor, called Randel's work "probably the most perfect thing of the kind."[14]

As street commissioner, Stilwell was deeply involved in the administration to execute the commissioners' grid plan. He oversaw the budget and noticed loopholes in the agreement between Randel and the city, which ultimately cost $30,000 in additional funds to set markers for every intersection up to 155th Street.[15] From 1811 to 1818, Randel and his crew installed marble monuments

8.2 Iron bolts, such as this one in an undisclosed location in Central Park, were placed by surveyor John Randel to demarcate the intersection of every street and avenue. If the corner was on rock, Randel placed a small one-inch bolt. If the intersection was on soil, he placed a three-foot-high marble monument inscribed with the street and the avenue. An original one can be seen in the Luce Center at the New-York Historical Society.

Source: Sara Cedar Miller, *Iron Bolt*. Courtesy of the Central Park Conservancy.

(when on soil) and drilled iron bolts (when on rock) to mark the future intersections of every street and avenue. In all they laid more than fifteen hundred marble monuments and nearly one hundred iron bolts.

One of the iron bolts had been discovered in the summer of 2004 by Reuben Rose-Redwood, a geographer from the University of Victoria conducting research on the 1811 plan for his master's thesis. Several more were discovered in Central Park in 2014 by archeologists working for the Central Park Conservancy. Randel's biographer, Marguerite Holloway, called it "a discovery akin to finding a marble statue submerged in a remote lake or a lamppost in the wild woods of Narnia."[16]

A few years before being appointed as a city surveyor, Stilwell was chosen by the state commissioners of taxes as an assessor for New York State, where he evaluated "lands and dwelling houses and the enumeration of slaves in the

State of New York." This research into enslavers "may have quickened his zeal for their emancipation, for soon after he manumitted all the slaves he owned."[17] Perhaps Stilwell had enslaved more than one person at an earlier time, but in the U.S. Census of 1790, only one, Rachel, was listed in his household. Ten years later, the census recorded one free person of color in his household. By 1808, he had officially manumitted Rachel, who remained with the Stilwells as an employee, "the presiding genius of the kitchen."[18] When Stilwell switched to the Forsyth Street Church he was approached by an enslaved woman named Day who "induced him to buy her time," which he did, along with that of her young son. She too became a domestic servant in the household, but died soon after.[19]

Day's son, Jem, succumbed to an all too common tragedy that befell children who were born into slavery. The Stilwells worried about him throughout his growing years, though they were reportedly frustrated at his willful personality. Devastated, undoubtedly, by his mother's death, he acted out in mischief often, including "astonishing feats of strength, agility and daring." Once, for example, he danced on a beam above a furnace in full blast. Stilwell found Jem a position at a Black barber shop, but he was fired after one too many mishaps with the customers. He was then apprenticed to a cotton factory in Paterson, New Jersey, but after a while ran off with a friend. They got lost and spent the night in a barn, which gave Jem severe frostbite. He returned to the Stilwells the next day and was treated by a doctor who saved his feet from amputation. From there, Jem wandered Long Island, taking odd jobs, everything from woodcutter to sailor. He would repeatedly return to the Stilwells, the only haven he had ever known. But after arriving one night intoxicated, he became enraged when the straitlaced and teetotaling couple turned him away. Doughty, who also lived with his in-laws, commented that Jem's "aspect had changed, the fun was gone out of his eyes, something diabolical had come into its place." They never heard from him again.[20]

ROBERT L. BOWNE

Despite his devotion to Methodism, Samuel Stilwell openly praised other faiths, particularly Quakerism, which he believed captured "the piety and the simplicity of the Gospel." When he divided his estate into small lots, he sold several of them to some Quakers from Long Island and New York.[21] When Oliver Delancey's daughter Charlotte had sold her father's property, the buyer, Joseph Orchard, took out a mortgage from two Oyster Bay Quakers, Daniel Cock and Daniel Underhill. It was Cock and Underhill who ultimately purchased Orchard's property and sold it to Stilwell.[22] In turn, Robert Latham Bowne, a member of the famous Flushing Quaker family, was Stilwell's first buyer.

Quakers, formally known as the Religious Society of Friends, were so named because they would "tremble in the way of the Lord." Their religious movement began in England, where they were persecuted for challenging and rejecting many tenets of the Anglican church. Quakerism attracted average people who felt the elite Church of England did not speak for or to them. They left England, and the first group of them came to New Amsterdam in 1657. But it was out of the frying pan and into the fire, for one year earlier, Director General Peter Stuyvesant had banned all religious meetings that were not part of the Dutch Reformed Church.

Stuyvesant immediately declared the Quakers outlaws. When one of their preachers was fined, flogged, and jailed, a group of Flushing Quakers petitioned Stuyvesant for religious liberty—known as the Flushing Remonstrance, a precursor to the Constitution's freedom of religion amendment. Stuyvesant denied the petition, dismissed much of the local government of Flushing, installed new Dutch Reformed leaders in its place, and imprisoned some signers of the petition. When a man named John Bowne, great-great-grandfather to Robert, allowed the Quakers to meet in his home, Stuyvesant expelled him from the colony. The banished Bowne went to Amsterdam, where he confronted the managers of the Dutch West India Company, who overruled Stuyvesant and ordered him to allow different religious beliefs in the Dutch colony.[23]

Robert L. Bowne may have gotten the idea to purchase uptown land from his cousin Walter Bowne, who had purchased a common land lot only three years earlier that today is a section of the Ramble. Walter, a wealthy merchant, was the mayor of New York from 1829 to 1833. Robert was not nearly as successful. By the time he died in 1821, he had defaulted on the $20,000 mortgage that he received

8.3 (*overleaf*) The West Meadow was once the property that Samuel Stilwell sold to Robert L. Bowne, a member of the celebrated Quaker family who lost his west side property due to foreclosure.

Source: Sara Cedar Miller, *West Meadow*. Courtesy of the Central Park Conservancy.

from land speculator William Edgar in 1809. For years, Bowne's wife, Naomi, and son, George, fought to hold on to the land, but ultimately the court ruled in favor of Edgar.[24] After a series of real estate exchanges, the land was briefly owned in the 1850s by Peter Augustus Jay, the son of John Jay, the first chief justice of the United States. Jay transferred it to Martin Zabriskie, who sold the land to the city for Central Park.[25]

THE DEMILTS

Summit Rock, at Central Park West and Eighty-Third Street, is the highest natural point in the park, and the only place in the park from which in winter you can see a tiny slice of the Hudson River and the New Jersey Palisades. Before the west side was built up, Egbert Viele, who named the rock, included this expansive view in the park's 1857 *First Annual Report*.[26] The mansions, crowded together and lining the Hudson River in the West 80s, show the desirability of a water view.

Originally the massive Summit Rock outcrop and surrounding landscape, now Central Park West, were two small lots belonging to Samuel Stilwell, part of a farm he had named Prospect Hill. In 1811, the Quaker Demilt brothers, Thomas and Benjamin, purchased it from him.[27] On the 1802 Goerck map of Stilwell's property, Eighth Avenue is labeled "Prospect Avenue," a strong indication that the promontory was one of the most outstanding features of Stilwell's huge estate.[28] The Demilt brothers paid $2,300, an enormous price for a small piece of land surrounding a large chunk of Manhattan schist. Why would anyone pay so much money—not to mention the associated annual taxes and assessments—for a property so costly to develop?

The eminently practical Demilts must have had a plan. The brothers were celebrated watchmakers and silversmiths, whose creations ranged from modest timepieces and silverware to jeweled works of art. A contemporary authority proposed that the Demilts were "perhaps the foremost horologists of New York City from approximately 1800 to 1845."[29] As cutting-edge entrepreneurs, they may have aspired to be the first Americans to sell British-made nautical chronometers and astronomical clocks, and to do that they would need an observatory.

The chronometer, invented in England by John Harrison in 1761, revolutionized sea travel in the Atlantic world. At sea, a sailor measures his location and progress by longitude and latitude. Latitude is easily determined. A sailor

8.4 The Demilt family that owned Summit Rock and environs were celebrated watchmakers and advertised their business on the watch paper that would be inserted into every timepiece.

Source: Demilt Watch Paper, Collection Stephen Manheimer.

simply observes the location of the North Star or the noonday sun and measures its angle relative to the horizon, which would tell him how far north or south of the equator he was. But longitude was much more difficult, because the earth spins, so there is no consistently located heavenly body by which to gauge longitude. Sailors would often take two clocks with them, one set to the time at the home port and one set to the local time on the ship. Because the earth rotates once per day, sailors knew that every hour difference was a fifteen-degree change in latitude, or about a thousand nautical miles. But the clocks of the seventeenth and early eighteenth centuries were pendulum timepieces, which were inaccurate aboard a rolling ship. Harrison's marine chronometer was instead a spring-driven escapement timekeeper, sealed in a vacuum and impervious to the movement of the outside world. With the ability to predict and guarantee a ship's course, the device remade world commerce and exploration and saved countless lives from shipwrecks or scurvy.[30] Watchmakers relied on astronomical observatories—generally sited on high altitudes with access to dark skies—to assess the precision of their chronometers. If the instrument passed exacting tests, it would be certified and valued as an observatory chronometer. Perhaps the Demilts purchased Summit Rock for its altitude and remote location, a perfect place for an astronomical observatory.

By 1818, Benjamin and Samuel Demilt established Demilt's Longitude Observatory, but it was located above their downtown shop on Pearl Street. They enjoyed the distinction of being the first American agents of nautical chronometers.[31] Though they never used their rock for an observatory—or for any other purpose—they held on to their property until it was taken for the park in 1856. Eventually a weather observatory was established in the park, first in the Arsenal and then on the tower of Belvedere Castle, where it has remained since 1920.

The Demilts were outstanding philanthropists. Benjamin was a founding member of the General Society of Mechanics and Tradesmen, a fraternal organization whose primary purpose was to aid fellow craftsmen who were ill or had financial troubles. It still exists today, headquartered on West Forty-Fourth Street.[32] In his will, Benjamin also left money to the widows of several silversmiths, many of whom named their children after him, such as Benjamin Demilt Ten Eyck and Demilt Gorsuch.

JOSEPH PEARSALL

Another Quaker and clockmaker, Joseph Pearsall, was the first owner of two of Stilwell's lots. These would eventually become an African American community known as Seneca Village.[33] In March 1787, Pearsall advertised the sale of his seventy-acre "valuable plantation" in Cow Bay on Long Island Sound, and by November he had purchased Stilwell's lots for a little more than $3,000.[34] The property was adjacent to Bowne's lots, and Pearsall would have known Bowne, as Hannah Bowne Pearsall was a relation.[35]

To give access to his lots from the Bloomingdale Road to the common lands at Seventh Avenue—roughly Broadway to the western edge of the Great Lawn—Stilwell, Pearsall, and Bowne petitioned the Common Council in 1798 to open a private east-west road through their adjacent properties. The council granted permission and named it Stilwell's Lane. Inside the prepark, the sixty-foot path connected with the north-south Spring Street—on later maps, "Old Lane"—that ran from Eighty-First Street to Eighty-Sixth Street, leading to "Tanner's Spring."[36] Promoted as a "never-failing spring" in real estate ads, it would have been a valuable asset for future residents of the area, including those in the densely populated Seneca Village.[37] By the twentieth century, park managers had boarded up Tanner's Spring. Today, it still exudes enough of a puddle to attract small birds.

SAMUEL OGDEN

Pearsall decided to pull up roots in New York and invest in property elsewhere. He sold his lots for $4,000 to wealthy ironmonger Colonel Samuel Ogden of Newark, New Jersey, netting $700 profit. Pearsall and his partner, Effingham Embree, both belonged to families that specialized in making timepieces, but many were also ironmongers, which may be how Ogden came to purchase Pearsall's lots. Samuel's father, Judge David Ogden, also had a farm in Flushing, the community of Quaker New York, another possible connection to Pearsall.[38]

When Judge Ogden died in 1798, he willed his Flushing farm to his son Nicholas, as he clearly had "unsettled affairs" with his son Samuel, who had not repaid the loan for his estate in Boonton, New Jersey. He stipulated in his will that if Samuel had not repaid it within the month, the executors would "proceed to collect by law." David Ogden may also have had a long-standing grudge against his son, an "ardent patriot" in the otherwise loyalist Ogden family. Samuel served as a colonel the New Jersey militia during the Revolutionary War.

Samuel Ogden also made one little-known but significant contribution to the life of Aaron Burr. When three-year-old Burr became an orphan, he and his sister were raised by his uncle and aunt, Rhoda Ogden Burr, Samuel's cousin. Rhoda's brothers, Matthias and Aaron Ogden, became Burr's lifelong friends. After the legendary duel that ended with the death of Alexander Hamilton, Burr was arrested and tried for treason in New York, the state where Hamilton died, but was acquitted for lack of evidence. But although Hamilton had died in New York, the duel had been fought in Bergen County, New Jersey. There Burr was indicted for Hamilton's murder by a grand jury in November 1804. At a critical moment in the state's Supreme Court trial, three years later, Colonel Samuel Ogden stepped in and "quashed" the motion, and Burr, the vice president at the time, was acquitted.[39] As is often the case, family came before country.

Ogden held on to his prepark property for only one year. In 1804 he sold it to Major James Fairlie at a loss.[40] This tiny parcel was small potatoes for Ogden, who was also a major land speculator in upstate New York, at one point selling over ninety thousand acres to Judge William Cooper, the father of author James Fenimore Cooper.[41] Judge Cooper was a witness to the Pearsall-to-Ogden conveyance, and on that same day Ogden also sold Cooper a house and lot on Pearl Street for $15,000.[42]

JAMES FAIRLIE

Major James Fairlie, a distinguished officer in the Revolution, was much sought after in New York's elite social circles for his amiable company and quick wit. He was one of the few to evoke genuine outbursts of laughter from the usually reserved General Washington. Count Casimir Pulaski, a Polish nobleman who joined the Continental Army during the Revolution, wrote to Benjamin Franklin about Major Fairlie: "for sagacity, wit, and knowledge of his profession, he has no superior: playful and satirical, or instructive, as he varies from one subject to another. I have taken much delight in his society, and think he has given me more instruction in pronouncing the English language than any other officer I have met with."[43]

Fairlie entered the army in 1776 at age nineteen. He was assigned first as an ensign to Colonel Alexander McDougall, possibly to guard McGowan's Pass.[44] Two years later, he became an aide-de-camp to General Baron Von Steuben. He fought in the Battle of Monmouth, and possibly he knew Colonel Ogden, who served in the New Jersey militia, from the war. He was described as "full

8.5 Artist Ralph Earl was allowed to paint several portraits like this one of Major
James Fairlie during the year he spent in debtor's prison, 1786–1787.

Source: Ralph Earl, *Portrait of Major James Fairlie*, 1786–1787. Courtesy of The Society of the Cincinnati,
Washington, D.C.

of courage, but tender-hearted"; Fairlie's most painful memory of the war was
when General Washington ordered him to witness the hanging of the unfortunate Major André, the British spy, who had colluded with the American traitor
Benedict Arnold.[45]

Fairlie, who was born in Albany, married Maria Yates, the daughter of New
York State Chief Justice Robert Yates. They lived in the First Ward, the enclave
of those in New York's highest social strata. He was a clerk of the state Supreme
Court, twice a member of the assembly, a presidential elector, an alderman, and
a delegate to the 1821 New York Constitutional Convention.

Fairlie kept his real estate investments to a minimum. His purchase in the
prepark seems to have been his only uptown property. He kept it for three years
and then sold it in June 1807 to a man named Naphtali Judah.

NAPHTALI JUDAH

Naphtali Judah, known around town as "quite the busy-body," bought Fairlie's property with a mortgage for $6,500—almost twice what Fairlie had paid Ogden.[46]

When he purchased his property, Judah was a wealthy partner in Benjamin S. Judah and Brothers, importers of products from the West Indies. Soon afterward, President Jefferson's embargo on exports to Britain hampered all Caribbean importation, and the business failed. Although Judah continued his social and political activities—he was a trustee and president of New York's prominent Shearith Israel Jewish congregation, a sachem of the Tammany Society, and an active leader of the Clintonian Democrats—he never recovered his pre-embargo wealth. He transitioned into auction, stationer, bookseller, and lottery manager enterprises, the last of which lost him his reputation and his mortgaged property.[47]

Just as the contemporary New York Lottery raises revenue for public education, the lotteries of the nineteenth century funded charitable and educational causes as well as government public projects, like the repair of roads, bridges, and canals or the construction of hospitals, schools, and libraries.[48] In 1810, for instance, the state legislature held a public lottery for the advancement of medical science, which contributed to the sale of Dr. David Hosack's Elgin Botanical Gardens to Columbia College. In 1818, another medical science lottery was held. This time, however, the advancement went directly into the pocket of lottery manager Naphtali Judah. Judah claimed he had received a letter from an anonymous friend advising him to buy lottery ticket number 15,468. The number had come to this so-called friend "in a dream." Everyone recognized this alibi as ridiculous, Judah's absurd attempt to cover up the pre-arranged winning ticket number from which he received a large share of the $100,000 prize.[49]

After the scam was uncovered, Judah's finances nosedived. He was forced into bankruptcy and defaulted on his mortgage, owing Fairlie nearly eight thousand dollars, which included the interest on the initial loan.[50] Fairlie held on to his land for four more years and then put it up for sale or lease once more. In March 1822, he placed a classified ad in the *National Advocate*, which ran for only four weeks. Presumably Fairlie had found his prospective buyer, John Whitehead.[51]

THE WHITEHEADS

John and Elizabeth Whitehead are frequently cited as the white couple who sold their property to a group of African Americans who founded a community that became known as Seneca Village. Yet with all the attention the community has received, scholars have shown little interest in the Whiteheads.[52] Given the speculative nature of New Yorkers, one historian assumed they were simply "real estate prospectors" and questioned whether their intentions were little more than "an opportunity for quick profit."[53] Another writer conjectured that the Whiteheads must have been surprised when Black New Yorkers purchased their land, an assumption that renders the couple into passive actors in the story.[54]

The Whiteheads were not the only landowners in the prepark to subdivide their property in 1825. That same year, Benjamin L. Benson sold off his family's long-held Harlem property, and two developers named Francis Price and Enoch Wiswall bought out the Harlem common lands. But unlike these others, the Whiteheads most likely divided their sixteen-acre plot as much in furtherance of a social cause as for financial gain.

We do not know for certain, but it is possible that the Whiteheads worked in tandem with the Black community to develop the settlement. No one has ever found any standard real estate advertisement in any New York newspaper for the Whitehead tracts. When Samuel Stilwell, Joseph Pearsall, and James Fairlie desired to sell their properties, they placed advertisements to attract buyers. But as far as we can tell, the Whiteheads did not. This suggests that they already knew the people to whom they would sell their land.[55]

Between 1825 and 1835, John Whitehead sold lots *solely* to Blacks or to the Black A.M.E. Zion Church to use as burial grounds. After his death from consumption in 1835, his family—widow, Maria (his second wife) (later Maria Palmer), daughter, Mary Whitehead Turner, and her husband, Richard Turner—continued the tradition of selling lots to Black buyers, with only one exception.[56] The Whiteheads also conveyed lots to African Americans on Bloomingdale property they owned on West Fifty-Third Street between Sixth and Seventh Avenue, the site of today's Hilton Hotel.[57]

The name John Whitehead is too common to trace with any certainty. Little is known about where he came from. One thing we know with some certainty:

a marriage between a John Whitehead and an Elizebeth Crandell took place at First Stanford Baptist Church in Duchess County on June 19, 1796. We know also that John Whitehead died in New York in 1835 at the age of sixty-two, making his birthdate 1773. A marriage at age twenty-three would have been appropriate.[58] To date, no record of Elizabeth or Elizebeth Whitehead has been found.

John Whitehead seems to have had several callings. Beginning in 1805, he was listed in *Longworth's City Directory* as a shoemaker, living at 31 Harmen Street (now East Broadway) on the Lower East Side. By 1816, he was listed as a cartman, still living at the same address, and one year later he moved to Orchard Street.[59]

Cartmen or carters were the truckers and movers of the nineteenth century. They were an elite group. Until the mid-century they were exclusively white, and proudly wore an identifiable uniform of "white frock, trousers, and farmer's hat and boots."[60]

8.6 *Moving Day (In Little Old New York)*, (detail), depicts May 1, the most lucrative day for New York City cartmen like John Whitehead. That day, every renter in New York moved from one home to another. The cartman in this 1825 painting wears the uniform of a white smock and top hat.

Source: Unknown Artist, *Moving Day (In Little Old New York)*, (detail), ca. 1827. Metropolitan Museum of Art. Bequest of Mrs. Screven Lorillard (Alice Whitney), from the collection of Mrs. J. Insley Blair, 2016. Accession Number: 2016.797.21.

Cartmen were the lifeblood of New York City, central to its social, political, and economic health. According to cartman Isaac Lyons, they were trusted confidants, free to go anywhere, "whether it be into the vaults of a bank or a lady's dressing-room, everybody supposes that *it is all right*."[61] The profession ranged from "catch cartmen," who hauled whatever came their way, such as firewood, farm produce, soil, or manure, to "fine arts" cartmen, who transported the paintings, sculpture, mirrors, and antiques of the wealthy—called by Lyons "the big bugs"—which required an expensive spring cart and other costly safety measures.[62] After the Revolution, more than one thousand cartmen were awarded the status of freemanship, giving them the right to work, vote, and hold local office.[63]

In 1819, of the nearly two hundred households on Orchard Street, nearly an eighth of the heads of them, John Whitehead included, were cartmen. But whereas the census recorded the other cartmen under the category of "Tenant Renting at $5 per Annum," Whitehead alone fell under the highest income grouping, "Freeholders of £100 and upwards." Of the households on Orchard Street, only 10 percent belonged to that monied group.[64] John Whitehead must have had much more than that minimum, as three years later he put down $1,100 (or approximately £238) for Alderman James Fairlie's seventeen-acre property. It was a significant amount for such a remote tract, roughly three quarters of a million dollars in today's money.[65]

The majority of white American-born cartmen held virulently nativist and racist sentiments, and they wielded enough political power to ensure that the city never granted a carting license to either foreign-born "aliens" or Blacks until the mid-nineteenth century.[66] The historian Graham Russell Hodges, author of *New York City Cartmen, 1667–1850*, speculated that John Whitehead's inclusive actions would have marked him as an outlier of his profession.[67]

By 1831, Whitehead had scaled the social ladder to assume the title of "Gentleman" in some of his deeds, a label generally applied to one whose income was derived from scholarly pursuits or from earned or inherited financial wealth—a man removed from the strain and vulnerability of manual labor.[68] An income of more than £100 and real estate investments were sufficient qualifications to be considered a Gentleman in *some* New York City circles, although the pedigreed "Gentlemen" born into the title would probably dismiss Whitehead as a wannabe.

And what of the Whiteheads' religion? Perhaps that might illuminate their involvement with the Black community. A clue to it is in their association with Reverend Edward Mitchell, who had married John and his second wife, Maria Burtsell, on May 17, 1828.[69] In 1801, Mitchell had joined the John Street Methodist Church, but later he became one of three prominent members who had questioned "the belief of limited future punishment, and a final restitution of all things," that is, being condemned to everlasting life in Hell. These "unpleasant" issues caused Mitchell and the others to withdraw from Methodism in 1796 and form the Society of United Christian Friends.

At the beginning, the United Christian Friends numbered only fourteen members.[70] According to their belief, God bestowed universal salvation to the entire human race, rather than granting it to a few exclusive adherents of any one particular faith.[71] This new church was born of a widening influence of democracy in political and social life that permeated spiritual life in the decades following the American Revolution. Historian Nathan O. Hatch viewed many of these movements as collective expressions that "challenged common people to take religious destiny into their own hands, to think for themselves."[72] Adopting the term "Friends" suggests that Marshall's society may also have been influenced by the Quakers, who were the first white religious group to denounce slavery in England and America.

By 1818, the Society of United Christian Friends had expanded and become the First Universalist Church.[73] A leader in that community, Henry Fitz, a preacher and editor of the Universalist Union's newspaper, the *Gospel Herald*, had a close business association with John Whitehead. Fitz was "a man of comprehensive and intensely active intellect, with remarkable independence of thought."[74] He witnessed several of the Whiteheads' legal conveyances of land for Seneca Village. Perhaps John and Maria shared in the broad-minded beliefs of their friends, Reverend Mitchell and Henry Fitz.[75] Their radical idea—that God's eternal salvation was granted to all, regardless of their faith—was not a far leap from the idea that dignity is granted to all, regardless of race.

In 1816, nine years before the establishment of Seneca Village, former members of the Manumission Society had formulated a plan to encourage all free Blacks to return to their "true home" in Africa.[76] Calling themselves the American Colonization Society, these white advocates for Black repatriation established the colony of Liberia on the coast of West Africa. Their goal was to ameliorate the restrictive and threatening situation of Black Americans by removing them from harmful racial injustice and assuring them the full rights they were currently denied. But the Black community identified the plan as a thinly veiled ploy to get rid of them. They had been in America for generations, and they stood their ground. America, not Africa, was their homeland, and they would fight for their right to stay and prosper on American soil. Seneca Village may have been the result. Many abolitionist whites were opposed to the colonization movement and joined in the Black community's growing rebuke of it.[77] Perhaps the free-thinking Whiteheads were among them.

chapter 9

Dividing Bloomingdale, Seneca Village

The Residents, 1825–1857

In their 1992 study *The Park and the People*, historians Roy Rosenzweig and Elizabeth Blackmar described the existence of Seneca Village, the once forgotten Black settlement located on what is now the west side of Central Park from Eighty-Third Street to Eighty-Ninth Street.[1] Their research celebrated Seneca Village as the longest and most stable African American property-owning community in America. The reaction to the information was immediate and overwhelming. Urban archeologists, historians, fiction and nonfiction writers, clergy, and artists all converged on the topic, and it was written into school curricula from kindergarten to college.[2]

This chapter of the Seneca Village story reviews the legal status of Black Americans in 1825, the year of the community's inception, and takes us through the earliest history of the residents up to the 1850s. With many important church records lost, only data from four censuses, city directories, a handful of court cases, and newspaper notices and articles at hand, our window into this community is small. The most available information appears in the real estate deeds, tax assessments, and wills, on which this study relies heavily. We can trace the changing population of the community through the buying and selling of property, their profits and losses, and perhaps discern some of the reasons they formed the community in the first place. Religion is central to Black social, political, and spiritual culture throughout America, and the three congregations in the community had a vital connection to the lives of the residents and to the congregants who came from farther away to worship. The following chapter will discuss those landowners who lived downtown, and whose records offer a much fuller picture of their public and personal lives.

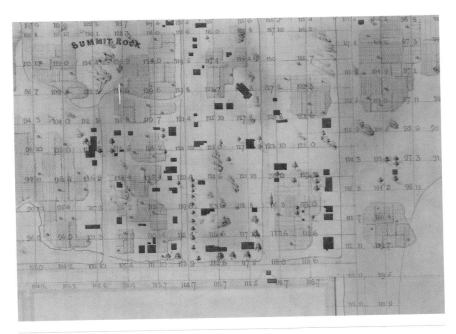

9.1 Seneca Village within Central Park, Seventh to Eighth Avenue, Eighty-Third Street to Eighty-Eighth Street, is detailed in Egbert Viele's *Map of Lands Included in The Central Park From A Topographical Survey*. Viele, a West Point-trained engineer, indicated over fifty houses and outbuildings, three churches, a school, rock outcrops, garden beds, and trees as they existed in 1855. The following year the landowners and a few renters received financial compensation. Many of the resident landowners left at that time, but those who remained or moved into the vacant homes became lessees of the city. In 1857, they were evicted to begin construction of Central Park.

Source: Egbert Viele, *Map of Lands Included in The Central Park from a Topographical Survey* (detail), June 17, 1855. New York City Municipal Archives.

The New York State Legislature began the process of gradually emancipating enslaved Blacks in 1799, and in 1817 the law added a provision that any child born to an enslaved mother between 1799 and 1827 was bound to serve their mother's enslaver and live on their property until they came of age: twenty-five for a woman and twenty-eight for a man.[3] It was not until July 4, 1827, that all Black New Yorkers received full freedom under the law. According to the groundbreaking work of historian Vivienne Kruger, in 1820—only five years before the inception of Seneca Village—30 percent of New York Blacks still lived with white families. This was still the case until 1848, for most of the years that Seneca Village existed.[4]

After slavery's long and painful legacy, a family together under one roof was perhaps the most cherished freedom of all. First-generation Seneca Villagers were old enough to have grown up in a white household, and for some of them, it was the first time their family enjoyed the most basic experience that white Americans took for granted.[5]

To date, Samuel Harding is the only resident of Seneca Village who can be identified as formerly enslaved. Harding was born in Staten Island in the 1760s and freed on June 12, 1810.[6] His master, John J. Glover, was a wealthy merchant and director of the New York branch of the Bank of the United States.[7] In 1809, when Glover fell on hard times, he was forced to sell his real estate and manumit some of his enslaved persons, including Sam Harding. At the time of his manumission, Harding would have spent his entire life from childhood to middle age in bondage. His daughter, Elizabeth Harding, was born while he was still enslaved, and possibly her mother, Diana, as well. Elizabeth Harding was one of the first buyers of John Whitehead's land.[8]

Shortly after purchasing James Fairlie's property, John Whitehead hired city surveyor Daniel Ewen—who later purchased adjacent land for himself—to subdivide his property into two hundred lots. This process was completed and and the survey filed with the city on September 16, 1825. The very next day, the Whiteheads conveyed their first twenty-seven lots to five members of New York's A.M.E. Zion Church. The buyers were Epiphany Davis, Andrew Williams, John Carter, James Newton, and Edward Hamilton.[9] For them, the dream of a safe and separate Black settlement as well as a good investment was at last a reality, though only Williams would ever live there.

From records, we can generalize that most of the village residents worked as unskilled manual laborers, porters, sailors, gardeners, service-industry workers, and domestics. Many of them had positions in one of the three churches besides their day jobs. They were hardworking, saving diligently until they could buy their own property. Most of the Whiteheads' early buyers purchased between one and three lots for an average of $40 each. This was a huge amount when the yearly earnings of unskilled workers hovered around $69. Scraping together the money for the land and erecting a home was beyond the reach of most Black families.

Those landowners who could afford it might have built their homes soon after they bought their property, but for most, it likely took time to amass the savings to do so. In the tax assessment records for 1828, John Whitehead owned thirteen acres and three houses. None of his buyers is listed in those records, though perhaps three

9.2 Both of William Pease's two houses were built atop flat elevated outcrops, the only documented placement in the entire village.

Source: Sara Cedar Miller, *Site of William Pease Home.* Courtesy of Central Park Conservancy.

families first rented the land and two of them built homes in anticipation of future sales. One house existed when John Whitehead purchased the property in 1824.[10]

The structures in the village ranged from modest one-story homes to three-story homes. A few buildings had basements.[11]

Many of the poorer residents, particularly those who rented their lots, probably constructed their own shanties. These structures proliferated throughout the prepark in the 1840s. One structure that housed A.M.E. Zion sexton Ishmael Allen and his family of seven measured just nine feet by ten, an unimaginably small space for so many people.[12] The 1865 Council of Hygiene described the shanties' construction:

built of rough boards, which form the floor, the sides, and the roof . . . either on the ground or little raised above it. It is from six to ten feet high, and . . . it contains no fireplace or chimney, but a stove pipe, the pipe from which passes through a hole in the roof. It has from one to three or four windows . . . Some shanties have but one room; others an additional smaller apartment, used as a bedroom. The better shanties are lathed and plastered . . . There is no sink or drainage.[13]

Our earliest visual account of homes in the village is the Colton Map of 1836. It depicts either twelve or thirteen dwellings, just under half of the twenty-nine homes in the entire prepark at that time.[14] The map matches the 1840 federal census, which listed thirteen Black households and one identifiable white renter, a man named Laurence McCaffrey, who leased the largest house in the community from Epiphany Davis. This brought the total village population to at least sixty-two. The number of structures would grow from eighteen in 1846 to approximately fifty-three in 1855.[15]

The landowners and lessees who lived in Seneca Village—similar to the Dutch families of prepark Harlem—intermarried, raised children together, prayed together, and helped each other in times of joy and in times of hardship.[16] Through deeds, wills, court records, and newspaper articles, we can now survey a landscape of multigenerational landowning families.[17]

Just consider the example of Samuel Harding and his extended family, some of the earliest landowners in Seneca Village. The year after his daughter Elizabeth bought her lot, she married Obadiah McCollin. Together they would purchase additional lots and build two adjacent homes along Eighty-Sixth Street. Diana Harding, Samuel's wife, would also buy a lot in 1826. Diana's sister Jane also purchased land as an investment in Seneca Village together with the Hardings.[18] We know from conveyances that Jane was married to Cornelius Henry, a Seneca Village landowner, who purchased his lots from John Whitehead only moments after Elizabeth Harding bought hers.[19] After Henry's death, Jane Henry probably married landowner Henry Harris.[20] Long-term renters Robert and Sarah Green, who built a home on a lot leased from Samuel Stilwell, were related Obadiah McCollin.[21]

SUFFRAGE

Per the New York State Constitution of 1777, all male residents over the age of twenty-one could vote for the state assembly as long as they paid taxes, owned property worth $50 or more, or rented a tenement for at least 40 shillings annually.[22] Black families of means embraced the idea of a communal sanctuary and an entrée into New York State's racially exclusive political system. Owning property meant one was literally invested in the community. In the words of Ezekiel Bacon, one of the federal convention delegates, owning property "furnished the most probable test of character and the greatest likelihood of finding united with it independence, sobriety, and safe intentions."[23]

By the first decades of the nineteenth century, however, ill winds began to blow and complicated paperwork was required for Blacks to vote. During the election of 1813, the united influence of a bloc of Black voters in New York City tipped the margin in favor of the Federalists, infuriating the Republican majority in the assembly.[24] The political status quo was in danger. Eleven years later during the 1821 New York State constitutional convention, Republican General Root reminded the assembled delegates of the power of the Black vote in 1813, "when a few hundred Negroes of the city of New York, following the train of those who ride in their coaches, and whose shoes and boots they had so often blacked, shall go to the polls of the election and change the political condition of the whole state."[25]

The convention became a bitter fight. Whereas owning property had been understood as a tacit example of character and a vested interest in the community, delegates to the conventions in 1821 and 1846 argued that the old "outward virtues" were to be supplanted by what legal historian Jacob Katz Cogan labeled "the look within," the shift toward new internal criteria required for a voice in the government. Dubious pseudoscientific theories on race contended that a qualified voter must now possess "innate and heritable traits" such as intelligence, competence, and moral discretion, qualities many believed were possessed only by the white man.[26]

A respected Black activist named Thomas Sipkins challenged the restrictions. At the 1821 convention, he read a proclamation from his New York community entreating the delegates to honor the same voting rights in the new constitution that Blacks had enjoyed for the past forty-four years.[27] Delegate Peter Augustus Jay—son of Supreme Court Chief Justice John Jay, a member of the New York Manumission Society, and a future owner of property adjacent to Seneca Village— boldly suggested striking out the word "white" as the qualification for suffrage.[28] For two months, the delegates debated. In the end, the majority arrived at a compromise: any Black male twenty-one years and older who had paid taxes on his estate, been a resident of the state for three years, and owned property valued at $250 "over and above all debts and encumbrances" could vote. It was as punitive a measure as the 1712 law that prohibited Blacks from owning property or gaining their freedom without an exorbitant £200 fee. Jay and eight others would not vote to ratify the constitution, and fifteen other delegates refused to sign.

Although Sipkins's appeal to the convention for universal male suffrage did not succeed, the rejection was a clarion call to those with financial means to form a landowning community in order to promote the franchise. Perhaps this was a call to Whitehead as well. The legislation stood with suffrage limitations until the end of the Civil War, though for the next four decades several Seneca Village landowners would be among the active leaders fighting against racial restrictions on voting, which were only lifted in 1870 by the passage of the Fifteenth Amendment.

New York was hardly alone in this. Restrictions were imposed on men of color in every new state that entered the Union after 1819. In 1807, New Jersey stripped voting rights from free Black men and all women. In 1821, voting rights were taken away from free Blacks in Massachusetts and New York, and in 1838 in Pennsylvania. By 1855, only Maine, Massachusetts, New Hampshire, Rhode Island, and Vermont granted the franchise to Black men without any restrictions.

GETTING TO $250

For most Black landowners, meeting the suffrage requirement of $250 was a long, frustrating road. Wealthy New Yorkers had historically pressured the city to underassess property so as to lower their tax rate.[29] That was a boon for white owners, but those few propertied Black Americans—though equally loathe to pay higher taxes—were political victims to a system that worked against them by undervaluing their property. In 1826, only sixteen Black New Yorkers had reached that bar of owning $250 of debt-free property.[30] It is likely that only Epiphany Davis and possibly Charles Treadwell owned enough property that year to vote.

But it seems that Seneca Village succeeded as an enfranchisement scheme. By 1829, the tax assessments in the village showed eight landowners had reached the $250 minimum. Several earned the franchise from the purchase of land with sufficient assessment, and others, like Andrew Williams and Charles Smith, had constructed homes that augmented their property's value.[31] In 1845, there were nearly 350 Black households taxed on their property in New York, and of them, only 26 percent were eligible to vote. A quarter of those were Seneca Village landowners.[32]

When the Erie Canal opened in October 1825, it "established the undisputed supremacy of New York City" as the nation's financial and commercial center.[33] Running 363 miles from Buffalo to Albany and merging into the Hudson River down to the bustling port of New York City, the canal carried agricultural produce and manufactured goods from upstate and the West faster and more efficiently than wagons or locomotives. Before, Philadelphia had been the premier port in America, but the new water route immediately elevated New York to a world-class port. The canal took eight years from start to finish, but New York City, with its modern grid plan under construction, watched its progress with great anticipation. When New York celebrated the canal's official opening on October 25, property values skyrocketed almost overnight.

In 1830, the total real estate value on the island of Manhattan was estimated at around $88 million. Just five years later, in 1835, that number had increased to $143 million. Just one year after that, it was worth $233 million. In June 1836, James Gordon Bennet, publisher of the *Herald*, summed up the speculative tornado blowing through New York: "All the haste, life, society, impulse, activity, force, steam power, and devil are now with the real estate operators."[34]

When historian Shane White pondered whether participating in the real estate boom might be "a widespread urge among African New Yorkers," he had to look no further than Seneca Village.[35] Although Blacks sat on the lowest rung of the economic ladder, thirty-eight members of the Black community purchased land from John Whitehead or his family during the boom years of 1825 to 1836. In the 1830s—and particularly between 1834 and 1836—many of Whitehead's original landowners sold their property for a profit that was probably more than they had earned in their entire working life. During these years, while the sellers profited, a group of new Black buyers entered the market to buy a home, a solid financial asset, and a vote.

Investing in real estate was a routine practice of the Black middle class, acknowledged by contemporary author Carla L. Peterson, the great granddaughter of Seneca Village landowner Joseph Marshall, whose family and similar Black

9.3 In her 1920s memoir, Maritcha Lyons, great granddaughter of Seneca Village landowners Elizabeth and Joseph Marshall, looked back on the prosperity that her Black middle-class family and their contemporaries enjoyed by investing in real estate in mid-century New York.

Source: "Maritcha Lyons." Schomburg Center for Research in Black Culture, Photographs and Prints Division, The New York Public Library, New York Public Library Digital Collections, https://digitalcollections.nypl.org/items/86ceccfb-3e62-d837-e040-e00a18064431.

families were "as savvy as white New Yorkers in understanding the value of real estate. They recognized that just as much as personal income, land was a good investment to be bought and sold for profit." [36] Writing in the 1920s, Maritcha Lyons, Marshall's granddaughter, looked back to an earlier time when "many of our people acquired real estate, accumulated and invested savings, and enjoyed a genuine, if not an extensive, prosperity."[37]

Property in Seneca Village was conveyed from seller to buyer regularly throughout the community's history. It would take an entire book just to trace the approximately two hundred exchanges of Seneca Village lots that took place between 1829 and 1855. Many of those transactions led to a dead end anyway, muddled by unresolved court cases over property, confusion over title, property loss, and poor record keeping. The best we can do is cite a few notable transactions—both profits and losses—from the boom of 1834 to 1836 and the depression that followed on its heels and lasted until 1844. After 1852, the planning for Central Park brought about a flurry of exchanges throughout the prepark, many by white speculators, that also included property in Seneca Village. But for Black landowners, unlike their white counterparts, real estate wasn't only a route to riches, it was the route to the ballot box and a community of their own.

The earliest of Whitehead's buyers to sell their property were Cloe and Benjamin Smith. When Richard Edman, a waiter, purchased their lot in 1829, the Smiths received a 100 percent return on the investment they had made four years earlier. Even greater profits would be had during the real estate boom of 1834 to 1836. A sixth of Whitehead's original buyers sold their land during those three years.[38]

Consider this example of how rapidly some owners flipped property for profit. In 1825, grocer Edward Hamilton purchased four lots on Eighty-Seventh Street for $140. Two years later he sold them to laborer Garrison Stewart for $175. Stewart held on to these lots for seven years until 1834, when he sold them to laborer David Blake for $190. Blake flipped the property *two hours later* to innkeeper Robert Frazer for an astonishing $410, more than doubling his money. The lots were assessed at $150 in 1836, but when Fraser built a house on one of them in 1841, it improved the property and increased the value of the land to $250 exactly, securing his right to vote in the next election.

The entrée of Blacks into the American capitalist system opened doors that had long been closed. Though they had little access to banks for a mortgage, an option always open to whites, a select group of private individuals gave many of the Seneca Village landowners a mortgage. As we shall see, that wasn't always a profitable transaction, but for most it was their first stepping-stone to a better life, one a little further removed from the urban perils that plagued them.

RIOTS

Although the real estate boom motivated many people of means to buy and sell property throughout the city and the nation, in New York those in the Black community were especially compelled to move away from downtown due to racial rioting, threats of fire and disease, and the most common dangers of the unhealthy and overcrowded wards.

Following emancipation on July 4, 1827, members of the white working class feared that the newly freed Blacks and their equally despised white abolitionist leaders would integrate their neighborhoods. This would lead to "amalgamation" or interracial marriage, take away their jobs, and grant the free Blacks political equality. The white working class—and the white middle-class press that stirred them up—could not have this. They were also provoked by the antiabolitionist newspaper *Courier and Enquirer*, the mouthpiece of the American Colonization Society, which pushed to rid the country of all free Blacks. The ACS, founded in 1816, had a resurgence in 1831. That year, Black New Yorkers held a public meeting that denounced colonization and opposed the lies and accusations that they were "a growing evil, immoral, and destitute of religious principles."[39]

These fears came to a head in eight days of riots in the first week of July 1834, said to be "the worst riots in antebellum New York."[40] On July 9, mobs of unruly white working-class journeymen and artisans ransacked the home of abolitionist Lewis Tappan. Then thousands stormed into what was meant to be an abolitionist meeting in the Chatham Street Chapel. Though the riot was eventually quelled, the hostility continued. On July 11, rioters burned down St. Philip's on Centre Street, the first Black Episcopal Church, which happened to be the church attended by several downtown Seneca Village landowners. They also burned an African schoolhouse on Orange Street. White families were told to place a light in their windows, because the mob would be directed to attack only those homes with darkened windows.[41]

FIRE

In 1839, Moses Beach, publisher of *The Sun*, called New York "the City of Fires!" He exclaimed: "No other metropolis can exhibit so imposing an array of conflagrations!"[42] Every night and in every ward, watchmen patrolled their neighborhoods on foot to watch for and report the fires that were constant in a city crammed with wooden buildings.

A few years earlier, on a night in December 1835 when temperatures had plummeted to seventeen degrees below freezing, a fire had broken out in a Wall

9.4 Fire was the greatest threat to both rich and poor New Yorkers, most of whom lived in wooden buildings. The Great Fire of December 1835 swept through downtown, destroying neighborhoods and displacing many. Seneca Village may have welcomed several new residents after the fire.

Source: "Burning of the Merchants Exchange, New York City. The great fire of December, 1835." The Miriam and Ira D. Wallach Division of Art, Prints and Photographs: Print Collection, The New York Public Library, New York Public Library Digital Collections, https://digitalcollections.nypl.org/items /510d47d9-7be4-a3d9-e040-e00a18064a99.

Street area warehouse. Within an hour, it had torn through the neighborhood we know today as the Financial District. The Great Fire of 1835, as it became known, raged for several days and smoldered for another two weeks. In total nearly seven hundred buildings were leveled, most of which had stored goods. The loss was estimated at between $20 to $40 million in 1835 dollars, and the loss in real estate values was far beyond that.[43]

No downtown resident escaped unscathed. Many had to relocate. The poor Blacks in the lower wards were the most frequent and vulnerable victims of fire, since they lived in overcrowded and shoddily constructed tinderbox homes. For those with means, Seneca Village—four miles from the city—may have been one reason behind the flurry of real estate activity in the months following the Great Fire.

Yet the wooden homes and outbuildings of Seneca Village were no more impervious to flames. On the 1855 condemnation maps, which detail the owners and renters of lots in the prepark, there is an unusual gray watercolored square on lot 19 on block 787 and another, more faded square on lot 21. All existing

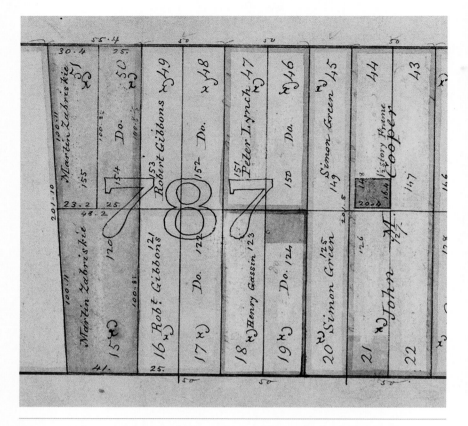

9.5 Lot 19 shows a gray square, the former home of the Landin family that may have been destroyed by fire or some other natural disaster. The house on Lot 21 may also have burned.

Source: Condemnation Map (detail). New York City Municipal Archives.

1855 structures on the Seneca Village maps—homes, barns, stables, and sheds—are painted in red, as can be seen on lot 44.

We know there was a fire on the south side of Eighty-Fifth Street between 1842 and 1843 on block 786, lot 41. In April 1846, Hannah Green, widow to landowner Cornelius Henry, transferred her dower right to her stepdaughter Sarah "Sally" Wilson. The conveyance to Wilson referred to the settlement that Green had received from the fire insurance company.[44] In the condemnation map of 1855, Wilson's house, built by her father in 1829, shows only a very slight change in the footprint of the two-story frame house, but the small attached room, probably

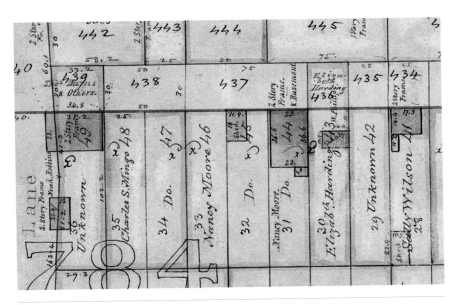

9.6 Houses along the south side of Eighty-Fifth Street depict a red footprint layered above a smaller, equal or greater gray footprint that most likely indicates a change in the size and/or shape of the home, possibly the result of a fire that we know happened to the home of Sally Wilson.

Source: Condemnation Map (detail). New York City Municipal Archives.

a kitchen and the backyard shed, must have been added during the reconstruction.[45] The map clearly depicts a larger home or a sizable addition onto the home of Wilson's neighbor Nancy Moore (lot no. 44).[46]

PLAGUE

In the 1820s, outbreaks of yellow fever, consumption, and smallpox plagued the Black population. A doctor researching an 1819 cholera outbreak compared the disproportion of illness and death between whites living above ground and Blacks living in basement rooms: "Out of 48 blacks, living in 10 cellars, 33 were sick, of whom 14 died; while out of 120 whites living immediately over their heads in the apartments of the same house, not one even had the fever."[47] In the cholera epidemics, Blacks succumbed at a rate as much as ten times that of their white counterparts. Cholera is a waterborne disease, but that was unknown at the time; and as historian Charles Rosenberg reasons, the river of New York's shallow and polluted wells served "Irish and Negroes [who] seemed its foreordained victims."[48] Eventually, in a bid to bring clean water to a desperate city, the Croton Aqueduct was constructed and included the receiving reservoir along the Seventh Avenue border with Seneca Village.

Even a move out of downtown did not guarantee escape from the disease. The 1849 cholera wave found many Black and white victims from Seneca Village and its neighboring areas, most of whom were buried in the Village's church cemeteries.

UNEMPLOYMENT

In May 1837, the nation's economic boom ended abruptly in a financial panic that would last for the next seven years. The depression was caused by a combination of factors: unbounded speculation, a disastrous wheat crop failure, a decline in cotton prices, and a breakdown in international trade, particularly with Britain. Across the nation, banks and businesses collapsed. The value of land plummeted, and inflation and unemployment went through the roof. After the flurry of real estate activity in the mid-1830s, property values dropped 16 percent. Seneca Village still saw a few profitable transactions, but several landowners could not sustain the financial responsibilities for their properties, likely because they had lost their jobs in the depression. By 1843, for example, seven village landowners were in default on their assessments to the city, and a few others were in default on their mortgages.[49]

In 1828, New York became the first state to adopt the lien theory of lending. This gave ownership of the property not to the lender but to the borrower or mortgagor for the term of the mortgage. Should the borrower default on his or her loan, judicial review was not always required. The lender could bid on the defaulted property and was often either the highest bidder or the only bidder, regaining the property for far below its actual market value. Many Seneca Village landowners found themselves victims of such foreclosures when they could no longer pay their mortgages or assessments. Prior to its abolition in 1847, the chancery court had the power to put the property in question up for auction. After that date, jurisdiction was transferred to the state supreme court, whose decision often mandated a public auction. The sheriff was charged with evicting debtors from their homes and putting the property up for auction, although the borrower could still regain possession of the property after a sale if the mortgage was repaid.[50] It was during these hard times that several mostly white mortgagees came into possession of foreclosed Seneca Village properties.[51]

Here are the stories of four village residents and the hardships they endured.

DANIEL ALDRIDGE

Though Daniel Aldridge only owned his lots on Eighty-Sixth Street for three years, his life warrants our attention because he was the father of Ira Aldridge, the most famous Black actor of the nineteenth century. The self-proclaimed "African Roscius"—after the renowned Roman actor—Ira Aldridge was celebrated through-out Europe, where his race did not bar him from performing as it did in America.[52]

Separating Aldridge fact from fiction is particularly difficult. There is an anonymous biographical pamphlet entitled *Memoir and Theatrical Career of Ira Aldridge, the African Roscius*, which historians believe was authored by Ira himself in 1848 or 1849. In it, Daniel Aldridge is said to be descended from the royal Fulah tribe of Senegal. The pamphlet claims Ira's forefathers were princes whose prisoners in battle were to be "exchanged, and not, as was the custom, sold for slaves."[53] It is quite possible that the Aldridge ancestors were from Senegal, shipped off to slavery in America.

In 1860, the Black physician and abolitionist Dr. James McCune Smith wrote an essay in *The Anglo-African Magazine* in which he mentioned that Ira's father, Daniel, had been a "straw-vender" in New York. He remembered him as "short in stature, with a tall, broad-brimmed white hat, mounted on a high cart filled with his merchandise, and dolefully crying 'Straw, s-t-r-a-w!' through the streets, especially on Saturday nights."[54] This account coincides with the *Longworth's Directory* almanac description of Daniel Aldridge as a "cartman black," and "Daniel Aldridge (colored), a huxter/huckster," or street vendor.[55]

While there is no record of Daniel receiving any financial support from his celebrated son, that is likely the source behind Aldridge's purchase in Seneca

9.7 Ira Aldridge was the most famous Black actor of the nineteenth century, here portrayed as Shakespeare's Othello. His father, Daniel Aldridge, owned land in Seneca Village.

Source: Henry Perronet Briggs, *Ira Aldridge as Othello*, c. 1830. National Portrait Gallery Collection.

Village. We know from future letters that Ira supported his sister, Susanna Peterson, and offered to pay for his nephew's education.

No record has been found that can verify Daniel as a "minister of the gospel," but we know he did not receive a Christian education at Schenectady College in upstate New York, as claimed in Ira's *Memoir*. Nonetheless, Smith confirmed that Daniel was "a strict member in high standing at 'Old Zion' " in lower Manhattan.[56] Ira's nephew, David I. Aldridge, regarded Daniel as "one of the founders of the A.M.E. Zion Church, and he helped turn over the sod for the first church."[57] Ira's biographer, Bernth Lindfors, called Daniel "an exhorter," meaning a licensed local public speaker or itinerant preacher.[58]

Daniel wanted his son to prepare for the ministry, which was the impetus behind enrolling the thirteen-year-old Ira in the African Free School. A natural talent led Ira to win prizes for declaration, and from there his passion for drama evolved. In the early 1800s, the only theater in New York that had a portion of the highest gallery set aside for a Black audience was The Park. This habitual exclusion inspired Black theater manager William Henry Brown and actor James Hewlett to found the African Grove Theater in 1821. Hewlett's sister, Elizabeth Hewlett Marshall, owned land in Seneca Village. Ira's first public performance was with the African Company.

But the limitations foisted upon ambitious and talented Black artists in nineteenth-century America were severe, so, like many other Black and female American artists, Ira turned to Europe. In London he found his first success, playing Othello in May 1825.

In 1824, Ira married Englishwoman Margaret Gill. They had a son, Ira Daniel, named for his father and grandfather. In a second marriage, years later, Ira would name a daughter Luranah, after his mother, who died in 1817 when Ira was only ten.

It was likely Daniel's connection to A.M.E. Zion that drew him in 1836, at the height of the real estate boom, to purchase two lots in Seneca Village, on Eighty-Sixth Street. He paid $80, believing that real estate values were only going to climb higher. He also took out a mortgage for $125 at 7 percent interest.[59] Sadly, Aldridge never profited from his investment. He died in 1840 at age 69, "after a painful and lingering illness."[60]

The name Howard Dresser, a famous abolitionist, activist, and lawyer for the New York Vigilance Committee, appears on several Seneca Village conveyances, including that of Daniel Aldridge. At Aldridge's death, Dresser instructed the transfer of Aldridge's mortgage and property to Josiah E. Landin, a fellow resident of the community, who had also purchased property in Seneca Village at the height of the boom in 1836.[61]

JOSIAH E. LANDIN

An ambitious man, Josiah E. Landin began a career in the 1830s selling trees to ornament estate gardens.[62] It is possible that Landin had something to do with the formal planting of mature trees on the east end of the block of Eighty-Fourth and Eighty-Fifth Street, to block the view of the reservoir's construction. After buying his first Seneca Village lot in the 1836 boom, Landin changed paths and became a real estate speculator. At the height of this career, he owned thirteen lots on four different blocks between Eighty-Fifth Street and Eighty-Ninth Street. By 1839, his property was assessed at $275, and he could finally vote. The Landins were popular in Seneca Village. Before the construction of the All Angels' Episcopal Church in 1849, they hosted neighborhood baptisms at their home on West Eighty-Seventh Street, in today's West Meadow.[63]

But Landin had bigger dreams than many of his village neighbors, dreams that didn't stop with just one lot. According to the tax assessment records, ten homes were on Landin's lots. A landowner turned developer, Landin took out five or six mortgages to finance his ambitious projects. After 1836, defaults on mortgages continued for the following four years. As Elizabeth Blackmar noted, "Manhattan real estate had (temporarily) lost its investment glow."[64] But while most investors retreated, Landin saw opportunity and took out several mortgages after the panic.[65] Slowly, though, he failed to honor his financial agreements. He was overcommitted and overleveraged, and his lots reverted to their mortgagees, including white restauranteur Henry Gassin; white Reverend James Hardenburgh; Mary Quinn, white heir of Joseph Quinn; and Black landowner Simon Green. Landin sold the other lots to white landowners: grocer Peter Lynch and wealthy New Jersey merchant Andrew C. Zabriskie.[66]

Yet inexperience and overcommitment may not have been the only cause of Landin's financial problems. The gray square on Landin's property indicated that his house no longer existed. If it had burned down, that alone would be devastating, but even more so if he carried no fire insurance. The Landins also likely experienced a tragic death in their family, as they adopted their grandsons, two-year-old Josiah and one-year-old Daniel Peterson. We know that in 1847, Sarah Landin married John Peterson in the Seneca Village home of sexton Henry Garnet. Sarah must have died in 1854 soon after giving birth to Daniel, which is why Josiah and Diana Landin took their grandsons into their home.

Eventually, Landin lost all but one of his homes and lots.[67] The family rented their former home from Zabriskie, but ultimately a court case decided in Landin's favor and he was awarded $510 for one of his properties.[68] The Landins were among the last of the long-tenured families forced to leave the community in October 1857.[69]

REVEREND LEVEN SMITH

In 1829, Reverend William M. Stilwell, the leader of the Methodist Society, gave a $1,100 mortgage to Reverend Leven (or Levin) Smith of the A.M.E. Zion Church for two separate properties, one of them for seven lots in Seneca Village. The purchase of these seven lots may have been an investment for a future

9.8 A.M.E. Zion Reverend Leven Smith and his family were forced to leave their home in Seneca Village due his unpaid mortgage commitments owed to his lender, Reverend William M. Stilwell.

Source: Leven Smith. Courtesy of A.M.E. Zion Church.

transfer to the church. His own lots were adjacent to the seven lots, originally purchased by Zion trustee Charles Treadwell, who sold them two years later to his church for a burial ground.

Smith's other mortgage agreement with Stilwell included a twenty-one-year lease on a Lower East Side property near the southeast corner of Christie and Delancey Streets—today, a part of Sara Delano Roosevelt Park. The lot, owned by Peter Gerard Stuyvesant, the great-great-grandson of the Dutch West India Company's infamous director-general of New Amsterdam, was leased to Smith, who then sublet it for $175 to two other lessees, guaranteeing an income for both Smith and Stuyvesant. The mortgage to Stilwell was officially discharged in 1837, but somewhere along the way Smith must have fallen short of his financial responsibilities. The U.S. Census of 1840 indicated that Smith and his family were living on his Seneca Village property at the time, but in a chancery sale their home and lots were auctioned off to Richard E. Stilwell, the Methodist reverend's son. The loss of the property must have been particularly devastating for Smith, one of the first Zion ministers Stilwell supported, and infuriating and humiliating too. His family had to vacate their home to make room for the family of John P. Haff—the elder Stilwell's daughter, son-in-law, and children.[70]

JAMES HUNT

Perhaps no one better illustrates the fallout from the speculative boom of 1836 than James and Marcy Hunt. The couple were unschooled players in the complex and often underhanded world of New York City real estate, even though James was said to have "acted as agent or had caused persons to buy property" in the village. In 1829, the Hunts purchased two choice lots on Eighty-Fourth Street and Seventh Avenue from John Scott for $240. By 1832 they had constructed a house on the corner lot, and they rented the house and lots two years later to John J. Washington, who paid $100 rent annually and probably planned to sublet the property.[71] The following year, James, "a respectable colored man," as he was described in a court testimony, was approached by Robert Ritter, a Black twenty-three-year-old in the shoemaking business, living farther south around Sixtieth Street and Seventh Avenue. He offered Hunt $1,500 for his house and two lots after paying off a $400 mortgage. That would be a profit nearly four times his investment minus the cost of the house construction. Despite Marcy's misgivings, the naïve James went through with the deal. Ritter paid him in wads of $50 and $100 "broken bank notes," which were no longer worth the ink used to print them. After months of trying to get his deed back from the con man, the defrauded Hunt pressed charges and Ritter was convicted of "false pretenses."[72]

THE RENTERS

Renters in New York were far more transient than they are today. Since the early nineteenth century, almost the entire rental population moved every May 1, which was known as Moving Day. The only people to benefit were the cartmen, who inflated their prices and clogged the streets on that day. The high turnover rate was probably no different in Seneca Village, yet we know that several renters—such as Samuel Stilwell's tenants, Robert and Sarah Green—built homes and arranged for long-term leases rather than wander nomadically every year.[73]

The renters in Seneca Village were African Americans, Irish, and German, first- or second-generation immigrants who likely moved there in the 1850s. Without recorded leases, we will never know many of the renters who passed through the community. Though the censuses recorded boarders living in households owned by others, the best records of renters are the city's assessment records, which often note the occupant of a dwelling who is not the owner. The records show at least sixteen likely rental households on the tax rolls, many of whom may even have constructed their dwelling, most likely a shanty. Today we think of the home or apartment as the rental property, but in the nineteenth century it was the land that was rented, and if the tenant built a home or farm buildings on it, the tenant owned the improvement.

Many landowners who did not live in Seneca Village might have constructed a dwelling on their property to acquire franchise rights more quickly. Though Epiphany Davis lived in and owned his home on Broome Street, he erected a substantial three-story dwelling on the south side of Eighty-Sixth Street and Seventh Avenue to provide a stream of rental income. He may have had an informal rental agreements prior to 1840, but that year he formalized a "farm let" to Irish grocer Laurence McCaffrey, who listed ten white residents there—two women and eight men—between the ages of twenty through thirty-nine, six of whom were engaged in agriculture.[74] The 1855 Viele topographic map indicates a large garden that spans the length and breadth of the block, and another large bed sits across Eighty-Sixth Street adjacent to the Davis property. Both plots may have been part of his rental agreement, though gardens were also plentiful throughout the adjacent Bloomingdale area.

In 1829, four years after he purchased his land from Whitehead, oysterman Cornelius Henry advertised in *Freedom's Journal* that he had "just finished a handsome two story frame house on the New African Burying ground, about five miles out of town and will rent on moderate terms."[75] In his 1855 petition to the commissioners, Charles Mingo noted that he had built his house four years earlier and rented it for $7 a month.[76] Brooklyn steam scourer (dry cleaner) and political activist John J. Washington bought three lots from William H. Webster and his wife, Hester. As owners, the couple had built two homes on their property, and they continued to live there after the sale to Washington. When Webster died, Hester married James Morgan, and the family continued to rent the land. When the city took the land for the park in 1856, Hester Morgan owned her homes and received $600. Washington, the landowner, received $2,476 for the three lots.[77]

Several residents lost their ownership for defaulting on a mortgage or on city assessments, but the new landowner—either the mortgagee or the highest bidder in a public auction—often allowed the former owners to stay on as renters, like Josiah Landin.[78]

All historians agree that almost all the landowners in Seneca Village before the 1850s were Black, but estimates vary as to the composition of the rental community.[79] The two most reliable sources are the U.S. Census of 1850 and the New York State Census of 1855. From those documents, the 1992 study estimated that between one-half and one-third of the community was composed of either Irish or German residents, and the rest were Black. The study counted that the community had approximately 264 residents.[80] A more recent study estimated the rental population as 38 percent white.[81]

The 1855 New York State Census has been the source for historians to determine the number of Seneca Village residents, but the records are confusing.[82] The listings don't include home addresses—a feature that had only been established in the denser downtown neighborhoods—so it is difficult to identify Seneca Village as a discrete community from its surrounding neighbors in the larger Ward 22.[83]

The census takers were instructed to number each visit to a home and record each family member within that structure.[84] Sometimes no one was at home, so the census takers would have to come back later. In 1850, the census taker visited Seneca Village four or five times on three separate days in September. In the 1855 census, he visited on five separate occasions to interview the head of the household or a relative who was at least twenty-one years old. It was easy to identify the Black residents, as the column for race denoted a "B" for Black and an "M" for mulatto, among the far more frequent blank spaces for whites.

To complicate matters, the census taker was instructed to continue the numbering system for both the house and the family without indicating a change of neighborhood, and—quite maddeningly— to leave no blank lines to separate information from a visit to a Seneca Village resident from, say, that from one living nearby on the Bloomingdale Road.[85] With one continuous stream of data, it is impossible to determine accurately the boundaries of the neighborhood and its respective residents. The Black Seneca Village residents tended to group together, but due to multiple census taker visits, many white families appear between visits to the African American residents.[86] The white household of John P. Paulison, for example, is entered in the 1855 census just before the Haff family of Seneca Village, yet the Paulison family lived quite a distance away on Eighty-Fourth Street and Ninth Avenue (now Columbus Avenue).[87] Where does one draw the line?[88]

This fluid and inexact system makes it impossible to know with any certainty the precise composition of the community. According to available records, therefore, one can best conclude that in September 1850, 108 Black individuals lived in the community alongside 30 known white renters. Just over one-quarter of the population would have been white renters. If we also include the unlikely possibility of 44 more whites, that would make the composition 40 percent white residents and 60 percent Blacks.[89]

Five years later, in July 1855, the number of Black individuals, both owners and renters, increased to 149. Of them, 12 Black landowning families—numbering 57 individuals—made up 38 percent of the Black resident population. The rest were renters.[90] Even assuming the highest number of white residents in Seneca Village, the community was still 70 percent Black.[91]

The 1855 condemnation map cited several vacant buildings, an indication that renters and owners alike saw the writing on the wall and were gradually leaving. Andrew Williams, who had constructed a small rental shanty on his property in 1851, stayed in his home until 1857, but according to the condemnation map, his shanty may have been empty in 1855, a loss of income and investment.[92] The composition of the community during the last sixteen months of its existence, from May 1856 to October 1857, changed radically when all residents of Seneca Village became tenants to a demanding new landlord: the City of New York.[93]

THE SPIRITUAL COMMUNITY

In order to survive the cruelty of slavery, Africans who were so brutally wrenched from their culture and their homeland created unique spiritual communities that merged native beliefs and practices with Christian worship. Whether adopted from missionaries in Africa or when they arrived in America, Christianity appealed to their desperate hope for deliverance from slavery in their earthly life and a rewarding future in their afterlife. The biblical captivity of the Israelites spoke to Black oppression, and the exodus from Egypt offered an uplifting story of freedom. When Moses declared, "Let my people go," that message wasn't just a metaphor, it was a cry from the deepest and darkest reality of Black lives.[94]

African Americans embraced the ecstatic forms of worship such as "the ring shout" that had come with them from Africa. Shouting, dancing, and music, elements that were deemed "brutish heathenism" by white Protestant sects, became more acceptable when the evangelical movement of the Great Awakening swept through America in the mid-eighteenth century. The connection to God through spontaneous personal, emotional, and physical manifestations appealed to free and enslaved Blacks and led to mass conversion. Passionate oratory of the preacher combined with uplifting and inspirational music, drumming, and dancing offered psychological relief and emotional release from the degradation of the virulent racism that devastated the lives of all Black people. The church offered members an identity, self-respect, and a sustained sense of continuity when even one's family could overnight be mercilessly torn apart.[95]

African Americans found a home in Methodist and Baptist churches, which accepted mixed-race congregations. Nonetheless, Blacks were prevented from receiving equal status within the organizations and felt the need to break away in order to control their spiritual, social, political, educational, and economic lives, all centered within the hub of the church. By 1796, the African Methodist Episcopal Zion Church, known later as "Mother Zion," was established in New York. Another Methodist denomination, the African Union First Colored Methodist Protestant Church and Connection, commonly called African Union, was founded in Delaware in 1813 and spread to New York soon after. Members of these two groups included most of the residents or landowners of Seneca Village, several of whom served as pastors, lay preachers, exhorters, and sextons. The third church, All Angels' Episcopal Church, stemmed from a missionary Sunday school that was established in the 1840s by rectors of St. Michael's, a west side white church.

Five generous Black landowners and four white sisters from the same family bought lots and donated or sold them for a small profit to their respective A.M.E. Zion, African Union, or All Angels' trustees.[96]

From the pulpit, Black religious leaders of every denomination across the city took a stand on the two most pressing political issues: universal suffrage and abolition. This was especially the case after the passage of the Fugitive Slave Act in 1850. Although New York had ended slavery on July 4, 1827—it was the last state in the North to do so—half the nation would still be enslaved for another thirty-six years. The churches in Black America were hubs of support, inspiration, action, and funding, and stops along the Underground Railroad.

THE AFRICAN METHODIST EPISCOPAL (A.M.E.) ZION CHURCH

For Black churchgoers, the long struggle to control how they worshiped was as much social and political as religious. The John Street Methodist Church was segregated in all its practices. Blacks, who made up 30 percent of the congregation, could receive communion only after white congregants and sit only in the back pews. And only white men were eligible for ordination as Methodist ministers.[97]

Beginning in 1796, the African Methodist Episcopal Zion Church in New York started holding separate services, though it remained under the aegis of white Methodist church leaders. Gradually, when white preachers were unavailable,

Black leaders took their place. In 1800, they built a church on the corner of Church Street and Leonard Street in today's Tribeca.[98]

The streak of religious independence that led to the founding of the church in 1796 coincided with the issue of slavery in the post-Revolution era. In 1785, New York State had begun to address gradual manumission. That same year, the New York Manumission Society was formed. The movements for political and spiritual equality were mutually reinforcing.

By 1818 the Board of Trustees of Zion Church, including future Seneca Village landowners Charles Treadwell, Tobias Hawkins, and Epiphany Davis, began to discuss the possibility of building a new house of worship downtown. With a growing vision of independence, Mother Zion looked forward to the day their deacons would be elevated to elders with the authority to ordain their own ministers. While they waited for approval, Reverend William Stilwell—the grand-nephew of Samuel Stilwell, the Seneca Village landowner, and the leader of a separatist movement—presided over their services.

In 1820, an irate group of white parishioners led by the Reverend William Stilwell left the Methodist Church to form the Methodist Society. The schism was born of financial matters and against the hierarchy of the church's leadership. Stilwell invited the John Street Black congregation to follow his group. They preferred their independence and chose to retain the ecclesiastical hierarchy of the Methodist Church.[99]

Mother Zion inched closer to independence. Although Reverend Stilwell still presided over the ministry, Abraham Thompson and James Varick were elected as the first Black elder candidates. After two more years, Stilwellite ministers finally ordained Thompson, Varick, and Leven Smith as elders. Mother Zion's ministry was at last established.[100]

Once the A.M.E. Zion church won its independence as an autonomous Black denomination, the members formed a separate community with its own institutions. One of its first needs was a burial ground. Starting in 1802, burial vaults were placed under the building. By 1807, the yellow fever epidemic forced the Common Council to demand the church cease burying its members there. Although the city gave the congregation a fifty-by-fifty-foot interment space in Potter's Field, it was "nearly filled" by May 1824. A.M.E. Zion trustees began searching for a burial ground.[101]

Six days after Zion trustees purchased Seneca Village land for personal use in 1825, the church bought eight of Whitehead's lots for a burial ground between

Eighty-Sixth Street and Eighty-Seventh Street. In 1823, only one year before Whitehead bought his property, the Common Council had ruled it unlawful to entomb a body in a vault or in the ground south of Canal, Sullivan, and Grand Streets.[102] Then, in 1851, the Common Council passed a law that forbade burials below Eighty-Sixth Street, suspicious that the "miasmas" of decaying bodies were behind the epidemics.[103] In 1827, the church had also acquired three larger lots from Whitehead, now in the Reservoir. Whitehead sold the lots to the church for less than lots he sold to private buyers: five dollars less in 1825 and ten dollars less in 1827.

That same year, Zion trustee Charles Treadwell, who had purchased his seven lots from Whitehead in 1825, sold them to Mother Zion.[104] The burial ground shows up on Treadwell's property in an 1836 map. Today it is the mound just east of the Spector Playground. Lucinda Lyons, the mother of future Seneca Village landowner Albro Lyons, was buried there in 1834, and four other family members would follow.[105] The Lyons family belonged to St. Philip's Episcopal Church, the Black part of Trinity Church, but it is likely there was no additional room in the St. Philip's burial ground.

Why the Treadwell lots were used for burials rather than the ones the church had purchased earlier remains a mystery, but the subterranean topography may have been the reason. In his submission to the park design competition of 1858, Superintendent of Draining George Waring noted that there was "a bed of excellent clay on the Park itself, north of 86th Street and west of the new reservoir." Perhaps the clay was not suitable for burials. The 1865 Viele topographical map of Manhattan also noted that the lots closest to Eighty-Eighth Street lay on marshland near a stream tributary that would have been too wet for burials. Roswell Graves's 1855 topography map of the same site shows a heavily wooded area, which suggests the area was never cleared for graves.[106]

When the city paid the trustees of the church for their burial ground in 1856, the Eighty-Eighth Street cemetery lots were awarded only half the price of the other burial ground to the south, possibly a rare attention to the topography.[107] Zion trustee Charles Treadwell's property was on dry land with only few rocks, which may have been the reason he sold it to the church for a cemetery. The 1848 tax records confirm that the Eighty-Fifth Street lots were used for an "African Cemetery."[108]

With more Blacks living in Harlem, Mother Zion was established to serve the uptown community. In 1822, the church planted a branch church called "Little

Zion," which soon counted sixty-six parishioners.[109] In 1830, they bought land for a new church on East 117th Street, sold to them by Isaac Adriance, the husband of Andrew and Margaret McGowan's granddaughter Margaret Eliza.[110] It was probably due to the founding of "Little Zion" that the smaller Seneca Village community took until 1853 to amass the resources needed for a church of its own.

Like many others, the Mother Zion trustees had problems paying the city's assessments that were targeted for the construction of Eighth Avenue. After repeated attempts to collect around seventeen dollars in back taxes for the years 1835 to 1837, the city seized and auctioned the seven Treadwell lots in 1842.[111] Dr. William A. Walters purchased the lease on the lands for a term of one thousand years and continued with new burials.[112] Dr. Walters was not only a physician, he was also the city's official coroner with an office in City Hall, and the terms of the lease confirm that the city intended to retain the land as a cemetery, under the city's jurisdiction. Walters personally reimbursed the city $150, canceling Zion's back rents, taxes, and assessments. That same day, he leased the property back to the Zion trustees for $150 for a term of one thousand years.[113]

This was also the time that Pastor Leven Smith had his own financial difficulties paying his mortgage to Reverend Stilwell. It is uncertain whether there was any connection between these two incidents. The conveyance from Walters to the church was witnessed by attorney Howard Dresser, one of several interventions he made to support the Seneca Village community, like Daniel Aldridge and Josiah Landin. Dresser was a well-respected abolitionist who was dedicated to helping free Blacks and enslaved people, and was even the first lawyer to advocate for an enslaved person in the New York courts.[114]

It took several years for the Mother Zion congregation to raise the money for a church in Seneca Village, but they did. The cornerstone was laid on August 4, 1853, just fourteen days after the New York State legislature took the land for Central Park. The church was a wooden structure, painted white. Church leaders anticipated a future school in the basement of the building and estimated about one hundred congregants.[115]

Today the landmarked Mother A.M.E. Zion Church on West 137th Street in Harlem has the distinction of being the oldest African American church in New York City and the "mother church" of the African Methodist Episcopal Zion conference.[116]

THE AFRICAN UNION CHURCH

The smaller of the two all-Black congregations was the African Union Church, a Methodist affiliate incorporated in Dover, Delaware, in September 1813. The church soon acquired followers in New York and Pennsylvania, and in 1826 was established downtown at Fifteenth Street and Seventh Avenue with only seven members.

In an 1846 book on the history of New York churches, the author noted that African Union members were meeting in Yorkville, "but has as yet no distinct organization."[117] That changed the following year, when the members erected the first church in Seneca Village. Their system of classes, doctrines, disciplines, and practices conformed to the Methodist tradition. As with Mother Zion, several members of the congregation purchased land in Seneca Village and gave it over to the church. For instance, in 1833, fourteen years before the church was built, Thomas and Hannah Green bought an oversized lot from church member Matilda Wigfall and conveyed it soon after to the trustees for $100. On July 1, 1853—only twenty days before the land would be taken for the park—landowner Elizabeth Townshend, who had purchased her lot from Eliza Wigfall for $1, also sold her lot to the Trustees of the African Union Church.[118] William Mathew, a trustee and the church sexton, reported in 1855 that he had lived in the village for twenty-three years. He purchased his home and lot from Marcy Hunt in 1847, which suggests that he had been a renter for the previous thirteen years.[119] Many residents in Seneca Village were born in Delaware, and many were likely attracted there by the church.[120]

The 1855 New York State census rated the African Union structure as "poor" and estimated the value of church and lot at $1,200. The building could seat one hundred worshippers, and the census taker estimated that about fifty usually attended.[121]

9.9 (overleaf) African Union, the first of the three churches to be erected in Seneca Village, and the attached school stood on the hill now the area surrounding the green horse chestnut tree in the center of the photograph.

Source: Sara Cedar Miller, Site of African Union Church and School. Courtesy of the Central Park Conservancy.

ALL ANGELS' CHURCH

According to Reverend Thomas McClure Peters of St. Michael's, a Protestant Episcopal church on Manhattan's west side, a mission Sunday School briefly began in "a village then called Seneca" in 1833 by Reverend James Richmond. After a thirteen-year hiatus, the school was reestablished in 1846. The following year Reverend McClure and Reverend William Richmond rented " an unfinished room in the centre of the settlement... rudely furnished with plank seats... [and] soon crowded with forty colored children." From that initial endeavor, the clergy then ministered informally to the whole community. The rented space was later identified as the home of "Miss Evers," who was a tenant of landowner Samuel Stilwell.[122]

In 1802, Samuel Stilwell conveyed a small portion of his prepark property to Gulian Ludlow, a wealthy New York cotton merchant and financier, who was a partner of his uncle Daniel Ludlow, the first president of the Manhattan Company, the earliest forerunner of JPMorgan Chase.

Gulian Ludlow's small parcel east of Eighth Avenue remained in the family until it became a part of Central Park. In 1848, Ludlow's four daughters—Arabella Ludlow, Emma Dashwood, Louisa Wright, and Frances A. Carroll—donated four of their lots to St. Michael's Episcopal Church on Ninety-Ninth Street and Amsterdam Avenue for worship, a Sunday school, and a burial ground for Methodist Society members. They also sold some of their lots to three Black families.[123]

With money collected from the St. Michael's congregation, All Angels' was consecrated in 1849. The church sat on a steep incline above Central Park West at Eighty-Fifth Street, a beacon to the surrounding community. Changing the traditional placement of the vestry from the north to the south side ensured the building could be seen and admired by passersby on Eighth Avenue.

The building sat on ground one hundred feet square and was surrounded on three sides by fencing with a front walk leading up to the west-facing porch. It had a quatrefoil window, a peaked gable, and a turret enclosing a small bell, a gift from a "gentleman of Boston."

Inside, the nave would have been flooded with light from the three windows flanking it on either side and the huge seven-by-nine-foot east window. The woodwork was pine but painted to resemble black walnut, a costlier material. Boston's newspaper, *The Christian Witness and Church Advocate*, saw the new building as

9.10 All Angels' Church was moved from Seneca Village to West Eighty-First Street and Eleventh Avenue (now West End Avenue) when the church was purchased by the congregation. The bell was used by the park staff until the church requested its return.

Source: All Angels' Church. Courtesy of All Angels' Church.

"proof positive" that limited resources should not deter a congregation from constructing an admirable edifice.[124]

In 1849, the year of the church's consecration, New York experienced a second wave of cholera. Several of its victims were buried in All Angels' adjacent cemetery. In total, there were thirty-four burials, two-thirds of whom were identified as "colored." In 1851, the city forbid burial grounds south of Eighty-Sixth Street. On February 3, 1852, Elizabeth Evers, age sixty-nine, a resident of Seneca Village, was the last to be interred. Most of the bodies were probably reinterred in the new St. Michael's Cemetery in Astoria, Queens. While workers were uprooting trees for the new entrance to the park at Eighty-Fifth Street and Eighth Avenue on August 10, 1871, they unearthed a black rosewood coffin. The engraved plate identified the body of sixteen-year-old Margaret McIntay, who died in February 1852. A second coffin, "enclosing the body of a negro, decomposed beyond recognition" was found nearby.[125]

But All Angels' was also a site of baptisms and marriages, not just burials. In 1848, Black church member Josiah Landin and William and Elizabeth Evers, white tenants of Samuel Stilwell, opened their village homes for these ceremonies while All Angels' was under construction.

In the 1855 New York State census report, All Angels' Church and lot were valued at $3,000. Two years later, the city paid the church a little more than $4,000 for the release of the property. The census estimated that the building could hold two hundred people, and thirty usually attended. The salary of the clergy was listed as "None." Thomas McClure Peters was salaried as rector for St. Michael's, not for his missionary duties (as his work at All Angels' was called). According to his son John Punnett Peters, the congregation was composed of Blacks and Germans, "all of whose houses were located in what was afterward the Central Park."[126]

Reverend McClure Peters seems to have been much beloved by many in the community. He offered a mortgage to resident Henry Garnet, and a church sexton, Ishmael Allen, named his first son after Peters.[127] The reverend may also have been the source for the mysterious name "Seneca Village," which will be discussed in chapter 17.

When the village disbanded, the old congregation scattered, and a new congregation included only one former Seneca Village resident, sexton William Godfrey Wilson. The building was in good condition, and the commissioners of Central Park considered moving it to their Seventy-Ninth Street offices on today's transverse road. All Angels' purchased the building from the city for $250 and removed it piecemeal to Eighty-First Street and Eleventh Avenue (today's West End).[128]

THE EDUCATIONAL COMMUNITY

Getting an education was a particularly important aspect of the Black community. Soon after its founding, A.M.E. Zion's leaders discussed a future school for its downtown church. In 1847, when the African Union built Seneca Village's first religious building, they attached a school to it, which likely initially met in the church's basement.[129] As a school in the public education system, it became known as Colored School No. 3. Catherine Thompson was the teacher and in 1857 Caroline W. Simpson was the principal. Thompson would have gotten her job most likely due to her family's connections to the African Union Church that was connected to the Seneca Village school. She lived a mile away in her family's home just inside what is today's park entrance at Sixty-Third Street and Central Park West. Her father, whitewasher Richard R. Thompson, had purchased his property in 1845. He was from Delaware, the birthplace of the African Union Church, and the family were likely members of African Union.[130] Two Irish public school educators also lived in Seneca Village after 1850: Catherine Geary, who was the principal of a white primary school on East Eighty-Fourth Street, and her daughter, Elleanor, a teacher. They were family members of John Geary, the reservoir keeper.[131]

An 1857 report by the New York Society for the Promotion of Education Among Colored Children described all the colored schools as "old," yet noted that Colored School No. 3 was "well attended." The report compared the "painfully neglected and positively degraded" conditions of the city's Black schools with "the splendid, almost palatial edifices, with manifold comforts, conveniences and elegancies which make up the school-houses for white children in the city of New York." Despite this disparity, the educational achievement by Black students in reading and spelling was "equal to that of any schools in the city." The report also noted that Blacks paid their "fair share of the school-taxes which has gone to improve schools for whites while "their own children are driven into miserable edifies in disgraceful localities.[132] Education, like almost every other component of daily life, had a racial divide.

THE LAND AND THE GARDENS

The land that became Seneca Village at the eastern edge of Bloomingdale passed through many owners before it became a Black community.[133] The densest blocks of Seneca Village, Eighty-Third Street to Eighty-Sixth Street, lay on a flat, mesa-like hilltop, relatively free of surface rock, a third of them in woodland, with a fine natural spring. This favorable topography made the area desirable real estate, and we know that Samuel Stilwell, a passionate fruit tree breeder, sold all of his Bloomingdale property with the exception of the tract that became a part of

Seneca Village. In 1803, a real estate ad offered "a small house on the premises and a variety of fine grafted fruit trees." By 1822, a small house, a barn, and spring on a survey map indicated the land was under cultivation.[134] The "old walls" depicted on the condemnation map of William Pease's Eighty-Fifth Street lot were probably vestiges of that farm. By the time John Whitehead purchased the land, it likely was arable soil.

Seneca Villager John P. Haff, whose family moved into the house of Reverend Leven Smith, was a serious gardener. In the 1850s, he won many prizes at the New York and New Jersey agricultural fairs for "a variety of culinary vegetables."[135] In the notation on the 1855 condemnation map, one can faintly read the partly erased inscription "Haff's Garden" scrawled across the lots with no planting beds. By 1855, Haff had become the innkeeper of the Elm Park Hotel, the former Apthorp mansion, and he no longer gardened in the prepark.

Several renters and owners listed their profession as gardeners. Most gardened right up to the taking of the land for the park. The Viele map is so detailed that one can easily count more than a hundred planting beds throughout the community. Almost all of the block between Eighty-Third Street and Eighty-Fourth Street was under cultivation. The Demilts, who never lived in the village, must have rented out their extensive property surrounding the base of Summit Rock. Daniel Aldridge was a huckster, a person who resold fruits and vegetables that he did not personally grow. With his access to Seneca Village produce, Aldridge joined the hundreds of street vendors who took advantage of the dearth of produce in stores due to the city's restrictions on private markets until 1843.[136] Perhaps others in Seneca Village did the same, although as street vending by Blacks and immigrants proliferated, threatened city merchants pushed the government to crack down on their activities.[137]

Growing one's own food in the nineteenth century was often as much a political message as an economic necessity. The free produce movement was a boycott against foods grown by enslaved labor. As Southern plantations produced cheaper fruits and vegetables and faster railroad transportation made them accessible to New York markets, the Seneca Village gardeners could protest slavery while eating their own homegrown food.[138]

Famed abolitionist and journalist David Ruggles, whose grocery store on Cortlandt Street was the venue for Josiah Landin's tree business, was also involved in the free produce movement. In newspaper ads, he proudly announced that his store sold "Canton and Porto Rican *sugars* . . . manufactured by free people, not by slaves."[139] This suggests that not only was Ruggles morally committed to selling free produce, but his business also benefited from increased sales through a network of like-minded customers.[140]

Modest kitchen gardens could never literally substitute for the cotton, rice, and sugarcane that were the symbols and substance of slave-driven agriculture. But the turnips, cabbages, and strawberries—sprouted in their own soil, and picked by their own free hands—nurtured the bodies and the souls of Seneca Village.

chapter 10

Dividing Bloomingdale, Seneca Village

The Black Leaders, 1825–1857

Many of the people who owned land in Seneca Village did not live there. Their homes and businesses, churches and social associations were in racially mixed downtown working-class wards. These were members of the Black elite of New York City, who counted for a large number of the most powerful Black leaders in the nation. In their private lives, they were entrepreneurial, well educated, and more economically stable than even the middle-class residents of the village.[1]

Among them were the reverends Theodore Wright, Charles B. Ray, and James N. Gloucester, leaders of Black Presbyterian and Congregationalist churches. Churches were central to the political issues of the day—suffrage, abolition, opposition to the colonization movement, and support of or participation in the Underground Railroad—and these Seneca Village landowners separately and collectively were powerful voices in the fight for equality and social justice. As historian Craig Steven Wilder has noted, "Religion was a perfectly human expression of social strife: the vessel of human sorrow. Politics were the means of channeling that sorrow into action."[2]

Some of them, like Wright, Albro Lyons, and Peter Guignon, had bonded at the African Free School founded by the New York Manumission Society. Many of the women—Elizabeth Marshall, her daughter Mary Joseph Lyons, and Elizabeth Gloucester—were indomitable forces in the struggle for Black causes and supporters of charities like the Colored Orphan Asylum, the Colored Home, the Association for the Benefit of Colored Orphans, and the African Dorcas Society, which collected clothing for poor children. The Lyonses and Guignons also socialized with New York intelligentsia at institutions like the literary Phoenix Society, the New York Female Literary Society, and the Philomathean Society lecture series.[3]

10.1 The famous civil rights leader Frederick Douglass was an acquaintance of many Seneca Village landowners. His statue by Gabriel Koren stands on Frederick Douglass Circle at the northwest corner of Central Park.

Source: Gabriel Koren, *Frederick Douglass*, photograph, Sara Cedar Miller. Courtesy of the Central Park Conservancy.

Once they had purchased their Seneca Village properties, these Black elites held on to their land or passed it to their heirs until it was bought by the city for Central Park. To this group of landowners, property was a long-term investment, not a means to quick profit. But like the village residents, they also used the value of their land as an entrée into the political system and a form of collective activism and community.[4]

THE MARSHALLS, THE GUIGNONS, AND THE LYONSES

Joseph and Elizabeth Hewlett Marshall came from very different backgrounds. Joseph was born in Maracaibo, Venezuela, date unknown, and was probably of Spanish and African descent. He ran away from home when his family pressed him "in continental fashion" to become a Catholic priest. This decision would cut him off from his family for the rest of his life. He moved to New York, joined the A.M.E. Zion Church, and became a house painter. Later he would suffer from a syndrome known as "painter's colic," severe intestinal problems from lead paint poisoning. He died in 1829.

Elizabeth was born in 1779 into "a poor white family of English heritage." She probably would not have been racially white but had very light skin. Her ancestor was George Hewlett, who emigrated from England in 1658 and founded the town of Hewlett, Long Island.[5]

Elizabeth had a brother, James Hewlett, who became an actor as a young man and identified as Black. He was the cofounder of the African Grove Theater, where he shared the stage with the young Ira Aldridge. James was charismatic and fond of quoting Shakespeare from memory. In his later years, he fell on hard times and was often jailed for a series of petty criminal acts. Known in the day as an "amalgamation," a mixed-race couple was not that unusual in lower Manhattan neighborhoods, where Blacks and whites lived cheek by jowl, but completely horrifying to the larger white world at the time. James was considered to have a "grossly depraved mind [to] induce a white woman to cohabitate with one of the negro race." Despite being unmarried, Elizabeth took Hewlett's name. When she fell out of the picture, he married Ann Haskins, who was "fond of a drink," and, more importantly, had a yearly annuity of $170. A handwritten note in the Williamson papers noted that Hewlett "was practically disowned by his family."[6]

10.2 James Hewlett cofounded the African Grove Theater and acted alongside the young Ira Aldridge. Hewlett was the brother of Elizabeth Hewlett Marshall, though the siblings do not seem to have been close.

Source: Colored drawing of African American actor James Hewlett (fl. 1821–1831) dressed as Richard the Third ("in imitation" of Mr. [Edmund] Keane). Cropped version. *Theatrical Portrait Prints (visual Works) of Men, Ca. 1700–1900*, 1700. Harvard Theater Collection, Houghton Library, Harvard University.

Elizabeth Hewlett and her sister Mary were apprenticed to a Quaker family, and later as an employee to the De Forrests, who were the first to discover coal in Pennsylvania.[7] Elizabeth herself had two earlier marriages that left her twice widowed; Joseph Marshall became her third husband. They had twelve children, though reportedly only four survived to maturity. Three of them—Rebecca, Gloriana Catherine, and Martha—died "in the first flush of maturity."[8]

The Marshalls were successful, and they built their own home on Collect Street, later called Centre Street. They had leased the land through the nearby St. Philip's Episcopal Church, of which they were devoted congregants. The area today is the site of the New York Criminal Court Building and the former prison, referred to as "the Tombs," which is now the Manhattan Detention Complex.[9]

In 1826 and 1827, the Marshalls purchased six lots in Seneca Village.[10] In 1829, when Joseph Marshall made out his last will and testament, he bequeathed one lot each to his four living daughters and two to his wife. By 1855, only Elizabeth, her daughter Mary Joseph Lyons, and the heirs of his late daughter Rebecca Guignon—husband Peter and daughter Elizabeth—were alive to inherit them.[11]

The year before he died, Joseph Marshall also invested in property in Canalville, New Jersey, which had fostered an enslaved and free Black population since the Revolution and had a Black Sunday school by the early 1820s.[12] A *New York Times* article noted that Canalville lots were sold to local people and to New York residents who wanted them "for country homes," a strong indication that the Marshalls intended their lots in Seneca Village not as a future residence but rather to ensure their right to vote and as a good investment.[13]

Elizabeth was strong, hard-working, a socially engaged entrepreneur, and a role model for her daughter and granddaughter. When Joseph died in 1829, she needed to support herself, so she converted her Centre Street home to a boardinghouse and the basement into a store, where she sold her own baked goods. As a respite from her hard work, she "indulged" annually in a Hudson River sailing vacation to Albany.

Elizabeth Marshall knew "personally or by reputation every colored person in the city," and also had acquaintances of English and Dutch heritage. She left a lasting impression on almost everyone she met, including her former employers, the coal mine owners, and they made sure she received a full supply of coal each winter. Their good fortune underscores the more comfortable life of the Marshalls and their family versus the harsher, more frigid conditions of those in poorer neighborhoods, including the shanties of Seneca Village.

By the 1850s, Elizabeth had sold her home and moved in with her daughter's family. "With Bible and spelling books" and with the "tender ministrations" of her family, Elizabeth passed her final years. She died at the age of eighty-two in 1861, just as the Civil War was unfolding. Near her death, her thoughts were less about her personal salvation than the salvation of her people from slavery; she prophesied, "Slavery will be abolished. I shall not live to see it, but God is just."[14]

THE LYONSES

Elizabeth Marshall's abolitionist sentiments carried through to her daughter Mary Joseph, the only one of the Marshalls' twelve children to enjoy a long life. [She would marry a man named Albro Lyons.] As a teenager, Mary Joseph learned about entrepreneurship and radical politics from her summers with her family's lifelong friends, the Remonds. During the summer months "Sir" Remond, as they called him, ran a confectionary store in the resort town of Newport, Rhode Island, where his daughter Susan, a culinary "genius," created her sought-after masterpieces. Mary Joseph, who had been trained as a hairdresser by Martel, a noted French practitioner, taught the art to the three Remond daughters, who went on to establish the Ladies Hair Works Salon of Salem, Massachusetts, and a wig business.[15]

Albro's grandfather, George Lyons 1st, was an African descendant from Long Island who married a "native squaw" from the local Shinnecock tribe. Albro's father, George 2nd, was born on Long Island in 1783 and married a woman

10.3 Albro and Mary Joseph Lyons were Seneca Village landowners and political activists for Black civil rights.

Source: "Double ambrotype portrait of Albro Lyons, Sr. and Mary Joseph Lyons." Schomburg Center for Research in Black Culture, Photographs and Prints Division, The New York Public Library, New York Public Library Digital Collections, https://digitalcollections.nypl.org/items/789776d0-0233-1efe-e040 -e00a18060ece.

named Lucinda Lewis from Dutchess County in upstate New York. Lucinda was of Dutch and Indian extraction, with "light hair, blue eyes, and the phlegmatic disposition of a Hollander. A thrifty, busy silent woman." She mothered eleven children and died in middle age. Albro, her fourth child, was born in 1814 in Fishkill, New York.[16] George Lyons was a whitewasher and "applied the first coat of paint on St. Philips P. E. Church . . . from which he contracted painter's colic." The Marshall and Lyons families were life-long congregants of the church, and the painter was Albro's father.[17]

Albro's parents were dedicated to giving him the best education possible. They enrolled him in the African Free School run by the New York Manumission Society at a time when emancipation in New York was becoming a reality, and most free Blacks believed education was the key to a better and more secure future. The Free School first opened in 1787 with forty students, including enslaved boys, and later welcomed girls, who for the most part were taught needlework and sewing. When their Cliff Street building burned down in 1814—the year Albro was born—the school raised enough money for a new building on Williams Street. Then, to satisfy the huge demand for education, they added another on Mulberry Street. Eventually their student body grew to five hundred.

The inculcation of elite white morality and social behavior was purposely engineered within the school to prevent what the members of the Manumission Society wrongly believed to be natural "habits of idleness" among Black people.[18] The curriculum included scientific subjects like astronomy and cartography, as it was assumed that most students would become sailors, a profession popular among many young Black men.

Albro, his future brother-in-law Peter Guignon, and many other students at the school became activists. Many became religious leaders, such as Reverends Theodore S. Wright and Peter Williams Jr., the celebrated head of St. Philip's. Williams married Amy Matilda, one of the Remond daughters. Several classmates became Seneca Village landowners, Timothy Seaman, Thomas Zabriskie, and Tobias Hawkins among them.[19]

The name of another schoolmate, Dr. James McCune Smith, appears on several Seneca Village deeds, indicating his role and possibly his financial backing in the community.[20] Smith was the first Black American to hold a medical degree. He was educated at the University of Glasgow in Scotland, after he was barred from American medical school because of his race. He became one of the central leaders and spokespersons for New York's Black community and delivered many

10.4 Dr. James McCune Smith—the first professionally trained Black physician in America and civil rights activist—was a friend and a colleague to several Seneca Village landowners.

Source: "Dr. James McCune Smith, first regularly educated Colored Physician in the United States," Schomburg Center for Research in Black Culture, Photographs and Prints Division, The New York Public Library, New York Public Library Digital Collections, https://digitalcollections.nypl.org/items/7896caac -e713-9809-e040-e00a18060b95.

of their children. He was the best man at the Albro Lyons wedding, delivered Maritcha Lyons, and later became her godfather.[21]

These well-educated students of the African Free School became the leaders of every political and social movement in Black New York. They fought for their rights to vote and to hold office, to end slavery, and to protect and assist enslaved runaways. They formed literary and scientific societies, their curiosity sparked by their formative years receiving the best education that Black children could at the time. They were the first truly cosmopolitan Black society, whose intellectual pursuits, as the Marshall's descendent Carla Peterson wrote, "gave them an opening onto a new world of culture, taste, and aesthetic appreciation that extended far beyond their racial group, their city, and even their nation."[22]

10.5 While living in Providence, Rhode Island, Albro and Mary Lyons sought admission to the best school for their daughters, Maritcha (left) and Pauline (right), but their rejection forced them to attend the "caste" school. Nonetheless, Maritcha persevered and had a successful career as a public school educator and administrator in the New York City school system.

Source: "Maritcha Lyons and her younger sister Pauline." Schomburg Center for Research in Black Culture, Photographs and Prints Division, The New York Public Library, New York Public Library Digital Collections, https://digitalcollections.nypl.org/items/a7d0e925-f88a-eff6-e040-e00a18060357.

Albro attempted to enroll his daughters in their ward's public school for white children, but he was rebuffed. They settled instead for the "caste" school far from home. Due to some unknown physical disability, Maritcha was homeschooled until the age of thirteen. Her parents indulged her with a piano, a luxury in any middle-class home, but one that demonstrates the Lyonses' cultural and educational priorities. Maritcha was admitted to the secondary academy Colored School No. 3, run by Charles L. Reason at Broadway and Thirty-Seventh Street. Her commute was stressful, as "riding for colored folks depended on the whims of stage drivers," who would often ignore or mock her, and she would then have to walk several miles to school.[23]

Albro became the proprietor of the Colored Seaman's Boarding House on Pearl Street and later combined it with the family's home on Vanderwater Street. Perhaps their close association with the Remond family introduced the Lyonses to the use of "free produce" in their boardinghouse. The free produce movement sought to use goods not produced by slave labor. At first the movement focused on sugar, molasses, chocolate, coffee, and tea—plants impossible to grow in the

New York climate. But food historian Michele Nicole Branch suggests that families like the Lyonses likely supported the program. An inventory of their staples revealed, for example, a barrel of brown sugar, indicating they avoided refined sugar, which was "the most-labor-intensive sugar." The Remonds even replaced cotton clothing with "free" textiles such as linen and wool.[24]

With their strong abolitionist sentiments, their free produce practices, and their boardinghouse that catered to a large transient population, it is perhaps no surprise that the Lyonses frequently offered shelter to enslaved fugitives on the Underground Railroad. Lyons took over the boarding house from William P. Powell, who had been a member of the short-lived abolitionist Committee of Thirteen. According to Maritcha's autobiography, her family helped thousands of fugitives escape to freedom. In 1861, a month before the outbreak of the Civil War, Lyons advertised his services as a broker for ship captains who needed "good stewards, stewardesses, cooks, and seamen." And he could supply them "at the shortest notice"—it was common to hide fugitives in the employ of ships at sea.[25]

10.6 The Lyons family's home was nearly destroyed during the New York City draft riots that took place over five days in July 1863 in protest to the conscription for the Union Army during the Civil War, during which eleven Black men were lynched.

Source: "The Riots In New York: The Mob Lynching A Negro In Clarkson-Street." 1863. The Miriam and Ira D. Wallach Division of Art, Prints and Photographs: Picture Collection, The New York Public Library, The New York Public Library Digital Collections, https://digitalcollections.nypl.org/items/510d47e1-2815-a3d9-e040-e00a18064a99.

The Lyonses themselves became fugitives during the New York City draft riot in the early years of the Civil War. After the Battle of Gettysburg, Lincoln knew he needed more soldiers, so he instituted a draft to fill the ranks. The only way out of the draft was to pay a steep conscription fee of $300 or find a replacement to serve in the Union Army. Blacks were excluded from the draft, as they were not considered citizens, and this enraged some of the vulnerable working-class whites. Racial tensions were already running high after the Emancipation Proclamation. White working-class Irish immigrants, already poor and desperate, feared that freed Blacks would take their low-paying jobs while they were at war.

For four days from July 13 to July 16, 1863, the tension erupted into violent riots. Maritcha Lyons described the rabble that attacked their house, "breaking window-panes, smashing shutters, and partially demolishing the front door." The family barricaded themselves inside using the stones that had been hurled through the windows. Later that night, a second gang attempted to break in. Albro Lyons bravely stepped to the front door and "fired point blank" into the menacing mob. Undeterred, they returned the third day and vandalized the house, ripping apart the furniture and lighting a fire in a room on the top floor. An officer from the nearby police station came to the Lyons home, and, sobbing openly, told them the few men in his unit could not protect them. With the police's help, Albro and Mary escaped after dark to the Williamsburg ferry. Terrified, Mary Lyons and her children braved a long and arduous trip to the Remonds in Massachusetts. By the time the riot was quelled by state militias and federal troops, at least 119 people had been killed. At least eleven of those were Blacks who had been lynched, stabbed, stoned, or mutilated.[26] On the first day of the riot, the Colored Orphan Asylum, home to more than 230 Black children, was ransacked and set on fire. The children were led to safety through a back entrance, while the bloodthirsty mob yelled, "Kill the monkeys." Not half an hour later, the four-story building was gone.[27]

Albro Lyons received $1,500 from the city for the damage to his home, but he was unable to revive his business in New York, and the family moved again to Providence, Rhode Island.[28] His family also chose to live in Providence for the reputation of its school system, though initially Maritcha was barred from attending the high school because she had only been previously educated in a "caste" school.[29] By 1870, the family returned to New York where Lyons had set up shop as a manufacturer of ice cream, a trade which he had learned as a young man.[30] Maritcha enjoyed a long and celebrated career as a teacher and a principal in the New York City school system.

THE GUIGNONS

Peter Guignon married Rebecca Marshall in 1840, the same year that his former schoolmate Albro Lyons married Rebecca's sister Mary Joseph. In 1803, Guignon's mother, a refugee from San Domingue, now Haiti, had arrived in America at the tail end of the Haitian Revolution, the massive bloody, decade-long revolt against the white slave-owning French plantation owners.[31] The Guignon family might have been among the free Blacks in Haiti or came to New York because they had family in America. Peter was born in 1813 and attended the African Free School, where he met his future brother-in-law. Rebecca, his wife, died at a young age, and Peter was left a widower with their infant daughter, Elizabeth.

Peter moved to Williamsburg when it was a small town in King's County and just before it became a city in its own right in 1851. He worked as a hairdresser from 1847 to 1854. Sometime before 1848, he married Cornelia Ray, who came from a well-heeled family of doctors and pharmacists. But Peter's luck would not last, and a series of "personal and familial travails" would follow him everywhere.[32]

In April 1859, an article from the *Brooklyn Daily Eagle* with the headline "Indecent assault By A Colored Man" described Guignon as "an obese cream-colored darkey," who was charged with "committing an indecent assault on a respectably dressed white girl named Sarah Lawrence, about 14 years of age." The article continues,

> The accused tends in the drug store of Dr. Ray, corner of Eleventh and South 1st sts., and the girl went in there to make some purchase, when she alleged, Guignon took some improper liberties with her. The girl's testimony was very direct, and no evidence was brought for the defence to disprove the charge made, yet the Justice seemed anxious on account of the "respectability" of the accused to suppress the publication of the case, and dismissed the charge.[33]

The *Brooklyn Daily Eagle* was notorious for its anti-Black attitudes. Judge Fox dismissed the charges against Guignon, but more sorrow was not far behind. Seven years later, he lost his sixteen-year-old son, Peter Jr., a student at Oberlin College, in a tragic accident.[34]

A member of the Black middle class, Peter was financially stable. We learn from the 1865 New York census that he had a home valued at four thousand dollars and owned his property.[35] The formal photographic portrait we have was

10.7 Peter Guignon, a classmate and brother-in-law of Albro Lyons, suffered many hardships in his life but was an avid civil rights activist and businessman.

Source: Peter Guignon. Courtesy of Carla L. Peterson.

probably taken at this time and shows Peter to be a light-skinned, handsome middle-aged man with a perfectly trimmed bushy graying mustache and head of silver hair tucked under a hat of Persian lambskin.

Despite his personal tragedies, Guignon took seriously his privilege to fight alongside his childhood friends for Black causes. In 1837, he and other "colored young men" petitioned the state legislature for Black enfranchisement, and their efforts grew into the New York Association for the Political Elevation and Improvement of the People of Color. He was active in Manhattan's St. Philip's Episcopal Church and elected as president of the American and Foreign Commercial Company, "for the purpose of foreign and domestic trade and commerce."[36]

Living in the close Black community of Brooklyn in the 1860s and '70s, Peter may have known Elizabeth Gloucester and her husband, James, who were also political activists living in Brooklyn Heights. Like him, Elizabeth owned a small property in Seneca Village close to his lots.

ELIZABETH GLOUCESTER AND REVEREND JAMES N. GLOUCESTER

Religion and politics were integral to the lives of Black New Yorkers, and no Seneca Village landowners better exemplified that concept than Elizabeth Gloucester and her husband, the Reverend James Gloucester.

In the fall of 1855, the Commissioners of Estimate and Assessment announced that financial compensation would be awarded to all landowners whose properties would be taken for Central Park. Most petitioners—Seneca Village owners included—protested the low estimates and requested more compensation, but one stands out. Though Elizabeth Ann Gloucester made "no objection to her said assessment," her lawyer wrote, she simply wanted to set the record straight that *she*, not her husband, was the legal owner of lot 194 on West Eighty-Eighth Street. Her petition states that Elizabeth held the title "free and clear and discharged of and from all debts, obligation and control of her said husband the said James N. Gloucester and to all intents and purposes as if she were a *feme sole* [an unmarried woman]."[37]

Her lawyer was quoting from New York State's Married Women's Property Act, passed on April 7, 1848, "for the effectual protection of the property of married women." Prior to that date, American law followed the dictates of *coverture*, described here by English jurist William Blackstone: "By marriage, the husband and wife are one person in the law: that is, the very being or legal existence of the woman is suspended during the marriage, or at least is incorporated and consolidated into that of the husband: under whose wing, protection, and cover, she performs everything." Or as contemporary historian Norma Basch has put it so succinctly, "In the eyes of the law the husband and wife were one person—the husband."[38]

Three months after the common property law was enacted, the Seneca Falls Convention gave official birth to the women's rights movement. Elizabeth Gloucester—though not in attendance—became an early embodiment of the modern, liberated woman, successful and in charge of her personal, business, and political life. That she was also a Black woman demanding her rights was extraordinary for her time. Even more extraordinary, she would become one of the richest Black women in America.

Elizabeth was born in Virginia in 1818 to a free Black woman who was servant to the Parkhill family of Richmond.[39] Before her mother died prematurely when Elizabeth was just six years old, she had arranged for Elizabeth to live in Philadelphia with the family of the late John Gloucester, formerly enslaved and a notable Presbyterian minister.[40] Although Gloucester had died two years before Elizabeth went to live with his family, the story of his struggle from slavery to freedom and his subsequent triumph as a religious and civic leader made a lasting impression on the young girl.

By twenty-one, Elizabeth was employed as a domestic by the prominent Philadelphia Quaker family of John Cook. According to most accounts, it was Mrs. Cook who taught Elizabeth the virtues of thrift, encouraging her to open a savings account to bring her security and independence. In time, Elizabeth left domestic service and used her savings to open a secondhand clothing shop in Philadelphia. It was also about this time that she became romantically attached to James N. Gloucester, one of the sons of her foster family. They married in 1830, and by 1838 the new Gloucesters and their infant daughter, Emma, had moved to New York. There, James, like his father and brothers, was ordained as a Presbyterian minister and planned a church in Brooklyn.[41]

With the profits from her Philadelphia store, Elizabeth opened another clothing shop in the Fifth Ward on Seventh Avenue in New York. She and her husband eventually expanded the business to sell furniture in a store they rented on West Broadway in today's SoHo. With her shrewd financial intuition, she began to buy real estate.

10.8 The beautiful kwanzan cherry allée on the west side of the Reservoir marks the site of Elizabeth Gloucester's first Seneca Village lot. It would be the first of a lifetime of real estate investments that made her one of the wealthiest Black women in America.

Source: Sara Cedar Miller, *Cherry Tree Allée*. Courtesy of the Central Park Conservancy.

Her career in real estate began with a humble lot in Seneca Village, but she would become the wealthiest Black woman mogul of her day. The deed lists James N. Gloucester, not Elizabeth, as the purchaser of the $100 property, but when the deed was officially recorded on November 12, 1849, two transactions took place simultaneously: attorney William Talmage purchased the property for a token ten dollars from both husband *and* wife, then resold it to Elizabeth alone for the same ten dollars. Despite the sweep of married women's property acts across the country, there was no system in place for the transaction of property from a husband to his wife, so Elizabeth's lawyer became the intermediary.[42] This three-way transaction was necessary to award Elizabeth sole rights to property that had legally belonged to her husband. According to common law practices as described in 1769 by Blackstone, "A man cannot grant anything to his wife, or enter into covenant with her: for the grant, would be to suppose her separate existence; and to covenant with her, would be only to covenant with himself."[43]

Despite the process necessary to secure Elizabeth title to her property, the deed from the Gloucesters to Talmage still required by law that Elizabeth, as all wives were required to do, submit to a "private examination separate and apart from her said husband" acknowledging that she was entering into the conveyance "freely and voluntarily without any threat or fear or compulsion of her said husband." Without this examination on record—dating back to a New York law of 1691—the deed could be nullified and declared illegal. This private intervention took place in every conveyance that involved a husband and wife in New York since 1691. In 1845, social reformer Elisha P. Hurlburt noted that though the intention of the interview was to protect the wife, it actually gave "legal right to inspire fear in the wife." He strongly promoted the abolition of the practice.[44]

Elizabeth Gloucester had no fear of her husband, though she did have a legitimate fear of laws that would favor her husband. The Seneca Village lot was not the only property transferred to Elizabeth Gloucester by her lawyer that day. The purchase of two lots in Brooklyn on Prince Street and Willoughby Street was also included in the contract. Three hours later, Talmage and the Gloucesters appeared in Brooklyn and repeated the same legal procedures that they had done in Manhattan. Perhaps Elizabeth had gained financial independence in exchange for purchasing the Brooklyn lots for James's Siloam (pronounced Shiloh) Presbyterian Church.[45] Whatever the arrangement, from there Gloucester's real estate career soared, though the family's bread and butter came from Elizabeth's successful boardinghouse business on Remsen Street in Brooklyn Heights. In 1856, Elizabeth received $460 for her Seneca Village lot to make way for Central Park. Immediately she used her award to buy a lot *near* Central Park, between Madison Avenue and Fifth Avenue around Ninety-Eighth Street, knowing full well that the value of the property would only increase because of the park.[46]

Elizabeth's transactions reveal a solid connection and commitment, along with her husband, to the inner circle of New York's Black religious and political community, which included prominent spiritual leaders, the Lyonses, and the Guignons.

In 1852, Elizabeth paid $450 for property from Dr. James McCune Smith on Sixth Avenue and Fifty-Third Street, not far from the Colored Orphans Asylum. At the time, this was a racially mixed neighborhood where the family of John Whitehead had sold several properties to Blacks a decade earlier. Elizabeth was "First Directress" of the asylum, Mary J. Lyons was "Second Directress," and Mrs. Charles B. Ray was Treasurer.[47]

Elizabeth made commitments throughout her life to financially assist other women, particularly widows. When James's colleague, St. Philip's Reverend Peter Williams, Jr. died, Elizabeth bought his small lot on West Broadway from his widow Sarah and assumed her mortgage of $3,000.[48]

The Gloucesters were active participants in the radical abolition movement. Siloam, the church that James founded in Brooklyn, became a common meeting ground for abolitionists, including Frederick Douglass and the white insurrectionist John Brown. James Gloucester first met Brown at a lecture on Leonard Street and invited him to stay at their home whenever he was in the city.[49] During the following years, Brown frequently stayed with the Gloucesters in their Brooklyn boarding house, and they often gave him money.

In September or October 1859, on the way to his failed attack on the federal armory at Harpers Ferry, Virginia, for which he would be tried for treason and executed, Brown stayed for a week with James and Elizabeth in their Brooklyn Heights home. James recalled the last conversation between Brown and his wife: "Brown said, 'Goodbye, Sister Gloucester. I've only sixteen men, but I'm to conquer.' 'Mrs. Gloucester said to him, 'Perhaps you will lose your life.' 'Well, my life,' he replied, 'is not worth much. I'm an old man. In Kansas, the balls flew around my head as thick as hail. I'll never be killed by a ball. If I fall, I'll open a ball in this country that will never stop until every slave is free."[50] Frederick Douglass met

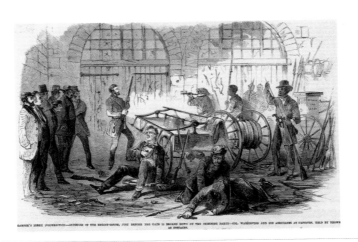

10.9 In 1859, just before leaving New York to lead an insurrection at the federal armory at Harper's Ferry in Virginia, abolitionist John Brown (center) was the guest of Seneca Village landowner Elizabeth Gloucester and her husband, Reverend James Gloucester. Elizabeth Gloucester aided Brown's rebellion by sending him $25 via Frederick Douglass.

Source: "Interior of the Engine-House, just before the gate is broken down by the storming party— Col. Washington and his Associates as captives." Schomburg Center for Research in Black Culture, Manuscripts, Archives and Rare Books Division, The New York Public Library, New York Public Library Digital Collections, https://digitalcollections.nypl.org/items/510d47da-70c3-a3d9-e040-e00a18064a99.

with John Brown just before the raid, and Douglass passed along a letter from Elizabeth Gloucester and a twenty-five-dollar contribution:

> Dear Friend,
>
> I gladly avail myself of the opportunity offered by our friend Frederick Douglass, who has just called upon us previous to his visit to you, to enclose to you for the good of the cause in which you are such a zealous laborer. A small amount which please accept with my most ardent-wishes for its, and your, benefit. The visit of our Mutual Friend Douglass has somewhat revived my drooping spirits in the cause but seeing such ambition & enterprise in him I am again encouraged. With best wishes for your Welfare and prosperity & the good of your cause. I subscribe myself your sincere friend,
>
> Mrs. E.A. Gloucester
>
> Please write to me—with best respects to your son.[51]

When Elizabeth bade respects to Brown's son, she was undoubtedly still in mourning over the loss of two of her sons, Alfred, who had died the year before, and the eldest son Stephen, who had died three years before that at age fifteen.

There was a hint of a rift in the marriage in Elizabeth's letter of November 1855 to the Board of Commissioners of Central Park, in which she claimed ownership of her property as a *"feme sole."* After her death in 1883, her last will and testament made her feelings for James perfectly clear. She left most of her properties to her surviving children, leaving only the rental income derived from his share of property to her husband.

The reports of Elizabeth's death and the subsequent fight over her estate captured newspapers across the country, many of whom were shocked to learn that a Black woman could attain such wealth. Her estate totaled $350,000, or about $4.5 million today. James claimed that all the business transactions were really purchased with his money and merely signed under Elizabeth's name. With the exception of eldest daughter Emma, who was disinherited and contested the will separately from her father, the five children sided with their mother's trustees, one of whom was James McCune Smith. To make peace in the family, the children eventually relinquished a portion of their estate to their father.[52]

In the meantime, James, no longer a pastor, had graduated from medical school and practiced a personal form of holistic medicine in Brooklyn. He marketed a new revolutionary panacea for almost all ills: a mixture of cider, salts, and water from his Long Island farms. He died of pneumonia at age seventy in 1890. With the exception of his son Charles, who squandered his inheritance and was wanted by the police for robbing his own family, the other Gloucesters passed quietly from the public eye.[53]

REVERENDS THEODORE S. WRIGHT AND CHARLES B. RAY

In 1852, Elizabeth Gloucester bought her second property in Seneca Village. It was a lot near Seventh Avenue and Eighty-Fourth Street, purchased from the widow of Reverend Theodore S. Wright, who had died in 1847, only a year after purchasing the property.[54] Wright was the second minister of New York's First Colored Presbyterian Church, who used his pulpit to advocate for the end of slavery and the rights of Blacks. The Gloucesters knew and worked frequently with Reverend Wright. The two men served on the New York City delegation to the National Convention of Colored Citizens, held in Buffalo.[55] Their Committee Upon the Condition of the Colored People reported out on the statistics of populations, churches, schools, institutions, and real estate values, an early sociological overview of urban Blacks in the country.[56]

Wright was born into a politically active family. His father, R. P. G. Wright, was a delegate and organizer in 1817 of the Negro Convention in Philadelphia, which formed in opposition to the American Colonization Society. As a child, Wright attended the African Free School with Albro Lyons and Peter Guignon. In 1828 he became the first Black graduate of Princeton Theological Seminary. Eight years later, he was the victim of a violent racial attack during a visit to the seminary's commencement exercises, described in a letter to his former professor Reverend Archibald Alexander. One of the students noticed Wright in the audience and shouted, "Out with the nigger—Out with the nigger!" Wright described how he was "seized by the collar by a young man, *who kicked me two or three times in the most ruthless manner*—at the same time saying, 'What do you do here? Don't let me see you here again.'"

No one came to Wright's aid, and Princeton President James Carnahan denied the attack. The letter was later published as "Outrage in Princeton," in the *Liberator*, yet Wright did not want the incident to tarnish the reputation of the school or defeat inroads made for the antislavery cause in the student body.[57]

10.10 Reverend Theodore S. Wright was an ardent abolitionist. He purchased land in Seneca Village shortly before he died. As an active conductor on the Underground Railroad at his home, today's 2 White Street in Tribeca, perhaps he was considering his prepark property for a similar purpose.

Source: G & W. Endicott, *Portrait of Rev. Theodore S. Wright*, ca. 1845. Randolph Linsly Simpson African-American Collection, Beinecke Rare Book and Manuscript Library, Yale University.

At the time of the incident Wright was already a distinguished minister and a formidable abolitionist leader. He set himself apart from the less radical spiritual leaders when he boldly challenged the hypocrisy of Christian churches for violating the morals and ethics of Jesus' teachings.[58] Wright asked the elders of his church, "Where is your consistency in talking about the heathen, traversing the ocean to circulate the Bible everywhere, while you frown upon them at the door?"[59]

His "bold stand in defense of militant, political action" increased in 1835 when he took over the leadership of the New York Committee of Vigilance, which helped fugitive slaves evade slave catchers. At the 1843 National Convention of Colored Citizens in Buffalo, twenty-seven-year-old activist Henry Highland Garnet delivered a "thinly-veiled call for revolt" in order to abolish slavery. They would later become radicalized, but at the time James Gloucester, Frederick Douglass, and Charles B. Ray denounced his call to action. But not Theodore Wright. He supported Garnet's militancy and has been credited as one of the two originators of the Underground Railroad in New York City.[60] Wright used his home at 235 West Broadway in today's Tribeca as a stop on the Underground Railroad.[61] Perhaps he bought his Seneca Village lot as an investment, but given his dedication to assisting enslaved fugitives, it is possible that he envisioned the vacant lot as a future stop along the railroad.

Elizabeth Gloucester was a cofounder of and generous donor to the Colored Orphans Asylum, along with Charles B. Ray's wife.[62] Ray was a Methodist minister who, with Wright, was cofounder and director of the New York Committee of Vigilance and an active member of the American Anti-Slavery Society.

Ray grew up in Massachusetts and was the first African American to be admitted to Wesleyan University, though he left after being the victim of student protests. He later studied at the Wesleyan Seminary and served as pastor of New York's Bethesda Congregational Church from 1845 to 1868. Ray also became the owner and editor of *The Colored American*, the New York newspaper that was a strong voice of Black politics and causes. On Ray's first visit to New York in 1832, he was introduced to Reverend Wright. From their first meeting, "like David and Jonathan, they became fast friends."[63]

Along with Wright, Ray had been an agent of the Underground Railroad assisting fugitives, many of them children, from his downtown home on Orange Street. In 1887, the year after their father's death, Ray's daughters wrote a biography that relayed many incidents of his personal bravery to assist runaways. A sixteen-year-old girl whose owner had reneged on her manumission agreement was sent to

10.11 In 1850, abolitionist Reverend Charles B. Ray bought two lots in what is now Strawberry Fields. That same year, he also began to pay taxes on a lot in Seneca Village owned by Elizabeth Gloucester. Given his active participation in the Underground Railroad and Gloucester's similar sentiments, it is likely that those lots might have become a stop on the railroad.

Source: "Portrait of Charles B. Ray." Schomburg Center for Research in Black Culture, Manuscripts, Archives and Rare Books Division, The New York Public Library,. New York Public Library Digital Collections, https://digitalcollections.nypl.org/items/7f57f98f-c629-98dd-e040-e00a1806352e.

Ray by her mother, who had recently bought her own freedom. The girl stayed with Ray and his family for three weeks, "so endearing to all that that parting was not without tears." Ray had secured a home for her farther away and had also arranged for the girl's mother to learn of her location for a happy reunion.[64]

Elizabeth Gloucester was also connected to Ray, who was listed in the tax records in the 1850s for her lot.[65] Before paying taxes on Gloucester's lot in Seneca Village, Ray had purchased two lots in what is now Strawberry Fields for $250, which secured his right to vote.[66] But there may have been another, more pressing reason. Ray purchased his property on October 23, 1850, about a month after

Congress passed the Fugitive Slave Act, which required the capture and return of all enslaved runaways, even within Northern free states. Perhaps the passage of the act impelled Ray to secure a home for himself in an outer ward and, like Wright, use it as a stop on the Underground Railroad. It is less clear if he and Gloucester intended to use her lot for the same purpose. It is possible that Ray, Wright, and Gloucester may have envisioned an Underground Railroad scheme that never materialized because the city took the land for Central Park.

In 1843, Ray served on the Committee Upon Agriculture at the Buffalo convention. The committee's primary focus was to encourage Blacks to attain wealth, dignity, and independence through farming. They believed "there is, and can be no real wealth, but in the possession of the soil." The committee recommended that those with a small amount of capital apply it to "the most honorable pursuits of the age."[67] To this end, in 1846 white abolitionist Gerrit Smith contacted Ray, Wright, and McCune Smith to help him transfer land he had inherited in upstate New York to poor Blacks. Though his plan failed for a variety of reasons, it may have been an inspiration to other urban dwellers to buy upstate land as an investment or future home. Porter Simon Green, a Seneca Village landowner, purchased forty acres in Hamilton County that he left to his wife, Huldah.[68]

Ray also belonged to a group of leaders who advocated for the attainment of Black wealth, a driving force behind the founding of Seneca Village. In 1850, he joined the short-lived American League of Colored Laborers, whose goal was to overcome the "one very great evil now suffered" by the Black community: "the want of money." As Leslie Harris noted, the display of a comfortable lifestyle and material achievements—including real estate investments—signified the same culture and moral values as those of middle-class whites while also helping the less fortunate of the Black community.[69]

THE WHITE LANDOWNERS

No discussion of the Black landowners of Seneca Village is complete without notice of the white landowners. Though the majority in Seneca Village were Black, a few whites saw an early investment opportunity in uptown real estate. The first of them was a counselor-at-law and philanthropist named Francis R. Tillou. In 1829, he purchased three lots on Eighty-Fourth Street from Andrew Roach's widow. The next was Archibald H. Lowery, a New Yorker who became a wealthy Washington real estate developer. In 1835, he purchased three lots from Thomas Jackson of Staten Island for $500. (After selling his property, Thomas Jackson, together with John Jackson—unrelated, as far as we know—purchased eight acres in Sandy Ground, a Black community on Staten Island.)[70]

The majority of the white landowners purchased their properties in the 1850s, when the park was an imminent reality.[71] Several were the mortgagors discussed in the last chapter. They did not choose to buy the land but came into it by default, foreclosure, or through a court-ordered auction. Most saw an opportunity to invest in the land. Only one buyer may have had plans to settle in the community, a butcher named Christian Tietjen. But he, as we shall see later in chapter 15, was the unwitting victim of two devious real estate speculators.

The succeeding generation of the Seneca Village families apparently forgot about the community once Central Park was built.[72] But at least one of them, George Washington Plunkitt—the crafty and corrupt Irish Tammany Hall politico—may have relished the idea of taking revenge on the park that obliterated his birthplace. According to his *New York Times* obituary, Plunkitt once pointed out to a reporter his birthplace, called "Nanny Goat Hill"—probably today's Summit Rock—"just inside the western wall of Central Park near Eighty-fourth Street." It was said to be located at "at a cluster of dwellings there at his birth . . . known as 'Nigger Village.'"[73] Although no documents have yet emerged of a Plunkitt family as owners or renters, the location could only be Seneca Village.

By 1892, Plunkitt had been elected to the state legislature, and there he sponsored a bill to enlarge and straighten Central Park's sinuous West Drive so wealthy financiers, powerful businessmen, and Tammany trotters could enjoy a "driveway for light wagons" to race along. The bill passed the senate in March, followed by a storm of public protest so profound that Plunkitt was forced to sponsor a second bill to kill the speedway that April. The movement of historic preservation was born when the racetrack died.[74]

Perhaps Plunkitt sought revenge. Slicing a destructive swath through the park would not have been too farfetched for the corrupt politician, who once suggested that his epitaph might read, "He Seen His Opportunity and He Took It."[75]

As we shall see in a later chapter, most prepark landowners received ample compensation for their land and their structures. Financial gain offered social, economic, educational, and political power, a road to independence. The right to own, buy, and sell property triumphed over centuries of *being* considered property by white enslavers.

But with few exceptions, the system did not amply reward renters, either in Seneca Village or in the prepark as a whole. Throughout the city, most renters were often pawns in a perpetual game of displacement, evicted at the whim of a landlord, uprooted by raised rental fees, victimized by what we now call gentrification or the march of civic progress: the opening of a street, the establishment of a school or hospital, the construction of a public utility, or the creation of a park.

chapter 11

Dividing Harlem, 1825–1843

THE HARLEM COMMONS

If the English had had their way back in 1666, we would all be taking the A train to Lancaster rather than Harlem. That year saw the fairly amiable charter between the English Governor Richard Nicholls and the freeholders and inhabitants of Harlem. The document recognized their rights to their "enjoyment and possession of their particular lots and estates," and their Dutch social customs and religious institutions.[1] But one of the governor's terms was ignored. They would live in Harlem, not Lancaster.

The charter established the border for Harlem's landowners and for its common lands, which—with regard to the prepark—sliced a diagonal line northwest through the land from East Eighty-Seventh Street to West 110th. Today's Reservoir was almost divided in two equal parts; one half would be owned by the city and the other was a part of the Harlem Commons.[2] Nicholls's patent fixed the Harlem property, but added a vague right of commonage, allowing Harlem inhabitants to go beyond the borders "for plowing, home pastures and meadow lands only."[3]

To prevent property disputes between the separate communities of New York and Harlem, the commissioners passed a law in 1669—not unlike that imposed on the ranchers of the American West—that required owners to brand their animals. The brands were either "N.Y." for New York or "N.H." for New Harlem, and an official was "sworn in each place to mark such horses and cattle as really do belong to the inhabitants, and none others."[4] Periodically the Harlem Commons were subdivided and land given to the freeholders, much of it to several prepark families, including the Montagnes, Dyckmans, Bensons, McGowans, and Kortrights.

The vague language in the royal charter defining the grazing boundary led to disagreements between Harlem and New York for over a century. Finally, the line was permanently set by an act of the Common Council on April 3, 1775. To make amends for the confusion about the grazing lands, Harlem freeholders were given an additional 290-acre tract of New York's common lands, which included much of the prepark.[5]

Although the "wasteland" of much of the Harlem Commons was considered unsuitable for farming, the areas was a rich place of daily exploration for a curious and adventurous boy. Samson Benson McGowan, Andrew and Margaret McGowan's younger son, fondly recalled his boyhood wandering what would be a part of today's North Meadow. In an 1857 trial in which McGowan was a witness, he described "the brush cedar, swamp alder, and scrub oak . . . huckleberry and blackberry bushes" and a small duck pond where the tennis courts are today. In the summer he shot ducks, and in the winter he ice skated. The pond also supplied local residents with fresh water, seasonal "muck" or compost, ice, and a pasture for their cattle.[6]

The terrain of the commons might have been useful to the locals, but as a whole it was hardly a bonus for the freeholders of Harlem. The city unloaded its unprofitable and untaxable common lands onto Harlem residents, who would be forced to pay future taxes and assessments on them. The total Harlem Commons property, aside from the prepark land, encompassed much of today's Upper East Side and East Harlem neighborhoods.

In 1820, when the city was ready to construct Third Avenue, Harlem Commons residents—less financially endowed than, say, wealthy Chelsea estate owner Clement Clarke Moore—were expected to pay stiff assessments to cover the costs. It became clear to the New York State Legislature that the community could ill afford the taxes, so on March 28, 1820, they vested the land to Harlem trustees. The trustees—among whom were Samson's older brother Andrew McGowan Jr.—were instructed to sell the commons, and the proceeds would benefit Harlem's library and certain schools.[7] Two years later, the trustees had the property resurveyed and took out a real estate ad, offering the land from Third Avenue to the Bloomingdale Road, "situated on elevated ground, susceptible of high cultivation and improvement, and consist[ing] of about three hundred acres." There were no takers.[8]

But things changed abruptly on April 13, 1825, when almost all of the Harlem Commons, totaling more than five thousand city lots, was bought for $25,000 by twenty-six-year-old Dudley Selden, an impressive beginning in the world of New York real estate speculation.[9] Every conveyance identified Selden as the official purchaser, and he reconveyed the land to more than seventy purchasers within the following two years.[10] It came as a complete surprise, therefore, when developer Francis Price revealed that Selden was a shell buyer. Price and his business partner, Enoch Wiswall, had "hired Dudley Selden to take title and give the deeds."[11] That same year Francis Price openly bought and developed property throughout the city, so one wonders, why did Price and Wiswall need to hide behind Selden in the Harlem Commons deal?

THE HARLAEM CANAL COMPANY

There was a push across America to create transportation routes and hubs that would enable the establishment of new cities and states, new markets, and new ports. Under Thomas Jefferson the country saw the greatest land acquisition with the Louisiana Purchase in 1803. That same year he commissioned the Corps of Discovery, better known as the Lewis and Clark expedition, in part to explore an intercontinental water route for the betterment of commerce. Five years later New York State funded a survey to see if a water route from Lake Erie in Buffalo to the port of New York City could be built. The result was the Erie Canal, finished in 1825, that established "the undisputed supremacy of New York City as a distributing agent for the commerce of the interior of the continent."[12] It also inspired an era of canal building throughout the country. Carried by that momentum, two entrepreneurial New Yorkers, Francis Price and Enoch Wiswall, had a vision. What if the Hudson River and the East River could be joined in the middle of Manhattan by a canal? Such a sea route would link New York's two rivers and continue on to Long Island Sound, New England, and Europe beyond.

The canal seemed almost preordained, as it would follow the course of the existing waterway. From a small pond on the heights of Manhattanville at Tenth Avenue and 124th Street, the water flowed across Harlem diagonally, heading southeasterly through the Muscoota flats of Henrick de Forest and Johannes de la Montagne until it reached the low-lying marshland of today's Harlem Meer, and from there ran east to the navigable Harlem Creek and the Harlem and East Rivers. Locks constructed at the Hudson River and at Third Avenue would make the journey possible for ships laden with cargo. The Harlem Creek could be deepened and enlarged to a sixty-foot-wide canal, lined with fifty-foot-wide streets, an incentive for both commercial and residential development. Harlem's canal would resemble those of Amsterdam, a fitting reminder of its Dutch roots.[13]

The New York State Legislature supported the new canal, and they passed the bill approving its construction in 1826. The City Council approved it too the following year.[14] Price and Wiswall most likely used Dudley Selden to conceal any connection between their canal scheme and the sale of the Harlem Commons. Had the Harlem trustees known about the plans of these well-known speculators to make a quick profit from lands they had held communally for over a century and a half, they would have either demanded a significantly higher selling price or prevented the sale altogether.

Together, Price and Wiswall (and sometimes Price alone) also bought out many private properties neighboring the proposed canal. In 1828, Price acquired a large tract from Benjamin L. Benson, the grandson of Adolph Benson, who owned much of the prepark land above Ninety-Sixth Street.[15] Benson probably saw the breakup of the Harlem Commons—290 acres adjacent to his property—as a sign that Harlem would no longer be the rural enclave of his youth. When Price arrived on the Harlem real estate scene, Benson sold him the land that had been in his family for four generations and watched as Price divided it into more than 500 25-by-100-foot lots.[16] Price now owned the prepark land that stretched from today's Conservatory Garden to the North Meadow and down to the Ravine and the Pool, and much of the Upper East Side and East Harlem.

While creating the canal, Price and Wiswall were also investing in the fledgling Yorkville community. They purchased property on either side of Third Avenue and Eighty-Sixth Street and divided it into 480 lots. The partners anticipated it would become as desirable a suburban community on the east side as Bloomingdale was on the west side.[17] By 1832, construction had begun on the world's first street railway, the New York and Harlem Railroad (today's Metro North), which would arrive in Yorkville and Harlem five years later. When it did, it heralded the end of an era for the old Dutch farms and their way of life.

While they were dividing great swaths of Manhattan Island, Price and Wiswall had another idea. That very same day, the New York Legislature named the two men as founding directors of the New-York Harlaem Spring Water Company, "for the purpose of providing fresh spring water to the people of New York from the Harlem Commons or such other high grounds north of seventy-fifth street." Before the creation of a municipal water system in the 1830s, New York had many private water companies, and the partners saw the potential to corner the market on Manhattan's abundant natural springs. Because that did not require approval from the Harlem trustees, they felt no need to conceal this aspect of their business venture.[18]

Many inland Harlem landowners were excited by the idea of owning waterfront property. Price and Wiswall had sold them on a vision of a canal lined with gold flowing through their sleepy rural neighborhood. Many sold their farms and marshland to the developers or else bought stock in the Harlaem Canal Company. The shareholders in the three-mile "Grand Canal," as one promotional ad called it, were promised "the usual privileges and revenues accruing from the stock itself." Buyers were also enticed by the offer of a free building lot—there would be 5,500 building lots in all—with the purchase of two shares. Accommodations for market boats and a "commodious square for an extensive Market" at both rivers would only enhance the three miles of charming residential neighborhoods. In a decade's time, the company promised, the $50 shares would be worth at the

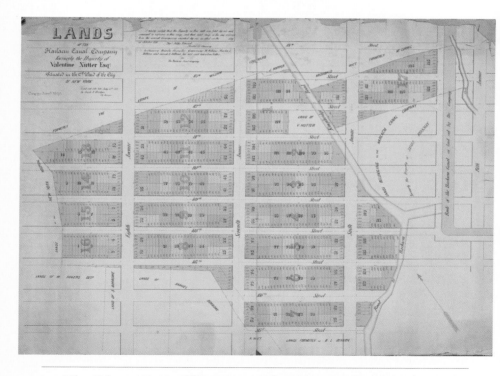

11.1 When Valentine Nutter sold his property to the Harlaem Canal Company, they divided it into nearly 1,200 saleable lots that were repurchased by the family at auction when the canal company failed in 1831. Note the adjacent canal at the top right of the map. It would have flowed through the northeast corner of today's Central Park.

Source: Joseph H. Bridges, *Lands of the Harlaem Canal Company formerly the Property of Valentine Nutter Esq. situated in the 12th Ward of the City of New York*, 1831, copy Jan. 1870. Lionel Pincus and Princess Firyal Map Division, The New York Public Library. Farm History, Map of the Harlem Commons, Municipal Archives.

lowest calculation, $500 per Lot. The company offered working-class New York-ers, "mechanics, tradesmen, ship-builders, carmen, industrious persons of every description" a piece of the American dream. These potential shareholders were assured that an investment in their company was "no visionary idea" and instructed them "to vest your money in a safe concern that immediately secures you one little spot of earth that you can exultingly point to, and say, 'This is mine.'"[19]

We have no record of how many people subscribed to the developers' project, but at least one resident—Valentine Nutter—knew *he* was sitting on a gold mine.[20] His strategically placed farm stood adjacent to the future waterway, and he was one of the first to jump in, selling all but one acre of his 110-acre estate in 1827. He sold it for $400 per acre, which meant $40,000 paid to him by Wiswall and Price in four installments. He also purchased 56 shares in the company, which gave him the bonus of 28 free building lots, which undoubtedly included a part of his own property that he could own once again.[21]

According to the company's charter, Price and Wiswall were to buy the land, pay for the construction of the canal, and bear all expenses. When they then acquired all of the capital stock, the developers would turn over both the land and the canal to the company. There was only one caveat. Keeping the protection of its property and its citizens in mind, the City of New York stipulated that construction of the canal could go forward *only* if and when the company had collected $40,000 worth of its stock and paid the city $30,000 as security.[22]

But before a shovel could break ground, problems arose. Many shareholders refused to honor their commitments, forcing the company to rely on those "respon-sible subscribers" who were then called upon to "advance moneys at the mere discre-tion of its officers."[23] But the call went unheeded, and the company trustees collected only $9,000 of the required $40,000 with the first installment. The second install-ment also faltered, garnering only $2,500, so the city prohibited construction from going forward. The Common Council—in lieu of cash—required that a sufficient amount of land be put up as security before construction could begin. Against the company's mounting debts, three Harlem Molenaor brothers put up two hundred acres of their Central Harlem, Manhattanville, and upper Harlem farmland, which included a part of today's Fort Tryon Park and possibly the site of the Cloisters.

That same month, the company's treasurer and real estate speculator, Archibald Watt, purchased over three hundred prepark lots from Benjamin L. Benson, the estate his family had owned for over a century. Watt also purchased more than a hundred Harlem Commons lots and nearly five hundred lots ranging from the East River to Fifth Avenue. One of them was the three-acre parcel that once belonged to Lanaw Benson, and more recently to the heirs of John Rankin, whose purchase of the small lot had secured Lanaw's manumission.[24] Watt mortgaged his newly acquired property to the city for $15,000 "as collateral security" against the failure of the canal scheme.[25] The company's charter was modified, and a new board of directors assumed ownership of all lands, transferred to the company. Wiswall and Price lost their command of the project.[26]

Infused with new funds and new hope, the city gave its approval. The new board proudly announced that the difficulties were behind them and urged those with capital to join in the scheme. The company held a celebratory luncheon at Harlem's Bradshaw Hotel, followed by a procession to the long-awaited groundbreaking.[27]

The shaky evolution of the canal venture caused tremendous concern to stockholders and mortgagees alike, and most importantly for us, to Valentine Nutter. The New-York Historical Society has in its collection a series of letters written to Nutter by his daughter Ann Livingston of Rochester during these stressful years. Nutter was already deeply concerned about the project even before he had sold his land to the developers, and Livingston assured him that a visit from her grandson Daniel D. Barnard would set his mind at rest and "compel those Canal men to do what is right."[28] But things did not go well for Nutter or any of the other landowners. Price and Wiswall stalled repeatedly in their payments to the landowners. When the company finally did pay Nutter, he received only $6,000 of the $10,000 they had agreed upon.[29] The company was foundering.

By May 1828, Livingston felt comfortable enough to invest fifteen acres of her choice property "along several windings" of the future canal.[30] But it wasn't long before Nutter was even more distraught. He became frantic about how and where he would live, and his daughter reminded him that as surely Price had made a payment, "he will expect to have the farm if he pays you interest, and charge for rent for the place." The aging Nutter would not or could not maintain his deteriorating property, and his daughter—extremely ill, in constant pain, bedridden, and soon to die—offered to set up housekeeping in the city for both of them. She implored her father to leave, but Nutter refused to budge from his familiar surroundings. Livingston wrote to him in frustration, "I must beg you to let me understand why you remain there or rather what late arrangements you have entered into with [the canal company]."[31]

Nutter's other daughter, Sarah, avoided all contact with her sister. She took their father to live on the Wilkins estate, Castle Hill, in Westchester, now the Bronx. When the Harlaem Canal Company went bust in 1831, Nutter and his family sued the company and the Molenaor brothers. The company-owned land was put up for auction, and much of it was purchased for far less than it was worth by Nutter, his daughter Sarah, his grandson Gouverneur Morris Wilkins, and Archibald Watt.[32] Price, Wiswall, the company directors, their stockholders, and the Molenaors were dragged through lawsuit after lawsuit by a host of irate investors and canal employees for years afterward.[33]

ARCHIBALD WATT AND MARY G. PINKNEY

Valentine Nutter's certificate for his fifty-six shares of the Harlem Canal Company is in the collection of the New-York Historical Society. The flip side of the stock certificate has a handwritten and itemized statement of money owed to Nutter by the company, signed by treasurer Archibald Watt. In 1827, the same year that the Harlaem Canal Company was incorporated, Watt married Mary Pinkney, the widow of Revolutionary War Colonel Ninian Pinkney of Maryland. Whether it was capital earned, inherited, or from Pinkney's dowry, Watt jumped into the canal headfirst, buying the land to use as collateral.

Archibald Watt was born in Dundee, Scotland, on July 8, 1790. It is uncertain when he emigrated to New York, though we know he began by importing

11.2 In 1828, Valentine Nutter sold most of his Harlem property to the Haerlem Canal Company and also invested in it, buying fifty-six shares of stock. When the company failed to meet its financial commitments, Nutter and his family sued and regained title to the property, then sold off some of it to speculator Archibald Watt.

Source: Stock Certificate of the Harlaem Canal Company, 1829, Valentine Nutter letters, 1798–1829, MS 2958.7232, New-York Historical Society.

Scottish goods to America. By 1826 he was listed, along with many prominent businessmen, as a director of the Howard Insurance Company. But Watt's restless, risk-taking personality drove him toward something more adventurous. Fellow New Yorkers scoffed when he purchased the remote Harlem farm of Oliver Delancey's nephew, John Delancey, in 1826. He had thrust himself into the covetous and fast-paced world of speculative real estate, forever driven by a lust that would one day almost destroy him.

Seven years after the Harlaem Canal Company failed to construct the canal, Watt and his brother, James, decided to make another go of it. As with Wiswall and Price, the financing was unsteady. But this time an environmental problem may have also accelerated the project's demise. According to the *Documents of the Board of Alderman* from March 1835, "The wells on the Harlem Heights have been drained by the Harlem Canal."[34] The failing water pressure irritated the surrounding residents, the final straw in an already troubled project. For almost a century, half-dug ditches filled with rainwater dotted the Harlem landscape, where children would "catch quantities of gold fish," and the long-forgotten stone embankments and locks could still be seen crossing the "desolate marshes and barren wastes of ground."[35]

Watt was overcommitted to the canal. He had purchased fifty-four acres of prepark land and vast amounts of Harlem real estate, and then came the financial Panic of 1837. Soon he was debt-ridden and "land poor," unable to meet his loan commitments. Later a lawsuit brought against him by his younger brother, James, "threatened to harass the old man to death." Watt had, however, a remarkable protégée by his side—his thirty-three-year-old stepdaughter, Mary Goodwin Pinkney. Mary's widowed mother had married Watt in 1827. Colonel Ninian Pinkney left his daughter $40,000, valued today at nearly half a million dollars. In 1843, she used that money to bail Watt out, covering his mortgages and mounting debts. In return, Watt turned his vast Harlem real estate holdings over to her.[36]

PInkney managed her new empire with an eagle eye and a tight fist. In 1872, for example, she sued the City of New York for awarding contracts for sewers just north of Central Park without complying with the open bid process, and exposed the inequitable shift of responsibility for funding the project from the government to the property owners. In the end, she won her case and lessened her assessment for the sewers from a million dollars to half that.[37]

Watt took great delight in mentoring his stepdaughter, who proved herself as shrewd and feisty as America's first multimillionaire, John Jacob Astor. It is said that as he lay dying, Astor remarked wistfully, "Could I begin life again knowing what I now know and had money to invest, I would buy every foot of land on the island of Manhattan."[38] Pinkney almost did just that. At her peak, she owned more land in the prepark than any other landowner, as well as most of central and part of East Harlem, including the former property of the McGowans, the Bensons, and even Valentine Nutter. Her property included an estate that at one time encompassed forty blocks from the East River to St. Nicholas Avenue. It covered today's Morningside Park, St. Nicholas Park, City College, and the old Polo Grounds between 110th and 112th Street between Fifth and Sixth Avenues. She sold all of it to the city for millions.

In the first, March 1868 edition of the *Real Estate Record and Builders' Guide* weekly, a reporter noted "one very curious fact": that although women were busily engaged in most aspects of real estate, it was not likely that they would get involved in speculation. That activity required "a certain kind of imagination, patience and foresight," which women did not possess.[39] That reporter had obviously not heard of Mary G. Pinkney, who had recently made close to half a million dollars for her prepark property.

As modern apartment buildings loomed over her block-wide neoclassical mansion on 139th Street between Seventh Avenue and Lenox Avenue, she lived a reclusive life, running one of America's most lucrative real estate empires while tending to her roses and her truck garden. The value of the land on which her garden beds lay caused one newspaper to call her asparagus, peas, and lettuce "the most expensive vegetables in the United States."[40]

In 1908, Mary G. PInkney's death at age ninety-eight was front-page news in the *New York Times*. Though the press always referred to the unmarried Pinkney as a "spinster," she wasted no time at a spinning wheel. Rather, she had become a real estate legend, one of the wealthiest women in America with an estimated worth around $50 million.[41]

In her obituary, the *New York Times* reported that for years Pinkney would delay paying taxes until her property had quadrupled in value, like Astor, making a huge profit on its sale that was significantly more than the taxes and the fines for her overdue payment. After her death, she left none of her fortune to charity but bequeathed all of it to her wealthy, spoiled, and irresponsible half-siblings and their children, who squandered it. Today, on the site of her historic Harlem mansion sits a McDonald's and its parking lot.[42]

The Harlem Commons abutted the southern area of Pinkney's estate and was only divided in 1825. The division of New York City's common lands, much of it to become Central Park, began much sooner, but the cause for the division was similar: the land was too valuable not to be exploited.

chapter 12
Dividing Yorkville, 1785–1835

Much of Manhattan Island, particularly what we now know as the Upper East Side, midtown, and what became much of Central Park, was original known as the city's common lands. Though this area was called "wastelands," as mentioned earlier, there were particular aspects of the topography that caused the common lands to lie uncultivated and uninhabited until James Amory and David Wagstaff transformed the intractable land into productive farms that today are many of the park's most celebrated landmarks.

THE COMMON LANDS

Perhaps the most outstanding horticultural feature in Central Park is the quadruple row of American elms that line the Mall. These trees were planted in 1922 after the sixty-year-old stand was found to be dying. City Forester J. S. Kaplan discovered that the mature elm roots were incapable of receiving nourishment due to the "hard and impenetrable stratum of clay" that lurked as close as two and a half feet below the surface of the park; by 1919, "hundreds" of the park's trees had already died for this reason. Kaplan suggested "a light blasting" of dynamite to loosen the unyielding crust, but the commissioners demurred, and the famous allées of elms, whose roots lay between a rock and a hard place, were chopped down.[1]

While the topography of Harlem and Bloomingdale favored settlement, investment, and military activity, the terrain under the Mall represented what for two centuries since the Dutch was considered "waste" land that covered most of the central, eastern, and southern sections of the prepark.

Eons of geologic actions conspired to create the landscape. Hundreds of millions of years ago, heat and pressure metamorphosed mud into shale, a fine-grained sedimentary stone. The same forces then turned shale into schist or gneiss, a much harder medium-grained rock. The collision of tectonic plates twisted, folded, and squeezed the rock upward into an ancient mountain chain, which many think eventually eroded and weathered in the Lower Cambrian and/or Late Proterozoic periods, from roughly 650 to 500 million years ago to a later period roughly 450 million years ago.[2] Manhattan schist is the bedrock of the island. Most of the outcrops that broke through the island's surface have been leveled to create the city's grid and its buildings. Today hints of those ancient formations remain in only a few of the city's parks, most famously, of course, in Central Park.

In the most recent period of glaciation in the Pleistocene, more commonly known as the Ice Age, New York experienced many cycles of glacial advancement and recession from over two and a half million to approximately eleven thousand years ago. The Laurentide ice sheet—a vast crystalline shield of frozen water two miles thick—scoured and leveled the Manhattan schist with its crushing weight. Its maximum glaciation peaked twenty thousand years ago, at which time the planet began warming and the glacier began to recede. The advancing ice was the main force that deepened the valleys of the Hudson and East Rivers, creating the hilly and undulating fourteen-mile island and one of the most extraordinary harbors on Earth, and the receding ice added to the process.[3]

The advancing and receding ice scrubbed the island of its soil cover, dug out valleys, and piled the earth into hills. Central Park's codesigners, Fredrick Law Olmsted and Calvert Vaux, called this rocky and uneven topography "broken." The local Lenape tribe called it "Manahatta"—"island of many hills."[4]

12.1 (*overleaf*) The magnificent elms that line the Mall are Central Park's most significant horticultural feature. These centenary trees were planted in 1922, when the roots of the 1859 plantings had become constricted by the layers of clay and hardpan that lay beneath the Park.

Source: Sara Cedar Miller, *Mall,* Courtesy of the Central Park Conservancy.

12.2 When global warming began to melt the Laurentide ice sheet over twenty thousand years ago, it dropped countless boulders on Manhattan—from small stones to others weighing hundreds of tons—that had been dragged by the ice from terrain as distant as the New Jersey Palisades. This photograph taken in 1862 shows the prepark landscape along Fifth Avenue strewn with tens of thousands of these stones, which were used by the park designers for substructure or as design elements.

Source: Victor Prevost, *5th Avenue*, October 23, 1862, from the album *Central Park*. Courtesy of the George Eastman Museum.

The melting ice deposited glacial till—unstratified mixtures of clay, silt, sand, gravel, and boulders—that received layers of the soft material in thicknesses as slight as a few inches or as thick as thirty feet.[5] The moving ice picked up and transported massive glacial erratics—boulders, some the size of a Subaru—from as far as the distant Palisades of New Jersey and dumped them across Manhattan's bumpy skin. Hundreds of them are captured in an early 1862 photograph of the park at Fifth Avenue that also shows two rock outcrops in the left foreground.

In 1855, when surveyor Roswell Graves created the topographic maps of the land that would become Central Park, he marked the locations where the glacier had dumped the erratics. They were later used to fill in depressions or as the underground foundation for the drives and retaining walls. Many became eye-catching "sculptures" or were used to control erosion throughout Central Park.

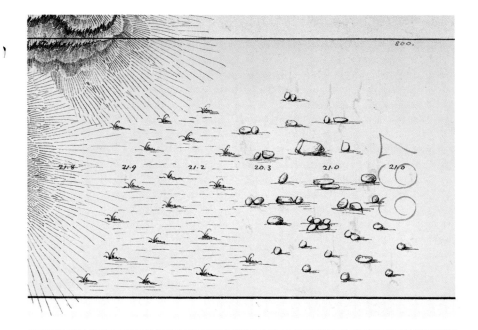

12.3 In his topographic survey, surveyor and draughtsman Roswell Graves captured groupings of the erratics throughout the landscape, these in the area just off Bethesda Terrace in the Lake.

Source: Roswell Graves, *Glacial Erratics* (detail), New York City Municipal Archives.

12.4 The southeast corner of the Sheep Meadow features a line of erratics that had been dumped by the glacier in an adjacent area. The designers used them throughout the park to shore up slopes and here kept the largest one as an eye-catching sculpture.

Source: Sara Cedar Miller, *Sheep Meadow*. Courtesy of the Central Park Conservancy.

12.5 (*overleaf*) Designers Olmsted and Vaux brilliantly used a group of erratics that were strewn across the bottom of the future Lake to line a steep slope in the Ramble, to prevent erosion and resemble a mountain rockslide.

Source: Sara Cedar Miller, *Gill.* Courtesy of Central Park Conservancy.

THE COMMON LANDS

With little promise for agriculture or human habitation, the jagged terrain of Manhattan Island's midsection—roughly three miles long and a half mile wide, running from roughly Second Avenue to Seventh Avenue and Twenty-Third Street to Ninety-Second Street—became the city's common lands. They were first granted in 1658 to the colony of New Amsterdam by the Dutch Assembly. The land was considered "waste, vacant, unpatented, and unappropriated." In 1686, after New Amsterdam had been turned over to the British and become

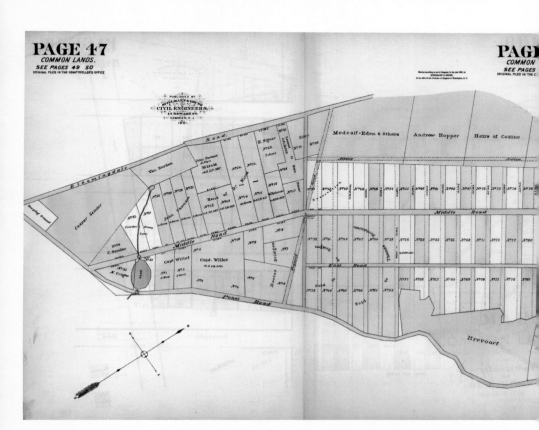

New York, Governor Thomas Dongan granted the vast and largely undesirable tract that now comprises midtown and much of Central Park to the Corporation of New York via royal charter. Overnight, the corporation became the largest property owner on Manhattan Island.[6]

The "diluvium" that was killing the elms on the Mall was everywhere. Issachar Cozzens described the barrier under today's Forty-Second Street as a fourteen-foot-thick "tough cement of clay, gravel, and boulders, very hard to dig." Roswell

---

12.6 Much of the southern, central, and eastern portions of the future park was the common lands that belonged to the city of New York. In the waning years of the eighteenth century the city, desperate for revenue, created five-acre lots in the common lands. The green and yellow blocks represent alternating lots for sale and lots for rent.

Source: Spielmann and Brush, (*Composite Map*) *Map of the Common Lands between the three and six mile stones belonging to the Corporation of the City of New York March 1st. 1796 (Sig) Casimir Goerck, City Surveyor.* Published by Spielmann & Brush, civil engineers, Hoboken, N.J., 1881. (to accompany) Certified copies of original maps of property in New York City. Courtesy of David Rumsey Map Collection, David Rumsey Map Center, Stanford Libraries.

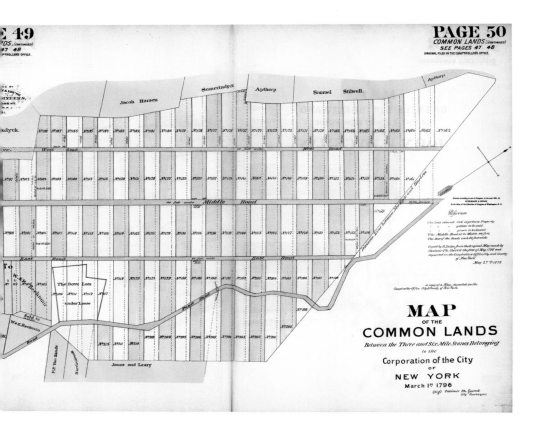

12.7 Quicksand, an unstable soil of clay, sand, or silt particles suspended in standing water, was discovered during the construction of Inscope Arch at the Pond.

Source: Sara Cedar Miller, *Inscope Arch*. Courtesy of the Central Park Conservancy.

Graves, the surveyor hired to undertake a thorough topographic study of the land in 1855, noted the "clayey, hard pan, degenerating in certain localities into a micaceous quicksand." The southern end of the park was particularly prone to bogs where rainwater was trapped between the underground rock and hardpan and fens that were fed by groundwater.[7] A detailed description of this soil and its resulting ecological effects came from Engineer-in-Chief Egbert Viele's entry into the 1858 design competition for the park.

> The soil of the Central Park contains an excess of clay, and this clay contains an excess of moisture, the consequence of which is that in damp weather, it is formed into a tenacious paste, from which the water will neither evaporate nor drain off. In dry weather, it bakes, becoming almost a solid substance through which the roots cannot penetrate. In very hot or very cold weather, it cracks open, either breaking the roots or exposing them. It attracts mechanically the nutritive juices essential to vegetation, and does not part with them to the plants.[8]

12.8 The prepark was covered with unhealthy, stagnant bodies of water—this image most likely the future Lake—that gathered because the thick layer of hardpan prevented proper drainage.

Source: Photographer Unknown, *"Looking southeast across Swan Lake, toward 59th St. between 6th and 7th Avenue,"* 1857, from PR020 (Geographic File),box 46, folder: Central Park In Preparation, prior to 1860 #283266d New-York Historical Society.

THE FIRST DIVISION OF PREPARK COMMON LAND

In the eighteenth century, the city would sell off pieces of this "useless" real estate from time to time. But as a rule, it was either leased for income or left fallow. Unlike the commons in other cities, New York prohibited its citizens from pasturing animals, gathering firewood, or removing plants or materials for personal use. As early as 1703, the Common Council mandated a punishment of forty shillings "for digging holes in Commons" or taking away earth, mould, sod, or turf. As late as 1788, their policy still held; the potter John Campbell was chastised for "digging & carrying away Clay from the Common Lands" necessary to manufacture his roof tiles.[9]

After the Revolutionary War, the city was debt-ridden, with few opportunities for a new revenue stream. The New York State Legislature withheld from the city any funds collected from the loyalists' confiscated property. Paralyzed, the city had no authority to collect sufficient taxes. The only funding came from wharf-age and ferry fees; the issuing of licenses; the recording of births, marriages, and deaths; and, important to our study, real estate conveyances and rental property. By 1785, the corporation was forced to sell its most tangible asset—roughly 1,200 acres of the common lands.[10]

That year the Common Council hired surveyor Casimir Goerck, a Pol-ish-born New Yorker, to divide the common lands starting from Forty-Second Street north to Eighth Avenue and Ninety-Third Street and diagonally across the prepark to Second Avenue into saleable parcels. He was further ordered to create a Middle Road that would bisect the lots. He did, and this eventu-ally became Fifth Avenue. The Goerck plan contained about 140 roughly five-acre irregular parcels, many with no access roads to the lots that lay beyond the Middle Road.[11] Some of the properties adjacent to the main roads sold, but the inaccessible parcels—the majority of them covered with clay, rock, fens, and bogs—did not.

In 1794 the council invited Goerck to modify his plan. After two years of surveying, he created a more uniform grid of 212 evenly rectangular five-acre lots, each roughly the size of a modern city block. He also added an East Road and a West Road, which allowed access to the outer lots. The East Road would become Park Avenue, and the West Road would become Sixth Avenue.[12]

Between 1790 and 1800, the city's population doubled, and the relentless push north continued. The economy was booming, and some pioneers were ready to invest in Goerck's reconfigured lots. Despite their immediate need for cash, however, the council took the long view, holding back the sale of each alternat-ing lot until the "barrenness and roughness" of the soil had first been improved for cultivation. Their decision was clear: "whatever tends to the improvement of the Lots immediately adjoining those belonging to the corporation will nearly in the same ratio improve those also, and render them at the expiration of the present lease, far more valuable than at present." The Finance Committee of the Common Council saw these improvements as a victory for everyone, "beneficial to the proprietors, ornamental to the suburbs of the City, and advantageous to the corporation."[13]

Until the sale, the city generally charged lessees a low annual rent either in cash—ranging from ten to thirty dollars—or, most often, an increasing number of "bushels of good merchantable wheat or the value of in good gold or silver coin of the State of New York." This was reminiscent of colonial leases when wheat was the city's most valuable commodity, as New York held an exclusive monopoly on the milling and exporting of flour. Barrels of flour and windmill blades can still be seen on the city's official seal along with the beaver, its first prized export.[14]

At the end of the eighteenth century, the developed areas of Manhattan suffered the pressures of a growing urban population. Downtown well water was polluted, and according to a 1799 report, even uptown water was "annually losing its purity." Most New Yorkers used rainwater collected in cisterns for washing, but for cooking anyone who could afford it had drinking water from uptown springs and streams brought in daily on water carts.[15] The water quality in the commons motivated more and more New Yorkers to invest in the city's cheap property. Poor soil could be improved, but a source of free, abundant, and pristine water was an incomparable magnet for aspiring farmers.

Right when the Common Council hoped to inspire a crop of new gardeners to improve the common lands, two helpful aids appeared in New York. The first was *The American Gardener's Calendar*, a comprehensive garden manual published in 1806 and written specifically for Americans. The author, expert horticulturist Bernard McMahon, brought the most up-to-date horticultural practices to the new or seasoned gardener with month-by-month detailed instructions on the best methods of growing every type of vegetation, from kitchen and ornamental gardens to orchards and vineyards. McMahon advised his readers of the ideal growing conditions for each situation, so important to common lands gardeners, whose poor soil would require much enrichment before it could bear fruit.

Coincident with McMahon's written guide, a living guide, the Elgin Botanical Gardens, was budding on the common lands, between the Middle and West Road from Forty-Seventh Street to Fifty-First Street (today the site of Rockefeller Center). Dr. David Hosack, a medical doctor, botanical scientist, and educator, founded Elgin as America's first botanical garden and conservatory, a place where nascent or experienced gardeners could admire new specimens or catch up on the most current practical methods. Prepark landowners or lessees would pass the new institution en route from downtown to their property, and it is quite likely that James Amory and David Wagstaff, two men who transformed their barren lots into productive farms, would have stopped many times to consult with Dr. Hosack or get inspiration from his Garden of Eden.[16]

JAMES AMORY

Many of Central Park's most beloved landmarks—the Mall and Concert Ground, Bethesda Terrace, the Dene, Rumsey Playfield, the East Green, and the former Center Drive, informally called "the Dead Road" by parkgoers—were once all a seventy-acre farm owned by James Amory.[17] Then as now, Amory's land was either gently rolling or fairly flat, with a few massive outcrops and only one steep slope that today runs through the Dene landscape. There were no deep depressions or swamps, and several streams and springs ran through the property, some feeding into a duck pond on the edge of the East Green.

Amory made just the kind of improvements that the Common Council was counting on to increase the value of its undeveloped adjacent properties. He dug a well of "never-failing water," which he claimed "washes better than rain."[18] And though his original landscape was layered with thin glacial till aboveground and

12.9 James Amory was the largest purchaser of common lands lots that his family and his descendants lived on, worked on and cultivated. Several of the park's most beloved landmarks, referred to as "the heart of the park," were on Amory's property: The Mall, Bethesda Terrace, Rumsey Playfield and surrounding landscapes, the Dene, and portions of the East Green, Sheep Meadow and the former Center Drive.

Source: Sara Cedar Miller, Aerial. Courtesy of the Central Park Conservancy

hardpan or schist below, after three decades he had transformed the poor soil into rich loam. For the most part, the composted earth was created from the city's unlimited supply of horse and cow manure. Even back in colonial New York, local farmers and gardeners purchased "street dirt" from the city. By 1830 the Common Council had standardized measures, set prices, and hired inspectors to keep records of this, one of the city's most abundant assets.[19] Decades later the Commissioners of Central Park also contracted with the railway companies and the city to create the park's greensward out of stable manure.[20]

Amory boasted that his farm was "the best cultivated on the island, planted with every kind of trees that can be procured, and every necessary planted in the garden for family use."[21] He grew gooseberries, currents, raspberries, wheat, oats, corn, and potatoes as well as cherry, pear, peach, and quince trees and a number of "elegant stately forest trees and ornamental trees, chiefly mountain ash."[22] Two unspecified lots—probably those at Cherry Hill and Bethesda Terrace— featured "a thrifty young wood," meaning "strong and healthy," that Amory suggested would pay for itself to clear.[23] By the time the park began clearing the land in 1857, Amory's land was "covered with a good soil, susceptible of a high state of cultivation." No other spot in the park below 106th Street was described so favorably.[24]

Amory's fertile garden plots were perfectly located for transporting his produce to downtown markets, as they were situated near Harsen's Lane, today's Seventy-First Street. In 1803, west side landowner Jacob Harsen Sr., had petitioned the Common Council to open a road to connect his property at Bloomingdale Road to the Middle Road (Fifth Avenue) and the Eastern Post Road (Third Avenue). The council saw the benefit to the sale of the city's adjacent common lands lots. The road was described as "passable for riders or for light wagons, but its bald edges of rock afforded poor foothold for horses dragging heavy carriages."[25] Today Harsen's Road meanders across the park at about Seventy-First Street, but lines up at the spot where the Seventy-Second Street cross drive intersects above the lower level of the Bethesda arcade.[26] The crossroad was particularly instrumental for the increased value of Amory's farm, which encompassed the land at the intersection of Harsen's Lane and the West Road (Sixth Avenue). Amory also boasted to prospective buyers of an academy and two churches near his property. St. James Church, on Madison Avenue and Sixty-Eighth Street, is still there.[27]

The Amorys luxuriated in a two-story house that was undoubtedly one of the finest dwellings in the area, featuring, "a handsome piazza." The home on a rise between the Mall and the Center Drive, surrounding the magnificent American elm dedicated in 1918 to poet Joyce Kilmer.[28] Among its eight rooms were two large kitchens with an oven in each, "a milk room secure from vermin," two Italian marble fireplaces, and a south-facing greenhouse. And for entertainment, the family also enjoyed a large, elegant barrel organ that played ninety tunes, the first music heard in the area that would later be famous for the concerts at the Bandstand and the Bandshell. The farm buildings included a large barn, a brick smokehouse, a stable, a chicken house, and a pig house.[29] A rough sketch of the family's dwelling and outbuildings is visible in an 1859 lithograph of ongoing park construction of the Mall and Dene, a section of the park that was a part of Amory's former farm (see figure 14.9).

The second of Amory's properties was located on the Middle Road and Seventieth Street—today the lawn that slopes down to the Mall from Rumsey Playfield, a memorial grove dedicated to veterans of World War I. The farm had enough cows to warrant a forty-by-thirty-foot cowshed and similar animal pens, a pond neatly enclosed for ducks and geese, and a two-story, six-room house—the one the Amory family probably occupied much of the time. The large garden plots were irrigated by a well with pumps and "a never-failing spring" for the animals.[30] The Amorys also owned property just beyond the park perimeter, east of the Middle Road, from Sixty-Third Street to Seventy-Seventh Street. It featured a large three-block cherry, pear, and apple orchard.

Despite these apparent riches, James Amory was dissatisfied with his lot in life—and his lots in the commons. He petitioned the Common Council constantly to exchange his lots for more desirable ones, or to own rather than rent them, or to sublease his lots to others.[31] The council repeatedly turned him down: most leased lots had more improvements than those for sale, and the city did not want to get stuck owning only "inferior" property, "as much as it tends to dry up the sources of Public Revenue and to impoverish the Corporation."[32]

In 1813 the city comptroller established the Sinking Fund, created to pay off the city's large debt. A major source of income was intended to be the sale of the last eighty-five-acre common lands lots, whose leases would expire in 1824.[33] The city's vacillation was frustrating to Amory, who wanted to either sell his land at a profit or expand his farm. In one of the city's only deals, Amory was allowed to purchase three previously leased lots in exchange for his "fireproof" store on Market Street Slip. The Common Council noted that Amory's lots were "greatly improved" and even offered Amory an extra thousand dollars.[34]

Another exception the city made for Amory was to sell him lot 110—Park to Fifth Avenue, Sixty-Seventh to Sixty-Eighth Street—which the Common Council deemed "wholly unproductive and incapable of being made otherwise being little else than a huge mass of Rock." Amory bought the lot from the city for $2,550 so he could erect a wall between his Dene property and the offending rock.[35] It has never been confirmed that he built the wall, and his taking offense seems odd, given that his adjacent lot also featured a massive rock, which today is graced by the charming rustic Dene Summerhouse. Before his death in 1836 and through negotiations with the city and other landowners, Amory had amassed over seventy acres, fifty in the land that would become Central Park and twenty between Fifth Avenue and Fourth (Madison) Avenue.

Though Amory farmed his land, he earned his living as a whip maker. For most of his life, he was the proud creator of exceptional horse whips for an exclusive clientele. His father, John, an acquaintance of Valentine Nutter, had established the business before the Revolution and made the "best and newest fashioned horsewhips" this side of the Atlantic.[36] Among many others, George Washington owned an Amory crop.

According to Jessie MacLeod, the curator at Mount Vernon, Washington chiefly purchased his riding equipment in England. So when the general ordered an American custom-made riding crop, it confirmed the superior quality and reputation of the Amory brand. Thought to possibly have been created as a whip, the silver-handled crop features the elegantly inscribed initials "GW" and "Amory & Johnson Makers New York." It is a prized treasure in the Mount Vernon Collection.[37]

In 1777, in the middle of the Revolution, James's father, John Amory, was himself a deserter from the Continental Army and later a professed loyalist. That year, he married the widow Mary Delamontagnie and left his whip business to run the tavern of her deceased husband, Abraham, the great grandson of Johannes de la Montagne.[38] Twenty years later, in June 1797, James reported to his family's close friend, Rufus King, a former member of the Continental Congress, the U.S. ambassador to Great Britain, and a former New York senator, that his father, "being tired of his folly," had come to live with him and supervise the business.[39] It is unclear whether James referred to the "folly" of running the tavern or owning a separate emporium from that of his son, but in 1797 father and

12.10 James and John Amory were celebrated whip makers for elite sportsmen. Their most famous client, George Washington, had the Amorys fashion a riding crop for him that is signed "Amory and Johnson" with the initials "GW" on the tip.

Source: Amory and Johnson, *Riding Crop*. Courtesy of Mount Vernon Ladies Association.

son were reunited in the family's whip manufactory and their exclusive sporting goods store on Broadway. They expanded the business to hand-carved whalebone, walking canes ("with and without swords"), and fishing and gun apparatus. The shop also featured luxury items imported from England: saddlery, fowling equipment, all the trappings in demand by the elite sporting clientele.[40] Amory, although not in elite circles, had a close connection to them through his association with Rufus King.

The correspondence between Amory and King during the years 1797 to 1802 reveals the anxieties and frustrations of American artisans who depended on raw materials and goods shipped from abroad. Vessels were constantly delayed with goods lost or misplaced, shipwrecked or captured by privateers or pirates. Catgut, a sturdy twine made from sheep intestines, was a vital part of the whip, and it was only made in Britain. The letters to King, who acted as his agent while in London, expose Amory's exasperation and impatience to procure his shipment of catgut to New York. Without the catgut, he couldn't finish thousands of whips, and without selling whips he couldn't pay his creditors. It was a downward spiral for the frustrated and frequently insolvent artisan.[41]

In November 1797, the situation was exacerbated when Amory's wife and their four children succumbed to "the prevailing fever" that ravaged New York from 1793 to 1803. Although the autumnal yellow fever season was fairly mild in 1796 and 1797, the Amory family fell victim to the disease. Symptoms began with "chills, intense back pain, and yellowing skin; then came a black crust on the tongue, delirium, and a diarrhea that resembled black molasses." Just before death, the victim would vomit a black bile "that had the look and feel of coffee grounds."[42] The disease was transmitted by urban-dwelling mosquitos like the *Aedes aegypti*, which today can carry the Zika virus.

Physicians of the day did not know the disease was borne by insects. Dr. Richard Bayley, for instance, blamed the urban filth. He connected such areas as Water Street—ground zero of the epidemic—to "a ridge just two feet high behind houses" that accumulated stagnant water. When that stagnant water containing "animal and vegetable matters" was exposed to the hot sun, the fever was the obvious result.[43] The Amorys lived at 71 Water Street, where they were bitten by the mosquitos that were drawn to the toxic soup brewing in their backyard.

The disease was assumed to be contagious, so James Amory could not hire a nurse, and no one dared to come near his infected family. He ministered to them himself. Later he would confess to Ambassador King that he "imprudently staid" in town, when normally he would, like most people, have left during the autumn fever season.[43] The Amory family was fortunate—they all lived—but the whip business suffered from James's absence. The following year, he lost his best apprentice to the fever. By November 1800, Amory wrote to King that, with "the thoughts of the Fever Coming this season, and staying in town one year had all my family down with it," he had decided to buy a lot in the commons and there build a small house and workshop.[44] By the time he had written the letter, Amory had already purchased a second common lands lot. The small house—later much expanded—is the one that was located on or near the Center Drive, near today's beach volleyball courts.[45]

An estimated fifty thousand people fled the city during the yellow fever epidemic of 1805. This was the year James Amory officially moved his whip manufactory to his new prepark home. He took out an ad in the *New-York Gazette* informing New Yorkers of his move and looking for two boys to be apprentices[46] A month later, he sought four more apprentices, between ten and sixteen and "of respectable parentage."[47] Business was improving. Six months later, Amory bragged that he was continuing "the business on a large scale," and this time sought two journeymen and four apprentices.[48]

Apprentices and salaried journeymen were not Amory's only help. We know he enslaved at least two people because of runaway ads he posted in 1813 and 1817, when most New Yorkers had already manumitted their enslaved people. The two who had run away were young George, a thirteen-year-old boy, who was "uncommonly afraid of dogs, having been severely bitten in his hand," and twenty-year-old Lue, who was "well-known . . . as he has drove a waggon for several years collecting dung." Amory's ad offered a reward of fifty dollars for their apprehension, and warned that anyone caught harboring them would be punished by the law.[49]

In 1790, one artisan out of every eight listed in the 1790 New York directory enslaved people. Ten years later, that number was only about one in seventeen. Many artisans began to substitute paid labor, as they would save on costs for food, shelter, and fuel.[50]

By February 1807, Amory placed an ad to sell his common lands property, hoping to move to a house downtown, and six weeks later he moved his workshop back to the Burling Slip building that Rufus King had sold to him. In the same ad, he announced that his prepark lots were for sale or lease, and he continued to advertise them for sale for the next two years.[51]

We know that Amory was building a family as well as a business, and by 1807 he had the first three of his seven children. But world events may have been the more immediate cause for his sudden turnabout, events that affected not just the New York economy but that of the entire nation. For James Amory—dependent on importing materials from England—the resumption of the Napoleonic Wars between Britain and France threw him, like countless other New York artisans and merchants, into economic crisis. His earlier letters to Ambassador King already showed the frustrations of an American manufacturer desperate for British goods, but by 1807 Amory's business was nearly destroyed by President Jefferson's embargo.

In 1818, Amory advertised his whip manufactory for sale. He sounded desperate. He pleaded "to some enterprising and industrious young man who has either money or friends" to buy his company. And if no whip maker should apply, Amory offered to "teach any person of Common abilities, especially be he a mechanic, viz. carpenter, turner, silver or black smith, in a short time, sufficient of the trade to enable him to carry it on with the help of journeymen."[52]

James Amory's ad represents the changing labor movement that began after the Revolution. Prior to the war, master craftsmen controlled the system, elevating former apprentices to paid journeymen before they left to open their own shops. In peace time, they transferred the political struggle to one demanding economic freedom and identified their employers with the tyrannous British and themselves with the American patriots.[53]

By 1807, the embargo pushed them to strikes in protest of master craftsmen who employed "half-trained apprentices" and foreigners rather than the higher-paid and skilled journeymen. The following years saw strife, strikes, and early violence stemming from labor arguments. Hundreds of journeyman carpenters smashed the windows of the General Society of Mechanics and Tradesmen, of which John Amory was a founding member. His son, James, was affected by the growing disenchantment and protests, and he attempted to solve his problems by appealing to a master craftsman of another trade to absorb his whip business.[54]

We don't know whether James Amory ever sold his business, but he was constantly beset with debt and constantly advertised for a buyer, including in one ad he placed in 1832 "To Farmers, Gardeners & Milkmen."[55] He died on February 15, 1835, at age sixty. Although he possessed valuable real estate, his last will and testament caused decades of problems for his wife and seven children.

DAVID WAGSTAFF

Cedar Hill, the steep meadow just inside the park at Seventy-Ninth Street and Fifth Avenue, the Seventy-Ninth Street Transverse Road, and a section of the Metropolitan Museum of Art were once a part of four common lands lots owned or leased by David Wagstaff, an English-born grocer, agriculturalist, and entrepreneur.[55] To grow high-quality produce for his downtown clientele, Wagstaff was attracted to the cheap and unimproved uptown city land. His large home stood on what is today the brink of Fifth Avenue entrance and the Seventy-Ninth Street Transverse Road. He described his property in an 1817 advertisement:

10 acres of good land, pleasantly situated on the Middle Road, 5¼ miles from City Hall. On the premises are a large well-built Dwelling House, two stories high, containing seven rooms; on the ground floor are two kitchens, three

bedrooms for servants, a dairy and a pantry, a pump of excellent water; a large Barn, and other out houses; a good bearing orchard; a very large Garden with half an acre of asparagus beds, which produces some of the largest that are brought to the market; a great variety of very best of fruit, and a quantity of shrubbery.[57]

In his 1857 report, park engineer James Sinclair noted that the top of the slope around Seventy-Eighth Street was grazing land on which grew a grove of cedars. Those eponymous trees gave the area its appearance, and it became one of the park's first mature plantations. Even today, a cedar grove still climbs along the northern slope. Wagstaff's pasture at the top of the hill features a display of blossoming cherry trees in the spring and one of the park's most magnificent elms. Sinclair also admired the "charmingly picturesque" view, which would have stretched across today's Upper East Side to the river, though now it is blocked by high-rise apartment buildings.[58]

Wagstaff's grocery business mushroomed to include shipping and a lucrative dry-goods trade, but despite his becoming one of New York's wealthiest citizens, his passion remained with farmers and their produce. Wagstaff was a prominent manager of the New-York County Agricultural Society, where he often judged the awards for best kitchen gardens, dairies, and dairy products to promote advancement in New York food production. In 1822, he was a judge for the best specimen of butter from a single dairy, with a first prize of fifteen dollars. Wagstaff's committee noted proudly that the offer of awards has "improved the character of the supply of butter in New York because of competition." The contest motivated greater care and neatness in manufacture, and some farmers were even "induced to furnish themselves with ice-houses" in express reference to the butter award.[59]

An activist and civic leader, Wagstaff joined his Yorkville neighbors in 1826 to petition the Common Council for a road from his land to the East River. The east side landowners—the upper-class Beekmans, Joneses, and Schermerhorns, whose families had owned the great river estates—charged people like Wagstaff for water access, if they permitted access at all. A road through their property was, they protested, intrusive and troublesome.[60] They might have felt it was an infringement on their privacy, but they may also have objected because of the material that the local farmers were hauling from the boat docks. It was customary for produce to be shipped by boats to the downtown markets and boatloads of fertilizing manure from the stables to come uptown in return. Whatever the cause of the conflict, the city agreed to open Seventy-Ninth Street to the East River.

Wagstaff owned a fine home near his store, but by 1820 the family had moved into their country house. From an 1821 jury census, we know that Wagstaff's twenty acres on Cedar Hill were in cultivation, and he pastured eleven neat cattle and two horses there.[61] When he made out his will in 1824, Wagstaff left all of his property and possessions, including his "farming utensils and cattle," to his family. He also, somewhat mysteriously, expressed a "wish" that his family "not remain in my country place after my decease but remove therefrom as soon as convenient thereafter."[62] He often petitioned the corporation, as had his neighbor James Amory, for the opportunity to purchase his leased land, and he was constantly rebuffed.[63] It's likely he was worried about the city's future plans for his rented land and didn't want his family's well-being to be interrupted by the city's indecision.

Wagstaff owned a substantial amount of farmland on the western side of the prepark. In 1796, he purchased seven acres of arable land from west side gentleman farmer Samuel Stilwell, and four years later he bought fifty acres of woodlands for around $5,500 from Rebecca Apthorp, who had inherited it from her father. Today Wagstaff's vast west side woodlands would include the American Museum of Natural History, the planetarium, and its surrounding parkland. Within the confines of Central Park, Wagstaff's farm stretched along the glades adjacent to the Great Lawn: Winterdale Arch and the bridle path, Shakespeare Garden, the Swedish Cottage, the Delacorte Theater, the Diana Ross Playground, the West Drive, and the Seventy-Ninth Street Yard maintenance facility.[64] The 1836 Colton map shows that the west side property was heavily wooded, while the 1855 Viele map shows large cultivated plots on Wagstaff's east- and west-side estates.

12.11 (*overleaf*) Cedar Hill was the property of grocer David Wagstaff, who lived in what is now the Seventy-Ninth Street Transverse Road and had a farm that specialized in asparagus beds.

Source: Sara Cedar Miller, *Cedar Hill*. Courtesy of the Central Park Conservancy.

His property also included Tanner's Spring, the park's most profuse spring, today inside Central Park West at Eighty-Second Street. It provided fresh water for irrigating crops and watering cattle for Seneca Village residents and other local residents.

The presence of the spring may have been the draw for a second small inter-racial community of renters that existed in 1855 between Seventy-Seventh and Seventy-Ninth Street, Sixth to Eighth Avenue. The New York State census for that year listed the Black households of the Johnsons, Connovers, Styers, and Ann McDonald living close to several German-born and French-born families. The Wagstaff heirs also rented to the Stones, a Black family living in a one-story house between Seventy-Ninth and Eightieth Street, today on the Transverse Road adjacent to the park's maintenance facility.[64]

Among the many marriages that occurred between neighbors in the prepark community, one was between David Wagstaff's daughter Ann and Benjamin Davis Craig, the son of lawyer Samuel D. Craig, who owned the common lands lots just south of the Wagstaffs. Unlike the Wagstaffs, Craig never lived on his prepark land. Instead, he leased it to several farmers, who built houses, farm structures, and a greenhouse. He also established an orchard on the property that may have been the grove of five hundred persimmon trees later noted in the 1857 plant inventory of the land that would become Central Park.[66]

When the city took the land by eminent domain in 1857, the Wagstaffs' country home became the headquarters of Egbert Viele and his superintendent, Frederick Law Olmsted.[67] In the commissioners' *First Annual Report*, the surveyor James C.S. Sinclair admired the potential of the Wagstaff and Craig farms, writing, "from the picturesque alterations of hill, vale, streamlet, dell, and precipice, it presents a series of topographical characteristics, which at little cost will render this division of the Park one of the most romantic spots on the island."[68] And it still is, particularly in winter when the slope becomes the largest sledding hill in the park.

SARAH "SALLY" WILSON

In the literature about Seneca Village, the Black community is set apart from any affiliation with other prepark residents. Yet an extraordinary relationship developed between the younger generations of the Wagstaff and Amory families and

Seneca Village resident Sarah "Sally" Wilson. Sally was the daughter of Cornelius Henry, who bought his three lots from John Whitehead in 1825. Sally was widowed twice to men from Seneca Village, first Joseph Thompson and then William Wilson. She must have walked across Eighty-Sixth Street to the Wagstaff home at Seventy-Ninth Street and Fifth Avenue, where she was probably employed as a domestic. It's possible that one of her parents had been enslaved by the Wagstaffs at the turn of the century, but no evidence has been unearthed.

In 1846, Wilson's widowed stepmother, Hannah Green, transferred ownership of Cornelius Henry's home and lot on Eighty-Fifth Street to her stepdaughter, including the insurance settlement Green received for the original house that had been destroyed by fire. Wagstaff's son-in-law, attorney William Lowerre, assisted Wilson with the conveyance and several other legal proceedings that followed.[69] In 1847, Wilson "sold" her property to David Wagstaff Jr., who subsequently reconveyed it to Wilson. As with Elizabeth Gloucester and Elizabeth McCollin, the conveyance ensured that a married woman would be guaranteed the "sole and separate use free from all control and debts or engagements of her husband" as if she were unmarried.[70] In 1852, after Wilson had attained sole ownership of her home and lot, she conveyed it mistakenly to the African Methodist Episcopal Zion Church of Yorkville. She had intended to leave it to the Yorkville church after her death, but because she could not read, she did not understand the terms of the deed. By a Special Term of the Supreme Court of New York, her deed was invalidated on the grounds that Wilson signed a document without full comprehension. The court documents reveal that James Amory Jr. acted as a "next friend," a position created when a litigant has a disability, which in Wilson's case was her illiteracy.[71] Again William Lowerre represented Wilson in the case and acted as the trustee to her estate to ensure she would retain her property for life. In 1854, Sarah Wagstaff, David Wagstaff Jr.'s widow, bequeathed "Sarah 'Sally' Wilson, a coloured woman," one hundred dollars.[72] But Wilson died a year later, at age fifty-seven, and became one of the first to be buried in the St. Michael's cemetery in Astoria. The city awarded her estate $795, which reverted to the Yorkville A.M.E. Zion Church.[73]

James Amory and David Wagstaff—like the generations before them—willed the farms to their heirs, neither dividing nor selling off the land they had worked so hard to nurture and transform. They were among the last who would purchase the land to improve and cultivate before the grid transformed it into a commodity for the cultivation of money.

BENJAMIN ROMAINE

The common lands of New York encompassed roughly half of the 106 acres that became today's Reservoir. The other half was part of the Harlem Commons. The Harlem Commons were divided into saleable lots after 1825, but the city-owned part of that property had only two owners. The first was Archibald McCullum, who built a home and gardens that today would be just inside the Reservoir's waters and near the beautiful cast-iron Bridge No. 27. The second and largest property owner was Benjamin Romaine, a well-known and colorful New Yorker, who owned one five-acre lot and leased the adjacent one from the city. Romaine's lots ran roughly from Fifth to Sixth Avenue and Eighty-Sixth to Eighty-Eighth Street and would today encompass part of the Reservoir, its running track, Rhododendron Mile, the East Drive, and part of the Bridle Path.

Romaine was no ordinary citizen. He was a Tammany Society member and protégé of the infamous Aaron Burr. In 1805, he was elected comptroller of the City of New York, a position that oversaw the accounting of the city's finances, including valuable information regarding common lands properties that were as yet unclaimed.[74] He served for less than two years, removed from office in December 1806 after being accused by the Common Council of acquiring water lots without paying for them.

In January 1807, Romaine petitioned the city for a stay of one year with interest to pay his debt, but his successor as comptroller, Isaac Stoutenburgh, demanded immediate payment. Four months later the council's attorney was still pursuing Romaine to pay for a lot he illegally held. He must have paid up, because in 1856 his heirs received a substantial award from the city—$74,555—for their father and grandfather's property in Central Park.[75]

Romaine's property malfeasance was not his only shifty escapade. In 1808, a year and a half after his dismissal as city comptroller, he became passionately dedicated to the Tammany Society's campaign to fund a monument memorializing the eleven thousand Revolutionary War patriots who died as inmates on the infamous British prison ships. Prior to their imprisonment, 2,828 captives were led by British soldiers through McGowan's Pass and down the Kingsbridge Road to the prison ships stationed in Wallabout Bay, Brooklyn.[76] Shallow graves had been dug for the dead along the shoreline, but the ocean tides had unearthed their bones. Some were never buried at all, and their bones still washed up on the shores of Brooklyn and Queens. Romaine, himself a prisoner of war in the Sugar

12.12 The common lands between Eighty-Sixth and Eighty-Eighth Street, Fifth Avenue into the Reservoir, an area that includes Rhododendron Mile, was the property of Benjamin Romaine, a colorful and corrupt character, whose grandson Robert J. Dillon was instrumental in the legalization of Central Park.

Source: Sara Cedar Miller, *Rhododendron Mile*. Courtesy of the Central Park Conservancy.

House Prison on Duane Street, felt strongly that the victims' remains, collected by Tammany and others, should be buried with honor, and their memory and valor consecrated in a fitting monument. On April 26, 1808, Tammany Society members, Romaine included, completed a vault in which the collected bones of the soldiers were interred on donated land on Jackson Street (now Hudson Avenue near the Brooklyn Navy Yard) on Wallabout Bay. Several associations and private individuals contributed to the monument. Tammany even induced the state assembly to contribute a thousand dollars. By 1821, the monument was yet unrealized, and all eyes turned to Tammany's treasurer, Benjamin Romaine. For five years, the legislature threatened Romaine to return the money or submit to legal procedures, but he never did, and he was never punished.[77]

Despite his wrongdoings, Romaine's vision was constructed The vault of bones and the monument today are in Brooklyn's Fort Greene Park, named for General Nathanael Greene, who called for the council of war meeting in

Mrs. McGowan's tavern. In 1867, Central Park's Frederick Law Olmsted and Calvert Vaux designed Fort Greene Park. In 1873, "twenty-two boxes, containing a mere fraction of total volume of remains, were interred into the newly created twenty-five by eleven-foot brick vault."[78] Benjamin Romaine, who died in 1844, is also buried inside.

Despite his checkered past, Romaine's greatest legacy was his descendants. His daughter Amelia married Gregory Dillon, the founder of the charitable Irish Emigrant Society and the president of the Emigrant Savings Bank. His grandson, Robert J. Dillon, became the corporate counsel of the City of New York, whose dedication and persistence made him the great advocate behind the legalization of Central Park in 1853 and later, when he became a Central Park commissioner, a major force behind its design in 1858.

Romaine's common lands property lay, as noted, within the confines of today's Reservoir, running track, bridle path, and East Drive.

Two decades before the Reservoir displaced Romaine's common lands property, the City of New York was planning a massive construction project on its common lands, the receiving reservoir, that lay between the Amorys, the Wagstaffs, and a growing number of other neighbors on the east side and the west side Seneca Village community. It promised to be a major panacea to the lives of residents living downtown, who were dying from the ravages of cholera and polluted water, but it was also guaranteed to be a major disturbance to the quiet prepark refuge.

chapter 13

The Receiving Reservoir, 1835–1842

Unbeknownst to the Fitzgerald family of 75 Cherry Street on the Lower East Side, the last day of their health and happiness together would be Sunday, June 25, 1832. The very next day, Mr. Fitzgerald suddenly took gravely ill. By Friday, his two young children, Jeremiah and Margaret, and his wife, Mary, were all dead. Only Mr. Fitzgerald recovered. They were New York City's first victims of Asiatic cholera (the bacterium *Vibrio cholerae*). Cholera was a horrifying and virulent disease of biblical proportions that had already killed millions worldwide, and in just two months taken the lives of over 3,500 New Yorkers.[1]

Symptoms began without warning. "Explosive-severe-voluminous" diarrhea, nausea, fever, stomach pain, and leg cramps beset victims who had seemed healthy just moments before. Within the next few hours, they "expelled immense quantities of bodily fluids, making their head, hands, and extremities turned cold, bluish in color, and death like in touch." After expelling all their fluids, victims cried for cold water. They were dehydrated, literally dying of thirst. Many died only hours after their first symptoms had appeared.[2]

Genteel New Yorkers chose to believe that the disease sought out people like the Fitzgeralds—poor, foreign-born, Catholic, and sinful, living "dissolute, alcoholic, drug related, sexually excessive, and filth ridden lives." They believed that cholera was God's punishment, "a scourge not of mankind but of the sinner." It seemed to Americans an irrefutable fact that cholera was most commonly found in those areas of the world, like India, least populated by Christians.[3]

Bottled spring water is not a recent phenomenon, and during the crisis wealthy New Yorkers protected themselves by receiving daily water deliveries from upstate and upper Manhattan natural springs. Still, the wealthy fled in great numbers, uncertain of the cause of the disease. Less than two weeks from the

13.1 Before John Snow discovered in 1854 that cholera was caused by contaminated drinking water, health officials believed could avoid the disease by avoiding drafts of air, raw vegetables, and unripe fruit. The disease caused a pandemic in the 1830s and 1840s.

Source: Notice: preventives of cholera, New York, 1849. U.S. National Library of Medicine, Digital Collections, http://resource.nlm.nih.gov/64730880R.

first cholera outbreak, over 100,000 New Yorkers—roughly half the population of the city—created a mass exodus. As in the yellow fever scares before it in 1795, 1799, 1803, and even as late as 1821, well-to-do New Yorkers moved to the less populated suburbs of Greenwich Village, Bloomingdale, Harlem, or Yorkville, or farther upstate. Philip Hone, the future mayor of New York and a famous diarist, would remain in his country home "until the destroying angel has sheathed his sword and our citizens have returned to their homes."[4]

The wealthy Stebbins family was no exception. They most likely fled to their country place in Ridgefield, Connecticut. During that first national outbreak in 1832, John Wilson Stebbins wrote to his family from New Orleans about the "apprehension for my safety on account of the cholera, that direful pestilence, which is now making its ravages in almost all our Southern and Western cities." Five years later, when New Orleans experienced another wave of the disease, Stebbins succumbed to it.[5]

When Stebbins's sister, the sculptor Emma Stebbins, was awarded the commission for Central Park's central fountain, she chose to memorialize the Croton water system that had eased cholera outbreaks in New York City. Instead of Hone's "destroying angel," Stebbins chose the healing angel who appeared at Jerusalem's natural pools of Bethesda. Unveiled in 1873, Stebbins's *Angel of the Waters* fountain celebrated "the blessed gift of pure, wholesome water, which to all the countless homes of this great city, comes like an angel visitant, not at stated seasons only, but day by day."[6]

In 1854, British physician John Snow discovered the real cause of the disease: polluted drinking water. But even before people knew to blame it, the piles of rotting garbage and the human and animal feces that seeped into the island's wells, underground springs, and rivers had been a source of anxiety for over a century. In 1829, researchers from the Lyceum of Natural History estimated that New Yorkers deposited over ten thousand tons of "excrementitious matter" annually that percolated down to the water table.[7]

The City Council adopted a few ordinances to solve the immediate sanitation crisis, but due to corruption, indifference, or inefficiency, garbage removal was ultimately left to the animals: the thousands of pigs, dogs, and goats who roamed the city's streets. From the eighteenth century, New Yorkers agreed that they desperately needed an abundant source of pure water. Other American cities relied on local rivers or lakes; Boston had Lake Cochituate and

13.2 Emma Stebbins's Bethesda Fountain was inspired by the biblical reference to an angel who blessed the pools of Bethesda in Jerusalem, which bestowed them with healing properties. The artist's brother died as the result of cholera, which influenced her to create a fountain dedicated to the healing properties of New York's Croton water.

Source: Emma Stebbins, *Angel of the Waters* (also known as Bethesda Fountain). Courtesy of the Central Park Conservancy.

Philadelphia had the Schuylkill River. But Manhattan's rivers were too close to the ocean to be potable.

After years of attempts to bring water from the Bronx River to Manhattan, the city finally chose instead the abundant waters of the Croton River in Westchester, forty miles away.[8] Through the force of gravity, the Croton's pristine water would flow southward through man-made dams, open channels, underground pipes, and a massive aqueduct over the Harlem River to a main distributing reservoir, from which it would flow to everywhere in Manhattan. But where to put the reservoir? Manhattan had an abundance of hills to ensure the gravitational flow of water, but not adequate table land. First the planners considered an elevated site between Eighth and Ninth Avenue and near the Bloomingdale Road, but they ultimately chose instead an elevated central site in Murray Hill on Forty-Second Street and Fifth Avenue, the site of today's New York Public Library.

13.3 After over a century of concern about the city's poor water, New York finally celebrated the completion of the Croton Aqueduct in 1842. The Egyptian-style distributing reservoir was constructed in an out-of-town location, Fifth Avenue and Forty-Second Street, the site of today's New York Public Library.

Source: "Croton Water Reservoir, New York City." The Miriam and Ira D. Wallach Division of Art, Prints and Photographs: Print Collection, The New York Public Library, New York Public Library Digital Collections,. https://digitalcollections.nypl.org/items/510d47d9-7cc0-a3d9-e040-e00a18064a99.

Engineer Major David Douglass, who conceived the initial route, felt the system would be best served by an intermediate receiving reservoir to hold the water before its distribution from the main tank at Murray Hill. Although Douglass and his successor, John B. Jervis, felt the storage facility was not absolutely necessary, they were cautious and preferred a safety valve, should anything go wrong, such as leaks in the thirty-eight-mile system. They first chose Harlem Heights from 133rd to 137th Street between Ninth and Tenth Avenues but eventually settled on York Hill, an elevated site encompassing six common lands lots between Sixth Avenue and Seventh Avenue from Seventy-Ninth Street to Eighty-Sixth Street.[9] The wider space would provide sufficient room for the reservoir's thick protective walls, and the city would save a lot of money because it already owned most of the land.

The engineers felt the vast open-air water body would provide several benefits to the system. The water would have a chance to regain its freshness after its thirty-eight-mile voyage in enclosed channels. The impurities collected on the long journey would have a chance to settle out before reaching the distributing reservoir two miles away. And when the future population arrived uptown, the receiving reservoir could serve them as well, though it would be years before pipes were laid above Forty-Second Street, due to the sparse population.

York Hill presented a challenge to the engineers. The hill was higher than necessary, and it stood on solid rock. Blasting would increase already escalating costs, so engineer Jervis came up with a solution that saved $50,000 in excavation costs. He designed two separate basins: the northern section would hold 20 feet of water, while the southern one, with higher walls, would hold 30 feet of water. In all, the reservoir would hold 180 million gallons. The creation of two tanks also controlled the sedimentation, which would be filtered out in the northern basin before the water flowed down to the lower one.[10]

As the work continued and costs escalated, the engineers were constantly pressured by the water commissioners to lower expenses. To cut costs they suggested reducing the two-basin reservoir to one, forecasting that "the 150-million-gallon storage tank could not be needed 'for a century to come, if ever required.'"[11] Ultimately the commissioners realized that the work had already progressed too far to stop, but they did shave off $75,000 by eliminating the blasting of the massive outcrop in the southwest corner of the lower basin.[12] Later park engineer Egbert Viele would name this Vista Rock, and it would become the site of the Belvedere. When the Croton Aqueduct Board turned the

rock over to the Board of Commissioners of Central Park in 1868, they stipulated that they retained the right to take it back if they ever needed it again.
They never have.

Out of the six required lots for the reservoir, the corporation had only sold two
and retained ownership of four, which saved the city great expense.[13] Common
lands lot 170 was originally owned by John Bradhurst and Moses Field, prominent
New Yorkers and partners in their families' drug company, and bequeathed to the
Heirs of Moses Field.[14] Lot 172 was purchased in 1799 by William Mathews, who
was either a merchant-tailor or a mason.[15] When Mathews's twenty-three-year-
old daughter Mary married merchant Tunis Van Brunt in 1815, Mathews transferred his common lands lot to him.[16] Unfortunately, five years after the marriage
Van Brunt became "indebted to sundry persons in divers sums of Money and by
reason of losses and misfortunes in trade" and was forced to convey his personal
estate and real estate to his lawyers to satisfy his debts. Nonetheless, on May 1,
1838, the corporation awarded him $11,000 for his lot.[17] In 1838, the construction
of the York Hill reservoir was set to cost more than half a million dollars, the
largest single Croton contract to date, plus the $22,000 additional expense to the
heirs of Moses Field and Van Brunt.[18]

Five years passed from the time the land was purchased until the reservoir was
finished in 1842. Once completed, it became a popular destination for those who
could get so far uptown. By 1846, schedules of the Third Avenue New York-Har-
lem railroad added frequent daily stops at the "receiving reservoir."[19] To soften
the look of the rigid walls, the designers created a grass-lined walkway around the
rectangular basin, an attraction to provide a pleasant country day trip for city
dwellers. In Nathan Currier's 1842 lithograph, *View of the Great Receiving Reservoir
Yorkville City of New York*, the artist drew a crowd gathered on the walkway and in
the foreground depicted a fashionable carriage, a couple arriving on horseback,
and a man and child on foot approaching the entrance to the promenade. The
foreground, a barren landscape with the exception of a small shrub in the lower
left-hand corner, depicts the west side. By 1842, that land—Seventy-Ninth to
Eighty-Second Street—was the future Seventh Avenue, owned by David Wagstaff.
Today it is the Delacorte Theater and the Winterdale Arch landscape. The shrub
may hint at garden plots within the Seneca Village community that stood just
outside of the picture's foreground, level with the basin. On the east side were
the home and barn of James Dobbin, who owned and leased the common lands
depicted on the reservoir's opposite side, today the site of the lawn and the statue

13.4 Until 1931, the Great Lawn in Central Park was the site of a receiving reservoir, a holding tank for the Croton water. The original site, known as York Hill, caused the water to flow by the force of gravity to the distributing reservoir on Murray Hill.

Source: "View of the great receiving reservoir. Yorkville City of New York." The Miriam and Ira D. Wallach Division of Art, Prints and Photographs: Print Collection, The New York Public Library, New York Public Library Digital Collections, https://digitalcollections.nypl.org/items/5e66b3e8-d471-e040-e00a180654d7.

of Alexander Hamilton, and farther east, the East Drive and the café in the American wing of the Metropolitan Museum of Art.[20]

The construction took five years, and it was no small inconvenience for the landowners nearby. Hundreds of workers and massive equipment created noise, dust, and damage to property and crops. The Amory farm was far from the immediate construction site, but rock blasting for Croton pipes on Fifth Avenue and Sixty-Eighth Street damaged the Amory family home.[21]

But even more threatening to neighbors were the violent labor strikes that shook the entire Croton system for two weeks in April 1840, halfway through construction. The dispute centered around the reduction of wages for thousands of Irish laborers. The depression that had begun with the Panic of 1837 had lingered, and contractors were paid less due to devalued city bonds. The city therefore would not extend the routine increase of one dollar for spring and summer work to its laborers or double the winter pay of six shillings. "The War of the Water Works" began in Westchester on Tuesday, March 31, and by Thursday, five hundred strikers, armed with clubs, beat laborers and destroyed tools and half-finished work from Harlem to York Hill, "making a clean sweep and allowing nobody the liberty to work who desired it." The disturbance continued throughout the week unabated, ignored by police.[22]

By Saturday the contractors—many receiving death threats—pleaded with Mayor Isaac Varian to quell the riot, lest workers lose their lives or the city lose its thirty-eight-mile investment. Reluctantly, Varian mounted his horse and led police and cavalry to put an end to the disorder in Manhattan. Near Yorkville, a mob of Irishmen, some with clubs, gathered momentum marching en masse to the reservoir site and threatening anyone who tried to work. From a nearby hill, impoverished Irish women and children looked on, "without hats and many without shoes."[23] At the receiving reservoir, where "some of the worst ring-leaders were gathered," the tension boiled over into a confrontation. The mob threatened to get five thousand men to oppose the military if attacked, but the police pursued, and two of the leaders were caught and thrown in jail.[24] After the showdown, the mayor invited his officers home for supper and champagne, while New Yorkers—already victims of frequent ethnic riots—worried that this protest was just the start of future unrest. The rioters kept up their protest in Westchester for a few more weeks, but police there finally arrested many of them. The wages would remain at six shillings.

One building in Seneca Village fronting Seventh Avenue may have been constructed due to the magnificent view of the receiving reservoir. After a series of many purchasers before him, wealthy cotton merchant George G. Root acquired ten lots along the avenue for $3,500 at the height of the real estate bubble.[25] Root started his career as a bookkeeper for shippers Dudley & Stuyvesant, and when Dudley died Root became a partner in the lucrative business, making him "one of the fashionable young men of the town."[26] It is a particular paradox that a white man so personally enriched by the cotton trade—a business built on the backs of enslaved laborers—invested in the Black community. Most likely he assumed the current residents would soon be priced out of the market.

But that did not happen. Instead, Root's company lost one million dollars in the Panic of 1837. By 1839, he was unable to pay his mortgage, and the property became the possession of his mortgagors, the Hudson Fire Company.[27] The author of *Old Merchants of New York* commented sardonically on Root's fleeting fame, "He who has negotiated his thousands, now has hard work to negotiate weekly $1.50 to pay for weekly lodgings somewhere on the Bowery. He passes along the streets scarcely known to the present race of wealthy citizens, and forgotten by most of those, who were his admirers and friends when fortune smiled upon him."[28]

In better days and with visions of the reservoir becoming a popular tourist attraction, it was most likely George Root who commissioned the design of a public house for the intended sightseers and promenaders. A real estate ad by architect William Hurry in 1846 boasted of the proximity to the reservoir: "situated on the Westerly side of the Receiving Reservoir between 84th and 85th Streets, Yorkville, consisting of 10 lots of land with house, stables, sheds, icehouse &c. The buildings are nearly new and will make a first-rate stand for a Public House, immediately opposite this attractive place of resort."[29]

All plans must have been canceled when Root declared bankruptcy. The insurance company who gave him the mortgage probably waited until the end of the recession to either commence or complete the building and put it up for sale.[30] After the future resort was finished, architect Edmund Hurry, his family, and his servants moved into the large new dwelling valued at $35,000 until the insurance company found the new buyer: the City of New York.[31] The lots and the structures were purchased to house the new Croton reservoir keeper, John Geary, one of six such Croton employee residences along the forty-mile aqueduct system.[32]

John Geary, an Irishman, came to America when he was only five years old. By 1855, at age sixty-two, he housed his wife, eight children, his cousin Fanny, who was employed as a domestic, and three boarders in the keeper's apartments. His wife, Catherine, was a school principal. The three oldest children were employed. John was a stonecutter; his daughter Eliza was a dressmaker and Mary a teacher. Croton records list Geary as keeper of the Eighth District until his death in May 1857. He was replaced by Ralph Ellis, who served as keeper until the 1870s.

John Wallace, an employee of the Croton Aqueduct Board, worked under Geary, earning between thirty and forty-five dollars per month.[33] Like Geary, Wallace was born in Ireland, and he lived in a home adjacent to Christian Tietjen. Unlike all other residents, Ellis and Wallace and their families were allowed to remain in place while the park was under construction. In May 1859, Wallace petitioned the commissioners that he and his family might take their Seneca Village home, which he had built only four years earlier, with them. He explained that he had been employed for thirteen years by the Croton system, during nine of which he was engaged on the Old Reservoirs at Eighty-Sixth Street. His home, he stated, "although comparably worthless to the authorities of the Park, is to me of considerable importance."[34]

The records of the Croton Aqueduct Board listed a Henry Meyer along with Geary and Wallace, as a vendor who supplied "oil," "oil and sundries," or "oil and cartage" to Geary and Wallace. Meyer, a grocer by profession, is listed as a resident of Seneca Village living with three other Germans: a clerk and two servants in both the 1855 New York Census and the 1856 list of prepark renters. This suggests that Meyer may have rented a home and opened it as a store in Seneca Village after 1850, when the Croton Aqueduct Board took over George Root's former property.[35]

Remnants of the receiving reservoir still exist in and around the park. Along the back wall of the Central Park Precinct on the Eighty-Sixth Street Transverse Road, a section of the massive schist walls can be seen. And throughout the park, especially within the former Seneca Village, are beautiful manhole covers that memorialize the path of the Croton Water.

13.5 The Croton Aqueduct Board decided not to blast the huge rock outcrop, later called Vista Rock, at the southwest corner of the receiving reservoir, in order to save $75,000. Today it serves as a commanding perch for the Belvedere, an Italian word for structures that have a "beautiful view."

Source: Sara Cedar Miller, *The Belvedere.*, Courtesy of the Central Park Conservancy.

13.6 Evidence of the Croton Water system is still found in Central Park. This manhole cover is one of several and can be found on the path of the former Seneca Village site, the settlement adjacent to the receiving reservoir.

Source: Diego Quintanar, *Croton Manhole Cover*. Courtesy of the photographer.

William Hurry's 1846 ad mentioned an ice house on the Eighty-Fourth Street lot. In the eighteenth century, ice was a luxury that only well-to-do people could afford. But proximity to the receiving reservoir provided an inexpensive source of ice to average New Yorkers, provided they had help to carry the heavy blocks and use of a wagon substantial enough to haul them away. In an ad entitled "Croton Ice," the public is informed that "Persons wishing Croton Ice can be supplied at the Receiving Reservoir. Arrangements will be made at convenient places on 86th Street so enable persons taking the ice to remove it from the water and to deliver it to their carts with facility; 25 cents per load will be charged for the ice in the water."[36]

In 1842 the Board of Aldermen prohibited New Yorkers from using unleased common lands "for ice ponds." Always paying attention to the bottom line, they probably wanted to profit from the new Croton ice rather than allow New

13.7 A view of the receiving reservoir from the tower overlooking Vista Rock, ca. 1865. Due to the city's growing population and the overuse of the Croton water, the system proved to be inadequate only eight years after construction was completed. Another reservoir was needed.

Source: Stereograph. Courtesy of the Central Park Conservancy.

Yorkers to remove it from the streams and ponds of the common lands as they had done illegally in the past.[37] The recent invention of the ice cutter—a horse-drawn device whose iron bars cut deep grooves into frozen lakes to free large blocks of ice—and the creation of the reservoir brought safe ice to those citizens and businesses able to collect the heavy blocks of ice.[38]

When the High Bridge aqueduct over the East River was completed in 1848, it increased the water pressure and enhanced the system, allowing for the greatest amount of water possible to come into Manhattan. New Yorkers, previously reluctant to pay for expensive plumbing, began to sign up in droves. Streets were cleaner, people were cleaner, public baths were created, fountains beautified the city parks, new manufacturing charged ahead, and pipes no longer froze, because homeowners kept the water running continuously all winter.

Whereas engineers had built a system that estimated allotted a "liberal" daily consumption of twenty-two gallons per person, by 1850 "lavish" use rose to ninety gallons per person.[39] That same year, water levels reached dangerous lows when New York experienced a serious drought. The city imposed stiff fines, and use was restricted in the same way that regulations are enforced today. In the summer of 1852, the lack of rain tested the means of supply more thoroughly than at any other time since the pipes were laid.[40] Though the Croton system was projected to be serviceable for decades, its creators did not foresee the population rise due to the influx of immigrants that stressed their new water system, only eight years after it was built.[41] New York needed another reservoir.

chapter 14
A Changing Land, 1845–1853

Before Central Park was created as an alternative to New York's cramped living conditions and crowded streets, the prepark had already become a refuge for many who were—to paraphrase poet Emma Lazarus—tired, poor, and yearning to breathe free. Before the mid-1840s, prepark settlement was sparse, with the exception of the few Harlem families, Seneca Village, and the east side farms of Wagstaff and Amory. But all that changed overnight when a flood of Irish and German immigrants exploded the population. With downtown bursting at its seams, these newcomers looked north, and in the decade before it would become Central Park, the land was transformed by new inhabitants and new uses.

IMMIGRATION

The arrival of its immigrant population changed the face of America. From the mid-1840s through the early 1850s, New York City's population changed from predominantly native-born residents to a European-born majority.[1] New York became the most populated Irish city in the world, larger than Dublin or Belfast. And only Berlin and Vienna could count more Germans than New York City.[2]

The economy was just recovering from the Panic of 1837 that precipitated a decade of unemployment, declining real estate values, and the devaluation of the dollar. American-born workers believed that these foreigners competed with them for jobs and housing, deflating their wages and inflating prices. As a consequence, nativism swept across the city. The 1842 summer election was a landslide victory for the new anti-immigrant American Republican Party. James Harper

14.1 The inhospitable low-lying swampland that became the lower park was once the site of Irish and German piggeries and shanties.

Source: Sara Cedar Miller, *Aerial Pond and Hallett Nature Sanctuary.* Courtesy of the Central Park Conservancy.

(founder of Harper & Row publishers) became the mayor, and he pledged to extend the naturalization period from five years to twenty-one years, a way to prevent the foreign-born from gaining citizenship, and attempt to hire only the native-born as public officials. Although Harper and his party lasted only a year in office, nativist sentiments crept into every part of New York life.[3]

By the mid-1850s, nativism had coalesced into secret societies for the American-born and even organized into the nationwide American Party, more commonly known as the Know-Nothings. The Know-Nothings were virulently anti-immigration and anti-Catholic. Although most members came from the working classes, the upper classes became members too, including artist and telegraph inventor Samuel F.B. Morse, whose statue stands at the entrance to Central Park at East Seventy-Second Street.[4]

The most fortunate immigrants arrived with money, skills, and education, or had family members who had already established themselves in the city. The poorest had nothing more than the clothes on their backs. Most were forced to live in overcrowded fire traps and rat-infested cellars. Others reluctantly chose the few municipal almshouses, and the very poorest slept in alleys and ate garbage they scrounged off the filthy streets. None of them was immune to the roving gangs of criminals and robbers.

But disease was the greatest enemy of the immigrant. During the years of greatest migration, typhus, typhoid, dysentery, diarrhea, and cholera killed more immigrants proportionally and caused the highest incidence of infant mortality. Almost two-thirds of the city's deaths in 1857 were of children under the age of five. Census Marshal William H. Aldis attributed the deaths of so many German children to "having no visible means of support except picking rags and gathering cinders" and "habits not at all calculated to promote health or to ward off disease."[5]

The vast majority of Irish immigrants came from rural areas, and they were adrift in the urban job market. Historian Robert Scally suggests that the mass exodus of Irish farmers to a wage-earning urban lifestyle "was a transformation which occurred to no other agrarian population with such speed and thoroughness, even in the revolutionary societies where it was the determined aim of totalitarian regimes."[6] With no marketable skills, appalling living conditions, and realistic fears, many Irish and German immigrants, particularly those from rural backgrounds, escaped to the fringes of the city to tend market gardens or raise pigs. To a large degree, their intended livelihood and economic situation determined where in the prepark they would settle.

THE IRISH

The first wave of Irish immigrants came in the eighteenth century. Middle-class and upper-class Irish Protestants and Catholics came to colonial America to take advantage of potential business opportunities. The working class often came as indentured servants, who exchanged up to five years of unsalaried work for a free passage across the Atlantic. Many Irish soldiers who had fought in the French and Indian War in the 1750s stayed to start a new life on American soil. Because sanctions imposed on Catholics prevented many of them from belonging to the culture at large, many married or baptized their children into a Protestant tradition.[7]

After the American and French Revolutions, the Irish were inspired to win liberty from their British oppressors. Their 1798 Rebellion became a five-month-long bloody insurrection, aided in part by French troops. But unlike the

Americans, the Irish were soundly defeated by the British army. It is estimated as many as thirty thousand Irish died. Many of the surviving rebels fled to America, including one named Gregory Dillon, who would go on to establish charities to help his people.

The second wave of Irish immigrants came in the 1830s, when Ireland suffered an agricultural crisis. Around 200,000 unskilled Irish immigrants came to New York in the 1820s and 1830s. Without skills ready-made for the urban economy, they were often put to backbreaking labor: digging the Erie Canal, clearing the land for the nation's first railroad tracks, and constructing New York's Croton Aqueduct system. They also laid the city's grid, and when their work was completed, it had ironically created new neighborhoods they were much too poor to afford to live in.[8]

And then, in 1845, a catastrophe struck the tenant farmers of Ireland.

The Famine

It is said that Sir Walter Raleigh first brought potatoes from the Americas to Ireland around 1589. The plants flourished in the moderate soil, and half an acre would yield a bountiful crop that could feed a family of six and their animals for a year. Potatoes are rich in life-sustaining proteins, carbohydrates, minerals, and vitamins. Potatoes and butter together have the necessary vitamins and minerals to sustain life.[9] With an occasional accompaniment of buttermilk, cabbage, and a seasoning of herring, three million Irish peasants ate approximately five pounds of potatoes per person per day. Irish farmers also grew other crops, but those were shipped off to England for the dinner tables of their wealthy British landlords, while day after day and year after year they survived on *práta*, the Irish word for potatoes.[10]

In a twist of fate, it was potatoes, a plant native to American soil, that ultimately brought the greatest wave of Irish immigration. Unbeknownst to potato growers, a fungus (*phytophthora infestans*) from the Peruvian fertilizer *guano* had attached itself to American seed potatoes that were shipped to Ireland for the 1845 harvest. Aboveground, the plant appeared to be healthy, but below the soil, the tubers grew black, slimy, and inedible. Overnight, 30 to 40 percent of the first year's crop was destroyed. For the following five years, successive catastrophic potato crop failures caused the starvation deaths of about 1.1 million Irish. About

1.5 million fled, emigrating to America, and most of those landed in the port of New York.[11]

The British and American ships that carried the Irish across the ocean were as traumatic as the starvation conditions the passengers had fled. Food and water were scarce. Three people were packed into one six-foot-berth that the victims likened to "coffins." Malnourishment and fatal illnesses like typhus and cholera, contracted in transit, killed about fifty thousand Irish during the exodus.

The Irish in the Park

In Ireland, extremely impoverished families lived in above-ground or semi-underground thatch-roofed clay dwellings, called *bothán scóir*, that have been likened by one historian to "smoking dung heaps."[12] At least one such abode near the "upper reservoir" was derogatorily described as "Jake's End": "It was mostly underground, being entered by a descent of several steps from a door which faced [east] . . . to the best of my recollections the den was windowless and all the light came through the door, which I certainly never saw closed. The cabin had a mud floor, with a small platform of broken plank on one side. There was an open fireplace with one iron fire-dog."[13] Particularly for the very destitute, the prepark had tracts of dry land that could provide squatters with this rudimentary shelter, similar to how the poorest of the early Dutch settlers lived on the Broad Way.[14]

Irish immigrants built crude shacks or a better grade of shanties wherever they found rock or dry land, and gradually the poor soil was transformed into small kitchen gardens and piggeries that put food on the table and provided an income. Many immigrants were talented at farming or animal husbandry in the Old World, and they brought those skills to the prepark. In 1856, a *New York Herald* reporter wrote that the gardens adjoining these shanties "furnish our markets with a portion of their supply of vegetables."[15] A natural spring near East Sixty-Third Street and Fifth Avenue might have provided fresh water to the residents.[16]

The streets of New York had been overrun with pigs since Dutch times. Any attempt to round up the pigs caused rioting in the streets by the poor people who owned them or captured them for food. By the deadly cholera epidemic of 1849, the filth of the pigsties was thought to be responsible for the return of the disease, and the piggeries and their owners were finally pushed uptown and into the previously uninhabited swampland of the lower park.[17]

14.2 This 1857 photograph shows a frame house, outhouse, kitchen garden, and surrounding orchard that was a typical home of many immigrants. This structure was located in what is today the west side of the Lake.

Source: Unknown photographer, *View from Point E*, (detail), New York City Municipal Archives.

A walk through the park below Sixty-Fifth Street still features that rippling landscape of massive high rock outcrops interspersed with low glades lying far below the grade of the surrounding streets. DeVoor's mill stream once ran through this land before it was transformed into today's Pond. The lowlands would have required costly filling and blasting before it could be developed into city streets. So, until Central Park was created, the bogs and fens attracted those who found them ideal for pigs and pigsties.

Poor families frequently raised hogs. They were cheap to care for because they ate table scraps or the gristle and flesh that clung to rotting slaughterhouse carcasses. They turned garbage into meat.[18] Pig farmers fed their hogs boiled offal and animal carcasses and sold the cleaned bones to the local bone-boiling factories. Though the profit was smaller for offal-fed hogs, these farmers could still make a living from butchers, who paid well for pork, an important staple of the nineteenth-century American dinner plate, including their own.[19]

These piggeries enriched the soil, which aided the future park. Frederick Law Olmsted, a farmer and the park's future superintendent, praised the by-product of the market gardens and piggeries at the southern end of the prepark: "Much of the land in the lower part of the park has been occupied by market gardeners and dealers in offal, and has in consequence been already enriched to some extent. In many places the surface is even now covered with a rich deposit of organic matter, as yet but partially incorporated with the soil."[20] Olmsted would have understood why this terrain of bogs, swamps, and mud was well suited to raising pigs. Of all domesticated mammals, pigs alone have no sweat glands, so they thrive in sheltered places away from the blistering sun. To keep cool, prevent sunburn, and rid themselves of nagging insects, hogs, like hippopotami, find protection by wallowing in mud. And mud was in plentiful supply in the low-lying areas of the park.[21]

For centuries, the challenging terrain below Sixty-Fifth Street had been described as "waste," a term applied to poor and uncultivated land. But by the 1850s, genteel New Yorkers conflated the condition of the terrain with a physical reaction to the uncultivated lifestyle of the poor. Most were repulsed by the noxious by-products of the lower park piggeries. The sight and smell of stewing offal in combination with the muddy ooze offended them. The reaction to smells is "culturally constructed" and subjective. The odor of horse manure was pervasive, unavoidable, and, by necessity, tolerated. Manure covered every neighborhood, both rich and poor, yet pigs and sties were the property of the lower classes and therefore deemed revolting to bourgeois New Yorkers.[22] Olmsted, on his first day as superintendent, wrote that "the stench was sickening." He understood that his job depended on removing offensive odors, but as a farmer, he would have appreciated both the practical realities and economic necessities of the piggeries and agreed with the sentiments of a present-day Iowa pig farmer, who said, "It smells like money to me."[23]

There were fifteen piggeries across the land that would become Central Park. The largest concentration of them were around Sixty-Fourth Street from Sixth Avenue to Seventh Avenue. Most of those lay along the landscape depression of Sixty-Fifth Street, which is a transverse road today. The topographic low point guaranteed the collection of rainwater, which was necessary for the pigs' external cooling system.

No records exist to indicate when the community may have formed or whether there was any sort of verbal or written agreement with the owner or leaseholder. Peter Amory, the son of James Amory, lived in the family homestead only a stone's throw from the Irish compound, and also had a pigsty.

Pig manure makes a fine fertilizer for plants, but it contains pathogens that make it hazardous as an amendment to vegetable gardens unless it is first composted. The runoff from storms contaminated nearby groundwater and may have contributed to a higher rate of illness in the area.[24] Although his view was undoubtedly biased, one contemporary noted that the lower park inhabitants looked emaciated, likely because of "the malarial state of the atmosphere which they breathed." This was confirmed by William H. Aldis, the marshall for the district of the prepark that encompassed the area west of Sixth Avenue and south of Eighty-Sixth Street, who reported many deaths of German children, who lived "in a 'Swamp' which is continually wet and subject to 'Fever and Ague.' "[25]

By 1853, the unsanitary environmental conditions threatened the already compromised terrain, and some downtown landlords began to refuse to rent for a piggery. One landowner, Walter Brady, rented a "farm let" to a twenty-five-year-old German tailor named Frederick Metzger and his wife, Regina. The let was a fourteen-year lease for a lot just south of today's Heckscher Playground. Based on the agreement, Brady made sure that his tenants would not use *his* land for a piggery, and he imposed strict guidelines in his lease prohibiting any work or business that would violate city ordinances or be considered a "nuisance" to the neighborhood. Brady also required his tenants to "dig and stone up a privy vault" four feet deep and four feet in diameter. If that was impossible due to rock, he required them to place "portable boxes or tubs," to be cleaned "at least once a year."[26]

When workers cut the deep swath for the Sixty-Fifth Street Transverse Road, they obliterated evidence of many of the former piggeries, which today include portions of the Sheep Meadow, Heckscher Ballfield, the Carousel landscape, and the Dairy landscape.

While the recent immigrant gardeners and pig farmers were settling in to the lower sections of the prepark, another community of first-, second-, and third-generation Irish Americans was establishing itself in Harlem. Though they were only a mere two miles distant, their living conditions were worlds apart.

The Sisters of Charity of Mount St. Vincent

The composting area of the park, just off the East Drive at 104th Street, is commonly referred to as "the Mount," a lasting reminder that it was once the home to two hundred Catholic schoolgirls and the order of the Sisters of Charity of Mount St. Vincent. Their stay in the park, from 1847 to 1859, was one solution to an educational dilemma for New York's Catholic children.[27]

In the already hot climate of anti-Irish feelings, nothing made nativist blood boil more than the subject of public funding for the education of Catholic children. Bishop John Hughes—the powerful Catholic leader known as "Dagger John"—understood that his people were not going to succeed in America without a proper education. To Hughes, Catholic doctrine was central to any curriculum, but Protestant New York abhorred the idea of funding schools that taught the "Romanist" catechism.[28]

In New York from 1812 to 1824, tuition-free charity schools for poor white children had been run by religious organizations that were, in part, funded by the common school fund. But in 1834, the state law providing for those schools was repealed, and the new Public School Society refused to funnel public funds to religious educational institutions.[29] All students were required to read from the Protestant King James Bible, which was anathema to Hughes and the faith. Hughes attacked a system in which no Catholic could send his child to the public schools "without wounding his own conscience, and sinning against God; and this he is not allowed to do for the whole world."[30]

He fought to fund religious schools, but in 1842, the state legislature passed a new law that banned all religious instruction in public schools and provided no funding for any school that taught a faith-based curriculum. On the night of the bill's passage, rabid nativists who blamed Hughes for being the instigator who destroyed their Protestant school system took to the streets and threw stones at his house.[31]

So, Hughes went to work. He spent years building a strong Catholic educational system in New York. First- or second-generation Catholics, mainly Irish, chose to send their children to schools connected with Catholic parishes, and the Sisters of Charity often operated the schools and taught the classes. Founded in Emmitsburg, Maryland, in 1809 by prominent former New Yorker Elizabeth Bayley Seton, the Sisters of Charity had been caring for orphan children and teaching in free schools and pay schools in New York since 1817. In 1846, a group of them formed an independent community under the leadership of Mother Superior Elizabeth Boyle. The first assistant mother was Hughes's sister Ellen, known as Sister Mary Angela.

The sisters sought to establish a Motherhouse large enough to accommodate a novitiate and a girls' boarding academy, which they believed would ensure the self-sufficiency of the order. First they opened a temporary novitiate at St. Joseph's School for Young Ladies, around East Broadway and Catherine Street, until they found a suitable and affordable location. It became the first institution to offer higher learning for women in New York.

As it happened, Harlem resident Tighe Davy—"an elderly gentleman of sterling piety," a long-standing political ally of Bishop Hughes, a park landowner, and a trustee of the Sisters of Charity—knew of a "handsome" property along the Kingsbridge Road. It was the old McGowan homestead, which had not been lived in for more than a decade.[32] In April 1847, Mother Boyle and her entourage embarked on a six-mile journey from St. Patrick's Convent on Prince Street to the McGowan property. They found the old house dilapidated and surrounded by pools of rainwater, and Sister Williamanna and one of the priests thought it so hopeless that they refused to leave the carriage. Inside, the scouting party found the front hall of the four-room building flooded, and the whole place presented "a most uninviting appearance."[33] Nonetheless, the purchase price was agreeable, the mortgage money was garnered, and by the end of the month the sisters had moved in.[34]

A wooden altar was the centerpiece of the chapel, a room that had once been the McGowans' parlor. As members of the Dutch Reformed Church, the McGowans would have been shocked to find their former home a center of Catholic devotion. There is no mention whether the sisters knew that their convent and school had been a former tavern.[35]

Sister Williamanna, who had refused to leave the carriage when she saw the shambles of the old tavern, recorded small details of daily religious life in her diary. It's a window into the life of a young novitiate, full of hard work and scarce resources. The one bed in the convent was reserved for Mother Boyle, who loaned it to any sister who took sick. They did the ironing outdoors on a board supported by two barrels. The stove was so small that dinner had to be cooked in shifts for the roughly seventy resident sisters and students. The sisters worked in the wash house and the bakehouse. Although the lower reservoir was only one mile away, the young women had to lug their water from a spring farther away, likely the former Montagne's Rivulet. In 1851, thanks to the connections of a generous church member, the Board of Aldermen passed a resolution to lay a pipe up Fifth Avenue to the sisters' compound, the first and only source of Croton water serving residents of the prepark.[36]

Today, the path north from the Mount still makes that precipitous sharp turn to McGowan's Pass, which likely caused the death of Jacob Dyckman a century earlier. Accidents were common. During their time at the convent, the dangerous incline once overturned a carriage full of sisters and injured Mother Boyle.[37]

The sisters had new wings added to the small house to accommodate the first forty students, all people "of good leaven" whose parents could afford private school, room, and board. The curriculum emphasized Catholic education and academic subjects. It was meant to turn the girls into "ornaments to society" by teaching the "sincere virtues" of true Victorian womanhood: piety, domesticity, charity, respect, obedience, and politeness. They were to become the mothers of "outstanding professional men, of scholars, educators, and clergy." One day, it was hoped they would make New York "the center of Catholicity."[38]

The curriculum emphasized skill in music, an important aspect of a young lady's development. The school put on performances for visiting parents and church dignitaries, and it was the students of the Mount St. Vincent Academy who held the park's first recorded concert on November 27, 1847, with such vocal and instrumental songs as "Rizzio's Lament" and operatic arias from *Lucia da Lammermoor* and *Hernani*.[39] Aside from the boarding students, the sisters also taught fifty or sixty local children at a day school on the site of today's Conservatory Garden, where the sisters and students also tended a garden.[40]

In 1856 the sisters had raised the money to build a beautiful new chapel, which they believed would be "the gem of the island." They erected it on the brow of the hill overlooking Yorkville and the East River. The steeple was topped by a bright golden cross that glittered above the academy, and the church could be seen for miles.[41]

14.3 The grounds of the former religious community of Mount St. Vincent became Central Park's first formal garden.

A few months before the chapel was consecrated, the sisters were informed by the city that their campus would be taken for the building of Central Park.[42] They moved to the former estate of actor Edwin Forrest on the border of Yonkers and the Bronx, where the College of Mount Saint Vincent is today. A few years later, the chapel became a hospital for Civil War soldiers attended by the sisters; later it became New York City's first uptown art museum within Central Park.[43] The chapel was demolished around 1915, but a remnant of its foundation still exists behind the composting operation.

Like nearly everywhere else in New York, the Mount St. Vincent community was separated by class. In 1855, seventy sisters ranging from nineteen to sixty lived there. All but four of them were born in New York. One of them, Sarah Stearns,

14.4 The elaborate interior of the Mount Saint Vincent chapel became Manhattan's first uptown art gallery and museum until it burned down in 1881.

Source: "Mt. St. Vincent statuary chapel." The Miriam and Ira D. Wallach Division of Art, Prints and Photographs: Photography Collection, The New York Public Library, New York Public Library Digital Collections, https://digitalcollections.nypl.org/items/510d47e1-f2a0-a3d9-e040-e00a18064a99.

was born in Massachusetts and was a member of the famous Brook Farm utopian community before she converted to Catholicism. Like their students, the women and girls came mostly from Irish families that had assimilated before the post-famine Great Migration. The convent employed nine men, almost all of whom were famine victims, born in Ireland, who had come to New York around 1850. They also employed eleven women servants, all first-generation Irish, although most had come to New York a few years earlier than the male employees. Life might have been difficult for these twenty servants, but unlike their countrymen at the other end of the prepark, they were fortunate to earn a regular salary from a trusted employer, and they had a clean room, nourishing meals, and purposeful work within a safe and loving community.

Irish Philanthropy

While the Catholic church provided alms and assistance to the needy, it was the elite Irish New York community that created private philanthropies to help their less fortunate countrymen adapt to America.

In 1817, many of the members of the former charitable organization, the Society of The Friendly Sons of St. Patrick, for the Relief of Emigrants from Ireland, established in 1771, formed the New York Irish Emigrant Association. Its members included prepark landowners William Edgar, John R. Skiddy, James McBride, and Daniel McCormick, a neighbor of Valentine Nutter.[44] Anti-Catholicism was mounting in New York, and the group saw it firsthand. They petitioned Congress to set apart a portion of unsold lands in the Illinois territory "for the purpose of being settled by emigrants from Ireland on an extended of term of credit." The concept had originated a year earlier with the founding of the American Colonization Society, a national organization that promoted manumitting enslaved people and sending them and other free Blacks back to Africa to found the colony of Liberia. When the Illinois plan did not pass the legislature, the New York Irish Emigrant Association disbanded.[45]

By 1841, leaders of the Irish community saw the need for a new charitable organization to offer social, medical, and financial assistance to the next wave of poor and unwelcome Irish immigrants. They founded the Irish Emigrant Aid Society and installed Gregory Dillon as its president. His organization was instrumental in providing the newly arrived with assistance in obtaining housing, jobs, and health services.

Irish Americans developed a system of "chain migration." One family member would arrive in America, find gainful work, and save enough money to bring over the next member. Dillon and his close associates realized that these immigrants needed a reliable bank to secure and protect their money as they saved it. In 1850, they incorporated the Emigrant Industrial Savings Bank.[46] By 1856, only six years after its incorporation, the bank held more than five thousand accounts totaling more than $1.3 million. After 1858, it was thousands of Irish immigrants who labored to build Central Park, and their paychecks would have been safely deposited in the Emigrant Savings Bank.[47]

Gregory Dillon and his equally eminent son, Robert J. Dillon—a trustee of both the bank and the Irish Emigrant Society—would have welcomed the opportunity to create a large municipal park to employ thousands of skilled and unskilled Irish immigrants. Robert J. Dillon, the grandson of common lands owner Benjamin Romaine, would later serve as corporation counsel of the City of New York from 1853 to 1856, and in this capacity he became the force behind the movement to legalize Central Park.[48]

THE GERMANS

Potatoes and politics brought over 50,000 Germans to America in 1848.[49] The failure of the crops in Ireland spilled over onto the continental farms as the fungus spread, and many Germans were starving. They also faced the consequences of a failed political revolution. In 1848, a wave of political disturbances spread across Europe, called the "Spring of Nations." In Germany, liberals rose up to replace the monarchies of several German states with republican governments. But they failed due to a split between the middle class and the working class, and by May 1848, dissenters from both classes were being rounded up by reactionary authorities. Inspired by the American Revolution, thousands of radicals left for America. Known as Forty-Eighters, these freethinkers railed against organized religion and slavery, and became outspoken critics of government.[50]

Several of the German gardeners who lived in the prepark arrived in New York after the rebellion. These young immigrants may have held similar political views to Professor Jupiter Zeus Hesser, an older park resident; he might have been a magnet to younger like-minded Germans with enough savings to build a home and form a farming community.

14.5 By the 1850s, the East Meadow, once the property of the Benson family, had become a community of about fifty German immigrants who resided on and farmed the land until it was taken for Central Park.

Source: Sara Cedar Miller, *East Meadow.* Courtesy of the Central Park Conservancy.

Jupiter Zeus Hesser, born Victor Hesser in 1799, was arguably the most colorful and eccentric of all the known park residents. He was a poet, published composer, music teacher, political activist, revolutionary thinker, and small-time real estate tycoon. He supported himself as a music professor around Sixth Avenue and Tenth Street, but characteristically chose an alternative lifestyle in the boondocks, away from the downtown scene. By 1852, he had leased or purchased property in today's North Meadow and some adjacent land west of Eighth Avenue.

Hesser had been in America since 1833. We can see the roots of his radical past in letters he wrote to President Abraham Lincoln in the 1860s. In one from March 19, 1861, Hesser referred to himself as "the lamb" of the biblical Revelations, who was forced out of his position by the government for his political stance. He ended his four-page tirade with a feverish commitment "to overthrow all unjust governments with their tyrants, to kill every Slaveholder, to break up all religious sects, and build up a new spiritual Jerusalem, a new Paradise where no Slavery, no marriage"—Hesser had just gone through a messy divorce from his wife, Licete—"no maliciousness, no Robbers, Thieves, Traitors, nor any falsehood will reign but God and his lamb all alone."[51]

Many immigrants after 1848 leased land inside what today is the East Meadow, from Ninety-Eighth Street to 101st Street between Fifth Avenue and Sixth Avenue. The land had originally been covered by a swamp in a chestnut grove, "a sort of meadow," but earlier tenants of the Benson family transformed the scruffy terrain into a more arable landscape before the arrival of the Germans.[52]

The largest area of cultivation in 1855 lay above Eighty-Seventh Street, on the northern edge of the present Reservoir. Much of it was owned by two of the largest real estate speculators, Courtlandt Palmer and Mary G. Pinkney. They both rented out their land to bide their time until selling would reap the highest possible return. To offset any mortgage interest, taxes, and incidental expenses, they gave short five-year leases to a group of German farmers. In addition, the presence of tenants prevented the habitual dumping of garbage and stable manure on unattended land.[53]

In 1851, Palmer rented a parcel to Henry Eilerman, a German farmer who paid an annual rent of $175 for his eight-acre garden, a two-story frame house, a stable, and sheds along the Kingsbridge Road. He lived there with his wife, their three children, and three immigrant boarders, all of whom had come to America the previous year. On the same day that Palmer leased the land to Eilerman, he also rented eighty lots to German farmer Andrew Bouck.[54]

Although Palmer did not stipulate that his tenants farm the land, Mary G. Pinkney required hers "to bring all lots under cultivation and so maintain them for garden purposes." The largest concentration of Germans rented Pinkney's land around Ninety-Ninth Street, which was flat and free of rocks. A few of PInkney's lessees had businesses—George Gramp was a "net manufacturer," and Gottlieb Gent a "manufacturer of mineral water"—but cultivation of the land was a condition of every lease. [55]

The majority of Pinkney's renters, approximately fifty German immigrants, counting wives, children, in-laws, and boarders, referred to themselves in the 1855 New York State Census as gardeners.[56] Harlem was served by a public market at 120th Street, offering prepark farmers a nearby venue in which to sell their highly perishable products or animals, easily accessible via the Kingsbridge and Harlem Roads.[57]

These families had saved enough money to lease a small plot of land and build a home and garden as the first step to prosperity. After a few productive years, the tenants might afford property upstate or out West. Others viewed farming as

14.6 German immigrant, music professor, and composer Jupiter Zeus K.M. Hesser owned
and leased farmland that he called "Jupiterville," located on today's East Meadow and
North Meadow.

Source: "The Musical Compositions of Jupiter Z. K. M. Hesser." Music Division, The New York Public
Library, New York Public Library Digital Collections, https://digitalcollections.nypl.org/items/510d47df
-9608-a3d9-e040-e00a18064a99.

a stopgap while they learned other skills. The rent was manageable, garden crops
provided income, and, like other ethnic groups who settled in the outer wards,
they could enjoy a peaceful life with their countrymen, miles from the bigotry,
disease, and crime of urban life.[58]

The German community built their homes and farm buildings quickly. In
1851, before the establishment of the settlement, there were only twelve buildings

in the stretch between Ninety-Sixth and 101st Street. Four year later, the Viele map shows thirteen more buildings.[59] Many gardeners could only afford to erect a shanty and a few sheds, while those with other occupations built substantial frame houses.[60]

Hesser called his uptown empire his "beloved Jupiterville." He built a large two-story house and barn with chicken coops and a goat stable. He cultivated twelve lots in all, seven of which he leased in 1853 from Pinkney and sublet. In the fall of 1855, Hesser told the Commissioners of Estimate and Assessment that his ground was "readied and manured for the Central Park."[61] The North Meadow, two connected plateaus of turf amounting to about eighteen acres, had been the former homestead to the German gardeners and was the first upper park landscape to be constructed.[62]

Hesser, more financially secure than many of his neighbors and a champion for the underdog, pleaded with the commissioners to consider that "A very great *number of poor families* who worked . . . a number of years on their squatter or lease ground, will be entirely ruined, when they must give up their cultivated land and move away without compensation," reminding them to "Please have mercy with the poor, then will the Lord have Mercy with you."[63] Scarcely a year earlier, urban gardeners had suffered an economic disaster. According to the 1855 census taker James Baldwin in the Twelfth Ward, "the Market Gardens are cultivated by Germans, and the products of last year was barely sufficient to pay expenses and support their families, drouth and disease being the principal cause of the failure."[64] Census taker A. C. Judson in the Twelfth Ward noted that "Germans cultivate small patches for gardens and make out to win enough to live upon, in their way, but nothing more."[65]

In June 1856, when renters were still allowed to live in the future prepark, a reporter for the *New York Herald* toured the lands, "through places where wheeled vehicles never dared venture." The touring party came across one of the "little plantations" of the German gardener who tended it. The reporter complimented his garden, but the gardener grew angry that his land would be taken away and pleaded with the reporter, whom he probably mistook for a city authority, not to do so.[66]

But to no avail. The German gardeners were eventually all driven out. Fredrick Reulein was the last immigrant to farm the land before it became a park. He leased land between Fifth and Sixth Avenue from 109th to 110th Street, within the site of the future extension of Central Park when it grew by four blocks north of 106th Street. In 1863, he petitioned the Commissioners of Estimate and

Assessment to increase his award. He claimed that the improvements he made to the property—a large greenhouse, a kitchen addition, and a substantial addition to the stable—warranted more compensation. The property also had a root house and a henhouse. All of these enhancements indicate that he had planned to live there and farm the land for many years. He had probably taken over the former property along the Post Road that had originally belonged to Valentine Nutter. In his petition, he estimated that he had $600 worth of vegetables growing in his plots.[67] As compensation, he was only awarded $150 for the buildings he created, although he was most likely allowed to harvest his produce.

The German Sugar Refiners

Not all Germans became gardeners. In the nineteenth century, New York City was the sugar refining capital of the world, and Germans were integral to the industry starting in the late eighteenth century.

Slavery was the backbone of the sugar industry, transporting millions of Africans to the sugar plantations of the Caribbean—Cuba, Barbados, and Jamaica— as well as Mexico, Guyana, and Brazil. New York became the chief refining center, as it was less dangerous and less costly to send the sugarcane to America than across the Atlantic to be processed in Europe. In the early eighteenth century many of the elite New York families—the Bayards, Van Cortlandts, Rhinelanders, and Roosevelts—owned the city's sugar refineries. The German immigrants brought unique refining skills to the city from England, where the first refining process had been patented in 1815.[68] By the 1840s publications on sugar manufacturing in America were available in the German language.

The raw canes were crushed into a viscous "dirty slurry" and shipped to New York, where the refineries converted the reddish-brown liquid into the pure "white gold" that was favored on the tables of refined diners around the world.[69]

The most offensive part of the refining process took place in bone-boiling works scattered along the fringes of the city. These establishments first removed fat, guts, and gristle from animal carcasses by boiling them in large cauldrons, which invariably smelled like rotting flesh. The cleaned bones were then burned in a furnace to create bone char, also called bone black. When the slurry was filtered through the crushed bone char, it produced a clear liquid that dried into perfect sugar crystals and could be formed into cubes, cakes, cones, or powder.

Not only was the bone-boiling process itself considered noxious, but the raw materials—dead cows, horses, and sheep—often sat outside in piles, which made bone boilers the city's most reviled industry.[70]

New Yorkers considered such industries a danger to public health, an affront to the genteel middle-class and upper-class life, and the biggest obstruction to lucrative real estate development. In 1849, just two years before bone boiling was banished from lower Manhattan, Francis Skiddy, landowner and wealthy sugar broker, exporter, and shipper, leased a few of his prepark lots at Eighth Avenue and Seventy-Fifth Street to German immigrant George H. Moller for a factory.

14.7 In an 1859 drawing of the Dene and Mall landscapes under construction, artist George Heyward depicted the furnace chimney from the bone-boiling factory, on the site of the Tavern on the Green Restaurant (see figure 14.8), formerly the Sheepfold, built in 1870.

Source: George Heyward, "View in Central Park, Promenade, June 1858 (detail)," in *Valentine's Manual, for 1859*. Stephen Manheimer Collection.

14.8 Tavern on the Green Restaurant, formerly the site of the bone-boiling works.

Source: Sara Cedar Miller, *Tavern on the Green*. Courtesy of the Central Park Conservancy.

Moller was a grocer, while others in the Moller family owned two sugar refining factories on Front and Vandam Streets.[71] The downtown ban must have been
the impetus for Moller to enter the family business and lease uptown land before
his family's factories were shut. The following year, he leased more land from
Jacob Harsen and created a second factory in the prepark around Sixty-Sixth
Street, today the site of the Tavern on the Green restaurant.[72] By 1855, only a year
before the city took the land for Central Park, he had enlarged his business with
fellow countryman William Menck.[73]

The 1855 New York State Census detailed the cost of running the two
steam-powered factories. Together, the two sites consumed "43,680 Bl. of
bones"—possibly "barrels." This was transformed into 13,400 Bl. of animal charcoal, worth more than $80,000. The factories employed twenty-one men whose
monthly salary was $24, not including board. Both properties included frame
houses or shanties in which the employees probably lived. Menck lived on
West Thirty-Fourth Street, away from the factory, but according to the census,
Moller lived on the grounds.[74]

Moller stayed in his family's sugar-refining business for the next thirty years as
a stockholder and secretary of the North River Sugar Refining Co. The Mollers
became extremely wealthy, but after consolidation in 1887 with seventeen other
refineries into the "sugar trust" monopoly—including the most powerful family,
the Havemeyers, which incorporated as Domino Sugar in 1900—the North River
company fell under investigation for antitrust violations by New York State, and
later the U.S. government.[75]

The Havemeyer family did not own any prepark land, but they did have a
connection through their patriarch William Havemeyer, who immigrated to the
United States in 1799 after learning sugar refining in England. Havemeyer was
hired by wealthy entrepreneur Edmund Seaman, who owned the first sugar boiler
in New York.[76] At the turn of the nineteenth century, Seaman's brother Henry
and sister-in-law Sarah Billopp Seaman bought several common lands lots. These
were passed down through intermarriage with the wealthy Kortright family, who
continued their connection to the sugar industry.[77] Sarah Billopp Seaman was
the child whose Staten Island mansion was the site of the failed peace conference
between the American congressmen and Admiral Howe during the Revolutionary War, now the landmark Conference House. The Seamans and their Kortright
heirs owned the land of today's Grand Army Plaza, part of the Sheep Meadow,
and the Ramble shoreline.

When the city bought the land for Central Park in 1856, sugar baron Nicolas Gouverneur Kortright was among a handful of descendants who had inherited and retained their family's property and prospered greatly when he received the award for his land.[78]

PHYSICAL CHANGES

As the people of New York City changed, the land changed with them. New Yorkers had new needs, and so they found new uses for the land over the decade of the mid-1840s to the mid-1850s.

In 1842, after a century of pollution, clean drinking water finally flowed into the city via the Croton Aqueduct. Immediately New Yorkers began to exploit the system. Of the thirty million gallons that streamed into the reservoirs over every twenty-four hours in 1855, the Croton Aqueduct Board estimated that a minimum of seventeen million gallons were being wasted. New Yorkers opened fire hydrants to wash buildings, coaches, and horses, or bottled and sold the water privately, or used it for "self-acting urinals." They installed fountains outside in private yards and indoors in hotels and restaurants, forcing the board to limit use to four months a year and four hours a day. During a cold spell in February 1851, the president of the board reported that the washline indicating the amount of water in the distributing reservoir was nine feet lower because New Yorkers kept their faucets running to prevent the pipes from freezing.[79]

By 1855, the stress on the system forced the Croton Aqueduct Board to lay more pipe from the receiving reservoir along Eighth Avenue from Eighty-First street to Forty-Second Street. The process injured people and property within the prepark, and the city was forced to compensate seventeen west side residents for damages, ranging from $201 for the damage to the house and stable of Michael Tracey to $9 due to broken glass and the death of a goat owned by William McCrudden.[80]

The abuse of the water coupled with the population explosion of the late 1840s and early 1850s strained the Croton system, a situation not foreseen a decade earlier. After searching several locations, the Croton officials decided to construct a new reservoir between Eighty-Sixth Street and Ninety-Sixth Street, directly north of the existing one. A diagonal line bisected the chosen site. One half of was owned by the city, and the other half—the former Harlem Commons—was privately owned.

By May 1854, the Croton Commissioners of Estimate and Assessment were tasked with assigning value to 1,360 lots, of which about 800 were owned or claimed by more than 100 different persons, societies, or corporations.[81] Dealing with 40 miles of landowners from the Croton River in Westchester to the distributing reservoir on Forty-Second Street had been such an arduous, litigious, and expensive ordeal for the aqueduct board in the 1830s that, twenty years later, they tried to quietly circumvent the process through some vaguely fraudulent measures. In a public document, they later admitted that they tried to save time and money "by employing some judicious person, unconnected with this Board, to make these purchases by private contract" before the public was aware of the reservoir's intended location. But the board was forced to give up their secret plan when they realized that the local community would be reasonably suspicious when a band of professional surveyors suddenly arrived on the scene and began measuring the uninhabited tract for some unknown purpose.[82]

By the 1850s, only a handful of the original 1825 landowners of the Harlem Commons still owned that property, the site of the future Reservoir.[83] Most bought the wasteland as an investment and resold it to other investors many times over. By 1857, when final awards were made, the cost to buy the land came to almost $730,000.[84]

THE BURIALS

Although the Croton Aqueduct Board described the future Reservoir landscape as "almost without erections or improvements of any kind—the few buildings standing upon it being of trifling value," they did not acknowledge another way the land had been used. Two large burial sites lay within its boundaries, containing the remains of more than three hundred Jewish adults and children.

Starting in 1825, the A.M.E. Zion Church bought land for burial grounds in Seneca Village. In the 1840s, four Jewish organizations acquired land for that same purpose, three of them on the east side of what is now the Reservoir and one on today's lawn of the Conservatory Garden.

In April 1847, New York State passed the Rural Cemetery Act, which sanctioned cemeteries as a commercial business for the first time. It replaced free burials in churchyards or private sites and moved the purchased burial plots to locations far from the built-up areas of downtown New York. Green-Wood Cemetery had already been established in Brooklyn in 1838. Before Central Park,

Green-Wood was a popular rural escape for New Yorkers, who toured in it their carriages or strolled its manicured grounds. But even before the legislature passed the Rural Cemetery Act, several Jewish congregations bought land in the sparsely inhabited rural ward north of Eighty-Sixth Street.

In 1654, an early group of Sephardic Jews came from Portuguese Brazil to New Amsterdam, then under the directorship of Peter Stuyvesant. He tried to deport them, on the basis that they would "infect and trouble this new colony,"[85] but the Jewish stockholders of the Dutch West India Company ordered him to accept them. For three years, he tried to deny them privileges extended to Dutch New Yorkers, but after continuous pressure from both the group and their representatives in Amsterdam, he relented and awarded them full rights in 1657.[86]

The community grew as Sephardic Jews started arriving from London and Amsterdam. Even if they were from Spain or Portugal, they first emigrated to London or the Netherlands, like the Walloons, the Huguenots, and the Pilgrims, who were all fleeing because of religious persecution in their homelands. Most were shopkeepers or merchants, and many settled in New York as their livelihood was in the transatlantic shipping trade. The first synagogue in New York, Shearith Israel, was built in 1728 and was the only Jewish congregation in New York until 1825. It is still strong and vibrant today in its fifth home on Seventieth Street and Central Park West.

Gradually the Ashkenazi Jews of Germany and Eastern Europe arrived, generally poorer than their Sephardic counterparts. Together they intermarried, formed Jewish enclaves, continued with Jewish ritual law, established Jewish cultural and charitable societies, and gradually built synagogues that reflected the culture of their original homelands.[87] Those congregations would also require their own burial grounds.

The idea to place a Jewish burial ground in the former Harlem Commons or common lands sites may have begun when the Hebrew Benevolent Society took possession of five lots between Ninety-Sixth and Ninety-Seventh Street in 1843. Though the deed did not mention their intentions, the lots were possibly slated for future grave sites.[88] In 1846, the Dutch congregation B'nai Israel bought two lots for a burial ground on the south side of Ninety-Fourth Street between Fifth Avenue and Sixth Avenue.[89] The Polish congregation of B'nai (Bikur) Cholim purchased three lots between Ninety-Third and Ninety-Fourth Street and Fifth Avenue that would be today be located on the running track. And in 1844, Alexander Frankland and others purchased two nearby lots on the south side of Ninety-Fifth Street, which they transferred in 1853 to the Trustees of Beth Israel for a cemetery, though it is not likely to have had any burials.[90] The cemeteries were on or near the Kingsbridge Road, conveniently accessible for funerals and for graveside visits.[91]

In 1853 the Croton Aqueduct Board hired James E. Serrell to survey the land for the rectangular reservoir. His report indicated a structure on two of the burial grounds.[92] Jewish burial practices generally erected a *Mataher*, a structure adjacent to the graveyard for funeral services and the performance of *taharah*, the ritual washing and wrapping of a body before burial.[93]

In 1885, Calvert Vaux designed a *Mataher* for the Sherith Israel congregation's Beth Olam Cemetery in Cypress Hills, Queens. Beth Olam is a rural-style cemetery that was shared by two other congregations, B'nai Jeshrun and Shaaray Tefila, when the prepark bodies were forced to be relocated and reinterred.

The Shaaray Tefila burials included the 156 bodies from the four lots on the central lawn of Conservatory Garden at Fifth Avenue between 104th and 105th Street. The site was fenced in and also included "a wooden tenement," possibly a *Mataher*.[94]

14.9 The Conservatory Garden lawn was the site of the burial ground for 156 members of Congregation Shaaray Tefila.

Source: Sara Cedar Miller, *Conservatory Garden.* Courtesy of the Central Park Conservancy.

After the second wave of cholera ravaged New York in 1849, many blamed its return on the "miasmas" thought to emanate from decaying bodies. In 1851, such fears moved the Common Council to forbid all burials on Manhattan Island south of Eighty-Sixth Street.[95] Before that ruling, many of the deceased buried in the Jewish burial grounds were probably victims of the epidemic.

According to Jewish law, a body could be removed only in order to be rein-terred in the Holy Land, near a relative, or due to the express wishes of the deceased. Eminent domain was not a good reason. So in 1853, when the city ordered them to disinter bodies from the Bnai Jeshrun cemetery on Thirty-Sec-ond Street, the Shaaray Tefila congregation opposed this vehemently and called upon other synagogues to protest and halt the removals. As a result, the mayor modified his demands and transferred to other areas of the cemetery only those few bodies that obstructed street improvements.[96] In his 1855 petition to the Commissioners of Estimate and Assessment for Central Park, Shaaray Tefila president Louis Levy beseeched them to consider one of Judaism's most sacred laws: that "the resting place of the dead is indivisible and under no circum-stances whatsoever for the purposes of public utility or the most urgent con-siderations that the human mind can conceive are those that faith permitted to disturb the graveyard."[97] Nonetheless, the commissioners and the mayor turned a deaf ear.

All three congregations were paid for the value of their property and the cost of reinterring the almost five hundred bodies of Jewish adults and children in Queens.[98] Many of the deceased must have perished during the 1849 cholera epi-demic, so it is ironic that those buried in the future reservoir were removed to make room for pure fresh water.

Today the Beth Olam Cemetery is situated in Cypress Hills in Queens. It was developed after the New York State legislature passed the Rural Cemetery Act. Because grave robbing for medical dissections was common in New York cem-eteries in the 1840s and 1850s, the board of trustees deliberated whether they should consider "supplying firearms to the keeper of the cemetery," given its dis-tant location.[99] Body snatching was easy in those days, as coffins were generally buried in shallow graves, especially in the prepark, where water, rock, or hardpan lay so close the surface.

The Shaaray Tefila section of Beth Olam sits on a hilltop with commanding views of Queens and Long Island. There lies the body of Reverend Samuel Myer Isaacs, who died in 1878. Isaacs, Shaaray Tefila's famed Netherlands-born leader of New York's first English-speaking Jewish congregation, would have presided over the burials of those who were once interred where the central lawn of Conservatory Garden is today.[100]

In 1847, Conservatory Garden's central lawn and surrounding allées were home to the future garden and public school of the Catholic Sisters of Charity, the Jewish cemetery, and the future home for a Black Protestant cemetery. The trustees of St. Philip's Episcopal Church also bought four lots for $500.[101] In 1795, St. Philip's dedicated a burial ground on today's Lower East Side, at Christie and Rivington Streets, "for the Interment of all Negroes who shall die within the City of New York." By 1820, the neighbors declared the cemetery a nuisance. But it was still operating in 1835, when Reverend Peter Williams Jr. complained to the rector, church wardens, and vestry of Trinity Church, "Our cemetery, which has been in use forty years, is now so full, that we cannot inter our dead as deep as the law requires, and for a violation of this law our sexton has recently been heavily fined."[102]

The old cemetery remained open until 1853, but in anticipation of its closing, the parish bought four lots in the prepark in 1847, purchased with money received from an insurance company for a fire in a building owned by the parish. When the 1851 ordinance banned burials south of Eighty-Sixth Street and forbade the creation of new cemeteries, except intramural burials, on Manhattan Island, the trustees sold their property the following year to Tighe Davy, a trustee of the Sisters of Charity. The St. Philip's property gained the church a profit of $250 over the purchase price of $500 they had paid five years earlier.[103] Some historians have suggested that "as Manhattan moved uptown, the cemetery land, as negotiable real estate, was viewed as potential income."[104]

Davy was possibly more certain that the land would be taken for the Central Park and anticipated a greater profit, while the trustees of St. Philip's took their substantial profit and bought a more reliable permanent resting place in Queens. In 1852, the reality of a park was still only a dream—or a nightmare, depending on which side of the political fence one stood.

PART III

The Idea of a Park

To most of us today, city parks are oases, retreats, sanctuaries, *rus in urbe*— the country in the city. But in nineteenth-century Manhattan, parks were battlegrounds that pitted public need against private interest. Landowners often refused to cede their property for public space, and the Common Council often refused to pay them for it. New York seemed unlikely to ever rival the great green cities of Paris and London.[1]

When the monotonous grid design, the Commissioners' Plan of 1811, was unveiled in 1811, New York only had two ten-acre green spaces: the Battery and City Hall Park. New Yorkers saw in the grid that their future would only include a few more postage-stamp–sized green squares: the plan proposed as the two largest parks the nineteen-acre Manhattan Square, today Theodore Roosevelt Park surrounding the American Museum of Natural History, and the twenty-five-acre Observatory Place in the East 90s that was never built. The plan relegated the banks of the rivers—which the commissioners called "those large arms of the sea"—as the places where New Yorkers could find fresh air, recreate, and commune with nature. Because "the price of land is so uncommonly great," the commissioners wrote, the island's interior blocks were earmarked for residential and commercial development, not for leisure. One proposed riverside park—the seventy-acre Harlem Marsh from Fifth Avenue to the East River and running three blocks from 106th Street to 109th Street—would have encompassed much of the property owned by the Benson and McGowan families. But those plans never materialized, and it too developed into a residential and industrial area.

In lower midtown, a fairly flat 260-acre expanse that had been part of the city's common lands was planned to become the Parade, the city's military parade ground. By default, that made it a public park. Several parcels of common land

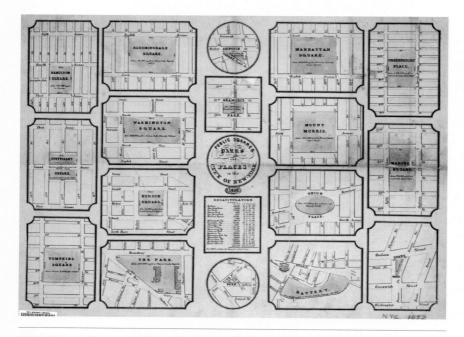

III.1 In 1852, the green spaces in the city totaled fewer than two hundred acres, less than a fifth the acreage of the future Central Park. Many landowners, taxpayers, and government officials strongly opposed adding costly public parks or squares to the city.

Source: "Public squares, parks, and places in the City of New York." Lionel Pincus and Princess Firyal Map Division, The New York Public Library, New York Public Library Digital Collections, https:// digitalcollections.nypl.org/items/3d7c42c0-f39f-0130-1867-58d385a7b928.

had been auctioned off in 1785 to a handful of investors, and in 1811, the angry landowners and the Common Council fought against taking this area for a public space. The owners wanted to retain their property as an investment, and the aldermen were reluctant to spend the exorbitant amount to repurchase it for parkland. By 1847, the political battle over the huge Parade whittled it down to today's six-acre Madison Square Park.[2]

The fight to create Stuyvesant Park, a small green patch on Second Avenue from Sixteenth Street to Eighteenth Street, raged for sixteen years. In 1836, Peter Stuyvesant, a descendant of the infamous Dutch director, donated seventy-two lots of his family's property to the city for a public park. When problems with street grading delayed the project for two years, the City Council finally appropriated funds to level the tract. In good faith, many investors bought surrounding land in anticipation of an elegant home and long-term investment fronting an exclusive leafy oasis. But by 1841, the park still had not surfaced, and an outraged Stuyvesant sued the city for breach of contract and an annual loss to him of $150,000. For over eight years, complaints from adjacent property owners to the Common Council were, according to one irate citizen, "permitted to sleep the sleep of death."[3]

Stuyvesant Park was just one municipal improvement that languished during the eight-year recession following the Panic of 1837. The devaluing of the dollar fueled serious unemployment, foreclosures, and a mass exodus from the city to the suburbs. During those same years, the social fabric of New York was rent, changing nearly every aspect of urban life.

From the 1840s through the early 1850s, New Yorkers saw a revolutionary shift in the city's demographics. Some of the new arrivals were native-born rural people who had chosen the factory over the farm. But the biggest influx came from the country's first great surge in foreign immigration. Between the years 1847 and 1854, nearly two million German and Irish immigrants landed at the port of New York. Many headed west or left for other cities, but by 1850 nearly half of New York City's population of 515,000 were foreign-born.[4]

Overnight, the fairly homogenous city exploded into a menagerie of cultures, customs, languages, behaviors, and expectations. The transition bewildered the city's social and economic hierarchies and brought massive anxieties about public space to New York's white upper and middle classes.[5] Creating public parks for *all* New Yorkers was the last thing on their minds.[6]

Dressed in their finery, polite society conducted their daily promenade every evening at six o'clock, a public confirmation of their elite status. The ritual had codes of behavior as rigid as dancing a minuet, and a proliferation of etiquette manuals guided the dancers' dress, posture, gestures, and facial expressions. As an example, to tip one's hat was an acknowledgment that the other person thus greeted was accepted into privileged society, but hat-tipping had rules. To do it properly, the hat must be lifted slightly from one's head. To merely touch the brim or raise one's arm toward it was considered "ostentatious." For a lady, it was only proper to lift one's hat just enough for a slight "inclination of the head . . . but the body need not be bent."[7] There was a prescribed pace, look, and attitude of self-containment. Talking while walking was frowned upon. It was "a curiously depersonalized form of sociability."[8]

III.2 This illustration from an 1857 issue of *Harper's Weekly*, "Broadway, opposite the St. Nicholas, at Four of the Afternoon," depicts the daily ritual of the fashionable promenade while attempting to ignore what were called "the dangerous classes." For some members of the genteel classes, the creation of a policed public park would provide a safe environment that the public streets could not.

Source: "Broadway, opposite the St. Nicholas, at four of the afternoon." The Miriam and Ira D. Wallach Division of Art, Prints and Photographs: Picture Collection, The New York Public Library, New York Public Library Digital Collections, https://digitalcollections.nypl.org/items/510d47e0-d791-a3d9-e040 -e00a18064a99.

But in the 1840s, when the lower classes began to invade the long-standing promenade at the Battery, the elite were forced to move the fashionable parade to their exclusive turf of upper Broadway. There, it also became targeted by brazen and rowdy boys and young men, "often travelling in packs of thirty or forty, who would overrun the sidewalks, driving respectable people into the gutters."[9] In his book, *The Dangerous Classes of New York, and Twenty Years' Work Among Them*, the reformer Charles Loring Brace singled out the Irish as the culprits. Walk down Broadway on a holiday, he wrote, when the Irish crowd the sidewalks, and one would see the "savagery gleam from those daredevil eyes. The materials of riot in the heart of the vast and populous city then strike one with terror," he continued.[10]

Brace's close friend, the future codesigner of Central Park Frederick Law Olmsted, also described the anxiety and alienation people felt on the city's crowded streets: "To merely avoid collision with those we . . . pass upon the sidewalks, we have constantly to watch, to foresee, and to guard against their movements. . . . [We see] thousands of fellowmen, have met them face to face, have brushed up against them, and yet have had no experience of anything in common with them."[11]

———◆◆———

Class riots and smaller clashes became more frequent and more terrifying. Several times in the 1830s, angry mobs took to the streets in riots, injuring people and damaging property. The largest disturbance, the Astor Place Riot of 1849, left an estimated twenty-two people dead and over a hundred injured, including many innocent bystanders.[12]

In response to this physical and psychological invasion, the genteel classes retreated from public outings to new private enclaves. In the decades following the late 1820s, small private parks had already been established far from working-class districts. In 1827, St. John's Park in today's Tribeca became the city's first exclusive green space, accessible only to those wealthy families living in the surrounding homes. In 1832, Gramercy Park, the brainchild of real estate developer Samuel Ruggles, transformed a swampy tract of common land into a two-acre gated park, opened with a key possessed only by the surrounding residents. Today it is still a gated private park.[13]

By 1838, without a space for rural recreation, New Yorkers began to frequent Brooklyn's new Green-Wood Cemetery and its nearly two hundred acres of shady groves, rolling green hills, and distant and extensive views. But soon that landscape filled with headstones, and it became obvious it was no permanent substitute for a public park.[14]

The fear of lawless public spaces led New Yorkers, particularly women, to retreat to the safety and sanctity of their private drawing rooms, which is itself shorthand for *withdrawing* rooms. While men inhabited both public and private spaces, women remained indoors, only venturing out when on the arm of their protective husband, tucked inside an enclosed carriage, or within the confines of the few private parks. Central Park codesigner Calvert Vaux took a swipe at the paranoia of the American woman, for whom even the parlor had become "a sort of quarantine": "one almost expects to see the lady of the house walk in with a bottle of camphor in her hand, to prevent infection, she seems to have such a fear that any one should step within the bounds of her real every-day home life."[15]

Because there were almost no parks, pleasure grounds, or shaded avenues, American women spent "many sedentary, listless hours" indoors. Even walking was "considered irksome and fatiguing."[16] And the Victorian woman's imprisonment in her home was mirrored in the entrapment of her clothing. Tightened whalebone corsets kept her from taking a deep breath. Off-the-shoulder dress sleeves constricted the free motion of her arms. The heavy skirt that "twists," about her knees doubles her fatigue, and arrests her locomotive powers." Multilayered crinolines, discovered to be flammable, were eventually replaced by a voluminous hoop or cagelike undergarment that made even simple movements awkward.[17]

Fearful concerns particularly for the safety of genteel citizens were expressed in a report by the Board of Aldermen, who questioned the merits of having a public park without the presence of a strong police force. They posed their concerns and fears in an 1851 report: "Would it be a safe resort for unprotected ladies—for their children and young persons—for the sick and infirm and the aged citizens of New-York? Could they sit down with their little family groups without danger of being insulted, run over, knocked down, perhaps robbed, and may be murdered? I think not."[18]

Despite these lingering fears, by the late 1840s several social and economic factors began to encourage many middle- and upper-class New Yorkers to look beyond their parlor windows for a protected public space in which to revitalize their promenade, commune with nature, and socialize with members of their class. The result would be the creation of Central Park, a park for all classes—but not before New Yorkers spent over a decade battling with each other about the site, the cost, the governance, the design, the use, and the users of this new American institution.

chapter 15

The Battle of the Parks, 1844–1852

n Asher B. Durand's 1849 painting *Kindred Spirits*, the late American landscape painter Thomas Cole stands on a rugged cliff amid the sort of picturesque woodland he often painted. Beside him is William Cullen Bryant, one of America's foremost romantic poets.

In July 1844, Bryant, in his "day job" as the editor of the influential *New-York Evening Post*, had painted for his readers a similar scene on Manhattan Island: a green landscape "covered with old trees, intermingled with shrubs, craggy eminences, a little stream, restless waters, and, in spring, the ground gay with flowers." Bryant was referring here to the Jones family's property, a picturesque patch of green along the East River from Sixty-Eighth Street to Seventy-Seventh Street. Bryant believed Jones Wood could be easily transformed into a city park, "an extensive pleasure ground for shade and recreation in these sultry afternoons." Other newspapers took up the cause, but it would be a few more years before New Yorkers would commit to a large—and costly—public park.[1]

The Gold Rush of 1849 had kickstarted an economic revitalization after a long depression. Thousands of young New York men, even those from "the best families," headed west to seek their fortune.[2] Many of them stayed in California, but the gold and its consequent riches flowed east, back home to New York. In the years from 1851 through 1854 alone, the city enjoyed the inundation of gold valued at $175 million. The flagging New York economy got the necessary increase it needed. Suddenly there was "more money, more credit, more investment, more production, more consumption, and more exchange."[3] This spurred the city government to open new streets, develop new neighborhoods, and construct new routes of transportation. New York began to look like its wealthy European counterpart cities, London and Paris. Except for one thing: it had no comparable park.

15.1 The painting *Kindred Spirits* by artist Thomas Cole shows him conversing in forested Catskill mountains with fellow Romantic, the poet William Cullen Bryant, who first proposed a large public park for New York that would evoke the woodlands in Cole's painting.

Source: "Kindred Spirits." NYPL Art Work, The New York Public Library, New York Public Library Digital Collections, https://digitalcollections.nypl.org/items/510d47da-32d4-a3d9-e040-e00a18064a99.

15.2 Inspired by the parks he saw in Europe, wealthy shipping magnate Robert Minturn, urged on by wife Anna Mary Wendell, became an important force behind the idea for a park in New York. His business partner, Moses Grinnell, became one of the Central Park commissioners.

Source: "The late Robert B. Minturn." The Miriam and Ira D. Wallach Division of Art, Prints and Photographs: Print Collection, The New York Public Library, The New York Public Library Digital Collections, 1861–1880, https://digitalcollections.nypl.org/items/510d47da-2888-a3d9-e040-e00a18064a99.

Amid the boom of 1849, Andrew Jackson Downing, the tastemaker of American homes and landscapes, echoed Bryant's plea. In his own magazine, *The Horticulturist*, Downing reminded his readers that parks in America were an embarrassment compared to those in European capitals.[4]

That same year, shipping magnate Robert Minturn and his family returned from a year-long European jaunt and were as appalled as Bryant and Downing had been about New York's lack of green space. Lyman Horace Weeks, writing a half century later in 1898, credited Minturn's wife, Anna Mary Wendell, for planting the idea of a park in the heads of her husband and his friends.[5] According to Minturn's son, that happened at a fateful meeting with the prominent men in his social circle, who echoed Bryant's rhapsodic vision to transform the Joneses' East River grove into New York's great new park.[6]

———

Mayor Caleb S. Woodhull thought otherwise. Although he considered open space important, "the great breathing places of the toiling masses," his idea of adding to the city's parks was simply an enlargement of the Battery. That would all change in 1851 when both candidates for mayor, Fernando Wood and Ambrose Kingsland, ran on a platform advocating a new park. When Kingsland won, he likely met with Minturn's group and had been following the newspapers that supported Jones Wood.

Jones Wood had the backing of many of the Common Council members and the New York State legislature, which passed the act authorizing the city to take possession of the lands for a new park on July 11, 1851.[7] The wealthy and influential Jones and Schermerhorn family, who owned the land, refused to give up their private enclave and went to court to protect it. They won a temporary injunction, and a New York County judge found the Jones Wood law unconstitutional, as it was determined the landowners were not given due process. The impetus to pass a second Jones Wood bill had lost several important backers who had shifted their interest to a new location.[8]

A growing number of detractors were opposed to Jones Wood. Andrew Jackson Downing again intervened. He argued that Jones Wood was "only a child's playground," much too small for New York's future park and too limited in vision to rival London's six thousand acres of green space. The Common Council, influenced by Downing's remarks, began to doubt their limited vision.[9]

In the meantime, a new park appeared on the horizon. Croton Aqueduct Board President Nicholas Dean and Alderman Henry Shaw proposed an alternative site: all the land between Fifth Avenue and Eighth Avenue between Fifty-Ninth Street and 106th Street. Dean was in the process of planning the construction of the new reservoir to be sited between Eighty-Sixth Street and Ninety-Sixth Street. He noted that the poor topography of the surrounding land, much of it part of the city's common lands, was its greatest asset. The same $1.5 million would buy a much grander space, and one that was more centrally located. Business leaders either leaned toward no park at all or preferred the more central site, while some social reformers thought one large park would be too inaccessible for working-class people and preferred the creation of many small parks in local downtown neighborhoods.[10]

The political fight turned on who would pay for it. The Jones Wood faction was led by State Senator James Beekman, whose east side estate was alongside the proposed park, and he was counting on a profound increase in the value of his property. But that would happen *only* if the new park was paid for by taxation rather than through heavy assessments placed on him and his neighbors.

The anti-Jones faction, composed of the majority of the aldermen, then threw a third space into the mix. They argued instead to add four acres of landfill to the existing ten-acre Battery at the southern tip of the island. They said it would most benefit those living and working downtown, especially the lower classes. By the 1850s the once fashionable playground of the well-to-do had become popular with the working class, who had no green space in the poorer neighborhoods. The Board of Aldermen did approve enlarging the Battery, but immediately a group of powerful merchants protested. They saw the plan as a threat to their shipping and commercial ventures, and they had the ear of the mayor. The Battery improvements were vetoed.[11]

By the summer of 1851, the Board of Aldermen created a Special Committee on Parks and charged them to answer the question: Would Jones Wood or Central Park become New York's answer to the Champs-Élysées?

Histories of Central Park have always emphasized its size as one of the reasons it won out against Jones Wood. But that's not how the committee saw it in their report. In recommending "the Central Park"—the first use of the name—the committee wrote that it was of "sufficient size" not for the appearance of a rural idyll, but so that land along its five-and-a-half-mile perimeter could be sold off for "rows of elegant private houses, the residences of wealthy citizens." The surrounding property, they reasoned, would command large prices and reduce the expense of the original cost, as was the case in Liverpool's Birkenhead Park. The assessments for these private villas would be sufficient to pay a large portion or even the entire cost of purchasing the land that would become Central Park, such that the expense "would scarcely be felt." The report also suggested that even

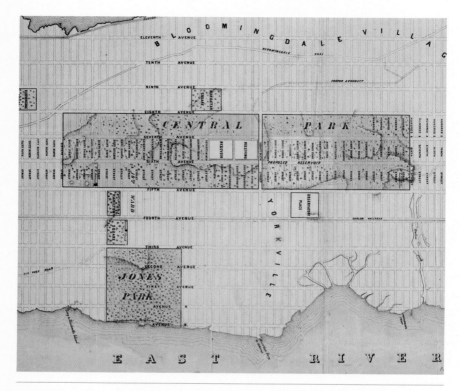

15.3 The decision about where to locate a new major New York park came down to two sites: Jones Wood on the east side, and the much larger central site surrounding the receiving reservoir and the proposed new and larger rectangular reservoir to its north.

Source: "New York city map." Lionel Pincus and Princess Firyal Map Division, The New York Public Library, New York Public Library Digital Collections, https://digitalcollections.nypl.org/items /d712f0a0-f3a1-0130-f212-58d385a7b928.

more parkland could be sold off or leased from time to time to pay for the park's upkeep and decoration.[12]

During their six-month investigation, the committee wondered whether they shouldn't simply eschew a park and build more city over the common lands. They conducted a study to determine how much it would cost the taxpayers to transform nearly eight hundred acres of Manhattan's roller coaster topography into a smooth and level grid of city blocks. Surveyors concluded that the cost of excavating earth and rock, filling in depressions, and creating the embankments for the streets would be much steeper than simply developing the land as a park.

The report determined, for example, that to continue to build Sixth Avenue from Sixty-Fifth Street to Seventy-Third Street, the area that today is the Mall and the Lake, would entail building an embankment "from twenty to forty feet in height." It would leave the low-lying adjacent lots utterly valueless unless they were filled in to nearly the same level. The undulating terrain, the Commissioners reasoned, would substantially benefit the design of a scenic landscape.[13]

Each side summoned gardeners and horticulturists, including the eminent botanist John Torrey, to testify about the suitability of their site for a park. The focus of the debate centered on whether the majestic stands of trees on the property of the Jones and Schermerhorn families could maintain their health after being thinned to make room for park paths. The underlying issue for Beekman and his Jones Wood backers was really the thinning of their wallets if they had to fork over the money for the park's potentially steep assessments.

On January 2, 1852, the Special Committee on Parks announced the results of its investigation and—to no one's surprise—chose the Central Park over Jones Wood. Weeks later, the Board of Aldermen passed a resolution requesting the state government to suspend action on Jones Wood until the Common Council could evaluate whether a central park "would not be more useful and acceptable to the people."[14] And by April, the second Jones Wood bill died when the legislative session ended.

THE AUCTIONS

Once the Special Committee announced its decision in the *Special Report on Parks* on January 2, the central site looked quite promising to become the future park, and by May a real estate ad was already hyping property near "the proposed New Central Park." But only two weeks before the ad was published, the city did something remarkable, confusing, and "odd."[15] That month and again in December, the corporation auctioned off 476 lots of its common lands property, already slated to become a significant portion of the new centrally located park.

The fiscal crisis of 1837 had emptied the city's coffers. Many New Yorkers had moved to the suburbs, which also eroded the tax base. The city's debt had skyrocketed to $14 million, largely due to the construction of the Croton Aqueduct. In 1844, fragile finances forced the city to begin selling off its greatest asset: eighty blocks of the common lands north of Forty-Second Street. It simply

330 The Idea of a Park

made more sense to sell the land than continue to rent it. The revenue from the purchase price, taxes, and assessments would lower the debt far more than the rental income could.[16] By May, 1852, the auctions for the land had arrived north of Fifty-Ninth Street.

SPECULATION

The prepark auctions coincided with the speculative fever for real estate that gripped New York and raised prices for the once undesirable common lands to record highs. In May and December of 1852, the city took in nearly half a million dollars from the inflated bids on its eight hundred prepark lots. At a New York State Senate interrogation, nurseryman James Hogg noted that the average common lands block sold for $67,876, "more than twice its more realistic worth."[17] The *New York Times* commented that "the prospect of the purchase for the contemplated object [Central Park] has made the land the subject of the most shameless speculation from which the city suffers perhaps to the extent of a half-million dollars."[18]

Speculation—a business transaction involving considerable risk with the promise of a spectacular and quick profit—ran counter to the core of Protestant America's values. The word comes from the Latin *speculum*, mirror. It was a universal symbol for self-love or pride, one of the seven cardinal sins. The amassing of easy money, often involving deception, rewarded profit-oriented individualism rather than the self-sacrifice of collective civic virtue.[19] The historian Karen A. Wyler wrote that admonishments about the evils of speculation were prevalent in early nineteenth-century literature. Abhorrence of this practice, for example, appeared in the epigraph to an 1801 novel, *Dorval; or The Speculator*,

> Tis avarice that suggests a thousand schemes,
> A thousand plans, and fills our waking dreams,
> With hopes of gain, bids speculation come,
> And forces ruin to a happy home
> And love of country turns to love of self,
> And centers all our pleasures in ourself.[20]

Speculation in land or currency was derided as a form of gambling taken up by those without the righteousness to pursue an honest trade. Long-term investments, on the other hand, exemplified the Christian virtue of patience.

But despite this, economist Edward L. Glaeser called America "a nation of gamblers," and real estate speculation was "a national pastime."[21]

Central Park was a speculative venture. In 1926, the historian Charles Beard argued that the concept of speculation was one of the driving forces behind its creation, "subjects not usually mentioned in polite society . . . themes that are as tabu in academic circles as sex at a Boston tea party."[22]

In 1848, the Tenant League formed as an organization to encourage a series of landlord-tenant reforms. Among their demands was that the city sell its common lands only to first-time homesteaders, to protect them against the greed of speculators.[23] One such speculator, the Prussian fur importer Sylvester Brush, had invested $4,700 in eight lots of common land on Fifth Avenue and Forty-Third Street that same year. Four years later, at the city's auction and after the publication of the 1852 *Special Report on Parks*, Brush saw the potential in purchasing another fifty lots within the lower prepark between Sixtieth and Sixty-Fifth Streets. This time he paid nearly $40,000, about 25 percent more per lot. His new property encompassed many choice Fifth and Sixth Avenue lots, including those that today contain the Pond, the Dairy, and the Kinderberg summerhouse. Brush and his fellow high-rollers rushed to amass large plots,; their value would skyrocket, and even if plans fell through, they would still be a surefire investment.[24]

In comparison, the fruit purveyor Daniel Gilmartin bought four lots at auction on the site of the Metropolitan Museum of Art, where he intended "to erect a dwelling house for himself and family," not "for speculation." A butcher named Diedrich Knubel acquired his lots adjacent to the receiving reservoir, and there he immediately planted two trees. By 1855, he had dug out his cellar and was ready to lay the foundation. He made it clear to the commissioners that his purchase too was "not for speculation."[25]

In choosing to auction the prepark's common lands, did the city anticipate a huge profit and assume it would buy back the inflated properties for much less? Were buyers ignorant, ill-informed, or in denial that the much-discussed Central Park would ever be built? Were the speculators so certain that they would reap an even greater profit by the time the city took back the land, even after mortgage, tax, and assessment payments? The answer to all of these is, basically, yes.

But in the end only the city was right. A small percentage of buyers flipped their property for a quick turnaround, but almost half the bidders walked away before paying the required 10 percent down payment, while others chose to forfeit their 10 percent rather than pay the balance. Most of the bidders held on to the land until they were forced to sell it back to the city just four years later, often at a loss.[26]

THE AMORY DIVISION

Whereas the City of New York divided its property purposely to make a profit, the surviving family of whipmaker and farmer James Amory were legally forced to sell the estate because of an error in Amory's will. Amory owned former common lands properties that are today some of the park's most famous landmarks: the Mall, Bethesda Terrace, the Dene, Rumsey Playfield, the East Green, the Center Drive, and part of the Sheep Meadow. When he died at the age of sixty in 1835, his last will and testament stipulated that his farm would pass first to his widow, then to his children, and subsequently to his grandchildren.[27]

Amory's will was dragged through the courts from 1846 to 1851 because of the Rule Against Perpetuities, created to impose limitations on a landowner's ability to control the future allocation of their property. Without that protection, James Amory's grandchildren would be impeded by restrictions and future buyers would have an unclear right to title.

There could be several reasons that James Amory wrote his will as he did: perhaps he thought his wife was too inexperienced and his children were too

15.4 The site of the former Amory homestead, today a memorial grove dedicated to heroes of World War I, was some of the most expensive lots sold in the prepark. Due to an error in their father's will, the Amory heirs were forced to auction off their property in 1851.

Source: Sara Cedar Miller, *Memorial Grove*. Courtesy of the Central Park Conservancy.

immature to manage the property. The property might not have been easily divisible, requiring trusts to manage it. Perhaps he thought his children would fight among themselves and sought to establish control to avoid later conflicts. It is also possible that Amory wished to control his property and his family from the grave.[28]

The answer seems to be all of the above. James Amory must have anticipated his family's dysfunction, as his son, Samuel, sued his mother and his six siblings in 1846, pressing the court to annul the will so he could partition and sell the property. After several trials, the case was turned over to Referee Philo T. Ruggles, who after hearing the arguments decided that the will was "invalid and void in certain respects."[29] In December 1851, the Supreme Court of New York ordered the sale of the entire farm, which spilled across the prepark boundary to the family's property between Fifth Avenue and Madison Avenue, Sixty-Third to Sixty-Seventh Street. The property was transferred to Ruggles and divided into more than a thousand lots, nearly eight hundred of which would eventually lie within Central Park. These were put up for sale by public auction. The auctioneers placed an advertisement in the *Evening Post*: "There probably has been no better opportunity offered to the citizens of New York for twenty years past to make selections in so desirable part of the island being on and in the vicinity of Hamilton [Square] and other contemplated squares, at their own prices either for investment or private residences."[30]

The March 1852 auction sold off all the property for close to $800,000, an unheard-of profit that made national headlines. The newspapers quoted $4,400 as James Amory's original purchase price thirty years earlier; however, one would be hard pressed to substantiate that, since he bought, sold, and repurchased his properties over so a long period of time. Even so, it was a huge profit during the high speculative year of 1852, only two months before the city began to auction off the common lands. One reporter commented that the increased profit on "so large a plot of ground is probably without a parallel even in this go-ahead city."[31]

Speculator Sylvester Brush, who had purchased fifty common lands lots for nearly $40,000, scooped up twenty-nine additional lots at the Amory auction for over $20,000, or approximately $750 per lot, a price reflected in his many choice corner and Fifth or Sixth Avenue properties.[32]

The individual Amory family members were forced to bid on their father's property along with speculators like Brush. Only one family member, broker Peter B. Amory, and his wife and seven children actually lived in the old family homestead near the present Mall and beach volleyball courts. He held a mortgage with Ruggles and held the most property within the prepark of any family member.[33] After the awards were assigned in 1856, the Amorys still retained the land across from Central Park, between Fifth and Madison Avenues, which they later sold for millions.

While the Amory offspring were waging war with each other, they stood loyal to brother James, who fought an additional battle with his wife, Angeline, for her share of his prepark property. *Amory v. Amory* dragged on for twenty years in New York and Wisconsin courts, and was based on the testimony of one suspect witness who claimed to have recently seen William Williams, Angeline's purportedly deceased husband. With the family's backing, the court nullified her marriage to Amory, despite the couple's thirty-year cohabitation and eight children, thus negating to her legitimate right to an estate worth approximately $750,000. They also secretly bribed Angeline's attorney to give her faulty legal advice.[34]

The three Amory brothers—Samuel, James, and John—moved to Fond du Lac, Wisconsin, where they became leaders in the community, real estate developers, and, like their father, sellers of saddlery and sporting guns. Amory Street to this day is a main thoroughfare of Fond du Lac.[35]

While plans for the future Central Park site were in the newspapers and discussed in the halls of government, businesses, and taverns, many landowners of parkland were less engaged and, in many cases, ignorant of the discourse. Hungry speculators circled them, and often tricked them out of their properties and profits.

MARY ANN PATRICK RECKLESS

If ever a name fit a situation, it was in the case of Mary Ann Reckless, a twice-widowed park landowner who was pounced upon by greedy businessmen. Her first husband, wealthy merchant John Patrick, purchased a common lands lot in 1801. Today, the property includes the two-hundred-foot Vista Rock tunnel on the Seventy-Ninth Street Transverse Road and the adjacent Ramble landscape to the south, with that magnificent tupelo tree, *Nyssa sylvatica*, and its adjacent meadow.[36]

Patrick, a native of Scotland, was related to the aristocratic Sheddens, who traced their heritage to the Royal House of the Stuarts and its vast estate in the Laird of Roughwood.[37] In America, John Patrick partnered with his uncle, William Shedden, to form Shedden, Patrick & Co., the largest and wealthiest commercial traders in New York, circulators of tobacco, rum, sugar, spirits, silks,

15.5 The Ramble meadow that features the magnificent tupelo tree was the former property of John Patrick and his widow, Mary Ann Reckless, the victim of an ill-intentioned speculation scheme in 1852.

Source: Sara Cedar Miller, *Ramble*. Courtesy of the Central Park Conservancy.

tea, glass, coal, tools, nails, and tropical fruits to and from Jamaica, Malaga, St. Petersburg, Manchester, Newcastle, China, and India.[38]

Before William Shedden died in 1798, he named three executors and trustees of his estate, one of whom was Patrick. When Shedden's son, William Patrick Ralston Shedden, came of age, he learned that the family's ancient lands were no longer his to inherit. The junior Shedden claimed in court that Patrick "secretly and fraudulently" appropriated a large portion of the Shedden children's property, worth in excess of sixty thousand dollars.[39] When, in 1852, Shedden learned the assessed value of Patrick's single block—sixty-four lots—of the future park, he sued Patrick's widow, Mary Ann, for it.

Mary Ann by that time was far from the New York gossip. She had remarried Joseph Reckless and lived with him in Burlington County, New Jersey, removed from the city's real estate ventures. Before Joseph Reckless died, he appointed a trustee for his wife's financial dealings, a typical practice to manage the affairs of a future widow. At the suggestion of John Bunting, supposedly a friend and advisor, Mary Ann Reckless changed her husband's trustee to Walter Townsend in the first week of May 1852, the same week of the first prepark common land auction.[40] With Townsend's assistance, Bunting then purchased her sixty-four lots for $1,000, far below the market value.[41] When she finally realized that she had been duped, she marched into the United States Court of Appeals to sue Bunting, but the court upheld his ownership. The 1852 report of the Special Committee on Public Parks to the Board of Alderman estimated that the value of the block was perhaps thirty times the value Bunting had paid Reckless.[42]

EPIPHANY DAVIS

The children of Seneca Village landowner Epiphany Davis were also victims of greedy speculators. Davis, a long-standing trustee of A.M.E. Zion Church, was the largest landowner in Seneca Village. In 1825, he paid John Whitehead $578 for his first twelve lots. He would eventually own six more.[43] Today, his largest parcel

15.6 The Pinetum in Central Park was the former the Seneca Village property of Epiphany Davis, a trustee of the A.M.E. Zion Church. The lots were sold by his heirs in a swindle that was perpetrated upon many unsuspecting landowners.

Source: Sara Cedar Miller, *Pinetum*. Courtesy of the Central Park Conservancy.

features a magnificent grove of pines now known as the Arthur Ross Pinetum. Davis was one of the wealthier property owners in Seneca Village and though he lived downtown, he would have seen his prepark property as a solid financial investment, a way to have a voice in the political process, and a contribution to the Black community. From his last will and testament, we know he possessed real estate, fine clothing, expensive jewelry, and luxurious household items, classic details of a nineteenth-century Black middle-class New York family. He also bequeathed his daughter Ann his framed print of a slave ship, a reminder than no matter how comfortable life could be for hardworking Black Americans, the evils of slavery were never to be forgotten.

In his will, he instructed his executors to sell his properties "with convenient speed."[44] And though his executors, including A.M.E. Zion Bishop Christopher Rush, were legally bound to dispose of his real estate, they decided not to do so until October 1852, nine years after Davis's death.

Under the auspices of the executors, Davis's children conveyed eight of their father's most valuable lots and two substantial three-story dwellings to Newell Bradner Smith, a New Orleans merchant, for the sum of $4,100. This may have seemed like a handsome profit for the family, but they received far less than it was worth. The eight lots were in a prized location along an avenue and a main thoroughfare, and only four years later the two homes alone were assessed at nearly $4,000. Smith offered the unsuspecting Davis heirs only slightly more for the structure and land combined.[45]

But why was a merchant from New Orleans buying property in New York City? Bradner Smith, it turns out, was the son-in-law of Don Alonzo Cushman, a well-known New York City developer whose great grandson founded today's real estate giant Cushman & Wakefield. Twenty-four hours after his purchase from the Davis family, Bradner Smith transferred the property to Don Alonzo Cushman for the same $4,100.[46]

Cushman, his sons, and N. Bradner Smith were looking to make a quick profit from the naïve heirs before they discovered that the land would be seized by the city for a park. If Cushman, a well-known developer, had made the Davis sale public, he might have been thwarted in the next phase of his scheme. Fifteen days after buying the lots, Cushman resold them to German butcher Christian Tietjen for more than double what he'd paid the Davises.[47]

The coming of the park and its ensuing rise in land values spurred eight more landowners in Seneca Village to sell their lots between 1853, the year the land was

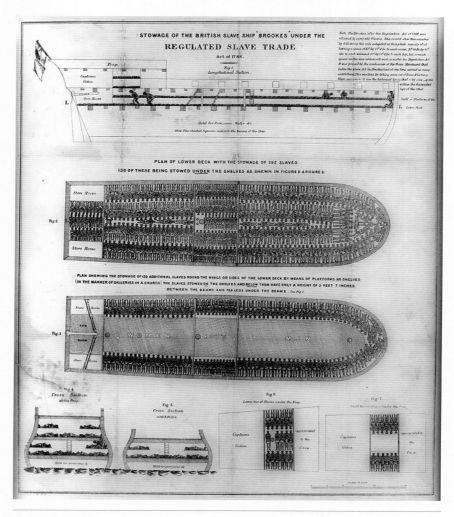

15.7 In his will Epiphany Davis bequeathed his daughter Ann his framed print of a slave ship; that may have been this popular 1788 image. It would have been a reminder than no matter how comfortable life could be for hardworking Black Americans, the evils of slavery were never to be forgotten.

taken by an act of the state legislature, and 1855, right before the Commissioners of Estimate and Assessment set the value of park properties.[48] All eight profited, although one landowner, Ann Eliza Derry, the daughter of Edward Wigfall, sold her late father's two lots for only ten dollars each. Perhaps she did not know the value of the property. Or perhaps her buyer, Samuel Thompson, was a relation, and the token twenty-dollar sale was an act of love.[49]

With so many new buyers and new speculators in the game, properties were changing hands at breakneck speed, while contention over the park had slowed the political process to a snail's pace. The Jones Wood versus Central Park factions in both Albany and the city remained frozen for a year and a half, until the warmth of the summer solstice in 1853 melted the ice.

chapter 16

Becoming Central Park, 1853–1856

The process to create Central Park was an almost endless battle, as complex and tedious as it was politically charged. Behind the scenes, commissioners debated and negotiated, cutting and breaking deals with one another. And out in public, the properties had to be evaluated, landowners' petitions had to be heard, the Supreme Court had to approve the commissioners' reports, and the City of New York had to take the land through eminent domain. In all, this took four years, from January 1852 to February 1856. It began with the Special Committee's report that favored the Central Park site and ended when the Supreme Court of New York approved the report of the Commissioners of Estimate and Assessment. And all the while, the anxious residents waited for the verdict, and the impatient public waited for their park.

The process began with the legalization of the park. Issues remained unresolved from the release of the Special Committee report in January 1852 through the spring of 1853. There were two main conflicts. The first was the choice of the park. Would it be Jones Wood, Central Park, or both? And the second was who would pay for the park's construction and maintenance. State Senator James Beekman, whose property was adjacent to Jones Wood, believed the park should be paid for by a general tax on all New Yorkers. But those citizens living far from either proposed park preferred that the bulk of the costs should be paid by taxing property owners, who, like Beekman, stood to benefit the most from a valuable asset next to their property.

With Beekman's forces mustered, the assembly passed another Jones Wood bill on April 2, 1853.[1] But in early June, the winds of change began to shift. The preference of the city's elite merchants, led by the Jones and Schermerhorn allies, and politicians including the Board of Aldermen moved toward "grudging acceptance" of the central site. The Common Council and the mayor all approved the central site by June 11, 1853, though oddly, the boundary of the park began four blocks north of Fifty-Ninth Street.[2] The bill then passed from City Hall back to the state capitol.

This highly influential bloc of city elite merchants and politicians convinced Whig Senator Edwin Morgan to switch his allegiance to Central Park. On June 21, 1853, Morgan introduced a bill to take the land from Fifty-Ninth Street to 106th Street. It stood to pass overwhelmingly. That same day Beekman, who saw the writing on the wall, proposed that the city's Common Council appoint a commission to choose the park, or perhaps both parks, following the next election in November. As June rolled into July, senate proceedings rehashed the debate of the special committee hearings two years earlier about the superiority of each site.[3] Anxious New Yorkers inundated the legislators with roughly twenty thousand petitions that favored one of the parks or none at all. Each side claimed the petitions of those opposing its park were fraudulent. The pro-Jones Wood alliance cited one pro-Central Park document in which 1,100 petitioners' names were entered with the same handwriting.[4]

By July 21, the last day of the legislative session, the fate of the park came down to a decision by that evening, lest the subject of a park for New York City be tabled until the next assembly. When the votes were cast before the dinner break, Central Park won overwhelmingly. The Jones Wood park was defeated. But a glitch in the system, some kind of constitutional technicality, called for another vote after dinner. And while no one was watching, Beekman snuck in an amendment that called for the city-appointed Commissioners of Estimate and Assessment to also include Jones Wood in their surveys. So in the end, the city went from a 150-acre park to a 750-acre park to a 900-acre park.[5]

But as we all know, New York wound up with only one park. The Schermerhorn family did not give up the fight for their property. In December, they had their second day in court before Judge James I. Roosevelt, the great uncle of future governor and president Teddy Roosevelt. The judge excoriated Beekman and his wealthy supporters in the Nineteenth Ward for their "private act" to benefit financially at the expense of the poorest citizens of the Fifth

16.1 Although Fernando Wood was arguably the most corrupt mayor in New York City's history, his one redeeming act was to veto a reduction of Central Park that would have had the park start at Seventy-Second Street rather than Fifty-Ninth Street and have lopped off eight hundred feet on either side, at Fifth Avenue and Eighth Avenue. This portrait by Charles Loring Elliott was painted in 1857, when he was both the mayor and the park commissioner.

Source: Charles Loring Elliott, *Fernando Wood*. Photograph by Glenn Castellano. Collection of the Public Design Commission of the City of New York.

Ward, and sent the potentially unconstitutional law back to the state and city legislatures. On April 11, 1854, the Albany lawmakers repealed the Jones Wood portion, just shy of a decade since Bryant had published his original call for a park.[6]

The loss of Jones Wood's acreage was a successful reduction of parkland, but it wasn't the only attempt. In the winter of 1854–55, an economic downturn caused many to question the need for such a large park, and in March the Board of Aldermen voted to remove the lower twelve blocks, begin the park on Seventy-Second Street, and chop off four hundred feet on the Fifth and Eighth Avenue sides of Central Park.

But Mayor Fernando Wood, who had won election in December, intervened. The wealthy Quaker had risen to power in late 1854 when many New Yorkers were desperate to end the dishonesty of the former administration. Wood ran on a reform platform, vowing to bring honesty back to the city government and improve the quality of life for his immigrant base. But in reality, he had attained his candidacy through a clandestine endorsement by the Know-Nothing Party, an affront to his foreign-born supporters, and squeezed into City Hall by winning only 33.6 percent of the votes. On the surface, it was noted, Wood had "changed the political game, but not its rules."[7]

In his entire notorious career—which included his effort to have New York secede from the Union during the Civil War—he did one good deed. His redeeming act came on March 23, when he vetoed the aldermen's plan to diminish Central Park. He considered the park an "intelligent, philanthropic and patriotic public enterprise" that would benefit future generations.[8] He was also a savvy politician, and he knew that more land meant more jobs for his working-class supporters. It has been suggested that he saved the park in order to ensure lining his pockets with bribes from future contractors.[9]

While the policing was in full force, the Commissioners of Estimate and Assessment had begun their work.

THE ESTIMATE AND ASSESSMENT PROCESS

The next step toward legalization of the park by the city was to assess the value of more than 7,500 lots and more than three hundred structures in planned Central Park land. The surveyors also had to assess 34,000 lots stretching from Thirty-Fourth Street to 120th Street and from Eleventh (now West End Avenue) to Second Avenue, whose owners would benefit from the park. In November 1853, corporation counsel Robert Dillon applied to the New York State Supreme Court to appoint five Commissioners of Estimate and Assessment. They in turn hired four surveyors, Gardener Sage, John Serrell, Roswell Graves, and Francis Nicholson, who took over two years to complete the exhaustive task.[10]

The long and arduous evaluation process made New Yorkers cranky and impatient. Their frustration can be summed up in this succinct plaint from the *Evening Post*, "THE CENTRAL PARK COMMISSIONERS—WHO ARE THEY? —WHAT ARE THEY? —WHERE ARE THEY? —Gentlemen: please inform a pent-up citizen what are the duties of the Central Park Commissioners—what is their pay, and, if *possible*, what they are about, and oblige," signed "A Father of Seven Young Children."[11] The assessments were executed in three different stages. First, the surveyors handwrote estimated values of the structures on preprinted templates that indicated the block and lot numbers and the type and size of the various buildings. Estimates fluctuated wildly from building to building, and without any photos or drawings of the houses, we cannot justify any individual appraisal. The size, age, and condition of a building—whether a piggery, a barn, or a three-story home—most likely accounted for the wide range of appraisals.

Most of the approximately three hundred structures in the prepark were wooden houses from one to three stories tall. There were also about a hundred shanties and an untold number of sheds, barns, pens, stables, and more primitive structures that went undocumented, as the city did not plan to compensate any squatters.

The size and placement of each structure from the surveyor's estimates were updated and transferred to the final bound book of condemnation maps, now in the collection of the Municipal Archives, and the names of the landowners and renters were added. In some instances, the names of the owners and lessees differ from those on the cadastral maps in the New-York Historical Society, as land and residences during this two-year time period were being transferred frequently.[12] Sales were at an all-time high, and it was also common for renters to move every May 1. Many of the lots were labeled "Unknown," due to financial and title issues and poor recordkeeping.

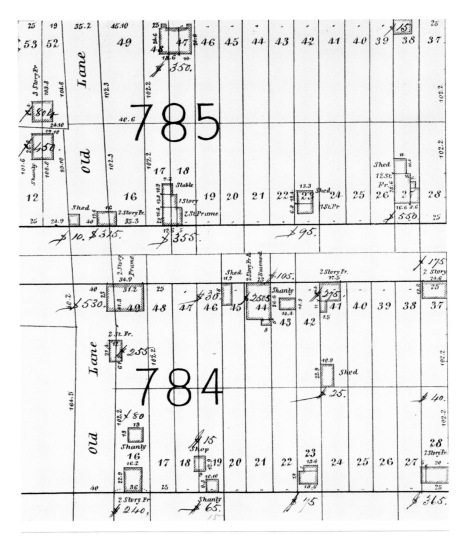

16.2 A page from the assessment report for structures within Seneca Village. It took from 1853 to 1855 to complete the surveys. The handwritten value was written onto printed templates that noted the type of structure and its dimensions. The value of the land was not indicated on these sheets.

Source: Structure assessment, blocks 783-785, Central Park Releases, New York City Municipal Archives.

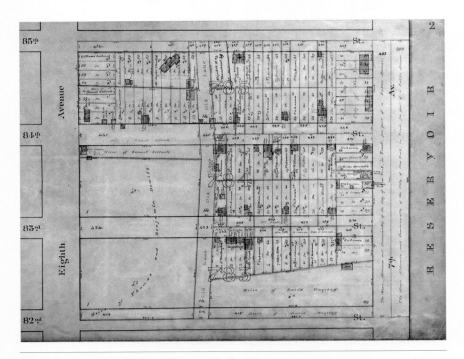

16.3 This condemnation map for three blocks in Seneca Village is one in a volume of forty bound maps, most of which include the names of the landowners or residents and the placement and size of their structures. In that time, ownership and rentals were constantly changing, but the maps offer some of the most authoritative visual documentation of the prepark populations.

Source: Condemnation Map. New York City Municipal Archives.

The surveyors Roswell Graves and Francis Nicholson executed exquisitely detailed, if somewhat fanciful ink drawings. The plans noted rock outcrops, placement of glacial erratics, swampland, elevations, and structures laid over block and lot numbers. Consider their topographic interpretation of Seneca Village. We can see rock outcrops—Summit Rock on the corner of Eighty-Third Street—and the placement of the homes in relation to these features. The homes of William Pease were unique in the village because he placed each of his houses on a high, flat outcrop, whereas all others are level with the ground. The rocks on what would become Eighty-Third Street are examples of features that would have required blasting if the street were to be opened.

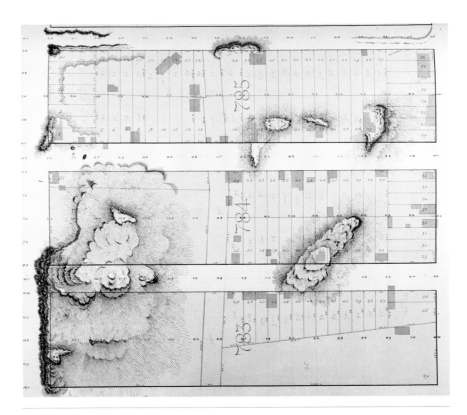

16.4 Surveyors Roswell Graves and Francis Nicholson combined the topographic features and structures for their 1855 prepark maps, here three blocks of Seneca Village, the prepark's most densely populated area

Source: Roswell Graves and Francis Nicholson, *Topographical Maps &c, In the Matter of Opening Central Park*, New York, July 1855. Commissioners of Estimate and Assessment and R. J. Dillon, counsel to the corporation, Municipal Archives. File No. 83.2 Accession No. 1653. New York City Municipal Archives.

THE PETITIONERS

The 1853 act charging the Commissioners of Estimate and Assessment with the authority to begin their process also stipulated that thirty days before the report was to go to the Supreme Court, the commissioners would present "the true copy or transcript" to the city's street commissioner, at which time it was to be publicized by advertisements in "at least two" local newspapers and posted in the street commissioner's office for inspection. The act further demanded that from the day the report was presented to the court, those with objections had twenty days to put their complaints in writing. These objections would then be reconsidered and "in case the same shall appear to them to require correction, but not otherwise, they shall and may correct the same accordingly."[13]

Among the many treasures in the New York County Court Division of Old Records are the seven bound volumes that include the petitions from dissatisfied landowners. For the most part, the petitioners protested what they considered low-ball offers from the commissioners. If, as the law stipulated, in some cases the commissioners were to reassess after receiving petitioners' objections, there is no record of those revaluations having been executed. And even if the estimates were undervalued and cause for a reassessment, the total cost for the parkland had already tripled from the original proposal of $1.5 million. Because of this increase, citizens were already beginning to question the need for such an expensive park. The city held fast to the limit of five million dollars allocated to buy the land. No additional funds would be forthcoming. The law also had a built-in inequity. We know that many of the landowners, particularly those in Seneca Village and foreign-born landowners, were either illiterate or did not read English, so the advertisements in newspapers may have been inaccessible to them.

Chief among the protestors was Harlem speculator Archibald Watt, in lieu of his stepdaughter Mary G. Pinkney, who wrote pages upon pages of petitions. They all came down to the same angry response: The creation of the park interfered with his jealously guarded money-making "adventure."[14]

Right behind Watt was Gouverneur Morris Wilkins, Valentine Nutter's grandson, who, like Watt, was horrified that the park would shortchange much of the land his grandfather had wheedled away from the Kortright heirs. Wilkins employed a common legal argument to oppose the commissioners: that the right of eminent domain was "too serious a matter to extend to *pleasure grounds*."[15]

Most petitions came from middle-class investors or speculators, whose assessments were far below the overinflated purchase prices they had paid in 1852 auctions at the height of the boom for the common lands. The feverish scramble to buy up property before it was seized for the park had many buying land at three or four times its market value. But the balloon popped, and now they faced sobering property estimates from the city commissioners. Many petitions claimed that they had been offered far more money for their property than the city was now offering them. Some brought in experts like builders and real estate agents or neighbors, who "verified" that the land was worth more. A builder named Joshua

M. Cooper, for example, wrote in support of William Mathew, trustee and sexton of the African Union Church, whose house and lot on Eighty-Fourth Street and Seventh Avenue he valued at $5,000 rather than the $1,500 that the city had offered.[16] Like most landowners, they based their estimate in 1855 on the overinflated, unrealistic prices of 1852 rather than the 1855 market values.

Many humbler middle- or working-class buyers in the 1852 auctions did not even know that their newly acquired lots were slated to become a park. These were not speculators but rather homeowners. They bid on average for between two and four lots so they might build a house and live there. Among them were leather dresser Benjamin Beaman, ropemaker Abraham V. Barbarie, and the countless gardeners throughout the prepark's nearly eight hundred acres. Others left out of the negotiations altogether were those, such as Gordon L. Ford of Ravenswood, Queens, who had leased lots for as long as thirty years. The majority of his leases, written between the years 1851 and 1854, were located in the future Reservoir, which had been chosen as a water body to be built *before* he leased the property from the city.[17]

When the Commissioners of Estimate and Assessment completed their report in July 1855, the next step in the legal process was to hold a hearing for petitioners and have the report approved by a Supreme Court judge. Because the taxpaying public were aghast at the five-million-dollar price tag for the park, many questioned the need for a park at all. Its legalization had become a political hot potato, and no Supreme Court district judge would agree to sit in approval of the commissioners' report. Dejected Central Park promoter, corporation counsel Robert J. Dillon, remarked that success with a hostile court was impossible: "The proceedings will be a farce."[18] But what seemed like a serious problem to Dillon was no problem at all to his most outrageous colleague, Daniel E. Sickles.

"THE FOUNDER OF CENTRAL PARK"

Though the notorious General Daniel E. Sickles appears often in accounts of nineteenth-century America, he is not a figure one usually associates with the history of the park. Yet, according to his eighteen-page undated manuscript in the Library of Congress, he considered himself to be "The Founder of Central Park."[19]

In 1852, a year before he turned his attention to the park, Sickles robbed a U.S. post office. Seven years later, while serving in the House of Representatives, Sickles

16.5 State senator Daniel E. Sickles, later a U.S. Congressman, helped to legalize Central
Park through many devious political maneuvers.

murdered the U.S. Attorney for the District of Columbia, a man named Philip Barton Key II. Key was the son of Francis Scott Key, the poet who wrote "The Star-Spangled Banner." The year before, Sickles's wife Teresa had begun an affair with Key. When Sickles caught his wife's lover signaling to her from outside the family home in Lafayette Square, he ran outside and shot Key several times with a pistol, killing him. Sickles was eventually acquitted of the murder on the grounds of temporary insanity—the first successful use of such a defense in American history.

A charismatic charmer, the dashing Sickles could comfortably schmooze with the movers of the city's upper crust as easily as he could with the shakers of its seamy underworld. In 1847, at age twenty-eight, he was elected to the New York State Assembly, where he made several key relationships that would benefit his future Central Park endeavors. He had an unrelenting devotion to his friends and stopped at nothing—even if it required breaking the law—to give them the boost they needed. So, when he learned through the grapevine that the campaign of his friend Robert J. Dillon for corporation counsel of the City of New York was in trouble, Sickles charged ahead without a second thought.

In 1852, Robert Dillon—the younger son of Gregory Dillon, the founder of the Emigrant Aid Society and Emigrant Savings Bank—was running on the Democratic ticket against Whig candidate Nelson Waterbury to be New York City's next chief attorney. Waterbury's supporters had stuffed anti-Dillon flyers into envelopes addressed to every voter on the electoral rolls. They were set to be mailed the next day.

When Sickles learned of these, he summoned his close associate, Captain Isaiah Rynders, the infamous leader of New York's underworld Empire Club gang, which most New Yorkers today remember as the Dead Rabbits. Rynders was particularly adept at interfering in elections. His rise to fame came during the presidential election of 1844, when he threatened physical violence to Whig voters as they arrived at the polls unless they promised to cast their vote for Democrat candidate James K. Polk. The success of Rynders's intimidation resulted in Polk's extremely narrow victory. It was the New York electoral votes that handed him the presidency.[20]

Sickles knew Rynders was the right man for the job, and on the night of October 30, 1852, "a half-dozen reckless ruffians"—Sickles and Rynders included—seized mail bags holding almost 40,000 circulars. "Sickles and another of the party seized Mr. Harriot [the proprietor], and a scuffle ensued, in which Harriot was choked and bruised in a brutal manner . . . Having accomplished this act of robbery, Sickles made all haste to Tammany Hall, and there boasted of his villainy."[21]

Sickles was prosecuted by the federal government for robbing the U.S. mail; nonetheless, his defense attorney was able to delay his appearance in federal court indefinitely. Not only did Sickles ultimately get off scot free, but Robert Dillon won the election, and as corporation counsel, he appointed Sickles to the post of corporation attorney; together they fought to legalize Central Park. With more than a little irony, three years after the robbery, Dillon's opponent, Nelson Waterbury, was appointed as the assistant to the postmaster of New York City.[22]

Given his devious nature, the following account from Sickles's autobiography about getting the report of the Commissioners of Estimate and Assessment approved seems quite plausible and smacks of Sickles's particular brand of both drive and deception.

State Senator Sickles knew the court calendars in the city were seriously overloaded, so he drafted a petition to Governor Horatio Seymour asking him to appoint an additional judge from another district until the backlog of cases was reduced. Sickles found around forty members of the bar to sign his petition and presented it to the governor. The governor responded favorably but cautioned Sickles that his "task will be a difficult one."[23]

In reality, Sickles cared only about finding a judge to confirm the commissioners' report, and he had just the judge in mind: Ira Harris of the Albany district court. When Sickles charged up to the Harris home in Albany, he learned from his wife, Pauline, that the judge was hearing a case out of town. This gave Sickles the perfect opportunity to charm Mrs. Harris and their three daughters, Clara, Louisa, and Amanda, plying them with "an alluring picture of a possible round of social pleasures" that awaited them in the city.[24] He convinced Mrs. Harris to pen a note to her husband, suggesting that a taste of cosmopolitan New York would be an exciting prospect for the family.

When he finally chased the judge down in a Monticello courtroom, Sickles described the New York City backlog to him, and said that "it was the unanimous wish of our bar that he would come to our relief." A later source of this story suggested that Sickles also dangled the promise of a governorship or senate seat in front of Harris, hinting that a move to the city would strengthen his chances with city politicians for a future nomination. Harris agreed.[25]

Shortly after Harris moved his family to New York, notice was given that a special term of the Supreme Court would sit for the confirmation of the report. On the day of the hearing, politicians, press, and the public all assumed that the case would be heard by antipark judge James Roosevelt, which guaranteed the report would be squashed. But Sickles had the governor and corporation counsel Robert Dillon, who would argue for report's confirmation, on his side. Sickles had outwitted the park opponents. He fancied he could already see Roosevelt's blade, "freshly sharpened, ready to cut out the vitals of the Central Park report and redden the carpets of the sanctuary with the blood of the victim." But then it was announced that Harris, not Roosevelt, would hear the case, and pandemonium broke out. After a month of Harris hearing the lawyers argue for the landowners, the exhausted Dillon closed the proceedings by saying to Harris, "Sign this report, and old age and prattling youth will thank you."[26]

While Judge Harris sat in court hearing arguments from lawyers representing the landowners, his wife and daughters were being showered with invitations. According to Sickles, the best houses in the city were after them "to attend breakfast parties, luncheon parties, dinner parties, receptions, theaters, balls and every sort of entertainment that could attract rural visitors." But when the judge learned that these solicitations came from opponents hoping to sway him on the matter of the park, he forbade his family to attend.[27]

Despite the many valid claims that the landowners were not receiving just compensation for their property, Judge Harris approved the report. He reasoned that only one in forty or less than three percent of the had landowners filed a petition, and for him that was satisfactory evidence that the commissioners had successfully calculated "the true value of so vast an amount of property." In his opinion, the estimates and assessments were professionally ascertained, and given the limits of his jurisdiction, he could only rule on the "judicious and equitable" nature of the report.[28]

After Harris sanctioned the awards, Central Park officially became a New York City park, and the Common Council proceeded to pay the damages awarded to the owners. Harris eventually realized that the excuse of an overloaded calendar had been a ruse by Sickles to secure a sympathetic judge, and he said he never would have come to New York had he known the truth.[29] In the end, Harris became a U.S. senator from New York, quite possibly due to the political connections he made in New York City during the hearing. He and Sickles were frequent visitors to the Lincoln White House. Lincoln once said that he looked underneath his bed each night to check if Senator Harris was there to seek another patronage favor.[30] Harris's daughter Clara and her fiancée Henry Rathbone were the Lincolns' guests in the presidential box at the Ford Theater the night of the president's assassination.[31]

16.6 New York State Supreme Court Judge Ira Harris moved to the city temporarily to officiate over the legalization of Central Park. He conducted the hearing of the protests of the petitioners who, for the most part, wanted a higher award for their properties. Harris would later become a U.S. senator, having made important political connections during the monthlong hearing.

Source: Hon. Ira Harris. [Between 1855 and 1865] Photograph. Library of Congress, https://www.loc.gov /item/2017896721/.

THE AWARDS

The commissioners surveyed and assessed the lots of the prepark as if they were intended to be incorporated into the grid system, not as a park.[32] The surveyors offered no written criteria for their decisions with regard to the lots, although those facing the four avenues and those at intersections were commonly assessed at higher values. The only clue we have is a letter from James J. Ruggles, clerk to the commissioners, back in November 1853 inviting surveyor Roswell Graves to discuss the process of assessment with them the following day, and to "furnish the maps including the necessary abstracts per foot & on an average for each block."[33]

The most valued properties were those closest to the developed city and along the four avenues, with corner lots garnering the highest awards. Lots along Fifth Avenue received the most money, followed by those lots along Sixth Avenue. Property on Eighth Avenue was generally given a higher value than comparable lots along Seventh Avenue. Midblock properties were valued less than those along the avenues, though on occasion and throughout the prepark, some lots were outliers and received awards inconsistent with their locations.[34]

The southern lots were the most prized properties, even though the area featured some of the most rocky and low-lying swampland. Yet in 1855, location trumped topography in determining a lot's financial destiny. On Eighth Avenue at the site of today's *Maine* monument, Ralph Marsh received $9,000 for his corner four lots. Similarly, the four lots on the northwest corner between Fifty-Ninth and Sixtieth Street and Fifth Avenue, today's Grand Army Plaza, wealthy sugar merchant Nicholas G. Kortright was awarded more than $9,100. He was a descendant of Lawrence Kortright Jr., who deeded his land to Sarah Nutter. He was also the descendant of Henry and Sarah Billopp Seaman, who acquired their common lands property in 1803, which also included lots that now encompass the beach volleyball courts and part of the Sheep Meadow and the Ramble shoreline. In total, Kortright received over $100,000 for his 109 lots.

Topographic features seem to have had little effect on the awards. In today's Dene landscape, on Fifth Avenue between Sixty-Seventh Street and Sixty-Eighth Street, the corner lots still commanded awards above $2,000, despite the massive rock outcrop that today features the Dene Summerhouse.[35] The properties that encompass today's Umpire Rock, which looms over Heckscher Ballfield, were also valued no differently than if the rock did not exist.[36]

When we get to the heart of James Amory's highly cultivated gardens, areas that today are the East Green and Rumsey Playfield and surrounding landscapes,

TABLE 16.1 Central Park Lot Values

Streets	8th Ave–7th Ave			7th Ave–6th Ave			6th Ave–5th Ave		
	Avenue Lots	Mid-block Lots	Avenue Lots	Avenue Lots	Mid-block Lots	Avenue Lots	Avenue Lots	Mid-block Lots	Avenue Lots
105th St–106th St		$373		$383	$261	$383			
104th St–105th St	$503	$320	$510	$328	$277	$416			
103rd St–104th St				$675	$543	$411			
102nd St–103rd St		$370			$304				
101st St–102nd St		$460			No Data				
100th St–101st St	$578	$361		$470	$374				
99th St–100th St		$408		$503	$369	$445			
98th St–99th St	No Data	$407	$650	$568	$340	No Data			
97th St–98th St		$398	No Data	$608	$385	No Data			
96th St–97th St					$438	No Data			
95th St–96th St		No Data			/$370/$458				
94th St–95th St	/$378/							No Data	
93rd St–94th St	/$412/				$860/$275/				
92nd St–93rd St		$510		$450/$357/	$330	$429			
91st St–92nd St					/$385/				
90th St–91st St				$580					
89th St–90th St	No Data				No Data				
88th St–89th St		$420							
87th St–88th St		/$438/							
86th St–87th St		/$515/			No Data				
85th St–86th St		$748 on 86 St. / $530 on 85 St.	$1,312		Receiving Reservoir				
84th St–85th St	$669	$507							
83rd St–84th St		/$530	$704						
82nd St–83rd St									
81st St–82nd St		No Data							
80th St–81st St									

Block									
78th St–79th St			$1,160		$447	$980	$947	$572	
77th St–78th St								$756	
76th St–77th St		No Data							
75th St–76th St					**$565**		$1,030	$623	$1,520
74th St–75th St		No Data			$739/$473/$1,058				No Data
73rd St–74th St	$909	$768					$888	$619	No Data
72nd St–73rd St	$1,164	$607	$879		$496	$1,131		$1,251	
71st St–72nd St	$1,142	$736	$716		$681	$1,138			
70th St–71st St	$1,104	$699	$1,010		$594	$1,203	$1,161	$761	$1,685
69th St–70th St	$1,038	$709	$734		$589	$1,201	$1,190	$762	$1,647
68th St–69th St	$1,156	$692	$773		$583	$1,125	$1,110	$762	$1,560
67th St–68th St	$1,197	$668	$799		$614	$1,219	$1,185	$726	$1,758
66th St–67th St	$976	**$700**	$893		$488	$1,176		$728	$1,785
65th St–66th St		**$848**	$991		$639	$1,220	$1,200	$605	$1,815
64th St–65th St		**$921**	$1,053		$662	State of New York			
63rd St–64th St			State of New York						
62nd St–63rd St	$1,823	$937	$1,245	$1,229	$718	$1,318	$1,172		$2,048
61st St–62nd St		$921	$1,213	$1,242	$759	$1,104		$826	
60th St–61st St		**$1,123**			**$959**		$1,937	$891	$2,197
59th St–60th St		$943	$1,485	$1,360	$900			$1,022	

Each block was laid out by the city in three zones: lots facing the eastern avenue, midblock lots, and lots facing the western avenue. Each zone is assigned a mean value per lot. The amounts in bold are for entire blocks purchased from a single owner. The blank cells represent awards for avenue lots and mid-block lots combined, the respective value of which is impossible to determine. Location appears to be the most important consideration in determining awards. Lots farther south and lots fronting an avenue or along Eighty-Sixth were worth more. Avenue lots between Fifth and Sixth Avenue were slightly longer, contributing to their value. More detailed data can be found on www.beforecentralpark.com.

Source: Compilation by Andrew Fox with the assistance of Maya Mau. Based on Releases in the Municipal Archives, City of New York

the pattern does not change: corner lots on Fifth and Sixth Avenues receive more than those midblock, suggesting that improved land did not receive a higher award than unimproved lots. Again, a lot's relationship to both the lower city and the avenues seems to have been the overriding benchmark.

Compensation for the lands taken in 1863 from 106th Street to 110th Street will be discussed in the last chapter, but it should come as no surprise that the value of those twelve blocks skyrocketed from the awards given seven years earlier for the park's lower terrain.

THE BOTTOM LINE

Across the fifteen hundred awards for Central Park land, let's revisit a few of those landowners—original buyers or their heirs—met in this study to see how they fared financially. From the compilation of the outcomes, one generalization can be made. With the exception of some landowners who paid inflated prices in 1852, most people made a profit, and a handsome one at that. Those who held a sizable amount of land for a significant length of time made the steepest profits.[37]

When Harlem landowner Archibald Watt was saved from bankruptcy by his shrewd stepdaughter, Mary G. Pinkney, she profited greatly from the sale of their property and received the highest personal award for her real estate. She received $77,545 for her portion of her land, which included parts of the North and East Meadows and the Reservoir. Her name also appears in the city's list of "Central Park Awards Unsettled, January 1, 1858," for $213,660. It is unclear if that is in addition to the first amount. If so, she would have received a total of $291,205.[38] She would make even more when the City bought the land above 106th Street.

As expected, the Corporation of the City of New York, which had been granted the common lands by royal charter in 1686, still retained many lots that were held in reserve for future profit. Many had been rented earlier by James Amory, David Wagstaff, or Sarah Billopp Seaman. The other chunk of city-owned property was the common land adjacent to the Harlem Commons, which today lies within the Reservoir. In total, the city received the highest award of almost $350,000, which it allocated to the Sinking Fund in order to, ironically, pay off the debt, much of which had been incurred from the building of the Croton Aqueduct system.[39]

The heirs of James Amory, David Wagstaff, and Benjamin Romaine, all long-term owners of the common lands, saw tremendous profit.

David Wagstaff, who owned not only his former common lands asparagus farm but also the west side woodland he had purchased from Rebecca Apthorp, received in total almost $125,000. The Dillon family, including Robert J. Dillon, the corporation counsel and Central Park commissioner, was heir to Benjamin Romaine and received almost $50,000 for their grandfather's common land lots, which encompassed a portion of today's running track, waters of the Reservoir, and Rhododendron Mile.

Mary Ann Reckless, the widow of John Patrick, who had purchased his common lands lots from the corporation in 1817 for $133, was one of the park's greatest losers, but she was not the only loser in the story. As you recall, in 1852 she was duped by her so-called friend and advisor John Bunting into believing that $1,000 total was the fair market value for her sixty-four lots in the Ramble. He grossly undervalued her property at the height of the real estate boom before the coming of the park. When she realized she was the victim of a con, she went to court but lost. The decision favored Bunting, who then sold the lots to Amasa S. Foster of Brooklyn three years later for a whopping $64,000—sixty-four times the price he had paid to Reckless and, without doubt, one of the largest profits for any single block of the park.[40]

That same day in 1855, Patrick's grandnephew William Ralston Shedden claimed that *he* was the rightful owner of the Patrick property and sued Reckless, Bunting, Foster, and the City of New York for the return of his "stolen" inheritance. Despite the litigation and devious behavior of all parties, with the exception of Mary Ann Reckless, the City of New York awarded Amasa S. Foster roughly half the inflated amount Foster had paid Bunting. For Bunting, who probably held a mortgage, and for Foster himself, it turned out to be quite a reckless scheme.[41]

Sarah Somarindyck and her husband, John Talman, were members of the family whose father, John Somarindyck, had purchased the forfeited "Little Bloomingdale" land of loyalist Oliver Delancey in 1785. Most of the family had sold off their parkland piecemeal, but the Talmans received nearly $205,000 for their southwest area blocks from Sixty-First Street to Seventy-Fifth Street. Their' profit was immeasurable, as Sarah Somarindyck had inherited her land.

The family of John C. Vanden Heuvel, Charles Ward Apthorp's son-in-law, was among the oldest families to hold on to their century-held land, which stretched from today's Wild West playground at West Ninety-Third Street to the Rudin Playground at West Ninety-Seventh Street and along the perimeter of the Reservoir. The outraged Thomas Gibbes Jr., married to Susan Annette Vanden Heuvel, petitioned the Commissioners of Central Park, claiming unfair assessment of his land. By 1856, Gibbes owned the largest share of the Apthorp prepark property through exchanges with family members. Like many other wealthy investors, Gibbes wanted to hold on to his real estate until its value had increased indefinitely. In his petition, he wrote to the commissioners, "I sincerely hope for my interest that the entire project for a Park may yet be abandoned."[42]

All told, the Apthorp heirs—the Gibbes, Hamiltons, and Vanden Heuvel great grandchildren—netted nearly $70,000, today worth approximately $212 million. Gibbes alone received over $40,000, worth more than $39 million in today's currency.[43]

In the nearby future Reservoir, the congregations of Bikur Cholim and B'nai Israel considered the disturbance of the burials in their cemeteries unspeakably sacrilegious and were less concerned about profiting from their awards. The commissioners did compensate them for their property and for the reinterment costs. B'nai Israel was awarded $825, a 106 percent profit, and an additional $1,138 for the removal of 207 bodies. Bikur Cholim received $1,885 for their three lots, a 371 percent profit, and an additional $660 for the removal and reinterment of 120 bodies.[44]

The only corporation still operating today that once owned land in the park is Tiffany & Co. The company's founder, Charles Tiffany, and his business partners, John B. Young and Jabez L. Ellis, purchased three lots for $900 in 1851, the same year that the illustrious jewelers introduced the iconic "Tiffany blue" box. The price of a "superior" gold watch was the same as for the company's three lots.[45] By 1856 when they received their award of $1,170, a 30 percent profit on their investment, it was less than even the less costly of their luxurious items.

With slight exception, this study does not trace the former renters. The renters scattered to other neighborhoods or other boroughs in their annual quest for a home. They are difficult to follow, unlike the landowners, most of whom had wealth even before their awards. Although the German immigrants living on the future North and East Meadows did not own their land they farmed—that award would go to Mary G. Pinkney—they did receive awards for their structural improvements, totaling $2,586.[46] Finding land for these gardeners would have been much more difficult, particularly if language was a problem. Land anywhere near the new park would be snapped up by speculators. The gardeners would be forced to move to the outer boroughs or New Jersey to find land to cultivate.

Many of the Irish piggeries moved south and west of Fifty-Ninth Street, where the press continued to disparage them: "The piggeries shanties in which the pigs and the Patricks lie down together while little ones of Celtic and swinish origin lie around miscellaneously, with billy goats" and so on.[47]

Thanks to correspondence from a descendant of piggery owner John Russell, we can trace the movement of one farming family. Russell had immigrated from Ireland in 1842, when he was nineteen years old. So in the 1855 census he would have been around thirty-two. His wife, Margaret Mary, was thirty-five. She was also born in Ireland, and their five children were born in New York. They rented a one-story house, labeled as a shanty on the 1855 condemnation map, and three lots with sheds located between Sixty-Second Street and Sixty-Third Street between Seventh Avenue and Eighth Avenue. After leaving the prepark, they moved with their hogs to the west Fifties in 1857 until they were the victims of the police's "hog raids" in August 1859 that demolished the piggeries to make way for real estate developers. Their pens were destroyed, and the Russell's hogs went to Brooklyn with his daughter and son-in-law. His son-in-law, whose name we do not know, was another farmer in the park piggery community around Sixty-Fifth Street, and he must have also been victims of the raids. The Russells moved to a one-story wood-frame house on Eighth Avenue between Sixty-Sixth and Sixty-Seventh Street, across from today's Tavern on the Green restaurant, where the next three generations of Russells lived until the late 1880s.[48]

Some landowners with smaller awards and smaller lots are traceable from wills in the Probate records. Their dying wishes stand as testament to their financial success and an increased quality of life. In his 1885 will, for example, William Menck, one of the owners of the bone-boiling works, left the confines of Central Park but moved nearby to West Fifty-Sixth Street. Among other investments both real and personal, he left his wife, Jane, and their daughter, Julia, securities worth $25,000.[49]

SENECA VILLAGE AWARDS

The eastern edge of Seneca Village ran along Seventh Avenue, properties along which most often received lower awards than those on the other three avenues. Yet, on occasion, those properties did garner higher awards regardless of the owners' race or economic standing. Black owner William Mathew's corner lot received $1,115—he received an additional $120 for his house—a large amount for Seventh Avenue and Eighty-Fourth Street. The receiving reservoir lay across the avenue from Mathew's property and may have offered an expansive water view, perhaps the reason for his higher award. In comparison, the other property owners on that block along Seventh Avenue, African Americans Isaac Pernell and Henry Garnett, received $700 and $650 respectively for their neighboring lots. White landowner Catherine Hennion also received $650 for her lot, while white

Know all Men by these Presents, WHEREAS:

in and by the Report of the Commissioners of Estimate and Assessment, duly confirmed by the Supreme Court, on the fifth day of February, in the year one thousand eight hundred and fifty-six, in a certain proceeding, entitled "In the matter of the Opening and laying out a Public Place, between 59th and 106th Streets and the Fifth and Eighth Avenues, in the City of New-York," an award for taking certain lands, to wit:

| DESCRIPTION. | WARD Nos. | | COMMISSIONERS' NUMBER. |
	BLOCK.	LOT.	
House Lot	786	37	

was made to *Elizabeth McCollin*
in the sum of *Fifteen Hundred and fifty*

Dollars,

as by reference to said Report and the Maps of said Commissioners, on file in the office of the Clerk of the city and county of New-York, will more fully appear.

Now Therefore, know ye, That I, *Elizabeth McCollin* the person named in and entitled to the said award, do hereby acknowledge to have received from the Mayor, Aldermen, and Commonalty of the city of New-York, the aforesaid sum of *Fifteen Hundred and*

fifty

Dollars,

in full payment and satisfaction of said award: And, in consideration thereof, I do hereby, for myself, my heirs, executors and administrators, grant and release unto the said the Mayor, Aldermen and Commonalty aforesaid, the said lots and parcels of land and all my right, title, and interest therein.

In Witness whereof, I have hereto set my hand and seal, this *Tenth* day of *June*, in the year one thousand eight hundred and fifty-six.

Sealed and delivered in the presence of

Wm van Hook

Elizabeth McCollin

16.7 The release from Elizabeth McCollin to the city of New York for her $1,550 award for her Central Park house and lot along Eighty-Sixth Street.

Source: Release of Elizbeth McCollin to the City of New York, Box 2870, New York City Municipal Archives.

real estate tycoon Archibald Lowery received on average roughly $700 for each of his three lots, one of which was a corner lot.

With the exception of the A.M.E. Zion Church, the awards to Seneca Village landowners for between one and six lots were significantly less than the holdings of the great landowning dynasties, who owned more land. Those who had purchased their lots from John Whitehead or his heirs made a large profit, minus the taxes and the cost of construction for any built structures. The percentage of their profits is for their land only and minus the award for their structures: the heirs of John Carter, 1566 percent; Elizabeth Harding McCollin, 1437 percent; Andrew Williams, 1375 percent; Sarah Wilson, heir of Cornelius Henry, 1187 percent; heirs of Diana Harding, 1122 percent; heirs of Nancy Morris, 987 percent; heirs of Joseph Marshall, 960 percent; William Pease, 941 percent; the Trustees of the A.M.E. Zion Church, 751 percent; heirs of Sarah Hunter, 312 percent.

Many later Seneca Village investors also made a profit: porter Simon Green bought his two lots on Eighty-Fifth Street for $700 in 1846 and received $1,280 for them in 1856, an 83 percent profit. He also had a house on his lot valued, which earned him rental income from Ada Thompson, who received $325 for the house she must have constructed on Green's property. In 1839, cooper James Hinson, a Seneca Village resident, purchased his two lots on Eighty-Fourth Street for $325; he was awarded $1,080, a 232 percent profit. After the death of James Moore in 1848, his executors sold Charles Mingo two adjacent lots for $600. The city awarded Mingo $1,250, a 108 percent profit, although he was not compensated for the house that had once been on his property but had probably burned down.[50] Christian Tietjen, who had been duped by Don Alonzo Cushman in 1852, received over $1,300 for each of his eight lots, a 61 percent increase over his four-year investment of $812 per lot.[51]

Albro Lyons's total real estate was worth $12,500. He received $1,080 for his two Seneca Village lots, and Peter Guignon received $1,455. He had a successful financial career after his second marriage and lived a financially comfortable life.[52] Elizabeth Gloucester began her legendary real estate career investing $100 in her single lot in Seneca Village, for which she received $460, an increase of 360 percent. Gloucester understood the value of investments. Without missing a beat, she used her award to buy a lot *near* Central Park between Madison and Fifth Avenues, Ninety-Eighth to Ninety-Ninth Street, knowing full well that the property would only increase in value because of its proximity to the park.[53]

In the late 1850s, it was reported that the wealthiest Blacks paid $1.4 million for the total value of their real estate and put $1.12 million into their savings account deposits. Some of them were most likely former Seneca Village landowners.[54] Seneca Village heirs Hannah S. Carter, widow of John Carter, and Huldah Green, widow of Simon Green, set up trust funds worth several thousands to manage the estates for the education and comfort of their most cherished loved ones. Simon Green had also purchased forty acres of land in upstate Hamilton County. The will of Elizabeth Harding McCollin may be the most touching, given our knowledge that as the daughter of Samuel Harding, she was born into an enslaved family. Elizabeth gave sizeable gifts to the Association for the Benefit of Colored Orphans, the Colored Home for the Aged and Indigent, and the Home Mission Society of the A.M.E. Church. She and her husband, Obadiah, had no children themselves, but they left several thousand dollars to Obadiah's Green relatives in Connecticut and one thousand dollars to Daniel Landin, who lost his mother at age two and was adopted by his grandparents Diana and Josiah Landin. Daniel must have meant more to Elizabeth than just the child of a Seneca Village neighbor. Elizabeth left the remaining money to her beloved Reverend Thomas McClure Peters of All Angels'. Her generous gesture belies the racist attitudes that were expressed in the writings of the minister and his son.[55]

Yet even though most prepark landowners accepted their awards, particularly when they made a generous profit, the reaction of the Seneca Village landowners would, at best, have been bittersweet. Yes, many short-term landowners made a profit that would enhance the quality of their lives materially, but for those long-standing families their emotional and spiritual connection to the community they had built could never be monetized. Some residents, like the children of Andrew Williams, Sarah Hunter, or Nancy Morris, had spent all or most of their entire lives in the community, and to them the loss must have been profound. And given all the inequities that Blacks experienced in every aspect of their lives, finding a new home and a new neighborhood that would promise the relative safety, security, and close-knit community that Seneca Village had been must have caused them anger, anguish and fear.[56] The villagers did not reassemble in another location.

After they received their award, Obadiah and Elizabeth McCollin moved nearby to the Nineteenth Ward, but the Landins and hundreds of other prepark landowners and renters remained while at the same time new families moved into Central Park as tenants of New York City under the watchful eye of the corrupt new Central Park Commission.[57]

chapter 17

The First Commission, 1855–1857

Once Judge Ira Harris sanctioned the report of the Commissioners of Assessment in February 1856, Central Park became a city park, and as such its governance fell under the jurisdiction of the city, though the legislature still had oversight and approval of appropriations. Not surprisingly, many people had their own idea of what that would mean: Robert Dillon, Daniel Sickles, Mayor Fernando Wood, the members of the Common Council, and the powers that be in Albany. Their tasks would include forming a board of commissioners, choosing a designer, funding and constructing the park, hiring police, managing the renters, and ultimately evicting them. That there was no money to pay for it all seemed to some a trifling detail.

Sometime after the Harris ruling, former corporation counsel Robert Dillon hatched a plan to prevent the corrupt Mayor Fernando Wood from taking the reins of power for the park that the conscientious attorney had so valiantly fought to legalize. Dillon wanted to confine the park's management to a board of commissioners made up of the city's literati and respected businessmen, people like Washington Irving, George Bancroft, William Cullen Bryant, and "others who had been to Europe and were competent to judge of such matters."[1]

Dillon's downfall was sharing his apolitical idea with Dan Sickles, who by January 1856 was a state senator. He introduced the idea in the Senate for a five-member commission headed by the mayor only days after Harris's confirmation. Sickles's bill for a commission passed, but only with an amendment that bypassed the mayor and his cronies and appointed five other commissioners.[2] With all the volleys back and forth between the Assembly and the Senate, the impatient Mayor Wood grew frustrated for the confirmation of Sickles's plan to install him as the chief commissioner.

The mayor also needed the approval of the city's Board of Aldermen. In the absence of state authority, he took matters into his own hands. As told by a *Herald* reporter, Wood approached Dillon to write a draft of his plan to put before the aldermen. "The Mayor received it, thanked the author, quietly drew his pen through Dillon's list of names, and substituted his own and that of Street Commissioner Joseph S. Taylor."[3] So when the first meeting of the new Central Park commission finally convened, its leadership was changed from a group of the city's most cultivated to two of its most corrupt.

Knowing he would still need the approval of New York's elite, Wood "gilded the pill" by appointing an advisory group composed of the very men that Dillon had envisioned as the actual commissioners.[4] The members of this bipartisan

---

17.1 Egbert Viele's *Map of Lands Included in The Central Park from a Topographical Survey* was initially an independent project. It depicts the prepark as it was in June 1855, showing homes, outbuildings, plantations, garden beds, rock outcrops, elevations, swamps, watercourses, roads, and paths.

Source: Egbert Viele, *Map of Lands Included in The Central Park from a Topographical Survey*, June 17, 1855. New York City Municipal Archives.

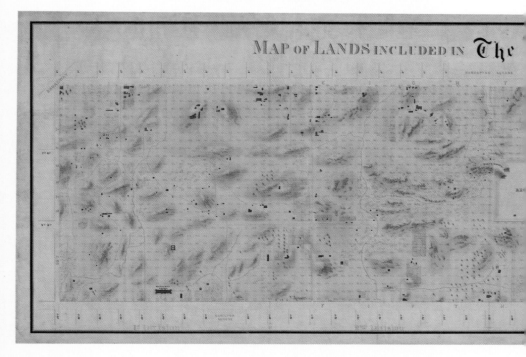

advisory group included the writer Washington Irving, who was elected president; the historian and statesman George Bancroft; Charles F. Briggs, the managing editor of *Putnam's Monthly*; Charles A. Dana, managing editor of the powerful Republican *New York Tribune*; William Cullen Bryant, editor of the *New York Evening Post* and the first to propose a large park for New York in 1844; and James E. Cooley, a former New York state senator and author of the special report of the majority committee that had first chosen Central Park over Jones Wood. Also on the board, and closer to Mayor Wood's heart, was real estate developer James Phelan, whom *The New York Times* identified as "the first man who made it a business to buy lots and sell them to builders, taking part payment and a lien on the property for the remainder."[5] Phelan owned fifty-seven lots from the former Amory property, a fact that eluded the *Herald* reporter and possibly everyone else.[6] Robert Dillon was invited to be on the committee, an obvious attempt to placate him after plagiarizing his idea. He declined.[7]

The group would soon realize, as a *Herald* reporter predicted, that their first—and only—responsibility was to be "ornamental appendages to the machine," and that if they asked questions or made trouble, "they would be shown the door."[8]

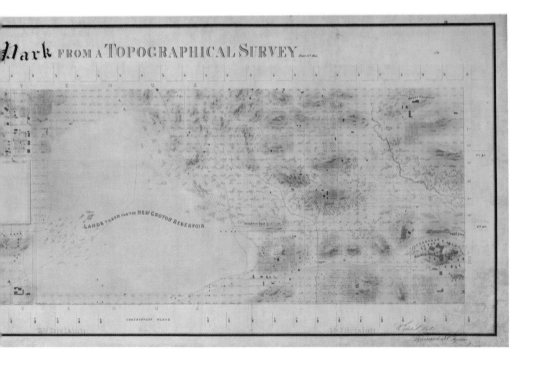

LIEUTENANT EGBERT VIELE

In 1854, while the four city-appointed surveyors roamed the lands to determine the value of nearly eight thousand lots for the Commissioners of Estimate and Assessment, Lieutenant Egbert Ludovicus Viele began his own unsolicited topographic survey.

History has not been kind to Egbert Viele, in part because he deserved it, but he also made significant contributions. He was born near Albany in Waterford, New York, and his father was a state senator. He graduated from the U.S. Military Academy at West Point as an engineer and spent his early adult life in the Mexican War. By the time of his resignation in 1853, he was a first lieutenant.[9] His first wife, socialite Teresa Griffin Viele, an early feminist, wrote *Following the Drum*—under the name "Mrs. Brigadier Gen. Egbert L. Vielé"—a vivid account of her life as an army wife on the Texas frontier. Their divorce in 1872 made national headlines. Each of them accused the other of adultery that also entailed issues of child custody. Their son, Francis Viélé-Griffin, became a famous French symbolist poet.[10] Despite his Knickerbocker heritage, Viele had a bad reputation in New York society for "poor manners, swearing, and insulting ladies."[11]

By 1855, Viele had set up shop on lower Broadway as a civil engineer. He was commuting from New Brighton, Staten Island, which was halfway between his day job conducting a statewide topographical survey for New Jersey and his office in Manhattan. He was also moonlighting in the future Central Park and waiting for the right moment and the right person to unveil his topographic plan.[12]

On February 4, 1856, one day before Judge Harris legalized Central Park, Taylor nominated Egbert Viele for a position as a city surveyor. The week following the Harris ruling, the Board of Aldermen—and undoubtedly the mayor—directed Taylor to furnish them with a detailed statement of "estimates, plans, and expenses for laying out and ornamenting the park" and authorized him to employ a surveyor to do that.[13] Taylor chose Viele, who had already been freely exhibiting his design for the park for six months by that time.[14]

The Board of Aldermen sanctioned Wood and Taylor as the two-man Central Park Commission on May 21, but three months earlier Taylor had unofficially received his orders to plan the park, and he had already hired Viele to do so. Now all Wood, Taylor, and Viele had to do was pretend that the selection process would be impartial, honorable, and democratic.

So it's no surprise that when the first board meeting convened to appoint a designer, only one contender showed up: Lieutenant Egbert Viele, with his twelve-foot-long topographic maps, park studies, and designs in tow. Not many noticed that his topographic survey was dated June 17, 1855, eight months before Judge Harris approved the commissioners' assessments, eleven months before Mayor Wood and Commissioner Taylor officially established themselves as park commissioners, and seven months before Viele himself was nominated for the

17.2 Lieutenant Egbert Viele, promoted to brigadier general during the Civil War, was the first designer of Central Park and made two significant contributions: the transverse roads and the shape of the new Reservoir.

Source: "Brig. Gen. Egbert L. Viele." The Miriam and Ira D. Wallach Division of Art, Prints and Photographs: Print Collection, The New York Public Library, New York Public Library Digital Collections, https://digitalcollections.nypl.org/items/510d47da-2293-a3d9-e040-e00a18064a99.

surveyor position.[15] Though we have his topographic survey, Viele's design plan for Central Park is lost to time. We know of it only from a slightly altered lithograph version printed in the 1857 *First Annual Report of the Improvement of the Central Park*, authored by Viele.[16]

VIELE'S PLAN

First and foremost, Egbert Viele was a competent sanitary engineer. He understood that before any park design could be implemented, it was necessary to remove the stagnant water that had created "a pestilential spot, where rank vegetation and miasmic odors taint every breath of air." The city had created a sewer system that, in his opinion, failed to address the deeper environmental problems. Viele proposed to protect the park's original watercourses by constructing a system of drainage that would empty the excess water into the East River.[17] It's hard to overstate the hazards of stagnant water. In October 1857, a report to the board of commissioners noted that nearly one-seventh of the laborers had suffered from intermittent fever while working the land, "unquestionably to be found in the tenacious and infiltrating condition of the soil."[18]

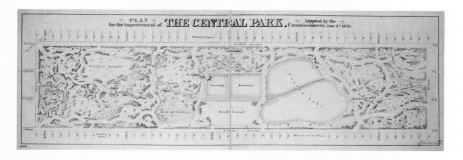

17.3 Egbert Viele's *Plan for the improvement of the Central Park* accepted the limitations of the existing topography as his guide and emphasized outward views from high points in the landscape. His design, like other entries to the design competition, relegated the park to a series of small spaces and little variety due, in part, to the requisite transverse roads on grade with parkland. Viele considered the Circuit Drive the most important feature of his plan, with all other features radiating from it.

Source: Lionel Pincus and Princess Firyal Map Division, The New York Public Library, New York Public Library Digital Collections, https://digitalcollections.nypl.org/items/6850fc74-5e61-8806-e040-e00a18067a2c.

17.4 Viele's plan for "Mount Prospect," later renamed the Great Hill, emphasized views of landscapes and waterways beyond the future park rather than delineating any scenes he would have envisioned within it.

Source: Aug. Ribstein, *View From Mount Prospect [Central Park] looking East*, engraving, Fred Mayer, in the *First Annual Report*, 1857. Courtesy of the Central Park Conservancy.

Viele subscribed to what was called the "modern" theory of landscape architecture in the eighteenth century, a way to integrate a park with its own natural topography, "nature's pencilings on the surface of the earth." Viele believed that to alter them would be a violation.[19] He acknowledged his debt to the major creators of English and German landscapes and based his design on their principles. He emphasized the importance of unifying the landscape's disparate features and put the Circuit Drive as the primary conduit to "embrace every feature of importance within the limits [of the park], and every prominent view without."[20] When his plan was first published in 1857, he chose to emphasize the sweeping views of the city and its surrounding waters from the park's highest points.

In the view from Mount Prospect—which today is called the Great Hill—a wide and rolling greensward plunges into a ravine. A couple, their small child, and a grazing cow take in the scene from the edge of the opposite precipice, looking out all the way to the Long Island Sound. In the distance sits the Mount St. Vincent convent and school, and beyond them lies the rapidly changing city: a railroad chugging up Third Avenue, the crowded shoreline of the East River, and sailing vessels on the river.

Following the praise heaped on the outward views of the park by the Senate bill in 1853, Viele's plan focused on these views to illustrate the public debut

17.5 *The North Gatehouse Construction Looking East* captures a ceremonial moment and offers a view of the workmen, the officials, and the equipment used to build this massive public works engineering project.

Source: Unknown Photographer (commissioned by Fairchild Walker Co.), *Reservoir North Gatehouse. New Reservoir (during construction). View of the North Wall of the Reservoir looking East.* Photograph. New-York Historical Society.

of his plan. To Viele, the highlight of his design was the opportunity to appreciate an overview of the contemporary city rather than presenting scenes that would evoke New York's forested past.[21]

THE BOTANICAL CATALOGUES

Viele may have had only a vague plan for the future park, but he carefully studied the elements that made up the physical terrain. In the *First Annual Report* from

January 1857, he expounded on Central Park's topography, geology, and botany. A year later, a second, more detailed botanical study conducted by Austrian gardener Ignatz Pilat and Prussian gardener Charles Rawolle added to Viele's list, documenting what plants grew on the land and the conditions in which they survived.[22]

For two hundred years, the Dutch, British, and then American governments had considered much of the land that became Central Park a wasteland. It is surprising, then, to read that Viele estimated 150,000 plants grew there. Viele reported forty-two species of trees or shrubs, while Pilat and Rawolle found 281, including herbs and vines. Most plants were native to North America, but a few were from Europe or Asia. Many of these had been imported to ornament homes and gardens, and some became invasive species. For instance, five hundred paper mulberry trees—a native of Japan that can grow in very dry situations that other trees find inhospitable—were found in the neighborhood of residences. The reports listed many foreign species that residents had purposely planted for ornament, shade, or fruit. Most species were also fast growing: hemlock spruce, white pine, and Lombardy and balsam poplar.

But most of the vegetation listed in Rawolle and Pilat's catalogue was native to North America. Perhaps their use evolved through the centuries by Native Americans, then was passed down to the Dutch and through successive generations of New Yorkers. Just west of Sixth Avenue and Seventy-Ninth Street, on the site of today's Ramble, there was a plantation of one hundred young honey locust trees. They might have been planted by the nearest resident, a leather dresser named Benjamin Beaman, who had purchased his lots in the city's common lands auction of 1852. The trees are ornamental, but also have pods whose sweet pulp can be used as a sugar substitute or fermented into a beer. Also, near the dwellings inside the park there were fifty fast-growing catalpa trees. The beanlike pods were used as a mild narcotic, as a tea to cure whooping cough, or as a laxative. *Saponaria officinalis* also grew nearby several homes, and its leaves provided households with a practical and important daily item, soap. When boiled and strained, the liquid produced a lather that dissolved fat and grease on cooking utensils and clothing.[23]

Another location in the park contained an orchard of five hundred persimmon trees, whose fruit can be eaten fresh or dried and made into loaves, puddings, and pies. The bark was used medicinally to treat conditions ranging from diarrhea and dysentery to diphtheria and venereal diseases. Or perhaps in this case it wasn't used medicinally, and the persimmon trees were there because the fruit can be fermented and distilled into a spirit. In 1771, the botanist Isaac Bartram suggested to the Philosophical Society of Philadelphia that farmers set aside fifty acres each on which they would plant three hundred persimmon trees to "become independent of the West-Indies for their expensive article of rum."[24]

In the parkland, Rawolle and Pilat found forty-two plants that Dr. David Hosack's 1811 *Hortus Elginensis* had noted for their medicinal uses. They estimated twenty thousand *Laurus sassafras* plants, which were said to act as a blood thinner and as a corrective for rheumatism and skin diseases, and a liniment for bruises. There was a profusion of certain shrubs, such as witch hazel, oxalis, and bittersweet, and among the trees were black cherry, slippery elm, red oak, tulip, and white pine. The toxic herb jimsonweed, *Datura stramonium*, was a popular and "widely distributed" treatment for the fitful coughing associated with asthma when it was burned and the smoke inhaled.[25] Many of the herbs they found had culinary uses: mint and mountain mint, wild marjoram, purslane, sorrel, and basil. There were also garden foods, like carrot, endive, yam, lettuce, lamb's quarters, and strawberries; and of course, fruiting trees and bushes like chestnut, hazelnut, catalpa, highbush blueberry, black raspberry, and blackberry.

This does not even account for the vegetables undoubtedly growing in the park residents' kitchen gardens, but those were outside the scope of the botanical reports. In 1857, as the city prepared to take the land for the park, Comptroller Azariah Flagg made a single sympathetic gesture, "in all fairness." He allowed the gardeners, who received no award for their plant material, fruits, and vegetables, to be "protected" while waiting for construction to begin.[26] Most of these people had garden beds on their property, while a few simply rented plots from the city.[27] The gardeners were assured that they could harvest their crops, in many instances their only livelihood. In total, there were a little more than a hundred acres under cultivation, approximately the size of today's Reservoir, or about 14 percent of the entire parkland, included the twenty-acre grassland just north of Seneca Village. In May 1857, the Committee on Buildings recognized the need for those "market gardeners who have spent considerable sums of money for manures and labor in preparing the ground . . . to have the privilege of taking off a crop in order to be reimbursed for their outlay." When five months later, the residents were forced to vacate the park, they were allowed to harvest their autumn crops.[28]

Gardener John Haff ripped out his grapevines when he left Seneca Village. He took up residence only blocks away as the innkeeper of the Elm Park Hotel, the former Apthorp mansion near today's Ninety-First Street and Columbus Avenue. The week after the assessments were posted in October 1855, Haff used an advertisement of the hotel to protest the mere $75 that he was awarded for his "Hot house, and [for] giving me the privilege of removing my Vineyard at my own cost and hazard, which for thirteen years I have labored to establish." But in his own version of sour grapes, he announced that in his new "abode" he would "serve up . . . those rich and luscious GRAPES, the product of my own hands," to enjoy along with "the best Turtle Soup ever made always on hand."[29] We know from Rawolle and Pilat that the prepark grew two species, *Vitis aestivalis* or summer grape, a red wine source, and *Vitis lambrusca*, a Concord grape. But those wild native species may not have been up to Haff's prize-winning standards. The Sisters of Charity were allowed by the commissioners to stay in the prepark for another two years and were permitted to remove their fruit, boxwood, currant, and gooseberry bushes when they left for their new Bronx campus.[30]

By October 1857, crews had begun ripping out the orchards and removing the shrubs, garden beds, and grape vines. They cleared the thickets beset with undergrowth of thorns and briars and tore up many valuable shrubs and young trees struggling for life. The staff was struggling too, often running afoul of the poison ivy that grew in great abundance in the landscape. One crew member was so badly stricken that he had to convalesce two weeks.[31]

***

Besides his natural history studies, Viele contributed two lasting features to Central Park's design: the placement of the transverse roads and the shape of the Reservoir. The four transverse roads, often cited as an idea of park designers Olmsted and Vaux, were first proposed by Viele. In his 1857 *Annual Report*, he included transverse roads that would provide for crossing the park "for business and other purposes."[32] The commissioners picked up on this suggestion and chose to include the transverse roads as a requirement in the later 1858 competition.

THE RESERVOIR

From space, astronauts see two things that they recognize as Central Park: the Reservoir's cloudlike undulating shape and the great green rectangle surrounding it.[33] The park's rectangle was created by the grid; the Reservoir's form was Egbert Viele's contribution.

Early promoters of the Reservoir imagined the future water body as "a picturesque, irregularly-shaped artificial lake, containing nearly one hundred acres of water in one placid sheet."[34] But when its location became official in 1852,

17.6 Egbert Viele converted the Reservoir from the original plan for a rectangle to this more pleasing naturalistic shape. His design also saved $200,000 that would have been required for rock blasting had the city decided to retain the original idea of a rectangular basin.

Source: Sara Cedar Miller, *Reservoir Aerial*. Courtesy of the Central Park Conservancy.

the unimaginative engineers of the Croton Aqueduct Board sketched a massive rectangular bathtub, an echo of the smaller receiving reservoir to its south (see figure 13.4).

The geometric rigidity offended the modern aesthetics of Viele, whose design for the future Reservoir rejected the ruler and embraced instead nature's sinuous curves. Viele's preference for the naturalistic style was not determined by abstract aesthetics alone, but by the topography: a deep valley surrounded on three sides by high ground and rocky outcrops. The site was obviously suited for the Reservoir. A reporter for the *New York Daily Times* wrote, "It seems as if Nature had scooped out this hollow in contemplation of the purpose to which it is to be applied."[35] Viele was also a shrewd observer of the bottom line, and he knew that exploiting the natural topography would save taxpayers more than $200,000 by avoiding the unnecessary and dangerous rock blasting required to construct the rectangular basin.[36]

Viele's design made sense to both the Croton Aqueduct Board and the Board of Commissioners of the Central Park, and the New York State legislature approved the transfer of lands required to accommodate the new curvilinear outline. In April 1857 the exchange was official, and the water commissioners declared that the Reservoir, by its shape and location, would become "the chief ornament of the park." They suggested naming it "The Lake of Manahatta."[37] At its completion, it was the largest man-made lake in the world.[38]

NAMING SENECA VILLAGE

The name "Seneca Village" may also be another possible contribution by Viele, an idea taken inadvertently from his original park plan, now lost to history.[39] Until 1873, sixteen years after the community's demise, no personal or public record, no legal document, no letter, deed, diary, will, court case, map, tax record, newspaper article, government document, or annual report by the Board of Commissioners of the Central Park ever used the term. It is fairly certain that Seneca Village was exclusively called such by outsiders, never by a landowner, renter, mortgagee, mortgagor, petitioner, or descendant of village landowners. In 1878, Ellen Williams, daughter of landowner Andrew Williams, referred to her community as "Yorkville," and in her 1928 memoir, Maritcha Lyons, the daughter of landowners Albro and Mary Lyons, describes her parents' property as "four lots of the ground now included in the domain of Central Park." If the community had a name, Williams and Lyons would have used it.[40]

The first published mention of "Seneca" was in an 1873 pamphlet, *The Growth of Charities*, authored in part by Reverend Thomas McClure Peters. In 1907, half a century after the demise of the community, Reverend John Punnett Peters repeated the name "Seneca" from his father's essay in *Annals of St. Michael's: Being the History of St. Michael's Episcopal Protestant Church for One Hundred Years 1807–1907*. According to Punnett Peters, in 1833 James Cook Richmond "had started a Sunday-school among the colored people, of whom there were many at Yorkville and Seneca village, a miserable settlement of low whites and colored people, on the site of the reservoir in Central Park."[41]

Frustrated in his research for historical accuracy, Punnett Peters admitted that the Reverend James Cook Richmond's and his brother Reverend William Richmond's "poorly kept records were rather characteristic of both brothers and resulted in many mistakes, dates included, under their combined thirty-eight-years of leadership."[42] So Punnett Peters did the best he could at reconstructing the past and took many of the Richmonds' "facts" with a leap of faith. The result has caused confusion and misunderstanding ever since.[43]

While The Reverends William Richmond and Thomas McClure Peters of St. Michael's Church on the west side were ministering to the All Angels' church members in Seneca Village from around 1854 until Richmond's death in 1858, they would likely have met Lieutenant Egbert Viele, who was at the time conducting his independent survey of the future park. Although Viele's printed plan for Central Park has been published many times, the original watercolor he presented at that commissioners' meeting has been lost. We only know its details thanks to the persistence of the *Herald* reporter who followed the story of the park's design. According to the reporter, Viele named the roads and avenues of the future park "after the different counties of the state, preference being given to Indian names." At the time, there were nineteen counties in New York state named for indigenous tribes. Seneca was one of them.[44]

Weaving these counties' names throughout his plan was a shrewd political move by Viele, who had to woo otherwise disinterested upstate legislators who might influence the choice of the park's designer. In a second *Herald* article, the reporter disclosed that Viele's park plan was New York state in miniature: it was to include "specimens of the entire flora of the State, so that the Park with its great lake, its noble public work, its miniature mountains, and fertile valleys will be as it were an epitome and exponent of the great State in which it lies."[45]

So perhaps the Reverends Richmond and McClure Peters, who were frequent visitors to Seneca Village, made the acquaintance of Viele as he surveyed the lands and shared with them his idea for Indian names. We know that some white New Yorkers, including former resident George Washington Plunkitt, called the settlement "Nigger Village," so the ministers may have seized on the more benign name Seneca for the road or avenue that Viele had placed right alongside their community. The word to those whites in middle-class antebellum culture may have been less a racist slur than, as historian Elizabeth Stordeur Pryor suggests, a distinction of one's class. If white lower classes used the derogatory term, the reverends would have sought a name for the community to distance themselves from "vulgar whites" and underscore their own "superior" status.[46]

Until Viele's original plan comes to light, we can never be absolutely certain that he chose "Seneca" for the road near that the former community or, for that matter, that his plan was absolutely the source for the name. The residents themselves have never been known to refer to their community as Seneca Village. Instead, all available evidence currently suggests that the name may have been the invention of two white rectors.

The community or its name did not appear again in print until 1911, and then not again until 1989, when Peter Salwen referred to it in his book, *Upper West Side Story*.

THE APPROPRIATIONS

When Judge Harris approved the report of the Commissioners of Estimate and Assessment in February 1856, it only provided for money to buy the land. It did not appropriate any funds to construct the park or hire police to watch over it. For that, the city was required to get approval for its budget and tax rate from the state's Board of Supervisors. Even the ever-optimistic Senator Daniel Sickles anticipated a major roadblock for the maximum of $1,500,000. Sickles's upstate supporters told him that if the board approved such a monumental outlay for a downstate park, "their constituents would be after them with sharp sticks and they would be run out of the county."[47]

Once again Sickles hatched a plan. For $500, he commissioned engineer Charles K. Graham, the future park surveyor and younger brother of Sickles's crafty attorney, to make two panoramas of the park, a sort of before-and-after juxtaposition. The before drawing was a barren landscape, all rocky and swampy; the after illustration was a breathtaking "Garden of Eden." In February, Sickles had them hung on the walls of the Senate antechamber, an attempt to persuade reluctant legislators to favor the funding of the park bill. But the senators were unmoved. The overall sentiment about the prospects for maintaining a beautiful park in a place like New York City was dubious. One disbeliever commented that one couldn't even grow flowers in New York City: "Every bud would require police protection, night and day!"[48]

When that didn't work, Sickles supplemented Graham's artwork with a $300 all-expenses-paid trip to the park site for a few opposing politicians from each party. According to Sickles, their visit to the desolate tract opened their eyes and upon their return, they made a favorable report.[49] Still, the legislators weren't buying it.

With resistance from the legislature, Wood bypassed the state's governing body and despite his questionable license to do so, forged ahead "without shadow or color of law, and of his own pure will and mere motive."[50]

In April, the city's Board of Supervisors passed a measure to tack a $200,000 tax onto the 1856 appropriations from the legislature, which they had no legal authority to do. The reform members of the board denounced the move, calling it "one of the blackest swindles ever attempted on the city."[51] A week later, corporation counsel Lorenzo Shepherd, the successor to Robert Dillon, won an injunction by the state supreme court against their proposal.[52] This didn't deter the commissioners, who continued on as though nothing had happened. They established two offices, one above the Shoe and Leather Bank on Chambers Street and one on Fifty-Ninth Street, at today's Columbus Circle. With no money in their coffers, they immediately hired staff and police to protect the city's property.[53]

By August 1856, the state supreme court had extended the injunction that barred the city from appropriating tax money for the park and confirmed that exclusive power resided with the state legislature. The judge railed against "the enormous extravagance and wasteful expenditures that have been so long indulged" and made it very clear that if the two commissioners continued to spend money without full and adequate authority, they might have to pay it back "out of their own pockets."[54]

When the mayor set up the commission, his first act was to create a twenty-man police squad to manage the residents and other locals who were using—and, according to several accounts, abusing—the city's property. The police were to curtail damage to the dwellings, trees, and shrubbery by citizens and cattle, goats, and swine that foraged on the city's property. These protections of the corporation's property began in the seventeenth century when the royal charter gave the city its common lands and not, as many have surmised, solely as a punitive measure for Central Park's renters.[55]

In a hostile and racist article in the *New York Daily Times* on July 9, 1856, it was reported that "the Ebon inhabitants"—obviously a reference to the Black families—had been notified to leave the prepark by the first of August, but that the police had trouble persuading "them and the poor Irish" that the commissioners were throwing them out.[56] The reason for the displacement was revealed less than two weeks later, when on July 17, 1856, police captain John Bennett issued a notice to all tenants that by the first of August, unless there was notification otherwise by the commissioners, members of the police and their families would be moving into their homes free of rent. The promise had not yet been fulfilled, but he also requested Commissioners Wood and Taylor to hire ten additional police for a night patrol to prevent night vandalism. The *Herald* reporter also noted that the officers had not been paid and were "complaining bitterly."[57] Two days later, the supervisor of the Committee on County Offices asked the mayor/commissioner if perhaps he would consider transforming the Sisters' convent to a prison due to the crowded condition of the Eldridge Street jail. This was a novel idea for the mayor, who said he would be willing to use it for a public institution, though he was "not then prepared to say."[58]

By November, the commission had spent an estimated $300,000 for expenses incurred on the park's improvements. The tight-fisted and responsible comptroller, Azariah Flagg, refused to add such a sum to the city's present burdens without an act of the legislature, and did not include it in the year's appropriations.[59] By December, the committee decided to allow the liabilities already spent but not to add $250,000, as Viele had suggested, for the following year.[60]

THE RENTERS

Desperate for money, the commissioners assumed that they could fund their operation by collecting rent from the tenants and profit from the sale of their homes and barns when they left. But again Flagg stopped them in their tracks. The rent or sale revenue of all real estate was legally directed to be deposited into the Sinking Fund, a law that had been established in 1813 to reduce the city's debt. But an exposé by several aldermen uncovered an even shiftier operation within Flagg's own department that placed rental money into the pocket of Joseph Rose, the City Collector of Revenue.[61]

On April 14, 1856, the Board of Aldermen directed the comptroller to report to them the names of the Central Park renters, the location of their property, and the amount of rent they agreed to pay the city. As all rentals in the city officially started on the first of May, Rose rushed to fulfill his mission. If any resident chose not to accept the city's rental terms, they would be forced to vacate their homes and replaced by "some careful person" to secure the premises. The homes were *not* automatically rented to the long-standing owners or lessees but rather auctioned off to the highest bidders, "except in a few cases, where there was a trifling difference" in the fee, in which case Rose accepted the current occupants. Rose's arrangement, no matter how "temporary," was a serious violation of the Reform Charter of 1853, which legally mandated a public auction to the highest bidders of all city property; public notice had to be given in newspapers for thirty days prior to the auction.[62]

The informal rentals—there were no written leases—were revealed to reporters by several angry aldermen who were tipped off that "a prominent citizen" had offered Joseph Rose $500 for the Wagstaff property, but Rose made a private deal and rented it for $250, subsequently subletting it for $500 while also removing attractive plantings. Rose did not receive a fixed salary but earned his wages from the collection of fees. Apparently some of the unrecorded deals were canceled when it was revealed that the rental agreements would be published.[63] In Rose's opinion, the arrangement had been "most advantageous to the city under the circumstances of the case."[64]

For the last sixteen months of its existence—from May 1856 to October 1857—the community that lived in the park numbered approximately 170 households, more than 400 adults and nearly 250 children.[65] Of these households, only 25 were former owners who had received their awards and remained in their homes.

In all, roughly 39 percent of the households were German, 35 percent Irish, 7 percent African American, 2 white American, and roughly 9 percent of unde-termined ethnicity.

May 16, 1856 is the date of the last count we have for the prepark residents in Seneca Village. Twelve Black families totaling fifty-five people were listed, not including the Scudder and Thompson families, who left before the final evic-tion.[66] Compared to the residents living in the community in 1855, the Black population had fallen by almost 70 percent. Approximately thirty whites resided in the community for the last sixteen months, an increase of about 30 percent.[67] It is possible that most of the Black landowners received their awards and left, but it's also possible that white renters offered a higher bid than former residents or bribed Rose to give them access to the rentals. In total, about eighty residents of Seneca Village were forced to leave the village in October.[68]

The condemnation maps for much of the rest of the park are not as com-plete as those of Seneca Village, so we do not have an exact count of the entire park population. When the Seneca Village residences are excluded, the remain-ing park residences totaled sixty-two houses and eighty-one shanties. There were other buildings too: at least fifteen piggeries, sixty-nine stables, twelve barns, two large bone-boiling establishments, the State Arsenal, the powder house, and a residence for the military guards.[69]

An incident regarding one of those stables gives us a window into how emo-tionally and physically stressful life in the park was under the domination of Captain Bennett and his police brigade, particularly for the poor, Irish, and Black residents, which is to say, most of the renters. The Seneca Village families of Maria Scudder and Catherine Johnson, daughters of the late longtime resi-dent Sarah Hunter, wound up in a series of events that culminated in the trial of *Scudder vs. John W. Bennett.*

Thomas Scudder sued the Captain of Police, John W. Bennett, for trespassing on his rental property, which had belonged to his mother-in-law, Sarah Hunter. Under Captain Bennett's orders, a few officers removed an old harness from the Scudders' Eighty-Fourth Street stable. Bennett claimed they did not trespass because the door was open and the building vacant. His men put several things in a wheelbarrow and locked them up until Scudder's teenage children could retrieve them.

Two witnesses testified that this wasn't true: they saw the captain kick in the locked door. Scudder, presumably with his wife, Maria, and their three children, had vacated their home days earlier as the situation devolved. Without asking questions, and following demands from city officials to leave no home vacant, Captain Bennett placed village resident Ada Thompson into the Scudders's home. Thompson had been renting her former home, but in the rental auction she must have underbid and therefore could not remain in it. Perhaps she was living with her relative Richard Thompson, a resident of the park, near Sixty-Third Street.

Once in the Scudder dwelling, the sixty-year-old Thompson testified to the deplorable conditions: "the rats were very thick; I could lay nothing down but the rats would get it." She left the following day. The Scudders must have vacated for the same reason. Likely the rats came from the attached stable, which was probably full of grain and hay that rats eat and nest in.[70]

Despite the uninhabitable conditions, Judge Maynard decided in favor of Captain Bennett, claiming that Scudder was not in possession and therefore there was no trespass. He dismissed Scudder's possessions as "old rubbish," worthless and not even proven to be his belongings.[71]

It is beyond the scope of this study to trace the next destination of the renters and residents when they left the park. We know many of the Irish and German piggery owners transferred their sties to the west side, and squatters probably followed the pattern of resettlement to areas farther north in Manhattan or to Brooklyn.

THE REPUBLICANS

Since the colonial charters of the seventeenth century, the Corporation of the City of New York had enjoyed the special status of home rule. All of that would change in the fall of 1856 when the new predominantly upstate Republican Party elected Governor John Alsop King, the son of Rufus King and a close friend of the Amory family. Together the governor and the Republican majority in the legislature crafted a new city charter that placed New York City under their total control. Oversight of Central Park by Commissioners Wood and Taylor and their Common Council cronies came to an end. On April 21, 1857, a nonpartisan board of eleven commissioners was put in place by the legislature to independently regulate and manage the building of Central Park.[72] Nine days later the new board of six Republicans, four reform Democrats and Wood Democrats, and one Know-Nothing met at the offices of Robert Dillon, the outgoing corporation counsel and one of their esteemed members. They would be charged with selecting the new designer of the park and overseeing its management and construction for the next twelve years.[73]

chapter 18

Designing Central Park, 1857–1858

The first battle for Central Park was the long and drawn-out five-year process to choose a site and to legalize it. The second battle was over its design. Before a design could be chosen, several steps had to be taken, many of them behind the scenes. The commissioners needed to hire a superintendent to oversee the construction. Architect Calvert Vaux had to get his two commissioners/friends to convince the other nine to hold a competition. Viele and his plan had to go; then Vaux had to get Frederick Law Olmsted, whom he had only met once, to agree to a partnership. The commissioners, frequently at odds with one another, had to manage a complex and fair competition. And once they chose the winning design, they had to appease the uncompromising artistic egos of the winners while balancing them with the hard-nosed demands of their opponents who preferred a different style. And that was just the beginning. All together, it took sixteen years to build Central Park, and then three additional years to build the perimeter wall.

In August 1857, only three months after the new independent commission was formed, Washington Irving, the author of *The Legend of Sleepy Hollow* and president of Mayor Fernando Wood's gentlemen advisory board, wrote a letter of recommendation to the board in support of Frederick Law Olmsted, an applicant for the position of superintendent. Olmsted later wrote that he believed Irving's letter "turned the balance" on his appointment.[1]

Until then, Olmsted had worked in a variety of careers and pursued interests that suited him for the job, and he had the political and social connections that made it happen. Six years later he would write of the job, "If a fairy had shaped it for me, it could not have fitted me better."[2] Thanks to his father's generosity—some might call it indulgence—Olmsted had invested in a publishing firm,

Photographs of some of the Beauties and Adornments, Natural and Artificial, of the great **CENTRAL PARK** as it is.

18.1 The cartoon "Beauties and Adornments, Natural and Artificial, of the great CENTRAL PARK as it is," published in the 1858 satiric magazine *Yankee Notions*, was a response to the public's impatience for the large and beautiful park they had been promised by the city. The artist lampooned the shanties and their poor Irish inhabitants.

Source: "Photographs of some of the Beauties and Adornments Natural and Artificial, of the great CENTRAL PARK as it is," *Yankee Notions*, vol. 7 (1858), 26–27. The Collections of The New York Public Library.

Dix and Edwards & Company, which went bankrupt only weeks earlier. He had published observations on his travels to England and the South in books titled *Walks and Talks of an American Farmer in England* (1852) and *A Journey in the Seaboard Slave States* (1856). He had been the managing editor of *Putnam's Monthly Magazine*, which brought him in close company with the literary leaders of the day, and he was a contributor to the *New York Times* under the pseudonym "Yeoman." His father had purchased two farms for him, one in Connecticut and one more recently on Staten Island. As a gentleman farmer, he had read and implemented the latest drainage theories and practices, and he possessed a firm

18.2 This photograph of architect-in-chief Frederick Law Olmsted was most likely taken in 1860, after his six-week trip to Europe. He had gone there to recuperate from the mental and physical pressures of his work on the park, though soon after his return a serious carriage accident fractured his upper left leg and left him lame.

Source: Olmsted Family Photographs, Olmsted Job #1 Frederick Law Olmsted, Sr., cap & cape c.1860. Courtesy of the National Park Service, Frederick Law Olmsted National Historic Site.

knowledge of soils and horticulture. Since his early childhood, he and his father had traveled together and shared their love for viewing picturesque landscapes "with ardor, affection, and industry."[3] He knew by heart the classic authors on the subject and admired and wrote about America's and Europe's natural terrain and man-made farms, gardens, estates, plantations, and parks. In his travels he studied park policing, a very important requirement for the management of a public park. And, not least, he was a member of the newly formed Republican Party, a not-too-subtle requirement for the chosen candidate.[4] Olmsted felt his ascendance to park superintendent was "normal, ordinary, and naturally out-growing from my previous life and history."[5]

With Washington Irving's support and a long list of other writers, journalists, scientists, and civic leaders behind him, Olmsted was elected by the board on September 11, 1857, just one vote shy of a unanimous consent.[6] He was charged with the supervision of the workforce to clear the land, drain the wetlands, get rid of noxious detritus from farms and factories, and remove the homes and structures purchased by the city from their former residents. And he had to do all of this under the disdainful eye of his arrogant and competitive new boss, chief engineer Egbert Viele, whose design for the park would soon be replaced by Olmsted's. Olmsted knew what he was up against. The day of his appointment, he wrote to his brother John, "It seems generally expected that Viele & I shall quarrel, that he will be jealous of me, & that there will be all sorts of Intrigues. I shall try the frank, conscientious & industrious plan, and if it fails, I shall have learned something more & be no worse off."[7]

Olmsted was right. Viele believed he was not the "practical man" the crews would have preferred, and so he put him through mental and physical trials that the biographer Laura Wood Roper equated with "hazing."[8] When Viele first met Olmsted, Viele flicked him away like a gnat. When he arrived for his first official day of duty, expecting it to be "a call of ceremony," Olmsted wore his best clothes, and Viele's foreman led him through the park's knee-deep puddles of slippery muck. Over the next several days, when introduced to the men he would oversee, he was cajoled and sometimes openly mocked. To Olmsted, a self-professed "unpractical man," it seemed "as if we were all engaged in playing a practical joke."[9] Little did they know that Olmsted, in his extensive journey throughout the antebellum South and Texas, had endured more hostile terrain and survived far more challenging circumstances than he would ever have in his new job.

Olmsted despised the spoils system that rewarded jobs to unqualified workers who were thrust upon the crews by New York's corrupt officials. But getting rid of them would be difficult given Viele's long-standing attachment to the Democratic bosses and their directives to hire the laborers whose votes had put and kept them in office.

Less than a month after Olmsted was appointed, the commissioners ordered a reduction of staff. The city had failed to appropriate the necessary funds to keep them on, and the jobs of roughly seven hundred Irish and German laborers were in peril. Two days later, the *New York Daily Times* reported that the Board of Aldermen resolved to begin work on the park as soon as possible, hoping to placate the hungry and desperate mobs who assembled in public carrying "Bread or Blood" banners. During one of these angry protests, a heated crowd estimated to be five thousand strong surrounded Wagstaff House—the offices of Viele and Olmsted near Seventy-Ninth Street and Fifth Avenue—demanding that Olmsted reinstate their jobs. As Olmsted watched anonymously from a distance, the speaker, a local politician, incited the crowd to violence. He held up a noose and pointed to a nearby tree, implying it was Olmsted's fate if the mob was not appeased. The protestors produced a list of ten thousand of the neediest men and demanded their immediate employment. When the funding was approved, the commissioners gave Olmsted the authority to hire a thousand men.[10]

In the same week, Olmsted wrote to his father in London, asking him a favor. Olmsted wanted his father to buy Viele "a nice, thin, light, silk faced, English Indian rubber over-coat," a kind that was only available in England. Viele must have admired Olmsted's and asked after it. It is one human gesture within a troubled relationship—these two adversaries, despite their differences, shared an appreciation for well-made work clothes. In this way, at least, it was Olmsted who was "the practical man."[11]

CLEARING THE LAND

Once Olmsted was directed by the board to hire and supervise the crews, he could proudly write to his father that he had "got the park into a capital discipline, a perfect system, working like a machine, a thousand men now at work."[12] He hired agricultural engineer George Waring to drain the wetlands, and the commission retained Samuel Gustin, the superintendent of planting, to oversee the horticulture.

The ground under the park was lined with impenetrable hardpan and viscous clay, which prevented the drainage of water into the soil. The deep standing pools, often infused with the waste of local pigsties or bone-boiling effluvia, putrefied the plant life on the ground into a noxious stew and brewed a host of diseases.

In his October 1857 report to the commissioners, George Waring noted that workers had already begun the removal of surface water, exposing the beds of all the swamps and ponds "to the action of the atmosphere," and planned to con-tinue work through the winter months.[13] These early drainage efforts were cap-tured in the only known photograph to exist from the joint efforts of Waring, Viele, and Olmsted.[14]

The image shows countless glacial erratic boulders, neatly stacked in rows before their removal to the perimeter of the park. After the shallow ditches drained the surface water, workers embedded a series of clay pipes below the park's soil to drain water on the surface and underground. The landscape in this photograph eventually became a water body—today's Lake looking northeast to the Ramble and the tower that would become Belvedere Castle—but before the design competition, it was assumed that the crews were executing Viele's idea to transform marshland into meadow.

Early on, Olmsted described his job as the implementation of "a barely tol-erable design." He was no less critical of the commissioners, whom he called "unmanageable, unqualified, and liable to permit any absurdity." Still, he enjoyed

18.3 The photograph was most likely taken in the winter of 1857 when Olmsted, Viele, and Waring were creating drainage ditches that would become the future Lake. The view is to the northeast and shows the future Lake and Ramble hillside on to the distant receiving reservoir and tower that is today's Belvedere.

Source: Photograph (detail) from Frederick Law Olmsted and Calvert Vaux, "Presentation Drawing No. 4 From Point D." Courtesy of the New York City Municipal Archives.

the work. He admitted as much in a letter to Harvard Professor Asa Gray, writing, "I like my place in it much."[15] He was becoming a landscape architect, though he didn't know it until Calvert Vaux entered his life.

CALVERT VAUX

Calvert Vaux is the unsung hero of Central Park history. Vaux—whose name rhymes with "hawks," not with "crow"—was an ambitious twenty-six-year-old British architect who had come to Newburg, New York, in 1850 at the invitation of Andrew Jackson Downing.[16] No architectural schools yet existed in America,

18.4 Codesigner Calvert Vaux was connected to two commissioners, and he convinced the board to hold a design competition. Once that was approved, Vaux invited Olmsted, who was at the time the superintendent of the park workforce, to join him in the competition. Though Olmsted turned him down at first, the two would go on to create the winning design.

Source: Olmsted Family Photographs, Olmsted Job #324 Calvert Vaux, From among J. C. Olmsted files. Courtesy of the National Park Service, Frederick Law Olmsted National Historic Site.

so Downing had gone to England to seek a designer who could assist him in building country homes and estates for his growing clientele in the Hudson Valley.

Downing began as a pomologist, a specialist in fruit trees, who evolved into the nation's "Apostle of Taste," an authority on the American way of life. In his periodical, *The Horticulturist*, he published designs of lifestyles, homes, and gardens for all classes of society. He also promoted the idea of a large New York City park, and if not for his unfortunate drowning in a steamboat accident, it would have been Downing and Vaux—not Olmsted and Vaux—who designed Central Park. By Downing's death at thirty-seven, he and Vaux had already begun to plan what was intended to be the first major public park in America: the Mall in Washington, D.C., which would hold the presidential park and the grounds of the Smithsonian Institution.[17]

After Downing's death, Vaux carried on their practice in Newburg until 1856, when he married. As a new bridegroom and a new American citizen, he moved to New York City, a place of better opportunity for a young architect at the forefront of his profession. Vaux was already a member of the Hudson Valley's literary and artistic circles. His new brother-in-law, Jervis McEntee, was the only student of renowned Hudson River School painter Frederic Church. In Manhattan, the same artists and writers were also members of the city's intellectual elite. Vaux became a founding member of the American Institute of Architects and an author. He published *Villas and Cottages*, a plan book of architectural residences dedicated to Downing and fashioned after his mentor's own book, *The Architecture of Country Houses*.

One of Vaux's first city clients was the banker John A. C. Gray, the director of the Bank of New York, who commissioned Vaux to design a new home for him at Fifth Avenue and Tenth Street. So impressed was Gray with Vaux's talent that a year later he hired him again to build a new bank on Wall Street and Williams Street. It was also around then that Gray became one of the new commissioners of Central Park. Vaux now knew two of the eleven commissioners. The other was Charles Wyllys Elliott, a writer and amateur horticulturist whom Vaux had met at the Downings' home and coincidentally a friend of Olmsted.

Vaux was perfectly positioned to influence the future plan for Central Park, but first he had to convince the commissioners of the inadequacies of Viele's plan. Years later, he wrote, "I pointed out whenever I had the chance that it would be a disgrace to the City and to the memory of Mr. Downing" to carry out Viele's plan for the park.[18]

With Gray and Elliott on his side, Vaux was able to realize his vision to decide the park's design through an open contest. On June 16, the commissioners voted to advertise a competition to design Central Park, open to everyone. None of them wanted to retain Viele's design. Vaux appears again in the minutes of their board meeting two months later, when the commissioners acknowledged the receipt of Vaux's new book, which was his subtle thank you for initiating the competition.[19] They would be hearing from him again soon.

The design competition had cash prizes attached. First prize was $2,000, a hefty sum for some fortunate designer—or even for a team of designers, for that is exactly what Vaux had in mind. After the competition was announced, Vaux invited Superintendent Frederick Law Olmsted to join him in creating a new design for Central Park. Vaux enjoyed partnerships. After Downing's death, he worked closely with colleague Frederick Clarke Withers and later with other architects too.

In a letter to Olmsted, he admitted his insecurities about working on landscapes alone: "I had no idea of competing because I felt my incapacity." The brief meeting at Downing's a few years earlier must have suggested to Vaux that he and Olmsted would make a winning combination. He must have seen in him a like-minded artistic spirit, not to mention a successful administrator and leader, with talents Vaux did not believe he possessed. And of course, Olmsted was more familiar with the park's topography than anyone else.[20] But Olmsted demurred.[21]

Olmsted was a gentleman first, and he would not have stepped on his boss's toes by submitting a competing design for Central Park, especially since he and Viele were already at odds with each other. Olmsted rightly assumed that the chief engineer would resubmit his rejected plan to the competition. But Vaux had a strong stubborn streak, and it seems he pushed and pushed Olmsted to confront Viele. We know from future incidents—the invitation to design Prospect Park, in particular—that Vaux could badger Olmsted until he yielded.

Eventually Olmsted agreed, and approached Viele to ask permission to enter the competition. Viele, in his typically brusque manner, waved him off, and the famous Olmsted-Vaux partnership began. Olmsted would later write, "I should have had nothing to do with the design of Central Park or Prospect Park had not Vaux invited me to join him in those works."[22]

Olmsted and Vaux spent their nights through that first winter of 1857–58 walking through the frozen swamps and rock-strewn fields of the parkland, envisioning the leafy meadows and crystalline lakes that would eventually overtake them.

JOHN AND MARY, FREDERICK AND MARY

In early 1858, Olmsted wrote to his father, "I am greatly interested in planning the Park with Vaux," but—at least to his financially supportive father—he emphasized his monetary prospects more than his artistic endeavor.[23] Olmsted was not just proud of his new prospects as a sign of accomplishment; he and his father were mourning the death of son and brother John Hull on November 24, 1857, in Nice, France, after a long bout with tuberculosis, and only three weeks after his wife, Mary Cleveland Perkins, gave birth to their third child, Owen.

John wrote a last letter to Fred "in a hand tremulous with weakness" two weeks before his death:

Dear dear Fred

It appears we are not to see one another any more—I have not many days, the Dr. says.

Well so be it since God wills it so, I have never known a better friendship than ours has been & there can't be a greater happiness that to think of that—how dear we have been & how long we have held out such tenderness.

I am kept wild with opium & am so weak that I suffer from many little things. I cannot comprehend this suddenness—but I see it. I can hardly be got out of bed & have no breath.

Give my love to the boys. I want you to keep something of mine—my watch or cane or something to C. & . . .* of some sort.

Don't let Mary suffer while you are alive,

God bless you,

John H.O.[24]

Olmsted took his brother's dying wish to heart. On June 13, 1859, with Mayor Daniel Tiemann officiating, Frederick and Mary married in the "Bogardus House" on "Bogardus Hill," the former Borrowe mansion and Elmwood boarding school, now the Great Hill.[25] Mary, Frederick, and his nephews and niece, soon to be his newly adopted children—John Charles, Charlotte, and Owen Frederick— lived in the former mansion until they moved across the park to the former McGowan/Mount St. Vincent convent complex with codesigner Calvert Vaux and his family. When the Olmsteds moved out, the Great Hill mansion became the home or office for park employees until its demolition in December 1897, the last remaining prepark residence.

18.5 Mary Perkins Olmsted, the widow of Frederick Law Olmsted's brother John, married her brother-in-law in a civil ceremony that took place on June 13, 1859, in the park's last remaining house on the Great Hill.

Source: Jesse L. Judd, *Half-length portrait of Mary Perkins Olmsted, facing three-quarters to the left, seated on a chair, holding papers*, 1863. Courtesy of Historic New England.

THE DESIGN COMPETITION

The deadline for submissions was April 1, 1858. More than thirty submissions were entered, so the commissioners gave themselves three weeks to review them and decide on the four prizes. Along with a hundred-foot-by-one-inch sepia or colored drawing, the entrants were required to submit a written description, which the commissioners had printed so they might better understand the motives and budgets behind each plan. Only five visual drawings have survived, so we must rely on the written descriptions for the rest.[26]

As a safeguard of the commission's objectivity, all plans were submitted anonymously. The authors' names were kept in sealed envelopes that were only opened after the votes were cast. Today we know who is responsible for most entries because there is a bound copy of the plans in the New York Public Library owned by Commissioner Dillon, who penciled in the names behind most entries. The second copy at the New-York Historical Society has Commissioner Charles H. Russell's handwritten notes and his opinions on most of the plans.[27]

On Tuesday, April 6, the board began to open the plans. With the exception of the clerk and a watchman, only the commissioners were allowed access to the locked exhibit room.[28]

A week later, they decided that all commissioners would arrive at 3:00 p.m. *daily* to review the submissions together. This gave them the opportunity to compare notes and form alliances during the eleven days before the election. It is probably fair to say that each commissioner had made his decision by Judgment Day on April 28.

On April 28, the Board of Commissioners of the Central Park gathered at a building on Broadway and Bleecker Street to determine the design for the future park. The eleven men assembled at 6:00 p.m. and remained there until 11:30 to debate and select the winners of the four prizes. The sole record of this meeting is the eight-page minutes cataloguing the motions and the votes, but not the commissioners' actual comments. For the politics and personalities behind those actions, we must read between the lines.[29]

The board had been formed by the legislature eleven months earlier, and the legislature had ensured that Republican commissioners held the majority: John F. Butterworth, Charles Wyllys Elliott, John A.C. Gray, James Hogg, Charles H. Russell, and William K. Strong. Five of these men were captains of industry or financial leaders and solid members of New York's cultural elite. James Hogg advertised himself as a "seedman" and belonged to the well-respected British horticultural Hogg family. He had been a staunch defender of Jones Wood, testifying in 1852 in favor of choosing it over Central Park. Hogg's contentious behavior toward his fellow commissioners and colleagues led to several internal investigations and lawsuits during his tenure.[30]

The Democrats represented a wider range of party affiliations, professional experiences, and personalities. Among them was attorney Robert Dillon, a reform

Democrat and well-respected leader of the New York Irish establishment. As corporation counsel, he was instrumental in the court fights to legalize Central Park.

Another Democrat was August Belmont, née Schöenberg, a German Jewish immigrant who had come to America as the agent of the wealthy Rothschild banking family. He soon formed his own successful firm and married into the prestigious family of Commodore Matthew Perry. When the commodore inquired whether his son-in-law planned to build a home near the new park, Belmont balked. Fearing the potential for neighbors that did not belong in his social milieu, he proposed that perhaps half a dozen families could "purchase a large block together and build at once." Belmont also suggested that the commissioners take thirty or forty acres apart for a zoological and botanical garden accessible only to subscribers. Belmont was the only European-born commissioner, and he noted that continental municipalities like Brussels and Antwerp had such institutions that took care of the upkeep and ran "without the aid of government."[31]

Belmont's suggestion for a private institution within the people's park would have horrified the most publicly minded commissioner, Andrew Haswell Green. Green was a prominent lawyer and president of the Board of Education, and he served as the commission's comptroller, treasurer, and, on occasion, its president. His eventual fights with Olmsted and Vaux are legendary, but he was also the great early supporter and defender of their masterpiece.

Thomas C. Fields, whom Tammany historian Gustavus Myers called "probably the most corrupt man that ever sat in the Legislature," was the complete opposite of Green. He represented the city's unique style of politicos, like Fernando Wood and Boss Tweed, and later he would be arrested and indicted for defrauding the city of nearly $200,000.[32]

Last was lawyer Waldo Hutchins, an anti-Catholic, anti-immigration, anti-abolition, anti-almost-anything-not-American member of the Know-Nothing Party. In 1872, Olmsted would refer to him and one other politician as "such dirty little steam tugs."[33] Fields and Hutchins often shared the same political outlook and voted together during the awards selection.

When the commissioners met on April 28, they did so to elect a winning design from the entrants. The first order of business, ahead of the award selection, was to discuss Viele's large surveys and drainage maps. Dillon moved to have them "properly backed and bound to secure them from further injury." Thanks to that request, the topographical and the drainage maps are preserved at the Municipal Archives. But though Commissioner Charles H. Russell believed that Viele's plan was worthy

18.6 The most prominent structure in the Old Cadet's Cemetery in West Point is a thirty-three-foot-high pyramid that is the tomb of General Viele and his second wife, Juliette Dana. The tomb and a drawing of a pyramid, submitted anonymously to the design competition soon after the commissioners rejected Viele's plan, may be more than a coincidence.

Source: Old Cadet's Cemetery, Stockbridge Collection. United States Military Academy Archives.

of either second or third place—he noted that it had "many valuable suggestions"—it won neither. According to Commissioner Thomas Fields, he did not vote for Viele's plan because "he would not accept second and therefore did not vote for it." It infuriated Viele, who understood the prizes to have been politically motivated.[34]

Next, the commissioners began reviewing the plans. When the envelope was opened for entry No. 2, it was "found to contain only a design for a pyramid." Was the author comparing the efforts of building, say, the Great Pyramid of Giza to that of Central Park? Perhaps, but it is worth considering a certain tomb in the West Point Cemetery. Even from quite a distance, the thirty-three-foot-high white granite pyramid mausoleum of Brigadier General Viele and his wife, Juliette Dana Viele, looms over the humbler tombstones of greater military heroes. Guarding the entrance are two sphinxes and a purportedly

Etruscan inscription over the lintel that reads EGBERT LUDOVICUS VIELE KIZI • ZILACHMKE • IMEANI • MUHIKLETH • JULIETTE • MUPPHZI KAMTHKE. The pyramid park submission was unsigned.[35] All fingers point to Viele. It appears to be the hasty and infantile gesture of a sore loser, whose accepted design had just been cast aside for an open competition.[36]

After reviewing all thirty-three entries, the commissioners began to vote. Each man was instructed to write his four choices on separate pieces of paper. Immediately, Commissioner Fields made a motion to disqualify entry No. 33, Olmsted and Vaux's "Greensward" plan, as it had been submitted after the midnight deadline. We cannot prove that Fields knew that No. 33 was their design, but, as with many other motions that evening, it seems that precious little was actually anonymous to the commissioners. Fields had cast the only vote against Olmsted when he was a candidate for the superintendent position. Olmsted explained that Fields's hostility was caused by a remark he once made that Fields was "the best partisan I ever knew, and he never forgave me for it."[37] The other commissioners voted down the motion.

Before they voted for first prize, motions flew about whether winning first prize constituted a commitment from the commission to build *all* of the winning design or only part of it. Robert Dillon argued that no plan was, "by reason of its marked superiority, entitled to the first prize." He moved that awards should only be given to second through fourth place. Perhaps he knew or surmised that Olmsted and Vaux's plan was the front runner. Charles Russell proposed that the four prizes be selected as planned, but that the board retain the liberty to amend the winning design. He considered that the majority of designs had "many suggestions of value." Andrew Haswell Green, the only true populist in the room, suggested delaying until the board could hear from the people, gathering "information from every source—through the press, from persons of taste, and from the criticism of the various competing artists" and the public. This motion did not pass.

Commissioner Waldo Hutchins asked to be excused from voting. Hutchins was a member of the Know-Nothing Party, and at an earlier meeting he and Fields had proposed that only American citizens should be hired as police for the park.[38] Whereas other commissioners voted for different design plans for each prize, Hutchins voted for only one plan for every slot. That was No. 26, the European-style design of Howard Daniels. Ironically, Hutchins is one of only two commissioners who are memorialized in Central Park. His elaborate marble bench lies just inside the park at East Seventy-Second Street.

Andrew Haswell Green is the other commissioner with a park bench. His is on the former site of Fort Fish in the northern end of the park. It is a smaller bench than the one that honors Hutchins, but it was Green's vote that put Olmsted and Vaux over the top on the first ballot. They won with seven votes (all six Republicans and Green) against four votes from the other three Democrats and Hutchins. Olmsted and Vaux split the $2,000 first prize, which would be about $33,000 each in today's currency.

Olmsted and Vaux's romantic landscape may have been the best, but there is no question that they were also favored insiders. Vaux was working with Commissioner Gray on his house and bank and must have discussed his night and weekend work moonlighting with Olmsted. Charles Wyllys Elliott, the one who had recommended Olmsted for the superintendent position, was his friend. And both designers were Republicans. But then again, they weren't the only insiders in the competition. Roughly a third of the submissions came from men employed on the park.[39]

Samuel Gustin, the superintendent of planting, won second place after four rounds of votes. Not only did he submit the requisite one-hundred-and-one-inch drawing, but he also created two three-dimensional models of the park: one of the existing topography and one of the park after his plan had been implemented. The topographic model was so useful that Commissioner Dillon proposed they purchase it for $1,000. Gustin was the favorite of most Democrats, so perhaps offering to buy his maps and models was a way of supplementing his second-place award.[40]

Plan No. 27 by Lachlan McIntosh, the disbursing clerk, and Michael Miller, the property clerk, took home third prize. Their plan was unremarkable, but according to Olmsted's chief biographer, Charles Beveridge, the commissioners saw the competition as a way "to reward 'their own.' "[41]

Fourth prize was awarded to "Manhattan," a design by landscape architect Howard Daniels, the only winner who was not employed by the park commission. But Daniels's continental style was out of step with the current preference for landscapes that blended into nature and disguised the handiwork of man. Daniels believed a park was "an artificial work," in which "art should everywhere be avowed and recognized." Hence he called his plan "Manhattan," and its main feature, the Central Avenue, mirrored the north-south arteries of the street grid and completely ignored the park's undulating topography. Daniels envisioned a broad and straight walk of two rows of tulip trees one hundred feet apart and two parallel rows of linden trees seventy-five feet away. These grand allées shot like an arrow up the center of the park from Fifty-Ninth Street to the base of Vista Rock at Seventy-Seventh Street, where they terminated in an elaborate water terrace.[42]

There were no votes for entry No. 16, by Susan Delafield Parish, a member of a wealthy New York family and the only woman to enter the contest. Nonetheless, the commissioners considered her plan of great value for its many original features. They deemed it so "beautiful and artistic" that they gave it a place of honor in the boardroom next to the four winning designs.[43]

Green got his wish for an exhibit. The commissioners voted to hold a public display of the plans, charging the public 25 cents each, "the proceeds from the entrance fee to be divided equally among the unsuccessful competitors."[44] In the end the exhibition was a success, and the remaining twenty-eight competitors each received $10.25.

The spirited session ended with a final vote, a simple procedural matter to pay the watchman, Charles F. Simmons, $16.50 for his service. It was the only unanimous vote of the night.

THE OTHER DESIGNERS

The board met again six days later, and a motion was put forward to have Russell, Dillon, and Fields form a three-man committee to work with Superintendent Olmsted on modifications to his plan. But Dillon and Fields refused to cooperate.[45] They were in denial that the Greensward plan was the final word on the subject. Fields made a motion to have the third- and fourth-place winners considered for first prize, but it was defeated ten to one.[46] Dillon proposed then to adopt Gustin's plan, but that motion was also defeated.[47] The board was torn, but it is fair to say that almost every commissioner assumed there would be *some* modification to Olmsted and Vaux's plan.

With revisions in mind, the board was eager to hear Olmsted's opinion on which elements from the thirty-one other plans *he* was considering adding to his own design.[48] It must have come as quite a surprise, therefore, to receive Olmsted's written reply the following day: "Many very interesting and artistic conceptions that are not introduced in plan 33 are, without doubt, to be found in the other plans exhibited, but they do not, it is believed, contain any desirable feature of prominent importance that is not already provided for in plan 33."[49]

Commissioners Dillon and Belmont must have been aghast at this insubordination. They would have regarded Olmsted as a mere employee of the commission, and they sought to put him in his place, especially since they disliked the romantic style of design. At two meetings in May, Dillon, backed by Belmont, decreed seventeen modifications to the Olmsted-Vaux plan that were inspired, for the most part, by Samuel Gustin's second-place plan. The two commissioners didn't just announce their ideas to the board—they created a public relations campaign in the newspapers, hoping to win over the public.[50]

August Belmont, the most famous horseman in America, pictured his afternoons in the park atop one of his thoroughbreds, coursing through miles of the leafy bridle paths or parading over the drives in one of his impressive carriages. When he learned that the winning prize would confine the horseback ride to a mere one-and-one-half-mile loop around the new reservoir, *and* that carriages and equestrians would be forced to share the drives, Belmont took the reins, so to speak, into his own hands. To Olmsted and Vaux, the park was meant to be a serene and meditative experience away from the urban bustle, so they designed serpentine roads to prevent the park from becoming a raceway and visitors from becoming rowdy spectators. But Dillon and Belmont demanded a six-mile ride throughout the entire park, and they were determined to get it.

Samuel Gustin's plan had many features that Dillon and Belmont fought to incorporate into the park's design. The Central Park Conservancy possesses the only known copy of the Gustin plan, folded into the printed description of entry No. 30. The most striking feature was a thirty-five-acre oval parade ground cut into six wedges, which must have pleased Belmont. Gustin explained that the unusual geometric field was "prepared especially with reference to equestrianism," and it was particularly advantageous for "trials of speed, displays of horsemanship, or the like." The Bois de Boulogne in Paris, constructed in the 1850s, included the Hippodrome de Longchamp, and Gustin took inspiration from the racetrack that became the subject of so many Degas paintings.

Gustin's plan also segregated pedestrians, equestrians, and carriages a feature similar to the entrance to the Bois de Boulogne, and Gustin incorporated it. So

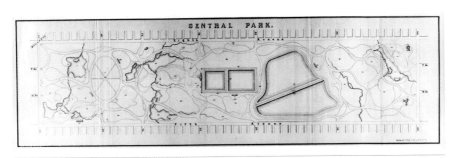

18.7 Samuel Gustin's plan for Central Park influenced the commissioners to adopt many of Gustin's features.

Source: Samuel Gustin, *Plan for Central Park*, Entry No. 31. Courtesy Central Park Conservancy.

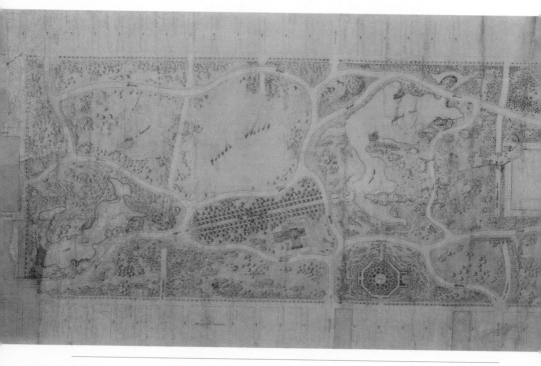

18.8 Calvert Vaux and Frederick Law Olmsted's "Greensward" was the winning entry in the 1858 design competition. Until the last four blocks were added in 1863, Central Park ended at 106th Street, and the receiving reservoir became the Great Lawn in the 1930s. Other than those major changes, Central Park retains the designers' plan for the most part.

Source: Calvert Vaux and Frederick Law Olmsted, *Greensward*, Entry No. 33. Courtesy of the New York City Municipal Archives.

enamored was Gustin with the new Parisian park that he attached a report by Chief Gardener Jean-Pierre Barillet-Deschamps describing the 2,200-acre landscape. Five months earlier, Dillon had offered a thousand dollars to "the engineer or other persons in chief" for information regarding the design and construction of the Bois, which he hoped would inspire New York's future park. The board approved Dillon's motion to seek out advice from the Bois de Boulogne designers, and they also approved a motion by Commissioner John Gray to invite experts from Birkenhead, a romantically landscaped park in Liverpool.[51] This was an early clue that Dillon would fight for the ancient geometric design over the modern naturalistic park that Olmsted had so admired in his 1850 visit to Birkenhead.[52]

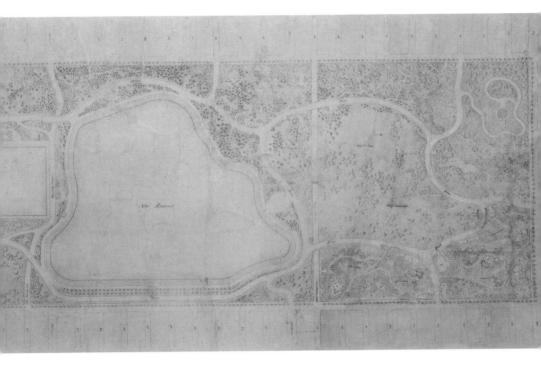

A WINNING COMPROMISE

Central Park's thirty-one ornamental bridges are part of what makes it Central Park, yet the original Greensward submission did not contain them. It featured only two footbridges and "a small but handsome stone arch" to span the declivity across McGowan's Pass at 106th Street and Sixth Avenue, the site of so many accidents, including the one that cost Jacob Dyckman his life.[53]

In their design, Olmsted and Vaux—like every other entrant in the competition—offered little to ensure pedestrians a safe crossing through the fast-moving horse and carriage traffic on the drives. But when the designers faced their next challenge—including Belmont's six-mile bridle path through the narrow

18.9 (*overleaf*) When forced to add a bridle path to the park, Calvert Vaux added the ornamental bridges as well. His elegant Bridge No. 28 anticipates the art nouveau style of the 1890s by nearly half a century.

Source: Sara Cedar Miller, *Bridge No. 28*. Courtesy Central Park Conservancy.

18.10 The sunken transverse roads that led city traffic—here a fire truck and a herd of sheep—under the park were the brilliant innovation of Olmsted and Vaux's Greensward plan.

Source: "Archway under Carriage Drive for Traffic Road Across the Park, 1859." Calvert Vaux, architect, W. H. Grant, engineer; Sarony, Major and Knapp, lithographers, *Third Annual Report if the Board of Commissioners of the Central Park*, January 1860. Courtesy of the Central Park Conservancy.

landscape—they solved both problems with a single brilliant solution. Vaux re-created the same over- and underpass system they had designed for commercial use *below* the park into a bilevel arch system for visitors *inside* the park.

Among the requirements stipulated for each design submission, the commissioners called for "four or more crossings from east to west." The Greensward plan proposed four sunken channels for the city's traffic run *across* and *below* the park, while maintaining an unobstructed rural idyll for visitors *inside* the park. It was the most innovative and creative concept, far and away superior to and unique from all the other plans in this regard. It was also, unwittingly, the prototype for the over- and underpasses of our modern highway system.[54]

Opinions differ on who conceived the partners' most creative idea. During an 1893 interview, Olmsted took credit for "the main elements" of their entire collaboration, including the sunken roads. According to Olmsted, the idea came to him from seeing a fire truck dash across the park on a path. Feeling guilty about his boast, he later backtracked about his claim, saying that although there was "nothing literally untrue . . . it was hardly just to Vaux." As a result, Vaux penned a memorandum the following year in which he claimed that he and Olmsted had "tacitly agreed" to share in the conception of the transverse roads. Some think Vaux contributed even more. Andrew Haswell Green threw his weight to Vaux, who he knew was the underdog. In his 1913 biography, written with his approval, Green attributed to Vaux "certain features of the park which have attracted the admiration both of the members of his profession and the public at large, there can be no doubt whatever."

> The transverse roads, which made the permanency of the Park in the midst of a great city possible, were especially his idea and his creation. Mr. Vaux was naturally a diffident man . . . a thinker and a designer, but not a talker or a writer [like Olmsted]. He therefore did not get the credit during his life-time that he earned and deserved, not because others wished to detract from hi[m] . . . , but because he was lacking in the self-assertion requisite to make his merits fully known to the world at large.[55]

Perhaps Green's animosity toward Olmsted caused him to challenge Olmsted's ownership of the idea, or perhaps Vaux did not receive the credit he deserved. Francis Kowsky has suggested that Olmsted and Vaux may have chosen to improve a weakness in Andrew Jackson Downing's 1852 plan for the Mall in Washington, D.C., in which several crosstown streets divide the landscape into small segments.[56]

Olmsted did give his partner credit for the architectural elements in their plan, including the arches and bridges that eliminated the perilous confrontation of pedestrians, carriages, and horseback riders, while offering each of them separate thoroughfares to provide for the safety and tranquility commonly associated with the pleasures of country life. They are also unique in their design and outstanding examples of Victorian decorative art.

But to Dillon and Belmont, the sunken roads were a blight, a deformity "forever to be deplored." They did not understand that sinking the transverse roads solved the puzzle of crosstown traffic and also hid the roads from view. It worked in the same way as a ha-ha—a deep trench alongside a wall that was found on many English estates—which allowed for a panoramic and unobstructed view of the countryside for property owners while preventing the escape of their grazing animals.[57] This same concept was, ironically, a feature in the Bois de Boulogne in Paris, so admired by Gustin, Dillon, and Belmont. The report by the chief gardener, which Gustin attached to his plan, described the eleven-and-a-half-foot deep "invisible fences" that were dug for the purpose of enclosing the woods on two sides of the Bois. Gustin never recognized the potential for digging similar trenches to avoid having the crosstown traffic pass through the park, and his greatest champions, Dillon and Belmont, dismissed the landscape device found in the French park they so loved. If they had gotten their way, the Seventy-Ninth Street crosstown bus would stop in the wooded Ramble and right at the door of Belvedere Castle rather than out of sight below it.

Dillon and Belmont were quintessential New Yorkers. They wanted to reach their destination via the straightest and fastest possible route. Among their seventeen demands, they proposed a wire suspension bridge to provide pedestrians a link from Bethesda Terrace to the walkway of the lower reservoir, avoiding a leisurely stroll through the Ramble woodlands.[58] They were also passionate modernists, who considered the reservoirs the "jewels of the park." Understandably, they were awed by the engineering feat of the Croton waterworks, but they also wanted an equally engineered conduit that bypassed nature and flew visitors directly to the park's technological gems.

When Olmsted challenged Dillon and Belmont's opinion that the reservoirs were the most important objects in the park, he declared them, in fact, "undesirable." He described walks around them as "perfectly comprehensible and uninteresting after one or two visits of examination." It was then that Olmsted—commenting on the reservoirs as monuments to modernity and urbanity—made his famous statement about "the one great purpose of the park": "to supply the hundreds of thousands of tired workers who have no opportunity to spend their summers in a country, a specimen of God's handiwork, that shall be to them what a month or two in the White Mountains or the Adirondacks, is, at great cost, to those in easier circumstances."[59] In this sense, Central Park embodied a democratic sentiment, even a social mission. Olmsted invoked the tired workers to remind the two wealthy commissioners that a visit to the Lake and the Ramble woodland—the landscapes under the purported suspension bridge—was the equivalent of a country vacation in the Adirondacks, so easily affordable to the Belmonts and Dillons of the world, and so far out of reach for working-class New Yorkers.

The wire suspension bridge was another affront to Olmsted. Using his professional connections, he fought back in the press. He placed a table tent on a rock in the future Ramble and invited New York's two most power newspapermen,

18.11 The transverse roads that led city traffic under the park—here, the Ninety-Sixth Street Transverse Road—were the brilliant innovation of Olmsted and Vaux's Greensward plan. They became the model for the under- and overpasses of our modern highway system.

Source: Sara Cedar Miller, *Aerial, Ninety-Six Street Transverse Road*. Courtesy of the Central Park Conservancy.

Charles A. Dana of the *Tribune* and Henry Raymond of the *Times*, to join him for breakfast. From the future shoreline of the Lake, he asked Dana and Raymond to picture the damage the intrusive suspension bridge would cause to his picturesque vision. The two newspapers stopped running articles in support of Dillon and Belmont's plan.[60]

In the end, Olmsted placated the commissioners by agreeing to construct a light bridge across the Lake "at as low a level as possible." By doing so, he and Vaux compromised one of their most important design decisions, to locate the

18.12 (*overleaf*) The most famous bridge in Central Park is Bow Bridge, designed as a compromise to replace a proposed suspension bridge. The span bisected the Lake and went against Olmsted and Vaux's design preference for unobstructed and limitless views.

Source: Sara Cedar Miller, *Bow Bridge and Lake*. Courtesy of the Central Park Conservancy.

18.13 The Pool, one of the most intimate and charming landscapes in the park, was influenced by Samuel Gustin's entry to the competition.

Source: Sara Cedar Miller, *Pool*. Courtesy of the Central Park Conservancy.

manmade structures in sites as visually inconspicuous as possible or, as with the park's arches and bridges, to camouflage them with vegetation.[61]

This light crossing became Bow Bridge, one of the park's most beloved icons. It has appeared in countless movies and advertisements, but Olmsted and Vaux designed the Lake to provide an illusion of infinity, intending visitors to imagine hidden coves and a limitless shoreline. This sense of unbounded space was a physical and psychological antidote to the visual bombardment of the cityscape. Bow Bridge, for all its beauty, focuses the eye of the visitor on a man-made object and severs the Lake into two smaller sections. Fortunately, the larger suspension bridge was never built.

Olmsted and Vaux, under pressure from Dillon and Belmont, enlarged the natural stream at Central Park West and 100th Street into the Pool, the park's most intimate water body. In his plan, Samuel Gustin chose to dam McGowan's Pass, and—with the help of locally fed streams and an overflow of the Reservoir—fashion

18.14 Conservatory Water, better known to park visitors as the Sailboat Pond or Model Boat Pond, was inspired by Samuel Gustin's plan for a water body on that site. The boats may have been inspired by the model yachts in Paris's Jardin du Luxembourg.

Source: Sara Cedar Miller, *Model Boating on Conservatory Water*. Courtesy of the Central Park Conservancy.

a thirty-foot-deep elongated lake that flooded the ravine and transformed the steep landscape into a far less dramatic experience. Olmsted and Vaux revised Gustin's idea by transforming the rivulet into a more expansive lake near Central Park West, merging it with additional city water that appeared to gush from the depths of a rocky grotto but was, in actuality, a man-made "cave" containing a hidden pipe.

The Gustin plan also contained a second water body, a small lake at Seventy-Fourth Street and Fifth Avenue that Olmsted and Vaux transformed into the Conservatory Water. The designers had originally created the requisite flower garden on the site, but they changed their plan to accommodate a reflecting pool for a two-story glass conservatory that was never built. It is better known as the Sailboat or Model Boat Pond, for the tradition of sailing model yachts across it. One French article attributed the start of this popular activity to Olmsted's visit to Paris's Jardin du Luxembourg, where the French have enjoyed a similar pastime since as early as 1832.[62]

Dillon and Belmont applauded the grand formal entrances at Sixth Avenue and Seventh Avenue, the parallel paths for carriages, horses, and pedestrians that terminated at the oval parade ground, today situated on Sheep Meadow and the Mall. Olmsted and Vaux had also placed a Promenade, the processional pathway at the centerpiece of their plan, to satisfy visitors' gregarious nature.

Curiously, there is no written explanation for the name change in 1859 from the "Promenade" to the "Mall." The answer may lie in the meaning that *promenade* had to mid-nineteenth-century New Yorkers. In the tradition of the evening promenade on Broadway in the 1840s and 1850s, the men and women of polite society would parade their fashions and their elite status while the lower classes looked on.[63] The designers and the commissioners intended the park to be inclusive, not class-conscious, and perhaps they realized that naming the walkway the Promenade took on an elite association that went against the park ideals. Caring deeply that Central Park serve all nationalities, races, and socioeconomic groups, the designers or possibly the commissioners chose to emphasize the *shape* of the main pathway rather than its *function*. The quarter-mile Mall was named after the seventeenth-century English game of pall-mall, a game played with a ball (a pall) and a mallet (a mall) on a long, straight alley. The term was already used for a straight tree-lined walkway in London, along Boston Commons, and in Pierre L'Enfant's 1790 plan for Washington, D.C.[64]

THE GREENSWARD CHALLENGE

With the underpinnings of the prepark's uses, Olmsted and Vaux's Greensward vision altered the terrain more than any other plan, as far as we can tell by their written descriptions. They transformed and expanded the limitations of its half-mile-wide broken topography into the illusion of a vast country estate.

Of the four other known visual plans, John J. Rink's geometric design could only have been constructed on the flats of Kansas. Its fanciful flower and shrub beds of circles, stars, and mazes would make a lovely scarf but would never work on the roller coaster landscape of Central Park.[65]

That left the three other known designs: those of Viele, Waring, and Gustin. They failed to challenge the landscape. In order to avoid filling depressions or

18.15 John J. Rink's entry to the design competition had no reference to the park's challenging topography but instead celebrated America's military past. Rink did, however, submit two plans. The other, perhaps a more naturalistic design, has been lost to history.

Source: John J. Rink, *Plan of the Central Park*, New York: Entry No. 4 in the competition, Ink and colored washes, March 20, 1858, Overall: 45 1/4 x 103 1/8 in. (115 x 262 cm), New-York Historical Society, (PR.003.234).

blasting rock outcrops, their paths, bridle trails, and drives formed a hodge-podge of small, disconnected glades and ponds that lacked any sense of expansiveness, variety, design intention, and surprise. Only the two reservoirs broke the repetitive pattern.

Olmsted and Vaux, on the other hand, rearranged much of the topography by filling, excavating, blasting, or clearing to create the seemingly infinite meadows and lakes, Greensward's vision of the sweeping and boundless views found in open country or on the canvases of the Hudson River School. Olmsted and Vaux called these "passages of scenery," a sequence of landscapes that varied in shape, size, and style and evoked a range of emotions. A visitor walks among the densely shaded and enclosed Ramble woodland out to the vast, sunny Lake, over a bridge to an elegant architectural terrace and the Mall, a walkway lined with a canopy of arching elm trees. To walk through Central Park is to walk through what Olmsted called "a gallery of mental pictures."[66]

Greensward was a plan set apart from the other four surviving visual entries to the design competition, so it came as a surprise to Olmsted and Vaux in 1864 when Egbert Viele claimed that they, among others, had stolen his design.[67] In his lawsuit against the city and Board of Aldermen, Viele won more than $9,000 based on three legitimate claims: he was owed his $2,500 salary for the year before he was dismissed; his preliminary surveys for the design competition; and the adoption of his plan by the former commission. In the trial, former Mayor Fernando Wood testified that Viele's plan had not been officially adopted. Viele himself claimed he had no written proof and was only "informed" of it by the mayor, but it had been printed in the city's *First Annual Report*, so the jury sided with Viele.

Viele's 1857 topographic survey was photographed and given to all the competitors to help them formulate their plans. Because the commissioners had offered Viele's survey as a baseline, Viele claimed that about half of the thirty-three submissions had copied it.[68] Given the limitations of the topography and the $1.5 million-dollar budget, most of the designs were indeed similar, but Viele, a spiteful loser, confessed that he had submitted *two* plans—not including No. 2, the pyramid plan that he may have put forward anonymously as a rebuff to the commission. He claimed that besides his signed entry—No. 28—he also created a second and secret submission, "a most absurd and impractical plan, not based upon any knowledge of the ground," and that had become No. 27, the third-place winner. He said that this was in reality *his* entry and not the creation of the property clerk Michael Miller and the disbursing clerk Lachlan McIntosh. Miller was the son-in-law of one of the commissioners, and the authorship of plan No. 27 was easily verifiable, even though Viele claimed to have purposely signed the entry himself. According to the vengeful engineer, his ploy was meant to "test the capacity of those men to judge" an inferior design and out them for injuring his reputation.[69]

In the trial, Viele took rightful credit for the design of the new reservoir, but he wrongfully compared the small lakes in his design to the sweeping water bodies of the Greensward plan. He noted that the placement of his drive entrances were similar, and he claimed (absurdly) that Olmsted and Vaux's transverse roads were "not materially" different from his own crossroads, even though Olmsted and Vaux's roads were depressed below the landscape and his were even with the ground. Most of all, he claimed that "the distinct characteristic" of his plan was his adaptation of the design to the park's topography, the basic foundation in the canon of landscape design.

Frederick Law Olmsted was in California at the time, so Calvert Vaux took the stand to testify against Viele. When asked by counsel, "In what respect does your plan differ from Viele?" Vaux replied, "In every respect."[70]

By 1864, the year of the Viele trial, Central Park had grown four blocks, now with a northern terminus at 110th Street rather than 106th Street. But even that small addition would entail several trials and travails before the last brushstroke on New York City's masterpiece was finally applied.

chapter 19

Extending the Park, 1859–1863

The four northernmost blocks of Central Park, between 106th Street and 110th Street, are unique.[1] The dramatic elevation changes in the topography at the northwest corner, Fort Clinton and Nutter's Battery to the forested woodlands sheltering the Blockhouse, and the sparkle of sunlight on the waters of the Harlem Meer—these are some of the outstanding natural features of the northern park. It was these attractions—most of which remain—that drew Hendrick and Isaac de Forest to the wilds of Manhattan Island in 1637. The lives of the Montagnes, Bensons, Kortrights, and Nutters and the military events at McGowan's Pass all took place on this Harlem landscape, a rich chapter of the park's prehistory. But those sixty-four acres—a total of twelve blocks—came very close to being excluded from Central Park.

The commissioners recognized the landscape's ruggedness and its successful contrast with the more manicured southerly grounds. Yet they also understood that adapting the ground to suit for millions of visitors would be both costly and challenging.[2] That was the reason that the park originally ended so abruptly at 106th Street. In the 1858 design competition, six entrants had the foresight to suggest the extension to 110th Street. Five of them were employees of the commission.[3] Olmsted and Vaux did not include the addition in their submission, though Olmsted later expressed his desire to do so. In December 1860, he wrote to Commissioner Fields that acquiring the extension "would add greatly to the value of the park, the line of 106th Street offering a most inconvenient and unseemly boundary, that of 110th Street a natural, convenient and beautiful termination of its scenery."[4]

In 1857, while Viele's plan was considered the accepted design, a map of Manhattan included his plan to 106th Street and left the space between the end

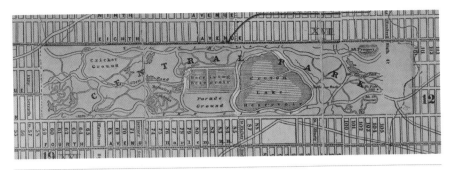

19.1 The extension of the park to 110th Street was envisioned as early as this 1857 map, two years before the commissioners petitioned the state legislature for the land. The map's creator used Viele's map and left a blank for the last four blocks.

Source: "New York city map." Lionel Pincus and Princess Firyal Map Division, The New York Public Library, New York Public Library Digital Collections, https://digitalcollections.nypl.org/items/d712f0a0 -f3a1-0130-f212-58d385a7b928.

of Central Park and 110th Street blank, which indicates that to some the extension seemed to be a foregone conclusion. In March 1858, six weeks before the design competition, Commissioner John A.C. Gray alerted the Common Council that the board was seeking cost estimates to purchase the northern rocky bluffs, "useless for any other purpose than that of the park."[5] By mid-May, the board asked Olmsted for a sketch of a plan to connect the drives above 106th Street with those already approved on the Greensward plan. For this task, they thought Olmsted should "call in the service of his associate," which was the board's first acknowledgment of Vaux's existence since the prizes were awarded.[6] By June the board commissioned photographs of the landscape, and in August they asked Olmsted to create a design and requested that the legislature acquire the land.[7]

In a letter to the *Journal of Commerce*, the author declared the exclusion of this acreage to be an "inexcusable mistake," and even suggested that some other portion of the park might advantageously be exchanged for it if the purchase price was too high.[8]

Recalling the battle between Central Park and Jones Wood, the same issue arose again: who would pay for it? Those who lived on and owned the surrounding properties were opposed to the increased assessments that they would have to pay as the result of the park's extension and sent a remonstrance against the extension to the legislature.[9] But on April 2, 1859, the legislature officially took the land for Central Park, under the assumption that the entire cost of the land and all the legal proceedings would not exceed $300,000.[10]

The next order of business was for the state supreme court, under the aegis of the board of park commissioners, to appoint "three suitable persons" as Commissioners of Estimate and Assessment. The assignment fell to the corporation counsel, Richard Busteed. The three parties—the landowners, the park commissioners acting on behalf of the corporation, and the mayor—had a vested interest in the appointments. So Busteed nominated Anthony J. Bleecker on behalf of the landowners, Hawley D. Clapp on behalf of the Central Park board, and Richard Kelly for the mayor.[11] Unlike the impartial and upstanding commissioners of 1853, two of the new commissioners were known to have a vested interest in the process.

Nine months before his appointment, auctioneer Anthony J. Bleecker had anticipated the extension of the park and auctioned some of the most valuable properties.[12] In choosing one of New York's most successful property auctioneers, the landowners were assured that their land would receive the highest possible appraisal. In fact, Busteed himself anticipated the potential for huge personal profit, so he paid $33,000 for joint ownership of thirty-one choice lots of the park extension within the year of leaving his position as corporation counsel.[13] Hawley D. Clapp lacked any professional qualifications to estimate and assess Harlem real estate. He was the proprietor of the Everett Hotel on Union Square, a five-star lodge that catered to the wealthiest and most discerning clients, people like Jay Gould, the Prince of Wales, and high-ranking Democratic politicians. It became the headquarters for New York's Democratic Party in the 1860s, which is the most likely explanation for Clapp's appointment.[14] And while the commissioners were estimating the value of the land, lots and mortgages were actively changing hands.

In 1858, the commissioners had written to the Common Council that the lots of the future extension were of "comparatively small value."[15] But for the next six years real estate speculation continued at a faster pace than it had in 1853. From 1858 to 1863, a fairly small circle of speculators and mortgagees had bought, sold, divided, and repurchased properties or transferred mortgages as the value of the land increased exponentially.

In May 1860, for example, real estate tycoon Mary G. Pinkney, who had already been awarded up to $375,000 for her property below 106th Street, sold one block in today's North Woods to Henry H. Elliot for $50,000, holding a mortgage of $40,000. As you may recall, in 1843 Pinkney had used the inheritance from her deceased father to bail out her stepfather, Archibald Watt, from financial ruin. Then she, his brilliant protégé, took over his real estate enterprise, which included much of the upper park.

Nine days after buying the property from Pinkney, Henry Elliott transferred his mortgage and the additional sum of more than $5,000 to Courtlandt Palmer.[16] Palmer and Elliott had been partners in a hardware business that had nearly folded after the Panic of 1837, and they used their few remaining resources to invest in real estate. At his death in May 1874, Palmer was reported to be worth "many millions," owning much of the land in Columbus, Ohio.[17] In 1863, when the city purchased his sixty-four lots for the park extension, he realized almost a 40 percent profit, which became a legal issue for him *and* the city of New York.

After eighteen months and much anticipation, Bleecker, Hawley, and Kelly issued their report to the Board of Central Park Commissioners. Their estimate for payment to the owners totaled a whopping $1.5 million, a sum far greater than the $300,000 the board had imagined. The shock of the new price tag was even more devastating than the increased cost for the lower park four years earlier. So although these lots were "very desirable" lands, the price-conscious board of commissioners aborted their proceedings. Central Park would end at 106th Street.[18]

The landowners were furious. Their much-anticipated profits had disappeared right in front of their eyes. They urged the three Commissioners of Estimate and Assessment to argue before the state supreme court that the Central Park board lacked the power to suspend the extension. The commissioners did just that in January 1861, but Supreme Court Judge Barnard sided with the board and refused to accept the three-man report. The judge ruled that as agents for the city, the commissioners of Central Park were legally sanctioned to buy the land on behalf of the city, and they were just as equally vested with the authority to cancel the purchase. In October, the judge dealt Bleecker, Clapp, and Kelly one more blow, reducing the inflated costs for their services by $43,000.[19]

Now the landowners were exasperated. Henry H. Elliott—the older brother of Olmsted and Vaux's good friend, commissioner Charles Wyllys Elliott—had a great deal invested in the area. He partnered with Commissioner Clapp to challenge Judge Barnard's decision, a scheme derided as "the big swindle embodied in

19.2 (*overleaf*) When the commissioners rejected the extension from 106th Street to 110th Street in 1860 due to the cost, it might have prevented such features as the cascade at Huddlestone Arch in the Ravine from being created.

Source: Sara Cedar Miller, *Cascade in the Ravine*. Courtesy Central Park Conservancy.

19.3 The last four blocks of Central Park, such as the lots in the North Woods pictured here, were subject to a frenzy of real estate speculation and skyrocketing prices. By 1863, when the land was officially taken for the park, the land was valued at nearly $19,000 per acre—more than double the $7,800 price per acre for the lower park in 1856.

Source: Sara Cedar Miller, *Aerial North Woods and Blockhouse*. Courtesy of the Central Park Conservancy.

the northern extension job." Elliott and Clapp advocated that Albany legislators switch from Republican state-appointed Central Park commissioners to Democratic city-appointed ones to "insure the acceptance of the $1,500,000 price tag for the park." At the same time, Elliott was working with Olmsted on the development of upper Manhattan, no doubt as a way to enhance his real estate portfolio[20] The Elliot-Clapp plan was defeated in the same way that the self-appointed mayoral commission of Fernando Wood and Joseph Taylor was overpowered by the Republican-led independent board of Central Park commissioners. That upstate/downstate drama would continue for much of the century.

The subject of the extension lay dormant for a year. In the interim, war came to America once again. On April 2, 1861, South Carolina militia artillery fired on the Union garrison at Fort Sumter, the first shots of the Civil War. While the war was devastating for the rest of the country, in its early days it brought an economic surge in industrial production to New York City.[21]

With more money in the city coffers, the time was ripe for another look at those twelve blocks. In March 1862, a committee was formed to investigate the repeal of the extension plan and to proceed with a new commission. Judge Daniel P. Ingraham of the state supreme court appointed three new commissioners. Two of them, Luther Bradish and Michael Uelshoffer, were well-respected men who had already served as commissioners for the lower park in 1853. The third man, Samuel B. Ruggles, was the real estate mogul responsible for the creation of Gramercy Park and the development of Union Square. He was there to act on behalf of the landowners.[22]

After a contested hearing, Judge Ingraham approved the report in April 1863.[23] The total purchase price, nearly $1.2 million, still exceeded the expectations of the board, though they had saved more than $300,000 from the previous commission. This was still a monumental increase in the price per acre of land taken for the park. In 1856, the cost for purchasing the 779 acres of land for the park and the new reservoir had averaged $7,800 per acre. In 1863, the sixty-four-acre extension rose to nearly three times that: around $18,750 per acre.[24] Tight-fisted treasurer Andrew Haswell Green expressed regrets that the city had not purchased the land before the creation of the rest of the park had caused real estate prices to soar.[25]

The greatest portion of these twelve blocks was held by three landowners: Gouverneur Morris Wilkins, who was Valentine Nutter's grandson, and the real estate tycoons Mary G. Pinkney and Courtlandt Palmer.[26] When the Harlem Canal Company foreclosed on its mortgages in 1830, Wilkins, Watt, and others bought back much of the Nutter estate and surrounding properties at greatly reduced prices.[27]

The aggregate sum of more than $585,000 for the property of Wilkins, Watt/Pinkney, and Palmer totaled half the awards given for the twelve blocks. The other thirty-seven owners and a few lessees were awarded the rest.[28] And during the time in which these forty speculators were playing musical chairs with the twelve-block properties, parallel transactions for the very same lots were taking place under an entirely different set of rules.

DR. MONTAGNE AGAIN

After the distribution of the awards in 1863, many people headed straight to court to contest the decisions. Some owners claimed that they, not those granted the award, held the legal title to the land and therefore deserved the money. These alleged titles occasionally went back a generation or two, but in one suit the deed supposedly proving rightful possession dated back more than two centuries, all the way to May 9, 1647.[29]

That was the day that New Amsterdam Director General William Kieft granted his loyal counselor Dr. Johannes de la Montagne two hundred acres that encompassed much of today's park above 106th Street, the Harlem flatlands from Morningside Park to Manhattanville, and much of East Harlem.[30] The story of the Montagnes had come full circle. In 1850, two hundred years later, an eighth-generation descendant of Dr. Montagne named John Montanye, a cooper, claimed title to that estate. He produced an English-language copy of Kieft's Dutch-language deed and waved it under the nose of a New York City official, who accepted it without reservation.[31]

Montanye was in cahoots with his second cousin, James A. Cosse, and he immediately "sold" Cosse his vast and valuable holdings for the unbelievably low price of $600, relying on the Kieft grant as legitimate proof of title. For two hundred years that property had been bought and sold through thousands of legal transactions. But the two descendants swore to the validity of their ownership via Kieft's deed as faithfully as they swore on their families' Bibles.[32] The Dutch playbook to keep the land in the family continued in the honored tradition.

James Cosse was a both comic and tragic figure. He was a shoemaker—or, in some documents, "a policeman"—who spent much of his youth dreaming and scheming about his legacy. His mother, Jane Montanye Truman, was descended in a direct line from Jean (or Jan) Mousnier de la Montagne, Dr. Montagne's oldest son. She must have filled her only child's head with tales of the family's former grandeur and position. Cosse confessed that as a young man he would travel uptown just to scope out his property, and he dreamed of making a claim to it as early as 1831 in the aftermath of the canal boondoggle.[33]

John Montanye died in 1862, but Cosse and his claims for Central Park property were dragged through hearings by the commissioners and through the courts from 1864 to 1871. The lawyers started by challenging Cosse's heritage, but he proved himself a legitimate Montagne descendant based on his family Bible.[34] There are bits and pieces of information on James Cosse in the documentary record. In 1850, he told a census taker that he was a forty-five-year-old farmer living around the Harlem Meer. We know also that he and his wife, Eliza Ann, had experienced marital problems as far back as November 5, 1834, when he placed an ad in the *New York Evening Post* after she had left him. The ad treated her departure as though she were a enslaved runaway. "LEFT—Eliza Cosse, the wife of J.A. Cosse left his bed and board without any cause or justification. All persons are forbid harboring or trusting her on my account. No charges paid."[35] They seemingly reconciled, and by the 1850 U.S. Census they lived together and had eight children. They gave their youngest son the first name of John De La Montagne, a way to underscore the family's legitimacy while they lived on Dr. Montagne's old Vredendal property, most likely in Valentine Nutter's house and property, as it was valued at $12,000.[36]

Prior to the purchase of his land in 1850, Cosse claimed that he had rented the Harlem property from John Montanye. In his 1864 and 1868 trial he produced a lease, dated in 1862 for a property purportedly leased in 1842, but it contained so many flaws and inaccuracies that its authenticity seems very doubtful.[37]

According to Cosse, he moved in 1842 into the first available vacant home in the Harlem Meer area. He had asked no questions about any ownership of lands or houses that he leased, sold, or inhabited. When the defense lawyer probed him for details, asking, "How did you get possession? Did you open the door?" Cosse replied, "The doors were open, the cattle could run through, and the pigs could run through," so he moved in. On the nearby McGowan's Pass property, Cosse claimed he took possession by letting his livestock graze there, turning "on it my cattle, horse, and cow."

Without any official survey or professional surveyor, he fenced in the land, guessing at the limits of the property. This itself was a serious legal offense. Fencing had been a legal requirement since 1647 to enclose one's cattle and, more importantly, to fix proper title. Ironically, Cosse's ancestor Dr. Montagne was present at a meeting in 1655 to discuss installing someone as fence viewer, an important Harlem position in partnership with the surveyor.[38]

Several of the six surveyors hired by Valentine Nutter over fifty years earlier testified at the trials. All but one of them—James E. Serrell, hired by Cosse—determined that the basis for Montagne's grant from Kieft was "so indefinite" that to fix an absolute location was "a mere piece of guess-work." But James E. Serrell was right. No other topography had the 200-acre flatlands in relationship to the kills and the hills of Harlem.

While Montanye never quit his day job as a barrel maker, Cosse tossed caution—and shoemaking—to the wind and entered the full-time occupation of Manhattan real estate. For more than two decades, Cosse conveyed his leased property as if he held the title legally. He carried on transactions with at least fifteen different tenants, renting houses, barns, and lots to a succession of gardeners, laborers, and fellow shoemakers, some through written leases and some through simple verbal agreements. In those days, all renters were transient. Homes in the area were abandoned and left vacant, fires were a constant, cycles of fallow land followed years of cultivation, and residents moved often. When a house or a lot became vacant on Cosse's "property," he shuffled the spaces and the people, himself and his family included.[39]

When the leases of his tenant gardeners, James Tracy and William Miller, ended, Cosse moved into their extensive farm complex. The complex contained a dwelling house, carriage house, root house, greenhouse, and sixty-four lots between 109th to 110th Streets around the site of today's East 110th Street playground. Cosse confirmed that this was the former Nutter property before he moved the house farther east in 1851 or 1852 in anticipation of the construction of Sixth Avenue. He removed the old frame, dug a new cellar and basement, and set the old frame on top.[40] His wife, Eliza Ann, sublet the old Nutter house in 1855 from its legal tenant, Stephen Dubois; she opened a hotel adjacent to the Kingsbridge Road, only steps from the old Half-Way House of Metje Cornelis. When Eliza Cosse didn't pay her rent, landowner John Pyne said her husband must step in and pay it for her.[41]

Cosse and Montanye were not the only descendants to claim ownership under the Kieft grant. The Montanye-to-Cosse deed had been recorded at the request of "A[nthony]. Feistel," the husband of another legitimate Montagne descendant, Cornelia Amerman Feistel. Other family members, it seemed, also relied on their Montagne bloodline as proof of ownership to a large chunk of Manhattan Island. The year following the conveyance of Montagne to Cosse, the Feistels, who rented land in the park, claimed ownership of six lots of land on today's East Meadow based on the Kieft grant. In an 1851 court case, the jury found in favor of plaintiff Charles Reade, who had sued Anthony Feistel when he claimed to be the rightful landowner. Reade noted that that specific property had been owned by the Bensons, *not* Dr. Montagne, and the judge ruled that the Feistels' claim was based on a "pretend" conveyance.[42] Reade won the case. In his own trial over a decade later, James Cosse admitted that he "took an active part" in the Feistel suits by taking copious notes of the testimonies and "obtaining witnesses."[43]

Cosse's series of sham transactions proved how little oversight the city had to validate legal titles. This was the era of the conman. Earlier, the speculators

Newell Bradner Smith and Don Alonzo Cushman shortchanged the heirs of Epiphany Davis, and con man Robert Ritter gave false bonds to Seneca Village landowner James Hunt. In the coming years, a fraudster named George C. Parker several times "sold" the Statue of Liberty, the Metropolitan Museum of Art, and the Brooklyn Bridge. Police had to remove the new "owners" when they were caught trying to erect toll booths.[44] Montanye and Cosse were early pioneers of this same trade. Even the term "confidence man" dates to 1849, when the cousins were illegally leasing houses and conveying land to unsuspecting people who were just looking for a place to call home.[45]

The two men were part of the growing class of swindlers who operated underneath the ever-increasing complexity of modern urban life. The creation of the park was plagued with flagrant corruption or self-promotion by such government officials as Fernando Wood and Daniel Sickles. A slew of tricksters and crooks preyed upon poor and ignorant immigrants, or, on the other end of the spectrum, the elite establishment like Clapp and Elliott tried to overturn the rule of law to turn a larger profit for themselves. Members of the aspiring middle class, caught up in the newly complicated world of buying and selling real estate, were frequent targets because of what historian David Scobey called the "mystification" of the real estate market, which was beset with "bogus sales, falsified deeds, and insider trading."[46] It was the middle class and working class on whom the descendants of Dr. Johannes de la Montagne plied their deceptions. By exploiting their ancestry, they devised a sophisticated scam to profit from their so-called inheritance.

But at last, the deceptions began to backfire. In 1849, David Randolph Martin, the president of Ocean Bank, had purchased twenty-seven lots above 106th Street from George Doughty and leased them to Patrick Daly. In 1856, John Montanye, claiming to be Daly's landlord, brought a suit against him in New York Superior Court for the "unlawful withholding" of his rent. To confirm Martin's ownership, Daly's lawyer called many long-standing residents and landowners to testify, including "a man upwards of 103 years of age, and a number of very old persons." Among them were Valentine Nutter's daughter, Sarah Wilkins; her son, Gouverneur Morris Wilkins; both McGowan brothers, Andrew Jr. and Samson B.; attorney Isaac Adriance, the husband of the McGowans' granddaughter Margaret Eliza; and Archibald Watt.[47] Trial documents do not detail Montanye's testimony, but from available records it appears that the Kieft grant did not make an appearance, probably because all the witnesses could recite the history of Harlem land transfers dating back to the Montagnes, and they would have laughed Montanye and Cosse out of court. The jury found in favor of Daly, and Montanye had to pay him for costs and expenses.[48]

The following year, Martin also won an ejectment suit—the legal means of recovering property and the legal means of determining title—forcing Cosse to abandon his claim to Martin's property.[49]

CAHILL & SEELEY V. PALMER AND THE MAYOR &C.

By 1862, the new Commissioners of Estimate and Assessment were evaluating the land once again, and James Cosse knew his chances to cash in on a Central Park windfall were slim. Undaunted, he hatched a new scheme. In September, knowing any deed under his name would likely be invalidated by the commissioners, he "sold" several lots of the prepark to two men, Sylvester Cahill, a fellow shoemaker, and Gilliam D. Seeley, a dealer of soda waters and sarsaparilla, a popular nineteenth-century medicinal and soft drink made from a tropical plant with a taste similar to root beer. They paid Cosse only one dollar each, plus "other good and valuable consideration." What they meant by "good and valuable consideration" was clarified ten days later in a notarized agreement among the three.

The document granted Sylvester Cahill three-fourths of the property on the condition that he "use his best endeavors and efforts" to obtain an award and compensation for the land within one year of the contract. To retain his so-called legal title to the property, Cahill agreed to negotiate with the current owners and lessees, showing them the Kieft deed and claiming ownership. If Cahill could meet these stipulations within the year, he would own three-quarters of the property and Seeley would own one-quarter. In other words, Cahill's seemingly insurmountable job was to convince all the legitimate owners that their title was in jeopardy and force them to negotiate based on the validity of the Kieft deed. If Cahill failed, his and Seeley's deed was null and void, and the property would be reconveyed to Cosse "free and clear of all encumbrances."[50]

It is not very clear what Seeley's role was in the plot, other than holding one-fourth of the potential award to be held in trust for the benefit of Cosse. Seeley was most likely Cosse's son-in-law, and his daughter was Amanda Seeley,[51] but there was an odd connection to John Montanye that turned up in the newspapers. It seems that since infancy Montanye's seventeen-year-old son, Charles, had suffered from an "aggravated case of scrofula," a serious form of tuberculosis affecting the lymph nodes and appearing as boil-like sores on the skin. Thanks to Bristol's Sarsaparilla, his son was apparently cured of scrofula, and Montanye began to evangelize on behalf of Seeley's product. He took out newspaper ads inviting anyone to his home on Hester Street to meet his son and see his healed scars for themselves.[52] Perhaps the land scheme was an indirect payment for Seeley introducing the sarsaparilla cure to Montanye's son.

When negotiations with the other landowners failed, Cahill and Seeley sued the legal owner, Courtlandt Palmer, and the city for $73,000 of his award money—equal in today's money to about $1.5 million—almost the exact amount the city had awarded Palmer for the one block of the North Woods that he had purchased from Elliott.[53] But that didn't work. After three trials, Cahill, Seeley, and most of all Cosse walked away penniless.

THE NEW GENERATION

In 1647, when Dr. Johannes de la Montagne received the deed for his distant and isolated tract of land, neither he nor his contemporaries could ever have predicted a day two centuries later when owning that much land on Manhattan would only be possible for a small clique of real estate barons, the likes of John Jacob Astor or, in our story, Courtlandt Palmer, Archibald Watt, and Mary G. Pinkney. The old Dutch family estates were quickly disappearing, and even such middle-class burghers as Dr. Montagne would have had to resign themselves to owning only one or two small twenty-five-by-one-hundred-foot plots.

In 1857, a financial expert writing for the *New York Times* shared the secret to "keeping money after you have made it"—investing in real estate in the city's undeveloped areas. Properties from Thirty-Ninth Street north, he claimed, were "tossed rapidly from hand to hand, in the market, making each time a profit for the seller, and insuring a quick return to the purchaser." With the coming of the park, lots in the remote 90s—once "taken only for debt by grumbling creditors"—now anticipated new centers of wealth. Though some businessmen might assume the inflated prices were merely speculative, the author wrote, he assured them that they reflected real and actual value. He ended his column with an encouragement to investors to enter real estate, as the commerce of the city was "rapidly becoming the commerce of the world."[54]

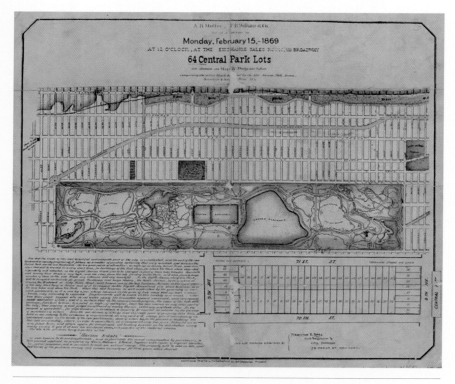

19.4 Once the park was established, real estate speculation went into high gear and the land surrounding Central Park became the most sought-after property in the city, a trend that continues to this day.

Source: "64 Central Park Lots, New York City." Lionel Pincus and Princess Firyal Map Division, The New York Public Library, New York Public Library Digital Collections, https://digitalcollections.nypl.org /items/9e9f4cba-dc7e-484e-e040-e00a18064cc8.

On March 21, 1868, the first issue of the *Real Estate Record and Builders' Guide* rolled off the presses, filling a need for the city's major preoccupation. A front-page article touted the money to be had, "At almost every sale which takes place, from 200 to 300 per cent, advance in prices over the fee brought five years ago is obtained. A feverish anxiety appears to prevail to secure property on the backbone of the city . . . above as well as below Central Park, say from 14th to 125th street; but the price of every inch of ground on the island is going up, and there is no telling at what point it will stop." Another article noted that a corner lot on Eighth Avenue and Eighty-Second Street, across from the park and a block from the former Seneca Village, sold at auction for about $4,200.[55]

The first issue of the *Real Estate Record* was published while Cahill was still in court defending his false claims against the legitimate owners. The editors let such "unprincipled dealers" know that they "intend to make war upon this nefarious practice."[56] In addition, leaders of the business and financial world soon developed protective measures to prevent such swindles. In 1871, the year of the second Cahill trial, a consortium of realtors, bankers, and businessmen formed the Real Estate Trust Company, "a joint-stock company to conduct surveys, do title searches, and manage the buying or transferring of mortgages." Five years later, the country's first title insurance company was formed in Philadelphia.[57]

By the end of our story in 1863, the ownership of the island had narrowed. Large chunks of Manhattan were now owned by just a few wealthy individuals. These men held the city and the country's economic and social power in their hands, and the class divisions in the city were yawning ever wider. Today, a similar small group of investors, now powerful international conglomerates, continues that trend. The investing and reinvesting, buying and selling, tearing down and building up show no sign of abating. Landfill has increased the size of Manhattan's natural shoreline, expanding the opportunity for the few to profit from this man-made property.

By 1858, the development of lower Manhattan had already eradicated much of the island's natural topography. In a prophetic letter to the commissioners, Frederick Law Olmsted lamented the loss of this landscape. He predicted that most of it would soon disappear beneath the paved city streets, and the only small vestige to survive would live on in Central Park: "The time will come when New York will be built-up, when all the grading and filling will be done, when the picturesquely varied rock formations of the island will have been converted into the foundations for rows of monotonous straight streets and piles of erect, angular buildings. There will be no suggestion left of its present varied surface, with the single exception of the few acres contained in the park."[58]

Epilogue: America's Park

For as long as anyone can remember, New Yorkers have asked each other, "Can you imagine the city without Central Park?"

I cannot. But, to me, the honor doesn't go far enough. The historian Kenneth T. Jackson once called Central Park "the most important public space in the United States."[1] And I agree. It is as much America's park as it is New York's.

The 843 acres that became Central Park witnessed the history of our nation more than any other single plot of American soil. The prepark was the staging ground for nearly every major theme and issue that we faced in our first two and a half centuries.

And the history of Central Park continued, as it saw our most fundamental conflicts, emotional struggles, and majestic triumphs reflected in its waters and played out on its fields.

Just as the prepark had its shameful incidents, so too, over the course of its history, the park also witnessed dark moments of muggings, assaults, and unjustified arrests of Communists, gay men, and the Central Park Five.

But through its history, the park has witnessed many more of our celebratory cultural events and civic milestones and been the platform for local, national, and international concerns.

Central Park saw firsthand the struggle over what a public space should be. It began as an apolitical space, a sanctuary from bustling city life for individuals and families—still its primary purpose and its psychological draw—but because of the power of nature in combination with its central location and its democratic mission, Central Park also became the city's most treasured space for communal gatherings.

Central Park has had rallies in support or in protest of every war or erected monuments to its fallen. Despite the prohibition of military use of park grounds, the New York State National Guard and other militias drilled and paraded on the

Green, now the Sheep Meadow, during the Civil War. The convent of the Sisters of Charity became a hospital for Union soldiers. After the war, the park memorialized the war heroes by erecting the Seventh Regiment Memorial, possibly the nation's first Civil War monument, that led to the installation of similar memorials in almost every city, town, and hamlet across America. The U.S.S. *Maine* National Monument at Columbus Circle memorializes the 260 American sailors who drowned in the 1898 attack on the *Maine*, which initiated the Spanish-American War. In 1917, a parade of military vehicles headed to Central Park, where a captured German submarine lay on the Sheep Meadow to raise money for Liberty Bonds. A memorial to the war's heroes lay on a slope just east of the Mall. In World War II, Mayor Fiorello LaGuardia sold war bonds at the nearby Naumburg Bandshell. That same spot in 1959 saw 16,000 Cuban Americans gather to hear Fidel Castro, while the following year both pro- and anti-Castro forces clashed at the dedication of the José Martí statue on Central Park South. On April 15, 1967, anti-Vietnam War activists Dr. Martin Luther King Jr., Dr. Benjamin Spock, and musician Harry Belafonte led hundreds of thousands of protesters from Central Park to the United Nations for the "Spring Mobilization to End the War in Vietnam." In April 1968, two weeks after her husband was assassinated, Coretta Scott King gave a speech in Central Park based on notes found in her late husband's pocket addressing the need to end the Vietnam War, poverty in America, and the power of women to effect social change. The following month, Reverend Ralph Abernathy held a rally at the Bandshell for Washington-bound protesters of the Poor People's Campaign going to fight for the War on Poverty. And on June 13, 1982, close to a million people marched from the United Nations into Central Park's Great Lawn for the largest antinuclear demonstration ever held.

The fields have been a platform for civil rights since the National Women's Suffrage Party mobilized in the 1920s, and a century later the monument to women's suffrage was installed on the Mall. In May 1940, the third Sunday in May was declared "I Am an American Day" to celebrate American citizenship across the nation. The most triumphant event took place in the midst of World War II, on May 21, 1944, when 1.5 million New Yorkers applauded the 150,000 people who took the oath of citizenship in Central Park.

In 1970, during the very first gay pride parade—then called Christopher Street Liberation Day—thousands again marched from Sheridan Square right back to the heart of Central Park. The unfurling in New York of one thousand panels of the national AIDS Memorial Quilt on the Great Lawn in 1988 commemorated the hundreds of thousands of lives lost to the devastating illness. The city mourned in December 1980 at a vigil after the death of John Lennon, and five years later commemorated his life by creating Strawberry Fields as an international garden of peace.

On July 20, 1969, thousands watched on huge movie screens in Sheep Meadow as Neil Armstrong took his first steps on the moon, and the park saw the "love-ins" and be-ins, gatherings that defined the Sixties in America. And on September 11, 2001, after the terrorist attack, and again in 2020 when the coronavirus shut the doors of every cultural institution in the city, the gates of Central Park remained open to welcome, to comfort, and to heal all who sought the refuge it was created to be.

A cornerstone of nineteenth-century Protestant American belief was that being in nature fostered a closer connection to God. In that way, a trip to Central Park was intended to be a spiritual experience. In the twentieth century, Central Park has been the site of services, gatherings, and celebrations for several religions: a reenactment of the crucifixion on Good Friday; the "Sunrise Meditation for World Peace" by Buddhist monk, the Dalai Lama; a rally by evangelist Billy Graham; a mass by Pope John Paul II; and the annual lighting of the world's largest menorah to celebrate the Jewish festival of Chanukah at Grand Army Plaza.

The park has also been a home for both art and science. Olmsted and Vaux considered Central Park "a single work of art," and it remains one of the most important works of art in this country. In 1871, it saw the city's first uptown art museum opened in the former chapel of the Sisters of Mount St. Vincent. A few years later, the Metropolitan Museum of Art was built on its eastern grounds. The park is a museum without walls for works from sculptural and decorative arts to the "The Gates" exhibit by Christo and Jeanne-Claude in 2005. The park has been a backdrop to countless films, from the first *Romeo and Juliet* filmed at Bethesda Terrace in 1908 to 1990's *Home Alone*, filmed in the same place. People flock to the park just to see that famous scene in person. Audiences have thrilled to the music from John Philip Sousa to Sinatra, Beethoven to Beyoncé.

The Central Park menagerie was the most visited attraction in the early park. Today the Central Park Zoo, part of the Wildlife Conservation Society, remains a popular scientific and educational attraction. In 1869, the American Museum of Natural History had its first home in the Arsenal, and the top floor became New York's branch of the United States Weather Service. In 1919 the weather service moved the instruments to Belvedere Castle, where they still measure the weather for New York City. And Central Park is one of the country's premier birding sites due to its prominent location on the Atlantic flyway migration route. America's famed ornithologist Roger Tory Peterson began his birding career as a boy in Central Park.

Perhaps most significant of all, Central Park was the birthplace of the American conservation movement. It was the first major landscaped urban park in America, and it inspired hundreds of others. The environmental and democratic vision of Central Park motivated Frederick Law Olmsted to conserve America's greatest natural wonders for public use. His 1864 groundbreaking report to Congress led to the protection of Yosemite Valley and later to the creation of both the state and national parks systems. In 1963, Central Park was declared a National Historic Landmark, and in 1974 it became New York City's first scenic landmark. In 2017, it was added to the Tentative List to become a UNESCO World Heritage Site.

But all was not always so celebratory. In the 1920s and again in the 1970s, the park fell prey to the vicissitudes of city politics and unstable economies. Without the funding and management needed to protect and maintain its landscapes and structures, Central Park, like most urban parks across America, began to deteriorate. By the mid-1970s vandalism was rampant, and crime was in the headlines daily. Reflecting the city's demographics, the park saw a racial divide at Ninety-Sixth Street: white New Yorkers and tourists below and Black and Hispanic visitors above. Central Park had become a national symbol of physical decay and social disgrace.

Inspired by the environmental movement of the 1970s and its annual celebrations of Earth Day, private citizens began to do what the city could not. And slowly, they reclaimed the park, creating a safe and welcoming landscape for all New Yorkers. Private funding was raised to manage daily operations and supplement the dwindling city budget allocations through the founding in 1980 of the Central Park Conservancy. The Conservancy joined a partnership with the City of New York, and this became the first public/private partnership in the country in support of an urban park. Today, park conservancies exist throughout New York City and in every other city in the nation.

When the Conservancy was still a fledgling organization, President Elizabeth "Betsy" Barlow Rogers knew she needed a photographer to document the existing conditions of the landscapes, the organization's early achievements, and fundraising events, and assist with the publication of a master plan. So, in 1984, she hired me.

For over thirty-five years I have photographed and led tours in Central Park. In all that time, though the park has been the stage for renowned events, those are not what I remember best. What stays with me the most are the personal moments, the moments when I have witnessed the deep emotional connection between the park and the people.

I have had the pleasure of meeting several descendants of Johannes de la Montagne, who have come from as near as Park Avenue and as far as Boseman, Montana, to pay homage to their ancestral land. And Ann de Forest of Philadelphia, who traces her lineage back to Isaac de Forest and fondly remembers her family's framed "beaver map," reproduced in chapter 1. I remember the eighty-one-year-old man who asked me to take a photo of him beside the statue of Balto. He had waited his whole life to visit it, ever since reading about the sled dog when he was a boy. And the Scottish man who traveled across the Atlantic to Central Park for the first time just so he could propose to his girlfriend in the Ramble. I stumbled upon the two while walking with my camera, right as the young man was down on one knee and lamenting that they wouldn't have a photo of the moment their lives changed. Now they do.

And I have my own personal memories of the park, memories that made me fall in love with it just like everyone else. It was in Central Park where I watched my seven-year-old daughter pretend to cross the New York City Marathon finish line, and then, thirty years later, I stood on the very same spot when I proudly watched her do it for real. I was with my grandson when he celebrated his first birthday in Central Park and tasted his very first ice cream cone on Sheep Meadow.

My grandson is eight now, so I dedicate this book, this backward look at Central Park's past, to him. And to the future memories that he too will one day make in Central Park.

To Nathaniel,
Love,
Nano

E.1 Central Park

Source: Sara Cedar Miller, *Aerial, Central Park*. Courtesy of the Central Park Conservancy.

Afterword

Elizabeth W. Smith, President and CEO, Central Park Conservancy

Before *Central Park* makes a remarkable contribution to the history of Central Park and New York City that expands our understanding of the 843 acres that form the center—and in many ways the hearT—of Manhattan Island.

The story of Central Park did not begin or end with the design by Frederick Law Olmsted and Calvert Vaux, although that has been the focus of much scholarship on the park. Sara's comprehensive and detailed account makes clear that this land has many layers and has many more stories to tell.

The new information in this book will be of great interest to the public and builds on the ongoing efforts of many researchers to uncover the history of this exceptional public space. One such layer of Sara's work, for example, provides new insight into the history of Seneca Village, which has also been the focus of the Conservancy's interpretive and research efforts in recent years as we have sought to not only share this history but also reveal its presence in the park. Sara's original research as well as the Conservancy's own continuing investigation into the history and impact of the park makes clear that stewardship of Central Park is multifaceted. Part of the restoration and care of its landscapes is also the interpretation of the park's many stories and layers, and the exploration of their connection to the purpose of the park.

My own personal connection to the park began when it was just climbing up from its nadir in the early 1980s. As a young mother, I would take each of my daughters into the park on weekend mornings and feel that I was in the most majestic place in the world. I soon joined the legions of New Yorkers who came to see Central Park as an essential aspect of life in the city, a sanctuary that offers us time and space to breathe. This was the original purpose of the park, a purpose that feels especially prescient and powerful today, when calamities and pandemics have put such strain on our lives.

The Conservancy's seemingly impossible mission is to care for Central Park forever. It was this almost quixotic mission, to ensure that the park and its purpose endure in perpetuity, that drew me to join the Conservancy in the first place. Having fallen in love with the park, I found myself equally drawn to its dedicated and determined guardian, which tirelessly oversees a place that, unknown to the public at large, is as complex and resource hungry as any major commercial endeavor.

My ongoing dedication to Central Park and to the Conservancy stems from my belief that the park will continue to play a tremendously important role in the city, not only as an essential respite but also as a venue for expressions of social justice and community spirit, as Sara has articulated in her epilogue.

Sara's "before and after" photographs attest to the almost miraculous rescue of Central Park over forty years. Today, with its restoration now largely complete, our challenge is to figure out how to sustain both the park and the Conservancy while the city, its prospects, and its politics continue to evolve.

New Yorkers of every stripe, including me, know that we must succeed in securing the future of Central Park. This can only be done by the Conservancy, in partnership with all its friends and supporters and the many civic leaders who see the city the way we do: as a headstrong, dynamic place that would be a mere shadow of its former self if the park were to be anything other than a magnificent refuge and a gathering place for us all.

A.1 Bethesda Fountain before restoration, 1980 (formerly the Amory farm).

Source: Courtesy of the Central Park Conservancy.

A.2 Bethesda Fountain and Terrace today.

Source: Sara Cedar Miller, Bethesda Fountain and Terrace. Courtesy of the Central Park Conservancy.

A.3 Cedar Hill, 1980 (formerly the Wagstaff farm).

Source: Courtesy of the Central Park Conservancy.

A.4 Cedar Hill today.

Source: Sara Cedar Miller, *Cedar Hill*. Courtesy of the Central Park Conservancy.

A.5 Harlem Meer, 1980 (formerly a part of the Kingsbridge Road and the farms of the Montagne, Benson, Kortright, Nutter, and Watt/Pinkney families).

Source: Courtesy of the Central Park Conservancy.

A.6 Harlem Meer and the Charles A. Dana Discovery Center today.

Source: Sara Cedar Miller, *Harlem Meer*. Courtesy of the Central Park Conservancy.

Acknowledgments

First and foremost, I owe my largest debt of gratitude to the late Margaret "Marge" Sullivan, board member of the Foundation for Landscape Studies and, more importantly, my beloved friend, for her generous support and also The Foundation for Landscape Studies for awarding me a David R. Coffin Publication Grant, for the color reproduction of the book.

This has been a journey of a lifetime, and its joy was as much about the people who supported me as the information they imparted or their editorial talents. None of this would have been possible without you. Sara Bedell and the staff of the Hampton Bays Library; Esme Berg and Ina Selden, New Amsterdam History Center; Sister Burk and the staff at the Family History Library, The Church of Jesus Christ of Latter-day Saints; Rev. Malcolm Byrd and Rev. Audrey Akins Williamson, African Methodist Episcopal Zion Church; Jennifer Carlquist, Boscobel; Marion Casey, Glucksman Ireland House, New York University; Emily Chapin, Museum of the City of New York; Molly Charboneau, family historian; Kimberly Diane Curtis, George Washington Papers, University of Virginia; Cara Dellatte, John Cordovez, and others, Manuscripts and Archives Division, New York Public Library; Mike Feller, naturalist and former chief naturalist for NYC Parks; Andrew Fox, Andrew Fox Tutors; Ellen Futter, Nicholas Tailby, and Steven Jaret, American Museum of Natural History; William J. Gallagher and Officer Jesse Cohen, Central Park Precinct, NYPD; Eddie Garcia, photographer; Aaron Goodwin, House Historian and Genealogist; Dr. Gilbert Hanson, SUNY, Stony Brook; Lesley Hermann, Gilder Lehrman Institute of American History; Graham Russell Gao Hodges, Colgate University; Marguerite Holloway, Columbia University; Richard Hunter and James Lee, Hunter Research, Inc.; Johnathan Kuhn, NYC Parks; Lauren Lean, Heather Shannon, George Eastman Museum, and Edna Claunch for setting up the wonderful private tour; Tom Lisanti, Nancy Kandoian, and Andrea Felder,

New York Public Library; Jessie McLeod and Dawn Bonner, Mount Vernon; Casey Madrick and Coleen McArdelle, West Point Military Academy; Leslie Matthaei, Architect of the Capitol; Julianna Monjeau, City of New York Public Design Commission; Emily Parsons, Society of the Cincinnati; Anne Petrimoulx and Whitey Flynn, Trinity Church Archives; Samar Qandi and Mark Sacha, NYC Department of Environmental Protection; Hector Rivera, Topographical Bureau Associate, Manhattan Borough President's Office; Jeff Rosenheim, Metropolitan Museum of New York; David Rumsey and Brandon Rumsey of the David Rumsey Map Collection; Rev. John Schmidt, Paul Johnson, Anne Kosmerl, and Micah Hauger, All Angels' Episcopal Church; Denice Shepherd and Thom Hoffman, Oyster Bay Historical Society; Laura Starr, Starr Whitehouse; Lois Stewart, Montagne family historian; Mark Tomasko, private collector; Joseph Van Nostrand, Division of Old Records; Kim Walker, Shelburne, Nova Scotia Historical Society; Thaisa Way, Dumbarton Oaks; Caroline Van Deusen, archivist; Vicken Yegparian, Stack's Bowers Galleries; the reference staffs: New York State Library and Archives, Albany; the Lionel Pincus and Princess Firyal Map Division, The New York Public Library; The New-York Society Library; the Rhode Island Historical Society, Providence; Library of the General Society of Mechanics and Tradesmen of New York; and the Blunt Library, Mystic Seaport, Mystic, CT. To my three homes-away-from-home where this book was birthed and nurtured, thanks to the holdings and the expertise of their respective staffs and especially for helping me remotely during COVID-19: the New-York Historical Society: Michael Ryan, Marilyn Kushner, Ted O'Brien, Mariam Touba, Crystal Toscano, Jill Reichenbach, Sophie Lynford, Emily Croll, Amanda Thompson, Eleanor Gillers, and postdoctoral fellow Alexander Manevitz; New York City Municipal Archives: Commissioners Pauline Toole and Kenneth Cobb and Cynthia Brenwall, Dwight Johnson, Marcia Kirk, Sylvia Kollar, Rossy Mendez, Julia Robbins, and Katie Ehrlich; and the Archives of the New York County Clerk: Joseph Van Nostrand, who, with the permission and support of Judge Milton A. Tingling, the New York County Clerk, went above and beyond his duties to provide me with access to the records during COVID-19 in an isolated and safe environment.

I am thankful for my readers who gave wonderful comments and edits: first and foremost the late and great Barry Lewis, who read every word, and Sr. Regina Bechtle and Mindy S. Gordon, Sisters of Charity of New York; Charles Beveridge, Olmsted Papers; Ann de Forest; New Netherland historian Frith Fabend; Nicole Fox; Eric Himmel, Abrams Books; Mike Feller; Jane Kirkwood; historia emerita Frank Kowsky, SUNY Distinguished Professor Emeritus Buffalo State College; Catherine McNeur, Portland State University; Alison Miller, Ellen and Jonathan Pearlman; Carla L. Peterson, University of Maryland; Eric Sanderson, Wildlife Conservation Society; Barnet Schecter, historian; Rebecca Shanor, historian; and Laurance Simpson, General Society of the Sons of the Revolution; Melanie Sokol, Asa Ryder Spurlock, and Shane White, University of Sydney; Rev. Audrey Akins Williamson, African Methodist Episcopal Zion Church; and Conservancy colleagues Lane Addonizio, John Reddick, and Marie Warsh. A special thanks to artist/historian Len Tantillo for his magnificent rendering of the de Forest-Montagne compound and his wealth of knowledge of early Dutch architecture, to artist Roxanne Panero for her typography expertise, and Melanie Belkin and Cynthia Brenwall for their help with the Index.

To my researchers, Maya Mau, Bobbi Oliner, and Valerie Thaler, and early editors, Andrea Danese, Bobbi Oliner, Carol Rial, and Deborah Wye, and special high fives to my talented New York Society Library writing group: Muffy Flouret, Lydie Raschka, Regina Toth, and Ina Yalof.

My deepest thanks to University of Virginia staff: Beth Meyer, Allison James, Chris Gist, Drew MacQueen, and graduate student Qinmeng Yu for georeferencing the maps and to map dealer and author Robert Augustyn and collector Larry Caldwell, also Mark Tomasko and Steven Manheimer, for the generosity of sharing their collections.

To attorneys Robert Ritter, and Ira Millstein and Phillip Rosen of Weil, Gotshal and Manges, who helped to unravel the complexities of legal documents.

To Andrew Fox and Maya Mau, who did the heavy lifting when it came to data analysis and calculating and illustrating the monetary awards for figure 16.6 Thanks to Maya, I now understand the difference between the mean and the median.

To Judith Heintz, my friend and former colleague, for her expertise as a landscape architect, and for the freezing day we ran around the park looking for glacial erratics; and to Stanley Zucker, who roamed through tombstones of Beth Olam Cemetery in Queens on the hottest day of the year; and to my colleague Marie Warsh as we, too, searched high and low for burials in Cypress Hills and St. Michael's Cemetery.

To Robin Karson and Jonathan Lippincott, Library of Landscape History, for their support and for the honor they bestowed upon me as "Preservation Hero."

My support groups have gotten me through the long haul: The Supper Club: Roberta Bernstein, Viki Sand, and Brady Littlefield; the Gotham Garden Club:

Rebecca Shanor, Judith Heintz, Joanne Morse, Mary O'Brien, and Anne Van Ingen; and the Manchester House History Group: Fay Radding and Mark Kleinman; the beach bums of Hampton Bays; and the Rash Guards of Riverhead; the docents of the Women's Committee; and friends and supporters: Adrian Sas, and Malcolm Pinkney, NYC Parks; Judy Bernstein, Cheryl Best, Debi Best and Eric Parker, Michael Cedar and Lauren Forman, Phyllis Cohen, Linda Cubitoso, Ann de Forest, Nancy Drosd, Paul Gangsei, and Susan Herman; Mike Grobstein, Rebecca and Bobby Kennedy, Maxine Liao, Laure and Steve Manheimer; Ira and Susan Millstein, Roxanne Panero, Dede Petri, Marie Ruby, Susan Urban, Patty Volk, and especially Jack Frieberg and Kevin Kiddoo for the countless hours they spent patiently listening to every saga and supporting every step of the process.

No words will ever be able to express my gratitude to my Central Park Conservancy colleagues and the trustees and donors, past and present, who have supported me personally and professionally since 1984. To my beloved friend Cynthia Larson Richard, who made that fateful phone call in May 1984 asking if I'd be interested in applying for the position of photographer of Central Park. To Betsy Rogers, who gave me her friendship and the most cherished gift of my professional life. To President Betsy Smith, who welcomed me into the president's office and has been a tremendous supporter of my work and reader of the manuscript. It is an honor to have her afterword complete this story and continue our dialogue and her important work. I am also grateful for my President's Office colleagues both past and present, and especially Chief of Staff Leah Van Horn, who is always there for me whether to listen, to advise, or to laugh. Salmaan Khan, Janie Kim, Anne Shutkin, and Shannon Spector, and consultant and longtime friend Gregory Long, have been a joy to work alongside. I am grateful to my colleagues Marie Warsh, John Reddick, and Lane Addonizio for the many years spent discussing aspects of the park's history, to Marisa Edwards and Elizabeth Gressel for the beautifully designed map of the park, to Bob Rumsey and Steve Bopp for pondering some mysteries of the landscapes with me and to archivists Rebecca Pou and Camille Lannan for their expertise and constant assistance. To Mary Caraccioli and the communication staff, and to Andrea Buteau, Erica Sopha and Kaitlin Holt of the Visitor Experience staff. There are no words that could ever capture my gratitude and love for the members of the Operations staff. It would take pages upon pages to name each one of them for the thirty-eight years of help and affection they have given me. They are the heroes of Central Park, A special thanks to colleagues past and present, Diandra Sarno, Joe Gamache, John

Dillon, Alan Clark, Josh Gaililey, John Harrigan, William Quansah, and Diane Schaub, for their assistance with aspects of my research, and to the ever-patient IT staff, Linda Heyward, Syed Hasib, Afridi Zaman, Josh Ehrlich, Jeff Connors, and Beth Haskell, whose expertise, and good humor is deeply appreciated. Here I also include Steve Krug, Steven Mau and the technology wizards at Apple and Microsoft who have rescued me during many meltdowns.

I am grateful to former editor Patrick Fitzgerald for the support that brought me to Columbia University Press. I am so blessed to have been assigned to the brilliant Stephen Wesley, who is far more than an editor; he is an alchemist who has transformed a jumbled and messy manuscript into a readable book, asked many insightful questions, and sprinkled the text with his beautiful writing and wonderful anecdotes such as the con man who "sold" many NYC landmarks. I am so thankful to have had such a great supporting team: Leslie Kriesel for her superb editing skills and coordination of the book's many elements; Julia Kushnirsky for her beautiful design, and Christian Winting and Ben Kolstad for their important contributions.

To the memory of my mentor, art historian Leo Steinberg. He was beside me in spirit every step of the way. And to scholars Sidney Horenstein and David Schuyler and park advocate Caroline Loughlin. To the memory of my parents, Sam and Sophie Cedar; my brother, Barry Cedar; and dear friends Joy Santlofer, Charles Schwartz, Barry Lewis and Marge Sullivan who brought beautiful colors to everything she touched, including this book.

Notes

ABBREVIATIONS

Assembly Docs	Documents of the New York State Assembly
Assembly J	*Journal of the New York State Assembly*
BA Docs.	Documents of the Board of Aldermen of the City of New York, vols. 1–32 (1835–1866)
BA Mins.	Minutes of the Board of Aldermen of the City of New York
BCCP *Mins.*	Board of Commissioners of the Central Park, Minutes 1858–1870
BCCP *Docs.*	Board of Commissioners of the Central Park, Documents, 1858–1870
CAB	Croton Aqueduct Board
MCC1675	Minutes of the Common Council of the City of New York, 1675–1776
MCC1784	Minutes of the Common Council of the City of New York, 1784–1831
Senate Docs	Documents of the New York State Senate

Repositories

DOF	Office of the City Registrar, New York City Department of Finance
DOR	Division of Old Records, New York County Court
LOC	Library of Congress
MANY	Municipal Archives, New York City Department of Records and Information Services.

MBP	City of New York, Borough of Manhattan, Office of the President, Topographic Bureau
NYHS	New-York Historical Society
NYPL	New York Public Library
NYSL	New York State Library

Newspapers

Brooklyn	*Brooklyn Daily Eagle*
Comm. Adv.	*New York Commercial Advertiser*
Her.	*New York Herald, New York Morning Herald*
NY Gaz.	*New-York Gazette & General Advertiser*
NYT	*New York Times* and *New York Daily Times*
Trib.	*New York Tribune*

Books

PFLO	Frederick Law Olmsted, *The Papers of Frederick Law Olmsted*, volume 3, "Creating Central Park," ed. Charles E. Beveridge and David Schuyler (Baltimore, MD: John Hopkins University Press, 1983)

Deeds, Mortgages, Probate

Extension	Central Park Extension, petitions for extension from 106th to 110th Streets, Department of Old Records, New York County Court
L	Liber (for deeds and mortgages in Block Indices of Reindexed Conveyances, pre-1917, Blocks 1107 to 1111, City of New York, Borough of Manhattan, Department of Finance, City Register; New York Land Records, familysearch.org)
Mortgages	New York Land Records, familysearch.org
NYS Census 1855	New York State Census, 1855, www.ancestry.com
P	Page (for deeds and mortgages in Block Indices of Reindexed Conveyances, pre-1917, Blocks 1107 to 1111, City of New York, Borough of Manhattan, Department of Finance, City Register; New York Land Records, familysearch.org)
Petitions	Volumes 1 to 7, Central Park Petitions, 1855–1868, Department of Old Records, New York County Court

Probate	New York Probate Records, Wills, www.ancestry.com
Releases	Central Park Releases from landowners to the City of New York, Municipal Archives
U.S. Census 1790 to 1860	U.S. Census, New York City, www.ancestry.com

People

AHG	Andrew Haswell Green
CV	Calvert Vaux
EV	Egbert Viele
FLO	Frederick Law Olmsted
FLO Jr.	Frederick Law Olmsted Jr.
JHO	John Hull Olmsted
JO	John Olmsted

PREFACE

1. Hunter Research, *A Preliminary Historical and Archaeological Assessment of Central Park to the North of the 97th Street Transverse, Borough of Manhattan, City of New York*. Prepared for the Central Park Conservancy, New York, 1990.

PART I: TOPOGRAPHY

1. Jan van Goyen, *View of Haarlem and the Haarlemmer Meer*, 1646. "The Haarlemmermeer Meer (Haarlem Lake), an inland body of fresh water was filled in during the nineteenth century." Online catalog entry adapted in 2011 from Walter A. Liedtke, " 'Pentimenti' in our Pictures of Salomon van Ruysdael and of Jan van Goyen," *Shop Talk: Studies in Honor of Seymour Slive*,. ed. Cynthia P. Schneider et al. (Cambridge, MA: Harvard University Art Museums, 1995), 156–157, note 35, figure 7, https://www.metmuseum.org/art/collection/search/436558.

2. In an 1868 trial long-tenured city surveyor James E. Serrell testified that the topography of the land from the "the kills"—the marshland along the East River that stretched intermittently from the East Ninety-Second Street shoreline to 109th Street and Fifth Avenue and the Harlem Creek along 107th and 108th Street—to "the hills"—the high ground across today's Central Park to the south and today's Morningside Heights to the west. The hills bordered the 200-acre flatlands that ran from 109th Street and Fifth Avenue to 124th Street and Tenth Avenue and occurred "no other place on the island of Manhattan, where there is 200 acres which lie between creeks and kills, answering that description except that particular place." *Sylvester Cahill and Gilliam B. Seeley agst. Courtlandt Palmer and The Mayor &c*, Supreme Court General Term (hereafter,

Cahill v. Palmer), vol. 83, (folio 111), 31, https://books.google.com/books?id=cDySrW -PGbGQC&pg=PA203&lpg=PA203&dq=benson+mcgowan&source=bl&ots=wNvn -TCwplJ&sig=7xR8TFIEZrco9XBuX4nM3G4Huoc&hl=en&sa=X&ei=2bKRVZPO -M4X8yQSSsZngAQ&ved=0CEYQ6AEwDA#v=onepage&q=benson%20 mcgowan&f=false. Part of the testimony is also transcribed in a handwritten document, *Central Park Extension, 106 to 110 St.*, 1863, no. 2 1862, 279 to 350, Division of Old Records (hereafter, DOR). My deep appreciation to ecologist Eric Sanderson, who confirmed the uniqueness of this area of Manhattan, and for his generous assistance with the manuscript.

3. W. H. Grant, "Map Showing the Original Topography of the Site of the Central Park, with a Diagram of the Roads and Walks now under construction," [*Second*] *Annual Report of the Commissioners of the Central Park, Board of Alderman Documents*, no. 8, (New York: W. C. Bryant, 1859).

4. Eric W. Sanderson, *Mannahatta: A Natural History of New York City* (New York: Abrams, 2009), 70; Eric W. Sanderson and Marianne Brown, "Mannahatta: An Ecological First Look at the Manhattan Landscape Prior to Henry Hudson," *Northeastern Naturalist* 14, no. 7 (2007): 545–570.

5. Email from Sanderson to author, Jan. 19, 2021; William T. Bean and Eric W. Sanderson, "Using a spatially explicit ecological model to test scenarios of fire use by Native Americans: An example from the Harlem Plains, New York, NY," *Ecological Modelling* 211 (2008): 301–308, welikia.org/wp-content/uploads/beansanderson2008lenapefireharlem.pdf.

6. Isaac de Rasieres to Blommaert, in J. Franklin Jameson, ed., *Narratives of New Netherland, 1609–1664* (New York: Charles Scribner's Sons, 1909), 104, https://archive.org/details /narrativesofnewno1jame/page/n1/mode/2up.

7. Charles E. Beveridge and David Schuyler, eds., "Descriptive Guide to the Arboretum," *Papers of Frederick Law Olmsted* (hereafter, *PFLO*), 12 vols. (Baltimore, MD: Johns Hopkins University Press, 1983), vol. 3, "Creating Central Park," 162.

8. David de Vries, *Short Historical and Journal Notes*, in Jameson, *Narratives of New Netherland*, 218–220.

9. De Vries, *Short Historical and Journal Notes* in Jameson, *Narratives of New Netherland*, 220–223.

10. Mrs. Robert W. [Emily Johnson] de Forest, *A Walloon Family in America: Lockwood de Forest and His Forbears, 1500–1848* (New York: Houghton Mifflin, 1914), vol. 1, 80–82. James Riker commented, "the future home [on] the rich flats of Muscoota promis[ed] to rival in productiveness the fertile meadows around their former homeland of Leiden," James Riker, *Revised History of Harlem (City of New York) Its Origin and Early Annals* (New York: New Harlem Publishing Company, 1904), 124–125. See also George Everett Hill and George E. Waring, Jr., *Old Wells and Water-courses of the Island of Manhattan* (New York: The Knickerbocker Press, c. 1897), 255.

11. John W. Pirsson, *The Dutch Grants, Harlem Patents and Tidal Creeks* (New York: L. K. Strouse & Co., 1889), 87, 107; E. B. (Edmund Bailey) O'Callaghan, *History of New Netherland, or New York Under the Dutch* (New York: D. Appleton, 1848), 43–46, https://

archive.org/details/historyofnewnetho10cal; Adrian Van Der Donck, *Description of New Netherland*, 1656, reprint, ed. Charles T. Gehring and William A. Starna (Lincoln: University of Nebraska Press, 2010); Sanderson, *Manahatta*, 104–135.

12. De Forest, *A Walloon Family*, 82–83. See also Hill, *Old Wells and Watercourses*, 256.

13. In 2014, Hunter Research, Inc., conducted archeological testing in the northern end of Central Park. In their assessment comparing the present-day park with the original topography, they noted, "In some respects the present-day topography in this section of Central Park broadly resembles that which prevailed prior to the Park's creation in the late 1850s and early 1860s. The principal rock outcrops and major slopes have changed little since the early 19th century and correlate well with the landscape shown on early maps, but in a more localized sense the topography today is much less rugged. Hollows and fissures have been filled, grading has been undertaken to facilitate the construction of roads and paths and the installation of utilities, and the creation of Lasker Pool and Harlem Meer has served to deemphasize the once sharply defined, pre-urban river valleys. McGown's Pass, where the Kingsbridge Road descended the bluffs to cross Harlem Creek, was formerly a much more obvious, ravine-like passage down the hillside" Hunter Research, Inc., *Archeological Testing and Monitoring Forts Landscape Reconstruction Project, Central Park, Borough of Manhattan, New York* (Trenton, NJ: July 2014, prepared for the Central Park Conservancy), 3-1, http://s-media.nyc.gov/agencies/lpc/arch_reports/1545.pdf.

14. For the known Lenape settlements, see Sanderson, "Lenape Sites and Place-Names," *Mannahatta*, Appendix B, 258–263.

15. I. N. Phelps Stokes, *The Iconography of Manhattan Island, 1498–1909*, 6 vols. (New York: Robert H. Dodd, 1915), vol. I, 67.

16. Riker explained the name Konaande Kongh as a term used in Dutch documents of 1669: "ko" translates as "cascade," "onde" as "hill," "kong" as "elevated place or locality," and "nunda" as "village." (Riker, *Revised History*, 122). See Reginald Pelham Bolton, *Indian Paths in the Great Metropolis* (New York: Museum of the American Indian, Heye Foundation, 1922), 68–71, 75.

17. Bolton, *Indian Paths in the Great Metropolis*, 109. Sanderson identified Munsee as the Lenape language; *Mannahatta*, 112. The interpretation by historian William Starna suggests that the Lenape, or more correctly "Lunáapeew," should more accurately be identified as Munsee, in "New Amsterdam Yesterday and Today," *New Amsterdam History Center Newsletter* 4, no. 1 (Spring 2021).

18. Sanderson, *Mannahatta*, 262.

1. THE FIRST SETTLERS, 1625–1664

1. Bernard Bailyn, "The Dutch Farrago," in *The Barbarous Years: The Peopling of British North America: The Conflict Civilizations, 1600–1675* (New York: Knopf, 2012), Apple Books edition, 637. My gratitude to historian and author Firth Fabend for her edits and suggestions for this chapter.

462 1. The First Settlers, 1625–1664

462 1. The First Settlers, 1625–1664

2. Eric W. Sanderson, *Mannahatta: A Natural History of New York City* (New York: Abrams, 2009), 184–189, 203; Julie van den Hout, "The Omnipotent Beaver in Van der Donck's *A Description of New Netherland*: A Natural Symbol of Promise in the New World." University of California, Spring 2015, https://escholarship.org/content /qt870174nb/qt870174nb_noSplash_506c26d948cab2db3fbcdf5c2c01a13f.pdf?t=nq1m8z.

3. Van den Hout, "The Omnipotent Beaver," 4, 9; Adriaen Van der Donck, "Of the Nature, Amazing Ways, and properties of the Beavers," in *A Description of New Netherland*, ed. Charles T. Gehring and William A. Starna (Lincoln: University of Nebraska Press, 2010), 73–114.

4. Edwin G. Burrows and Mike Wallace, *Gotham: A History of New York City to 1898* (New York: Oxford University Press, 1999), 12. Originally the Dutch West India Company took all the profits from the fur trade, but eventually relaxed its strict monopoly and allowed others to profit from trade, though it still controlled prices for noncompany traders; Van den Hout, "The Omnipotent Beaver," 12. See also note 55.

5. Burrows and Wallace, *Gotham*, 12.

6. The Lenape presence on Manhattan Island was divided into three main communities based on location: the Wickquasgeck in northern Manhattan; the Rechgawawank in Harlem, and the Manahate in lower Manhattan and the islands; see, Sanderson, *Mannahatta*, 110.

7. Sanderson, *Mannahatta*, 202–203. See also https://welikia.org.

8. James Riker, *Revised History of Harlem (City of New York) Its Origin and Early Annals* (New York: New Harlem Publishing Company, 1904), 86–87. See also Joannes De Laet and George Folsom, *Extracts from the New World, or, A Description of the West Indies* (New York: George Folsom, 1841), a translation of Book III, chapters VII–XI, 282–316, LOC, https://www.loc.gov/item/11022409/.

9. Riker, *Revised History*, 88; De Laet and Folsom, *Extracts from the New World*, chapter XI, 312–314. An extensive bibliography of ecological sources can be found in Ted Steinberg, *Gotham Unbound: The Ecological History of Greater New York* (New York: Simon & Schuster, 2014), 394–401.

10. Bailyn, *The Barbarous Years*, 688.

11. Burrows and Wallace, *Gotham*, 9–10.

12. Bailyn, *The Barbarous Years*, 64–66.

13. Burrows and Wallace, *Gotham*, 3–11.

14. Pieter Schagen Letter, 5 November 1626, received 7 November 1626, reproduced and translated by the New Netherland Institute, http://www.newnetherlandinstitute.org /history-and-heritage/additional-resources/dutch-treats/peter-schagenletter; see also E. B. O'Callaghan, *Documents Relative to the Colonial History of the State of New York, Procured in England Holland, and France by John Romeyn Brodhead, Esq.*, ed. E. B. O'Callaghan (Albany, NY: Weed, Parsons, and Company, 1856), "Mr. Peter Schagen to the States General; the Island of Manhattans purchased," vol. 1, 37–38, https://archive.org/details/documentsrelativo1brod /page/n49/mode/2up.

15. Riker, *Revised History*, 126; Mrs. Robert W. [Emily Johnson] de Forest, *A Walloon Family in America: Lockwood de Forest and His Forbears, 1500–1848* (New York: Houghton Mifflin, 1914), vol. 1, 80–81.

16. David Steven Cohen, "How Dutch Were the Dutch of New Netherland?" *New York History* 62, no. 1 (January 1981): 44–60. For a history of Walloons' struggle for religious freedom, see John Howard Abbott, *Descendants of Bastiaen Van Kortryk: A Native of Belgium who Emigrated to Holland about 1615* (New York: Tobias A. Wright, 1922), 9–15, https://archive.org/details/courtrightkortri00abbo/page/8/mode/2up.

17. Riker, *Revised History*, 79, and 78n on the various spellings of Montagne, as La Montagne, Montanye, Delamontagnie, Mousnier de la Montagne.

18. Riker, *Revised History*, 85–86.

19. De Forest, *A Walloon Family*, 14, 17–31.

20. Riker, in *Revised History*, 80n, suggested that Montagne had finished his degree before coming to Leiden and over the course of seventeen years was enrolled at the university to continue "the common practice for professional improvement." Riker noted that Montagne's enrollment was "three times severed and as often renewed"; I. N. Phelps Stokes, *The Iconography of Manhattan Island, 1498–1909* (New York: Robert H. Dodd, 1916), vol. II, 117.

21. De Forest, *A Walloon Family*, 68–71.

22. De Forest, *A Walloon Family*, 64–69.

23. Arnold J. F. Van Laer, *New York Historical Manuscripts: Dutch, Translated*, ed. with added indexes by Kenneth Scott and Kenn Stryker-Rodda, vol. 1, *Register of the Provincial Secretary, 1638–1642* (Baltimore, MD: Genealogical Publishing Co., 1974), doc. no. 19, 31n3. https://www.newnetherlandinstitute.org/files/6514/0151/8811/Volume_I_-_Register _of_the_Provincial_Secretary_1638-1642.pdf.

24. Riker, *Revised History*, 126.

25. Riker, *Revised History*, 126, 129; Hunter Research, *A Preliminary Historical and Archeological Assessment of Central Park to the North of the 97th Street Transverse Borough of Manhattan, City of New York*, Vol. I, D–68, 69, http://s-media.nyc.gov/agencies/lpc /arch_reports/444_A.pdf.; de Forest, *A Walloon Family*, 84, 87, 96; Stokes, *Iconography*, vol. II, 194; vol. IV, 88, 90.

26. The two versions of the Manatus map are the Castello in Italy and the Harrisse map in the Library of Congress, Washington, D.C. The Italian map cites Montagne's property as "18: Bon. van Loein ontangle," and the Library of Congress map has "19: bouwerij van Loen ontangele." These two names are corruptions or misspellings of "La Montagne," who owned the property after de Forest. The *bouweries* are listed in John A. Kouwenhoven, *The Columbia Historical Portrait of New York: An Essay in Graphic History* (New York, Harper & Row, 1953), 36–37.

27. The site of the homestead cannot be definitively located. In 1922, archaeologist Reginald Pelham Bolton suggested that the homestead would have been sited near fresh water, the agricultural fields, and the Native trail, and suggested 115th Street and Fifth Avenue. Siting it closer to 109th Street would have had an even greater advantage, being closer

to the Harlem Creek and Rechewanis. See *Indian Paths in the Great Metropolis*, Part 1 (New York: Museum of the American Indian/Heye Foundation, 1922), 68–76 (and see Bolton map, figure I.4). For the 1647 deed from Kieft to Montagne, see Charles T. Gehring, trans. and ed., *New York Historical Manuscripts: Dutch*, Volumes GG, HH, I, Land Papers (Baltimore: Genealogical Publishing Co. Inc., 1980), 60–61. Historian Edmund Bailey O'Callaghan, writing in 1858, just before the creation of Central Park, noted, "The original La Montagne farm was situated on New York Island, east of the Eighth Avenue, and north of Ninety-third st, whence it extended to the Haerlem River." By "north of Ninety-third st," O'Callaghan was referring to the marshlands that ranged from the East River at Ninety-Third Street to approximately Second Avenue. He was not suggesting that Montagne's farm extended west to Eighth Avenue at Ninety-Third Street. In E. B. O'Callaghan, *History of New Netherland, or New York Under the Dutch* (New York: D. Appleton, 1848), vol. 2, book II, chapter VII, 186n1, https://archive.org /details/historyofnewneth01ocal; Riker, *Revised History*, 122, 124–126; de Forest, *A Walloon Family*, 81–83, 105; H[enry] Croswell Tuttle, *Abstracts of Farm Titles in the City of New York, between 75th and 120th Streets: with maps* (New York: The Spectator Company, 1878). Stokes placed the homestead on a high point on today's composting operation overlooking today's Harlem Meer; see Hunter Research, *A Preliminary Historical and Archeological Assessment*, vol. 1, D-67, D-69 for sources. Stokes based his opinion on a later deed (1669 rather than the 1647 deed) and incorrectly sited Konaande Kongh. See I. N. P. Stokes, *Iconography of Manhattan Island*, 1498–1909 (New York: Robert H. Dodd, 1916), Vol. II, 194–195, also Vol. IV, 110. The Native settlement was not located in the prepark but rather on the high ground that encompassed today's Madison, Park, and Lexington Avenues, Ninety-Eighth Street to 100th Street, confirmed in Sanderson, *Mannahatta*, 261. Archeologist Reginald Pelham Bolton first identified the location in 1922 (see figure I.5).

28. Tantillo's painting is based on a description of the de Forest/Montagne homestead in Riker, *Revised History*, 126, 145, and de Forest, *A Walloon Family*, 83–86. According to Riker, the house, built in the Dutch rural style, was surrounded by a high fence of "heavy round palisades or pickets" for protection against the Natives. The farmhouse measured forty-two feet long by eighteen wide, and had two doors. Emily de Forest noted the entrance had "a well-secured gate or gates." The barn featured long narrow stables that were called *uytlaeten* between the outer walls and the posts that supported the roof. Above the two stables was a loft for the fodder. The open area between the flanking stables was the threshing floor. The house had a thatched roof made from nine hundred bundles of reeds.

29. Lois Stewart, *The Ancestors and Descendants of James Montaneÿ (1799–1857): The Montana Branch of the Montayne Family* (Baltimore, MD: Gateway Press, 1982), 7.

30. The overseer of the slaves also must have been in charge of the indentured servants because the March 22, 1639, council minutes were concerned with payment by Montagne to his two indentured servants, not an issue involving enslaved people. Van Laer, "Deposition of Jacob Stoffelsen, overseer of Negroes, as to the employment of said Negroes

during the administration of Wouter van Twiller," vol. 1, *Register of the Provincial Secretary*, doc. no. 83, 112–113; Riker, *Revised History*, 134; Stokes, *Iconography*, vol. IV, 89.

31. Enslaved people also labored on the tobacco plantations as early as 1626. De Forest, *A Walloon Family*, 121.

32. E. B. O'Callaghan, trans., *Voyages of the Slavers St. John and Arms of Amsterdam, 1659,1663; together with Additional Papers Illustrative of the Slave Trade under the Dutch* (Albany, NY: J. Munsell, 1867), https://archive.org/details/voyagesofslavers03ocal. For contemporary histories of slavery in the Dutch colonial era, see Jaap Jacobs, *The Colony of New Netherland: A Dutch Settlement in Seventeenth-Century America* (Ithaca, NY: Cornell University Press, 2009); Ira Berlin and Leslie M. Harris, eds., *Slavery in New York* (New York: New-York Historical Society, 2005); Graham Russell Hodges, *Root and Branch: African Americans in New York and East Jersey, 1613–1863* (Chapel Hill: University of North Carolina Press, 1999); Edgar J. McManus, *A History of Negro Slavery in New York* (1966; reprint, Syracuse, NY: Syracuse University Press, 1970); Joyce Goodfriend, "Black Families in New Netherland," https://www.newnetherlandinstitute.org /files/3513/5067/3660/6.1.pdf; Leslie M. Harris, *In the Shadow of Slavery: African Americans in New York City, 1626–1863* (Chicago: University of Chicago Press, 2004), 14; Riker, *Revised History*, 134; Burrows and Wallace, *Gotham*, 31–32.

33. Harris, *In the Shadow of Slavery*, 17.

34. Van Laer, "On the 5th of December 1641," vol. IV, *Council Minutes, 1638–1649*, doc. no. 110, 130; de Forest, *A Walloon Family*, 87.

35. O'Callaghan, *History of New Netherland*, vol. 1, 187.

36. Van Laer, "Promissory note of Johannes la Montagne to the deacons of New Netherland," vol. I, *Register of the Provincial Secretary, 1638–1642*, doc. no. 122, 170; James Riker, *Harlem: Its Origins and Early Annals* (New York: New Harlem Publishing Company, 1904), 185.

37. Van Laer, "On the 26th of August 1638," vol. IV, *Council Minutes, 1638–1649*, doc. no. 18, 22–23.

38. Van Laer, "Lease from Cornelis van Tienhoven to Claes Cornelissen Swits and Jan Claes sen Alteras of the farm previously occupied by Jacob van Curler," *Register of the Provincial Secretary*, doc. no. 69, 93; Stokes, *Iconography*, vol. II, 193.

39. Riker, *Revised History*, 129; Burrows and Wallace, *Gotham*, 35.

40. Riker, *Revised History*, 129–134. Emily de Forest (*A Walloon Family*, 93) was probably in error when she noted that Geertruyt Bornstra had not traveled to New Amsterdam with Hendrick in 1637 and remained there until she arrived as the new bride of Andries Hudde in 1638.

41. Van Laer, "Agreement about the cultivation of a tobacco plantation on Manhattan Island," vol. 1, *Register of the Provincial Secretary*, doc. 19, 30–32.

42. "Specification of what Johannes la Montaenje has paid and disbursed to divers persons on account of debts and for the maintaining of the house and plantation of the late Hendrick de Foreest, deceased on the 26th July, August, 1637, 'First, the purchaser shall

be bound to tender and pay the proceeds of the hereinafter mentioned property within the period of 12 months, commencing on the date hereof, and that in three installments: the first, cash down; the second in six months; and the third and past payment as above. Johannes la Montaenje remains the purchaser for ƒ. 1800," Van Laer, "Public sale of the house and effects of the late Hendrick de Forest," Van Laer, *Register of the Provincial Secretary*, doc. no. 59, 82–83; doc. 19, 31n3; Stokes, *Iconography*, vol. IV, 88.

43. Van Laer, "Quitclaim from Andries Hudde to Johannes la Montagne of his Interest in the farm Vredendal left by the late Hendrick de Forest," Van Laer, *Register of the Provincial Secretary*, doc. nos. 216–217, 296–298; doc. no. 139, 193. See also Riker, *Revised History*, 129–135.

44. Van Laer, "Receipt of Andries Hudde for part payment of the amount due by Johannes la Montagne to the estate of Hendrick de Forest," Van Laer, *Register of the Provincial Secretary*, doc. no. 57, 78–82; see also *James Riker Papers, 1660–1989*, Series 2. Colonial Papers 1660–[1880s], box 3, folder 6, Archives & Manuscripts, NYPL.

45. See figure 4.6, "Unidentified girl drinking at Montaigne's Spring, McGown's Pass, Central Park, New York City, July 23, 1898," of Montaigne's Fonteyn by James Reuel Smith. The earliest nineteenth-century source, George Everett Hill and George E. Waring Jr.'s *Old Wells and Water-courses of the Island of Manhattan* (New York: The Knickerbocker Press, c. 1897), 256, references the stream, now the reconfigured Loch, as "Montanye's Rivulet," but the earlier *fonteyn* was the term used. "Montanye" became the more modern spelling of "Montagne," beginning with Johannes de la Montagne's grandson Abraham Montanye (see Riker, "The Montanye Family," *Revised History*, 545n), but Riker uses "Montanye" even for Dr. Montagne, so it is confusing. Historian Edward Hagaman Hall used the term in his 1905 *McGown's Pass and Vicinity* (New York: The American Scenic and Historic Association), 9, which probably sourced Hill and Waring. Hall has many errors and omissions in his discussion of the Montagne family's land. "Montagne's Rivulet" was not noted in any of the six volumes of Stokes's *Iconography of Manhattan Island*, which collected every known map and document of New York City to 1928. It is used in this study only as a point of reference.

46. Riker, *Revised History*, 134, 137.

47. Van Laer, "Disbursements by Johannes La Montagne for maintenance of the plantation of the late Hendrick de Forest," Van Laer, *Register of the Provincial Secretary*, doc. no. 57, 79.

48. Riker, *Revised History*, 138.

49. David P. de Vries's comments about duffels is quoted in Riker, *Revised History*, 127n, 137.

50. For a discussion of the politics behind replacing Van Twiller with Kieft, see Jaap Jacobs, "A Troubled Man: Director Wouter Van Twiller and the Affairs of New Netherland in 1635," *New York History* 85, no. 3 (2004): 225–227; http://www.jstor.org/stable/23185831.

51. Jacobs, *The Colony of New Netherland*, 68.

52. Charles Burr Todd, *The Story of the City of New York* (New York: G. P. Putnam's Sons, 1888); Riker, *Revised History*, 137ff.

53. Jameson, *Narratives of New Netherland*, 332–337.

54. O'Callaghan, *Documents*, vol. 1, Holland Documents I–VIII, 1603–1656, vol. 6, 496; Russell Shorto, *The Island at the Center of the World* (New York: Vintage, 2005), 114.

55. Before 1838, the company held a monopoly on all beaver pelts, but that year it opened the trade to private individuals. Susanah Shaw Romney, *New Netherland Connections: Intimate Networks and Atlantic Ties in Seventeenth-Century America* (Chapel Hill: University of North Carolina Press, 2017), 48, 50; see also Ann M. Carlos and Frank D. Lewis, *Commerce by a Frozen Sea: Native Americans and the European Fur Trade* (Philadelphia: University of Pennsylvania Press, 2010), 15–35.

56. Van Laer, *Council Minutes, 1638–1649*, 4, 8; O'Callaghan, *History of New Netherland*, vol. 1, 185–186.

57. Shorto, *The Island*, 118–120; Riker, *Revised History*, 138.

58. Jacobs, *The Colony of New Netherland*, 77.

59. O'Callaghan, *History of New Netherland*, vol. 1, 240–241; Van Laer, *Council Minutes, 1638–1649*, "Articles submitted by the honorable director and council of New Netherland to the heads of families or householders residing here under the jurisdiction of the honorable West India Company," doc. no. 104–105, 124–125; Riker, *Revised History*, 138–139.

60. O'Callaghan, *History of New Netherland*, vol. 1, 242, 243n1. See Van Laer, *Council Minutes, 1638–1649*, doc. no. 106, 125–126, for the opinions of eight of the twelve men.

61. O'Callaghan, *History of New Netherland*, vol. 1, 241–249; see also Jacobs, *The Colony of New Netherland*, 77–78.

62. O'Callaghan, *History of New Netherland*, vol. 1, 265–269.

63. O'Callaghan, *History of New Netherland*, vol. 1, 266–269. De Vries's account was later retold in a pamphlet, *Broad Advice*, to the authorities in Amsterdam, assumed to be written by Cornelis Melyn, an enemy of Kieft. Shorto, *The Island*, 124; Bailyn, *The Barbarous Years*, 707–713.

64. David P. de Vries, "Voyages from Holland to America, A.D. 1632 to 1644," Collections of the New-York Historical Society, 2nd ser., vol. 3, pt. 1 (1857), 78, 129, in Bailyn, *The Barbarous Years*, 664.

65. Shorto, *The Island*, 127.

66. Riker, *Harlem*, 159; de Forest, *A Walloon Family*, 104.

67. O'Callaghan, *History of New Netherland*, vol. 1, 287.

68. Riker, *Revised History*, 142–143.

69. Stokes, *Iconography*, vol. IV, Mar. 5, 1644, 101.

70. Stewart, *The Ancestors and Descendants of James Montaney*, 13 .

71. Bailyn, *The Barbarous Years*, 717–718; O'Callaghan, *History of New Netherland*, vol. 1, 299–300; O'Callaghan, *Documents*, Holland Documents, vol. 5, 413; Jameson, *Narratives of New Netherland*, 282; Burrows and Wallace, *Gotham*, 39.

72. Shorto, *The Island*, 230.

73. O'Callaghan, *History of New Netherland*, vol. 1, 273.

74. E. B. O'Callaghan, *A Brief and True Narrative of the Hostile Conduct of the Barbarous Natives Towards the Dutch Nation* (Albany, NY: J. Munsell, 1863), Appendix, "Treaty of Sixteen Hundred and Forty-five," 21–24; Riker, *Revised History*, 145.

75. A portion of today's East Harlem stretched from the East River west to Fifth Avenue and was bordered on the north by the Harlem Creek and on the south by a smaller kill at approximately Ninety-Third Street. Riker, *Revised History*, 150; de Forest, *A Walloon Family*, 115.

76. Jameson, *Narratives of New Netherland*, 287.

77. Much of the negative assault on Kieft was propaganda put out by his enemies; see Willem Frijhoff, *Fulfilling God's Mission: The Two Worlds of Dominie Everardus Bogardus, 1607–1647* (Leiden: Brill, 2007), chapter 13, 453–454.

78. Shorto, *The Island*, 185.

79. Shorto, *The Island*, 231.

80. Jameson, *Narratives of New Netherland*, 333.

81. Shorto, *The Island*, 245–249; Bailyn, *The Barbarous Years*, 737–764.

82. Jaap Jacobs, " 'Hot Pestilential and Unheard-Of Fevers, Illnesses, and Torments': Days of Fasting and Prayer in New Netherland," *New York History* 96 (3–4): 284–300, https://www.jstor.org/stable/newyorkhist.96.3-4.284; Stokes, *Iconography*, vol. I, 56.

83. Stokes, *Iconography*, vol. I, 57; Riker, *Revised History*, 181.

84. "A Tour of New Netherland: Harlem," https://www.newnetherlandinstitute.org/history-and-heritage/digital-exhibitions/a-tour-of-new-netherland/manhattan/haarlem/.

85. Riker, *Revised History*, 181–185, 188–189, 290–292.

86. Riker, *Revised History*, 794.

87. Riker, *Revised History*, 200–202. The house survives today as the historic Mattewis Persen House Museum & Cultural Heritage Center in Kingston. https://www.dutchcultureusa.com/event/a-reflection-of-1665-dutch-life-in-wiltwyck.

88. Jacobs, *The Colony of New Netherland*, 95–96.

89. Emily de Forest claimed that the Dutch captive was Isaac de Forest, but no documentation corroborates her narrative. De Forest, *A Walloon Family*, 135–139.

90. Shorto, *The Island*, 296.

91. Shorto, *The Island*, 140; John Christopher Schwab, "History of the New York Property Tax," *Publications of the American Economic Association* 5 (1890): 19n2, https://archive.org/metadata/jstor-2485701.

2. ALONG THE KINGSBRIDGE ROAD, 1683–1845

1. Hunter Research, *Archeological Testing and Monitoring Central Park Forts Landscape Reconstruction Project, Manhattan, New York* (prepared for the Central Park Conservancy, July 2014), 3-1 to 3-58; 4-1, 4-2, http://s-media.nyc.gov/agencies/lpc/arch_reports/1545.pdf; Hunter Research, Inc., *Archival Research and Historic Resource Mapping North End of Central Park Above 103rd Street, Borough of Manhattan, New York City,*

Summary Narrative (prepared for the Central Park Conservancy, July 2014,), 2-2 to 2–9, http://s-media.nyc.gov/agencies/lpc/arch_reports/1617.pdf.; *NYT*, Sept. 25, 2014, A 29.

2. Hunter Research, *Archeological Testing and Monitoring*, 4-2; email, Hunter to author, Dec. 18, 2020.

3. Edwin G. Burrows and Mike Wallace, *Gotham: A History of New York City to 1898* (New York: Oxford University Press, 1999), 184.

4. According to I. N. Phelps Stokes, *The Iconography of Manhattan Island, 1498–1909* (New York: Robert H. Dodd, 1918), vol. III, 554, McGowan's Pass was first noted as named for the family in 1756 when Daniel McGowan purchased the nine-acre tract. The pass was part of Harlem Commons until the first division of Harlem communal land in 1712.

5. Edward Hagaman Hall, *McGown's Pass and Vicinity* (New York: The American Scenic and Historic Preservation Society, 1905), 6–46. In a note on page 7, Hall explained that he chose to use the spelling "McGown" based on a mortgage executed by Daniel McGown in 1758 (an error; the deed was dated 1757) and documents by his heirs when they sold the property in 1845. This study employs "McGown" whenever it is spelled as such in historic documents, but uses "McGowan" as is used interchangeably by family members and in documents that describe "McGowan's Pass."

6. John Randel Jr., "City of New York, north of Canal Street in 1808–1821," in David Thomas Valentine, *Manual of the corporation of the city of New-York* (New York, 1864), 847–856.

7. James Riker, *Revised History of Harlem (City of New York) Its Origin and Early Annals* (New York: New Harlem Publishing Company, 1904), 67; John Howard Abbott, *Descendants of Bastiaen Van Kortryk: A Native of Belgium who Emigrated to Holland about 1615* (New York: Tobias A. Wright, 1922), 13–15, https://archive.org/details /courtrightkortriooabbo.

8. In the Dutch naming system a child got his or her name by adding the suffix "son" or "sen" meaning "child of" to their father's Christian name. According to this system, Jan Bastiaensen's father was named Bastiaen (short for Sebastian). His son became Jansen, that is, Jan's son. Riker, *Revised History*, 67n.

9. Riker, *Revised History*, 390.

10. Harrison Bayles, *Old Taverns of New York* (New York: Frank Allaben Genealogical Company, 1915), xv, https://archive.org/details/oldtavernsofnewyoobayl.

11. E[dmund] B[ailey] O'Callaghan, *Laws and Ordinances of New Netherland 1638–1674* (Albany: Weed, Parsons and Co., 1868), 61, 80, 95, 110, 262, 364, https://babel.hathitrust. org/cgi/pt?id=cool.ark:/13960/t83j4269t&view=1up&seq=6.

12. Mary E. Woolley, "Early History of the Colonial Post Office," *Publications of the Rhode Island Historical Society, 1892–93* (Providence, 1893), vol. 1, 270–279, quoted from James Wilson Grant, ed., *Memorial History of New York: From Its First Settlement to the Year 1892* (New York: New York History Co., 1892), vol. 1, 355–356: Eric Jaffe, *The King's Best Highway: The Lost History of the Boston Post Road, the Route that Made America* (New York: Scribner, 2013); Riker, *Revised History*, 285.

13. Richard J. Koke, "Milestones Along the Old Highways of New York City: A Record of the Silent Sentinels of the Stagecoach Era," in *The New-York Historical Society Quarterly* 34, no. 3 (1950): 165–234. According to Koke, by 1801 the milestones were reconfigured; his map shows the three such markers along the west side of the Middle Road, today's Fifth Avenue: the fifth milestone at Sixty-Sixth Street, the sixth between Eighty-Fifth and Eighty-Sixth Street, and the seventh between Ninety-Seventh and Ninety-Eighth Street. The milestone 7½ was in the prepark between Ninety-Third and Ninety-Sixth Street, marking the intersection of the Bloomingdale Cross Road (Apthorp or Jauncey's Lane) and the Post Road (180, 182, 200, 229). Most milestones have been lost to history, but the New-York Historical Society has several in its collection, though not the one from the prepark.

14. Stokes, *Iconography*, vol. IV, 385; Hunter Research, Inc., *A Preliminary Historical and Archeological Assessment of Central Park to the North of the 97th Street Transverse, Borough of Manhattan, City of New York. For: The Central Park Conservancy and The City of New York*, 2 vols., 1990, http://s-media.nyc.gov/agencies/lpc/arch_reports/444_B.pdf, Vol. I, D-183. Metje was also known as Mettje or Mettye with a surname of Jansen or Bastiaensen.

15. Sarah Kemble Knight and Rev. Mr. Buckingham, *The Journals of Madam Knight and Rev. Mr. Buckingham from the Original Manuscripts*, (New York: Wilder & Campbell, 1825), 56, https://catalog.hathitrust.org/Record/001268169.

16. Abbott, *Descendants*, 27; Riker, *Revised History*, 563, 803.

17. Dyckman's Black Horse Tavern is not to be confused with the downtown tavern of the same name that was an important New York meeting place as early as 1727. Bayles, *Old Taverns of New York*, 91.

18. The Bensons followed the Dutch system of naming a male child after their paternal grandfather, but by the eighteenth century the Dutch began to copy the English, naming the son after the father, which resulted in a succession of similar names. See David Steven Cohen, *The Dutch-American Farm* (New York: New York University Press, 1992), 146–147.

19. Cohen, *The Dutch-American Farm*, 138–142. George Dyckman (no relation to Jacob Dyckman) acquired the land from his father-in-law, Teunis Ides van Huyse. George Dyckman later bought adjacent land from his brother-in-law Abraham de la Montagne, the grandson of Johannes (see chapter 7). In 1742, George Dyckman then sold the land to Jacob Dyckman Jr. and Jacob's brother-in-law Adolph Benson; see Riker, *Revised History*, 592. See also Hunter, *A Preliminary Historical and Archeological Assessment*, vol. I, D-588-3, D-36–38.

20. For a history of Samson Benson's conveyances, see Riker, *Revised History*, 430.

21. For the division of Samson Benson's property among his children, see Riker, *Revised History*, 435; H[enry] Croswell Tuttle, *Abstracts of farm titles in the city of New York, East side, between 75th and 120th streets* (New York: The Spectator Company, 1878), 274.

22. Riker, *Revised History*, 438. Adolph Benson's original will is in "Harlem papers, 1660–1879," NYHS, Mss Collection (Harlem Papers).

23. After the Common Council became aware of Adolph Benson and Jacob Dyckman's encroachment onto the corporation's common lands in 1748, they petitioned the council to lease forty acres of common land. *Minutes of the Common Council of the City of New York 1675 to 1776* (hereafter, *MCC1675*), Mar. 18, 1748, 370; Riker, *Revised History*, 803.

24. Stokes, *Iconography*, vol. IV, 607. A 1757 mortgage between Daniel McGown and Benjamin Benson, June 6, 1793; "United States, New York Land Records, 1630–1975," familysearch.org. *Mortgages*, Liber 1 Page 52, 1757 (hereafter, "L" and "P") also included two other properties: "twelve acres of land, Lot Number five in the Town of Harlem . . . and also a Dwelling house and Lott of Ground Scituate Lying & being in the City of New York in . . . Maiden Lane." The entire loan was for £350 with interest at 7 percent.

25. The Dyckmans emigrated from Westphalia in northwest Germany and owned a large farm at Spuyten Duyvil, at the border of Manhattan and the Bronx. The family's homestead—today the Dyckman Farmhouse Museum—built about 1785, on Broadway at 204th Street, remains the oldest house in Manhattan.

26. *New York Mercury*, Mar. 8, 1756, quoted in Stokes, *Iconography*, vol. III, 555. Jacob Dyckman is listed in 1757 as having obtained a tavern license and is also listed in 1759, when he opened his second tavern at Spuyten Duyvil. There is no mention of the McGowan family in any tavern lists from 1756 to 1766; however, Benjamin Benson, who held the McGowan mortgage, is listed as having a tavern license in 1759. *Tavern Keeper's license book, 1756–66*, NYHS (BV New York City—Mayor's Office).

27. Riker, *Revised History*, 282, 290, 447. The garden was a part of the property that Jan de la Montagne sold to Jan Louwe Bogert in 1673 on Montagne's Point, whose northern point was in the vicinity of Fifth Avenue and 103rd Street. See John W. Pirsson, *The Dutch Grants, Harlem Plains and Tidal Creeks* (New York: L. K. Strouse & Co., 1889), 92–97, https://books.google.com. The garden was also discussed in great detail in the printed transcript of the 1868 trial *Cahill v. Palmer*, folio 360–362, 96.

28. "*Chapter II: An Act Entitled an Act to regulate the gauging of rum brandy and other distilled liquors, and molasses . . . and Chapter VII: An Act to let Farm the Excise on Strong Liquors, retailed in this Colony . . . ,*" *Laws of New-York from The 11th Nov. 1752, to 22d May 1762: The Second Volume*, Digested by William Livingston, And William Smith, jun., New York, MDCCLXII; "The Twentieth Assembly, held in the Twenty Sixth Year of the Reign of King George the Second, begun the Twenty-Fourth of October, 1752." Patricia U. Bonomi, *A Factious People: Politics and Society in Colonial New York* (New York: Columbia University Press, 1971), lists the members and their districts, appendices, n.p.; James Thomas Flexner, *States Dyckman: American Loyalist* (Boston: Little, Brown, 1980), 11.

29. Jacob and Catalina's son States Morris Dyckman appears to have been the only Loyalist in the Dyckman or Benson family. Flexner, *States Dyckman*, 14.

30. Koke, "Milestones," 173n8.

31. Thomas F. De Voe, *The Market Book: Containing a Historical Account of Public Markets in the Cities of New York, Boston, Philadelphia and Brooklyn*, Vol. 1 (New York: Hall, Clayton and Medole, 1862), 64–66.

32. Catherine Benson was previously married to Swede Luke Shourd, also a seafaring man, lost at sea ten years before she married Daniel McGowan in 1740. The history of the McGowan property is detailed in Stokes, *Iconography*, vol. III, 554–555. Stokes also cites a memo by James Riker that noted the mortgage between Benjamin Benson and Daniel McGowan was in the possession of the late Isaac Adriance, a member of the Benson family. Daniel was still alive in 1761, being named the poll for the Assembly elections in February; see John Daniel Crimmins, *Irish-Americans Historical Miscellany: Relating Largely to New York City and Vicinity* (New York: author, 1905), 60.

33. See Crimmins, *Irish-Americans Historical Miscellany*, note 31, for McGowan's Irish heritage. For his Scottish heritage see Hopper Striker Mott, *The New York of Yesterday: A Descriptive Narrative of Old Bloomingdale* (New York: G. P. Putnam's Sons, 1908), 77; and John Flavel Mines, *A Tour Around Manhattan and My Summer Acre* (New York: Harper & Brothers, 1893), 469, https://babel.hathitrust.org/cgi/pt?id=loc.ark:/13960/tonsox74v&view=1up&seq=5&skin=2021.

34. "Dr. Wood was personally acquainted with McGowan's son Andrew. Riker states that in 1745 Daniel bought from David Devoor the property now comprising the part of Central Park now the Harlem Mere," in Riker, *Revised History*, 287. In 1749, as a freeholder and inhabitant of New Harlem, Daniel McGowan voted to authorize Jacob Dyckman Jr. and two other men to represent New Harlem in the conflict with the Corporation of New York concerning the Harlem Commons legal boundaries. Carl Horton Pierce, *New Harlem Past and Present: The Story of an Amazing Civic Wrong, Now at Last to be Righted* (New York: The Harlem Publishing Company, 1903), 252–253.

35. The Old Testament source is "Cursed be he that perverteth the judgment of the stranger, fatherless, and widow. And all the people shall say, Amen," Deuteronomy 27:19. The tale is misrepresented in Flexner, *States Dyckman*, 12, 16–17. Flexner cites the source of Catherine's quote as a manuscript memorandum by Thomas F. DeVoe that is located in NYHS Mss Collection (Harlem Papers), 220. H. Dorothea Romer and Helen B. Hartman, "The Black Horse Tavern," in *Jan Dyckman of Harlem and His Descendants* (New York: J. A. Thompson, 1981), 24n3; *Rivington Gazette*, February 17, 1774, quoted in Flexner, *States Dyckman*, 17. The McGowan tract was originally a part of lot No. 7 of the first division of the Harlem Common Lands, which in 1712 was awarded to Samuel Waldron. The next owner was Abraham de la Montague, who then passed it in 1729 to George Dyckman. In 1748, George Dyckman sold a twenty-acre tract to Jacob Dyckman. Stokes, *Iconography*, vol. III, 554; Hunter, *A Preliminary Historical and Archeological Assessment*, vol. 1, D-36-38.

36. "Ordered that Aldn Bayard direct Road Master to put Rails along the Road on the side Hill [editor: McGowens Pass (*sic*) indicted in note below] to prevent accidents to Horse & Carriages. And also that Mr. Aldn direct the sides of the Arch in the middle of the

Road to be raised on a level with said Road," *Minutes of the Common Council, 1784–1830* (hereafter, *MCC1784*), vol. 1, 295, https://catalog.hathitrust.org/Record/001150706; John Flavel Mines, *A tour around New York, and My summer acre; being the recreations of Mr. Felix Oldboy* (New York: Harper & Brothers, 1893), 271.

37. *New-York Journal*, or, *The General Advertiser*, "Notice," June 18, 1772, 3.

38. Samson Benson, Jr. married Mary Sickels, Dec. 10, 1763.

39. Michael J. O'Brien, "Irish Property Owners of NYC," *The Journal of the American Irish Historical Society* 15 (1916): 288. The letter referred to an article written by Wood to James Riker in 1880 in the Riker papers of the New York Public Library. To date, the author was unable to locate it.

40. Esther Singleton, *Dutch New York*, (New York: Benjamin Blom, 1968), 207.

41. Edward Hagaman Hall, "History of Central Park in the City of New York," *Sixteenth Annual Report of the American Scenic and Historic Preservation Society*, (Albany: J. B. Lyon Company, 1911), Appendix G, 429, https://babel.hathitrust.org/cgi/pt?id=wu.890 72985211&view=1up&seq=11.

42. Historical Society of the New York Courts, August 1816, https://history.nycourts.gov /case/in-re-waldron/. John P. Waldron was issued a tavern license in 1809. *Tavern Licenses 1809*, NYHS.

43. "New York, U.S., Wills and Probate Records, 1659–1999," www.ancestry.com, (hereafter *Probate*), Last Will and Testament of Andrew McGowan, L56, P166–172, 1820.

44. Adriance was related to Mary Benson's deceased brother John Sickles, making Margaret Eliza both a grandniece on her Sickles side and a great granddaughter on her Benson side.

45. Last Will and Testament of Mary Sickles, *Probate*, L74, P474–77, 1834.

46. In the tax assessments for 1814, Samson Benson Jr. owned two houses and one hundred acres, assessed at $36,000, in Record of Assessments for 1814, Ninth Ward, Harlem Division, unpaginated, microfilm roll no. 45, MANY.

47. Riker, *Revised History*, 438. Andrew McGowan was assessed in 1808 as having real estate valued at $5,000 and personal worth of $1,000. He was listed as one of New York's richest men with a personal estate tax of $10,000, in 1815 and in 1820; in D. T. Valentine, ed., "Comparative Wealth of Citizens of New York," *Manual of the Corporation of the City of New York*, 761; Henry Croswell Tuttle, *Abstract of Farm Titles in the City of New York; East Side Between 75th and 120th Streets* (New York: The Spectator Company, 1878), vol. 3, 265–401; *Farm Histories*, "The Margaret McGown Farm," MANY (unpublished).

48. According to Andrew and Margaret's son, Samson Benson McGowan, the nuclear family only lived on the prepark homestead until 1824 or 1825, but Margaret Eliza gave birth to her son John Adriance "at McGowan's Pass" on October 6, 1832, so Margaret must have lived there until she moved in with the Adriance family. See Albert Winslow Ryerson, *The Ryerson Genealogy* (Chicago: private printing, 1916), 296, https://books .google.com/books?id=YSVPAAAAMAAJ&q=John+Adriance#v=onepage&q=McGow &f=false. See also testimony of Samson B. McGowan, *Cahill v. Palmer*, 203. Testimony of Henry Post McGowan, Andrew's son, during a trial, New York State Court

of Appeals, *Dunham v. Townshend*, in *Reports of Cases Decided in the Court of Appeals of the State of New York*, vol. 118 (Albany, Jan. 1890), 285. *US Census 1850*, New York City, 19th Ward, 132. In *Trow's New City Directory*, vol. 94, May 1, 1881, Samson B. McGown was listed as living at East 106th and Third Avenue. Andrew Jr. died in 1870. According to Riker, *Revised History*, 439, Alderman Samson Benson McGowan was born in 1797 and died in 1884.

49. "By Anthony Bleecker & Co," *Comm. Adv.*, May 16, 1844, 1. The New York City Tax Assessments for 1846 still list Andrew McGowen (and McGown) as owning property from 102nd to 107th Street, valued at $4,600. Maybe not all of it was transferred to the Sisters. The largest portion of the property, 36 lots between 104th and 105th Streets was valued at $3,000; see Tax Assessments 1846, 82–83, microfilm roll np. 67, MANY. By the time the brothers sold their home, the property had been much improved since Jacob Dyckman built it. On the Randel farm map of 1818–20, the structures had grown to five buildings, including what must have been a large barn. On close inspection, there seems to have been a large wrap-around porch added, from which the McGowans could admire the eastward-facing views mentioned in the ad. A comparable architectural drawing of a porch on a Randel map is the one built in 1799 at Gracie Mansion, still in existence today. The McGowan porch probably deteriorated by the time of the sale, since it is not mentioned.

50. See chapter 14.

51. "Destruction in the Park: Buildings at Mt. St. Vincent Ruined by Fire," *NYT*, Jan. 3, 1881. The article contains many errors regarding the McGown family.

52. In March 1757, a year after the sale to Daniel McGowan, Jacob Dyckman is listed as having a license; New York (N.Y.) Office of the Mayor, *Tavern Keeper's License Book 1756–66*, Book 42, 198, NYHS (BV New York City—Mayor's Office noncirculating).

53. In 1882, Samson B. McGowan confirmed that the tavern on the Kingsbridge Road on the north side of the present Ninety-Seventh Street between Fifth and Sixth Avenues, marked on the Colles road map in 1789 as Leggett's Tavern, was the Black Horse tavern of the Revolution. He noted that he had been in it many times in his boyhood and that it burned down in 1808. *The Magazine of American History with Notes and Queries* 8 (1882): 46, https://archive.org/details/magazineofamerico8stev. See "Letter from General Clinton to the Committee of New-York Convention, King's Bridge, September 18, 1776," in *Peter Force's American Archives*, Fifth Series, vol. 2, col. 383, https://babel.hathitrust .org/cgi/pt?id=iau.31858027039449&view=1up&seq=256&q1=Committee%20of%20 NewYork%20Convention,%20King%E2%80%99s%20Bridge,%20September%20 18,%201776; Riker, *Revised History*, 592, 710; Hall, *McGown's Pass*, 20.

54. *New-York Historical Society collection of New York tavern licenses, 1783–1797* (Box 1, Folder 4, John Leggett 1783–97, 1862, NYHS Ms. 443 28). For the Christopher Colles map, see Stokes, *Iconography*, vol. V, Plate 51b, 1150; also reproduced in Hunter, *A Preliminary Historical and Archeological Assessment*, vol. 2, Illustration 14. Illustration 15 is a drawing of Leggett's Tavern.

55. Kimmel's tavern license in *Tavern Licenses 1809*, New York Historical Society: John C. Kemmel, Ward 9, Harlaem Post Road. Office of the Mayor, and in *Tavern Keeper's License Book 1808–1809*; License of John C. Kemmel, Ward 9 Harlaem. Mar. 19, 1789. In the *Cahill v. Palmer* trial, Kimmel's son, William J.W. Kimmel, testified that his father ran the tavern in 1806 and 1807, though tavern licenses issued though the Mayor's Office also gave John C. Kemmel a license for the years 1808 and 1809. The next occupant was Robert Latimer, who lived there until 1815 or 1816, but possibly did not operate it a tavern. The next occupant, Joshua Tuttle, lived in and ran it as a tavern until 1823 or 1824. After Tuttle, "two or three persons" occupied it until it was either burned down or town down. See *Cahill v. Palmer*, handwritten testimony *Central Park Extension*, 355. The tavern appears on surveyor John Randel's farm map No. 54, http://thegreatestgrid .mcny.org/greatest-grid/randel-composite-map.

3. THE ENSLAVED BENSONS, 1754–1846

1. James Riker, *Revised History of Harlem (City of New York) Its Origin and Early Annals* (New York: New Harlem Publishing Company, 1904), 429.

2. *U.S. Census, 1790*, 130; *U.S. Census, 1800*, 927; *U.S. Census, 1810*, 783; *U.S. Census, 1820*, 941. McGowan's drop in enslaved people in the decade between 1790 to 1800 reflects a trend in New York slavery; see Shane White, *Somewhat More Independent: The End of Slavery in New York City 1770–1810* (Athens: University of Georgia Press, 1991), 32–38; Vivienne Kruger, "Born to Run: The Slave Family in Early New York, 1626 to 1827" (Ph.D. diss., Columbia University, 1985), table 1, 891; Hopper Striker Mott, *The New York of Yesterday: A Descriptive Narrative of Old Bloomingdale* (New York: G. P. Putnam's Sons, 1908), 280.

3. *New-York Manumission Society records, 1785–1849. Volume 2, Register of Manumissions of Slaves in New York City, June 18, 1816–May 28, 1818*, BV Manumission Society, vol. 2, 57, Mss Collection, NYHS nyhs_nyms_v-02_001, https://digitalcollections.nyhistory.org /islandora/object/islandora%3A132423#page/17/mode/1up.

4. Leslie M. Harris, *In the Shadow of Slavery: African Americans in New York City, 1626–1863* (Chicago: University of Chicago Press, 2004), 11, 50, 70–73, 94–95; Ira Berlin and Leslie M. Harris, *Slavery in New York* (New York, New-York Historical Society, 2005), 16–17, 124–130; Graham Russell Gao Hodges, *Root and Branch: African Americans in New York and East Jersey, 1613–1863* (Chapel Hill: University of North Carolina Press, 1999), 170; Kruger, "Born to Run," 818–822; White, *Somewhat More Independent*, 46,–54, 147–49; Eric Foner, *Gateway to Freedom: The Hidden History of the Underground Railroad* (New York: Norton, 2015), 39–44; Edgar J. McManus, *Black Bondage in the North* (Syracuse, NY: Syracuse University Press, 1973), 177–179.

5. White, *Somewhat More Independent*, 38, 51, 55.

6. White, *Somewhat More Independent*,149; Rhoda G. Freeman, *The Free Negro in New York City in the Era Before the Civil War* (New York: Garland, 1994), 6.

7. "Runaway from the Subscriber," *The New-York Journal or the General Advertiser*, Oct. 3, 1771, 4; "Runaway from the Subscriber," *The New-York Gazette* and *The Weekly Mercury*, Aug. 10, 1772, 5.

8. "Ten Dollar Reward," *The Columbian*, May 20, 1812, 3; also in Graham Russell Hodges and Alan Edward Brown, *Pretends to be Free: Runaway Slave Advertisements from Colonial and Revolutionary New York and New Jersey* (New York and London: Garland, 1994), 163.

9. In the last will and testament of Susan Benson, Charlotte, "a colored servant woman in my family," is bequeathed a feather bed; *Probate*, L 60, P48/61, Dec. 27, 1825. See also H[enry] Croswell Tuttle, "The Samson Benson Tract," *Abstracts of farm titles in the city of New York, East side, between 75th and 120th Streets* (New York: The Spectator Company, 1878)," 395. In the Record of Assessment for 1826, "Widow" Combs was listed as residing in the home and four lots left to her by her former enslaver; "Old Harlem Road," microfilm, roll no. 66, unpaginated, MANY.

10. In *U.S. Census, 1810*, widows made up the largest category of female –heads of white households and had the most enslaved servants; see White, *Somewhat More Independent*, 40, table 3 and table 10.

11. For the transfer of Central Park at Fifth Avenue at 110th Street to the city, see "Supreme Court, In the Matter of One Hundred and Tenth Street, for Order Appointing Commissioners," May 17, 1899, 223, in *Block Indices of Reindexed Conveyances, pre-1917, Blocks 1107 to 1111, City of New York, Borough of Manhattan, Department of Finance, City Register*. "The Harlem Road" that ran along the southeast border of the property was originally an indigenous trail that branched off from the Kingsbridge Road at 109th Street and headed northeast to a Native settlement that became the village of Harlem. See figure I.6.

12. Waldron to Benson, L 56, P361, 1763, "New York City Land Conveyances 1654–1851," microfilm, Milstein Division, NYPL; vol. 1110–1111, Office of the City Registrar, City of New York, DOF. The property was first common lands of the Town of Harlem and sold to Aaron Bussing on May 30, 1753. It was then sold by his executor, Adolph Meyer, to David Waldron on May 1, 1788; Riker, *Revised History*, note, 801–802n819. See also Tuttle, "The Lanaw Benson Tract," *Abstracts of farm titles in the city of New York, East side, between 75th and 120th Streets* (New York: The Spectator Company, 1878), 383–386.

13. Lanaw's birthplace is unknown. In an online search for a location in Africa named "Lanaw," only one instance was found: Shai, Greater Accra, Ghana; its geographical coordinates are 6° 2′ 0″ North, 0° 10′ 0° 2′ 0″ East and its original name (with diacritics) is "Lanaw," www.maplandia.com. From 1737 to 1771, 70 percent of the enslaved people imported to New York were from Africa, Lanaw probably among them; Kruger, "Born to Run," 437–441. The name Lanaw does not appear in the African Names Database on www.slavesvoyages.org. I am grateful to William Quansah, my Ghanaian American Conservancy colleague, who traveled to Shai Hills Preserve research the name or place of Lanaw. A sign in the preserve listed the Ga-Dangmes tribes of Se, Klo, Ada, Osudoku, Gbugla, and Ningo who once resided in the area.

14. Maps differ as to the amount of land on the western edge of the property, which was the Harlem Creek. Some show the property ranging from the perimeter between 109th and 110th Streets, possibly including a strip of land inside the wall, or as little as the crescent of land at the southwest corner that was cropped to create a road on the edge of the traffic circle at 110th Street and Fifth Avenue; see John Randal Farm map no. 58, 1818–1820, BMP; Otto Sackersdorff, *Maps of farms commonly called the Blue book, 1815, drawn from the original on file in the street commissioner's office in the City of New York, together with lines of streets and avenues* (New York: Court of the Southern District of New York, 1868), 16; Lanaw Benson Farm, Farm Histories, folder no. 7, MANY.

15. Eric Foner, *Give Me Liberty!: An American History,* 3rd ed. (New York: Norton, 2012), vol. 1, 2. Thanks to Stephen Wesley for sharing the Foner quote with me.

16. Jill Lepore, "The Tightening Vise: Slavery and Freedom in British New York," in Berlin and Harris, *Slavery in New York*, 81; Freeman, *The Free Negro in New York City*, 8. Harris, *In the Shadow of Slavery*, 39; New York State, *The Colonial Laws of New-York From the Year 1664 to the Revolution*, vol. I (Albany: James B. Lyon, 1894), chapter 250, December 10, 1712, 761–762, https://babel.hathitrust.org/cgi/pt?id=umn.31951002158537d&view=1up&seq=8; *Public Laws of the State of New-York, Passed at the Thirty-Second Session of the Legislature*, chapter XLIV (Albany: Websters and Skinner, 1809), Feb. 17, 1809, 450, https://babel.hathitrust.org/cgi/pt?id=nyp.33433090878202&view=1up&seq=11.

17. Benson to Rankin, L56, P362–363, Apr. 9, 1799.

18. The equivalent of £221 was roughly $909 in 1799. The consumer price index of $909 in 1799 was roughly equal to $20,000 in 2021 dollars. Conversion calculated using https://www.measuringworth.com/calculators/exchange/result_exchange.php. For the consumer price index for 1799 dollars converted to the 2021 value, see http://www.in2013dollars.com/us/inflation/1799?amount=550.

19. Rankin to Watt, L259, P451, 1830.

20. New York State, *The Colonial Laws*, chapter 250, 764–765; Lepore, "The Tightening Vise," 81; Harris, *In the Shadow of Slavery*, 39.

21. Lepore, "The Tightening Vise," 81.

22. It may be a coincidence that a different John Rankin was an Ohioan Presbyterian minister who became a famous abolitionist. No evidence of a connection between the two Rankins has turned up yet, but research is ongoing.

23. Harry B. Yoshpe, "Record of Slave Manumissions in New York During the Colonial and Early National Periods," *The Journal of Negro History* 26, no. 1 (January 1941): 92; Freeman, *The Free Negro in New York City*, 9. Hodges, *Root and Branch*, 169n17, 323.

24. David Waldron in *U.S. Census, 1790*, City and County of New York, Harlem Division, 130; David Waldron in *U.S. Census, 1800*, City and County of New York, Seventh Ward, 927; Last Will and Testament of Elizabeth Rankin, *Probate*, L44, P244, 1803.

25. White, *Somewhat More Independent*, 107.

26. In 1828, John Rankin's niece, Margaret Gosman, sold her uncle's three-acre property for $1,525 to speculator Archibald Watt. Gosman to Watt, L234, P5, 1828.

27. Later maps show that the house on the Rankin property had been moved to Lanaw's smaller tract. See Randal Farm Map No. 58, ca. 1814, MBP, https://thegreatestgrid .mcny.org/greatest-grid/randel-map-gallery/164. The house is also depicted in William James Proctor and John Joseph Holland, "Military Map of Haerlem Heights with Landscape Vignette at Upper Right," 1814, NYHS (see figure 6.1).

28. *Tax Assessments 1799, Wards 1–2, 4–7 & Harlem Division*, MANY. My thanks to Ken Cobb for bringing to my attention the colored map in the Farm History "The Lanaw Benson Farm" that confirmed Lanaw Benson owned a section of the prepark.

29. Last Will and Testament of Ellenor Waldron, *Probate*, L52, P185, 1815. Sam Waldron was described as "now or late, the property of Lewis Morris, deceased." Morris, probably Lewis Morris III, lived on his family's vast estate in Westchester, today's Morrisania neighborhood in the Bronx. He died in 1798, one year before the formerly enslaved, Sam, appeared in the tax assessment records. For the history of the enslaved people by Morris family, see Kruger, "Born to Run," 126nn103, 104. "Ellenor, a Black" was listed in the Record of Assessments, Ninth Ward, 1808, as owner of the property with house and lot valued at $200 (microfilm, roll no. 44, 1808, 7); 1809 records: "Ellenor/A Black," house and lot valued at $150 (microfilm, roll no. 44, 1809, 7); 1813 records: "Ellenor/A Black," house and lot valued at $100 (microfilm, roll no. 44, 1813, 15), MANY.

30. The only other possibility is Jannetje Bensen, who was born a member of the Coeyemans or Ten Eyck family. On September 17, 1722, Tanneke Waldron, daughter of Samuel Waldron, born in 1703, married Johannes Benson, born in 1700, the older brother of Adolph, Benjamin, Catherine, and Catalina. Riker, *Revised History*, 430. Margaret Kelly and Ted O'Reilly both noted the similar sound of the names "Lanaw" and "Ellenor" in conversation with the author.

31. Photocopies of the Last Will and Testament of Adolph Benson, July 10, 1754, and the Last Will and Testament of Tanneke Benson, 1773, in the notebook "The Dyckman Papers, box 7," Boscobel, Garrison, NY. I am grateful to Jennifer Carlquist, executive director and curator, for assistance with the papers. See Last Will and Testament of Adolph Benson, *Probate*, L44, P252, Feb. 26, 1803; Tanneke Benson, *Probate*, L33, P4, June 2, 1780; Riker, *Revised History*, 705. The original wills are located in the collection's "Harlem Papers, box 2, folder 2, 1751-1775, NYHS. In the same folder is a second will by Adolf Benson dated September 19, 1768 in which there is no mention of Len and only mentions a "servant" to be bequeathed to his wife. I am grateful to Ted O'Reilly for locating the documents.

32. Riker, *Revised History*, 705.

33. Sylvester to Combs, L202, P127, 1815. In the will, the granddaughters are noted as Grace Delsworth and Sana (or Lana) Laversley. Documents mentioning Grace Sylvester, Grace Delsworth, or Sana Laversley have not been found in either New York City or Philadelphia records.

34. Last Will and Testament of John Rankin, *Probate*, L43, P189, Feb. 6, 1800; Last Will and Testament of Elizabeth Rankin, *Probate*, L44, P257, 1803; Last Will and Testament of

Henry Rankin, *Probate*, L83, P169, 1841. In her will, Ellenor Waldron stipulated that the house and property were to be sold, one half to John Combs and Grace Delsworth, and the other half to Sana Laversley; *Probate*, L52 P156. See, "John Combs, a Black," in *U.S. Census, 1800*, New York City, Ward 7, 929; Sarah Combs to Charlotte Lawrence, L480, P134, 1846. A Black woman named Charlotte Lawrence, age 31, in *U.S. Census 1850*, New York, Ward 8, 901, may be the grantee, see also, *The New York City Directory for 1851–1852* (New York: Doggett & Rode, 1851), 314. Lawrence sold the small lot to Reverend Richard M. Abercrombie of St. Andrew's, a Protestant Episcopal Church in Harlem for $2000. Given the proximity of the church to the property, Lawrence may have been living in Sarah Combs' house and attending the Harlem church. Lawrence to Abercrombie, L577, P65. 1851. For information on St. Andrew's see, http://anglicanhistory .org/usa/misc/draper_harlem1889.html. Last Will and Testament of Susan Benson, *Probate*, L60, P61,1825. I am grateful to Shane White for reading this chapter and agreeing with my conclusions (email, June 22, 2020).

35. Bennett Liebman, "The Quest for Black Voting Rights in New York State," *Albany Government Law Review* 11 (2018): 389, see also note 23; Dixon Ryan Fox, "The Negro Vote in Old New York," *Political Science Quarterly* 32, no. 2 (1917): 252–275, https://www .jstor.org/stable/2141732.

36. Hodges, *Root and Branch*, 168.

37. Fox, "The Negro Vote," 257; Freeman, *The Free Negro in New York City*, 91 .

4. THE WAR AT MCGOWAN'S PASS, 1776–1784

1. Joseph J. Ellis, *Revolutionary Summer: The Birth of American Independence* (New York: Knopf, 2013), 113-126; Rick Atkinson, *The British Are Coming: The War for America, Lexington to Princeton, 1775–1777* (New York: Henry Holt, 2019), 376–379.

2. Barnet Schecter, *The Battle for New York: The City at the Heart of the American Revolution* (New York: Walker & Co., 2002), 396n19; see I. N. Phelps Stokes, The *Iconography of Manhattan Island*, vol. V (New York: Robert Dodd, 1926), 1114. I am grateful to historian Barnet Schechter and to Dr. Laurence Simpson, general president of the General Society of the Sons of the Revolution, for reading and editing the manuscript. Schecter, email to author, October 5, 2020.

3. Ellis, *Revolutionary Summer*, 35; Rick Atkinson, *The British Are Coming: The War for America, Lexington to Princeton, 1775–1777* (New York: Henry Holt, 2019), 352.

4. Philander D. Chase and Frank E. Grizzard Jr., eds., *The Papers of George Washington*, Revolutionary War Series, 27 vols. (Charlottesville: University Press of Virginia, 1994), vol. 6, *13 August 1776–20 October 1776*, 199–201; "From George Washington to John Hancock, 2 September 1776," *Founders Online*, National Archives, https://founders.archives .gov/documents/Washington/03-06-02-0162.

5. "To George Washington from John Hancock, Sept. 3, 1776," *Founders Online*, National Archives, https://founders.archives.gov/documents/Washington/03-06-02-0168. Original

source: Chase and Grizzard, eds., *The Papers of George Washington*, Revolutionary War Series, vol. 6, 207; Ron Chernow, *Washington: A Life* (New York: Penguin, 2011), 252.

6. Ellis, *Revolutionary Summer*, 137; Joanne B. Freeman, *Affairs of Honor: National Politics in the New Republic* (New Haven: Yale University Press, 2001), xx.

7. "To George Washington from Major General Nathanael Greene, 5 September 1776," *Founders Online*, National Archives, https://founders.archives.gov/documents/Washington /03-06-02-0180. Schecter, *The Battle for New York*, 170; Ellis, *Revolutionary Summer*, 35; Atkinson, *The British Are Coming*, 388.

8. Chase and Grizzard, eds., *The Papers of George Washington*, 288–289n3; Chernow, *Washington*, 253; Schecter, *The Battle for New York*, 171.

9. Charles Farmar Billopp, *A History of Thomas and Anne Billopp Farmar, and some of their Descendants in America, 1846–1907* (New York: The Grafton Press, 1907), 60.

10. Ellis, *Revolutionary Summer*, 131–133.

11. Walter Isaacson, *Benjamin Franklin: An American Life* (New York: Simon & Schuster, 2004), 319–320.

12. Chase and Grizzard, eds., *The Papers of George Washington: Revolutionary War Series*, vol. 6, August–October 1776 (Charlottesville and London: University Press of Virginia, 1994), 279–280.

13. Chase and Grizzard, eds., *The Papers of George Washington: Revolutionary War Series*, vol. 6, 288n1.

14. Roger J. Champagne, *Alexander McDougall and the American Revolution in New York*, (Schenectady, NY: Bicentennial, 1975), 113. 113.

15.

"To reconsider		To adhere
Gen. Beall REZIN	Gen. McDougal ALEXANDER	Gen. Spencer JOSEPH
Gen. Scott JOHN MORIN	Gen. Parsons SAMUEL H.	Gen. Clinton GEORGE
G. Fellows	Gen. Mifflin THOMAS	Gen. Heath WILLIAM"
G. Wadsworth	Genl Green [sic] NATHANAEL	
Gen. Nixon JOHN	Gen. Puttnam [sic] ISRAEL	

In Chase and Grizzard, eds., *The Papers of George Washington*, 288–289n1. "Footnote D, in Joseph Reed writing: The mutilated text within angle brackets is supplied from the documents in the McDougall Papers, which are certified by Richard Varick as true copies of Reed's manuscript, one made on 13 Feb. 1782 and the other made on 15 Mar. 1782." See Champagne, *Alexander McDougall*, 113; Edward Hagaman Hall, *McGown's Pass and Vicinity* (New York: The American Scenic and Historic Preservation Society, 1905), 14–15.

16. Rufus Rockwell Wilson, *Heath's memoirs of the American war, reprinted from the original edition of 1798; with introduction and notes* (New York: A. Wessels Company, 1904), 69.

17. *George Washington Papers, Series 4, General Correspondence: Alexander McDougall to George Washington, with Court Martial Charges*, 1782, https://www.loc.gov/item/mgw431243/.

18. Champagne, *Alexander McDougall*, 113. See also *The Papers of George Washington*, 288n1. McDougall papers, microfilm reel no. 4, 1782–1795, NYHS.

19. Champagne, *Alexander McDougall*, 177.

20. "From George Washington to Alexander McDougall, March 2, 1782," *Founders Online*, National Archives, https://founders.archives.gov/documents/Washington/99-01-02-07904.

21. "From George Washington to Alexander McDougall, February 3, 1782," *Founders Online*, National Archives, accessed Sept. 29, 2019, https://founders.archives.gov/documents /Washington/99-01-02-07769; Champagne, *Alexander McDougall*, 177.

22. Nathanael Greene to Alexander McDougall, August 18, 1782: "We hear much about a dispute between you and General Heath and a duel to be fought between you and the noble Earl. I wish to learn the cause of all the rumours. You will oblige me much in detailing the particulars." Microfilm, reel no. 4, 1782–1795 Alexander McDougall Papers, NYHS.

23. "To George Washington from Alexander McDougall, June 15, 1782," *Founders Online*, National Archives, https://founders.archives.gov/documents/Washington/99-01-02-08696.

24. "To George Washington from Alexander McDougall, August 23, 1782," *Founders Online*, National Archives, https://founders.archives.gov/documents/Washington/99-01-02-09219.

25. In volume 14, folio 77 of "Manuscripts of the Colony and State of New York in the Revolutionary War," in Edward Hagaman Hall, "History of Central Park, in the City of New York," Appendix G, Sixteenth Annual Report, 1911, of the American Scenic and Historic Preservation Society (Albany, NY: J. B. Lyon Company, 1911), n412. In 1893, it was noted, "The place is of some historic repute, too, as the main building is known to have been Washington's headquarters for a while." A further detail mentions "a large Franklin stove, then in one of the parlors, has been removed to the new Mount St. Vincent [in the Bronx] and is said to have been there in the General's time," A.M.M.G., ed. James J. Doherty, *Life of Mother Elizabeth Boyle: One of Mother Seaton's Companions, the Assistant Mother Under Her for Eight Years and First Superioress of 'The Sisters of Charity of St. Vincent de Paul' of New York City* (Mount Loretto, Staten Island: Mission of the Immaculate Virgin, 1893), 186.

26. Wilson, *Heath's Memoirs*, 69.

27. Worthington Chauncey Ford, ed., *The Writings of George Washington*, "1776," vol. 4 (New York: G. P. Putnam's Sons, 1889), 402–404, https://oll.libertyfund.org/title/ford-the-writings-of -george-washington-vol-iv-1776. The letter was read in Congress on Sept. 16th; 404n1.

28. Chernow, *Washington*, 253; Ellis, *Revolutionary Summer*, 148–149, and sources 205n33, Schecter, *The Battle for New York*, 186; Atkinson, *The British Are Coming*, 389–394.

29. Smallwood quoted in letter "From George Washington to John Hancock, September 16, 1776, note 4, https://founders.archives.gov/documents/Washington/03-06-02-0251. For Smallwood's account and other witnesses, see editors' notes in "To George Washington from Major General Nathanael Greene, 5 September 1776," *Founders Online*. *George Washington: A Biography* (New York: Charles Scribner & Sons, 1951), vol. 4, 194n118; see also Chernow, *Washington*, 253–254; Ellis, *Revolutionary Summer*, 149.

30. Ellis, *Revolutionary Summer*, 149; Atkinson, *The British Are Coming*, 392.

31. The British under General Henry Clinton advanced unopposed until they reached the east/west cross road at approximately Ninety-Sixth Street connecting the Bloomingdale

Road with the Kingsbridge Road, where they were met by Maryland troops under Colonel Smallwood, to cover the retreat of the rebels who were guarding the fortifications at Horn's Hook on the East River at Eighty-Ninth Street (now the site of Gracie Mansion).

32. Henry P. Johnston, *The Campaign of 1776 Around New York and Brooklyn* (Brooklyn: Long Island Historical Society, 1878), 244.

33. "Letter from Colonel Smallwood to Maryland Convention," October 12, 1776, in *Peter Force's American Archives*, Fifth Series, vol. 5, column 1013; Henry P. Johnston, *Battle of Harlem Heights* (New York: The Macmillan Company, 1897), 41.

34. Hall, *McGown's Pass and Vicinity*, 22–23.

35. Frederick Mackenzie, *Diary of Frederick Mackenzie: Giving a Daily Narrative of His Military Service as an Officer of the Regiment of Royal Welch Fusiliers During the Years 1775–1781 in Massachusetts, Rhode Island and New York*, ed. Allen French (Cambridge, MA: Harvard University Press, 1930), vol. 1, 49; "M'Gown's Pass Chosen for Historic Pageant," *New York Sun*, July 7, 1912, 14.

36. Michael Cohn, "Fortifications of New York During the Revolutionary War 1776–1782" (unpublished paper, New York City Archeology Group, 1962), unpaginated, confirms the location and construction of the fortifications and cites sources. See also Claude Joseph Sauthier, *A map of part of New-York Island showing a plan of Fort Washington, now call'd Ft. Kniphausen with the rebels lines on the south part, from which they were driven on the 16th of November 1776 by the troupes under the orders of the Earl of Percy*, LOC, https://www.loc.gov/item/gm71000653/. The map, "Advanced Posts—New York Island," dated October 12, 1776, shows the fortifications on what became known as Fort Clinton and Nutter's Battery as well as the advanced posts that guarded the Kingsbridge Road on the flats, in *Diary of Frederick Mackenzie*, 76, reproduced in Hunter Research, *A Preliminary Historical and Archeological Assessment of Central Park to the North of the 97th Street Transverse, Borough of Manhattan, City of New York. For: The Central Park Conservancy and The City of New York*, 1990, http://s-media.nyc.gov/agencies/lpc/arch_reports/444_B.pdf, vol. 2, illustration 4. I am grateful to Richard Hunter and James Lee of Hunter Research, Inc. for confirming the evidence in the Robertson drawing. Hunter, emails to author, March 18, 19, 21, 2021.

37. Hall, *McGown's Pass and Vicinity*, 21–22.

38. Hunter Research, Inc. *Archival Research and Historic Resource Mapping North End of Central Park Above 103rd Street, Borough of Manhattan, New York City, Summary Narrative*, prepared for the Central Park Conservancy, July 2014, http://s-media.nyc.gov/agencies/lpc/arch_reports/1617.pdf, 5–6.

39. BCCP, *Eighth Annual Reports of the Board of Commissioners of the Central Park* (New York: Wm. C. Bryant & Co., 1864), 8; Hunter, *Archival Research*; Hall, *McGown's Pass and Vicinity*, 22.

40. David M. Griffen, "To Huts: British Winter Cantonments Around New York City," *Journal of the American Revolution*, Feb. 25, 2019, https://allthingsliberty.com/2019/02

/to-huts-british-winter-cantonments-around-new-york-city/; Reginald Pelham Bolton, "The Military Hut-Camp of the War of the Revolution on the Dyckman Farm in Manhattan," *The New-York Historical Society Quarterly Bulletin* 2, no. 3 (1918): 89–97; Smith, *Springs and Wells*, 22. James Reuel Smith, *Springs and Wells of Manhattan and the Bronx* (New York: New-York Historical Society, 1938), 19–21.

41. Mackenzie, *Diary of Frederick Mackenzie*, 80.

42. John Charles Phillip von Krafft, *Journal of John Charles Phillip von Krafft: Lieutenant in the Hessian Regiment Von Bose 1776–1784*, ed. Thomas Edsall (New York: New-York Historical Society, 1882), 42, https://babel.hathitrust.org/cgi/pt?id=c001.ark:/13960/t4xh0628p&view =1up&seq=7.

43. Thomas Jones, *History of New York During the Revolutionary War and of the Leading Events in the Other Colonies at that Period*, ed. Edward Floyd de Lancey (New York: New-York Historical Society, 1879), 185–187.

44. Eric W. Sanderson, "Mannahatta: An Ecological First Look at the Manhattan Landscape Prior to Henry Hudson," *Northeastern Naturalist* 14, no. 4 (December 2007): 558; Ted Steinberg, *Gotham Unbound: The Ecological History of Greater New York* (New York, Simon & Schuster, 2014), 36, 406n28. A comparison of the 1777 Sautier map north of McGowan's Pass with the British Headquarters Map of 1782 shows how stretches of once lush vegetation turned barren.

45. Ezra Stiles, *The Literary Diary of Ezra Stiles, D.D., LL.D*, ed. Bowditch Dexter, M.A. (New York: Charles Scribner's Sons, 1901), vol. 3, Jan. 1, 1782–May 6, 1795, 36, https:// babel.hathitrust.org/cgi/pt?id=uc1.b3335180&view=1up&seq=13.

46. William Cronon, *Changes in the Land: Indians, Colonists and the Ecology of New England* (1983; reprint, New York: Hill and Wang, 2003), 160.

47. Von Krafft, *Journal*, 167, 169.

48. Von Krafft, *Journal*, 185.

49. Thomas F. De Voe, "The Benson House at Harlem," *The Magazine of American History with Notes and Queries* 5 (1880): 219, https://archive.org/details/magazineameri -ca19stevgoog/page/n240/mode/2up. W. H., "The Old Benson House," *The Magazine of American History with Notes and Queries* 8 (1882): 229, https://archive.org/details /magazineofamerico8stev/page/228/mode/2up.

50. "Destruction in the Park: Buildings at Mt. St. Vincent Ruined by Fire," *NYT*, Jan. 3, 1881, 8.

51. James Riker papers, 1660–1989, series 2; Colonial Papers, box 3, vol. 3, "Harlem Chronology," folder 8; NYPL, Archives & Manuscripts; see also James Riker, *Revised History of Harlem (City of New York), Its Origin and Early Annals* (New York: New Harlem Publishing Company, 1904), 434.

52. The Empire Society of the Sons of the American Revolution Membership Applications 1889–1970, Membership number 51970, www.ancestry.com; James A. Roberts, ed., *New York in the Revolution as Colony and State*, 2nd ed. (Albany, NY: Press of

Brandon Printing Co., 1898), "Lists and Indexes: Sundry Persons Not in Regular Organizations," 270, https://catalog.hathitrust.org/Record/008729813. Erastus C. Knight, comptroller, *New York in the Revolution as Colony and State, Supplement*, ed. Frederic G. Mather (Albany, NY: Oliver A. Quale, 1901), 65, https://catalog.hathitrust.org /Record/100010263.

53. De Voe, "The Benson House at Harlem," 219; "The Benson House in Harlem where I was born was built by my great grandfather and is more than 100 years old. [The house was located at Third Avenue and 121st Street; see Riker, *Revised History*, 172n.] In September, 1776 when the British fired at Jacob Walton's house, my father became alarmed for his family, and putting a few valuable and necessaries in a waggon took his wife and children to the country expecting to return in a fortnight, but we remained there, till after peace was proclaimed. First we settled in Fishkill and afterwards lived at Salisbury in Connecticut," "Recollections of Mrs. Benson McGowan of Harlem," in Johnston, *Battle of Harlem Heights*, 185. Johnston's information comes from papers in possession of the late Mr. Moore, librarian of Lenox Library, dated 1847 [not located to date in the NYPL Manuscript & Archives Division]; Howard Pashman, "The People's Property Law: A Step Toward Building a New Legal Order in Revolutionary New York," *Law and History Review* 31, no. 3 (2013): 596, https://www.jstor.org/stable/23489504?seq=1.

54. De Voe, "The Benson House at Harlem," 219.

55. John Flavel Mines, *A Tour Around Manhattan and My Summer Acre* (New York: Harper & Brothers,1893),469–447,https://babel.hathitrust.org/cgi/pt?id=loc.ark:/13960/t0nsox74v &view=1up&seq=5&skin=2021; Hall, *McGown's Pass and Vicinity*, 19–20. This myth was repeated by Hopper Striker Mott, but in this 1908 iteration, the author further confused Andrew McGowan with his son Andrew McGowan Jr. See *The New York of Yesterday: A Descriptive Narrative of Old Bloomingdale* (New York: G. P. Putnam's Sons, 1908), 316–317.

56. "Tablet is Unveiled at Old Fort Clinton, Children Whose Pennies Bought It Attend the Exercises, McGown's Pass in History," *NYT*, Nov. 25, 1906, 9. The article has several errors about the Benson and McGowan families.

5. VALENTINE NUTTER, 1760–1814

1. Lawrence Kortright to Sarah Nutter, L 340, P 545, Apr. 5, 1760, recorded at the request of G. W. Wilkins, Sept. 7, 1835, that is, Gouverneur Morris Wilkins, Valentine Nutter's grandson. Sarah Nutter is never referred to as a widow, implying that her husband was still alive when the deed was issued. The title of the Nutter farm came into question on or before 1835 when Silas M. Stilwell wanted to purchase parts of the property. In an undated letter from Wilkins to his grandfather, Wilkins noted that he needed "to satisfy him [Stilwell] about the title." Due to this requirement, Wilkins had the deed from Lawrence Kortright to Sarah Nutter recorded by the city seventy-five years after the original transaction took place (correspondence in AHMC, Valentine Nutter

Collection, folder 1, New-York Historical Society). See also Gouverneur M. Wilkins, "Abstract of Title of Gouverneur M. Wilkins to Lands Situate in Harlem in the 12th Ward of the City of New York as shown herein," *Central Park Extension 106th Street–110th Street*, no. 2, 1862, 249–253, 398–402. James Riker, *Revised History of Harlem (City of New York), Its Origin and Early Annals* (New York: New Harlem Publishing Company, 1904), 568. To date, no other records have been found of Sarah Gilmore or Gillmore Nutter. I am grateful to Kim Walker, Archivist, at the Shelburne County Archives & Genealogical Society, Shelburne, Nova Scotia, for her help researching Valentine's Nutter's life in Shelburne and sharing the contents of the archives, hereafter referred to as Nutter File.

2. Last Will and Testament of Laurens Kortregt, *Probate*, L 22, P 508, old 450–452, November 8, 1761. Rebecca, a daughter of Theunis Idens (see chapter 7), was married to Abraham Delamontagnie, also known as Abraham Montanye, the great grandson of Johannes de la Montagne. Catalina, Idens's youngest daughter, married George Dyckman, who bought out Delamontagnie's land, thus increasing his tract that stretched from Ninety-Ninth to 107th Streets or, in park terms, from the Tarr Family Playground at 100th Street to the Great Hill. Sometime before 1726 Dyckman sold the eastern section of this holding to Lawrence Kortwright Sr. When he died in 1726, the property passed to his son, Lawrence Kortwright Jr., and daughter, Eve Kortwright Benson, the wife of Adolph Benson and mother of Lawrence Benson, who inherited the largest property in the northern end of the prepark. See *Cahill v. Palmer*, 803–815, 217–219; Riker, *Revised History*, 568. There is no record of this deed in the city records, often the case when property was passed between family members. For the practice of testators who drafted their own will, see David E. Narrett, *Inheritance and Family Life in Colonial New York City* (Ithaca, NY: Cornell University Press, 1992), 25.

3. I am grateful to attorney Robert Ritter for unraveling the mystery and explaining the difference between a will and a deed. Email to author, March 8, 2018. Riker noted that Kortright gave a deed to Sarah Nutter, and referred to the renunciation as "another will." See also Riker, *Revised History*, 568. Thanks to Ira Millstein and his colleague Phillip Rosen of Weil, Gotschal & Manges, both of whom confirmed the interpretation of the Kortright documents.

4. Printed in the 1868 court case, *Cahill v. Palmer* (folios 619–621), 166–167, the deed/will and with it a Memorandum said to be "at the request of Sarah Nutter" and noted to be a "true copy" of the original deed, was produced in which John Keenan, a witness to the first Kortright will, validated the document to Commissioner John Van Cortlandt on August 25, 1760, four months after the first will was written and three months before Kortright revoked it. The following day, August 26, 1760, the memorandum noted that the deed to Sarah Nutter was recorded by "Geo Banyar, Sec'y." Without any other corroborating record of the memorandum, a Liber and Page, it is impossible to verify its authenticity.

5. *The Burghers of New Amsterdam and the Freemen of New York, 1675–1866* (New York: New-York Historical Society, 1885), 183.

6. *Tavern Keeper's License Book, 1756–66*, BV New York City–Mayor's Office, NYHS. In ancestrycom (https://www.ancestrylibrary.com/family-tree/person/tree/152384307/person /232083000398/facts?_phsrc=TBY546&_phstart=successSource) his death is said to be 1760, but no source exists for the information, which also incorrectly notes that his death occurred in "Manhattan Kings New York," that is, both Manhattan and Brooklyn In "A List of Farms on New York Island 1780," surveyor Evert Banker noted that Lawrence Kortright owned in total 159 acres of land in Harlem; *The New-York Historical Society Quarterly Bulletin* 1, no. 1 (April 1917): 10.

7. Riker, *Revised History*, 568.

8. "Records of the First and Second Presbyterian Churches of the City of New York," in *The New York Genealogical and Biographical Record*, vol. 11 (New York, 1880), 32, https:// archive.org/details/newyorkgenealog00socigoog/page/n256/mode/2up?q=Nutter; Nutter was noted as a bookbinder; *The Burghers of New Amsterdam*, 183.

9. Isiah Thomas, "The History of Printing in America, With a Biography of Printers and an Account of Newspapers in Two Volumes," vol. 2 (Albany, NY, 1874); *Archaelogia Americana; Transactions and Collections of the American Antiquarian Society* 6 (1874): 236, https://babel.hathitrust.org/cgi/pt?id=hvd.32044014618060&view=1up&seq=11.

10. *New York Journal or General Advertiser*, Nov. 2, 1775, 4.

11. On January 13, 1777, Nutter was enlisted by Major-General James Robertson as Ward Watchman for the East Ward, in David Thomas Valentine, *Manual of the corporation of the city of New-York* (New York, 1863), 635.

12. *NY Gaz*, "Valentine Nutter," Nov. 25, 1776, 4; Dec. 9, 1776; see also Ruma Chopra, *Unnatural Rebellion* (Charlottesville: University of Virginia Press, 2011), 53, 66n85.

13. Richard D. Pougher, " 'Averse . . . To Remaining Idle Spectators': The Emergence of Loyalist Privateering During the American Revolution 1775–1778," Ph.D. diss., University of Maine, 2002, vol. II, 366n68, https://digitalcommons.library.umaine.edu/etd/208/.

14. Harvey Amani Whitfield, "The American Background of Loyalist Slaves," *Left History: An Interdisciplinary Journal of Historical Inquiry and Debate* 14, no. 1 (2009): 62, lh.journals.yorku.ca/index.php/lh/article/download/24905/23099; *Book of Negroes*, Guy Carleton Papers, RG 1, NSARM; see note 14, http://novascotia.ca/archives/africanns /BN.asp. *The Book of Negroes* contains the names and identifying information of African Americans departing with the loyalists; such information was the basis for any future compensation claims from patriot slave owners. A copy was sent to Congress. The transcript is taken from the original document held in the National Archives of the United Kingdom. See http://www.blackloyalist.info/sourcedetail/display/79, Nutter image, 115–116. Robert Ernst, "A Tory-eye View of the Evacuation of New York," *New York History* 64, no. 4 (October 1983): 388, https://www.jstor.org/stable/123174022.

15. "Five Guineas Reward," *Royal Gazette* (New York, May 20, 1783); see Whitfield, "The American Background of Loyalist Slaves," 67n85.

16. The name Roseway is probably an Anglicized version of the original site, Port Razior. Lord Shelburne was the English prime minister, William Petty-Fitzmaurice, 1st

Marquess of Lansdowne, 1782–1783, who succeeded in securing peace with America in the final months of the war.

17. For Nutter's role as keeper of the subscriber rolls, see http://globalgenealogy.com/news /articles/00098.htm. The Dragoons "were to remain in their regiments as a militia and their officers were to continue in their respective ranks and were to be obeyed as such until the Governor of Nova Scotia made other arrangements"; Marion Robertson, *King's Bounty: A History of Early Shelburne* (Halifax: Nova Scotia Museum, 1983), in Nutter File, 76.

18. United Empire Loyalists Association of Canada, http://www.uelac.org/.

19. *Nova Scotia Packet and General Advertiser*, Feb. 9, 1785, in Bonnie Huskins, "Shelburnian Manners: Gentility and the Loyalists of Shelburne, Nova Scotia," *Early American Studies: An Interdisciplinary Journal* 13, no. 1 (Winter 2015):167n31, https://muse.jhu.edu /journal/322.

20. "In consequence of discontents at Shelburne as to discontents of the allotment of land, the governor and council appointed the following persons there as agents to assign lands to the settlers, according to the king's instructions, and to report to the governor . . . Isaac Wilkins, and any four of the rest to form a quorum," in council August 5, 1784. Nutter was one of the listed members. In Beamish Murdoch, *A History of Nova-Scotia, or Acadie* (Halifax: James Barnes, 1867), vol. 3, issue 11, Appendix, chapter 3, 40, https://electriccanadian.com/history/novascotia/historyofnovasco03murdiala .pdf. Nutter owned the building that acted as a temporary courthouse, charging the province fifty pounds annually; Captain William Booth, "Remarks and Rough Memorandums," Shelburne, Nova Scotia, 1787–1789, ed. Eleanor Robertson Smith, Shelburne County Archives & Genealogical Society, 2008, Nutter File.

21. *Register of Marriages in the Parish of St. George and St. Patrick in the County of Shelburne in the Province of Nova Scotia*, "Marriages (Anglican) of Shelburne, N.S. by the Rev. Dr. Walter," London, n.d., Nutter File.

22. Ernst, "A Tory-eye View of the Evacuation," 394. Nutter was a member of the grand jury to work with Commissioners Colonel Thomas Dundas and Jeremy Pemberton, appointed by Parliament to examine the claims of the loyalists' property losses; "Shelburne," *The Royal American Gazette*, June 26, 1786, 3, Nutter File. He heard the case of Jonathan Pell; see "Estimate of the Losses suffered by the within named Jonathan Pell during the late unhappy Dissentions in America in consequence of His Loyalty to His Majesty and Attachment to the British Government," in *Revolutionary War Claims for Losses of the Niagara Settlers and the Long Point Settlers*, https://sites .google.com/site/niagarasettlers/revolutionary-war-claims/revolutionary-war -claims-p.

23. "Mowatt Street Chronicles," compiled and researched by Karen Grovestine Powell, edited by Kimberly Robertson Walker, Shelburne County Archives & Genealogical Society, 2009, 2, Nutter File.

24. See "Canada's Historic Places, Ryer-Davis House," https://www.historicplaces.ca/en /rep-reg/place-lieu.aspx?id=7540&pid=0.

25. Aaron N. Coleman, "Loyalists in War, Americans in Peace: The Reintegration of the Loyalists, 1775–1800," Ph.D. diss., University of Kentucky, 2008, 280, http://uknowledge .uky.edu/gradschool_diss/620/.

26. Although loyalists were legally supposed to petition the state for permission for reentry, many refugees trickled back into the city with no consequences. An act was passed April 11, 1792, that allowed all banished Tories to return to the state provided they took an oath of loyalty to the new government. No documentation exists that indicates a petition by Nutter, who reentered unofficially. Oscar Zeichner, "The Loyalist Problem in New York After the Revolution," *New York History* (July 1940): 298. Nutter is listed as "bookseller and stationer" in *The New-York Directory and Register for the Year 1791*, 94. He placed his first advertisement in the *Daily Advertiser*, "Just opened and for sale," June 20, 1791, 3.

27. *Cahill v. Palmer*, folios 834–846, 225–228; Riker, *Revised History*, 568.

28. *Cahill v. Palmer*, "Points of Plaintiffs," 8–10, "Points of Defendants," 10.

29. "Two Stray Cows," *American Minerva and the New-York Advertiser*, Oct. 24, 1795, 3. He had not moved into the house as he gave 114 Water Street as his address; "Beef," *Daily Advertiser*, Dec. 20, 1796.

30. *Cahill v. Palmer*, folio 765, 206.

31. "For Sale," *American Minerva and the New-York Advertiser*, Nov. 25, 1795, 2; "Stock in Trade," *Comm. Adv.*, Oct. 16, 1797, 3. The business sold to Brown and Stansbury in Apr., 1798; *NY Gaz.*, Apr. 24, 1798, 4.

32. *Cahill v. Palmer*, folios 752–756, 203–204.

33. *Cahill v. Palmer*, folio 665, 180.

34. Nutter enslaved five people. *US Census, 1800*, New York, Seventh Ward, 929.

35. Elegant Country Seat, *EP*, Mar. 19, 1810, 3; Nutter had six cows and three horses, and his grandson also kept two horses on Nutter's Harlem Lane property. Jury List, 1819, roll 1, New York City Census M.N. no. 10774 1821, MANY.

36. *Cahill v. Palmer*, folio 512, 137.

37. "The Old Wilkins Mansion," Henry Collins Brown, ed., *Valentine's Manual of Old New York*, No. 5. New Series, (New York: Valentine's Manual, Inc., 1921), 234–235, https:// archive.org/details/valentinesmanua1921brow/page/n11/mode/2up?q=%22the+old +Wilkins+Mansion%22; Robert Bolton Jr., *Bolton's History of the Church in West Chester County, From Its First Settlement to the Present Time*, vol. 1 (New York: Alexander S. Gould, 1855). Letter, Livingston to Nutter, NYHS, Mss Collection (AHMC—Livingston, Ann), Non-circulating.

38. "Ninth Ward," *Comm. Adv.*, Nov. 12, 1807.

6. THE WAR OF 1812, 1805–1814

1. Thanks to Joshua Galiley and Alan Clark of the Central Park Conservancy tree crew for identifying the tree's species in the database, Jan. 15, 2019.

2. Upon completion of the archeological recording, geotextile fabric and a thin cover of soil were placed over the exposed remains. Hunter Research, Inc., *Archeological Testing and Monitoring Forts Landscape Reconstruction Project, Central Park, Borough of Manhattan, New York*, prepared for the Central Park Conservancy by Hunter Research, Inc., January, 2014 http://s-media.nyc.gov/agencies/lpc/arch_reports/1545.pdf, chapter 3. Previous to the contractors' work, mentioned in chapter 2, Hunter Research was hired to do exploratory work. Richard Hunter and James Lee "dug a small exploratory trench first (2.5x10) and found the eastern footing of the gatehouse. The western footing and the roadbed were actually encountered during the course of monitoring a long trench being dug by the contractors when they were installing drainage. The drainage work was modified somewhat to minimize the impact to the road and gatehouse foundations, which are still largely preserved there underground." Noted in an email, Richard Hunter to author, May 9, 2019. Having confirmed that the works at Nutter's Battery and Fort Clinton stood on fortifications from the Revolutionary War (see chapter 4), Hunter felt that "the larger blocks probably date from the War of 1812 period," email, Hunter to author, April 21, 2021.

3. Hunter Research, *A Preliminary Historical and Archeological Assessment of Central Park to the North of the 97th Street Transverse Borough of Manhattan, City of New York*, Vol. I, D-115-116, Vol. 2 Illustrations 41, 72, 75, and 76)http://s-media.nyc.gov/agencies/lpc/arch_reports/444_A.pdf. Committee of Defence, *Proceedings of the Committee of Defence,1814 July–1815 Oct.*, NYHS, Mss Collection (BV New York City Committee of Defense Non-circulating), August 31, 1814, 50.

4. Hunter, *Archeological Testing*, 3–2; David Dunlap, "Excavated in Central Park: Traces of Anti-Redcoat Fortifications, Never Needed," *NYT*, Sept. 24, 2014, 29.

5. I. N. Phelps Stokes, *The Iconography of Manhattan Island*, vol. V (New York: Robert Dodd, 1926), 1445–1446.

6. Stokes, *Iconography*, vol. V, 1471.

7. Paul A. Gilje, " 'Free Trade and Sailors' Rights'; The Rhetoric of the War of 1812," *Journal of the Early Republic* 30, no. 1 (spring 2010): 1–23; Edwin G. Burrows and Mike Wallace, *Gotham: A History of New York City to 1898* (New York and Oxford: Oxford University Press, 1999), 409.

8. Herbert Heaton, "Non-Importation, 1806–1812," *The Journal of Economic History* 1, no. 2 (1941): 178–98, http://www.jstor.org/stable/2113472.

9. See John Stevens, Esqr. T. Pope del. 1807, *Plan of Fortifications for the Defence of the Harbour of New York*, 1807, NYHS, https://digitalcollections.nyhistory.org//islandora/object/nyhs%3A69921.

10. Burrows and Wallace, *Gotham*, 409–415, 423–427; "The War of 1812: An Essay Collection, American," https://weta.org/press/war-1812-essay-collection-american.

11. R[ocellus] S. Guernsey, *New York City and vicinity during the war of 1812: being a military, civic, and financial local history of that period, with incidents and anecdotes thereof* (New York: C. L. Woodward, 1889–1895), vol. 2, 212–213, quoted in Steven H. Jaffe,

New York at War: Four Centuries of Combat, Fear, and Intrigue in Gotham (New York: Basic Books, 2012), Apple Books edition, 302, 772n43.

12. Burrows and Wallace, *Gotham*, 428.

13. *EP*, "Proceedings of the Common Council in relation to the Defense of New-York," July 30, 1814; J. G. Swift, *Report on the defence of the City of New York, accompanied with maps, views, and topographical plans, Addressed to the Common Council* (New York: 1814), NYHS, https://digitalcollections.nyhistory.org/islandora/object/islandora%3A115181#page/4/mode/2up.

14. Committee of Defence, *Proceedings*, Aug. 6, 2–6.

15. Burrows and Wallace, *Gotham*, 427.

16. Committee of Defence, *Proceedings*, Aug. 13, 17–19, Aug. 17, 23–25. The appendix in the *Proceedings* (243–295) lists every group who donated their time and every financial donor, though not every volunteer group is identified by the location (Brooklyn or Harlem) of their labor. The apprentice butchers are identified as 100 "Young Butchers," assigned on Aug. 25, 1814, to work in Harlem on Aug. 31, 1814 (258–259).

17. Committee of Defence, *Proceedings*, Aug. 18, 25–26, Aug. 25, 35, and "by the regiment of Col. van Beuren's militia (comprising all the companies from Spring Street to Kingsbridge); and Capt. Messeroe [who] attended with a piece of his flying artillery to fire a salute on the occasion," *The Columbian*, Aug. 18, 1814. "On Friday, Aug. 19th, sixty men employed by Robert Macomb, Esq., in the construction of his mill-dam, turned out for work on the Heights. This stone dam was finished and opened to the public Dec. 23." See Hopper Striker Mott, *The New York of Yesterday: A Descriptive Narrative of Old Bloomingdale* (New York: G. P. Putnam's Sons, 1908), 67.

18. Thomas F. De Voe, *The Market Book: Containing a Historical account of the Public Markets in the Cities of New York, Boston, Philadelphia and Brooklyn*, Vol. I (New York: Self-published, 1862), 431–433. Original letter from Daniel Burtnett to Thomas DeVoe in Thomas DeVoe Papers, unmarked folder, NYHS. See Roger Horowitz, Jeffrey M. Pilcher, and Sydney Watts. "Meat for the Multitudes: Market Culture in Paris, New York City, and Mexico City Over the Long Nineteenth Century," *The American Historical Review* 109, no. 4 (2004): 1064.

19. In an email dated May 5, 2019, to this author, Richard Hunter and Jim Lee of Hunter Research confirmed that the ramparts built by the apprentice butchers were the same ramparts uncovered by Hurricane Sandy.

20. "Camp at Harlem Heights," *EP*, Aug. 27, 1814, 3.

21. Committee of Defence, *Proceedings*, Sept. 3, 1814, 57–58; Oct. 11, 1814, 103–104; Oct. 28, 1814, 182; Fairlie's contribution in "Committee of Defense," *EP*, Aug. 20, 1814, 3; "Committee of Defense," Lemuel Wells, Sept. 1, 1814, 3.

22. Mott, *The New York of Yesterday*, 69. See "Ten Dollar Reward," *Mercantile Advertiser*, Aug. 24, 1814, 3.

23. Chairman Fish offered the company $25 a day for the boats. *Proceedings*, Aug. 19, 1814, 28–19; Sept. 1, 1814, 52–53.

24. "Committee of Defence," *NY Gaz*, Aug. 20, 1814; "Committee of Defence," *NY Gaz*, Aug. 19, 1814, 10; "Harlem Heights," *EP*, Aug. 24, 1814, 2, "Tallow Chandlers," Aug. 24, 1814, 3; "Detail of Duty for Aug. 25," *The National Advocate*, Aug. 25, 1814, 2; Oct. 26, 1814, 3, Oct. 28, 1814, 3; Nov. 3, 1814, 3; *The Columbian*, Aug. 22, 1814, 3; *Comm. Adv.*, Aug. 26, 1814, 2; "Committee of Defence, *National Advocate*, Aug. 29, 1814, 2.

25. "People of Color," *The Columbian*, Oct. 29, 1814, 3; "Test of Patriotism," *EP*, Aug. 30, 1814, 3; "The New York African Society," *The National Advocate*, Aug. 20, 1814, 3; Robert J. Swan, "John Teasman: African-American Educator and the Emergence of Community in Early Black New York City, 1787–1815," *Journal of the Early Republic* 12, no. 3 (Fall 1992): 331–356, https://www.jstor.org/stable/3123834. John Marander was one of the group of Black parishioners to request that Trinity Church form a Black congregation that later became St. Phillip's Episcopal Church. For information on Teasman and Marander, see Ira Berlin and Leslie M. Harris, eds., *Slavery in New York* (New York: New-York Historical Society, 2005), 186, 226–227. Committee of Defence, *Proceedings*, Aug. 25, 1814, 262. Another fifty men worked on Harlem Heights on Nov. 1, 1814, 266.

26. Swift to Nancy, L108 P161, Oct. 31, 1814.

27. *Laws of New York*, Thirty-Eighth Session, Chapter 18, in Leo H. Hirsch, "The Slave in New York," *The Journal of Negro History* 16, no. 4 (1931): 383–414, doi:10.2307/2713870.

28. *The Memoirs of General Joseph Gardiner Swift, LL.D, U.S.A.* (Worcester, MA: F. S. Blanchard, privately printed, 1890), 135, https://catalog.hathitrust.org/Record/010938918.

29. Guernsey, *New York City and vicinity*, 317ff.

30. "General Orders," *National Advocate*, Oct. 24, 1814, 3.

31. Hunter, *Archival Research*, 6.

32. Committee of Defence, *Proceedings*, Oct. 19, 1814, 111–112.

33. Discharged Sept. 25, ret. Oct. 10, served until Dec. 3, New York, War of 1812, Payroll Abstracts for New York State Militia, 1812–1815, New York State Archives.

34. Hugh Hastings, State Historian, ed., *The Papers of Daniel D. Tomkins, Governor of New York 1807–1817*, Military, vol. 3 (Albany: State of New York, 1902), 743ff, mistook his last name for Ward. In the military documents, his surname is Worth. The Payroll Abstracts for New York State Militia, 1812–1815, New York State Archives, listed him as Barzillai Worth. He lived in Poughkeepsie and served with the Sea Fencibles (Fowler's).

35. Hastings, *The Papers of Daniel D. Tomkins*, vol. 3, "The Movement of Troops Toward New York, Necessaries for the troops," Albany, Aug. 7, 1812, 63.

36. Committee of Defence, *Proceedings*, Sept. 24, 1814, 87.

37. Hastings, *The Papers of Daniel D. Tomkins*, 746–747. Macomb is most likely the son of William Macomb, a British colonial merchant and fur trader in Detroit. William Macomb Sr. was a Loyalist during and after the Revolutionary War, and was elected as a member of the first parliament of Upper Canada. His son, the quartermaster, followed the Macomb family business, Macomb, Edgar and Macomb, who dealt in Revolutionary War "trading in scarce merchandise and military supplies." David B. Dill, "Portrait of an Opportunist: The Life of Alexander Macomb, Part I," *Watertown*

(NY) *Daily Times*, Sept. 9, 1990, C2, http://www.mlloyd.org/gen/macomb/text/amsr/wt.htm.

38. The word "magazine" comes down to us from the Turkish meaning a "collection"—be it either a fortification with a collection of weapons, a bound volume with a collection of articles and pictures, or the French *magasin*, a store, which is collection of items for sale.

39. *MCC1784*, vol. 4: 364, 467, 479; Stokes, *Iconography*, vol. V, 1455. For the decision to erect a powder house in 1747, see D. T. Valentine, *Manual of the Corporation of the City of New York* (New York: McSpedon & Baker, 1856), 427.

40. *Digest of Special Statutes of the City of New York, February 1, 1778 to January 1, 1931*, "Statutes Not Specifically Repealed," Laws 1808, Ch. 118, 38, "provides for the purchase by the state of land, not to exceed half an acre, in the city of New York." The city "have sold to the State all the right of this Board, in the Lots of land purchased by Adam Fink, bounded on Manhattan Avenue, commonly called the Common lands: no. 103. subject to a rent of Ten Dollars per an. for Twenty years from the 1st May 1803 and Lot no. 102. subject to a quit rent of 4. Bushels of Wheat forever. The above lots of land have been sold for the sum of Seven hundred Dollars, to be paid to this Corporation on delivery of a good and sufficient title from them to the people of the State of New York," *MCC1784*, vol. 5: 136, 144. See also George Ashton Black, *The History of Municipal Ownership of Land on Manhattan Island* (Ph.D. diss., Columbia University, 1889), 54, https://archive.org/details/ldpd_6626214_000/page/n5/mode/2up.

    Property owner Adam Fink received a tavern license on March 9, 1791, for a tavern in the Out Ward; see *New York City Tavern Licenses 1783–1797*; box 1, folder 5, Ms. 443 28, NYHS.

41. Hastings, *The Papers of Daniel D. Tomkins*, vol. 2, Nov. 1, 1808, 152; Nov. 4, 1808, 159–160.

42. State of New York, *Digest of Special Statutes Relating to the City of New York, February 1, 1778 to January 1, 1921*, Statutes Not Specifically Repealed, 1807, Chapter 118; Laws, 1808, 38. Stokes, *Iconography*, vol. V, 1501, from *Assembly J*, 32nd Session, 222. A photograph of the building appears in "Bridge No. 7 from the North," from the album *Central Park*, by Victor Prevost, dated Sept. 22, 1862, in the collection of George Eastman House, Rochester. The structure has a sign, "Arsenal House," and is adjacent to Denesmouth Arch under construction.

43. Hastings, *The Papers of Daniel Tomkins*, vol. 3, 506. In his address to the legislature, Tomkins noted, "The powder magazine and the dwelling house for the superintendent will be completed in a few days," vol. 2, "The Governor's Address to the Legislature," Nov. 1, 1808, 152. In volume 1, Tomkins mentioned a soldier stationed in the powder magazine, Private Andrew Whitford. He was one of those who "apprehended a jaundice which he attributed to his exposure while on duty with his Company at the State powder magazine." His doctor, John Gamage, Surgeon of the 1st Regiment, 10th Brigade, was charged and dismissed from service after he caused the death of another patient and "wholly neglected" Whitford, who was forced to pay for a private physician. *The Papers of Daniel Tomkins*, vol. 1, 758–759.

44. BCCP *Min.*, May 24, 1858, 43.

45. BCCP *Min.*, May 24, 1858, 43.

46. Mahan, *Complete Treatise on Field Fortifications*, 58–60.

47. Guernsey, *New York City and vicinity*, 395.

48. Committee of Defence, *Proceedings*, Aug. 26, 1814, 36; Aug. 27, 1814, 37.

49. Blockhouse No. 2: 1814, NYC, South side of 114th Street west of Morningside Avenue; Blockhouse No. 3: 1814, NYC, South side of 121st Street west of Morningside Avenue; Blockhouse No. 4: 1814, NYC, South side of 123rd Street near Tenth Avenue in Morningside Park. Today large boulders from the Blockhouse are embedded in the surrounding wall of P.S. 36, built in 1967. Swift: "a chain of almost perpendicular rocks, and wooded heights, of difficult ascent, except in one place, and accessible only to the lightest of troops. On these heights, have been erected block houses . . . within supporting distance of each other, and near enough for the interchange of grape shot; all of them to mount heavy cannon on their terrace," Hunter Research, *A Preliminary Historical and Archeological Assessment of Central Park to the North of the 97th Street Transverse, Borough of Manhattan, City of New York. For: The Central Park Conservancy and The City of New York*, Volume I and II, 1990, http://s-media.nyc.gov/agencies/lpc/arch_reports/444_B .pdf, 809–2, D-315; Guernsey, *New York City and vicinity*, 395; Edward Hagaman Hall, *McGown's Pass and Vicinity* (New York: The American Scenic and Historic Preservation Society, 1905), 33–35.

50. BCCP, *Eighth Annual Report for the Year Ending December 31, 1864* (New York, Wm. C. Bryant & Co., 1864), 8. The last volunteer party worked on the Harlem line on November 12, and the defenses were essentially complete by this time. Hermance's brigade was mustered out on November 21. Guernsey, *New York City and vicinity*, 389, 379–380. On November 29, General Swift, upon the suggestion of the Committee, directed Major Horn to "dismiss this day, all the hands now employed at the public works at Haerlem." *Proceedings*, Nov. 29, 1814, 142.

51. Sara Cedar Miller, "Central Park's Sunken Treasure," *New-York Journal of American History* 65, no. 3 (Spring 2004): 93–97; Sara Cedar Miller, "A Case of Mistaken Identity: A Historian's Hunt for Buried Treasure," *Site/Lines* (Spring 2019): 11–13, https:// www.foundationforlandscapestudies.org/pdf/sitelines_spring19.pdf. My colleague at the Central Park Conservancy, John Harrigan, proved after extensive research that the guns were from the HMS *Hussar* and that the smaller gun was one of the first carronades ever made, and one of two earliest carronades still in existence.

52. *Military Topographical Sketch of Haerlem Heights and Plain Exhibiting the Position and forms of Field Works and Block Houses which have been constructed in that Neighbourhood [sic] for the Defence of the City of New York by Genl Swift Chief Engineer copied from a Survey Made by Lieut. Renwick of the 82nd Regt New York Militia by T.E. Craig Lt. Artillery*, NYHS, Manuscript Division, https://digitalcollections.nyhistory.org/islandora/object/nyhs%3A69936.

53. Committee of Defence, *Proceedings*, Sept. 15, 1814, 77; Sept. 20, 1814, 83; Jan. 24, 1814, 168–169.

54. The letter from General Morton to General Scott dated Feb. 25, 1823, requesting the removal of the gatehouse (called the "Block House" in the document) was brought to my attention by Richard Hunter in an email, May 5, 2019.

55. Hall, *McGown's Pass*, 34. According to Hopper Striker Mott, *The New York of Yesterday*, 69, "On Feb., 22, 1900, the United States Daughters of 1812 caused to be erected one of a series of bronze tablets intended to mark points which gained historic interest during that war. It had been decided to place it on Blockhouse No. 1 but owing to the isolated position of this tower and the likelihood of the memorial being hidden from view by foliage, the plan was changed. The Board of Trustees of Columbia University then sanctioned its being affixed to the wall of Fayerweather Hall, on Amsterdam Avenue facing 117th Street." *Cahill v. Palmer* (folio 733–734), 198.

56. BCCP *Min.*, Apr. 8, 1858, 182. The company is listed in *Trow's New York City Directory* of 1857 and 1862 at 89 Wall Street, but the powder magazine is not listed. "The occupants of the Arsenal and the Powder House are given notice that the Park Commissioners wish to take possession of the buildings," *BCCP Min.*, Aug. 5, 1858, 98. In the expenses by the commissioners for 1858, the Hazard Powder Company billed them for powder on July 15, 1858, for $527.50; Oct. 7, 1858, for $1035; Feb. 3, 1895, for $1887.50; and Apr. 21, 1859, for $3,445. BCCP *Min.*, Jan. 31, 1859, 88, 131, 204, 250. The Powder House is also mentioned in the *First Annual Report*, Oct. 27, 1857, 81, "when all buildings on the Park are to be sold, including the Powder House." The *First Annual Report*, Oct. 30, 1857, 83, announces plans for a plant nursery to be sited on two acres of ground north of the Arsenal; presumably that would have been after the Powder House was demolished.

57. Elizabeth Blackmar and Roy Rosenzweig, "Central Park," *Encyclopedia of New York City* (New Haven: Yale University Press, 1995), 198.

58. Jonathan Kuhn, "History of the Arsenal," https://www.nycgovparks.org/about/history /the-arsenal.

PART II: REAL ESTATE

1. Tammy La Gorce, "Why is Houston Street Not Pronounced Like the City in Texas?" *New York Times*, Jan. 26, 2017, MB, 4; Gerard Koeppel, *City on a Grid: How New York Became New York*, (New York: Da Capo Press, 2015), 14.

2. Ira Rosenwaike, *Population History of New York City* (Syracuse, NY: Syracuse University Press, 1972), 15, table 2, 16.

3. Marguerite Holloway, *The Measure of Manhattan: The Tumultuous Career and Surprising Legacy of John Randel Jr., Cartographer, Surveyor Inventor* (New York, Norton, 2013), 48, 310n43. My deep gratitude to Marguerite for being an early and enthusiastic supporter of the project.

4. Catherine McNeur, *Taming Manhattan: Environmental Battles in the Antebellum City* (Cambridge, MA: Harvard University Press, 2014), 48–52.

5. Holloway, *The Measure of Manhattan*, 60; Koeppel, *City on a Grid*, 117–128; Edwin G. Burrows and Mike Wallace, *Gotham: A History of New York City to 1898* (New York and Oxford: Oxford University Press, 1999), 420, Reuben Skye Rose-Redwood, "Rationalizing the Landscape: Superimposing the Grid Upon the Island of Manhattan" (MS thesis, Pennsylvania State University, 2002), http://beyondcentralpark.com/Rationalizing _the_Landscape_FINALCOPY.pdf.

6. Rose-Redwood rejected the notion of "crass commercialism and utilitarian motivation," and stressed instead the cultural and religious underpinnings of Cartesian aesthetics and Protestant theology. For this study, it is important that Rose-Redwood also challenged the notion that the island's topography had been flattened by the grid. He compared the topography of Manhattan before the grid with a survey of the modern island, and made the surprising discovery that Manhattan was still an island of hills. Reuben Skye Rose-Redwood, "Re-Creating the Historical Topography of Manhattan Island," *Geographical Review* 93, no. 1 (January 2003): 124–132, www.jstor.org /stable/30033893.

7. Walt Whitman, "Murray Hill Reservoir, Nov. 25, 1849," in *Empire City: New York Through the Centuries*, ed. Kenneth T. Jackson and David S. Dunbar (New York: Columbia University Press, 2002), 208; Henry James quoted in Sam Roberts, "200th Birthday for the Map that Made New York," *NYT*, Mar. 21, 2011, A18. Frederick Law Olmsted showed his disdain for the grid by commenting sarcastically that it "was hit upon by the chance occurrence of a mason's sieve . . . that was taken up and placed upon the map [of the ground]," in Frederick Law Olmsted and J. James R. Croes, "Preliminary Report of the Landscape Architect and the Civil Topographical Engineer, upon the Laying Out of the Twenty-third and Twenty-fourth Wards," Nov. 21, 1876, *PFLO*, vol. VII, "Parks, Politics and Patronage, 1874–1882," 244.

8. Hillary Ballon, *The Greatest Grid: The Master Plan of Manhattan 1811–2011*, https:// thegreatestgrid.mcny.org/; Richard Howe, "A Little Pre-History of the Manhattan Grid," The Gotham Center for New York History, https://www.gothamcenter.org/blog /a-little-pre-history-of-the-manhattan-grid; Burrows and Wallace, *Gotham*, 419–422.

9. Burrows and Wallace, *Gotham*, 579; Louis P. Tremante III, "Agriculture and Farm Life in the New York City Region, 1820–1870" (Ph.D. diss., Iowa State University, 2000), 28–32; Elizabeth Blackmar, *Manhattan for Rent, 1785–1850* (Ithaca, NY: Cornell University Press, 1989), 94–108.

10. Clement C. Moore, *A Plain Statement Addressed to the Proprietors of Real Estate in the City and County of New-York, by a Landholder* (New York: J. Eastburn and Co., 1818), 39; Moore to Mayor, Aldermen, and Commonalty of New York, L227, P213, 1827; L231, P210, 1828.

11. Roy Rosenzweig and Elizabeth Blackmar, *The Park and the People: A History of Central Park* (Ithaca, NY: Cornell University Press, 1992), 7.

12. Rose-Redwood, "Rationalizing The Landscape," 108.

13. Rose-Redwood, "Rationalizing The Landscape," 25n40.

14. Martha J. Lamb, *The History of the City of New York: its Origin, Rise, and Progress* (New York: A. S. Barnes and Company, 1896), vol. 3., 569–572, quoted in Rose-Redwood, "Re-Creating the Historical Topography of Manhattan Island," 111–112. See also Holloway, *The Measure of Manhattan*, 60.

15. Koeppel, *City on a Grid*, 11; Blackmar, *Manhattan for Rent*, 30–33.

16. Blackmar, *Manhattan for Rent*, 35–36.

7. DIVIDING BLOOMINGDALE, 1667–1790S

1. Reverend John Punnett Peters, *Annals of St. Michaels: Being the History of St. Michael's Episcopal Protestant Church for One Hundred Years 1807–1907* (New York: G. P. Putnam's Sons, The Knickerbocker Press, 1907), 3; Hopper Striker Mott, *The New York of Yesterday: A Descriptive Narrative of Old Bloomingdale* (New York: G. P. Putnam's Sons, 1908), 2; Peter Salwen, *Upper West Side Story: A History and Guide* (New York: Abbeville Press, 1989), 13–14.

2. I. N. Phelps Stokes, *The Iconography of Manhattan Island*, vol. VI (New York: Robert Dodd, 1928), 125. "The allotments to Wouterse and Vigne have not been absolutely proved from the records. It is possible that Vigne got lots 7 and 8, and that Wouterse got lots 9 and 10, But there are indications that the list is correct" (94, 126).

3. Stokes, *Iconography*, vol. VI, 172; see Franklin Jameson, ed., "Answer to the Representatives of New Netherland, 1650," in *Narrative of New Netherland, 1609–1664* (New York: Charles Scribner's Sons, 1909); J. H. Inness, New *Amsterdam and Its People: Studies, Social and Topographical, of the Town under the Dutch and Early English Rule* (New York, Charles Scribner's Sons, 1902), vol. 2, 326–327.

4. Stokes, *Iconography*, vol. IV, Sept. 6, 1640, 92.

5. Stokes, *Iconography*, vol. VI, "The Charles Ward Apthorp Farm," 68–69.

6. Stokes, *Iconography*, vol. VI, "The Charles Ward Apthorp Farm," 68–69. Theunis's surname had many spellings: Ides, Idens, Eidesse, Idesse, Van Huyse; see James Riker, *Revised History of Harlem (City of New York), Its Origin and Early Annals* (New York: New Harlem Publishing Company, 1904), 609.

7. James Bartlett Burleigh and J. Franklin Jameson, eds., "The Trials and Conversion of Theunis Idenszen," in *Journal of Jasper Danckaerts 1679–1680* (New York: Charles Scribner's Sons, 1913), xxiii, 190-194, ; see also Joyce Goodfriend, *Who Should Rule at Home?: Confronting the Elite in British New York City* (Ithaca, NY: Cornell University Press, 2017), 21.

8. James, *Journal of Jasper Danckaerts*, 194–196, 223; Riker, *Revised History*, 592n.

9. Stokes, *Iconography*, vol. VI, 69; Riker, *Revised History*, 394.

10. Riker, *Revised History*, 394. The division between Idens's land and the Harlem Commons was established in 1690. "Beginning at the Harlem line, the western boundary of the commons is for some distance the eastern line of Theunis Ides' land, run in 1690 . . . This

line extended from 106th to 89th street, about half way between 7th and 8th avenues. It does not seem to have been questioned by the city of New York, though I [George Aston Black] find no mention of the patent under which it was held," in George Aston Black, "The History of Municipal Ownership of Land on Manhattan Island" (Ph.D. diss., Columbia University, 1889), 50, https://archive.org/details/ldpd_6626214 _000/page/n5/mode/2up.

11. Idens's daughter Rebecca was married to Abraham Delamontagnie, the great grandson of Johannes de la Montagne. Delamontagnie sold his portion to brother-in-law George Dyckman, the husband of Idens's youngest daughter, Catalina. Dyckman bought out Delamontagnie's land, increasing his own tract from Ninety-Ninth to 107th Street or, in park terms, from the Tarr Family Playground to the Great Hill. The Delamontagnie land included the portion sold by Dyckman in 1748 to Adolph Benson and Jacob Dyckman (no relation), later the Black Horse and McGowan taverns. Sometime before 1726, George Dyckman sold the eastern section of his holding to Lawrence Kortwright Sr. When Kortwright died in 1726, the property passed to his son, Lawrence Kortwright Jr., and his daughter, Eve Kortwright Benson, the wife of Adolph Benson and mother of Lawrence Benson, who inherited the largest property in the northern end of the prepark. Lawrence Kortright Jr.'s portion became Valentine Nutter's land. Stokes, *Iconography*, vol. VI, 69–70; Riker, *Revised History*, 545n.

12. The deed to Delancey has not been found; see Stokes, *Iconography*, vol. VI, 139.

13. Stokes, *Iconography*, vol. VI, 96; Edwin G. Burrows and Mike Wallace, *Gotham: A History of New York City to 1898* (New York and Oxford: Oxford University Press, 1999), 266.

14. Stokes summarized Oliver Delancey's conveyances and moves: "The descriptions are long, evidently drawn from an accurate survey, though no surveyor's name is given. As protracted to the scale of the Randel Map, they are found to be contiguous and to agree with the Randel survey, 153 acres more or less. As Charles Ward Apthorp already owned the large farm to the north of De Lancey, on which there was a good house, it is useless to conjecture which house he occupied. However, he chose the upper farm for a country seat, built there the Apthorp mansion in 1764, and sold the old house to Gerrit Striker, the house on the De Lancey farm he sold to his brother-in-law, James McEvers." Stokes, *Iconography*, vol. VI, "The Oliver Delancey Farm," 93–96; Delancey Farm Maps, MANY.

15. For a history of Fraunces Tavern, 1785–1795, see https://www.frauncestavernmuseum .org/history.

16. Philip Ranlet and Richard B. Morris, "Richard B. Morris's James DeLancey: Portrait in Loyalism," *New York History* 80, no. 2 (1999): 185–210, http://www.jstor.org/stable /23182484.

17. Stokes, *Iconography*, vol. IV, Feb. 17, 1749, 614. All of the incidents are recounted in Leo Hershkowitz and Isadore S. Meyer, eds., *Letters of the Franks Family (1733–1748)* in The Lee Max Friedman Collection of American Jewish Colonial Correspondence (Waltham, MA: American Jewish Historical Society, 1968), 116–118n4.

18. Burrows and Wallace, *Gotham*, 135.

19. David Franks to his brother Naphtali "Hertsy" Franks, Apr. 1, 1743. Hershkowitz and Meyer noted that the "Country house" was Oliver Delancey's estate in Greenwich Village. He had not yet built the Bloomingdale house. *Letters of the Franks Family*, 116.

20. Franks Family Papers, Center for Jewish History, New York, box 1, folder 31, June 7, 1743.

21. Hershkowitz and Meyer, eds., *Letters of the Franks Family*, 116–118. Stokes, *Iconography*, vol. IV, 614, 616; Stephen Birmingham, *The Grandees: America's Sephardic Elite* (New York: Dell, 1972), 163–165. James Grant Wilson, *Memorial History of the City of New-York, from Its First Settlement to the Year 1892* (New York: New-York History Co., 1892), vol. II, 274.

22. Sir Henry Clinton to William Howe, Nov. 28, 1777, in Clinton Papers, Clements Library, cited in Ruma Chopra, *Unnatural Rebellion: Loyalists in New York City During the Revolution* (Charlottesville: University of Virginia Press, 2011), 163.

23. Charlotte Delancey, born in 1761, moved to England and married Sir David Dundas in 1807. Elizabeth Floyd Delancey was the daughter of Richard Lloyd of Mastic, Suffolk County, the wife of John Peter Delancey of Mamaroneck, and grandmother of Edward Floyd de Lancey (often spelled Delancey or De Lancey). The incident is recorded in two sources: Thomas Jones, *History of New York During the Revolutionary War and of the Leading Events in the Other Colonies at that Period*, ed. Edward Floyd de Lancey (New York: New-York Historical Society, 1879), vol. I, 185–187, and note 57, "The Plundering and Burning of the Seat of General De Lancey at Bloomingdale, and the Barbarous Treatment of the Ladies of His Family by the Americans, November, 1777," 669–670, and Edward de Lancey's personal, handwritten account of the incident in the Edward Floyd de Lancey papers, Delancey Family Collection of Family Papers Circa 1660–1904, in the Delancey Family Record, extended, box 3, no. 4, MCNY. In note 57 of the Jones book, Edward de Lancey wrote a detailed account of the incident that he got firsthand from an 1835 interview with Charlotte de Lancey Dundas. In the account that mentions Central Park, it is unlikely that Charlotte could have been able to identify her hiding place well enough to have Edward de Lancey determine that it was in Central Park. The interview was conducted nearly thirty years before Edward de Lancey would have visited the Park. See also the entry in the journal of Lieutenant Stephen Kemble, who reported that "this night between the hours of 12 and 2, a party of Rebels landed from Jersey at Bloomingdale ransacked and burnt Brig. Gen. using his wife and daughter extremely ill," Nov. 25, 1777, in "Journal of Lieut. Col. Stephen Kemble," *The Kemble Papers*, Vol. I, *The Collections of the New York Historical Society for the Year 1883*, (New York: New-York Historical Society, 1844), 144. See Delancey genealogy, www.ancientlydelancey.com. Elizabeth Floyd Delancey is buried near her grandson Edward Floyd Delancey in the Delancey Family Cemetery, Mamaroneck, NY. With deep appreciation to Eddie Garcia for photographing the Delancey cemetery. See also Stokes, *Iconography*, vol. VI, 96. He noted that the Randal Farm map, no. 44, although drawn thirty years later, showed a dock, which he surmised might have been "the landing place of the troops on that November night in 1777."

24. Phila Delancey poem, Delancey Family Record, extended, box 3, no. 176, MCNY.

25. Marcus Gallo, "Property Rights, Citizenship, Corruption, and Inequality: Confiscating Loyalist Estates during the American Revolution," Carroll Collected, John Carroll University, 2019, 2, https://collected.jcu.edu/cgi/viewcontent.cgi?article=1067&context=fac_bib_2019.

26. The entire title was "Act for the Forfeiture and Sale of the Estates of Persons who have adhered to the Enemies of this State, and for declaring the Sovereignty of the People of this State, in respect to all Property within the same." Laws of The State Of New York, Passed in The Third Session of The Legislature, Held at Kingston, In Ulster County, Chap. XXIV, Passed Oct. 22, 1779. For Delancey's forfeiture of his Lower East Side farm, see Burrows and Wallace, *Gotham*, 267–268. For all loyalist forfeitures, see "New York, U.S., Sales of Loyalist Land, 1762–1830," https://www.ancestrylibrary.com/search/collections/5368/. See also Gregory Palmer, *Biographical Sketches of Loyalists of the American Revolution* (Westport, CT: Meckler Publishing, 1994), for amounts claimed and awards given.

27. Just north of the Somarindyck prepark property, descendants of Theunis Idens had intermarried with the Somarindycks and another old Dutch family, the Harsens, in 1763. The Harsen descendant, physician and philanthropist Dr. Jacob Harsen, also kept a portion of his land until it became Central Park. Dr. Harsen was nominated for a seat on the Board of Commissioners of the Central Park to replace Robert Dillon in 1858, *BCCP Mins*, Dec. 23, 1858, 167. See Mott, *The New York of Yesterday*, 11, 81. Today the Harsen land encompasses Strawberry Fields, Wagner Cove on the Lake, Mineral Springs, the Croquet and Lawn Bowling Greens, the Seventh Regiment Memorial, Tavern on the Green, and parts of western portion of the Sheep Meadow. Harsen House at 120 West Seventy-Second Street memorializes Harsenville.

28. Today the house would be located just south of Eighty-Ninth Street and east of Riverside Drive. Stokes, *Iconography*, vol. VI, 96. See also Howard Pashman, "The People's Property Law: A Step Toward Building a New Legal Order in Revolutionary New York," *Law and History Review* 31, no. 3 (2013): 587–626.

29. Orchard received a mortgage from Long Island Quakers Daniel Cock and Daniel Underhill; *Mortgages*, L4, P60, 1785.

30. Idens gave one-sixth of his property to his daughter Dinah and her husband, Marinus Roelofse van Vieckcren. They sold their land to Stephen Delancey, whose son Oliver, as we have seen, acquired the land from Seventy-Ninth to Eighty-Second Street. That same year, Oliver Delancey conveyed 153 acres of Idens's original parcel to Charles Ward Apthorp (L57, P245, 1763, also L209, 259, 1826), who also consolidated 85 additional acres from Theunis Idens's son Eide and his daughter Sarah (L57, 241, 1762).

31. Stokes, *Iconography*, vol. VI, 95.

32. Apthorp and others to Jauncey, L72, P450, 1799.

33. This and other less prominent roads in the Apthorp tract would become a source of lawsuits between Apthorp heirs and subsequent landowners until 1910. See "The Famous Apthorp Farm Litigation Finally Ended," *NYT*, July 31, 1910, Magazine, 7.

34. Charles Ward Apthorp Papers, June 13, 1797, Charles Ward Apthorp collection, 1756–1908, NYHS, Mss Collection AHMC-Apthorp, Charles Ward.

35. See Map of the area later bounded by 93rd and 99th Streets, Central Park West and Broadway, Manhattan, New York (N.Y.), NYHS, Maps (M2.1.24); Gardener Sage, Map of the area later bounded by 88th and 99th Streets, Central Park near the proposed 7th Avenue, and the Hudson River, Manhattan, New York (N.Y.), NYHS (M2.1.24). Maria Williamson died in 1789 after the birth of their second son. Her husband, Hugh, died in 1819 at the age of 85. The two Williamson boys died in their twenties, and their land reverted to Maria Williamson's niece Maria Hamilton.

36. Delancey to Apthorp, L57, P245, 1763; Apthorp to Wagstaff, L75, P90, 1806; Stokes, *Iconography*, vol. VI, 95.

37. Last Will and Testament of Grizzel Shaw, *Probate*, L53, P356, Sept. 5, 1809; codicil Dec. 5, 1818.

38. Handwritten transcription of the sworn testimony of Francis Barretto [Jr.], "Supreme Court, In the Matter of the Central Park, Isaac Adriance, Petitioner," *Petitions*, vol. 7, 631–637. No conveyance has come to light between Francis Barretto Jr. and John Shaw.

39. Richard C. McKay, *South Street: A Maritime History of New York* (New York: Haskell House Publishers, 1971), 23.

40. From the Diary of Elisabeth De Hart Bleecker, NYPL, quoted in Stokes, *Iconography*, vol. VI, Chronology Addenda, Dec. 27, 1799, 50, https://digitalcollections.nypl.org /items/f500a030-7f4d-0133-c4a4-00505686d14e. John Shaw is also depicted as inhospitable to a British visitor in Thomas Twining, *Travels in America 100 Years Ago* (New York: Harper & Brothers, 1894), 148.

41. "Demarara Sugar, Rum &c.," *Morning Chronicle*, Sept. 20, 1803, 3.

42. Stokes, *Iconography*, vol. VI, 48, 95.

43. *Petitions*, testimony of prepark resident Catherine Coggery, vol. 7, 531.

44. Vanden Heuvel to Price, L225 P212, 1827.

45. Ron Chernow, *Alexander Hamilton* (New York: Penguin, 2005), 2–3.

46. "The Statue of Hamilton: Crowds Witness Its Unveiling in Central Park," *NYT*, Nov. 23, 1880, 1; see also Sara Cedar Miller, *Central Park, An American Masterpiece: A Comprehensive History of the Nation's First Urban Park* (New York: Abrams, 2003), 198–199. The author mistakenly attributed James as the commissioner of the statue, but it was John Hamilton; Gerald Koppel, *Water for Gotham* (New York: Princeton University Press, 2000), 174–177.

47. *Releases*, Blocks 780 to 805, Box 2870, MANY.

48. The Apthorp/Vanden Heuvel heirs never divided their property, as they planned to keep it indefinitely; however, their prepark land ran up against the common lands that were divided into many lots. *Petitions*, vol. 3, 80.

49. $100 in 1856 dollars equals $3,126.20 today, according to www.measuringworth.com.

8. DIVIDING BLOOMINGDALE, 1790-1824

1. Le Roy to Borrowe, L69, P121,1796; See Hunter Research, Inc., *A Preliminary Historical and Archeological Assessment of Central Park to the North of the 97th Street Transverse, Borough of Manhattan, City of New York. For: The Central Park Conservancy and The City of New York.* Volume I and II, 1990. http://s-media.nyc.gov/agencies/lpc/arch_reports /444_B.pdf, 804–1 to 807–1a–p, D–278–289; I. N. Phelps Stokes, *The Iconography of Manhattan Island*, vol. VI (New York: Robert Dodd, 1928), 116.

2. Ron Chernow, *Washington: A Life* (New York: Penguin, 2011), 806–809.

3. An 1811 map shows a lane that connected Borrowe's property with the Bloomingdale Road. By 1819, the property was depicted on the Randel map with an L-shaped building, later identified as a carpenter's shop, and two other outbuildings, a barn and a chicken coop, at the north side of the hill's crest between 105th and 106th Street. Hunter Research, *A Preliminary Historical and Archeological Assessment*, 804-1-3, D–278–283.

4. Watt to Bushnell, *Mortgages*, L173, P341,1834; transferred to James Watt Jr. to Bushnell, L354, P599, 1836. Sands and Griffen to Bushnell, L328, P490, 1835, for $30,000. Lewis Seymour and Benjamin North to Orsamus Bushnell, L199, P276, 1836.

5. "Elmwood Hill Juvenile Institute," *EP*, May 25, 1832, 3. The cost, which included "board, tuition and washing," ranged in 1830 from $80 to $120, and by 1836, tuition was raised from $150 to $200 per year, depending on the chosen course of study. *New York Daily Express*, Mar. 6, 1837.

6. "Elmwood Hill Boarding School," *EP*, Dec. 3, 1832; "A Prospectus of Elmwood Hill Collegiate and Commercial Institute," *EP*, July 16, 1835, 1; "Elmwood Hill Collegiate and Commercial Institute," *New York Daily Express*, Apr. 22, 1839, 4.

7. By 1843, Whitney North Seymour owned the property, though the deed has not been found. He may have lived there, but by January 1843, he was advertising for a tenant: "A beautiful country seat on the 8th Avenue, just above the upper reservoir with about six acres first quality land. The house is large and very convenient, in perfect order the grounds well arranged with suitable out houses. One of the most delightful situations for beauty of scenery on this island, and everything requisite for making it a pleasant residence for a genteel family." "To Let," *Comm. Adv.*, Jan. 19, 1843, 3.

8. Seymour held onto the tract for eight more years until 1851, when it was purchased by manufacturer Benjamin Sutton for $12,000. Seymour to Sutton, L577, P227, 1851. A year later, Sutton sold it to John Purple Howard for $18,000; Sutton to Howard, L619 P216, 1852. "John P. Howard's Estate; How an Old New York Hotel Keeper Disposed of His Fortune," *Her.*, Dec. 6, 1885, 9. Howard received nearly $30,000 for the property. For Olmsted's residence, see chapter 18.

9. Samuel Stilwell Doughty, *The Life of Samuel Stilwell: With Notices of Some of His Contemporaries* (New York: Brown & Wilson, 1877), 23.

10. Doughty, *The Life of Samuel Stilwell*, 21–22.

11. Doughty, *The Life of Samuel Stilwell*, 24.

12. Doughty, *The Life of Samuel Stilwell*, 24.

13. *The Daily Advertiser*, New York, June 8, 1799, 2.

14. Doughty, *The Life of Samuel Stilwell*, 31–33. In *City on a Grid: How New York Became New York* (New York: Da Capo Press, 2015), 90, historian Gerald Koeppel acknowledged Stilwell's expertise and mused on why he or another well-known local surveyor, Benjamin Taylor, were not chosen over Charles Loss to survey for the Commissioners' Plan of 1807 after Loss had made "several errors of a serious nature" in his work (35).

15. Doughty, *The Life of Samuel Stilwell*, 34–35.

16. Marguerite Holloway, "Unearthing the City Grid That Would Have Been in Central Park," Jan. 8, 2011, https://www.newyorker.com/news/news-desk/unearthing-the-city-grid-that-would-have-been-in-central-park.

17. Doughty, *The Life of Samuel Stilwell*, 26.

18. Doughty, *The Life of Samuel Stilwell*, 38; Stilwell to Rachel, L106, P472, 1814.

19. Doughty, *The Life of Samuel Stilwell*, 38–40. The record of the transaction has not been found and is not listed in any slavery manumission records.

20. Doughty, *The Life of Samuel Stilwell*, 38–40.

21. Kyle T. Bulthuis, "Preacher Politics and People Power: Congregational Conflicts in New York City, 1810–1830," *Church History* 78, no. 2 (June 2009): 261–282n38; Doughty, *The Life of Samuel Stilwell*, 43.

22. Cock and Underhill to Stilwell, L46, P549, 1791.

23. Stilwell to Piersall [transcription misspelled for "Pearsall"], L69, P400, 1797.

24. "In Chancery," *EP*, Feb. 3, 1846, 4.

25. LeRoy Edgar to Jay, L576, P329, P331, 1850; Jay to Zabriskie, L647, P643, 1852.

26. Commissioners of the Central Park, *First Annual Report*, opp. 10.

27. Stilwell to Robinson, L63, P256, 1803; Robinson to Burling (unrecorded), L73, P15, 1806; Burling to Demilt, L92, P296, 1811. William Wade Hinshaw, et al., compilers, *Encyclopedia of American Quaker Genealogy*, vol. 3 (Ann Arbor, MI: Edwards Brothers, Inc., 1940), Demilt, 99; Robert L. Bowne, 42; Joseph Pearsall, 250, https://babel.hathitrust.org/cgi/pt?id=mdp.39015028799719&view=1up&seq=257&skin=2021.

28. Untitled Map, surveyed by Casimer Th. Goerck, 1796, for Samuel Stilwell, "80th to 86th Street, E. & W. of 8th Ave. (Formerly Prospect Ave.)," No. 610, Microfilm, DOF.

29. Theodore Crom, *Horological and Other Shop Tools 1700–1900* (Florida: self-pub., 1987), 60.

30. Dava Sobel, *Longitude: The True Story of a Lone Genius Who Solved the Greatest Scientific Problem of His Time* (New York: Penguin, 1995).

31. For an image advertising the Demilt Observatory on Pearl Street, see http://www.westsea.com/captains-log/scrimshaw03.html. The chronometers were manufactured by the celebrated London firm Parkinson & Frodsham. Jonathan Betts, *Marine Chronometers at Greenwich: A Catalogue of Marine Chronometers at the National Maritime Museum, Greenwich* (Oxford: Oxford University Press, 2018), 375–376; Edmund M. Blunt, *The Nautical Almanac and Astronomical Ephemeris for the Year 1821 Published*

Annually, April 1819; Marvin E. Whitney, "American Chronometer Makers, Part 6," *Horological Times*. 5, no. 4 (April 1981): 21.

32. *Catalogue of the Apprentices' and Demilt Libraries, New York, July 1, 1855*, Apprentices' Library, (New York: John W. Amerman, 1855), "Catalogue of the Demilt Library," 113–160. For a history of the Demilt Library, see Thomas Earle and Charles T. Congden, eds., *Annals of the General Society of Mechanics and Tradesmen of the City of New York 1785–1880* (New York: The Society, 1882), 178, 187–189. After the death of Samuel Demilt, Elizabeth Demilt bequeathed $5,000 in 1850 "for its general purposes," and an additional $5,000 "for the enlargement and improvement of the Demilt Library." Another sister, Sara Demilt, bequeathed $2,000 for the same purposes in 1850. In 1874, the Demilt Library was incorporated with the Society's Apprentices' Library.

33. A house and a stable are on an 1803 Goerck map; map file, microfilm, no. 78, *Inventory of Register's Office Filed Maps*, Block 1111, Section 4, DOF.

34. Stilwell to Pearsall, L69, P400, 1797.

35. Originally Pearsall and his younger brother Thomas were partners, but Thomas went on to become a successful merchant on his own and Joseph joined with fellow Quaker Effingham Embree, as Pearsall & Embree, from 1781 to 1789. Embree, a relation to Pearsall, became the more celebrated craftsman, even having a fine example of his work in the White House. Nonetheless, online photographs of a stately "grandfather" clock, once owned by the Museum of the City of New York, attest to Pearsall's elegant craftsmanship. https://adamsbrown.com/wordpress1/antique-clocks -for-sale/early-american-tall-case-clocks/new-york-tall-case-clocks/joseph-pearsall -new-york-chippendale-mahogany-tall-case-clock-c-1770/.

36. *MCC1784*, vol. 2, Apr. 2, 1798, 429.

37. A map by Casimir Th. Goerck for Samuel Stilwell to Joseph Pearsall in 1803 shows a spring at about Eighty-Third Street, giving the road the name "Spring Street. A house and a stable can also be seen on the map," map file, microfilm, no. 78, *Inventory of Register's Office Filed Maps*, Block 1111, Section 4, DOF; see Tanner's Spring. James Reuel Smith, *The Springs and Wells of Manhattan and the Bronx* (New York: New York Historical Society, 1938), 15–16.

38. Pearsall to Ogden, L63, P440, 1803. Pearsall & Pell, ironmongers, 205 Queen Street; 1789, *The New-York Directory and Register for the Year 1789* (New York: Hodge, Allen and Campbell, 1789), 68. For information on David Ogden and William Ogden Wheeler, see Lawrence Van Alstyne and Charles Burr Ogden, eds., *The Ogden family in America, Elizabethtown branch, and their English Ancestry* (Philadelphia: J. B. Lippincott, 1907), 67–69.

39. *Centinel of Freedom*, Nov. 24, 1807, cited in Charles H. Winfield, *History of the County of Hudson, New Jersey: from its Earliest Settlement to the Present Time* (New York: Kennard & Hay Stationery M'fg and Printing Co., 1874), 220; Nancy Isenberg, *Fallen Founder: The Life of Aaron Burr* (New York: Penguin, 2007), 8.

40. Ogden to Fairlie, L75, P259, 1804.

41. Alstyne and Ogden, *The Ogden family in America*, 105.

42. Ogden to Cooper, L63, P442, 1803.

43. James Grant Wilson, *The Memorial History of New-York: From Its First Settlement to the Year 1892* (New York: New-York History Company, 1893), vol. 3, n118; Alstyne and Ogden, *The Ogden family in America*, 155.

44. See notes on the reverse of a reproduction of the painting of Fairlie in the Frick Art Reference Library, https://imagesdigitalcollections.frick.org/media/id/dfb89e36cca322631 -8377eb0efd23797/large. I am grateful to Emily Parsons, Deputy Director and Curator of the Society of the Cincinnati, for her information on James Fairlie.

45. Alstyne and Ogden, *The Ogden family in America*, 155.

46. Fairlie to Judah, L173, P142, 1807; *Mortgages*, Fairlie to Judah, L16, P286, 1807.

47. Robert W. Reid, *Washington Lodge, No. 21, F. & A.M., and Some of Its Members* (New York: Washington Lodge, 1911), 173–174.

48. Victoria Johnson, *America's Eden: David Hosack, Botany, and Medicine in the Garden of the Early Republic* (New York: Norton, 2018), 232, 234.

49. *Report of the trial of Charles N. Baldwin, for a libel: in publishing, in the Republican chronicle, certain charges of fraud and swindling, in the management of lotteries in the State of New-York* (New York: C.N. Baldwin, 1818); *City-Hall Recorder*, vol. 3, no. 11, Nov. 1818, 161.

50. On the 1815 survey by Otto Sackersdorff, *Maps of Farms Commonly Called the Blue Book*, map page 13, the property is owned by "Naphtali Judah (James Fairlie)" possibly indicating a mortgage between the two. On map drawn as part of a conveyance from Robert Lenox to Mayor, Aldermen and Corporation of the City of New York, L131, P205, 1818 (property map on page 207), Naphtali Judah is cited as owner of the land. According to the Randel Farm Maps—the surveys of which were drawn from 1819 to 1820—Fairlie, not Judah, was cited as the owner.

51. *National Advocate* March 16, 1822, Volume X, 2; Fairlie to Whitehead, L173, P108, 1824.

52. See chapter 9, note 2 for sources.

53. Alexander Manevitz, "Seneca Village, Central Park, Manhattan," a recording for Open House New York, https://ohny.org/sites/Seneca-village.

54. Leslie M. Alexander, *African or American? Black Identity and Political Activism in New York City, 1784–1861* (Champaign: University of Illinois Press, 2008), 155; Alexander, "Seneca Village," in Ira Berlin and Leslie M. Harris, *Slavery in New York* (New York: New-York Historical Society, 2005), 268.

55. With his first transfer of property Whitehead's total profit came to $1,328, which was more than enough to repay the $1,200 mortgage held by Jameson Cox, canceled the same day, *Mortgages*, February 6, 1824; L409, P6, 1824.

56. Turner to Philip, L344, P379, 1835.

57. John Whitehead did not have a will, as his death was unexpected, but records indicate that Maria Whitehead estimated the value of her husband's estate at $2,500; *Probate*, Letters of Administration, L33, P170, 1835. In 1824, Henry Fitz and Jacob Peterson bought land from Cornelius Harsen, a member of the prominent west side landowning family, who also

owned land in the prepark. By December 1825, Whitehead gave a mortgage to Henry Fitz for two separate properties: $700 for thirteen lots between Fifty-Third and Fifty-Fourth Streets, between Sixth Avenue and the Bloomingdale Road, and $400 for one house and lot, later known as 399 Fourth Street and Avenue D, that would become the Whiteheads' home in 1830 after Fitz defaulted on his loan. Whitehead to Fitz, L90, P314, L90, 317, 1826. There are no conveyances from John Whitehead to grantees for his midtown property, though he may have leased property. Whitehead's heirs (Maria Whitehead Palmer and her second husband, Abram Palmer) sold lots to at least two Black men, Peter Wilson and John Parker. Palmer to Wilson, L451, P165, 1844; Palmer to Parker, L452, P263, 1844.

58. In the 1790 *U.S. Census*, there were eight John Whiteheads living in the country, none from New York City. It is possible that he was a naturalized citizen. There were twenty-two John Whiteheads born in England in 1773. For the marriage see "Records of First Stanford (Baptist) Church at Bangall," *The New-York Genealogical and Biographical Society Record*, vol. 38 (New York, 1907), 97.

59. *Longworth's American Almanack and New-York Register and City Directory* (New York: David Longworth), 1805, 409; 1816, 450; 1816: 450; 1818, 448.

60. Graham Russell Hodges, *New York City Cartmen, 1667–1850*, rev. ed. (New York: New York University Press, 2012), 4.

61. Isaac Lyons, *Recollections of an Old Cartman: Boonton, New Jersey, From the Newark Journal*, Newark, NJ, 1872, Article No. 1, 1, https://archive.org/details/recollectionsofoolyon/page/n5.

62. Lyons, *Recollections of an Old Cartman*, article no. 1, 2.

63. Graham Russell Gao Hodges, interview by author, May 5, 2016. Cartmen held such "petty political offices" that included "constable, collector and assessor" and "part-time positions, which provided additional income such as watchman and inspectorships." Hodges, *New York City Cartmen, 1667–1850*, 73.

64. *New York County Jury Census*, 1819, Ward 10, box 8, vol. 15, unpaginated; http://nycma .lunaimaging.com/luna/servlet/detail/NYCMA~10~10~15~1206205?sort=identifier %2Ctitle%2Cdate%2Cvolume_number&qvq=sort:identifier%2Ctitle%2Cdate%2Cvolume _number;lc:NYCMA~10~10&mi=14&trs=2158-59.

65. Fairlie to Whitehead, L173, P108, 1824. It was one-third the sum that Judah had paid for it and less than the $3,250 that Fairlie paid when he had purchased nine of his sixteen acres from Ogden in 1804. *Mortgages* $1,200 from Cox to Whitehead L67, P409, 1824. Whitehead could have known Cox as a member of the Committee of Public Officers charged with investigating "A Law to regulate Carts and Cartmen." The website www .measuringworth.com was used for all the values in the chapter.

66. During the War of 1812 many newly arrived Irish immigrants replaced the cartmen who joined the military. After the war, they demanded their jobs and the return of their privileged status. The Common Council was forced to bow to their political power, and rescinded the "aliens' " licenses. Blacks had been excluded from the profession since 1684 and for the most part were only able to obtain a license in the 1850s under

Mayor Fernando Wood. Hodges, *New York City Cartmen*, 171. See also Graham Russell Hodges, "Desirable Companions and Lovers: Irish and African Americans in the Sixth Ward, 1830–1870," in *The New York Irish*, ed. Ronald H. Bayor and Timothy J. Meager (Baltimore, MD: Johns Hopkins University Press, 1996), 116–117. See also Rhoda G. Freeman, *The Free Negro in New York City in the Era Before the Civil War* (New York: Garland, 1994), 213, 215. It is uncertain if Aldridge was a licensed cartman.

67. Hodges, interview by author, May 5, 2016.

68. Whitehead to Scudder, L288, P289, 1831; Whitehead to Harris, L339, P354, 1831.

69. *Comm. Adv.*, "Marriages," May 17, 1828, 2.

70. Diana Bertolini, "Biographical Note," *Mitchell Family Papers 1706–1957*, NYPL, Manuscripts and Archives Division, Nov. 2009, v; Jonathan Greenleaf, *A history of the churches, of all denominations, in the city of New York, from the first settlement to the year 1846* (New York: E. French, 1846), 344–348, https://catalog.hathitrust.org/Record/001408135.

71. Edward Mitchell, *The Christian Universalist* (New York: Clayton & Van Norden, 1833); see also Sean Wilentz, *Chants Democratic: New York City and the Rise of the American Working Class, 1788–1850* (New York: Oxford University Press, 1984), 79.

72. Nathan O. Hatch, *The Democratization of American Christianity* (New Haven, CT: Yale University Press, 1989), 58. Historian Sean Wilentz singled out the society as being a "rowdier popular impiety," along with other Universalist sects that attracted "craftsmen" and many working-class followers; Wilentz, *Chants Democratic*, 79.

73. Greenleaf, *A history of the churches*, 344–348.

74. "Death of Henry Fitz, the Telescope Maker," *Scientific American* 9, no. 20 (Nov. 14, 1863): 311; Thomas Whittemore, *Life of Rev. Hosea Ballou: With Accounts of His Writings, and Biographical Sketches of His Seniors and Contemporaries in the Universalist Ministries*, vol. 2 (Boston: James M. Usher, 1854), 171, https://www.google.com/books/edition /Life_of_Rev_Hosea_Ballou/E6gl-iLCYz8C?hl=en&gbpv=1&dq=Thomas+Whittemore, +Life+of+Rev.+Hosea+Ballou:&printsec=frontcover.

75. Whitehead to Hamilton, L197, P443, 1825.

76. Leslie M. Harris, *In the Shadow of Slavery: African Americans in New York City, 1626–1863* (Chicago: University of Chicago Press, 2004), 134, 190–202.

77. Bella Gross, "Life and Times of Theodore S. Wright, 1797–1847," *Negro History Bulletin* 3, no. 9 (June 1940): 135–136, https://www.jstor.org/stable/44212030.

9. DIVIDING BLOOMINGDALE, SENECA VILLAGE: THE RESIDENTS, 1825–1857

1. Roy Rosenzweig and Elizabeth Blackmar, *The Park and the People: A History of Central Park* (Ithaca, NY: Cornell University Press, 1992), 65–73. This study considers Seneca Village as the former Whitehead, Stilwell, and Ludlow properties between Seventh and Eighth Avenues. Although many documents refer to Seneca Village as "Yorkville," this study includes the settlement as an area of Bloomingdale, as all prior owners of the land considered it to be so.

2. Peter Salwen, *Upper West Side Story: A History and Guide* (New York: Abbeville Press, 1989), 46–47; Douglas Martin, "Before Park, Black Village; Students Look Into a Community's History," *NYT*, Apr. 7, 1995, B1; *Before Central Park: The Life and Death of Seneca Village*, an exhibition at The New-York Historical Society, Grady T. Turner and Cynthia R. Copeland, co-curators, 1997; Douglas Martin, "A Village Dies, A Park Is Born," *NYT*, Jan. 31, 1997; Edwin G. Burrows and Mike Wallace, *Gotham: A History of New York City to 1898* (New York and Oxford: Oxford University Press, 1999), 747–748; Hope Lourie Killcoyne, *The Lost Village of Central Park*, Mysteries in Time Series (New York: Silver Moon Press, 1999); Leslie M. Harris, *In the Shadow of Slavery: African Americans in New York City, 1626–1863* (Chicago: University of Chicago Press, 2004), 75, 86; Craig Steven Wilder, *In the Company of Black Men: The African Influence on African American Culture in New York City* (New York: New York University Press, 2001), 101–102; David Dunlap, "Under Central Park, And Now on Radar," *NYT*, Aug. 10, 2005, B1; Diana diZerega Wall, Nan A. Rothschild, and Cynthia Copeland, "Seneca Village and Little Africa: Two African American Communities in Antebellum New York City," *Historical Archaeology* 42, no. 1 (2008): 97–107; Education Department, *Seneca Village: A Teacher's Guide to Using Primary Sources in the Classroom* (New York: New-York Historical Society, 2010); Lisa Foderaro, "Unearthing Traces of African-American Village Displaced by Central Park," *NYT*, July 28, 2011, A26; Carla L. Peterson, *Black Gotham: A Family History of African Americans in Nineteenth-Century New York City* (New Haven, CT: Yale University Press, 2012); Marilyn Nelson, *My Seneca Village* (South Hampton, NH: Namelos, 2015); Tonya Bolden, *Maritcha: A Nineteenth-Century American Girl* (New York: Abrams, 2015); "The People Before the Park," written by Keith Josef Adkins, dir. John J. Wooten, Premiere Stages, Kean University, Union, NJ, Sept. 3–20, 2015, http://www.keanstage.com/event/0fd64444f7362d1d158fa396df04a0b1; Brent Staples, "The Death of Black Utopia," *NYT*, Nov. 28, 2019, A26; Leslie M. Alexander, "Seneca Village 1825–1857," in *African or American? Black Identity and Political Activism in New York City, 1784–1861* (Champaign: University of Illinois Press, 2008). Mapping the African American Past, "Seneca Village," Columbia Center for New Media Teaching and Learning, http://maap.columbia.edu/place/32.html; Antoinette Mullins, "A Village Vanished: Seneca Village," Harlem Live, http://www.harlemlive.org/community/parks/senecavillage/seneca.html; Diana diZerega Wall, Nan A. Rothschild, Meredith B. Linn, and Cynthia R. Copeland, Institute for the Exploration of Seneca Village History, Inc., "Seneca Village, A Forgotten Community: Report on the 2011 Excavations," NYC Landmarks Preservation Commission, 2018, http://s-media.nyc.gov/agencies/lpc/arch_reports/1828.pdf; Alexander Manevitz, " 'A Great Injustice': Urban Capitalism and the Limits of Freedom in Nineteenth-Century New York City," *Journal of Urban History*, January 23, 2021, https://journals.sagepub.com/doi/10.1177/0096144220976119. The Institute for the Exploration of Seneca Village History has done research and archaeological investigation with the Central Park Conservancy, since 1998, and in 2011 they both conducted excavations there. Then, in 2019, the Conservancy did an exhibit on Seneca Village in the park. The New York City Archaeological Repository (Nan A.

Rothschild Research Center) has the archaeological collections; see Nan A. Rothschild, Amanda Sutphin, H. Arthur Bankoff, and Jessica Striebel MacLean, *Buried Beneath the City: An Archaeological History of New York* (New York: Columbia University Press, 2022).

3. New York State Archives, New York (State), Dept. of State, Bureau of Miscellaneous Records, Enrolled acts of the State Legislature, Series 13036–78, Laws of 1817, Chapter 137, Section 4, passed March 31, 1817, https://digitalcollections.archives.nysed.gov/index .php/Detail/objects/10817.

4. Vivienne Kruger, "Born to Run: The Slave Family in Early New York, 1626 to 1827" (Ph.D. diss., Columbia University, 1985), table 1, 891. As Harris notes, under these circumstances, "slave parents might gain full freedom before their children," Harris, *In the Shadow of Slavery*, 94.

5. Kruger, "Born to Run," 852–858.

6. Glover to Harding, L87, P509, 1810, in Harry B. Yoshpe, "Record of Slave Manumissions in New York During the Colonial and Early National Periods," *The Journal of Negro History* 26, no. 1 (January 1941): 84. Harding is listed as age 81 in *U.S. Census, 1850,* and age 94 in *New York State Census, 1855.*

7. *U.S. Census, 1800,* Ward 3, 700.

8. In *U.S. Census, 1850,* Ward 12, Samuel Harden, age 81 and living in Seneca Village with the Thompson family (visit no. 1564), was listed as a pauper, a term that may indicate he was manumitted with no annuity after the age of 45. Whitehead to Harding, L191, P447, 1825.

9. Whitehead to Davis, L197, P344, 1825; Whitehead to Williams, L197, P346, 1825; Whitehead to Carter, L197, P348, 1825; Whitehead to Trustees of the Methodist Episcopal Church, L197, P350, 1825; Whitehead to Hamilton, L197, P443; Whitehead to Newton, L238, P252, 1825.

10. "Middle Road," Tax Assessment 1826–1836, microfilm roll no. 66, MANY. In 1824, the property was listed as owned by James Fairlie, with one house, and valued at $1,600. For the existing house, see chapter 8n37 and John Whitehead property survey map, microfilm map file 38, *Inventory of Register's Office Filed Maps*, Block 1111 Section 4, DOF.

11. The houses with basements are on Block 784, lots 44 and 32; Sylvan to Cooper, L587, P601, 1851.

12. The 1855 condemnation map depicted the size of the shanty. There was also a nine-by-eleven-foot "shop" on the premises. The figures are from *New York State Census, 1855.*

13. Citizens' Association of New York, Council of Hygiene and Public Health, *Report of Hygiene and Public Health of the Citizens' Association of New York Upon the Sanitary Condition of the City* (New York: D. Appleton and Company, 1865), quoted in Richard Plunz, *A History of Housing in New York City* (New York: Columbia University Press, 2016), 54.

14. *The Topographical Map Of The City and County Of New-York, and the adjacent Country: With Views in the border of the principal Buildings and interesting Scenery of the Island*

(New York: J. H. Colton & Co., 1836), in the collection of David Rumsey, https://www
.davidrumsey.com/maps2268.html.

15. Tax Assessment, Twelfth Ward, 1846, vol. 2, 22–23, microfilm, roll no. 67, MANY; Matthew Dripps, *Map of that part of the city and county of New-York north of Fiftieth St.*, https://digitalcollections.nypl.org/items/a93bb462-3e41-cf04-e040-e00a1806ra3f. Condemnation Maps, Blocks 783 to 789, MANY; Davis to McCaffrey, L405, P455.

16. Rosenzweig and Blackmar, *The Park and the People*, 67–68.

17. The Marshall/Lyons/Guignon family; the Harding/McCollin/Green family; the Undrill/Pease/Richerson family; the Thomas Green and Hannah Greene (who later married Cornelius Henry)/Sarah Henry Wilson/Matilda Wigfall/Edward Wigfall family; the Thompson/Johnson/Scudder/Morris family; the Hunter/Moore/Riddles/Wilson/Bennett family; and the William and Hester Webster (who later married James Morgan) family.

18. Whitehead to Elizabeth Harding, L191, P445, 1825, Whitehead to Diana Harding, L218, P131, 1827; marriage of Elizabeth Harding to Obadiah McCollin, Feb. 25, 1826.

19. Whitehead to Cornelius Henry, L191, P447, 1825.

20. Whitehead to William Henry, L265, P202, 1829; Jane Harris (Henry) to Wallace, L466, P361, 1845.

21. The release to the city for lot no. 37 on block 784 was signed by Robert and Sarah Green and Elizabeth and Obadiah McCollin, noted as heirs of Diana Harding.

22. Dixon Fox, "The Negro Vote in Old New York," *Political Science Quarterly* 32, no. 2 (1917): 256–257.

23. New York (State), *Reports of the proceedings and debates of the New York Constitutional Convention, 1821* (New York: Da Capo Press, 1970), 285; C. Edward Skeen, John Armstrong, and A. Spencer, " 'A Political Bear-Garden . . .': Four Letters on the New York Constitutional Convention of 1821," *New York History* 59, no. 3 (1978): 326–342, http://www.jstor.org/stable/23169747.

24. Fox, "The Negro Vote," 256–257, see note 9, "An Act to prevent frauds at election and slaves from voting"; *Laws of New York*, Revision of 1813, vol. 2, 253.

25. New York (State), *Reports of the proceedings*, 186.

26. Jacob Katz Cogan, "The Look Within: Property, Capacity, and Suffrage in Nineteenth-Century America," *The Yale Law Journal* 107, no. 2 (1997): 473–498, doi:10.2307/797262.

27. *Journal of the Convention of the State of New-York* (Albany: Cantine & Leake, 1821), Sept. 12, 1821, 49, 51.

28. *Journal of the Convention*, 91. Peter Augustus Jay's property was formerly owned by Robert L. Bowne, and extended from the Bloomingdale Road and Eighty-Sixth Street to the boundary of Seneca Village, Eighty-Ninth Street. See chapter 8, note 26.

29. Edward Pessen, "Did Fortunes Rise and Fall Mercurially in Antebellum America? The Tale of Two Cities: Boston and New York," *Journal of Social History* 4, no. 4 (1971): 339–357, www.jstor.org/stable/3786475.

30. Bennett Liebman, "The Quest for Black Voting Rights in New York State," *Albany Government Law Review*, August 28, 2018, https://papers.ssrn.com/sol3/papers.cfm?

abstract_id=3240214. The tax assessments for Seneca Village residents are found in the Municipal Archives on microfilm and catalogued by years and wards. Seneca Village was in Ward 12. In 1853 the land below Eighty-Sixth Street became Ward 22.

31. Edmund Cosby, Epiphany Davis, Edward Hamilton, James Moore, John Scott, Charles Smith, Isaac Wallace, and Andrew Williams. Two others, George Howell and Edward Wigfall, were assessed at $240, just under the minimum amount for voting.

32. Village residents: Samuel Benben, Thomas Jackson, Josiah Landin, Obadiah McCollin, James Moore, William Pease, John Scott, Charles Smith, Isaac Wallace, William Webster, William Wilson, Andrew Williams and possibly Charles Sylvan. Nonresidents: John Carter, Epiphany Davis, Robert Fraser, Peter Guignon, Edward z, George Howell, Albro Lyons, William Smith, Charles Treadwell, William Undrill. Tax Assessments, Nineteenth Ward and Twelfth Ward, microfilm roll no. 67.

33. The Real Estate Record Association, *A History of Real Estate, Building and Architecture in New York City During the Last Quarter of a Century* (New York: Record and Guide, 1898), 36.

34. *Her*, June 15, 1836, quoted in Shane White, *Prince of Darkness: The Untold Story of Jeremiah G. Hamilton, Wall Street's First Black Millionaire* (New York: St. Martin's Press, 2015), 133–134. My thanks to Shane White for bringing the Hunts and his book, *Prince of Darkness*, to my attention, and for reading the two Seneca Village chapters.

35. White, *Prince of Darkness*, 138; 138–142.

36. Peterson, *Black Gotham*, 64, 167.

37. Maritcha Lyons, "Memories of Yesterday, All of Which I Saw and Part of Which I Was—An Autobiography," Harry Albro Williamson Papers, Reel 1, Schomburg Center, New York Public Library," 27. In 1843, the Agriculture Committee of the National Convention of Colored Citizens acknowledged land ownership by Blacks as the most attainable route to wealth: "there is, and can be no real wealth, but in the possession of the soil. The soil alone possesses a real value—all other things have only a relative value: their value is to be computed from the amount of land they will purchase." Though the committee was in that instance referring to farming as a livelihood, the head of the committee was Reverend Charles B. Ray, who would become a future prepark landowner seven years later (see chapter 10); *Minutes of the National Convention of Colored Citizens; Held at Buffalo; on the 15th, 16th, 17th, 18th, and 19th of August, 1843; for the purpose of considering their moral and political condition as American citizens*, 30.https://omeka.coloredconventions.org/items/show/278.

38. Transactions between 1825 and 1836: Whitehead to Hamilton, L197, P443, 1825; Hamilton to Stewart, L227, P330, 182, 1827; Stewart to Blake, L316, P139, 1834; Blake to Frazer, L316, P442, 1834; Whitehead to Smith, L220, P299–300, 1827; Smith to Moore, L316, P616, 1834; Diana and Samuel Harding to Smith, L327, P538, 1835; James Mack to Harding/McCollin. L312, P412, 1834; Harding/McCollin to Isaac Tyson, L314, P319, 1834; Tyson

to Thomas Zabriskie, L370, P194, 1836; Harding/McCollin to Diana Harding, L315, P305, 1834; Whitehead to Irish, L200, P478, 1826; Irish to Thompson, L334, P414, 1835; Whitehead to Black, L271, P498, 1831; Black to Johnson, L288, P115, 1832; Johnson to Frazer, L345, P3, 1835; Whitehead to Waters, L253, P552, 1829; Waters to Allen, L340, P327, 1835; Allen to Philip, L358, P335, 1836; Philip to George W. Smith, L366, P245, 1836; Whitehead to Hamilton, L281, P373, 1832; Hamilton to Smith, L315, P433, 1834; Harding to Nancy Smith, L327, P358, 1835; Whitehead to Russell, L290, P41, 1832; Russell to Cummings, L318, P444, 1835; Cummings to Washington, L352, P327, 1836; Washington to Landin, L380, P596, 1837; Whitehead to Cosby, L211, P168, 1826; Cosby to Webster, L318, P537, 1835; Whitehead to Jackson, L215, P31, 1826; Jackson to Lowery, L335, P33, 1835; Whitehead to Wallace, L252, P232, 1829; Wallace to Brinkerhoff, L339, P408, 1835; Whitehead to Scott, L288, P578, 1832; Scott to Hunt, L257, P109, 1830; Hunt to Washington (rental), L365, P293, 1836.

39. Harris, *In the Shadow of Slavery*, 142.

40. Harris, *In the Shadow of Slavery*, 170–173, 190–202.

41. Sean Wilentz, *Chants Democratic: New York City and the Rise of the American Working Class, 1788–1850* (New York: Oxford University Press, 1984), 263–267; Paul Gilje, *The Road to Mobocracy: Popular Disorder in New York City, 1763–1834* (Chapel Hill: University of North Carolina Press, 1987), 163–170; Linda K. Kerber, "Abolitionists and Amalgamators: The New York City Race Riots of 1834," *New York History* 48, no. 1 (1967): 28–39, http://www.jstor.org/stable/23162902.

42. *The Sun*, Mar. 29, 1839, quoted in White, *Prince of Darkness*, 64.

43. White, *Prince of Darkness*, 60; Eugene P. Moehring, *Public works and the patterns of urban real estate growth in Manhattan, 1835–1894* (New York: Arno Press, 1981), 5.

44. Today that lot with the gray square is the West Meadow landscape. The rental agreement between James Hunt and John J. Washington stipulated that the renter must insure against fire with a $1,000 policy on the property; L365, P293, 1836; Green to Wilson, L475, P537, 1846.

45. The 1846 tax assessment for the Twelfth Ward indicates a house on William Wilson's lot, Ward 12, Tax Assessment, 1846, vol. 2, 22, microfilm roll no. 67, MANY. The homes with basements do not have a gray wash underneath them, canceling that feature as an explanation for the layers. Though these cadastral maps—maps that name property owners—were done for the entire prepark to 106th Street, only the Seneca Village maps employ this detail of color coding.

46. A faint—almost invisible to the naked eye—rectangle on Charles Mingo's property, lot 48. In his petition to the Commissioners of Estimate and Assessment, Mingo noted that he had just constructed a rental house on his property only four years earlier and therefore demanded a higher reward before releasing it to the city for Central Park. *Petition*, vol. 5, 103. The neighboring house on lot 49 also shows a similar enlargement to the Moore dwelling on lot 44.

47. Plunz, *A History of Housing in New York City*, 141; Kyle T. Bultheis, *Four Steeples Over the City Streets: Religion and Society in New York's Early Republic Congregations* (New York: New York University Press, 2014), 59, 159.

48. Charles Rosenberg, *The Cholera Years: The United States in 1832, 1849, and 1866* (Chicago: University of Chicago Press, 1987), 58–59.

49. The seven were Charles Silvan, Thomas Jackson, George G. Root, Mrs. Black, Edward Wigfall, John Carter, and George Howell; see "Non-Payment of Assessments," *New-York Commercial Advertiser*, Apr. 23, 1843, 1.

50. Andra Ghent, *Special Report: The Historical Origins of America's Mortgage Law*, Research Institute for Housing America, 2012, http://www.housingamerica.org/RIHA/RIHA/Publications/82406_11922_RIHA_Origins_Report.pdf; Andra Ghent, "How Do Case Law and Statute Differ? Lessons from the Evolution of Mortgage Law," *The Journal of Law & Economics* 57, no. 4 (November 2014): 1095, https://www.jstor.org/stable/10.1086/680931. See the laws regarding the taxation and assessments of real estate passed by the State of New York in D. T. (David Thomas) Valentine, *A Compilation of the Laws of the State of New York* (New York: Common Council, 1862), 1161–1162, 1241–1270.

51. Reverend James Hardenberg, Reverend William Stilwell and Richard E. Stilwell, Henry Gassin, Mary Quinn, Andrew C. Zabriskie, and the Hudson Fire Insurance Company. Other possible mortgage lenders include Robert Marshall, George T. Taylor, and John M. Cooper. See Elizabeth Blackmar, *Manhattan for Rent, 1785–1850* (Ithaca, NY: Cornell University Press, 1989), 201–203.

52. Bernth Lindfors, *Ira Aldridge: The Early Years, 1807–1833* (Rochester, NY: Rochester Studies in African History and the Diaspora, 2011), 4; Bernth Lindfors, ed., *Ira Aldridge: The African Roscius* (Rochester, NY: University of Rochester Press, 2010), See also Bernth Lindfors, "Ira Aldridge's Relatives in New York City," *Afro-Americans in New York Life and History* 31, no. 1 (January 2007), https://go.gale.com/ps/i.do?id=GALE%7CA158529010&sid=googleScholar&v=2.1&it=r&linkaccess=abs&issn=03642437&p=AONE&sw=w&userGroupName=nysl_oweb&isGeoAuthType=true. The article continues: "Ira Aldridge's life in New York City," *Afro-Americans in New York Life and History* 32, no. 1 (January 2008), https://go.gale.com/ps/i.do?p=AONE&u=nysl_oweb&v=2.1&it=r&id=GALE%7CA173646757&inPS=true&linkSource=interlink&sid=bookmark-AONE. These articles also give a history of the Black theater and the African Free School.

53. *Memoir and Theatrical Career of Ira Aldridge, the African Roscius* (London: Onwhyn, 1849), 8. Autographed copy, https://babel.hathitrust.org/cgi/pt?id=udel.31741113286852&view=1up&seq=11.

54. Lindfors, *Ira Aldridge: The Early Years*, 18.

55. Aldridge is listed in *Longworth's American Almanac, New-York Register, and City Directory, 1803* (New York,: D. Longworth, 1803), 25, as a "laborer." He disappears for a few years and reappears in 1813 as a "grain measurer" in *Longworth's*, 4. From 1820 to 1835

he is a "cartman, black," in *Longworth's*, 55; in 1834–35, he is listed as a "huckster," *Longworth's*, 91.

56. Lindfors, *Ira Aldridge: The African Roscius*, 18.

57. Lindfors, *Ira Aldridge: The African Roscius*, 19, quoted in David I. Aldridge, "About Ira Aldridge," *New York Age*, Jan. 25, 1890, 4.

58. Lindfors, *Ira Aldridge: The Early Years*, 12.

59. Whitehead to Aldridge, L354, P292, 1836. Thomas Mildeberger to Daniel Aldridge, Aug. 17, *Mortgages*, L198, P510, 1836.

60. *Colored American*, 10 October 1840, 1. Lindfors, *Ira Aldridge: The Early Years*, 20.

61. Hester Walgrove gave a $500 mortgage to Daniel Aldridge, L200, P103, 1836. On May 7, 1839, Chancery Court awarded Dresser the Aldridge property for his $1,200 bid in a public auction of the Aldridge lots, L396, P307, 1839. That same day Dresser transferred the Walgrove mortgage and the property to Josiah E. Landin, L395, P552, 1839. Reverend James B. Hardenburgh to Landin, *Mortgages*, L274, P207, 1844. On Feb. 3, 1847, Court of Chancery First Circuit of the State of NY, "pending in court between William McLean Jr. (Executor of Will of Samuel Walgrove) and other complainants and Horace Dresser, lawyer, and other Defendants mortgaged premises sold at public auction for ten hundred and ten dollars" to Rev. James B. Hardenburgh, L487, P43, 1847.

62. "For Sale—Fruit and Forest Trees," *EP*, Mar. 4, 1830. Though he gave no address for himself, he advised interested clients to leave orders with David Ruggles, the future journalist and activist, who owned a grocery at 1 Courtland Street.

63. Baptized in the home of Josiah Landin "near 87th Street: William Henry, b. Dec. 18, 1845 son of Elizabeth Harris; Josiah, b. June 18, 1847, and baptized Mar. 31, 1848, the son of David Shipley and Elizabeth Harris," in Thomas McClure Peters, "Baptisms, Confirmations, Marriages and Burials for the years 1847 to 1865," *All Angels' Church, New York City, Parish Record Book, 1847–1874*, All Angels' Church, Office of the Rector.

64. Blackmar, *Manhattan for Rent*, 203.

65. Bonner to Landin, *Mortgages*, L215, P485, 1837; Clayton to Landin, *Mortgages*, L211, P197, 1838; Gassin to Landin, *Mortgages*, L221, P233, 1838; *Mortgages*, L233, P401, 1839; Green to Landin, L258, P466, 1842.

66. Scudder to Landin, L414, P347, assumes mortgage to Scudder from Joseph Quinn. Lease of Aldridge's lots 110 and 111, Mayor, Aldermen, and Commonalty to Doherty, L469, P598, 1840; Lease from Doherty to Landin, L469, P600, 1844, for $30 for one hundred years. There is no record of a renter for this property.

67. "Non-Payment of Assessments," *EP*, Apr. 9, 1844, 1. In 1844, several owners were on the city's list for nonpayment of assessments on lots 150 and 151. The average tax on property per individual was $2.90 in 1820, $2.40 in 1830, $4.33 in 1840, $5.80 in 1850, and $12.10 in 1860; in John Christopher Schwab, "History of the New York Property Tax," *Publications of the American Economic Association* 5, no. 5 (September 1890): 84, www.jstor.org/stable/2485701; "Mortgage Sale," *EP*, Aug. 18, 1853; Master of Chancery to Hardenbergh, L487, P43, 1847. Landin's conveyances: Maria Whitehead, L369, P229, 1836 (four

lots: 123–124, 150–151); James S. Bonner, L378, P183, 1837, lot 78 (from Jesse Russell); John J. Washington, L380, P596, 1838, lot 77 (from Jesse Russell); Horace Dresser, L395, P552, 1839, lots 110–111 (from Aldrich); Scudder to Landin, L414, 347, 1841, lot 80 (mortgage from Joseph Quinn); Simon Green, L430, P534, 1843, lots 125 and 149 (see court case 580 392, 1851, involving J .B. Hardenburgh, John Cleinger, Carstin Engle, and Landin), Hamilton W. Robinson, L447, P386, 1844.

68. Sheriff to Gassin, L657, P381, 1854; Sheriff to Lynch, L649, P229, 1854; Hardenburgh to Zabriskie, L609, 475, 1853. Lyman Horace Weeks, ed., *Prominent Families of New York* (New York, The Historical Society, 1898), 636. *BA Docs.*, May 16, 1856, Doc. No. 25, 24.

69. As for most residents, no record has been found indicating the location of their next home after leaving the community, though there is a record of the Landins of Staten Island who had come from Maryland early in the century and were later connected to the community's A.M.E. Zion Church of Sandy Ground/Rossville. Rossville A.M.E. Zion Church, 584 Bloomingdale Road, Staten Island, Landmarks Preservation Commission, Feb. 1, 2011, Designation List 438 LP-2416, 3, http://s-media.nyc.gov/agencies /lpc/lp/2416.pdf.

70. Chancery to Richard E. Stilwell, L412, P559, 1841, includes the seven lots in Seneca Village; Mortgagee William Stilwell to Mortgagor Leven Smith for $1,100, *Mortgages*, L122, P547, Jan. 13, 1829, included a lot at 23 Broad Street as well as the lots in Seneca Village. The mortgage was discharged June 27, 1837. See also Peter Gerard Stuyvesant to Smith, L279, P405–407, 1824, lease for lot southwest side of Christie and Delancey Streets; Smith leased to James R. Hicks and Levin Williams for a term of twenty-one years, Feb. 7, 1832; see also L453, P627, 1844, lease from Stuyvesant to Smith to Hicks to Williams, $175, 1844, for a term of twenty-one years. Leven Smith (spelled Leben Smith), *U.S. Census, 1840*, New York County, Twelfth Ward, 142. The *New York State Census, 1855*, noted that John P. Haff had been a resident of New York City for thirteen years, placing his move to Seneca Village in 1842, two years after his brother-in-law bought the property. *New York State Census, 1855*, Ward 22, E.D. 3, 44.

71. Hunt to Washington, L365, P293, 1836.

72. Scott to Hunt, L257, P109, 1829. White, *Prince of Darkness*, 141.

73. Blackmar, *Manhattan for Rent*, 213–214.

74. *U.S. Census, 1840*, Twelfth Ward, 142.

75. Though the ad mentions his property, "on the new African Burying ground," Henry's two lots were not on the same block as the established cemeteries; *Freedom's Journal*, Jan. 2, 1829.

76. *Petitions*, vol. 5, 103, DOR.

77. Washington to Webster, L555, P83, 1848; *Releases, Blocks 780 to 805*, box 2870, MANY.

78. After their eviction, the new owner Anthony Bell rented to the Hunts. At some point James died and Marcy regained possession of her property, and rented her home and corner lot to William Mathew, who purchased it in 1847. Wealthy New Jersey merchant Andrew C. Zabriskie, who had purchased Landin's foreclosed property from Reverend

Hardenburgh, allowed the Landins to stay in their former home as renters until 1857. Hardenburgh to Zabriskie, L609, P475, 1853.

79. The white landowners before 1850 were: Francis R. Tillou (Roach to Tillou, L251, P408, and L252, P490, 1829), Archibald Lowery (Jackson to Lowery, L335, P33, 1835), Elias L. Philip (Turner to Philip, L344, P379, 1835; Moses to Philip, L358, P335, 1836), Elbert Brinkerhoff (Wallace to Brinkerhoff, L339, P408, 1835) to Ebenezer Monroe (L383, P580, 1837), Richard E. Stilwell (Chancery to Stilwell, L412, P559, 1841), and John Whitehead's widow, Maria Whitehead, and his daughter and son-in-law, Mary and Richard Turner, who inherited the Whiteheads' land. Other whites owned the property due to mortgage foreclosures. The racial identity of Robert Marshall (1844) is undetermined.

80. Rosenzweig and Blackmar, *The Park and the People*, 66.

81. The 1855 population has been estimated at 225 residents by Meredith Linn of the Institute for the Exploration of Seneca Village History and Marie Warsh of the Central Park Conservancy. Their study determined that "62 percent of the population was African American or 139 people. The remaining 83 residents were thought to be mostly Irish and some Germans as well." Email, Warsh to author, December 5, 2021.

82. Education Department, *Seneca Village: A Teacher's Guide*, 41–44.

83. For the history of street numbering, see Gerard Koeppel, *City on a Grid: How New York Became New York* (New York: Da Capo Press, 2015), 106–107.

84. Both the New York State Legislature and the United States Congress created the instructions for the census process, and still do today. *Chap. XI An Act providing for the taking of the seventh and subsequent Censuses of the United States, and to fix the Number of the Members of the House of Representatives, and provide for their apportionment among the several States*, Thirty-First Congress, Sess. I. Ch. 11, 1850, May 23, 1850, 428–130; https://www.census.gov/history/pdf/1850instructions.pdf. Secretary of State, *Instructions for Taking the Census of the State of New-York In the Year 1855* (Albany: Weed, Parsons & Co., 1855), 12–24, http://www.nysl.nysed.gov/scandocs/documents/nycensusinstruct1855.pdf.

85. "As each page of schedule No. 1 has 45 lines . . . every page (except the last, which must necessarily be incomplete) should contain that number of names, and that no lines be omitted or entries made, except in the spaces having a number printed in the margin," *Instructions for Taking the Census*, 12.

86. We can compare most Black residents and some white residents on the censuses, as their names also appear on maps, deeds, assessment lists, and newspaper accounts. But many of the other white families grouped between the known Seneca Village families do not appear on any other documents. An example of boundaries can be found in the *U.S. Census, 1850*, page 198a: fifteen Black residents are listed living in three separate households. Residents Thomas Jackson and his family were identifiable Seneca Village renters. Another Black family, Isaac Smith and his wife, Margaret—unknown to any other documents—were listed on page 198b. Between the Jacksons and the Smiths,

eight white households with a total of fifty-two residents are listed. The Smiths are then followed by one eight-member household *before* listing the seven Haffs, who are the first *confirmed* white family in Seneca Village, known by other documents. Should we consider the people listed between the Jacksons and the Haffs as residents of Seneca Village?

87. *The New-York City Directory for 1854–1855* (New York: Charles R. Rode, 1854), 554.

88. The most reliable identification of an otherwise undocumented white family occurs when their name appears between known residents and is listed during the same visit. In the 1850 federal census, for example, it seems fair to count the five-member Irish family of John Carrigan (visit number 1563) as they were listed after known Black landowners William and Sally Wilson (visit number 1562) and before the known Black renters of the Thompson family (visit number 1564); the interviews all took place on Sept. 21, 1850. The Carrigan family was not listed in the 1855 *New York State Census*.

89. This figure would include all white households that were bookended between the known Black households—and it is unlikely that all of them would have lived in Seneca Village. In 1850, resident Blacks totaled 108 people and known whites totaled 24 people (Hurry, 6 people; Gallagher, 6 people; Dunn, 3 people; Eversi, 2 people; Haff, 7 people). The seventeen household members of the Croton employees are excluded.

90. According to the Dripps map of 1851 (https://www.davidrumsey.com/maps5090.html), Seneca Village had thirty-eight dwellings. According to the 1855 condemnation maps, the number had increased to a total of fifty-four houses, though at least two had disappeared. The increase in housing is most likely due to fourteen rentals, almost all of them rented by Black tenants. The households of new Black renters account for twenty-five residents: Pleasant Smith, family of four; Ishmael Allen, family of seven; John Lane, family of seven; John White, family of seven.

91. Of those acknowledged white renters, 24 of them would comprise only about 14 percent of the total Village population. A possible maximum of 14 other whites would bring the total of whites to 38 individuals or 18 percent of the total population. Known white residents include: Haff, family of 7; Meyers, 4 unrelated persons; Riley, family of 2; Barlow, family of 2. Possible whites listed in the 1855 census include: Casey 5, Carey 4, Glynn 4, Renahan 3, Foley 2, Collins 1, McPotter (possibly McFarlane) 5.

92. It is unclear how long Williams's shanty was vacant, as noted on the condemnation map. Ellen Williams Butler and her husband were living there in 1855, as recorded in *New York State Census*.

93. To be discussed in chapter 18.

94. Henry Louis Gates, Jr., *The Black Church: This Is Our Story, This Is Our Song* (New York: Penguin, 2021), 35–36.

95. Douglas A. Jones, Jr., "Shouting, and the Beginning of African American Writing," *Early American Literature* 53, no. 1 (2018): 74. Wilder, *In the Company of Black Men*, 36–53; Dennis C. Dickerson, "Liberation, Wesleyan Theology and Early African Methodism, 1766–1840," *Wesley and Methodist Studies* 3 (2011): 109–120; Kyle T. Bulthuis,

"Tobacconist, Methodist, African, Patriot: Uncovering the Real Peter Williams in Early Republic New York City," *New York History* 99, no. 2 (Spring 2018): 209–226; Kyle T. Bulthuis, "Preacher, Politics and People Power: Congregational Conflicts in New York City, 1810–1830," *Church History* 78, no. 2 (June 2009): 261–282.

96. Treadwell to A.M.E. Zion Trustees, L225, P263, 1827; Green to African Union Trustees, L377, P430, 1833; Townshend to African Union Trustees, L663, P28, 1854. The Ludlow sisters gave the property to Cornelius R. Duffie, Minister of the Gospel; Abraham V. Williams, Physician; and John Jay and John A. King, Jr., who were most likely the trustees of All Angels'; L531, P208, 1849.

97. Kyle T. Bultheis, *Four Steeples Over the City Streets: Religion and Society in New York's Early Republic Congregations* (New York: New York University Press, 2014), 59; Wilder, *In the Company of Black Men*, 45; The Methodist Society records of Baptisms and Marriages 1818 to 1851, NYPL, Manuscripts and Archives Division.

98. "Records were kept of Negro members as far back as 1801 when [Samuel] Seaman in his Annals [*The Rise of Methodist Society in the City of New York* (New York, 1821)] states that in New York City there were 685 white members and 150 colored. These 150 members evidently belonged to the Chapel." David Henry Bradley, Sr., *A History of the A.M.E. Zion Church* (Nashville, TN: The Parthenon Press, 1956), 62.

99. Bulthuis, "Preacher, Politics and People Power," 272–281.

100. Christopher Rush, *A Short Account of the Rise and Progress of the African M. E. Church in America* (New York: self-pub., 1866); Harris, *In the Shadow of Slavery*, 84.

101. *MCC1784*, vol. 4, 522, 525, vol. 11, 700. Carole Inskeep, *The Graveyard Shift: A Family Historian's Guide to New York City Cemeteries* (Orem, UT: Ancestry Publishing, 2000), 4.

102. The AME Zion Church first bought eight lots in block 787 from Whitehead in 1825 (L197, P350) and then acquired three oversized lots in Block 789 in 1827 (L226, P211). For Common Council rulings, see *MCC1784*, vol. 11: 811; *MCC1784*, vol 14: 633. See also Nancy Dickinson and Faline Schneiderman, "Methodist Episcopal Cemetery: Intensive Documentary Study Second Avenue New York, New York Second Avenue Subway," Historical Perspectives, Inc., Westport, CT, June 2003, 17, http://s-media.nyc.gov/agencies/lpc/arch_reports/436.pdf. 8.

103. Inskeep, *The Graveyard Shift*, xi.

104. Treadwell to African Methodist Episcopal Church, L225, P263, 1827. Levin Smith, Zion preacher, bought six lots adjacent to Treadwell, 113–118 (L242, 504, 1828), but did not sell them to the church. The deed from Whitehead to Levin Smith, baker, for six lots, was "Recorded for Wm M. Stilwell"; the Reverend, who ordained Smith, held his mortgage (see note 70). Smith's first name, Levin, is also spelled Leven, Leben, or Neven.

105. Theodore Lyons, age 2 years, 7 months, 1 day, died July 11, 1835, and was buried in "Zion's Church buriel [*sic*] ground, 85th Street between 7th and 8th aves, New York City"; Colden Lyons, age 19 years, 2 months, 3 days, died October 16, 1838, and Maria Lyons, age 29, 15 days, died January 6, 1841; their parents, Lucinda Lyons, age 44, died December 22, 1834, and George Lyons 2nd, age 60, died in 1843; all were recorded as buried

in the Eighty-Fifth Street Zion lots. Harry Albro Williamson papers, roll 1, "Family Record of George Lyons," NYPL, Schomburg Center for Research in Black Culture, 9–11. Zion Burial Ground at Eighty-Fifth Street between Seventh and Eighth Avenues is noted in the 1848 edition of *Doggett's New York City Directory, Illustrated with Maps of New York and Brooklyn, 1848–1849*, 7th ed. (New York: John Doggett, Jr., 1849), 21.

106. Entry No. 29, "Art the Handmaid of Nature," 31, in *Catalogue of Plans for the Improvement of Central Park, 1858*, NYHS. See also, Viele, *Topographical Map of New York Showing Original Water Courses and Made Land*, 1865, LOC, and also Block 789 (Eighty-Eighth to Eighty-Ninth Streets, Seventh to Eighth Avenues), in Roswell Graves, *Topographical Maps &c. In the Matter of Opening Central Park*, New York, July 1855.

107. City to Trustees of the African Methodist Episcopal Church, signed for by Isaac Pernell, vol. 780 to 805, box 2870, MANY.

108. Tax Assessments, 1848, MANY.

109. Christopher Moore and Andrew S. Dolkart, "Mother African Methodist Episcopal Zion Church," Landmarks Preservation Commission, Designation List, 252 LP-1849, July 13, 1993, 3, 8, n. 8; http://s-media.nyc.gov/agencies/lpc/lp/1849.pdf.

110. Adriance to Trustees of the African Methodist Episcopal Church, L273, P490, 1830.

111. Mayor, Aldermen and Commonalty of the City of New York to William A. Walters, L475, P615, 1846; William A. Walters to the Trustees of the African Methodist Zion Church, L475, P615, 1846.

112. Bulthuis, "Preacher, Politics and People Power," 272–281.

113. The Zion burials listed in McClure's All Angels' record book do not specify which of the Zion burial grounds were used.

114. Horace Dresser obituary, *NYT*, Jan. 24, 1877, 5; see Eric Foner, *Gateway to Freedom: The Hidden History of the Underground Railroad* (New York: Norton, 2015), 69. It's not clear that ownership of the property was returned to Zion when the conveyance from Walters to Zion was for a lease. For the years 1841 to 1845 Treadwell was listed as the person responsible for paying the taxes, and may have been so named because he was a church trustee rather than because he was the former owner. By 1846, the "African Church" was paying the taxes, and when the city bought the land for the park in 1856, the Trustees of the A.M.E. Zion Church received the award. No known documents record the change in status from lessee to ownership.

115. The 1855 *New York State Census* does not list the church in the "Churches, Schools, &c." category in the 22nd Ward, unless it was misnamed the "84th Street Presb." Church, but that seems unlikely given the noted size of accommodation (350 people), the value of the church ($10,000), and the salary of the clergy ($1,000); see Part 5, "Churches, Schools, &c." 22nd Ward, E.D. 3, 85.

116. My deepest gratitude to the Reverends Malcolm Byrd and Audrey Akins Williamson for giving me a tour of the church and the archives, and to Reverend Williamson for reading the manuscripts for chapter 3 and both Seneca Village chapters.

117. Jonathan Greenleaf, *A history of the churches, of all denominations, in the city of New York, from the first settlement to the year 1846* (New York: E. French, 1846), 328, https://catalog .hathitrust.org/Record/001408135.

118. Green to African Union Trustees, L377, P430, 1833; Townsend to African Union Trust- ees, L663, P28, 1853. John Whitehead to Edward Wigfall, L213, P94–96, 1826; Ann Eliza Wigfall to Elizabeth Townshend, L643, P192, 1852; Townsend to African Union, L663, P28,1853. According to tax records ranging from as early as 1832 to as late as 1854, Matilda Wigfall (or Widow Wigfall) was charged as the responsible party for paying the assessments on lots 47 and 48, the lots of the African Union Church. The tax records do not mention Elizabeth Townshend or the African Union Church, though they list the "African Church" or "Zion African Church" in the assessment records.

119. *Petitions*, vol. 5, 92.

120. The church was mentioned in a condescending and probably inaccurate manner by All Angels' Reverend Thomas McClure Peters in in his 1873 pamphlet: "A small Methodist church, the only place of worship from Fifty-ninth to One Hundred and Tenth Street, was on Sunday scantily attended by a few blacks. There was no service for the children, no Bible class or Sunday-school in which they might be taught of Jesus." [Thomas McClure Peters], New York Protestant Episcopal City Mission Society, *The Growth of Charities* (New York: Julius Schlueter, 1873), 9. McClure Peters's negative description of the African Union Church was purposely omitted when the text from *The Growth of Charities* was copied by his son John Punnett Peters, in *Annals of St. Michael's: Being the History of St. Michael's Protestant Episcopal Church, New York for One Hundred Years 1807–1907* (New York: G. P. Putnam's Sons, 1907), 446.

121. *New York State Census, 1855*, Section 5, "Churches, Schools, &c," 85.

122. [McClure Peters], *The Growth of Charities*, 8–10. This is the first publication of the name "Seneca." Many facts have been fused and confused about the establishment in 1833 of a Sunday school by Reverend James Richmond of St. Michael's Church. Reverend John Punnett Peters in *Annals of St. Michael's* (248) noted that the mission school was first located "on the site of the reservoir in Central Park." This was later echoed in *The Park and the People* (66). Authors Rosenzweig and Blackmar noted that the York Hill community most likely merged with those already living in Seneca Village due to the construction of the receiving reservoir. The assertion may rest on a case of mistaken identity of the York Hill landowner. It was assumed that a Black man named William Mathew, who did own property in Seneca Village, first owned property on York Hill. The property was, in fact, owned by a white man with a different name spelling, William Mathews, who bought the prereservoir land from the city in 1799 (see chapter 13, n15). The assumption that York Hill was only located within the confines of the prepark adds to the misunderstanding. York Hill continued to Third Avenue between Sixty-Sixth and Sixty-Ninth Street—known today as Lenox Hill—and on its "crest," St. James Church was built and consecrated in 1810 (29, 239). It was an Episcopal church closely associated with St. Michael's. St. James

remains on Sixty-Ninth Street and Madison Avenue. It had a Sunday school for Black children that was mentioned in an 1815 diocesan report. The Yorkville community was located "below" St. James Church; Peters noted that *later* a community of "free blacks" also was located in what we now know as the prepark (41). This earlier and more populated Black neighborhood of Yorkville would have been more fitting for a Sunday school that served thirty children after 1815 (87, 393, 446). In his *A Tour Around Manhattan and My Summer Acre* (New York: Harper & Brothers, 1893), John Flavel Mines confirmed that circa 1825 a preacher from St. Michael's in Bloomingdale—most likely James Cook Richmond—would come on summer Sunday mornings to St. James (425). In 1833—the year that Richmond was said to have started the Seneca Village school—a Methodist Sunday school "for colored persons" was established by Reverend James Floy in conjunction with the Bowery Village (later the Seventh Street) Church of the Methodist Episcopal Church, in William B. Silber, *A History of the St. James Methodist Episcopal Church at Harlem, New York City, 1830–1880* (New York: Phillips & Hunt, 1882), 57.

123. Ludlow's mother, Ann Verplanck, was also from a socially prominent family, and his uncle Gulian Verplanck was president of the Bank of New York. Gulian Ludlow was himself a member of the exclusive Belvedere Club, a society for wealthy loyalist-leaning businessmen. His father had much of his property confiscated after the war, property that his son would have otherwise inherited. Despite his wartime loyalist sentiments, Ludlow remained in New York after pledging loyalty to the new United States. William Seton Gordon, *Gabriel Ludlow (1663–1736) and His Descendants* (reprinted from the New York Genealogical and Biographical Record, 1919), 10, https://archive.org /details/GenealogyGlh232968997/page/n3/mode/2up?q. Ludlow to Hampton, L580, P573, 1849; Ludlow and others to Angeline Riddles, L529, P399, 1849; Ludlow and others to William G. Wilson, L572, P200, 1850.

124. "Churchman," *Christian Witness and Church Advocate* (Jan. 4, 1850), 2.

125. Margaret McIntay is not listed in Peters, "Baptisms, Confirmations, Marriages and Burials for the years 1847 to 1865," 15. *Her*, Aug. 11, 1871, 4, cited in Rosenzweig and Blackmar, *The Park and the People*, 89n70, 551; Education Department, *Seneca Village: A Teacher's Guide*, 29.

126. *New York State Census, 1855*, 85; Peters, *Annals of St. Michael's*, 396 Rosenzweig and Blackmar, *The Park and the People*, 72.

127. *Mortgages*, McClure Peters to Henry Garnet, L407, P284, 1852, transferred to Eliza Garnet, L624, P287, 1853.

128. In 1858, Wilson petitioned the Commissioners of Central Park, though what he was requesting was not recorded. It is possible that he was writing on behalf of the church, but more likely the petition pertained to his dwelling. Peters, *Annals of St. Michael's*, 396; *Releases*, Blocks 780 to 805, box 2870, MANY.

129. According to the authors of "Seneca Village and the Making of Central Park" (https:// www.nyhistory.org/seneca/village5.html), Colored School No. 3 was located in the basement of African Union, although no source is given. The condemnation map shows it attached to the church.

130. Shiells to Thompson, L461, P259, 1845, block 62–63, lots 39 and 40; *New York State Census, 1855,* Ward 22, E.D. 3.

131. *New York State Census, 1855,* Ward 22, E.D. 3; Yorkville, Colored School No. 3, Caroline W. Simpson, principal. Caroline Simpson is probably the woman listed as "mulatto," age 30, having no listed occupation and living in the Tenth Ward with a Black relation, William Simpson, a servant, age 19, in *U.S. Census, 1850,* Tenth Ward, 23. Catherine Geary, Principal, Primary School 55, East Eighty-Fourth Street and Fourth Avenue, H. Wilson, compiler, *Trow's New York City Directory for the Year Ending May 1, 1858* (New York: John F. Trow, 1857), 50.

132. "Report on The Improvement of Schools for African American Children in New York City," *The Anglo-African Magazine* [New York City], July 1859, including the 1857 report submitted by the New York Society for the Promotion of Education Among Colored Children to a state commission appointed to evaluate the city schools, in http://nation-alhumanitiescenter.org/pds/maai/identity/text8/equalopportunity.pdf.

133. Oliver Delancey, Joseph Orchard, Daniel Cock and Daniel Underhill, Samuel Stilwell, Joseph Pearsall, Samuel Ogden, James Fairlie, Naphtali Judah, and John Whitehead; see chapters 7 and 8.

134. See note 10.

135. New York State, *Documents of the Assembly of the State of New York,* vol. 6, 1846, 62. It is noted that Haff's residence was Bloomingdale, the neighborhood that encompassed both the Elm Park Hotel and Seneca Village. Haff's twenty-one-year passion for grape cultivation was attributed to his father, who was "something of a *connoisseur* of the article." In the 1840s Haff lived in Fort Lee, New Jersey, where he won awards for his "superior specimens of field grapes" and for "two bunches of Sweet Water and a bunch of Isabella grapes."

136. Thomas David Beal, *Selling Gotham: The Retail Trade in New York City from the Public Market to Alexander T. Stewart's Marble Palace, 1625–1860* (Stony Brook: State University of New York at Stony Brook, 1998), 48.

137. Beal, *Selling Gotham,* 52. In table 2.3, "African American Agriculturists in New York's Twelfth Ward, 1850," Louis Tremante identified eight Black men listed in the U.S. Census as farmers and one as a gardener. Tremante suggested that they might live "in and around" Seneca Village, though none of their names is entered in the U.S. Census near the community, nor do they appear on any documents; in Louis P. Tremante III, "Agriculture and Farm Life in the New York City Region, 1820–1870" (Ph.D. diss., Iowa State University, 2000), 61, https://lib.dr.iastate.edu/cgi/viewcontent.cgi?article=13289&context=rtd.

138. Lawrence B. Glickman, "Buy for the Sake of the Slave: Abolitionism and Origins of American Consumer Activism," *American Quarterly.* 56, no. 4 (2004): 889–912, doi:10. 1353/aq.2004.0056. Michele Nicole Branch, "Just Provisions: Food, Identity, and Contested Space in Urban America, 1800–1875" (PhD diss., University of California, Berkeley, 2012), 104, https://digitalassets.lib.berkeley.edu/etd/ucb/text/Branch_berkeley_0028E_12752.pdf.

139. Graham Russell Hodges, *David Ruggles: A Radical Black Abolitionist and the Underground Railroad in New York City* (Chapel Hill: University of North Carolina Press, 2010), 43–44, 211n21. Ruggles ads: *New-York Freedom's Journal*, "Fresh Goshen Butter," May 9, 1828, 16; "Groceries," Aug. 22, Sept. 5, 25, Oct. 10, 1828, and Dec. 12, 1828–Mar. 9, 1829.

140. Hodges, *David Ruggles*, 43.

10. DIVIDING BLOOMINGDALE, SENECA VILLAGE: THE BLACK LEADERS, 1825–1857

1. Carla L. Peterson, *Black Gotham: A Family History of African Americans in Nineteenth-Century New York City* (New Haven, CT: Yale University Press, 2012); see also Carla L. Peterson, "Black Life in Freedom," in Ira Berlin and Leslie M. Harris, eds., *Slavery in New York* (New York: New-York Historical Society, 2005), 181–213.

2. Craig Steven Wilder, *In the Company of Black Men: The African Influence on African American Culture in New York City* (New York: New York University Press, 2001), 64.

3. See Leslie M. Harris, *In the Shadow of Slavery: African Americans in New York City, 1626–1863* (Chicago: University of Chicago Press, 2004), chapters 4, 5, and 6; see also Carla L. Peterson, *Black Gotham: A Family History of African Americans in Nineteenth-Century New York City* (New Haven, CT: Yale University Press, 2012), 127–138.

4. For an interview with Carla Peterson on Black elite families, see https://thegrio .com/2011/03/01/black-gotham-review.

5. Maritcha Lyons, "Memories of Yesterday, All of Which I Saw and Part of Which I Was—An Autobiography," Harry Albro Williamson Papers, Reel 1, Schomburg Center, New York Public Library, 27; Peterson, *Black Gotham*, 41–42.

6. Shane White, *Prince of Darkness: The Untold Story of Jeremiah G. Hamilton, Wall Street's First Black Millionaire* (New York: St. Martin's Press, 2015), 122–124. White can also be heard on the Gotham Center podcast "The African Grove," https://www.gothamcenter .org/podcasts/ohny-weekend-podcasts. Harry Albro Williamson Papers, 11.

7. Lyons, "Memories of Yesterday," 1–3.

8. Lyons, "Memories of Yesterday," 2, 44. According to Peterson, Edward was a schoolmate of Albro Lyons; *Black Gotham*, 67, 118, 141; confirmed in Peterson, interview by author, June 19, 2020.

9. In 1818, wealthy land speculator George Lorillard acquired swampland on Collect Street that was auctioned off by the City of New York. In 1819, the African Episcopal Society, renamed the St. Philip's Episcopal Church, acquired a sixty-year lease, and in 1820 Joseph Marshall leased a lot and later built a house it, valued at $900. By 1829, the property was worth $1,200. After Joseph Marshall's death, the property belonged to Elizabeth, who built a structure on the rear of the lot that housed a bakery, valued by 1838 at $2,000. Peterson, *Black Gotham*, 41.

10. Whitehead to Marshall, L208, P121, 1826; L220, P190, 1827. Maritcha wrote that her parents owned four lots ("Memories of Yesterday," 2); they owned six lots.

11. Albro Lyons sold the Marshall's sixth lot, no. 23, block 788 to his former schoolmate Timothy Seaman. Lyons to Seaman, L410, P40, 1840.

12. Graham Russell Gao Hodges, *Black New Jersey: 1664 to the Present Day* (New Brunswick, NJ: Rutgers University Press, 2019), 7, 42, 71.

13. Mildred Jailer, "Map to Tell Story of Passaic's Past," *NYT*, Jan. 4, 1976, 67. It was referenced in Marshall's will as "Acquackanonk." In 1828, Canalville was a residential subdivision on the Morris Canal in today's Clifton, New Jersey. See *Probate*, Joseph Marshall, last will and testament, L63, P99, 1829.

14. Lyons, "Memories of Yesterday," 2–3, 43–44.

15. See Sarah Parker Remond in https://www.encyclopedia.com/women/encyclopedias -almanacs-transcripts-and-maps/remond-sarah-parker-1826-1894; Sirpa Salenius, *An Abolitionist Abroad*: Sarah Parker Remond in Cosmopolitan Europe (Amherst, MA., University of Massachusetts Press, 2016).

16. The notes in the Williamson Papers, possibly written by Albro Lyons, noted that George Lyons was born in 1783. The New York City Death Records note that he died in 1843 at the age of sixty-four, and estimate that his birth was in 1779. He was buried in Zion's cemetery on Eighty-Fifth Street in Seneca Village.

17. Maritcha noted that her father was born in "Fishkill-on-Hudson," a misnomer for Fishkill Landing, which became Beacon, New York, in 1913. The genealogical booklet, probably written in 1851 and authored by Albro Lyons (Harry Albro Williamson Papers, Reel 1, 4, also noted in Harris, *In the Shadow of Slavery*, 309n36) says he was born in Fishkill, which is an inland city four miles northeast of Beacon. According to the *U.S. Census, 1810*, George Lyons and his three family members lived in Beekman, twelve miles northeast of Fishkill. According to genealogist Aaron Goodwin, "when Albro was born in 1814, the Town of Fishkill abutted the Town of Beekman . . . a birth in Fishkill could have been anywhere in the area that is now Fishkill, East Fishkill, Wappinger, or LaGrange. Either George Lyons moved between 1810 and 1814, or he was very close to the border between Fishkill and Beekman," Goodman, email to author, June 1, 2021.

18. The history of the Free School: Schomburg Center for Research in Black Culture, Manuscripts, Archives and Rare Books Division, The New York Public Library. "The history of the New-York African free-schools, from their establishment in 1787, to the present time," New York Public Library Digital Collections, accessed August 11, 2021, https://digitalcollections.nypl.org/items/510d47e4-123b-a3d9-e040-e00a18064a99; Harris, *In the Shadow of Slavery*, 128–144; Peterson, "The Mulberry Street School," *Black Gotham*, 76–92. John L. Rury, "Philanthropy, Self Help, and Social Control: The New York Manumission Society and Free Blacks, 1785–1810," *Phylon (1960–)* 46, no. 3 (1985): 231–241, doi:10.2307/274831.

19. In 1837, several village landowners or friends—Albro Lyons, Timothy Seaman, Edward V. Clark, and Peter Guignon—joined "A Call to Colored Young Men" for Black men of their age "to form a regular organization with a view to systematic effort . . . in petitioning the legislature . . . a right which they had enjoyed uninterruptedly for 40 years."

In "For the Colored American Important Meeting a Call to Colored Young Men," *Colored American*, Aug. 19, 1837, 3.

20. Smith's name appears on the conveyance of widow Martha Wright: Martha [written Martin M.] Wright, City of New Haven widow of Theodore S. Wright, Minister of the Gospel to Elizabeth A. Gloucester, wife of James N. Gloucester, Minister of the Gospel $100 lot 47, L612, P448, 1852.

21. Lyons, "Memories of Yesterday," 4; Jessie Carney Smith, ed., "Maritcha R. Lyons," *Notable Black American Women*, Book 2 (Detroit: Gale Research, 1996), 417–420.

22. Peterson, *Black Gotham*, 30.

23. Lyons, "Memories of Yesterday," 6.

24. Michele Nicole Branch, "Just Provisions: Food, Identity, and Contested Space in Urban America, 1800–1875" (Ph.D. diss., University of California, Berkeley, 2012), https://escholarship.org/uc/item/4gk6g2v8, 104–105.

25. Eric Foner, *Gateway to Freedom: The Hidden History of the Underground Railroad* (New York: Norton, 2015), 106; "Albro Lyons (successor to Samuel Gloyne) Seamen's General Outfitting Store, 37 Water Street," *The Weekly Anglo-African* (New York), Mar. 9, 1861, 4.

26. Lyons, "Memories of Yesterday," 8–11a; Peterson, *Black Gotham*, 223–258; Edwin G. Burrows and Mike Wallace, *Gotham: A History of New York City to 1898* (New York and Oxford: Oxford University Press, 1999), 887–902; Harris, *In the Shadow of Slavery*, 280–286; Iver Bernstein, *The New York City Draft Riots: Their Significance for American Society and Politics in the Age of the Civil War* (New York: Oxford University Press, 1990), 27–31. Bernstein noted (page 33) that a Central Park laborer named Doherty incited a group of fellow Irishmen to burn down the house of lawyer Josiah Porter for refusing to allow Doherty to erect a shanty on his land.

27. White, *Prince of Darkness*, 295–303. Though the riot took place downtown, fear of violence affected the city's residents even in Central Park, three miles away. Weekly statistics taken for all boats that circled the Lake showed roughly two-thirds fewer boaters the week of the riot. The rowboats saw the most dramatic dip in use, 77 percent. Overall, an estimated 30,000 fewer people came to the park on the four Sundays in July than had come in June, and nearly 45,000 fewer visitors came in July than had returned in August. The rise in attendance following the riot may signify that the public considered the park as the refuge as it was intended to be. *BCCP Seventh Annual Report* (New York: Wm. C. Bryant & Co., 1864), 21–24, 39.

28. *Communication from the Comptroller Relative to Expenditures and Receipts of the County of New York, on Account of the Damage by Riots of 1863*, Vol. 2 (New York: The New York Printing Company, 1868), 18, https://digitalcollections.nypl.org/items/409d92c0-cb9c-0130-03e4-58d385a7bbd0/book#page/5/mode/2up.

29. Lyons, "Memories of Yesterday," 8–11.

30. Lyons, "Memories of Yesterday," 8; *U.S. Census, 1870*, New York City, Eighth Ward, 125.

31. Peterson, *Black Gotham*, 35–37, 122–123; Harris, *In the Shadow of Slavery*, 68, 73; Burrows and Wallace, *Gotham*, 317; White, *Prince of Darkness*, 16–18.

32. Peterson, *Black Gotham*, 283–305; Peterson, "Black Life in Freedom," 182–214.

33. "Indecent assault By A Colored Man," *Brooklyn*, Ap. 13, 1859, 2.

34. Peterson, *Black Gotham*, 303, 305–309. In an interview with Peterson on June 19, 2020, she was unfamiliar with the article and the incident.

35. *New York State Census, 1865*, Brooklyn, Ward 16, 91.

36. Peterson, "Black Life in Freedom," 211. "Laws of New York—By Authority, Ch. 770, "An Act to Incorporate the American and Foreign Commercial Company," Passed May 8, 1869, *Morning Express*, Albany, Sept. 10, 1869, www.fultonhistory.com, Albany NY *Morning Express* 1869–0882.pdf.

37. *Petitions*, vol. 4, 178-180. William A. Smith of Franklin Township, to James N. Gloucester, L529, P244, 1849.

38. William Blackstone, *Commentaries on the Laws of England*, Vol. 1, Oxford, 1765, 442–445; Norma Basch, *In the Eyes of the Law: Women, Marriage and Property in Nineteenth-Century New York* (Ithaca, NY: Cornell University Press, 1982), 42.

39. According to the 1855 *New York State Census*, Elizabeth's age of thirty-seven indicates that she was born in 1818. According to this and several other records, throughout her life Elizabeth was classified as "mulatto." Much of the information on the Gloucesters is from the series of articles in Brownstoner.com: http://www.brownstoner.com/history /walkabout-the-gloucester-family-of-brooklyn-part-1/ by Suzanne Spellen (aka Montrose Morris); http://www.brownstoner.com/history/walkabout-the-gloucester-family -of-brooklyn-part-2/ by Suzanne Spellen (aka Montrose Morris); http://www.brownstoner .com/brooklyn-life/walkabout-the-gloucester-family-of-brooklyn-part-3/ by Cate Corcoran.

40. After being deeply moved by the "gifted" abilities and ardent spirituality of his enslaved person, Gideon Blackburn, a Presbyterian minister and John Gloucester's enslaver taught him to preach the gospel and form a congregation for his Black Tennessee community. When Gloucester was able to buy his freedom, he was ordained as a minister in 1811 and moved to Philadelphia, where he founded the First African Presbyterian Church. He raised the money to buy the freedom of his wife and his then four children; see Anthony B. Pinn, ed., *African American Religious Cultures*, Volume 1, A–R, "African Americans in the Presbyterian Church" (Santa Barbara, ABC-CLIO, LLC, 2009), 39. For the influence of Gloucester on Samuel Cornish, see Graham Russell Hodges, *David Ruggles: A Radical Black Abolitionist and the Underground Railroad in New York City* (Chapel Hill: University of North Carolina Press, 2010), 37.

41. It took almost ten years until Gloucester founded the Shiloh Presbyterian Church. Perhaps he led another group at an earlier date. From about 1847 "the group led by Rev. Gloucester had been holding religious services as a mission under the supervision of the New School branch of presbytery. In the beginning, these were held in the Hall Buildings at the corner of Fulton and Cranberry Streets." http://www.siloam-brooklyn .org/history.

42. James and Elizabeth Gloucester to Talmage, L531, P601–603, 1849; Talmage to Elizabeth Gloucester, L531, P600, 1849. Ten years earlier Obadiah and Elizabeth Harding McCollin conducted the same the same legal process so she could hold the title as *feme sole*—legally transferring one of their two lots to Elizabeth by first selling the lot to

lawyer Augustus Floyd, who then conveyed it to Elizabeth alone. Obadiah and Elizabeth McCollin to Augustus Floyd, L401, P160, 1839; Floyd to Elizabeth McCollin, L401, P161, 1839.

43. Blackstone, *Commentaries on the Laws of England*, 442.

44. The laws & acts of the General assembly for Their Majesties province of New-York, as they were enacted in divers sessions, the first of which began April, the 9th, annoq; Domini, 1691 (Printed and sold by William Bradford, printer to Their Majesties, King William & Queen Mary, 1694); Joan R. Gundersen and Gwen Victor Gampel, "Married Women's Legal Status in Eighteenth-Century New York and Virginia," *The William and Mary Quarterly* 39, no. 1 (1982): 125, doi:10.2307/1923419. Deborah A. Rosen, "Women and Property Across Colonial America: A Comparison of Legal Systems in New Mexico and New York," *The William and Mary Quarterly* 60, no. 2 (Ap. 2003): 365, https://0-www-jstor-org.library.nysoclib.org/stable/pdf/3491767.pdf?ab_segments=0%2Fbasic_SYC-5187_SYC-5188%2Fcontrol&refreqid=fastly-default%3Acfde36ad565d6-326fb95d793f9d2da58; E[Lisha] P. Hurlburt, *Essays on Human Rights and their Political Guaranties* (New-York: Greeley & McElrath, 1845), 166–167, quoted in Lori D. Ginzburg, *Untidy Origins: A Story of Woman's Rights in Antebellum New York* (Chapel Hill, NC: University of North Carolina Press, 2005), 66.

45. James and Elizabeth Gloucester to Talmage, L204, P296, 1849, and Talmage to Elizabeth Gloucester, L204, P299, 1849, County of Kings. The indenture took place on July 21, 1848, shortly after the case of Thomas Baylis against James N. Gloucester and wife. The judgment in the Supreme Court ordered Sheriff Daniel Van Voorhis to sell the Prince and Willoughby lots that were eventually purchased by Elizabeth Gloucester; *Brooklyn*, July 20, 1849, 4. In 1849 Gloucester moved his congregation to Myrtle Avenue, and the following year Elizabeth purchased the site at 106 Prince Street, between Myrtle and Willoughby Avenues, where it was to remain for the following sixty years; http://www.siloam-brooklyn.org/history.html.

46. Jackson to Gloucester, L719, P212, 1856. See Ellen Hartigan-O'Connor. "Gender's Value in the History of Capitalism," *Journal of the Early Republic* 36, no. 4 (2016): 613–635.

47. Smith to Gloucester, L619, P65, 1850, with Gloucester assuming $250 of the mortgage toward the purchase price. The Colored Orphan Asylum was burned down in the Draft Riots in 1863; "The Colored Orphan Asylum," *The Weekly Anglo-African*, March 24, 1860, 2.

48. Williams to Gloucester, L525, P395, 1849. Lot 123 was in the Fifth Ward, the interracial working-class neighborhood bounded by West Broadway (then called Chappell Street), Hudson, and Leonard Streets, today's Tribeca. Williams had cofounded *Freedom's Journal*, the first African American owned and operated newspaper in the United States. He also founded the Phoenix Society, a mutual aid organization for African Americans, and he was a board member of the American Anti-Slavery Society that assisted runaway slaves. The Williamses' daughter, Amy Matilda, had a second marriage to Charles Lenox Remond, the Rhode Island Black abolitionist who was an intimate friend of Albro and Mary Joseph Lyons. He was a delegate to the Convention of 1843 in Buffalo.

49. *Brooklyn*, "Underground: The Remains of Mrs. E. A. Gloucester," Aug. 11, 1883, 4; https://www.brownstoner.com/history/walkabout-the-gloucester-family-of-brooklyn-part-2/

50. The historian Benjamin Quarles wrote, "Of the Blacks who corresponded with Brown, none spoke in more militant tones and sent him more money than clergyman James Newton Gloucester, whose donations were supplemented by those of his wife Elizabeth, a successful businesswoman." See Quarles, *Allies for Freedom & Blacks on John Brown* (Cambridge, MA: Da Capo, 2001), 3. Quarles also reproduces the complete text of the two letters from James N. Gloucester to John Brown in 1858. The original letters are in the John Brown Papers, 2–5, Kansas Historical Society, Topeka, https://www.kshs.org/archives/225810, https://www.kshs.org/archives/225811. Noted in Brown's diary that he wrote to J. N. Gloucester, Sept. 9, *Her.*, Oct. 25, 1859, 4.

51. The letter is in the Historical Society of Philadelphia, Digital Library, https://discover.hsp.org/Record/dc-8633; Quarles, *Allies for Freedom*, 2.

52. "The Funeral of a Colored Woman who was Said to Have Been the Richest of her Race in America: Beautiful Floral Tributes and Costly Trappings," *Brooklyn*, Aug. 11, 1883, 4; "Dusky Ducats," *Brooklyn*, Sept. 14, 1883, 4; "Mrs. Gloucester's Will to be Contested," *New York Globe*, Sept. 22, 1883, 3; "A Bone of Contention. Dr. Gloucester's Family Fight Over the Rich Colored Woman's Will," *Truth*, Sept. 16, 1883, 7; "Colored Croesuses," *Huntsville Gazette* (Huntsville, AL), Oct. 1, 1887, 2; "Events of Importance on Both Sides of the Atlantic," *Irish Nation*, New York, Aug. 18, 1883, 3; "Death of a Wealthy Colored Woman," *The Sun*, Baltimore, MD., Aug. 11, 1883, 3.

53. "The Literary Enterprise, " *New York Globe*, Dec. 15, 1883, 2. *Brooklyn*, Apr. 27, 1890, 12; May 16, 1887, 6; "Died," *Brooklyn*, Mar. 22, 1890; "Dr. Gloucester Left Two Wills," *Brooklyn*, Apr. 3, 1890; "Revocation of an Irrevocable Will," *Brooklyn*, July 18, 1890, 6; "A Will Contest," *Plaindealer*, Detroit, MI, Apr. 11, 1890, 4; "Dr. Gloucester's Two Wills," *New York Age*, Apr. 12, 1890, 2; "Mrs. Gloucester's Son in Trouble," *Trib.*, May 16, 1887, 1; "For Robbing His Father," *Kansas City Star*, Kansas City, MO, May 16, 1887, 1. James and Elizabeth Gloucester and six of their children are buried in Green-Wood Cemetery; they purchased plots in 1856 (L475, P67) and buried their son Alfred in 1859.

54. Wright to Gloucester, L612, P488, 1852; Foner, *Gateway to Freedom*, chapters 3 and 4, 63–118.

55. See *Minutes of the National Convention of Colored Citizens, held at Buffalo; on the 15th, 16th, 17th, 18th, and 19th of August, 1843; for the purpose of considering their moral and political condition as American citizens*, New York, 1843, 37–39, https://omeka.coloredconventions.org/items/show/278.

56. The New York City report was compiled by Gloucester and Wright and gives an overview of Black New York in 1843: "Colored inhabitants 16,000—churches 10; Methodist 6; Presbyterian 1; Baptist 2; Episcopalian 1—communicants 3000, including those attached to other churches—Sabbath-schools 13—district schools 5, one of which embraces 4 departments, and another 2 departments, with 12 colored teachers—select

schools 2—benevolent societies, male 13, female 15—temperance societies 4—literary societies, male 3, female 1—education societies 2—1 public library, with—volumes—public property, including churches, burying-grounds, and one public hall, 120,000 dollars— real estate difficult to estimate," *Minutes of the National Convention of Colored Citizens,* 39, https://omeka.coloredconventions.org/items/show/278.

57. Bella Gross, "Life and Times of Theodore S. Wright, 1797–1847," *Negro History Bulletin* 3, no. 9 (June 1940); Correspondence, Wright to Archibald Alexander, 11 Oct. 1836, published in *The Liberator,* Nov. 5, 1836; see also https://slavery.princeton.edu/stories/white-supremacy-at-commencement#ref-2.

58. Gross, "Life and Times of Theodore S. Wright," 133. Though William Lloyd Garrison opposed Wright after the split with the American Anti-Slavery Society, he still wrote a tribute to Wright after his untimely death in 1847; see Gross, 135.

59. Gross, "Life and Times of Theodore S. Wright," 135.

60. Wilder, *In the Company of Black Men,* 167–169; Foner, *Gateway to Freedom,* 99.

61. See Alexander Nazaryan, "New York City Would Really Rather Not Talk About Its Slavery-loving Past," *Newsweek,* Apr. 15, 2015, http://www.newsweek.com/2015/04/24/new-york-city-would-really-rather-not-talk-about-its-slavery-loving-past-321714.html.

62. "The Colored Orphans Asylum," *The Weekly Anglo-African,* Mar. 24, 1860; see Rosenzweig and Blackmar, *The Park and the People,* 73.

63. Henrietta Cordelia Ray and Florence Ray, *Sketch of the Life of Rev. Charles B. Ray,* 1887, https://archive.org/details/9342f943-b613-491a-9d22-1f733a906f7c/page/n33/mode/2up, 62; Foner, *Gateway to Freedom,* 86–87.

64. Ray, *Sketch of the Life of Rev. Charles B. Ray,* 27, 46–47.

65. The 1854 and 1855 assessments for Lot 47 indicated a house on the property, valued at $300 in 1854 and $400 in 1855, most likely a shanty. No house or remnant of a house appeared on the 1855 condemnation map, though if correct, the assessment would reinforce the idea of the property as a stop on the Underground Railroad. MANY, microfilm roll no. 177, 22nd Ward, 1849–1857.

66. McCormick to Ray, L557, P242, 1850.

67. *Minutes of the National Convention of Colored Citizens,* 31–36.

68. Harris, *In the Shadow of Slavery,* 275–277. Probate, Will of Huldah Green, L125, P332, 1858.

69. Harris, *In the Shadow of Slavery,* 239–240.

70. Whitehead to Jackson, L215, P31, 1827; Jackson to Lowery, L335, P33, 1835; *U.S. Census, 1830,* New York, Richmond, Southfield, Staten Island census and residential business directories at the NYPL; Call no. *ZI-497, reel 1. *New York State Census,* Richmond County, Westfield, Northfield, Southfield, Castleton. Thomas Jackson, perhaps a renter, still appears on the assessment rolls for lots 30 and 31 owned by Lowery, and also on lot 32 owned by Charles Sylvan that he sold to Joshua Cooper (L587, P601, 1851), though ownership is "Unknown" on the condemnation map. There are garden plots on the property, and Jackson may have farmed them himself or subleased them to someone in the community.

71. White landowners: Peter C. Doremus, Henry Gassin, Catherine Hennion, Peter Lynch, David R. Martin, Ebenezer Monroe, John Orser, John Pitts, Mary Quinn, George G.

Taylor, Christian Tietjen, William J. Sherwood, and Andrew C. Zabriskie. The racial identity of landowners Robert Marshall, Robert Gibbens, and Jeremiah Judson has not been determined at this writing.

72. For the extraordinary story of Andrew Williams and his family after Seneca Village, see Aaron Goodwin, *New York City Municipal Archives: An Authorized Guide for Family Historians* (New York: New York Genealogical and Biographical Society, 2016), 157–164.

73. "George W. Plunkitt Dies at 82 Years," *NYT*, Nov. 20, 1924, 16; "Plunkitt of Tammany Hall," *NYT*, Nov. 20, 1924, 22; see Rosenzweig and Blackmar, *The Park and the People*, 66, 547n15.

74. Rosenzweig and Blackmar, *The Park and the People*, 367–369.

75. George Washington Plunkitt, *Plunkitt of Tammany Hall: A Series of Very Plain Talks on Very Practical Politics, Delivered by Ex-senator George Washington Plunkitt, the Tammany Philosopher, from His Rostrum—the New York County Court House Bootblack Stand*, William L. Riordon, ed., Chapter 1, https://www.gutenberg.org/files/2810/2810-h/2810-h.htm.

11. DIVIDING HARLEM, 1825–1843

1. James Riker, *Revised History of Harlem (City of New York), Its Origin and Early Annals* (New York: New Harlem Publishing Company, 1904), 226.

2. *Conveyances on Record in the Registrar's Office by Dudley Selden, From the 1st January, 1825, to the 1st January, 1838* (New York: Alexander S. Gould, 1838), 69–73, https://babel.hathitrust.org/cgi/pt?id=nnc2.ark:/13960/t7rn6gz54&view=1up&seq=9. James Riker, *Harlem: Its Origins and Early Annals* (New York: self-pub., 1881), 413–414.

3. George Ashton Black, "The History of Municipal Ownership of Land on Manhattan Island" (Ph.D. diss., Columbia University, 1889), 25, citing Riker, *Revised History*, 252.

4. Riker, *Revised History*, 253.

5. *Conveyances on Record in the Registrar's Office by Dudley Selden*, 168–169; George Ashton Black, "The History of Municipal Ownership of Land on Manhattan Island" (PhD diss., Columbia University, 1889), 33. I. N. Phelps Stokes, *The Iconography of Manhattan Island*, vol. IV (New York: Robert Dodd, 1922), 842, 880. In 1806 (April 14), the Common Council appointed a committee to demarcate the boundaries with at least four monuments with "New York" on one side and "Harlem" on the other; Stokes, *Iconography*, vol. V, 1445, quoting the *MCC1784*, vol. 4: 178–179, https://babel.hathitrust.org/cgi/pt?id=nyp.33433081924841&view=1up&seq=189. The Harlem Commons covered a wedge of land in the prepark heading northwest from East Eighty-Seventh Street and Fifth Avenue to West Ninety-Third near Eight Avenue, north to 107th Street between Seventh and Eighth Avenues and southeast to Ninety-Sixth Street and Fifth Avenue. See map, Spielmann & Brush, in their very rare atlas, *Certified Copies of Original Maps of Property in New York City* (1881), copied from the original 1824 map by Charles Clinton, https://www.raremaps.com/gallery/detail/59385/harlem-map-of-the-harlaem-commons-surveyed-agreeably-to-t-spielmann-brush-clinton.

6. Transcription of Samson Benson McGowan testimony during the dispute concerning the Waldron family property of Edward Byrne, Dec. 26, 1857, *Petitions*, vol. 7, 594–626.

7. "Harlem Commons," *New-York Columbian*, Feb. 4, 1820, 2. Black, "The History of Municipal Ownership of Land on Manhattan Island," 33.

8. "Harlem Commons," *The National Advocate*, Oct. 8, 1824, 3. The ad ran almost daily until January 22, 1825. The New York common lands and the Harlem Commons line was surveyed in 1796 by Casimir Goerck and resurveyed in 1822 by Isaac Ludlum and Samuel Doughty.

9. Moses Yale Beach, *Wealth and Biography of the Wealthy Citizens of The City of New York City*, 12th ed. (New York: Sun Office, 1855), "Dudley Selden," 66, http://www.columbia.edu/cu/lweb/digital/collections/cul/texts/ldpd_6316657_000/ldpd_6316657_000.pdf.

10. Black, "The History of Municipal Ownership of Land on Manhattan Island," 34; Trustees for the Freeholders and other Inhabitants of Harlem to Selden, L194, P45, 1825; L214, P4,1826.

11. *Petitions*, vol. 7, folio 75–80.

12. The Real Estate Record Association, *A History of Real Estate, Building and Architecture in New York City During the Last Quarter of a Century* (New York: Record and Guide, 1898), 36.

13. Thanks to Muffy Floret for suggesting this connection.

14. Stokes, *Iconography*, vol. V, 1668; *MCC1784*, vol. 16: 228; vol. 17: 43–44; vol. 20: 110–111.

15. See agreement between Dudley Selden and Benjamin L. Benson, L383, P294, Apr. 3, 1828, 160; Benson to Watt, L230, P555, 1828; L241, P513, 1828; see also "Map of a tract of land belonging to Francis Price and Formerly of Benjamin L. Benson situated at Harlem," file no. 83, *Inventory of Register's Office Filed Maps*, Block 1111 Section 4, DOF.

16. Price and Wiswall notified the subscribers to lots on the "Benson Tract" to pay for their deeds or forfeit their claims, in "Notice," *Comm. Adv.*, Sept. 1, 1825, 4.

17. Anthony Lofaso, *Origins and History of the Village of Yorkville in the City of New York* (New York: Xlibris, 2010), 21–23.

18. *Laws of the State of New York Passed at the Forty-Ninth Session of the Legislature Begun and Held at the City of Albany the Third Day of January, 1826*, Chapter 290, "An Act to Incorporate the New-York Harlaem Spring Water Company," Apr. 18, 1826 (Albany: William Gould & Co., 1826), 337ff.

19. "Harlem Canal," *Comm. Adv.*, Oct. 30, 1827, 1.

20. Andrew McGowan, Jr., was on the board as was Archibald Watt, elected as Treasurer, *Comm. Adv.*, May 22, 1828.

21. Nutter to Price and other, L235, P278, July 17, 1827; Nutter to Harlem Canal Company, L246, P185, Dec. 9, 1828.

22. *Report of the Board of Directors of the Harlaem Canal Company*, Dec. 20, 1828 (New York: Grattan's Office, 1828), 7–8, NYHS.

23. *Report of the Board of Directors of the Harlaem Canal Company*, 8.

24. Gosman to Watt, L 234, P5, 1828; L259, P451, 1830. Although Watt had amassed almost all the real estate in the area of the proposed canal by the 1830s, he failed to gain title to the three-quarter-acre of Sarah Combs's property, a strong indication that they must have refused all offers.

25. Mayor, Aldermen and Commonalty of the City of New York to Watt, *Mortgage*, L114, P252, 1828; see *MCC1784* vol. 16: 387–391, 228; 549; vol. 17: 43–44, 110.

26. *Report of the Board of Directors of the Harlaem Canal Company*, 9.

27. *Report of the Board of Directors of the Harlaem Canal Company*, 8–10; Memorandum between David, William and Clinton Molenaor to Wiswall and Price, L232, P21, 1826; see also *Mortgages*, McKay to Price, L97, P293, also L232, P23; see also the invitation to Isaac Adriance, Esq., for the groundbreaking ceremony in "Harlem Papers, Misc.," folder 1820s, NYHS, Mss Collection (Harlem Papers).

28. Livingston to Nutter, May 27, 1827, NYHS, Mss Collection (AHMC-Livingston, Ann).

29. Nutter to Price and Wiswall, L235, P278, 1827. "Articles of Agreement, July 17, 1827, conveyed 110 acres [reserving one acre between 111 and 112 on west side of the line] for $400 per acre, payable $10,000 on or before Nov 16, with interest and remainder in three equal payments with interest, and with first payment received a Bond and mortgage or said premises to secure the payment of the residue of said purchase money. The second party have the privilege of entering the premises for purpose of surveying and laying out lots for contemplated canal which may pass across the same." The first payment was extended to December 26, then to February 15, 1828, and it was stipulated that "parties of second part are only required to pay $6,000 and the $4,000 remaining sum on first day of March." Nutter to Harlaem Canal Company, L246, P185, 1828.

30. Livingston to Nutter, L241, P110, 1828.

31. Livingston to Nutter, undated, NYHS, Mss Collection (AHMC-Livingston, Ann).

32. Chancery to Wilkins, L278, P366–371, 1831; Chancery to Wilkins L322, P385–393, 1834.

33. *William Smith vs. Enoch Wiswall and Francis Price*, in Jonathan Prescott Hall, *Cases argued and determined in the Superior court of the City of New-York*, vol. 2 (New York: Oliver Halstead, 1833), 469; "Mr. Pascalis, Mr. Kelly, Harlaem Canal Company," *New-York Spectator* 33, no. 48 (Jan. 29, 1830): 4; "Meant to Cut Manhattan in Two," *Her.*, Jan. 3, 1892, 10. On Molenaor property, see "Sheriff's Sale," *Morning Courier and New-York Enquirer*, Oct. 28, 1931, 2; "Chief Justice Decision," *EP*, May 17, 1832, 2.

34. *BA Docs, 1834/35*. vol. 1. doc. no. 45, Mar. 4, 1835, 521https://babel.hathitrust.org/cgi/pt?id=nyp.33433062753649&view=1up&seq=589&skin=2021.

35. Robert E. Deitz, *A Leaf from the Past: Deitz Then and Now: Origins of the Late Robert Edwin Deitz* (New York: R. E. Dietz Company, 1914), 45; John Flavel Mines, *A Tour Around Manhattan and My Summer Acre* (New York: Harper & Brothers, 1893), 456.

36. "A Rich Farm in Manhattan," *Kansas City Star*, Kansas City, MO, Jan. 23, 1904, 7.

37. "The Courts: Objections to a Sewer Assessment," *Trib.*, Apr. 9, 1875, 9; "Real Estate Derelicts Worth Fortunes: Romance of Un[k]nown Property in Greater New York," *Dallas Morning News*, Dallas, TX, Nov. 16, 1902, 19.

38. Quoted in Matthew Hale Smith, *Sunshine and Shadow in New York* (Hartford, CT: J. B. Burr and Company, 1868), 117.

39. *Real Estate Record and Builders' Guide* 1, no. 1 (Mar. 21, 1868): 2.

40. *Kansas City Star*, Jan. 23, 1904, 7; *NYT*, Dec. 9, 1908, 1. The *New York Times* (Apr. 9, 1911, 99) stated that Watt made his earliest purchase of real estate in 1810 in what would become Central Park. Research has not been able to support this statement.

41. "Miss Pinkney Dead, Leaving Millions," *NYT*, Dec. 9, 1908, 1; "Pinkney Millions Go to Watt Family," *NYT*, Dec. 16, 1908, 18; "Pinkney Estate in Auction Market," *NYT*, Apr. 9, 1911, 99.

42. For a more detailed discussion of her family and photographs of the mansion, see, https://daytoninmanhattan.blogspot.com/2019/07/the-lost-watt-pinckney-mansion-139th.html.

12. DIVIDING YORKVILLE, 1785-1835

1. Kaplan noted that they were already using "small blasts of dynamite" to plant new trees in the park. "Dynamite to Promote Tree Growth," *Twenty-Fifth Annual Report of the American Scenic and Historic Preservation Society*, 1920, Legislative Document No. 117 (Albany, NY: J. B. Lyon Company, 1920), 149–151; *Yale Forest School News* 8, no. 1 (January 1920): 12. The elms on the Mall today date from the planting in 1922.

2. I am grateful to Eric Sanderson for his help with this chapter and specifically for alerting me to more recent studies on the USGS (United States Geological Survey) website that date the schist to the "Lower Cambrian and or Late Proterozoic" (https://mrdata.usgs.gov/geology/state/sgmc-unit.php?unit=NJCAZm;10), and for the Ullman citation in the following note. Thanks also to Nick Tailby and Steven Jaret of the American Museum of Natural History and Professor Gilbert Hanson of the State University of New York at Stony Brook for the geological and ecological information they provided for this study. My deepest and most profound thanks to and fond memories of the late Sidney Horenstein, the genius of all things geologic in New York City. I enjoyed many years of his friendship and tutelage and regret our time together was much too short.

3. See David Ullman, "The retreat chronology of the Laurentide Ice Sheet during the last 10,000 years and implications for deglacial sea-level rise," in Vignettes: Key Concepts in Geomorphology, https://serc.carleton.edu/vignettes/collection/58451.html.

4. For a reference to the "broken" landscape, see, Frederick Law Olmsted and Calvert Vaux, "A Review of Recent Changes, and Changes which have been Projected, in the Plans of the Central Park, Letter I, A Consideration of Motives, Requirements and Restrictions Applicable to the General Scheme of the Park," in Frederick Law Olmsted, Sr., *Forty Years of Landscape Architecture: Central Park*, ed. Frederick Law Olmsted, Jr. and Theodora Kimball (Cambridge, MA: MIT Press, 1973), 251. Eric W. Sanderson, *Mannahatta: A Natural History of New York City* (New York: Abrams, 2009), 10. For an alternative interpretation of the name "Manahatta" see Ives Goddard, "The Origin and

Meaning of the Name 'Manhattan,' " *New York History* (Fall 2010): 277–291. https://repository.si.edu/bitstream/handle/10088/16790/anth_Manhattan.pdf?sequence=1.

5. "Probably not a square rood could be found, throughout which a crow-bar could be thrust its length into the ground without encountering rock. Often in places where no rock was visible, it has been found, in the progress of the work, to be within from three inches to two feet of the surface, for long distances together." *BCCP, Third Annual Report of the Board of Commissioners of the Central Park*, Jan. 1860 (New York: W. C. Bryant & Co., 1860), 35. For a diagram of the strata of geologic material, see *First Annual Report of the Improvement of the Central Park*, Doc. No. 5, January 1, 1857 (New York: Chas. W. Baker, 1857), opp. 24.

6. George Ashton Black traces the encroachments over time of private and common property on both the east and west sides in "The History of Municipal Ownership of Land on Manhattan Island," 49–52. Ownership was confirmed again in 1730 by the Montgomery Charter. I. N. Phelps Stokes, *The Iconography of Manhattan Island*, vol. III (New York: Robert Dodd, 1918), 869; James Riker, *Revised History of Harlem (City of New York), Its Origin and Early Annals* (New York: New Harlem Publishing Company, 1904), 413; Russell Shorto, "Laying the Groundwork, 1640 to 1800," in *New York Rising: An Illustrated History from the Durst Collection*, ed. Kate Ascher and Thomas Mellins (New York: The Monacelli Press, 2018), 18; Gerard Koeppel, *City on a Grid: How New York Became New York* (New York: Da Capo Press, 2015), 18; Richard Howe, "Notes on Casimir Goerck's 1785 and 1795 Surveys of the Common Lands of the City of New York," Gotham, A Blog for Scholars of New York City History, The Gotham Center for New York City History, https://www.gothamcenter.org/blog/notes-on-casimir-goercks-1785-and-1795-surveys-of-the-Common-Lands-of-the-city-of-new-york.

7. Issachar Cozzens Jr., *A Geological History of Manhattan or New York Island Together with a Map of the Island and a Suite of Sections, Tables and Columns, for the Study of Geology, Particularly Adapted for the American Student* (New York: W. E. Dean, 1843), 25, https://www.biodiversitylibrary.org/item/124972#page/33/mode/1up; Roswell Graves, Entry No. 25, *Descriptions for Designs for Improvement of Central Park, 1858; Third Annual Report of the Board of Commissioners of the Department of Public Parks for the Period of Twenty Months, From May 1st, 1872, to December 31st, 1873* (New York: William C. Bryant & Co., 1875), 57.

8. Viele, Entry No. 28 in Board of Commissioners of Central Park, *Catalogue of Plans for the Improvement of Central Park*, s.n. 1858, NYHS, Main Collection (Y1800 Boa Cat), 15.

9. *MCC1675*, vol. 2: 1697–1711, 258. See also other offenses to the city's property, *MCC1784*, vol. 1: 384, vol. 2: 174, vol 3: 205, vol. 19: 125. Many sources beginning with Roy Rosenzweig and Elizabeth Blackmar, *The Park and the People: A History of Central Park* (Ithaca, NY: Cornell University Press, 1992, 91, suggested that cutting firewood on city property was only deemed a "crime" in order to harass prepark residents. That may be so, however, the removal of natural resources from city owned property had been illegal since its earliest days.

10. George Ashton Black, "The History of Municipal Ownership of Land on Manhattan Island," 23–26.

11. *MCC1784*, vol. 1, 145; vol. 2, 216; Marguerite Hollowell, *The Measure of Manhattan: The Tumultuous Career and Surprising Legacy of John Randel Jr., Cartographer, Surveyor Inventor* (New York: Norton, 2013), 49–50; Koeppel, *City on a Grid*, 25–28.

12. See Stokes, *Iconography*, vol. III: Plate A. PL. 9 for Goerck's original drawings of the common lands of 1785 and 1796, 216.

13. "The Common Lands embrace a property which it is presumed will hereafter add much to the resources of the Corporation, every encouragement ought therefore to be offered to render them as valuable as possible. The [Finance] Committee [of the Common Council] are not acquainted with any measure more likely to produce that result than the general improvement of the adjoining land." *MCC1784*, vol. 8: Mar. 25, 1816, [354–356], 461–462.

14. The city sold 58 lots for a total of £17,600. The terms of the sale required "four bushels of wheat per annum forever," 10 percent of the money to be paid on the day of sale with an additional 10 percent on delivery of the deed and the remainder to be paid in four annual payments at 6 percent interest and secured by a mortgage. *MCC1784*, vol. 2: 304–306 includes a list of purchasers to November 22, 1796, the numbers of their lots, and the cost; see also list of purchasers in notes to *Map of the Common Lands from 59th to 76th Street Showing the Old Street and Mapped in 1796 by Cassimer T.H. Goerck, City Surveyor and Resurveyed by Isaac T. Ludlam in 1822*, https://earthworks.stanford.edu/catalog /princeton-z89orw67f.

15. Report of William Weston, Esq., "On the practicability of introducing the WATER of the River Bronx into this City," to be printed at the request of the Common Council, held on Saturday, the 16th day of March, 1799, *BA Docs.*, Doc. 61, 281–291; *New-York As It Is, in 1837: Containing, A General Description Of The City Of New-York, List Of Officers, Public Institutions, And Other Useful Information Including The Public Officers, Accompanied By A Correct Map* (New-York: J. Bisturnell, 1837), 15, https://babel.hathitrust.org /cgi/pt?id=hvd.32044009523366&view=1up&seq=9.

16. Victoria Johnson, *America's Eden: David Hosack, Botany, and Medicine in the Garden of the Early Republic* (New York: Norton, 2018), 175–191; Louis P. Tremante III, "Agriculture and Farm Life in the New York City Region, 1820–1870" (Ph.D. diss., Iowa State University, 2000), 207.

17. Mayor, Aldermen and Commonalty to Amory: L155, P14, 1804; L320, P268, 1825; L320, 294, 1827; L320, P297, 1823; L659, P132, 1800; L659, P137, 1799; L659, P139, 1816; L659, P140, 1815; L659, P142, 1816; Costard to Amory, L283, P500, 1832; Chancery to Amory: P178, P326, 1824; L320, P268, 1825; L320, P294, 1827. Chancery to Amory, L320, P264, 1823; L320, P267,1830; L178, P326, 1824. For Amory's common lands issues with the Common Council, see *MCC1784*, vol 3: 155, 462, 479, 501, 502, 729, 745; vol 8: 21, 638; vol. 9: 476, 569; vol. 11: 689, 749; vol. 12: 694; vol. 13: 15, 179, 251, 292; vol. 14: 336, 557, 558; vol. 15: 1, 53, 131; vol. 16: 141, 260, 516, 517, 561, 579.

18. "Auction," *NY Gaz.*, July 7, 1814, 4.

19. Catherine McNeur, *Taming Manhattan: Environmental Battles in the Antebellum City* (Cambridge, MA: Harvard University Press, 2014), 101–109.

20. BCCP, *Second Annual Report*, 1859 (New York: Wm. C. Bryant & Co., 1859), 4.

21. "Sales by Auction: By Martin Hoffman," *Morning Chronicle*, May 14, 1807, 6.

22. *NY Gaz.*, Dec, 24, 1811, 4; *EP*, May 16, 1831, 3.

23. "To Farmers, Gardeners & Milkmen," *EP*, Jan. 21, 1832, 4. See *Topographical Map of the City and County of New-York, and the adjacent Counties*, J. H. Colton, 1836, in Robert T. Augustyn and Paul E. Cohen, *Manhattan in Maps, 1527–2014* (New York: Rizzoli, 2006), 106–107; see also https://www.loc.gov/item/2007627512/.

24. Charles K. Graham, "Report of the First Division," *First Annual Report*, 46–53.

25. John Punnett Peters, *Annals of St. Michael's: Being the History of St. Michael's Episcopal Protestant Church for One Hundred Years 1807–1907* (New York: G. P. Putnam's Sons, The Knickerbocker Press, 1907), 92.

26. See the Colton map georeferencing, https://davidrumsey.georeferencer.com/maps /069f470a-8e8a-5488-8299-f481c69461fb/view

27. "Elegant Farm, " *EP*, July 24, 1820, 1.

28. The "Kilmer" elm, dedicated to the poet of "Trees," Joyce Kilmer, after his death in World War I. The tree is located inside the railing on the western side of the northwest quadrant of the Mall. There is a plaque dedicated to Kilmer at the base.

29. "To Land Speculators," *American*, Nov. 17, 1827, 2.

30. *EP*, Jan. 23, 1832, 4. The pond is still depicted in 1855 on lot 555 (between Seventieth and Seventy-First Street and Fifth to Sixth Avenue, now the East Green) in Roswell Graves, *Topographical Maps &c. in the Matter of Opening Central Park* (New York, July 1855), unpaginated, MANY.

31. *MCC1764*, vol. 3, Apr. 23, 1804, 501.

32. *MCC1764*, vol. 8, 461–62; vol. 11, July 28, 1821, 749.

33. "Only five of the 52 lots, the leases of which expired in 1833, were leased again in that year, though meanwhile two others had been leased for 21 years in 1832. After 1833 and until 1842 only six more were leased, none of them longer than to 1846. Beginning with 1842 the lots were let out in bulk from year to year in anticipation of sales on account of the sinking fund. Not one had been sold since 1827," Black, "The History of Municipal Ownership of Land on Manhattan Island," 45.

34. Amory was the highest bidder at the 1822 auction for the three-story brick store for $1,875. The following year the city purchased it from Amory for $3,000; Amory to Mayor, Aldermen and Commonalty, L170, P28, 1823. *MCC1764*, vol. 14: Apr. 1823, 15. As an example of the price of common lands property versus downtown property, Robert Lenox bought his three common lands lots, 125, 128 and 131, today's Seventy-First to Seventy-Fourth Street, Fifth to Madison, in 1818 for $500 (L125, P569). Three years later he bought three lots, 8, 9, and 11, near fashionable Bowling Green for $8,250.

35. The Common Council was willing to sell lot 110 in 1820 but had no buyers until Amory made his proposal in 1825; see *MCC1764*, vol. 10: 741; vol. 15: 1, 53, 131; vol. 16: 141–142, 516, 561, 579.

36. *NY Gaz.*, May 15, 1780, 2.

37. The inscription "Amory & Johnson Makers New York," most likely refer to the makers John Amory, whipmaker, and Samuel Johnson, silversmith; see *The New York Directory and Register for the Year 1790* (New York: Hodge, Allen and Campbell, 1790), 27, 56). In the 1792 directory (page 7), James Amory was also listed separately from his father, and Samuel Johnson (spelled Johnston) was listed as a goldsmith. Thanks to Assistant Curator Jessie MacLeod for her help in trying to determine a date for the crop's purchase (MacLeod to author, Dec. 14, 2017). The whip is described as "Silver-headed riding crop with a tapered wooden shaft or stock. Handle is spiral wrapped with a narrow, channeled strip of horn and silver braid or twisted wire; horn is secured at lower end with an iron nail or brad. Central section is spiral wrapped with a double-ply natural fiber (possibly hemp) woven in a herringbone pattern. Stitched leather loop (modern) attached at tapered end. Silver head is engraved on top with script initials or monogram: 'GW' bordered by scrolls, and around ferrule with geometric bands along top and bottom." http:// www.mountvernon.org/preservation/collections-holdings/browse-the-museum -collections/object/w-1213. The "natural fiber" mentioned in the entry was most likely the catgut that Amory used in his whips. John Amory, whipmaker at 27 Broadway, first appears in *The New York Directory and Register for the Year 1790*, 7.

38. Loyalist John Amory married Mary Delamontagnie in 1777. Her first husband, Abraham Delamontagnie, a patriot, was the grandson of Johannes de la Montagne.

39. Amory to King, June 8, 1797, letter no. 112, NYHS, Rufus King Papers, Mss collection (BV King Rufus).

40. As early as September 1791, James Amory placed an ad in the *New-York Gazette:* "James Amory Whip & Cane Manufactory No. 99 Broadway opposite Trinity Church. He also cuts whatever whalebone [scrimshaw] in the best and most approved manner." *NY Gaz.*, Sept. 1, 1791, 3.

41. Amory to King, Nov. 16, 1798, letter no. 113; Amory to King, Nov. 16, 1798, letter no. 120, Dec. 4, 1798: Rufus King Papers, Mss collection (BV King Rufus).

42. Johnson, *America's Eden*, 84.

43. Bob Arnebeck, "Yellow Fever in New York City, 1791–1799," paper presented at the 26th Conference on New York State History, June 9–11, 2005, Syracuse, NY. Bayley quotes from *An Account of the Epidemic Fever which prevailed in the City of New York*, 1796; http://bobarnebeck.com/yfinnyc.html.

44. Amory to King, Nov. 16, 1798, letter no. 120, NYHS, Rufus King papers (Mss collection) BV King Rufus).

45. Amory to King, Nov. 12, 1800, letter no. 122, NYHS, Rufus King Papers, box 32, (Mss collection) BV King Rufus).

46. "James Amory, Whip Maker," *NY Gaz.*, Oct. 27, 1806, 2.

47. "James Amory, Whip Maker," *NY Gaz.*, Nov. 4, 1806, 4. He continued this ad almost daily until January 29, 1807.

47. "James Amory, Whip Maker," *NY Gaz.*, May 1, 1807, 4.

49. "Fifty Dollar Reward," *NY Gaz.*, Aug. 4, 1813, 2; "Twenty Dollars Reward," *NY Gaz.*, Aug. 15, 1817, 4.

50. Shane White, *Somewhat More Independent: The End of Slavery in New York City 1770–1810* (Athens: University of Georgia Press, 1991), 35–36.

51. "James Amory, Whip Maker," *NY Gaz.*, Feb. 2, 1807, 4; Mar. 13, 1810, 4.

52. "Old established Whip Manufactory for Sale," *NY Gaz.*, Jul 25, 1818, 3.

53. Howard B. Rock, "The American Revolution and the Mechanics of New York City: One Generation Later," *New York History* 57, no. 3 (July 1976): 392; http://www.jstor.org/stable/23169485.

54. "Old established Whip Manufactory for Sale," *NY Gaz.*, July 24, 1818; Edwin G. Burrows and Mike Wallace, *Gotham: A History of New York City to 1898* (New York and Oxford: Oxford University Press, 1999), 413–414; Rock, "The American Revolution and the Mechanics of New York City," 367–394.

55. "To Farmers, Gardeners & Milkmen," *NY Gaz.*, Jan. 23, 1832, 4.

56. *MCC1784*, vol. 2: 304, for lease to David Wagstaff of lot 150; vol. 3: 18, 155, 463. *MCC1784*, vol. 2: 744, purchase of David Wagstaff of lots 141 and 143; see also vol. 13: 180, 249, 657, 685; vol. 15: 617; *New York Gazette* March 14, 1817 Vol XXVII, 1.

57. *NY Gaz.*, Mar. 14, 1817, 1.

58. James C.S. Sinclair, "Report on the Progress in Second Division," Dec. 31, 1856, *First Annual Report*, 55.

59. *Spectator*, May 21, 1822, 2; see also, *New York Daily Advertiser* June 20, 1820, 2; *EP*, Mar. 6, 1824, 3.

60. Anthony Lofaso, *Origins and History of the Village of Yorkville in the City of New York* (New York: Xlibris, 2010), 25–26.

61. Wagstaff, *Jury Census for 1821*, MANY

62. Last Will and Testament of David Wagstaff, *Probate*, L62, P327, 1824.

63. *MCC1784*, vol. 2: 744; vol. 3: 18, 155, 463; vol. 13: 180, 249, 657, 685; vol. 15: 617.

64. Apthorp to Wagstaff, L75, P90, 1807.

65. The *New York State Census* for July 6, 1855, Ward 22, E.D. 3, listed four Black or "mulatto" families: Abraham and Jane Connover and their grandchild; Daniel and Margaret Johnson and their three children, all described as "mulatto"; Egbert Styers, Black, and his wife, Catherine, a mulatto; and a single Black woman, Ann McDonald. The Black family of John and Margaret Stone and their three children are listed in the *New York State Census, 1855*, Ward 12, E.D. 3, and on the condemnation map as living in the house on block 780, belonging to the Wagstaffs. According to the census, these families lived near the German-born households of Elizabeth Rusket, Mary Peach, and Stephen Close (or Clark), who lived between Sixth and Seventh Avenues, Seventy-Seventh to Seventy-Ninth Streets. The white families were still living there ten months later when they were included in the city's list of renters of May 21, 1856, though the four Black families were no longer listed (see chapter 17, "The Renters").

66. Scott to Craig, L186, P130, 132, 1825; lease of lot 133 to Samuel D. Craig, *MCC1784*, vol. 17: 729; see *Petitions*, vol. 3, Samuel D. Craig claims he is the "unknown owners"

of lot 41, with a "substantial stone wall and cultivated and improved as an orchard." He also claimed the properties of Fred Vanderpoel, John Garcia, States Wilkins, and Henry Dol, who were his tenants.

67. Charles E. Beveridge and David Schuyler, eds., *Papers of Frederick Law Olmsted* "Creating Central Park," Vol. III (Baltimore, MD: Johns Hopkins University Press, 1983), 116.

68. James C.S. Sinclair, *First Annual Report*, 54.

69. Green to Wilson, L475, P537, 1846; Wilson to Wagstaff, L494, P277, 1847; Wagstaff to Wilson, L547, P69, 1847.

70. The Wagstaffs were also connected to Seneca Village through their membership in St. Michael's Church. Even though they lived in Yorkville, three generations of Wagstaffs are recorded: David and Sarah Ann, his wife from 1769 to 1854; second generation David and Sarah Ann, and a granddaughter, baptized in 1820. The family had a vault in St. Michael's, which "kept the Wagstaffs in touch with that church, where, however, they were baptized and married as well as buried." Peters, *Annals of St. Michael's*, 119.

71. Wagstaff to Wilson, L611, P120, 1852. Gratitude to attorney Robert Ritter, for an explanation of "next friend"; email to author, Nov. 3, 2017.

72. Last Will and Testament of Sarah Ann Wagstaff, Court of the Surrogate, County of New York, *Probate*, L109, P373, Apr. 7, 1854; for fire, see chapter 10.

73. Thomas McClure Peters, "Baptisms, Confirmations, Marriages and Burials for the years 1847 to 1865," *All Angels' Church, New York City, Parish Record Book, 1847–1874* (All Angels' Church, Office of the Rector). The Wagstaffs may have also known James and Marcy Hunt, as their mortgage was from William Wagstaff, the executor of his father's estate; see Shane White, *Prince of Darkness: The Untold Story of Jeremiah G. Hamilton, Wall Street's First Black Millionaire* (New York: St. Martin's Press, 2015), 140.

74. Gustavus Myers, *The History of Tammany Hall*, 2nd ed. (New York: Boni & Liveright, 1917), 13, 23.

75. Tax Assessments, 1812–1840; Ninth Ward for years 1813, 1814, and 1815, microfilm roll no. 45, MANY.

76. Edward Hagaman Hall, *McGown's Pass and Vicinity* (New York: The American Scenic and Historic Preservation Society, 1905), 22–23.

77. Robert E. Cray, "Commemorating the Prison Ship Dead: Revolutionary Memory and the Politics of Sculpture in the Early Republic, 1776–1808," *The William and Mary Quarterly* 56, no. 3 (1999): 565–590. doi:10.2307/2674561; Myers, *History of Tammany Hall*, 22.

78. "Prison Ship Martyrs Monument," Historic signs, New York City Department of Parks & Recreation, https://www.nycgovparks.org/parks/fort-greene-park/monuments/1222.

13. THE RECEIVING RESERVOIR, 1835-1842

1. Charles Rosenberg, *The Cholera Years: The United States in 1832, 1849, and 1866* (Chicago: University of Chicago Press, 1987), 25–26; Benjamin Miller, *Fat of the Land: Garbage of New York the Last Two Hundred Years* (New York: Four Walls Eight Windows, 2000),

17–21; Catherine McNeur, *Taming Manhattan: Environmental Battles in the Antebellum City* (Cambridge, MA: Harvard University Press, 2014), 109–119.

2. Rosenberg, *The Cholera Years*, 3.

3. Rosenberg, *The Cholera Years*, 40–54.

4. Hone Diary, 71, quoted in Carla L. Peterson, *Black Gotham: A Family History of African Americans in Nineteenth-Century New York City* (New Haven, CT: Yale University Press, 2012), 95–96.

5. John Wilson Stebbins to Henry Stebbins, Nov. 13, 1832, unpublished, private collection.

6. Ralph Stebbins Greenlee and Robert Lemuel Greenlee, *The Stebbins Genealogy*, 2 vols. (Chicago, 1904), vol. I, 497; https://archive.org/stream/stebbinsgenealog01gree#page/496/mode/2up/search/John+Wilson+Stebbins; See also Sara Cedar Miller, *Central Park, An American Masterpiece: A Comprehensive History of the Nation's First Urban Park* (New York: Abrams, 2003), 62–67.

7. McNeur, *Taming Manhattan*, 119. Calculations based on cubic yards to tons, in https://scdhec.gov/sites/default/files/Library/CR-011175.pdf.

8. Charles King, *A Memoir of the Construction, Cost, and Capacity of the Croton Aqueduct: compiled from Official Documents: Together with an Account of the Civic Celebration of the fourteenth October, 1842, on Occasion of the Completion of the Great Work: preceded by a Preliminary Essay on Ancient and Modern Aqueducts* (New York: self-pub., 1843); John Bloomfield Jervis, *Description of the Croton Aqueduct* (New York: Slam & Guion, 1842); John Bloomfield Jervis Papers, Jervis Public Library, Rome, NY; Fayette B. Tower, *Illustrations of the Croton Aqueduct* (New York: Wiley and Putnam, 1843); Theophil Schramke, *Description of the New-York Croton Aqueduct: in English, German and French* (New York: self-pub., 1846); Edward Wegman, *The Water Supply of New York, 1658–1895* (New York: John Wiley and Sons, 1896); *Reduced Copies Of Measured Drawings Written Historical And Descriptive Data Photographs, Historic American Engineering Record, New York-120, Old Croton Aqueduct*, Historic American Engineering Record, National Park Service, Department of the Interior, Washington, D.C.; Nelson Manfred Blake, *Water for the Cities: A History of the Water Supply Problem in the United States* (Syracuse, NY: Syracuse University Press, 1956), 121–171; Gerard T. Koeppel, *Water for Gotham: A History* (Princeton: Princeton University Press, 2000); https://crotonhistory.org/resources/.

9. "Report of Mr. D.B. Douglass to the Commissioners for Supplying the City of New-York pure and wholesome Water," *BA Docs.*, Doc. no. 44, Feb. 1, 1835, 403–433; Doc. no. 84, Dec. 19, 1836, "The Commissioners have deemed a property belonging to the Corporation in the 12th Ward is in all respects suitable." They estimated that five-sevenths of the tract belonged to the corporation.

10. King, *A Memoir of the Construction*, 193, 198.

11. Blake, *Water for the Cities*, 158–159, quoted in Koeppel, *Water for Gotham*, 254.

12. King, *A Memoir of the Construction*, 182.

13. Wealthy merchant Robert Lenox leased two common lands lots and purchased two others from Andrew Ogden on the site of the future receiving reservoir, but by 1818, he

conveyed all four lots back to the Mayor, Aldermen and Commonalty of the City of New York, L131, P205, 1818.

14. Joseph Alfred Scovill [Walter Barrett], *The Old Merchants of New York* (New York: Thomas R. Knox, 1864–70), vol. 3, 117. Bradhurst and Field also owned three other common lands lots that are today's Conservatory Water, from Seventy-Fourth to Seventy-Sixth Street, Fifth to Sixth Avenue. For their reservoir property, the Heirs of Moses Field was awarded $11,000.

15. See William Mathews, listed in *Longworth's American Almanac New-York Register and City Directory* 1801, 230. William Mathews has been confused with William Mathew, who was a resident of Seneca Village, and conjectured to be among the residents of a Black community on York Hill that was displaced due to the construction of the receiving reservoir. There is no documentation that this community existed; the idea was based on a misunderstanding of Peters's text. (See chapter 9, note 122.)

16. Teunis G. Bergen, *The Bergen Family; Or: The Descendants of Hans Hansen Bergen, One of the Early Settlers of New York and Brooklyn, L.I.* (New York: Bergen & Tripp, 1866), 294. Roy Rosenzweig and Elizabeth Blackmar refer to his name as "Tums" in *The Park and the People: A History of Central Park* (Ithaca, NY: Cornell University Press, 1992), 547n13, probably a typo. It is spelled correctly in *BA Docs.*, 4, no. 10, "Semi-Annual Report of the Water Commissioners," Jan. 1–June 30, 1839, 139, https://books.google.com/books?id=CmI-AAAAYAAJ&pg=PA115#v=onepage&q=tunis&f=false.

17. Mayor, Aldermen, and Commonalty of the City of New York to Tunis Van Brunt, L368, P350, 1838.

18. Koppel, *Water for Gotham*, 231.

19. New York and Harlem Railroad fare to receiving reservoir from City-Hall 3¼ miles 12½ cents; Edward Ruggles, *A Picture of New York in 1846; With a Short Account of Places in its Vicinity; Designed as a Guide to Citizens and Stranger* (New York: Homans & Ellis, 1846), 86.

20. Chancery to Dobbin, L213, P199, 1827; *MCC Proceedings Asst. Ald.*, 1846, vol. 28: 204, 252, 254. See Last Will and Testament of James Dobbin, *Probate*, L80, P443, 1839.

21. "Board of Aldermen: Petitions," *Comm. Adv.*, Aug. 1, 1843, 1.

22. "Wars of the Water Works!" *Comm. Adv.*, Apr., 10, 1840, 1; Koeppel, *Water for Gotham*, 249–253, 335n11.

23. "Another Great Excitement," *Morning Herald*, Apr. 7, 1840, 2.

24. "Another Great Excitement," *Morning Herald*, Apr. 7, 1840, 2.

25. Whitehead to Scott, L288, P578, 1827, for eleven lots and lot 198. Scott to Pitcher, L309, P314, 1834; Pitcher to Root, L337, P96, 1835; *Mortgages*, L187, P176, 1836, canceled May 11, 1836. In 1840, the city assessed the property at $1,600.

26. Scovill, *The Old Merchants of New York*, vol. 1, 319–320.

27. Root was on the Board of Directors of the Hudson Fire Company. See Hudson Fire Insurance Company to Root, *Mortgages*, L225, P276, 1838.

28. Scovill. *The Old Merchants of New York*, vol. 1, 319–320.

29. "Reservoir House," *Comm. Adv.*, New York, Mar. 23, 1846, 4, signed W. Hurry, 13 Wall Street, the same address as architect Edmund Hurry, who placed an ad in the *New York Journal of Commerce* (May 11, 1848, 2) announcing the move of the office from 13 Wall Street to 14 Wall Street. William and Edmund are listed as architects at 13 and 14 Wall Street, respectively, in *Doggett's New York City Directory, 1848–1849* (New York: John Doggett, Jr., 1848), 212.

30. Root declared bankruptcy on January 31, 1843, but he was still on the rolls of tax assessments for 1843. The Hudson Fire Company paid the taxes from 1842 to 1848.

31. Edmund Hurry lived on the premises with his wife, Eliza; children, Edmund and Sophia; and servants or boarders, Pat Quigley and Ellen Hollington; *U.S. Census, 1850*, New York City, 19th Ward.

32. By 1850 the property was given over to the Corporation of the City of New York for the reservoir keeper's home, barn, and stable, see Tax Assessments for the years 1842 to 1848, microfilm rolls nos. 66 and 67, MANY.

33. New York (N.Y.) Commissioners of the Croton Aqueduct Board, *New York City Croton Aqueduct records, 1835–1884*, Disbursements 1854–1864, Manuscript Division, NYPL.

34. Education Department, *Seneca Village: A Teacher's Guide to Using Primary Sources in the Classroom* (New York: New-York Historical Society, 2010), 12; Wallace's letter is in the Library of Congress.

35. See entry for Feb. 27, 1857, *New York City Croton Aqueduct records, 1835–1884*, in "Mss Coll 2163, Disbursements 1854–1864, New York (N.Y.) Commissioners of the Croton Aqueduct Department," Manuscripts & Archives, NYPL.

36. "Croton Ice," *Comm. Adv.*, Mar. 7, 1843, 2.

37. "Report of Committee on Lands and Places, on leasing lands in Twelfth Ward," *BA Docs.*, Doc. no. 49, Dec. 5, 1842, 447–451.

38. Cindy R. Lobel, *Urban Appetites: Food and Culture in Nineteenth-Century New York* (Chicago: University of Chicago Press, 2014), 46–47.

39. Lazarus White, *The Catskill Water Supply of New York City: History, Location, Sub-Surface, Investigations and Construction* (New York: John Wiley & Sons, 1913), 8.

40. *BA Docs.*, June 1851 to Jan. 1852, vol. 18—Part 2, Doc. no. 81, Dec. 31, 1851 (New York: McSpedon & Baker, 1852), 1421; *Abstract of Corporation Ordinances, And Rules and Regulations adopted by the Croton Aqueduct Board in relation to Water, to which the attention of Consumers, and all others is earnestly invited* (New York: Collins, Browne & Co., 1855).

41. *CAB, Annual Report of the Croton Aqueduct Department made to the Common Council of the City of New York*, Jan. 3, 1853 (New York: McSpedon & Baker, 1853), 15–16.

14. A CHANGING LAND, 1845–1853

1. Ira Rosenwaike, *Population History of New York City* (Syracuse, NY: Syracuse University Press, 1972), 16, 33–54; Robert Ernst, *Immigrant Life in New York City, 1825–1863*

(Syracuse, NY: Syracuse University Press, 1994), 20; Edward K. Spann, *The New Metropolis: New York City 1840–1857* (New York: Columbia University Press, 1981), 23–24, tables, 430, 432; Frederick M. Binder and David M. Reimers, *All the Nations Under Heaven: An Ethnic and Racial History of New York City* (New York: Columbia University Press, 1995), 33–93; Sean Wilentz, *Chants Democratic: New York City and the Rise of the American Working Class, 1788–1850* (New York: Oxford University Press, 1984), 109–110. I am grateful to Catherine McNeur for reading the chapter and making many valuable edits and suggestions.

2. Sister Marie de Lourdes Walsh, *The Sisters of Charity of New York 1809–1959*, vol. 1 (New York, Fordham University Press, 1960), 150. Tyler Anbinder, *City of Dreams: The 400-Year Epic History of Immigrant New York* (New York: Houghton Mifflin Harcourt, 2016), "Kleindeutschland," 173.

3. Tyler Anbinder, *Nativism and Slavery: The Northern Know Nothings and the Politics of the 1850s* (New York: Oxford University Press, 1992), 11.

4. Robert Ernst, "Economic Nativism in New York City During the 1840s," *New York History* 29, no. 2 (1948): 170–186, http://www.jstor.org/stable/23149135. Morse authored *Conspiracy Against the Liberties of the United States*, where he charged the Vatican of sabotaging the values and ideals of Protestant America. Roy Rosenzweig and Elizabeth Blackmar, *The Park and the People: A History of Central Park* (Ithaca, NY: Cornell University Press, 1992), 98.

5. *New York State Census, 1855*, New York City, Ward 22, E.D. 3, Part 4, "Marriages and Deaths," unpaginated.

6. Robert Scally, "Liverpool Ships and Irish Emigrants in the Age of Sail," *Journal of Social History* 17, no. 1 (Autumn 1983): 5–30.

7. Joyce Goodfriend, "Upon a bunch of Straw: The Irish in Colonial New York City," in *The New York Irish*, ed. Ronald H. Bayor and Timothy J. Meagher (Baltimore, MD: Johns Hopkins University Press, 1996), 35–47; Patrick McGrath, "Secular Power, Sectarian Politics: The American-Born Irish Elite and Catholic Political Culture in Nineteenth-Century New York," *Journal of American Ethnic History* 38, no. 3 (Spring 2019): 36–75. www.jstor.org/stable/10.5406/jamerethnhist.38.3.0036.

8. Edwin G. Burrows and Mike Wallace, *Gotham: A History of New York City to 1898* (New York and Oxford: Oxford University Press, 1999), 743.

9. My thanks to Stephen Wesley for this information.

10. Cormac Ó Gráda, *Famine: A Short History* (Princeton, NJ: Princeton University Press, 2009), 77. Kerby A. Miller, *Emigrants and Exiles: Ireland and the Irish Exodus to North America* (New York: Oxford University Press, 1985), 281; "Food in Ireland 1600–1835," https://www.dochara.com/the-irish/food-history/food-in-ireland-1600-1835/.

11. Arthur Gribben, ed., *The Great Famine and the Irish Diaspora in America* (Amherst: University of Massachusetts Press, 1999), 181. Anbinder, *City of Dreams*, 129–148; Kerby A. Miller, *Emigrants and Exiles: Ireland and the Irish Exodus to North America* (New York: Oxford University Press, 1985), 280–344; Jay P. Dolan, *The Irish Americans:*

A History (New York: Bloomsbury, 2008), 78; Hasia R. Diner, " 'The Most Irish City in the Union': The Era of the Great Migration, 1844–1877," in *The New York Irish*, ed. Ronald H. Bayor and Timothy J. Meagher (Baltimore, MD: Johns Hopkins University Press, 1996), 87–106.

12. Marion McGarry, Galway Mayo Institute of Technology, "Room to improve: the homes of Ireland's 19th century rural poor," January 8, 2019, https://www.rte.ie/brainstorm/2019 /0107/1021775-room-to-improve-the-homes-of-irelands-19th-century-rural-poor/. For a description of the construction of these huts, see "Earthen homes stuck with muddy image," *Irish Times*, Aug. 23, 1997, https://www.irishtimes.com/news/earthern -homes-stuck-with-muddy-image-1.99733.

13. John Punnett Peters, *Annals of St. Michael's: Being the History of St. Michael's Episcopal Protestant Church for One Hundred Years 1807–1907* (New York: G. P. Putnam's Sons, The Knickerbocker Press, 1907), 93. Peters suggested that the structure was the remnant of a former "imposing timber structure, but was now far advanced in ruin." If so, it is more likely that the earthen structure was built into the old foundation.

14. Jean Zimmerman, *The Woman of the House* (New York: Harcourt, 2016), 36.

15. "The Central Park," *Her.*, June 5, 1856, 1.

16. James Reuel Smith, *The Springs and Wells of Manhattan and the Bronx* (New York: New York Historical Society, 1938), 13.

17. Catherine McNeur, *Taming Manhattan: Environmental Battles in the Antebellum City* (Cambridge, MA: Harvard University Press, 2014), 128–129.

18. Joel Tarr, "The Search for the Ultimate Sink: Urban Air, Land, and Water Pollution in Historical Perspective," *Records of the Columbia Historical Society, Washington, D.C.* 51 (1984): 22, http://www.jstor.org/stable/40067842.

19. McNeur, *Taming Manhattan*, 165.

20. Beveridge, *PFLO*, vol. 3, "The Greensward Plan: 1858, Particulars of Construction and Estimate for a Plan of the Central Park," 153.

21. Chris Mayda, "Pig Pens, Hog Houses, and Manure Pits: A Century of Change in Hog Production," *Material Culture* 36, no. 1 (2004): 18–42; Enrique Alonso and Ana Recarte, *Pigs in New York City: A Study on 19th-Century Urban "Sanitation,"* Friends of Thoreau Environmental Program Research Institute of North American Studies, University of Alcalá, Spain, http://www.institutofranklin.net/sites/default/files/fckeditor/CS%20Pigs %20in%20New%20York.pdf.

22. Melanie A. Kiechle, "Preserving the Unpleasant: Sources, Methods, and Conjectures for Odors at Historic Sites," *Future Anterior: Journal of Historic Preservation, History, Theory, and Criticism* 13, no. 2 (Winter 2016): 23–31; McNeur, *Taming Manhattan*, 161. My gratitude to Catherine McNeur for suggesting that I research the history of odors and specifically recommending the work of Kiechle as well as Connie Chang's *Shaping the Shoreline*. Her own work, *Taming Manhattan*, discusses the class differentiation of odors.

23. Frederick Law Olmsted Jr. and Theodora Kimball, eds., *Forty Years of Landscape Architecture: Central Park* (Cambridge, MA: MIT Press, 1973), 215; Charles Bethea, "Flooding

from Hurricane Florence Threatens to Overwhelm Manure Lagoons," *The New Yorker*, Sept. 15, 2018. Iowan quote by Ina Yalof offered in conversation.

24. "Agriculture: Water, Air Quality Fears Conflict with Pig Farms," Feb. 16, 2015, https://www.cnbc.com/2015/02/16/water-air-quality-fears-conflict-with-pig-farms.html

25. *BCCP Docs.*, Doc. no. 16, Mar. 16, 1858, Egbert Viele, "The Drainage of the Central Park," 1; *New York State Census, 1855*, Ward 22, E.D. 3, IV. Marriages and Deaths, unpaginated, quoted in Rosenzweig and Blackmar, *The Park and the People*, 74.

26. Brady to Metzger, L649, P96, 1853; Brady to Stroh and Hess, L646, P243, 1853.

27. I am grateful to Sr. Regina Bechtle and Mindy S. Gordon of the Sisters of Charity of New York for reading and editing this chapter of the manuscript.

28. Ernst, *Immigrant Life in New York City*, chapter 12, 135–149; E. K. Spann, *The New Metropolis: New York City 1840–1857* (New York: Columbia University Press, 1981), 28–34.

29. Joseph J. McCadden, "Bishop Hughes versus the Public School Society of New York," *The Catholic Historical Review* 50, no. 2 (1964): 188–207.

30. "Bishop Hughes Reply to the Address," *Freeman's Journal*, Sept. 4, 1841, 4.

31. John Hughes, *Address of the Roman Catholics to fellow citizens of the city and state of New York* (New York: H. Cassidy, 1840). Leo Hershkowitz, "The Irish and the Emerging City: Settlement to 1844," in *The New York Irish*, ed. Ronald H. Bayer and Timothy J. Meager (Baltimore, MD: John Hopkins University Press, 1996), 11–34: John Loughery, *Dagger John: Archbishop John Hughes and the Making of Irish America* (Ithaca, NY: Cornell University Press, 2018), 121–138.

32. James J. Doherty, *Life of Mother Elizabeth Boyle: One of Mother Seaton's Companions, the Assistant Mother Under Her for Eight Years and First Superioress of 'The Sisters of Charity of St. Vincent de Paul' of New York City* (Mount Loretto, Staten Island: Mission of the Immaculate Virgin, 1893), 224.

33. Walsh, *The Sisters of Charity*, vol. 1, 138; Doherty, *Life of Mother Elizabeth Boyle*, 186.

34. Elizabeth Boyle to Sisters of Charity, L527, P462, 1849, for $6,000; "The cathedral trustees had loaned Mother Elizabeth ten thousand dollars to purchase the property. It was to be refunded with interest dating from July, 1849, 'provided that the institution could pay such interest with convenience and justice to other creditors.' " "One of the other creditors was Thomas McGowan, who held a mortgage of four thousand dollars, bearing interest at seven percent," Walsh, *The Sisters of Charity*, vol. 1, 140. The said "Thomas McGowan" was more likely either Thomas Odell or Andrew McGowan. There was no Thomas McGowan in the family, but Catherine McGowan's sister was Anne Odell, married to John Odell of Westchester.

35. In 1881, a fire claimed the old convent and the remains of the McGowans' home. *NYT*, Jan. 2, 1881. Two years later, a second restaurant, the Mount St. Vincent Tavern, arose on the site. Justifiably, the sisters insisted their name not be associated with a tavern, and by the time the second structure was torn down in 1915, it had been renamed McGowan's Pass Tavern. By 1859, the sisters had moved their new campus to the border of Yonkers and the Bronx. Today it is the College of Mount St. Vincent. A tribute to the sisters' history is on a plaque affixed to a boulder north of Conservatory Garden.

36. Walsh, *The Sisters of Charity*, vol. 1, 154.

37. Doherty, *Life of Mother Elizabeth Boyle*, 194.

38. Doherty, *Life of Mother Elizabeth Boyle*, 145.

39. Doherty, *Life of Mother Elizabeth Boyle*, 143.

40. Handwritten testimony of laborer James Fitzpatrick, who had worked for the sisters until they left the park in 1859; *Central Park Extension, 106–110*, no. 2, 1862, 332b, DOR; *New York State Census, 1855*, Twelfth Ward, E.D. 2, lists the sisters and employees of the Sisters of Charity and their place of birth" 83.

41. Walsh, *The Sisters of Charity*, vol. 1, 156, quoting *Freeman's Journal and Catholic Register*, Mar. 24, 1855, 5.

42. The chapel was "blessed but not solemnly consecrated," on March 19, 1855; see Walsh, *The Sisters of Charity*, vol. 1, 155.

43. Ernest A. McKay, *The Civil War in New York* (Syracuse, NY: Syracuse University Press, 1991), 124.

44. A previous organization, the New York chapter of the Society of the Friendly Sons of St. Patrick, was an American charitable and social organization, formed in 1771 before the Revolution for the relief of emigrants from Ireland. At that time, the majority of New York Irish were Protestants, who had emigrated before the war, and assimilated easily into American culture.

45. Ernst, *Immigrant Life*, 33. James McBride, a wealthy Irish merchant of predominantly Irish-made imports, owned land between Seventh and Eighth Avenue at Eighty-Second Street, adjacent to the land of David Wagstaff and the Demilts. William Edgar Jr. purchased the large property that had once been owned by Robert L. Bowne, adjacent to Seneca Village.

46. Marion Casey, "Refractive History: Memory and the Founders or the Emigrant Savings Bank," in *Making the Irish American: History and Heritage of the Irish in the United States*, ed. J. J. Lee and Marion R. Casey (New York: New York University Press, 2006), 305–309. I am grateful to Marion Casey for generously sharing her information on the Dillon family. It is probably no coincidence that the following year Black leader James McCune Smith proposed a Mutual Savings Institution for the Black community, "The Meetings of the Colored People," *The Liberator*, Apr. 4, 1851, 4.

47. Tyler Anbinder, "Moving Beyond 'Rags to Riches': New York's Irish Famine Immigrants and Their Surprising Savings Accounts," *The Journal of American History* 99, no. 3 (December 2012): 746. The archives of the Emigrant Savings Bank are located at the New York Public Library. The library has scanned and put online records of 19,000 depositors and the "Test Books" that give valuable information the depositors entered about their family history; see http://archives.nypl.org/mss/925#detailed.

48. See chapter 18 for Dillon's role as commissioner in the park's design; see also Sara Cedar Miller, *Central Park, An American Masterpiece: A Comprehensive History of the Nation's First Urban Park* (New York: Abrams, 2003), 100, 102, 106, 134, 137, 146, 173–174, 234.

49. Richard J. Purcell, "The New York Commissioners of Emigration and Irish Immigrants, 1847–1860," *Studies: An Irish Quarterly Review* 37, no. 145 (March 1948): 32, http://www.jstor.org/stable/30100186.

50. LaVerne J. Rippley, *The German-Americans* (Boston: Twayne, 1976), 49–54. See also Charlotte Brancaforte, ed., *The German Forty-Eighters in the United States* (New York: Lang, 1989).

51. Abraham Lincoln papers: Series 1. General Correspondence. 1833–1916: Jupiter Hesser to Abraham Lincoln, Tuesday, Mar. 19, 1861, 1–4, LOC, Manuscript Division, https://www.loc.gov/resource/mal.0823500/?st=gallery.

52. Ryer Van Blaerken and a Mr. Kemble in the 1830s, signed twenty-one-year leases from the Benson family. Van Blaerken built a small stone house along the Kingsbridge Road. Two Irish tenants, one named Morrissey, lived in a shanty with mud walls and a thatched roof from 1839 or 1840 until 1842, followed by Anthony Feistel and his wife, who lived in another structure. Benson testimony, New York Superior Court, *Charles Reade, Respondent against Anthony Feistel, Appellant* (New York: W. C. Bryant, 1851), Sept. 13, 1850, 29–30, 89. For additional information on the Feistels, see chapter 19.

53. Louis P. Tremante III, "Agriculture and Farm Life in the New York City Region, 1820–1870" (Ph.D. diss., Iowa State University, 2000), 28–29, 69–70.

54. Palmer to Eilermann and other, Palmer to Bouck, L611, P521, 1850.

55. Porter to Hesser, L600, P506, 1852 (land between Eighty-Ninth and Ninetieth, Eighth to Ninth Avenue); Firth and Hall to Hesser, L620, P167, 1852; Fay to Hesser, L665, P407, 1854; Pinkney to Hesser (see note 12). According to the *New York State Census, 1855*, Eilerman had been in New York eight years, Grams, Fukerer, and Tieman for six years, Weise for five years, Kuntz for three years.

56. All conveyances except Alless were dated in March 1853. George Grams, a net maker, L646, P381; John McLaughlin, the sole Irishman, a city lamplighter, L646, P375, and Jupiter Z. K. Hesser, a music professor, L646, P374. Those listed as "city gardener" in Pinkney leases: Gottleib Gent, L646, P378; Casimer Kuntz, L646, P380; Henry Folz and John Bonner, L646, P386; John Fukerer, L646, P395; Gottfried Kern, L646, P387; Conrad Keiffer, L646, P389; Catherine Alless, L646, P384, 1853.

57. Thomas F. DeVoe, *The Market Book: Containing a Historical Account of Public Markets in the Cities of New York, Boston, Philadelphia and Brooklyn*, Vol. 1 (New York: Printed for the Author, 1862), 500.

58. Tremante, "Agriculture and Farm Life," 34, 58, 65.

59. See the 1855 Viele topography map that shows the growth of the community and compare with Dripps Map of 1850, https://davidrumsey.georeferencer.com/maps/281278200268/view.

60. Rosenzweig and Blackmar, *The Park and the People*, 74. George Grams, Christian Gent, Casimer Kuntz, and Jupiter Hesser had frame houses.

61. *Petitions*, Vol. 2, 100–103. Hesser's other five lots were leased from wealthy landowner Seth Grosvenor and the Heirs of Henry A. Fay.

62. BCCP, *Third Annual Report*, 41.

63. *Petitions*, Vol. 2, 103.

64. *New York State Census, 1855*, Ward 12, E.D. 4, IV. Marriages and Deaths, unpaginated, as quoted in Tremante, "Agriculture and Farm Life," 62.

65. *New York State Census, 1855*, Ward 12, E.D. 1, "II. Agriculture and Domestic Manufacturing," unpaginated; Rosenzweig and Blackmar, *The Park and the People*, 74.

66. McNeur, *Taming Manhattan*, 205–207.

67. *Central Park Extension*, 77. No lease between Reulein and his landlord, probably Daniel Lord, has been found.

68. Ernst, *Immigrant Life*, 79–80; McNeur, *Taming Manhattan*, 161–162; Burrows and Wallace, *Gotham*, 118–137; American Sugar Refining Company, *A Century of Sugar Refining in the United States*, 3rd ed. (New York: The De Vinne Press, 1918), 6; Brendan Cooper, "The Domino Effect: Politics, Policy, and the Consolidation of the Sugar Refining Industry in the United States, 1789–1895" (Ph.D. diss., CUNY Graduate Center, 2018), https://academicworks.cuny.edu/cgi/viewcontent.cgi?article=3937&context=gc_etds.

69. Khalil Gibran Muhammad, "The Sugar that saturates the American diet has a barbaric history as the 'white gold' that fueled slavery," *The 1619 Project, NYT Magazine*, Aug. 14, 2019, https://www.nytimes.com/interactive/2019/08/14/magazine/sugar-slave-trade-slavery.html.

70. Joy Santlofer, Joy Santlofer, "Sweet Apple," May 7, 2003 (unpublished); *Food City: Four Centuries of Food-Making in New York* (New York: Norton, 2017), 148–152; The American Sugar Refining Company, *A Century of Sugar Refining in the United States, 1816–1916* (New York: The De Vinne Press, 1916), 10–12; "Bone-Boiling and Fat-Melting Establishments," *NYT*, Sept. 5, 1865, 2.

71. *Doggett's New-York City Directory, Illustrated with Maps of New York and Brooklyn, 1848–1849* (New York: John Doggett Jr., 1848), 290.

72. Francis Skiddy and the Commonwealth Fire Insurance Co. to George H. Moller, L517, P654, 1849. Jacob Harsen to George Moller L 548, P169, 171, 1850. In 1857, Menck paid $50 rent to the commissioners, an indication that he was still either working or living in the park; *BCCP, Third Annual Report*, 55.

73. George H. Moller, age 37, occupation, "Bone Factory (crossed out) Animal Charcoal," *New York State Census, 1855*, Ward 22, E.D. 3; "William Menck bone black, Eighth Ave corner W.66, h[ome] 173 West 34th Street," *Trow's New York City Directory for the Year 1855/56* (New York: John F. Trow, 1856), 571.

74. *New York State Census, 1855*, New York City, Ward 22, E.D. 3, III. "Industry Other Than Agricultural," George H. Moller and Brothers, 78; William Menck, 78.

75. District Court of the United States for the Southern District of New York, *United States of America, Petitioner, against The American Sugar Refining Company Et. Al, defendants*, Vol. 6 (New York: The J.W. Platt Company, 1913), 3160–3182.

76. John Craig Havemeyer, *Life, Letters and Addresses of John Craig Havemeyer* (New York: Fleming H. Revell Co., 1914), 19, https://catalog.hathitrust.org/Record/000969951/Cite.

77. Sarah Billopp Seaman was the daughter of loyalist Christopher Billopp; see Charles Farmar Billopp, *A History of Thomas and Anne Billopp Farmar, and some of their Descendants in America, 1846–1907* (New York: self-pub., 1907), 60. Edmund Seaman's daughter Catherine married John Kortright, and their son, Nicholas G. Kortright, and Sarah and Henry Seaman's daughter, Frances Townsend, inherited much of the sugar business

under Seaman, Tobias & Co. and all the Seamans" prepark land. See also chapter 17 for the release of property from the city to N. G. Kortright.

78. Besides the Seaman/Kortrights, the other long-standing eighteenth-century landowning families below 106th Street were the descendants of Charles Ward Apthorp, John Somarindyck, David Wagstaff, James Amory, Isaac Jones, and Jacob Harsen.

79. Myndert Van Schaick, *Abstract of Corporate Ordinances, And Rules and Regulations adopted by the Croton Aqueduct Board in relation to Water, to which the attention of Consumers, and all others, is earnestly invited* (New York: Collins, Bowne & Co., 1855), 1–4.

80. *BA Docs.*, Doc. no. 2, vol. 23 (New York: Chas. W. Baker, 1856), 33.

81. Central Park Reservoir, City of New York, Department of Water Supply, Gas, and Electricity, Borough of Manhattan, Real Estate Division, Sheet No. 3, in the Archives, New York City Department of Environmental Protection. My thanks to Samar Qandil, archivist at the Department of Environmental Protection, for sharing her vast knowledge of the city's water system.

82. Croton Aqueduct Department, "Report of the Croton Aqueduct Department made to the Common Council of the City of New York," *BA Docs.*, Doc. no. 81, Dec. 31, 1851 (New York: McSpedon & Baker, 1852), 1408.

83. The only remaining purchasers from Selden were Archibald Watt/Mary G. Pinkney, Daniel West, William D. Murphy, Joseph Fletcher, Henry Van Solingen, and Isaac Adriance, a relative of the McGowan family, who retained some of his pre-Reservoir land until he released it to the city.

84. *Annual Report of the Comptroller of the City of New York of the Receipts and Expenditures of the City Government for the Year 1857* (New York: Chas E. Baker, 1857), Doc. no. 10, 25, https://babel .hathitrust.org/cgi/pt?id=nyp.33433069110181&view=1up&seq=604&q1=Central%20Park.

85. Patricia U. Bonomi, *Under the Cope of Heaven: Religion, Society, and Politics in Colonial America*, updated ed. (New York: Oxford University Press, 2003), 25.

86. Eli Faber, "America's Earliest Jewish Settlers, 1654–1820," in *The Columbia History of Jew and Judaism in America*, ed. Marc Lee Raphael (New York: Columbia University Press, 2008), 25, 28–35. David de Sola Pool, *The Mill Street Synagogue (1730–1817) of the Congregation of Shearith Israel* (New York: n.p., 1930).

87. Hyman Bogomolny Grinstein, *The Rise of the Jewish Community of New York, 1654–1860* (Philadelphia: Jewish Publication Society of America, 1945), 3–99, https://babel.hathitrust .org/cgi/pt?id=uc1.32106014036500&view=1up&seq=9.

88. Chancery to Hebrew Benevolent Society, L434, P574, 1843.

89. Hiram B. Gray to Congregation B'nai Israel, L491, P435, June 30, 1846, lots 45 (700) and 46 (701) in block 579.

90. There were two different congregations at the time, B'nai Israel and Beth Israel. Hiram B. Gray to Bikur Cholim, L527, P563, Nov. 22, 1849. See Congregation Beth Israel, New York Office of the Comptroller, Power of Attorney, 1857 Synagogue property purchase of documents 1857–1870, Box #CB1, Folders 1–3 I-257, American Jewish Historical Society, Center for Jewish History, New York. The copy of an undated Central Park Reservoir map in the archives of the New York City Department of Environmental

Protection has cited four lots to Jewish organizations: block 578, lot 46 to B'nai Israel, lot 48 to Bikur Cholim, and block 579, lot 49 to Beth Israel and a blank space on the adjacent lot 51. The owners on the DEP map and the lot numbers are not the same as the archival releases in the American Jewish Historical Society, which should be considered the documents of record. Merges or transfers between congregations may be the cause for the confusion regarding the lots and their owners. Research on the two Reservoir cemeteries is still in progress. Bikur Cholim and Beth Israel are now a part of the Park Avenue Synagogue. B'nai Israel no longer exists. Alexander Frankland, Aaron Joseph, Pincas Davis, and Myer Goldman to Trustees of Beth Israel, July 3, 1844, block 579, lots 752 (49), 753 (47), recorded L626, P151, 1853. I am grateful for research assistant Bobbi Oliner, who found the deeds at the Center for Jewish History.

91. Central Park assessment for the cemetery lot adjacent to the future Reservoir site and belonging to Congregation Shaaray Hashamayim (the Rivington Street Synagogue), between Fourth and Fifth Avenue at Eighty-Ninth Street, received $310.78, "passed and approved by City Council, for a reimbursement to said congregation for moneys paid for assessments on their property adjacent to Central Park, the amount to be charged by the Comptroller to the account of 'Donations.' " See Folder 3, "Congregation Sharaay Hashamayim, Miscellaneous Papers, 1866–1870, paid May 10, 1866," American Jewish Historical Society.

92. James E. Serrell, *Maps & Profiles of Ground for New Reservoir Situated Between 86th and 96th Streets and Between 5th and &7th Avenues* (New York, 1853), NYPL, Lionel Pincus and Princess Firyal Map Division, 11 (Block No. 578), 12 (Block No. 579). Beth Israel's *Metaher* would have been on lot 701 (46) and Bikur Cholim's on lot 753 (49).

93. Grinstein, *The Rise of the Jewish Community*, 313–329.

94. Although a map of the area (Municipal Archives) labeled structures B and C as barns. It is possible that Building C was a *Metaher* attached to the barn that would have been owned by the Sisters of Charity. The lots, 459–462 between 104th to 105th Streets Fifth to Sixth Avenues, were originally transferred from Louis Levy to Shaaray Tefila L668, P256, 1848 for $1.00. Levy to Hinton L485 P207, 1846 "For Congregation not yet Incorporated," and recorded at the Request of J[ohn]D. Phillips on June 14, 1854. Phillips also owned land above 106th Street. See, *Releases, Extension 106th to 110th Streets*, MANY. I am grateful to Conservancy colleagues Diane Schaub and Joseph Gamache for measuring the lawn to locate the former lots.

95. Inskeep, *The Graveyard Shift*, xi; Nancy Dickinson, "St. Phillip's Episcopal Church Cemetery, Intensive Documentary Study, Christie Street, New York, New York, Second Avenue Subway," prepared by Historical Perspectives, Inc., Westport, CT, June 2003, 12; http://s-media.nyc.gov/agencies/lpc/arch_reports/437.pdf; Rev. B.F. De Costa, *The Story of St. Phillips' Church, New York City, A Discourse*, (Printed by the Church, 1889), Appendix, 3. http://anglicanhistory.org/usa/misc/decosta_philip1889.html.

96. Grinstein, *The Rise of the Jewish Community*, 327.

97. *Petitions*, vol. 3, 116–118. In a separate petition from Shaaray Terfila to the Commissioners of Estimate and Assessment, the congregation included undertaker David J. Polak's

list for labor removal of coffins, transportation, and reinterment: $3.00 for the removal of coffins and opening new ground, new coffins, sexton's fee; $3.50 for shrouds; $4.00 for ropes, pulleys, and removal of headstones; and $5.00 each for hearse and coach. See *Petitions*, vol. 5, 79–80.

98. Beth Israel received $825 for lots 752 and 753 in block 759 and also $1130.50 for the removal of 207 bodies from the graves, March 2, 1857, to Ellis Joseph, President, see folder no. 1; Bikur Cholim received $1,885 for lots 697, 698, and 699 in block 578 and also $660 for 120 bodies to Raphael Lowenthal, President, see folder no. 2, both in box no. CB1, folders 1–3 I-257, in "Synagogue property purchase documents, 1857–1870, from the New York City Office of the Comptroller," American Jewish Historical Society Archives, Center for Jewish History. There is no release in the folders for B'nai Israel, and their lots were recorded in the release to Beth Israel. Congregations Beth Israel and B'nai Israel were given permission by the board of aldermen to remove the dead from the site for the new reservoir; "Public Meetings," *Trib.*, May 15, 1856, 6.

99. David de Sola Pool, *Portraits Etched in Stone: Early Jewish Settlers 1682–1831* (New York: Columbia University Press, 1952), 142, Grinstein, *The Rise of the Jewish Community*, 322–324.

100. For a map of the Sharaay Tefila lots, see Joseph F. Bridges, *Real Estate Survey Books*, ca. 1826–1851, Mss Col 390, Manuscripts and Archives Division, NYPL. For a biography of Isaacs and the Shaaray Tefila congregation, see Robert P. Swierenga, "Samuel Myer Isaacs: The Dutch Rabbi of New York City," *American Jewish Personalities* in *The American Jewish Archives Journal* 44, no. 1 (1992): 607–618, http://americanjewisharchives.org /publications/journal/PDF/1992_44_02_00_swierenga.pdf. My deepest gratitude to Stanley Zucker, who chauffeured me through the maze of Queens on the hottest day of the year to visit Beth Olam.

101. Pollard to the Trustees of St. Philip's Episcopal Church, L493, P127, 1847.

102. Dickinson, "St. Philip's Episcopal Church Cemetery," 8.

103. The Rector, Churchwardens and Vestrymen of St. Philip's Church to Tighe Davy, L621, P45, 1852.

104. Dickinson, "St. Philip's Episcopal Church Cemetery," 13.

PART III: THE IDEA OF A PARK

1. The story of Central Park's early development is told in greater detail by Ian R. Stewart, "Politics and the Park: The Fight for Central Park," *New-York Historical Society Quarterly* 61, nos. 3–4 (July/October 1977), and in Roy Rosenzweig and Elizabeth Blackmar, *The Park and the People: A History of Central Park*, (Ithaca, NY: Cornell University Press, 1992), chapters 1 to 4.

2. Catherine McNeur, *Taming Manhattan: Environmental Battles in the Antebellum City* (Cambridge, MA: Harvard University Press, 2014), 48–56. In conjunction with the Parade, a fight also ensued to save the continuation of Broadway beyond Twenty-Third

Street. The former cow path and Wickquasgeck trail that led diagonally uptown from the Battery offended the pure Cartesian aesthetics of the grid. In their plan, the commissioners had little regard for the meandering thoroughfare, truncating it at the Parade's perimeter. But New Yorkers have always fought for their beloved landmarks, and in 1817 the state legislature gave its regards to Broadway, achieving what most likely was New York's first historic preservation victory.

3. Anon., *An Earnest Plea for Justice: Addressed to the Honorable Members of the Common Council of the City of New York Individually* (New York: self-pub., 1845). Stuyvesant Square was opened to the public in 1851.

4. Ira Rosenwaike, *Population History of New York City* (Syracuse, NY: Syracuse University Press, 1972), 42; E. K. Spann, *The New Metropolis: New York City 1840–1857* (New York: Columbia University Press, 1981), 430, table 4.

5. Spann, *The New Metropolis*, 139–173; Lawrence W. Levine, *Highbrow/Lowbrow: The Emergence of Cultural Hierarchy in America* (Cambridge, MA.: Harvard University Press, 1988), 202–205; Karen Halttunen, *Confidence Men and Painted Ladies: A Study of Middle-Class Culture in America, 1830–1870* (New Haven, CT: Yale University Press, 1982), 114–116; John F. Kasson, *Rudeness and Civility: Manners in Nineteenth-Century Urban America* (New York: Hill and Wang, 1990), 123–124.

6. John Evelev, "Rus-Urban Imaginings: Literature of the American Park Movement and Representations of Social Space in the Mid-Nineteenth Century." *Early American Studies* 12, no. 1 (Winter 2014): 174–201. Evelev's article cites the recent literature on this wide-ranging subject.

7. Kasson, *Rudeness and Civility*, 143.

8. David M. Scobey, "Anatomy of the Promenade: The Politics of Bourgeois Sociability in Nineteenth-Century New York," *Social History* 17, no. 2 (May 1992): 212. www.jstor.org /stable/4286016.

9. *Trib. Semi-Weekly*, Feb. 4, 1853, 3, quoted in Scobey, "Anatomy of the Promenade," 217; McNeur, *Taming Manhattan*, 59–61.

10. Charles Loring Brace, *The Dangerous Classes of New York, and Twenty Years' Work Among Them* (New York: Wynkoop & Hallenbeck, 1872), 30, quoted in David M. Scobey, *Empire City: The Making and Meaning of the New York City Landscape* (Philadelphia: Temple University Press, 2002), 148; Scobey, "Anatomy of the Promenade," 212.

11. Frederick Law Olmsted, *Public Parks and the Enlargement of Towns* (Cambridge, MA: The American Social Science Association, 1870), 11, quoted in Scobey, "Anatomy of the Promenade, 212; Sara Cedar Miller, *Central Park, an American Masterpiece: A Comprehensive History of the Nation's First Urban Park* (New York: Abrams, 2003), 20.

12. Edwin G. Burrows and Mike Wallace, *Gotham: A History of New York City to 1898* (New York and Oxford: Oxford University Press, 1999), 761–766; Leo Hershkowitz, "An Anatomy of a Riot: Astor Place Opera House, 1849," *New York History* 87, no. 3 (2006): 277–311. www.jstor.org/stable/23183493; Levine, *Highbrow/Lowbrow*, 61–69; Spann, *The New Metropolis*, 234–239.

13. Burrows and Wallace, *Gotham*, 577–579.

14. Jeffrey Richman, *Brooklyn's Green-Wood Cemetery: New York's Buried Treasure* (Lunenburg, VT: Stinehour Press, 1998), 16; see also David Schuyler, "The Didactic Landscape: Rural Cemeteries," in *The New Urban Landscape: The Redefinition of City Form in Nineteenth-Century America*, 2nd ed. (Baltimore, MD: Johns Hopkins University Press, 1988), 37–56.

15. Evelev, "Rus-Urban Imaginings," 191, citing Calvert Vaux, *Villas and Cottages* (1857; reprint, DaCapo Press, 1967), 97.

16. Andrew Jackson Downing, "A Talk About Public Parks and Gardens," *The Horticulturist and Journal of Rural Art and Rural Taste* 3 (October 1848): 156–157, https://babel .hathitrust.org/cgi/pt?id=uc1.b2928285&view=image&seq=173.

17. Helene E. Roberts, "The Exquisite Slave: The Role of Clothes in the Making of the Victorian Woman," *Signs* 2, no. 3 (Spring 1977): 554–569, https://www.jstor.org/stable/3173265.

18. Board of Aldermen, Aug. 5, 1851, quoted in *Senate Docs.*, 76th sess., vol. 3, nos. 71 to 86 (Albany, NY: C. Van Benthuysen, 1853), doc. 83, June 21, 1853, 16, https://babel.hathitrust .org/cgi/pt?id=nnc1.cu08231141&view=1up&seq=7.

15. THE BATTLE OF THE PARKS, 1844–1852

1. "A New Public Park," *EP*, July 3, 1844, http://nyshistoricnewspapers.org/lccn/sn83030384 /1844-07-03/ed-1/seq-2/. For the initiation for a new park and its political history, see Roy Rosenzweig and Elizabeth Blackmar, *The Park and the People: A History of Central Park* (Ithaca, NY: Cornell University Press, 1993), 15–22; Ian R. Stewart, "Politics and the Park: The Fight for Central Park," *New-York Historical Society Quarterly* 61, nos. 3, 4 (July/October 1977): 125–129.

2. E. K. Spann, *The New Metropolis: New York City 1840–1857* (New York: Columbia University Press, 1981), 281–284. It was estimated that one in five adults living in California in 1860 were born in New York (281n1).

3. Spann, *The New Metropolis*, 283.

4. [Andrew Jackson Downing], "A Talk About Public Parks and Gardens," *The Horticulturist and Journal of Rural Art and Rural Taste*, ed. Andrew Jackson Downing vol. 3, No. 4, (October 1848): 153–158, https://babel.hathitrust.org/cgi/pt?id=uc1.b2928285&view=page &seq=169&skin=2021; Stewart, "Politics and the Park," 130–133; Rosenzweig and Blackmar, *The Park and the People*, 29–30.

5. Lyman Horace Weeks, *Prominent Families of New York* (New York: The Historical Company, 1898), 406, quoted in Rosenzweig and Blackmar, *The Park and the People*, 15–17; Robert Bowne Minturn Jr., *Memoir of Robert Bowne Minturn* (New York: Anson D.F. Randolph, 1871), 146, Appendix, 313–314, https://archive.org/details/memoirof -robertbooomint. It seems odd that Robert Minturn Jr., a generation closer to the source, would mention his father's acquaintances but fail to address any role his mother might have played in the conception of Central Park.

6. Minturn, *Memoir of Robert Bowne Minturn*, 146.

7. "An Act Relative to the Powers and Duties of the Mayor, Alderman, and Commonalty of the City of New York in the Matter of Taking Possession of the Laying Out Certain Lands for a Public Park in the Nineteenth Ward of the City," passed July 11, 1851, in Doc. 5, *First Annual Report on the Improvement of the Central Park, New York*. Doc. No. 5, Part I (New York: Chas. W. Baker, 1857), 81–87; Rosenzweig and Blackmar, *The Park and the People*, 20–22.

8. Rosenzweig and Blackmar, *The Park and the People*, 44–45; See, correspondence about Jones Wood from State Senator Edwin D. Morgan to Mayor Ambrose Kingsland and Robert B. Minturn, both dated April 1, 1852.

9. Andrew Jackson Downing, "The New York Park," *Horticulturist and Journal of Rural Art and Rural Taste* 6, no. 7 (August 1851): 345–349.

10. Rosenzweig and Blackmar, *The Park and the People*, 37–42, 45–50; Stewart, "A Talk About Public Parks," 138–140.

11. Rosenzweig and Blackmar, *The Park and the People*, 31–36, 44–45n12.

12. Daniel Dodge and Joseph Britton, "Report of the Special Committee on Public Parks," Doc. 83, 137–158, and Doc. 5, in *First Annual Report*, http://nyc.gov/html/records/pdf/govpub/4055annual_report_manhattan_central_park_1857.pdf. Rosenzweig and Blackmar, *The Park and the People*, 47; see also correspondence of James W. Beekman (1815–1877), Beekman family papers (Mss Collection (Beekman papers), NYHS.

13. Table 1, "Report of the Special Committee on Public Parks"; Rosenzweig and Blackmar, *The Park and the People*, 46, consider the findings in the table "somewhat questionable."

14. "In regard to the Jones Wood park," *New-York Observer*, Feb. 19, 1852, 2.

15. "Public Sales, Anthony J. Bleecker, auctioneer," *EP*, May 21, 1852, 1. See ad, "Corporation Sale of Real Estate," *The Evening Mirror*, Dec. 16, 1852, 4; Rosenzweig and Blackmar, *The Park and the People*, 80, call the city's auction "odd," which indeed it was.

16. George Ashton Black, "The History of Municipal Ownership of Land on Manhattan Island" (Ph.D. diss., Columbia University, 1889), 54.

17. *Senate Docs.*, 76th Session (1853), vol. 3, 32–33.

18. "The Middle Park," *NYT*, June 21, 1853, 4; see also *Yankee Notions* 7, no. 1 (January 1858): 26, 27, https://babel.hathitrust.org/cgi/pt?id=nyp.33433095180216&view=1up&seq=7.

19. Sarah Wood, *Dorval, or The Speculator, A Novel, Founded on Recent Facts* (Portsmouth, NH: 1801), 49, quoted in Karen A. Weyler, " 'A Speculating Spirit': Trade, Speculation, and Gambling in Early American Fiction," *Early American Literature*, vol. 31, no. 3 (1996): 207.

20. Weyler, " 'A Speculating Spirit,' " 227–228.

21. Edward L. Glaeser, "A Nation of Gamblers: Real Estate Speculation and American History," *The American Economic Review* 103, no. 3 (2013): 1–42, www.jstor.org/stable/23469700; Charles Lockwood, *Manhattan Moves Uptown: An Illustrated Book* (New York: Barnes and Noble Books, 1976), 75.

22. Quoted in Rosenzweig and Blackmar, *The Park and the People*, 17–18 (see 538n7), from Charles A. Beard, "Some Aspects of Regional Planning," *American Political Science Review* 20 (May 1926): 276–279.

23. Edwin G. Burrows and Mike Wallace, *Gotham: A History of New York City to 1898* (New York and Oxford: Oxford University Press, 1999), 767.

24. The Mayor, Aldermen and Commonalty of the City of New York to Brush, L561, P232, 234, 236, 1848; The Mayor, Aldermen and Commonalty of the City of New York to Brush, L637, P187–199, 1852; *Mortgages*, Ruggles to Brush, L672, P362.

25. The Mayor, Aldermen and Commonalty of the City of New York to Knubel, L618, P677, 1852. *Petitions*, vol. 3; The Mayor, Aldermen and Commonalty of the City of New York to Gilmartin, L670, P139, 1852; *Petition*, vol. 3, 120; Rosenzweig and Blackmar, *The Park and the People*, 81.

26. Judge Ira Harris, "In the Matter of the Application of the Mayor, &c, of the City of New York, Relative to the Opening and Laying Out of A Public Place, Between Fifty-Ninth and One-Hundred and Sixth Streets and the Fifth and Eighth Avenues, in the City of New York," *First Annual Report*, Doc. No. 5, Appendix I, 106; Rosenzweig and Blackmar, *The Park and the People*, 83.

27. Last Will and Testament of James Amory, *Probate*, L72, P356, 1835.

28. Ritter, email to author, May 14, 2017.

29. "Legal Record, Court of Appeals," *EP*, Jan. 4, 1854, 2, traces the history of the Amory case from 1846 to 1854.

30. "Adrian H. Miller, auctioneer," *EP*, Mar. 9, 11, 13, 15, 1852, 3.

31. "Extraordinary Increase," *New-York Evangelist*, Mar. 25, 1852, 3.

32. *Mortgages*: Ruggles to Brush, L437, P322–337; L 473, P 540–555; Amory to Brush, L677, 544–547, 1852; Amory to Brush, L672, P362, 1852.

33. In 1852, one of the new landowners, Samuel Lord, was ordered by the referees to complete his purchase after the auction, which he refused to do, questioning the validity of the title. He appealed to the Supreme Court, which reversed the decision of the referee and decided that the will was valid. The plaintiff appealed to the Court of Appeals, which unanimously reversed the decision in 1854, affirming the correctness of the referee's original decision.

34. "Important Decision: The Amory Will Case," *Madison Daily Democrat* (Madison, WI), July 23, 1874, 1.

35. Ruth Shaw Worthington, "The history of Fond du Lac County, as told by its place-names," (1976), https://digicoll.library.wisc.edu/cgi-bin/WI/WI-idx?type=turn&id=WI.FondHistory &entity=WI.FondHistory.p0009&isize=text.

36. The Mayor, Aldermen and Commonalty of the City of New York to Patrick, L120, P341, 1817.

37. "The Romance of the Sheddens," *The Spectator: A Weekly Journal of News, Politics, Literature and Science* (London, Joseph Clayton) 33 (Dec. 1, 1860): 1144.

38. Joseph Alfred Scoville [Walter Barrett, pseud.], *The Old Merchants of New York City* (New York, 1870), vol. 2, part 1, 69–72.

39. *William Patrick Ralston Shedden, David Oliphant, and Harriet Turner, his wife against Amasa S. Foster, Samuel P. Townsend, Mary Ann Reckless, The Mayor, Aldermen and Commonalty of the City of New York*, New York Supreme Court, City and County of New-York, 1856, 3.

40. Reckless to Townsend, L429, P523, 1852.

41. Reckless to Bunting, L600, P603, 1852; *Petitions*, vol. 4, 126–130.

42. Dodge and Britton, "Report of the Special Committee on Public Parks," Table No. 1.

43. Whitehead to Davis, L197, P346, 1825; Whitehead to Davis, L235, P483, 1828; Whitehead to Davis, L262, P287, 1830.

44. Last Will and Testament of Epiphany Davis, *Probate*, L101, P68, Jan. 10, 1851.

45. There were two attached three-story houses: the one at the corner of Eighty-Sixth Street and Seventh Avenue was assessed for $2,005, the adjacent house was assessed at $1,824; see *Releas*es, Block 786, Lot 36, MANY. A series of detailed maps printed by the city in 1853 noted each lot and structure in the future park. They were created to assist surveyors in the assessment of each property. A blank copy is in the NYPL. One copy featuring handwritten values for many properties throughout the prepark area exists in a private collection and agrees, for the most part, with the copy in the *Release* volumes in MANY. On the 1855 condemnation map for block 786, the name John Wallace is written within the adjacent structure. John Wallace probably first rented the building from Davis's heirs. Wallace was an employee of the Croton Aqueduct Board and was allowed to stay in the park when the prepark residents were forced to move and the homes were torn down in 1857. Wallace then must have erected his own small house on Seventh Avenue between Eighty-Fourth and Eighty-Fifth Streets that contained "two rooms and a cooking shed." In a letter to the Commissioners of Central Park dated May 2, 1859, he asked for "the privilege of removing the little house." See Education Department, "Seneca Village: A Teacher's Guide to Using Primary Sources in the Classroom" (New York: New-York Historical Society, undated), 13.

46. Davis heirs to Smith, L612, P420, 1852; Smith to Cushman, L620, P233, 1852. In a "Notice" in the *New York Journal of Commerce*, Jan. 25, 1848, 1, announced that N. Bradner Smith and Don Alonzo Cushman were no longer with the firm of Cushman & Co., and Smith was now "General Commission Merchant" of New Orleans, https://infoweb-newsbank -com.i.ezproxy.nypl.org/apps/readex/results?page=20&p=EANX&fld-base-0=alltext &val-base-0=%22N.%20Bradner%20Smith%22&sort=YMD_date%3AA&val-database -0=&fld-database-0=database&fld-nav-0=YMD_date&val-nav-0=.

47. Cushman to Tietjen, L619, P105, Oct. 30, 1852; see Tietjen's petition, *Petitions*, vol. 3, 107.

48. Bennett to Webster, L696, P 255, 1855; J. B. Hardenburgh to Andrew C. Zabriskie, L609, P475, 1853; Reeds to Mulvaney, L645, P 436, 1854; Reeds to Stuart, L658, P379, 1854; Howell, Jr. to D. R. Martin, L685, P263, 1855; Barton Francis to Judson, L630, P597, 1853;

Court Referee to John M. Cooper, L680, P75, 1854; Sheriff to Lynch, L603, P611, 1852; Sheriff to Lynch after Landin, L649, P229, 1854; Edman to Zabriskie, L628, P319, 1853; Palmer to Joshua M. Cooper, L587 P604, 1853 (after default from Sylvan).

49. Derry to Thompson, L624, P285, 1853; Whitehead to Wigfall, L213, P96, 1826.

16. BECOMING CENTRAL PARK, 1853–1856

1. Ian R. Stewart, "Politics and the Park: The Fight for Central Park," *New-York Historical Society Quarterly* 61, nos. 3, 4 (July/October 1977): 143–144.

2. *First Annual Report on the Improvement of the Central Park, New York* (New York: Chas. W. Baker, 1857), Doc. No. 5, Part I, 167; Senate Docs., Doc. 82, June 21, 1853, 4, https://babel.hathitrust.org/cgi/pt?id=nnc1.cu08231141&view=1up&seq=7.

3. "Necessity of a Central Park: Two Reports to the Legislature," in *BA Docs*, vol. 24, no. 1–21 (1857), Doc. No. 5, Daniel Dodge and Jos. Britton, "Central Park Report," 165–183e; James W. Beekman and Henry E. Bartlett, "The Jones' Park Report," June 21, 1853, 184–192, https://babel.hathitrust.org/cgi/pt?id=nyp.33433062757616&view=image&seq=409&q1=Central%20Park; Roy Rosenzweig and Elizabeth Blackmar, *The Park and the People: A History of Central Park* (Ithaca, NY: Cornell University Press, 1992), 49–50.

4. Stewart, "Politics and the Park," 144.

5. Rosenzweig and Blackmar, *The Park and the People*, 52–54.

6. Stewart, "Politics and the Park," 147–149, Rosenzweig and Blackmar, *The Park and the People*, 53.

7. Jerome Mushkat, *Fernando Wood: A Political Biography* (Kent, OH: Kent State University Press, 1990), 31–36; Rosenzweig and Blackmar, *The Park and the People*, 56–58; Stewart, "Politics and the Park," 151.

8. *First Annual Report*, 130–134.

9. Mushkat, *Fernando Wood*, 47–48; Rosenzweig and Blackmar, *The Park and the People*, 56; Stewart, "Politics and the Park ,"153.

10. "Deposited today Oct. 3 and posted in the Street Commissioners office—upwards of 7500 parcels. James F. Ruggles examined the legal titles, J. Mansfield Davies, Esq., computed the values of the lands taken and of those assessed. Surveyors Sage, Serrell, Nicholson, Graves each taking a division have executed the surveys and voluminous maps, which accompany the report," "The Central Park, The Assessment Completed," *NYT*, Oct. 4, 1855, 4.I. N. Phelps Stokes, *The Iconography of Manhattan Island*, Vol. III (New York: Robert Dodd, 1918), 723, credits Egbert Viele as being one of the surveyors hired by the Commissioners of Estimate and Assessment in 1853, but Viele was hired later by the first commission; see chapter 18.

11. "City Intelligence," *EP*, Aug. 14, 1855, 2.

12. A series of cadastral maps of the prepark by Gardener Sage, dated 1853 to 1855, are in the New-York Historical Society (maps M.27.3.49a—M.27.3.17–49a).

13. *First Annual Report*, Doc. No. 5, Appendix E, "In the Matter Of the Application Of The Mayor, &c., Of The City Of New York, Relative To The Opening And Laying Out of a Public Place, Between Fifty-Ninth and One Hundred And Sixth Streets and the Fifth And Eighth Avenues, In The City Of New York," passed July 21, 1853, 93–94.

14. Archibald Watt, *Petitions*, Vol. 2, 206ff; Mary G. Pinkney, Vol. 3, 129; Rosenzweig and Blackmar, *The Park and the People*, 79–81.

15. Gouverneur M. Wilkins, *Petitions*, Vol. 4, 33ff.

16. Joshua M. Cooper, *Petitions*, Vol. 5, 91.

17. Beaman, *Petitions*, Vol. 3, 92; Ford, *Petitions*, vol. 3, 25; Ravenswood, *Petitions*, Vol. 3, [page].

18. Daniel E. Sickles, "The Founder of Central Park, New York," Sickles Papers, Library of Congress, Manuscript Division, undated, 7.

19. The life of Daniel Sickles is covered in three biographies: W. A. Swanberg, *Sickles the Incredible* (New York: Charles Scribner's Sons, 1956); Nat Brandt, *The Congressman Who Got Away with Murder* (Syracuse, NY: Syracuse University Press, 1991); Thomas Keneally, *American Scoundrel: The Life of the Notorious Civil War General Dan Sickles* (New York: Doubleday, 2002). Rosenzweig and Blackmar, *The Park and the People*, 545n39 and 550n59.

20. Tyler Anbinder, *Five Points: The Nineteenth-Century New York City Neighborhood* (New York: Simon & Schuster, 2010), 143–144.

21. "Politicians Taking to the Highway," *EP*, Nov. 1, 1852, 2 (from *The Sun*); "The Broadway Post Office Robbery," *EP*, Nov. 2, 1852, 2; "The Broadway Post Office Robbery," *NYT*, Nov. 2, 1852; "Daring Loco-Foco Outrage, Dan Sickles Robbing a Private Post Office, Assaulting the Proprietor and stealing his Papers," *Trib.*, Feb. 24, 1852; Keneally, *American Scoundrel*, 20, 23.

22. "Ex-Judge Nelson J. Waterbury Dead," *NYT*, Apr. 23, 1894, 1.

23. Sickles, "The Founder," 7.

24. Edward Hagaman Hall, "Central Park, in the City of New York," *Sixteenth Annual Report of the American Scenic and Historic Preservation Society* (New York: American Scenic and Historic Preservation Society, 1911), appendix G, 461. Many details in this report differ from the Sickles narrative.

25. Sickles, "The Founder," 8–9; Rosenzweig and Blackmar, *The Park and the People*, 559n59; Keneally, *American Scoundrel*, 47–48.

26. Sickles, "The Founder," 9–10; Hall, *Sixteenth Annual Report*, 461.

27. Kenneally, *American Scoundrel*, 48; Hall, *Sixteenth Annual Report*, 461.

28. *First Annual Report*, Doc. 5, Jan. 19, 1857, Appendix I; J. Harris, "In the Matter of the Application of the Mayor &c., of the City of New York, Relative to the Opening and Laying Out of a Public Place, Between Fifty-Ninth and One-Hundred and Sixth Streets and the Fifth and Eighth Avenues, in the City of New York," 103–111; Rosenzweig and Blackmar, *The Park and the People*, 84–85; Stewart, "Politics and the Park," 154.

29. Hall, *Sixteenth Annual Report*, 461.

30. Glyndon Van Deusen, *Thurlow Weed: Wizard of the Lobby* (Boston: Little, Brown, 1947), 264.

31. Gene Smith, "The Haunted Major," *American Heritage* 45, no. 1 (February/March 1994).

32. The award figures are based on information in seven bound volumes in the Municipal Archives, discovered in the department's storage facility in 2017. I am grateful to Aaron Goodwin, who first alerted me to their discovery, and to Deputy Commissioner Ken Cobb and his staff for allowing me access to this treasure trove of information. A deep debt of gratitude also goes to Andrew Fox, for designing the programs to calculate and analyze the award data for figure 16.6, and to Maya Mau, for her early research and contributions.

33. Ruggles to Graves, Nov. 29, 1853, NYHS, Mss Collection (AHMC—Ruggles, James Francis), Non-circulating. A second set of maps, dated between 1853–1855, were signed by City Surveyor Gardener Sage and are located in the map collection of the New-York Historical Society. These cadastral maps do not assign value, but note the size of each lot, structures, and the name of each owner or lessees.

34. As late as January 1858, many awards were unsettled due to title issues, unpaid taxes, or missing data. Comptroller of the City of New York, *Annual Report of the Comptroller of the City of New York, of the Receipts and Expenditures of the Corporation for the Year 1857* (New York: Chas W. Baker, 1857), "Awards Unsettled as of Jan. 1, 1858," Doc. No. 10, 99.

35. Stephen Roberts received $2,135 for his Sixty-Eighth Street corner lot, while Thomas McKnight received $2,025 for his Sixty-Ninth Street corner lot; *Releases*, "Abstract of Damages South Eastern Division," box 2871, MANY.

36. Block 763, lots 29–36, William S. Wright award for $9,965 for six lots and the two corner lots along Seventh Avenue; *Releases*, box 2871, MANY.

37. Rosenzweig and Blackmar, *The Park and the People*, 85.

38. Comptroller of the City of New York, *Annual Report of the Comptroller. . . for the Year 1857*, Doc. No. 10, Statement No. 23, 100.

39. Comptroller of the City of New York, *Annual Report of the Comptroller of the City of New York, of the Receipts and Expenditures of the Corporation for the Year 1855* (New York: McSpedon & Baker, 1856), Doc. No. 11, 13. https://books.google.td/books?id=uQgAAAAAMAAJ&printsec=frontcover&hl=fr&source=gbs_ge_summary_r&cad=0#v=onepage&q=Central%20Park&f=false.

40. Corporation to Patrick, L120, P341, 1817; Reckless to Townsend, L429, P523, 1852; Reckless to Bunting L600, P603, 1852; Foster to Townsend, L629, P456, 1853; Foster to Townsend, L676, P485, 1854; Bunting to Foster, L681, P119, 1855; Townsend to Bunting, L685, P41, 43, 45, 1855.

41. In comparison, an adjacent Ramble lot between Seventy-Seventh and Seventy-Eighth Streets, Sixth to Seventh Avenue, owned entirely by the Estate of Walter Bowne, a wealthy businessman and the former mayor of New York, brought $34,262. Block 669 that was between Sixth and Seventh Avenues and Seventy-Fourth to Seventy-Fifth Streets and belonged to the Corporation of the City of New York garnered in total $36,165. *Releases*, Blocks 544–671, Box 2871, MANY.

42. The Apthorp/Vanden Heuvel heirs never divided their prepark property, as they planned to keep it indefinitely, Thomas S. Gibbes, *Petitions*, vol. 3, 80.

43. $100 in 1856 dollars equals $3,126.20, according to www.measuringworth.com.

44. B'nai Israel had purchased their two lots on Ninety-Fourth Street from congregation member Hiram B. Gray for $400; L491, P435, 1847. Two years later Bikur Cholim also purchased three lots from Gray for $400; L527, P563, 1849.

45. Edwin G. Burrows and Mike Wallace, *Gotham: A History of New York City to 1898* (New York and Oxford: Oxford University Press, 1999), 723; Murray to Tiffany, Young and Ellis, L619, P394, 1851; *National Police Gazette* (New York), Jan. 26, 1856.

46. Catherine Alless, $230; Conrad Keiffer, $400; Casimer Kuntz, $125; Gotfried Kern, $125; Jupiter Z. M. Hesser, $1,451; Gottleib Gent, $30; John Fukerer, $100; George Grams, $425.

47. *NYT*, June 5, 1858, 2, quoted in Catherine McNeur, *Taming Manhattan: Environmental Battles in the Antebellum City* (Cambridge, MA: Harvard University Press, 2014), 161.

48. Email to Central Park Conservancy, Apr. 10, 2005. The author has not been successful in making contact with the Russell descendant.

49. Last Will and Testament of William Menck, *Probate*, L335, P400, 1885.

50. Charles Mingo, *Petitions*, Vol. 5, 103.

51. Christian Tietjen, *Petitions*, Vol. 3, 107. In 1855 his house was valued at $2,005, with a remainder of $1,312 per lot, for which he paid Cushman on average $812 per lot in 1852.

52. William Henry Boyd, *Boyd's Tax Book: Being a List of Persons, Corporations and Co-Partnerships, Resident and Non-Resident, Who Were Taxed According to the Assessors' Books, 1856 And '57* (New York: New-York Historical Society, 1857); also listed: Nancy Morris ($200), Charles B. Ray ($3,100), William Pease ($5,500), Landin ($200), E. Gloucester (personal value $554); Geo T. Taylor ($800); Zion Church ($21,500); Andrew Williams ($1,100); John Mulvaney ($450).

53. Jackson to Gloucester, L719 P212, 1856.

54. Carla L. Peterson, *Black Gotham: A Family History of African Americans in Nineteenth-Century New York City* (New Haven, CT: Yale University Press, 2012), 176, 402n31 cites Moses Yale Beach, *Wealth and Pedigree of the Wealthy Citizens of New York City: Comprising an Alphabetical Arrangement of Persons Estimated to Be Worth and Upwards, with the Sums Appended to Each Name; Being Useful to Banks, Merchants and Others*, 3rd ed. (New York: Sun Office, 1842), 49; Rhoda G. Freeman, *The Free Negro in New York City in the Era Before the Civil War* (New York: Garland, 1994), 205–208.

55. Last Will and Testament of Hannah S. Carter, *Probate*, L127, P445, 1859; Last Will and Testament of Huldah Green, *Probate*, L125, P332, 1858; Last Will and Testament of Elizabeth McCollin, *Probate*, L204, P452, 1872.

56. My deep appreciation to Reverend Audrey Akins Williamson for sharing with me her insight into the profound loss that Seneca Village residents would have felt.

57. See *U.S. Census, 1860*, 19th Ward, E.D. 3, 21. The ward included the East River to Sixth Avenue, Fortieth Street to Eighty-Sixth Street. Obadiah McCollin's profession was listed as milkman. Their real estate was valued at $6,000 and personal wealth at $200.

17. THE FIRST COMMISSION, 1855–1857

1. "More Central Park Developments," *Her.*, June 13, 1856, 4.
2. *Senate Journal*, 79th Session, Feb. 6, 14, Mar. 7, 10, 24, 25, 28, 1856, https://books.google.com/books?id=xroaAQAAIAAJ&pg=PA1#v=onepage&q&f=false. The appointed commissioners were William Kent, Peter Cooper, James F. Freeborn, James Harper, and James E. Cooley; *Senate Journal*, March 28, 465.
3. "More Central Park Developments," *Her.*, June 13, 1856, 4. *First Annual Report on the Improvement of the Central Park, New York* (New York: Chas. W. Baker, 1857), Doc. No. 5, Part I, 8.
4. "More Central Park Developments," *Her.*, June 13, 1856, 4.
5. "James Phalen's 1851 No. 88 Bedford Street," http://daytoninmanhattan.blogspot.com/2017/08/james-phalens-1851-no-88-bedford-street.html.
6. *Abstract of Damages South Eastern Division*, Blocks 544–672, MANY.
7. "Central Park," *Evening Mirror*, May 27, 1856, 2.
8. "The Dark Lantern Conspiracy on the Central Park," *Her.*, June 11, 1856, 6.
9. Beveridge and Schuyler, eds., *PFLO*, vol. 3, 69–71.
10. Chase Viele, "Knickerbockers of Upstate New York," *De Halve Moon, Quarterly of the Dutch Colonial Period in America* 47 (October 1972): 1–2. On the divorce and child custody cases: "The Viele Divorce Suits," *Trib.*, Oct. 7, 1870, 2; "The Viele Divorce Suits," *Trib.*, Oct. 8, 1870, 11; "The Suit of General Viele," May 21, 1871, 2; "The Viele Divorce Suit," *Trib.*, June 19, 1871, 2; "City Intelligence. The Viele Divorce. Custody of the Children," *Comm. Adv.*, June 22, 1871, 4.
11. Roy Rosenzweig and Elizabeth Blackmar, *The Park and the People: A History of Central Park* (Ithaca, NY: Cornell University Press, 1992), 102, note 20, 552.
12. Charles R. Rode, *The New-York City Directory for 1854–1855* (New York, 1854); "Egbert L. Viele, civil engineer, 13 Broadway, h[ome], New Brighton (Staten Island)," 846.
13. *BA Mins.*, vol. 61, Jan. 1–Mar. 25, 1856, 261.
14. "A Good Beginning," *NYT*, June 10, 1856, 4.
15. "Meeting of the Central Park Commissioners," *Her.* , 5, 1856, 1. The topographic map is the possession of the Municipal Archives and hangs prominently in the Reading Room at 31 Chambers Street. It was first published in I. N. Phelps Stokes, *The Iconography of Manhattan Island*, Vol. III (New York: Robert Dodd, 1918) 722–723. The Municipal Archives also has Viele's drainage map that he had prepared.
16. *First Annual Report*, 10–35.
17. *First Annual Report*, 12–13.
18. *BCCP Docs.*, Doc. No. 10, Oct. 6, 1857, Olmsted to BCCP, 4.

19. *First Annual Report*, "The Plan," 36–45.

20. *First Annual Report*, "The Plan," 39.

21. *Senate Docs.*, 76th Session, 20–21, 27.

22. *First Annual Report*, Doc. No. 5, "Botany," 25–35; Charles Rawolle & IG[natz] A. Pilat, *Catalogue of Plants: Gathered in August and September 1857, in the Ground of the Central Park*, Part First (New York: M. W. Siebert, 1857).

23. David Hosack, *Hortus Elginensis: or A Catalogue of Plants Indiginous and Exotic, Cultivated in the Elgin Botanic Garden in the Vicinity of the City of New-York*, 2nd ed. enlarged (New York: T. & J. Swords), 1811.

24. C. H. Briand, "The common persimmon (*Diospyros virginiana* L.): The history of an underutilized fruit tree (16th–19th centuries)," *Huntia* 12, no. 1 (2005): 71, 77–78. http://faculty.salisbury.edu/~chbriand/pdfs/huntia05.pdf.

25. Michael C. Bonasera and Leslie Raymer, "Good for What Ails You: Medicinal Use at Five Points," Becoming New York: The Five Points Neighborhood, *Historical Archaeology* 35, no. 3 (2001): 56–57, https://www.jstor.org/stable/2561693. Bonasera and Raymer's study of the plants grown in the Five Points neighborhood of the Sixth Ward shows a similar demographics to much of the prepark, but remarkably absent in both the Viele and the Rawolle and Pilat lists is wormseed or Jerusalem oak, *Chenopodium ambrosoides*, popular in both the eighteenth and nineteenth century for the treatment of worms in humans and animals and the most omnipresent plants found by the archeologists in the Five Points.

26. *BA Docs.*, Doc. No. 25, May 16, 1856.

27. In 1853, the push for kitchen gardening drove many gardeners, such as Anthony and Mary Uhll and their son, Anthony Jr., to buy one lot for farming before it was taken for the park. They spread their gardens across two blocks, owning the one lot on Block 763 and renting both a house and garden plots on Block 762; Wilson to Uhll, L627, P398–401, 1853; Chancery to Anthony, Uhll, Jr., L646, P621, 1854.

28. *BCCP Docs.*, May 26, 1857, 1. The Committee on Buildings was William K. Strong and James Hogg.

29. *The New-York Atlas*, Oct. 14, 1855, 3. According to Stokes, Elm Park was "an inn and pleasure resort" in 1860; Stokes, *Iconography*, Vol. IV, 742.

30. *BCCP Mins.*, Jan. 5, 1858.

31. *First Annual Report*, 59, 52.

32. *First Annual Report*, 39.

33. NASA Commander Curt Brown, *New York Daily News*, Nov. 17, 1998.

34. Daniel Dodge and Joseph Britton, "Report of the Special Committee on Public Parks," Doc. 83, in *First Annual Report*, 1473; *EP*, July 22, 1853, 2.

35. "New-York City: The Present Look of Our Great Central Park," *NYT*, July 9, 1856, 3.

36. *Report of the Croton Aqueduct Department made to the Common Council of the City of New York, December 31, 1851* (New York: McSpedon & Baker, 1852), 18. The total cost for buying the land for the Reservoir, including the city land, was $708,000; *Trib.*, Feb. 22, 1856, 3.

37. *MCC*, Doc. No. 2, "The Croton Water Works Extension," Jan. 5, 1858, 8–9. The name "The Lake of Manahatta," was one of many suggestions, including "Croton Lake." In 1994, the water body was officially named the Jaqueline Kennedy Onassis Reservoir in memory of the former first lady, who lived nearby and jogged around it frequently; "Central Park Honor for Jacqueline Onassis," *NYT*, July 23, 1994, sec. 1, 23.

38. "The New Reservoir," *The Constitution* (Middletown, CT), Aug. 27, 1862, 3.

39. Suggestions range from a connection to the Roman poet Seneca, the country of Senegal, the Seneca Falls Convention of Women's Rights, and the indigenous peoples of the Seneca Nation. In a 1995 interview. this author postulated that the term could have been a racial slur aimed at Blacks and Native peoples; see Rosenzweig and Blackmar, *The Park and the People*, 546n11; Douglas Martin, "Before Park, Black Village; Students Look Into a Community's History," *NYT*, Apr. 7, 1995, B1; Jasmin K. Williams, "The Village in the Park," *New York Post*, Aug. 13, 2007.

40. Aaron Goodwin, *New York City Municipal Archives: An Authorized Guide for Family Historians* (New York: New York Genealogical & Biographical Society, 2016), 159; Maritcha Lyons, "Memories of Yesterday, All of Which I Saw and Part of Which I Was—An Autobiography," Harry Albro Williamson Papers, Reel 1, Schomburg Center, New York Public Library, chapter 1, 2.

41. New York Protestant Episcopal City Mission Society, *The Gradual Growth of Charities* (New York: Julius Schlueter, 1873), in NYHS Mss Collection, F128 BV2805.N4 A1, box 1, 148, 8–9. John Punnett Peters, *Annals of St. Michael's: Being the History of St. Michael's Protestant Episcopal Church, New York for One Hundred Years 1807–1907* (New York: G. P. Putnam's Sons, 1907), 248. The next use of the term appears in a history of Central Park dating to 1911 in Edward Hagaman Hall, *Sixteenth Annual Report of the American Scenic and Historic Preservation Society* (New York: American Scenic and Historic Preservation Society, 1911), 443–445. It was not mentioned again until 1989 by Peter Salwen in *Upper West Side Story: A History and Guide* (New York: Abbeville Press, 1989), 46–57; and then in 1992 by Rosenzweig and Blackmar, *The Park and the People*, 546n11.

42. Peters, *Annals of St. Michael's*, 261.

43. See chapter 9, note 122.

44. "Meeting of the Central Park Commissioners," *Her.*, June 5, 1856, 1.

45. "The Central Park," *Her.*, June 9, 1856, 2.

46. Despite the use of the racist slur "Nigger Village," the reporter at the *New York Daily Times* described the community positively as "a neat little settlement," and complimented "their habits and the appearance of their dwellings" as "pleasing"; "New-York City: The Present Look of Our Great Central Park," *NYT*, July 9, 1856, 3. Craig Steven Wilder, *In the Company of Black Men: The African Influence on African American Culture in New York City* (New York: New York University Press, 2001), 101. See Elizabeth Stordeur Pryor, "The Etymology of Nigger: Resistance, Language, and the Politics of Freedom in the Antebellum North," *Journal of the Early Republic* 36, no. 2 (Summer 2016): 210, https://o-muse-jhu-edu.library.nysoclib.org/article/620987; and Patrick Rael, *Black*

Identity and Black Protest in the Antebellum North (Chapel Hill, NC: University of North Carolina Press, 2002), 102–107, cited in Pryor.

47. Daniel E. Sickles, "The Founder of Central Park, New York," Sickles Papers, Library of Congress, Manuscript Division, undated, 12.

48. The exhibit was confirmed in an article by "Sentinel," *New York Morning Courier*, Feb. 15, 1856, www.fultonhistory.com, 1856–0151.pdf.

49. Sickles, "The Founder," 14–15; Sickles's letter, June 13, 1856, "The Central Park," Letter to the Editor, *Her.*, June 16, 1856.

50. "More Central Park Developments," *Her.*, June 13, 1856, 4.

51. "Board of Aldermen," *Frank Leslie's Illustrated Newspaper*, May 31, 1856, 3

52. "The Central Park Appropriation," *Her.*, July 18, 1856, 8.

53. "New-York City: The Councilmen's Committee—Mayor Wood on the Central Park Question," *NYT*, Dec. 10, 1856, 8; "Mayor Woods' Central Park Policemen Defeated," *Trib.*, March 2, 1858, 8.

54. "Law Intelligence: The Central Park Appropriation," *NYT*, Aug. 25, 1856, 6.

55. See chapter 12, note 9.

56. "New-York City: The Present Look of Our Great Central Park," *NYT*, July 9, 1856, 3.

57. "The Central Park Police Matters," *Her.*, July 18, 1856, 8.

58. "Eldridge Street Jail," *Her.*, July 22, 1856, 8.

59. "The Tax List of 1857," *Morning Courier and New-York Enquirer*, Nov. 22, 1856.

60. "New-York City: The Councilmen's Committee—Mayor Wood on the Central Park Question," *NYT*, Dec. 10, 1856, 8.

61. "Lands and Tenements in Central Park—Collector of the City Revenue," *New-York Atlas*, June 1, 1856, 2.

62. "Lands and Tenements in Central Park-Collector of the City Revenue," *New-York Atlas*, June 1, 1856, 2.

63. "The Central Park," *New-York Atlas*, May 18, 1856, 2; "Lands and Tenements in Central Park-Collector of the City Revenue," *New-York Atlas*, June 1, 1856, 2.

64. "To the Editor of the Herald," *Her.*, May 26, 1856, 8.

65. Because of the illegality and the lack of a written lease, we cannot be absolutely certain that the renters on the list in May 1856 were the same renters who were evicted from the park in October 1857. However, with no new list published after that date, we can only surmise that these were the last residents of Central Park. The figures are based on the May 21, 1856, list sent to the Board of Aldermen. No public auction was listed to overturn Rose's actions and install new renters.

 The figures are based on the 1855 *New York State Census*. When no information was found for the household, two adults were assigned. The number of children would most likely have been greater. A male or female child with a job was counted as an adult. Adult boarders would also have fluctuated. The article "City Items: Central Park Lands," *Trib.*, May 28, 1856, gives "the present number of Tenants" as 180.

66. Seneca Village's Black households: Morgan, Mathew, Hinson, Jacobs, Wallace, Wilson, Lane, Pease, Robert Green, Williams, Landin. The Scudder and Thompson families left earlier.

67. Irish households: McFenliss (may be McFarlane), Gallagher, Barlow, Dulady (may be Duliddy), and Dunn; German households: Hillman, Meyer. The ten members of the Benjamin Dubois family rented a two-story house and shed on Eighty-Fourth Street, most likely the former home of Sally Wilson, who had died in 1855. The Duboises moved there from their home in a different area of the Twelfth Ward; *New York State Census, 1855,* Twelfth Ward, E.D. 1; Renters, *BA Docs.,* No. 19, May 16, 1856.

68. The condemnation maps noted thirty-three houses and ten shanties in Seneca Village in 1855. On May 1, 1856, when the renters and their dwellings were counted, the city-owned structures were nineteen houses and three shanties. Seven shanties were probably destroyed, and fourteen of the houses had either been consolidated in the city's tally, moved to another location, or destroyed.

69. These figures do not include the ninety nuns, students, and employees of Mount St. Vincent, who were allowed to stay until 1859; see chapter 14.

70. https://www.farnam.com/stable-talk/how-to-banish-rats-and-mice-from-your-barn; https://stablemanagement.com/articles/problems-mice-rats-caution-baits-23513.

71. "Marine Court before Hon Judge Maynard: Action Against the Central Park Police for Trespass," *Her.,* Aug. 5, 1856, 3.

72. Edwin G. Burrows and Mike Wallace, *Gotham: A History of New York City to 1898* (New York and Oxford: Oxford University Press, 1999), 835–837.

73. *BCCP Mins.,* Apr. 30, 1857, 1.

18. DESIGNING CENTRAL PARK, 1857–1858

1. Charles E. Beveridge and David Schuyler, eds., *PFLO,* Vol. III, "Creating Central Park, 1857–1861" (Baltimore, MD: Johns Hopkins University Press, 1983), "Passages in the Life of an Unpractical Man," 84–90.

2. Victoria Post Ranney, Gerard J. Rauluk, and Caroline F. Hoffman, eds., *PFLO,* Vol. V, "The California Frontier, 1863–1865" (Baltimore, MD: Johns Hopkins University Press, 1990), FLO to CV, Nov. 26, 1863, 146.

3. Beveridge, Hoffman, and Hawkis, eds., *PFLO,* Vol. VII, "Parks, Politics and Patronage, 1874–1882," 629.

4. Beveridge and Schuyler, eds., *PFLO,* Vol. III, 2. The major biographies and writings on Olmsted in order of publication date: Frederick Law Olmsted, *Forty Years of Landscape Architecture,* ed. Frederick Law Olmsted Jr. and Theodora Kimball (Cambridge, MA: MIT Press, 1973); Laura Wood Roper, *FLO: A Biography of Frederick Law Olmsted,* (Baltimore, MD: Johns Hopkins University Press, 1973); Elizabeth Barlow and William Alex, *Frederick Law Olmsted's New York* (New York: Praeger, 1972); Kalfus, *Frederick Law Olmsted,* 1990; Charles Beveridge and Paul Rocheleau,

Frederick Law Olmsted: Designing the American Landscape (New York: Rizzoli, 1995, updated edition, 2022);); Witold Rybczynski, *A Clearing in the Distance: Frederick Law Olmsted and America in the Nineteenth Century* (New York: Scribner, 1999); Frederick Law Olmsted, *Civilizing American Cities, Writings on City Landscapes*, ed. S. B. Sutton (New York: DaCapo Press, 1997), Justin Martin, *Genius of Place: The Life of Frederick Law Olmsted* (New York: DaCapo Press, 2011); Tony Horowitz, *Spying on the South: An Odyssey Across the American Divide* (New York: Penguin, 2019). The twelve-volume series, The Frederick Law Olmsted Papers Project, initiated by its first editor-in-chief, Charles Capen McLaughlin, and led since 1980 by series editor Charles E. Beveridge, was completed in 2021.

5. Ranney, Rauluk, and Hoffman, eds., *PFLO*, Vol. V, 146.
6. Democrat Thomas C. Fields voted for Edwin Smith, a city surveyor. See *BCCP Mins.*, Sept. 11, 1857, 50; Beveridge and Schuyler, eds., *PFLO*, Vol. III, 80. In an invitation to Roswell Graves, Smith was also named as an invitee to participate in the survey by the Commissioners of Estimate and Assessment; see chapter 16, note 32, He did not ultimately participate.
7. FLO to JHO, Sept. 11, 1857, in Beveridge and Schuyler, eds., *PFLO*, Vol. III, 81.
8. Roper, *FLO*, 129.
9. Roper, *FLO*, 130.
10. BCCP *Mins.*, Nov. 10, 1857, 93. Beveridge and Schuyler, eds., *PFLO*, Vol. III, 15, 105, 116n1. , 286; "Hard Times in the City," *NYT*, Oct. 8, 1857, 1; "Board of Aldermen," *NYT*, Oct. 9, 1857, 1.
11. Beveridge and Schuyler, eds., *PFLO*, Vol. III, FLO to JO, Oct. 9, 1857, 104.
12. Beveridge and Schuyler, eds., *PFLO*, Vol. III, FLO to JO, Jan. 14, 1858, 113.
13. BCCP, *Docs. for the Year Ending April 30, 1858* (New York: Wm. C. Bryant & Co., 1858), Doc. No. 12, Oct. 30, 1857, 6–11.
14. Heckscher conversation with author, May 2008. The photograph is part of Greensward plan presentation board No. 4 From Point D, in the collection of MANY. A second print is in the New-York Historical Society folder "Central Park—Park in preparation prior to 1860." The caption written on the photograph is, "The old farm that was flooded to make Central Park Lake. Looking north, toward the Ramble, from the Bethesda Fountain site. 1857." The site of the caption is incorrect. The date is also incorrect, as the pools of Bethesda were first revealed by Stebbins on May 31, 1873, at the unveiling of the fountain.
15. FLO to Asa Gray, Beveridge and Schuyler, eds., *PFLO*, Vol. III, 102.
16. For Vaux biographies and work, see William Alex and George B. Tatum, *Calvert Vaux, Architect and Planner* (New York: Ink, Inc., 1994); Francis R. Kowsky, *Country, Park and City: The Architecture and Life of Calvert Vaux* (New York: Oxford University Press, 1998).
17. David Schuyler, *Apostle of Taste: Andrew Jackson Downing, 1815–1852* (Baltimore, MD: John Hopkins University Press, 1996; new edition, Library of Landscape History, University of Massachusetts Press, 2015); Judith K. Major, *To Live in the New World: A. J.*

Downing and American Landscape Gardening (Cambridge, MA: MIT Press, 1997). A marble urn, designed by Calvert Vaux and dedicated in 1856 to the memory of Downing, is today a centerpiece in the Enid A. Haupt Garden of the Smithsonian Institution in Washington, D.C.

18. Kowsky, *Country, Park and City*, 96n11.

19. BCCP *Mins. for the Year Ending April 30, 1858* (New York: Wm. C. Bryant & Co., 1858, 18, 40.

20. Kowsky, *Country, Park and City*, 96–97.

21. Kowsky, *Country, Park and City*, 97n14; CV to FLO, June 3, 1865, in Ranney, Rauluk, and Hoffman, eds., *PFLO*, Vol. V, 387; Letter from Frederick Law Olmsted to the Editor of the *American Architect*, May 19, 1877, "The Central Park," *American Architect and Building News* 11 (June 2, 1877): 175, https://babel.hathitrust.org/cgi/pt?id=msu .31293108047212&view=1up&seq=377&size=125.

22. Beveridge and Schuyler, eds., *PFLO*, Vol. III, 67.

23. "I am greatly interested in planning the Park with Vaux. If successful, I should not only get my share of the $2000 offered for the best, but no doubt the whole control of the matter would be given me & my salary increased to $2500." Beveridge and Schuyler, eds., *PFLO*, Vol. III, 114.

24. JHO to FLO, Nov. 3, 1857, in Roper, *FLO*, 133.

25. Beveridge and Schuyler, eds., *PFLO*, Vol. III, 60–61; Roper, *FLO*, 142.

26. The existing visual plans are those of Olmsted and Vaux, Samuel Gustin, George Waring, Egbert Viele, and John J. Rink. See Sara Cedar Miller, *Central Park, An American Masterpiece: A Comprehensive History of the Nation's First Urban Park* (New York: Abrams, 2003), chapter 3, 70–86. The bound pamphlets are available as *Catalogue of Plans for the Improvement of Central Park, 1858*, NYHS, and *Descriptions of plans for improvement of the Central Park*, NYPL.

27. For an in-depth discussion of the commissioners, the entrants, and the competition, see Roy Rosenzweig and Elizabeth Blackmar, *The Park and the People: A History of Central Park* (Ithaca, NY: Cornell University Press, 1992), 95–149, 553–554n38. For a discussion of the competition and visual images of the known plans, see Miller, *Central Park, An American Masterpiece*, 82–85; Morrison H. Heckscher, *Creating Central Park* (New York: The Metropolitan Museum of Art and Yale University Press, 2008), 22–23, 26–35; Cynthia S. Brenwall, *The Central Park: Original Designs for New York's Greatest Treasure* (New York: Abrams, 2019), 13–39. The best reproduction of the restored Greensward plan is a foldout in Brenwall, 34–36. Commissioner Charles H. Russell's collection of the written plans and his handwritten comments are in the collection of the NYHS.

28. BCCP, *Mins.*, Apr. 6, 1858, 178; Russell notations in *Catalogue of Plans*, 4.

29. BCCP, *Mins*, Apr. 28, 1858, 187–194; Heckscher, *Creating Central Park*, 20–24.

30. Thomas Hogg Sr., a British-born horticulturist, owned a well-known plant nursery on East Seventy-Ninth Street and First Avenue in New York City. His two sons, Thomas Hogg Jr. and James Hogg, continued the business. James Hogg was also a member of the Torrey Botanical Club. See also Beveridge and Schuyler, eds., *PFLO*, Vol. III, 103n5.

31. David Black, *The King of Fifth Avenue: The Fortunes of August Belmont* (New York: Dial Press, 1981), 141.

32. Gustavus Myers, *The History of Tammany Hall*, 2nd ed. (New York: Boni & Liveright, 1917), 244: *NYT*, Nov. 8, 1871, 2; Jan. 26, 1885, 1, in Beveridge and Schuyler, eds., *PFLO*, Vol. III, 93n18.

33. Roper, *FLO*, 340.

34. Russell quote in *Catalogue of Plans*, on blank pages at the front of the bound volume; "The Central Park," *Her.*, May 22, 1858, 8; "The Central Park Job," *Her.*, May 31, 1858, 4.

35. See Miller, *Central Park, An American Masterpiece*, 234.

36. Rosenzweig and Blackmar called No. 2 the "mocking gesture" of "someone unhappy with the outcome of the political struggle," but they did not name Viele specifically. *The Park and the People*, 95.

37. Ten commissioners voted for Olmsted; only Fields voted for his competitor Edwin Smith. Beveridge and Schuyler, eds., *PFLO*, Vol. III, 88.

38. BCCP, *Mins.*, April 12, 1858, 187.

39. Lachlan McIntosh, the disbursing clerk, Michael Miller, the property clerk; Samuel Gustin, superintendent of planting; George Waring, superintendent of draining; surveyors Charles Graham and John Bagley; surveyor Roswell Graves; engineer John J. Rink; Chief Engineer Egbert Viele; and Superintendent Olmsted.

40. BCCP, *Mins.*, Dec. 1, 1859, for $300. On that same day Viele requested his plan be returned to him. He filed suit on Jan. 21, 1860. At about the same time, Viele filed charges against John A.C. Gray for words spoken by the Commissioner about Viele's qualifications requesting his appointment as engineer.

41. Beveridge and Schuyler, eds., *PFLO*, Vol. III, 27n74; Rosenzweig and Blackmar, *The Park and the People*, 119, called it a "bonus."

42. *Catalogue of Plans*, Plan No. 29, 5–6.

43. *BCCP Mins.*, Sept. 9, 1858, 115–116.

44. *BCCP Mins.*, Apr. 28, 1858, 188, 194.

45. *BCCP Mins.*, May 4, 1858, 1–2.

46. *BCCP Mins.*, May 10, 1858, 15.

47. *BCCP Mins.*, May 13, 1858, 23–24.

48. FLO to BCCP, May 14, 1858. The quote is repeated again in Doc. 3, May 17, 1858; BCCP, *Documents of the Commissioners of the Central Park for Year Ending April 30, 1859* (New York: Evening Post Steam Presses, 1859), 1–2.

49. "Amendments to the Central Park Plan," *Her.*, June 2, 4; "The Central Park," *Her.*, June 8, 3, 4; "The Central Park, Mssrs. Dillon and Belmont to the Public," *Her.*, June 11, 8. For charges of corruption of the commissioners, see "The Central Park Job," *Her.*, May 31, 1857, 5.

50. Miller, *Central Park, An American Masterpiece*, 86.

51. *Explanatory Notices of a Design for Laying Out the Central Park, No. 30* (New York: Baker & Godwin, 1858); BCCP *Mins.*, Dec. 18, 1858, 113; Commissioner Gray moved to also pay $100 to officials at Birkenhead Park in Liverpool; BCCP *Mins.*, Dec. 29, 1858, 119.

52. Fredrick Law Olmsted, *Walks and Talks of an American Farmer in England* (New York: G. P. Putnam, 1852), 78–81, (reprint, Amherst, MA: Library of American Landscape History, 2002), chapter 8, 86–96.

53. The first footbridge was located on a cross drive designed to cut a swath through the heart of the wooded Ramble and the second footbridge was designed to cross the Ninety-Seventh Street Transverse Road. Beveridge and Schuyler, eds., *PFLO*, Vol. III, 121. For Jacob Dyckman's accident, see chapter 2.

54. Beveridge and Schuyler, eds., *PFLO*, Vol. III, 159–160, 187n35.

55. Miller, *Central Park, An American Masterpiece*, 95, 245n26; see typed manuscript in the papers of Andrew Haswell Green (1843–1911), attributed to Henry Mann and "received and corrected" by biographer John Foord and Green, Mar. 7, 1903, NYHS, Mss Collection Andrew Haswell Green Papers Non-circulating, MS 264.

56. Beveridge and Schuyler, eds., *PFLO*, Vol. III, 180–181n14. For English influences on the separation of roadways and the influence on Downing's plan for Washington, D.C., see Kowsky, *Country, Park and City*, 47, 100. See also I. N. Phelps Stokes, *The Iconography of Manhattan Island*, Vol. III (New York: Robert Dodd, 1918) 722–723.

57. Elizabeth Barlow Rogers, *Landscape Design: A Cultural and Architectural History* (New York: Abrams, 2001), 516.

58. A suspension bridge was a feature in the design submission by Charles K. Graham and John Bagley. Graham was an engineer working for Viele. He was also the purported draughtsman of the two drawings presented by Daniel Sickles that hung in the Albany legislature in 1856. He was also the younger brother of John Graham, Sickles's attorney. John Bagley was the city engineer and surveyor of the Central Park extension. See the Central Park Extension maps, 1859, in the collection of the Manhattan Borough President's Office.

59. *BCCP Docs.*, Doc. No. 5, May 31, 1858, 6.

60. FLO to William A. Stiles, Mar. 10, 1895, in Frederick Law Olmsted, *Frederick Law Olmsted Papers: Correspondence, –1928; General Correspondence, –1928; 1895, Jan.–Dec. 1895*. Manuscript/Mixed Material. https://www.loc.gov/item/mss351210198/

61. Frederick Law Olmsted and Calvert Vaux, "A Review of Recent Changes, and Changes which have been Projected, in the Plans of the Central Park, Letter I, A Consideration of Motives, Requirements and Restrictions Applicable to the General Scheme of the Park," and "Letter II, Examination of the Design of the Park and of Recent Changes Therein," in Olmsted, *Forty Years of Landscape Architecture*, 240–270. In the Greensward plan, Olmsted and Vaux objected to "causeways carried over high arches . . . since it puts an abrupt limit to the view," in Beveridge and Schuyler, eds., *PFLO*, vol. III, 122.

62. "The Story of Pierre Paudeau and the Paris Pond Yachts and Paris Pond Boats!" in which is included a scan of an article, "Pond Boats of the Luxembourg Garden," https://www.modelsailboat.com/paris2.html. To date, research cannot confirm this attribution to Olmsted.

63. See part III, note 9.

64. https://www.britannica.com/sports/pall-mall-game.

65. According to the handwritten commentary by Charles H. Russell, the original owner of the bound volume of the written descriptions, Rink (entry No. 4) also submitted a second plan, now lost, that was probably done in sepia. Much of Rink's text does not match the colored submission in the New-York Historical Society bound volume.

66. FLO to BCCP, Jan. 22, 1861, in Olmsted, *Forty Years of Landscape Architecture*, 310.

67. "The Facts in the Viele Case," in Olmsted, *Forty Years of Landscape Architecture*, Appendix 3, 554–556.

68. The only known copy of the Viele topographic map, photographed by the studio of Matthew Brady, is in the collection of the New-York Historical Society and was bound with the *Catalogue of Plans*. It is a small version of the large plan in the MANY collection.

69. "The Facts in the Viele Case," in Olmsted, *Forty Years of Landscape Architecture*, 556 and 556n3.

70. "The Facts in the Viele Case," in Olmsted, *Forty Years of Landscape Architecture*, 559.

19. EXTENDING THE PARK, 1859–1863

1. See part I.

2. *BCCP Seventh Annual Report for the Year Ending with December 31, 1863* (New York: Bryant & Co., 1864), 5–10.

3. Roy Rosenzweig and Elizabeth Blackmar, *The Park and the People: A History of Central Park* (Ithaca, NY: Cornell University Press, 1992), 113, 554n40 cites entry no. 9 (by Augustus Fitch), entry no. 21 (by Charles Graham and John Bagley), and entry no. 27 (by Lachlan McIntosh and Michael Miller) as the three plans suggesting an extension to 110th Street. Additional plans include entry No. 25 (Roswell Graves), entry No. 29 (Waring), entry No. 30 (Gustin), and entry No. 31 (Hoffman and Wehle). The extension is discussed in BCCP *Mins.*, Jan 26, 1858.

4. In "Objections offered by Mr. Tappen in the matter of extension of Central Park case," Tappen mentioned the quote "in a letter addressed to Mssr Fields & others, Central Park Commrs,," Dec. 12, 1860; *Petitions*, vol. 7, 210–211.

5. BCCP *Docs.*, May 4, 1858, to April 30, 1859, Doc. No. 15, Mar. 16, 1858, 5.

6. BCCP *Docs.*, Doc. No. 2, May 10, 1858, 3–4.

7. BCCP *Mins.*, May 4, 1858, to March 17, 1859, June 24, 1858, 73; Aug. 5, 94; Beveridge and Schuyler, eds., *PFLO*, Vol. III, 289. For a timeline and expenditures of the extension, see BCCP, *Seventh Annual Report*, 5–10. The photographs have not been found.

8. "The Central Park," *NYT*, Jan. 7, 1858, 4, quoting the *Journal of Commerce*. This substitution was also put forward by Roswell Graves, who suggested buying the land to 110th Street and selling "a few blocks taken off the southerly end of the park"; see Board of Commissioners of Central Park, *Catalogue of Plans for the Improvement of Central Park*, s.n. 1858, NYHS, Main Collection (Y1800 Boa Cat), Entry No. 25, 6.

9. *New York Sun*, Mar. 2, 1858.
10. Rosenzweig and Blackmar, *The Park and the People*, 554n40.
11. "Law Reports," *NYT*, July 14, 1859, 3. The other men nominated were Samuel B. Ruggles and Prosper M. Wetmore by the property owners and Moses Taylor and Simeon Draper by the board of commissioners.
12. "A.J. Bleecker, Auctioneer," *New York Morning Courier*, Oct. 11, 1858. Bleecker's ad promoted "the following valuable Lots on Fifth Avenue, near the CENTRAL PARK, viz. 8 LOTS, comprising the entire east front of 5th avenue, between 100th and 110th streets . . . [a]lso, 11 LOTS adjoining, (6 on 109th and 5 on 110th street). The proposed extension of Central Park will make these lots all front on the Park," www.fultonhistory .com, New York NY Morning Courier 1858–1950.pdf.
13. Tappen to Busteed, L848, P388, 1860.
14. "The Lost 1853 Everett House," Sept. 18, 2017, http://daytoninmanhattan.blogspot .com/2017/09/the-lost-1853-everett-house-37-east.html.
15. BCCP, *Documents for the Year Ending April 30, 1859*, Doc. No. 12., Sept. 16, 1858, 7.
16. Pinkney to Elliott, L810, P290, 1860; Elliott to Palmer, L837, P501, 1860; also, Elliott to Palmer, L837, P500, 1861, for eight lots on Eighth Avenue between 106th and 107th Streets, for $6,000 and the $20,000 mortgage from Pinkney.
17. "Obituary: Courtlandt Palmer," *NYT*, May 12, 1874, 1.
18. BCCP, *Fourth Annual Report of the Board of Commissioners of the Central Park for the Year 1860* (New York: Bryant & Co., 1861), 12–13.
19. "Central Park Extension," *New-York Atlas*, Dec. 30, 1860, 4; "The Central Park Extension Enormous Valuation of Property," *NYT*, Jan. 8, 1861, 3; "Central Park Extension—Alleged Over Valuation," *NYT*, Jan. 16, 1861, 3.
20. "Matters at Albany," *New-York Atlas*, Mar. 10, 1861, 5. Henry H. Elliott also served with Olmsted on the commission to develop Manhattan above 155th Street. Olmsted's letter to Elliott in 1860 is cited as the only clear document in which Olmsted explains his design concepts for the northern end of Manhattan; see Beveridge and Schuyler, eds., *FPLO*, Vol. III, letter from FLO to Elliott, Aug. 27, 1860, 259–267. See also, Gail K. Addiss, "The Critique Became the counter-Narrative: Planning Manhattan North of the Grid," CUNY Academic Works, Sept., 2019, https://academicworks.cuny.edu/cgi /viewcontent.cgi?article=4524&context=gc_etds.
21. Edwin G. Burrows and Mike Wallace, *Gotham: A History of New York City to 1898* (New York and Oxford: Oxford University Press, 1999), 876; Miller, *Central Park, an American Masterpiece*, 55, 243n16.
22. "General News," *NYT*, Mar. 1, 1862, 3; for more on Ruggles, see Catherine McNeur, *Taming Manhattan: Environmental Battles in the Antebellum City* (Cambridge, MA: Harvard University Press, 2014), 61–73.
23. It was first passed by the state legislature on April 1, 1859; "New York Legislature," *NYT*, Apr. 2, 1859, 1; "The State Legislature," *NYT*, Apr. 22, 1863, 4. "Subscribers," *New York Evening Telegram*, Feb. 14, 1871. *Objections with an Appeal for a Review and Increase of Award*

in the Matter of Extension of Central Park (New York: Wm C. Bryant & Co., Feb. 21, 1863); *Central Park Extension*, 83–90.; BCCP, *Seventh Annual Report*, "*Decision of Hon. D.P. Ingraham, Justice of the Supreme Court, On the motion to confirm the report of the Commissioners of Estimate and Assessment of the land between the south side of One Hundred and Sixth and One Hundred and Tenth streets, and Fifth and Eighth Avenues*," 65–73.

24. Based on the total purchase price to the city of $5,402,637.50 for 779 acres in 1856 (including areas owned by the corporation and the state arsenal and grounds and in addition to the $708,000 for the new reservoir) and the total purchase price of $1,179,590 for sixty-four acres.

25. BCCP, *Seventh Annual Report*, 5–10; The Real Estate Record Association, *The History of Real Estate, Buildings, and Architecture in New York City: During the Last Quarter of the Century*, 2nd ed. (1898; reprint, New York: Arno Press, 1967), 43 claims the 1856 price as $7,800 and the 1863 price as $20,000.

26. See "Index to Central Park assessment district map series: North eastern division," Gardner A. Sage, NYHS, also noted on file, "Also indexes two consecutively numbered companion series, one entitled Damage maps Central Park. North eastern division; the other, Damage maps Central Park. North western division. These cover part of Central Park proper." See also *Releases*, "Extension," MANY.

27. Chancery to Wilkins, L278, P366–371, 1831; L322, 385, 1834; L322, P393, 1834; Chancery to Watt, L278, P88, 1831; L278, P236, 1831; L328, P105, 1834; L328, P 112, 1834.

28. The top six owners were Gouveneur Wilkins, $353,932; Mary G. Pinkney, $126,749; Courtlandt Palmer, $104,487; D. Randolph Martin, $62,708; Arthur Tappen, $63,334; Daniel Lord, $54,673; Henry H. Elliott, $11,400. *Releases*, "Extension," MANY.

29. James Riker, *Revised History of Harlem (City of New York), Its Origin and Early Annals* (New York: New Harlem Publishing Company, 1904), 145, 150; Mrs. Robert W. de Forest, *A Walloon Family in America: Lockwood de Forest and His Forbears, 1500–1848* (New York: Houghton Mifflin, 1914), 115; *Cahill v. Palmer*, see part I, note 2.

30. The division by the Harlem freeholders of Johannes de la Montagne's Flats (109th to 124th Streets) into "parcels from four to six morgen each, by an actual survey; running in narrow strips from the little creek (Montagne's) due west to the hills [Morningside] Heights, and 'numbered from south to north,'" in Carl Horton Pierce, *New Harlem Past and Present: The Story of an Amazing Civic Wrong, Now at Last to be Righted* (New York: The Harlem Publishing Company, 1903), 26–27.

31. No record of a deed exists recognizing Montanye's specific ownership of the land. For an explanation of the Montagne groundbrief after 1664, see Riker, *Revised History*, 290–292. In 1858, Edmund O'Callaghan noted that the Montagne property "has wholly passed out of the hands of the family," *History of New Netherland, or New York Under the Dutch.* New York, D. Appleton, 1848), vol. 2, 211n2.

32. John Montanye, George F. Montanye, John Montanye, and James A. Cosse had already petitioned the Commissioners of Estimate and Assessment for their purported land in the lower park in November 1855, though no action was taken and they received no

compensation. *Petitions*, vol 4, 78–79. They claimed 'northerly half of Block No. 583 and the whole of Blocks 584–590 and middle line of the block between 98 and 99 Streets, on the north by 106 and on the west by 6th Avenue. Also all those portions of Blocks 686 to 692. This claim was not mentioned in the 1864 suit.

33. The auction for the properties affected by the folding of the Harlaem Canal Company occurred in 1831. The handwritten testimony of the 1864 trial is contained in *Central Park Extension*, 277–365, DOR. The transcriber is not identified.

34. Johannes Mousnier de la Montagne, b. 1595 in France; Jean Mousnier de la Montagne, b. 1832 in Leyden; Vincent de la Montagne, b. 1657 in New Amsterdam; Thomas de la Montagne, b. 1691 in New York City; Vincent Montanye, b. 1721 in New York City; Rebecca Montanye, b. 1752 in New York City, m. Peter Truman c. 1752; Jane Montanye Truman, b. 1780 in Fishkill, NY, m. Peter Cosse c. 1797; James Alexander Cosse, b. 1805, d. 1878, m. 1832 Eliza Ann Grant b. 1816, https://wc.rootsweb.com/cgi-bin/igm .cgi?op=GET&db=delamontagne&id=I18430.

35. "Left," *EP*, Nov. 7, 1834, 3.

36. *U.S. Census, 1850*, New York City, Twelfth Ward, household no. 611. Cosse was listed as a farmer; John Montanye, Fourteenth Ward, household no. 218, was listed as a cedar cooper, born in New York in 1805. See https://wc.rootsweb.com/cgi-bin/igm .cgi?op=GET&db=delamontagne&id=I1913; Montanye.

37. There were three trials: 1864, 1869, and 1871. The 1864 trial has only a handwritten transcription in *Petitions*, vol. 7; that was heard by the Commissioners of Central Park. The 1868 and 1871 trials were in the Supreme Court, *Cahill v. Palmer*; see part I, note 2. Cosse produced the lease, Montagne to Cosse, L850, P155, 1862. A copy of the lease was dated February 16, 1842, but only recorded in New Jersey on Jan. 2, 1862, six weeks before the termination of the purported twenty-year agreement, and only sixteen days before John Montayne died in Hoboken, New Jersey. Coincidentally, the lease was recorded in New Jersey's Hudson County by John White Jr., who had been "personally acquainted" with both cousins and as the county's commissioner of deeds, afforded him the legal authority to file the document. In this highly questionable document, John Montanye was misspelled in three different ways—Montangie, Montagnie, and Montagne—none of them how he spelled his name; the lease was also witnessed by a C. Montagne; Kieft was twice misspelled as Reift. At the beginning of the lease, the terms were for "$1.00" a year for twenty years and "One hundred dollars" at the end of the same lease. In the hearing in 1864, Cosse testified that the lease was for three years, not twenty, at $1.00 per year, not one hundred dollars.

38. *Cahill v. Palmer*, (folio 473), 127; *Central Park Extension*, 286, 298–301. "Minutes of the Court of Burgomasters and Schepens, 1653–1655," ed. Berthold Fernow, Mar. 21, 1655, in *The Records of New Amsterdam from 1653 to 1674 Anno Domini*, vol. I, 295. See also a discussion of fencing in, David Steven Cohen, *The Dutch-American Farm*, (New York: New York University Press, 1992), 77.

39. *Cahill v. Palmer*, "Points for Defendants," 5, Serrell testimony, *Cahill v. Palmer*, (folio 111), 31. Cosse first "sold" the block on which the Nutter farm stood to mason Richard C. Ackley for $6,000, L495, P292, 1847. Three months later, Ackley, who probably uncovered

Cosse's plot, reconveyed the block back to him for the same amount. On August 14, 1848, an odd alliance of fourteen "owners," seemingly all legitimate Montagne descendants, conveyed the block between 109th and 110th Streets and also eight lots on the east side of Sixth Avenue between 109th and 110th Streets to Cosse for $2,400 (L510, P127, August 14, 1848). The group included Andrew Thomson, Mary B. Freeman, Mary Ann Collings, Sarah Jane and Mary B.T. Downe, Catherine Clark, George De La Montanye, Sarah Ann Bogert, Mary Blauvelt, Ann Sparry, Eliza Thompson, John de la Montagne, Eliza Rogers, and John M. Fountain. Most of the above were confirmed as Montagne descendants by Cosse in the trial of December 1, 1864 (see *Extention*, 316–317). In 1848, Cosse continued to sell land he did not own, conveying segar manufacturer and real estate tycoon William Henry Hall (L495, P468, 1848), and turner Gilbert Sherwood addition property for a total of $17,500 (L495, P468, 1847). Tenants with leases from Cosse included: Thomas Gibson, Maria Gibson, Charles Ludike, Henry Spahn, John L. Henry, Alexander Clark (shoemaker), John Myer, James Tracey (gardener), Terence Moran (laborer), John Harris, William Miller (gardener), Mr. Newdike, Mr. Sweeney, Leonard Lewis (shoemaker), Anthony Turnbull (shoemaker), John Hutchinson (who rented land on 110th to 111th Streets), and, according to Cosse, "Clarence or some such name. He worked up at Sisters of Charity." *Cahill v. Palmer, Central Park Extension*, 287–297.

40. *Central Park Extension*, 268–310; Hunter Research, Inc., *A Preliminary Historical and Archaeological Assessment of Central Park to the North of the 97th Street Transverse, Borough of Manhattan, City of New York. For: The Central Park Conservancy and The City of New York*, Volumes I and II, 1990, http://s-media.nyc.gov/agencies/lpc/arch_reports/444_B .pdf, Vol. I, D-234, concurs that the house conforms to the dimensions of the Nutter dwelling. This property was probably the same lots and buildings leased by Daniel Lord to German immigrant Frederick Reulein, who received a release of $125 from the commissioners in 1863 (see chapter 15).

41. John Pyne testimony, Jan. 25, Jan. 31, 1865, *Central Park Extension*, 320–324.

42. New York Superior Court, *Charles Reade, Respondent against Anthony Feistel, Appellant*, (New York: W. C. Bryant, 1851), Sept. 13, 1850. The Feistels were confirmed as living on the Bensons' former property.

43. *Central Park Extension*, 307–308.

44. Gabriel Cohen, "For You, Half Price," *NYT*, Nov. 27, 2005, Section 14, 4.

45. John F. Kasson, *Rudeness and Civility: Manners in Nineteenth-Century Urban America* (New York: Hill and Wang, 1990), 103.

46. David M. Scobey, *Empire City: The Making and Meaning of the New York City Landscape* (Philadelphia: Temple University Press, 2002), 82.

47. "Superior Court—Part First. Before Hon. Judge Woodruff. an Ejectment Suit under an Old Dutch Deed, *John Montanye agt. Patrick Daly*,' " *Her.*, Oct. 30, 1856, 5.

48. *John Montanye agst. Patrick Daly*, New York Superior Court, filed Nov. 7, 1856, DOR. In the 1865 trial, Cosse testified that Daly claimed to own the land; Daly owned two lots purchased from Abel Tinker (L606, P448, 1852) for $90. See *Central Park Extension*, 310.

49. According to the testimony of James Cosse, D. Randolph Martin filed a suit in the Court of Common Pleas for an injunction of disputed land between Fifth Avenue and McGowan's Pass and 107th to 109th Streets. See, *Central Park Extension*, 284–285.

50. Cosse to Cahill and Seeley, "Agreement," L864, P74, Sept. 26, 1862.

51. See, death notice for Amanda Seeley, https://www.familysearch.org/ark:/61903/1:1:2 W6R-N5W.

52. Letter from John Montanye to Mr. C.C. Bristol, New York, Feb. 4, 1843, in "Aggravated Case of Scrofula," *New York Morning Chronicle*, Feb. 10, 1843.

53. Block 809, house and lot 1 to 64, to Courtland Palmer, $76,040, *Release*s, "Extension" MANY; 1863 (Box 2870) values converted to 2019, see https://www.officialdata.org/us /inflation/1863?amount=1.

54. "All Business Men Ought to Know Something about Real Estate," *NYT*, Aug 14, 1857, 5.

55. *The Real Estate Record and Builder's Guide*, vol. 1, no. 1, March 21, 1868, 1, 3.

56. *The Real Estate Record and Builder's Guide*, vol. 1, no. 1, March 21, 1868, 3.

57. Scobey, *Empire City*, 112.

58. Olmsted to BCCP, in Beveridge and Schuyler, eds., *PFLO*, Vol. III, May 31, 1858, 196.

EPILOGUE

1. Kenneth T. Jackson, preface, in Sara Cedar Miller, *Central Park, An American Masterpiece: A Comprehensive History of the Nation's First Urban Park* (New York: Abrams, 2003), 7.

Selected Bibliography

Abbott, John Howard. *Descendants of Bastiaen Van Kortryk: A Native of Belgium who Emigrated to Holland About 1615*. New York: Tobias A. Wright, 1922.

Alex, William, and George B. Tatum. *Calvert Vaux, Architect and Planner*. New York: Ink, Inc., 1994.

Alexander, Leslie M. *African or American? Black Identity and Political Activism in New York City, 1784–1861*. Champaign: University of Illinois Press, 2008.

American Sugar Refining Company. *A Century of Sugar Refining in the United States*. 3rd ed. New York: The De Vinne Press, 1918.

Anbinder, Tyler. *City of Dreams: The 400-Year Epic History of Immigrant New York*. New York: Houghton Mifflin Harcourt, 2016.

——. "Moving Beyond 'Rags to Riches': New York's Irish Famine Immigrants and Their Surprising Savings Accounts." *The Journal of American History* 99, no. 3 (December 2012).

Atkinson, Rick. *The British Are Coming: The War for America, Lexington to Princeton, 1775–1777*. New York: Henry Holt, 2019.

Augustyn, Robert T., and Paul E. Cohen. *Manhattan in Maps 1527–1995*. New York: Rizzoli, 1995.

Bailyn, Bernard. *The Barbarous Years: The Peopling of British North America: The Conflict Civilizations, 1600–1675*. New York: Knopf, 2012, Apple Books edition.

Ballon, Hillary. *The Greatest Grid: The Master Plan of Manhattan 1811–2011*. New York: Columbia University Press, 2012.

Basch, Norma. *In the Eyes of the Law: Women, Marriage and Property in Nineteenth-Century New York*. Ithaca, NY: Cornell University Press, 1982.

Bayles, W. Harrison. *Old Taverns of New York*. New York: Frank Allaben Genealogical Company, 1915.

Beach, Moses Yale. *Wealth and Pedigree of the Wealthy Citizens of New York City: Comprising an Alphabetical Arrangement of Persons Estimated to Be Worth and Upwards, with the Sums Appended to Each Name; Being Useful to Banks, Merchants and Others*. 3rd ed. New York: Sun Office, 1842.

Beal, Thomas David. *Selling Gotham: The Retail Trade in New York City from the Public Market to Alexander T. Stewart's Marble Palace, 1625–1860*. Stony Brook: State University of New York at Stony Brook, 1998.

Berlin, Ira, and Leslie M. Harris, eds. *Slavery in New York*. New York: New-York Historical Society, 2005.

Bernstein, Iver. *The New York City Draft Riots: Their Significance for American Society and Politics in the Age of the Civil War*. New York: Oxford University Press, 1990.

Beveridge, Charles E., and Paul Rocheleau. *Frederick Law Olmsted: Designing the American Landscape*. New York: Rizzoli, 1995.

Beveridge, Charles E., and David Schuyler, eds. *The Papers of Frederick Law Olmsted*. Vol. III, "Creating Central Park, 1857-1861." Baltimore, MD: Johns Hopkins University Press, 1983.

Beveridge, Charles E., Carolyn F. Hoffman, and Kenneth Hawkins, eds. *The Papers of Frederick Law Olmsted*. Vol. VII, "Parks, Politics, and Patronage, 1874–1882." Baltimore, MD: Johns Hopkins University Press, 1983.

Billopp, Charles Farmar. *A History of Thomas and Anne Billopp Farmar, and some of their Descendants in America, 1846–1907*. New York: self-pub., 1907.

Binder, Frederick M., and David M. Reimers. *All the Nations Under Heaven: An Ethnic and Racial History of New York City*. New York: Columbia University Press, 1995.

Black, David. *The King of Fifth Avenue: The Fortunes of August Belmont*. New York: Dial Press, 1981.

Black, George Ashton. "The History of Municipal Ownership of Land on Manhattan Island." Ph.D. diss., Columbia University, 1889, 54. https://archive.org/details/ldpd_6626214_000 /page/n5/mode/2up.

Blackmar, Elizabeth. *Manhattan for Rent, 1785–1850.*, NY Ithaca: Cornell University Press, 1989.

Blackstone, William. *Commentaries on the Laws of England*. Vol. 1. Oxford: 1765.

Board of Commissioners of the Central Park. *Catalogue of Plans for the Improvement of Central Park*, s.n. 1858, NYHS, Main Collection (Y1800 Boa Cat). Handwritten notations by Commissioner Charles H. Russell.

Board of Directors of the Harlaem Canal Company. *Report of the Board of Directors of the Harlaem Canal Company*, Dec. 20, 1828. New York: Grattan's Office, 1828.

Bolton, Reginald Pelham. *Indian Paths in the Great Metropolis*. New York: Museum of the American Indian, Heye Foundation, 1922.

Bonasera, Michael C., and Leslie Raymer. "Good for What Ails You: Medicinal Use at Five Points." *Historical Archaeology* 35, no. 3 (2001): 49–64. http://www.jstor.org/stable/25616938.

Bonomi, Patricia U. *A Factious People: Politics and Society in Colonial New York*. New York: Columbia University Press, 1971.

Boyd, William Henry. *Boyd's Tax Book: Being a List of Persons, Corporations and Co-Partnerships, Resident and Non-Resident, Who Were Taxed According to the Assessors' Books, 1856 and '57*. New York: New-York Historical Society, 1857

Brace, Charles Loring. *The Dangerous Classes of New York, and Twenty Years' Work Among Them.* New York: Wynkoop & Hallenbeck, 1872.

Bradley Sr., David Henry. *A History of the AME Zion Church.* Nashville: The Parthenon Press, 1956.

Branch, Michele Nicole. "Just Provisions: Food, Identity, and Contested Space in Urban America, 1800–1875." Ph.D. diss., University of California, Berkeley, 2012. https://escholarship.org/uc/item/4gk6g2v8.

Brenwall, Cynthia S. *The Central Park: Original Designs for New York's Greatest Treasure.* New York: Abrams, 2019.

Bultheis, Kyle T. *Four Steeples Oover the City Streets: Religion and Society in New York's Early Republic Congregations.* New York: New York University Press, 2014.

Burleigh, James Bartlett, and J. Franklin Jameson, eds. "The Trials and Conversion of Theunis Idenszen." In *Journal of Jasper Danckaerts 1679–1680.* New York: Charles Scribner's Sons, 1913.

Burrows, Edwin G., and Mike Wallace. *Gotham: A History of New York City to 1898.* New York and Oxford: Oxford University Press, 1999.

Cantwell, Anne-Marie, and Diana diZerega Wall. *Unearthing Gotham: The Archaeology of New York City.* New Haven: Yale University Press, 2001.

Casey, Marion. "Refractive History: Memory and the Founders or the Emigrant Savings Bank." In *Making the Irish American: History and Heritage of the Irish in the United States,* ed. J. J. Lee and Marion R. Casey. New York: New York University Press, 2007.

Champagne, Phillip J. *Alexander McDougall and the American Revolution in New York.* Schenectady, NY: Bicentennial, 1975.

Chase, Philander D., and Frank E. Grizzard Jr., eds. *The Papers of George Washington.* Revolutionary War Series, vol. 6, *13 August 1776 – 20 October 1776.* Charlottesville: University Press of Virginia, 1994.

Chernow, Ron. *Washington: A Life.* New York: Penguin, 2011.

Chopra, Ruma. *Unnatural Rebellion: Loyalists in New York City During the Revolution.* Charlottesville: University of Virginia Press, 2011.

Cohen, David Steven. *The Dutch-American Farm.* New York: New York University Press, 1992.

Coleman, Aaron N. "Loyalists in War, Americans in Peace: The Reintegration of the Loyalists, 1775–1800." Ph.. diss., University of Kentucky, 2008. https://uknowledge.uky.edu/gradschool_diss/620.

Comptroller of the City of New York. *Annual Report of the Comptroller of the City of New York of the Receipts and Expenditures of the City Government for the Year 1857.* New York: Chas E. Baker, 1857, Doc. No. 10. https://babel.hathitrust.org/cgi/pt?id=nyp.33433069110181&view=1up&seq=604&q1=Central%20Park.

Conveyances on Record in the Registrar's Office by Dudley Selden, From the 1st January, 1825, to the 1st January, 1838. New York: Alexander S. Gould, 1838.

Cooper, Brendan. "The Domino Effect: Politics, Policy, and the Consolidation of the Sugar Refining Industry in the United States, 1789–1895." Ph.D. diss., CUNY Graduate Center, 2018. https://academicworks.cuny.edu/cgi/viewcontent.cgi?article=3937&context=gc_etds.

Corcoran, Cate. "The Gloucester Family of Brooklyn." http://www.brownstoner.com/brooklyn -life/walkabout-the-gloucester-family-of-brooklyn-part-3/.

Cozzens Jr., Issachar. *A Geological History of Manhattan or New York Island Together with a Map of the Island and a Suite of Sections, Tables and Columns, for the Study of Geology, Particularly Adapted for the American Student.* New York: W. E. Dean, 1843. https://www .biodiversitylibrary.org/item/124972#page/33/mode/1up.

Crimmins, John Daniel. *Irish-Americans Historical Miscellany: Relating Largely to New York City and Vicinity.* New York: self-pub., 1905.

Cronon, William. *Changes in the Land: Indians, Colonists and the Ecology of New England.* 1983; reprint, New York: Hill and Wang, 2003.

Croton Aqueduct Department. "Report of the Croton Aqueduct Department made to the Common Council of the City of New York." *Documents of the Board of Aldermen of the City of New York*, Doc. No. 81, Dec. 31, 1851. New York: McSpedon & Baker, 1852.

De Forest, Mrs. Robert W. [Emily Johnson]. *A Walloon Family in America: Lockwood de Forest and His Forbears, 1500–1848.* New York: Houghton Mifflin, 1914.

DeVoe, Thomas F. *The Market Book: Containing a Historical Account of Public Markets in the Cities of New York, Boston, Philadelphia and Brooklyn.* Vol. 1. New York: Hall, Clayton and Medole, 1862.

Dickinson, Nancy. "St. Philip's Episcopal Church Cemetery, Intensive Documentary Study, Christie Street, New York, New York, Second Avenue Subway." Prepared by Historical Perspectives, Inc., Westport, CT, June 2003. http://s-media.nyc.gov/agencies/lpc/arch _reports/437.pdf.

Diner, Hasia R. " 'The Most Irish City in the Union': The Era of the Great Migration, 1844– 1877." In *The New York Irish*, ed. Ronald H. Bayor and Timothy J. Meagher. Baltimore, MD: Johns Hopkins University Press, 1996.

Doherty, James J. *Life of Mother Elizabeth Boyle: One of Mother Seaton's Companions, the Assistant Mother Under Her for Eight Years and First Superioress of 'The Sisters of Charity of St. Vincent de Paul' of New York City.* Mount Loretto, Staten Island: Mission of the Immaculate Virgin, 1893.

Doughty, Samuel Stilwell. *The Life of Samuel Stilwell: With Notices of Some of His Contemporaries.* New York: Brown & Wilson, 1877.

Edsall, Thomas, ed. *Journal of John Charles Phillip von Krafft: Lieutenant in the Hessian Regiment Von Bose 1776–1784.* New York: 1888. https://babel.hathitrust.org/cgi/pt?id=coo1.ark :/13960/t4xh0628p&view=1up&seq=7.

Eldredge, Niles, and Sidney Horenstein. *Concrete Jungle: New York City and Our Last Best Hope for a Sustainable Future.* Oakland: University of California Press, 2014.

Ellis, Joseph J. *Revolutionary Summer: The Birth of American Independence.* New York: Knopf, 2013.

Ernst, Robert. *Immigrant Life in New York City, 1825–1863.* Syracuse, NY: Syracuse University Press, 1994.

Evelev, John. "Rus-Urban Imaginings: Literature of the American Park Movement and Representations of Social Space in the Mid-Nineteenth Century." *Early American Studies* 12, no. 1 (Winter 2014).

Foner, Eric. *Gateway to Freedom: The Hidden History of the Underground Railroad.* New York: Norton, 2015.

Ford, Worthington Chauncey, ed. *The Writings of George Washington.* Vol. 4, "1776." New York: G. P. Putnam's Sons, 1889.

Fox, Dixon. "The Negro Vote in Old New York." *Political Science Quarterly* 32, no. 2 (1917).

Freeman, Joanne B. *Affairs of Honor: National Politics in the New Republic.* New Haven, CT: Yale University Press, 2001.

Freeman, Rhoda G. *The Free Negro in New York City in the Era Before the Civil* War. New York: Garland, 1994.

Frijhoff, Willem. *Fulfilling God's Mission: The Two Worlds of Dominie Everardus Bogardus, 1607–1647.* Trans. Myra Heerspink Scholz. Leiden, Boston: Brill, 2007.

Gates Jr., Henry Louis. *The Black Church: This Is Our Story, This Is Our Song.* New York: Penguin, 2021.

Ghent, Andra. "How Do Case Law and Statute Differ? Lessons from the Evolution of Mortgage Law." *The Journal of Law & Economics* 57, no. 4 (November 2014). https://www.jstor.org/stable/10.1086/680931.

——. *Special Report the Historical Origins of America's Mortgage Law.* Research Institute for Housing America, 2012. http://www.housingamerica.org/RIHA/RIHA/Publications/82406_11922_RIHA_Origins_Report.pdf.

Gilje, Paul. *The Road to Mobocracy: Popular Disorder in New York City, 1763–1834.* Chapel Hill: University of North Carolina Press, 1987.

Glickman, Lawrence B. "Buy for the Sake of the Slave: Abolitionism and Origins of American Consumer Activism." *American Quarterly* 56, no. 4 (2004).

Goddard, Ives. "The Origin and Meaning of the Name 'Manhattan.' " *New York History* (The New York State Historical Association), Fall 2010.

Goodfriend, Joyce. *Who Should Rule at Home?: Confronting the Elite in British New York City.* Ithaca, NY: Cornell University Press, 2017.

Goodwin, Aaron. *New York City Municipal Archives: An Authorized Guide for Family Historians.* New York: New York Genealogical and Biographical Society, 2016.

Greenleaf, Jonathan. *A history of the churches, of all denominations, in the city of New York, from the first settlement to the year 1846.* New York: E. French, 1846. https://catalog.hathitrust.org/Record/001408135.

Griffen, David M. "To Huts: British Winter Cantonments Around New York City." *Journal of the American Revolution*, February 25, 2019.

Grinstein, Hyman Bogomolny. *The Rise of the Jewish Community of New York, 1654–1860.* Philadelphia: Jewish Publication Society of America, 1945. https://babel.hathitrust.org/cgi/pt?id=uc1.32106014036500&view=1up&seq=9.

Gross, Bella. "Life and Times of Theodore S. Wright, 1797–1847." *Negro History Bulletin* 3, no. 9 (June 1940).

Guernsey, R[ocellus] S. *New York City and vicinity during the war of 1812: being a military, civic, and financial local history of that period, with incidents and anecdotes thereof.* Vol. 2. New York: C. L. Woodward, 1889–1895.

Hall, Edward Hagaman. "Central Park, in the City of New York." *Sixteenth Annual Report of the American Scenic and Historic Preservation Society*, appendix G. New York: American Scenic and Historic Preservation Society, 1911.

——. *McGowan's Pass and Vicinity*. New York: The American Scenic and Historic Preservation Society, 1905.

Halttunen, Karen. *Confidence Men and Painted Ladies: A Study of Middle-Class Culture in America, 1830–1870*. New Haven, CT: Yale University Press, 1982.

Harris, Leslie M. *In the Shadow of Slavery: African Americans in New York City, 1626–1863*. Chicago: University of Chicago Press, 2004.

Hartigan-O'Connor, Ellen. "Gender's Value in the History of Capitalism." *Journal of the Early Republic* 36, no. 4 (2016): 613–635. doi:10.2307/jearlyrepublic.36.4.613.

Hastings, Hugh, State Historian, ed. *The Papers of Daniel D. Tomkins, Governor of New York 1807–1817*. Military Vol. III, State of New York. New York and Albany: Wynkoop, Hallenbeck, Crawford Co., 1902.

Hatch, Nathan O. *The Democratization of American Christianity.* New Haven, CT: Yale University Press, 1989.

Heaton, Herbert. "Non-Importation, 1806–1812." *The Journal of Economic History* 1, no. 2 (1941): 178–198. http://www.jstor.org/stable/2113472.

Heckscher, Morrison H. *Creating Central Park*. New York: The Metropolitan Museum of Art and Yale University Press, 2008.

Hershkowitz, Leo. "The Irish and the Emerging City: Settlement to 1844." In *The New York Irish*, ed. Ronald H. Bayer and Timothy J. Meager. Baltimore, MD: John Hopkins University Press, 1996.

Hershkowitz, Leo, and Isadore S. Meyer, eds. *The Lee Max Friedman Collection of American Jewish Colonial Correspondence: Letters of the Franks Family (1733–1748)*. Waltham, MA: American Jewish Historical Society, 1969.

Hirsch, Leo H. "The Slave in New York." *The Journal of Negro History* 16, no. 4 (1931). doi:10.2307/2713870.

Hodges, Graham Russell Gao. *Black New Jersey: 1664 to the Present Day*. New Brunswick, NJ: Rutgers University Press, 2019.

——. *David Ruggles: A Radical Black Abolitionist and the Underground Railroad in New York City*. Chapel Hill: University of North Carolina Press, 2010.

——. *New York City Cartmen, 1667–1850*, rev. ed. New York: New York University Press, 2012.

——. *Root and Branch: African Americans in New York and East Jersey, 1613–1863*. Chapel Hill: University of North Carolina Press, 1999.

Hodges, Graham Russell, and Alan Edward Brown. *Pretends to Be Free: Runaway Slave Advertisements from Colonial and Revolutionary New York and New Jersey.* New York and London: Garland, 1994.

Holloway, Marguerite. *The Measure of Manhattan: The Tumultuous Career and Surprising Legacy of John Randel Jr., Cartographer, Surveyor, Inventor.* New York: Norton, 2013.

——. "Unearthing the City Grid That Would Have Been in Central Park." January 8, 2011. https://www.newyorker.com/news/news-desk/unearthing-the-city-grid-that-would-have -been-in-central-park.

Hosack, David. *Hortus Elginensis: or A Catalogue of Plants Indiginous and Exotic, Cultivated in the Elgin Botanic Garden in the Vicinity of the City of New-York.* 2nd ed., enlarged. New York: T. & J. Swords, 1811.

Howard, Nathan. *Howard's Practice Reports in the Supreme Court and Court of Appeals of the State of New York.* Vol. 30. Albany, NY: William Gould & Son.1866.

Howe, Richard. "A Little Pre-History of the Manhattan Grid." Gotham, A Blog for Scholars of New York City History, The Gotham Center for New York History, March 13, 2011, https://www.gothamcenter.org/blog/a-little-pre-history-of-the-manhattan-grid.

——. "Notes on Casimir Goerck's 1785 and 1795 Surveys of the Common Lands of the City of New York." Gotham, A Blog for Scholars of New York City History, The Gotham Center for New York City History, October 20, 2015. https://www.gothamcenter.org /blog/notes-on-casimir-goercks-1785-and-1795-surveys-of-the-Common-Lands-of-the -city-of-new-york.

Hunter Research, Inc. *Archeological Testing and Monitoring Forts Landscape Reconstruction Project, Central Park, Borough of Manhattan, New York.* Prepared for the Central Park Conservancy, January 2014. http://s-media.nyc.gov/agencies/lpc/arch_reports/1545.pdf.

——. *Archival Research and Historic Resource Mapping North End of Central Park Above 103rd Street, Borough of Manhattan, New York City, Summary Narrative.* Prepared for the Central Park Conservancy, July 2014. http://s-media.nyc.gov/agencies/lpc/arch_reports/1617.pdf.

——. *A Preliminary Historical and Archaeological Assessment of Central Park to the North of the 97th Street Transverse, Borough of Manhattan, City of New York. For: The Central Park Conservancy and The City of New York.* Volumes I and II, 1990. http://s-media.nyc.gov /agencies/lpc/arch_reports/444_B.pdf.

Huskins, Bonnie. "Shelburnian Manners: Gentility and the Loyalists of Shelburne, Nova Scotia." *Early American Studies: An Interdisciplinary Journal* 13, no. 1 (Winter 2015).

Inskeep, Carolee. *The Graveyard Shift: A Family Historian's Guide to New York City Cemeteries.* Orem, UT: Ancestry Publishing, 2000.

Isenberg, Nancy. *Fallen Founder: The Life of Aaron Burr.* New York: Penguin, 2007.

Jacobs, Jaap. *The Colony of New Netherland: A Dutch Settlement in Seventeenth-Century America.* Ithaca, NY: Cornell University Press, 2009.

——. "Hot Pestilential and Unheard-Of Fevers, Illnesses, and Torments: Days of Fasting and Prayer in New Netherland." *New York History* 96, no. 3–4 (Summer/Fall 2015): 284–300. https://www.jstor.org/stable/newyorkhist.96.3-4.284.

Jaffe, Eric. *The King's Best Highway: The Lost History of the Boston Post Road, the Route That Made America.* New York: Scribner, 2013.

Jaffe, Steven H. *New York at War: Four Centuries of Combat, Fear, and Intrigue in Gotham.* New York: Basic Books, 2012, Apple Books edition.

Jameson, Franklin, ed., *Narratives of New Netherland, 1609–1664.* New York: Charles Scribner's Sons, 1909.

Jervis, John Bloomfield. *Description of the Croton Aqueduct.* New York: Slam & Guion, 1842.

John Brown Papers, Kansas Historical Society, Topeka: James N. Gloucester to John Brown, February 19, 1858 (https://www.kshs.org/archives/225810), March 9, 1858(https://www.kshs.org/archives/225811).

Johnson, Victoria. *America's Eden: David Hosack, Botany, and Medicine in the Garden of the Early Republic.* New York: Norton, 2018.

Johnston, Henry P. *Battle of Harlem Heights.* New York: The Macmillan Company, 1897.

Jones, Thomas. *History of New York During the Revolutionary War and of the Leading Events in the Other Colonies at that Period,* New York, 1879. In *Eyewitness Accounts of the American Revolution.* Vol. I. Ed. Edward Floyd de Lancey. New York: New-York Historical Society, 1879.

Kalfus, Melvin. *Frederick Law Olmsted: The Passion of a Public Artist.* New York: New York University Press, 1990.

Kasson, John F. *Rudeness and Civility: Manners in Nineteenth-Century Urban America.* New York: Hill and Wang, 1990.

Keneally, Thomas. *American Scoundrel: The Life of the Notorious Civil War General Dan Sickles.* New York: Doubleday, 2002.

Kerber, Linda K. "Abolitionists and Amalgamators: The New York City Race Riots of 1834." *New York History* 48, no. 1 (1967). http://www.jstor.org/stable/23162902.

Kiechle, Melanie A. "Preserving the Unpleasant: Sources, Methods, and Conjectures for Odors at Historic Sites." *Future Anterior: Journal of Historic Preservation, History, Theory, and Criticism* 13, no. 2 (Winter 2016).

King, Charles. *A Memoir of the Construction, Cost, and Capacity of the Croton Aqueduct: compiled from Official Documents: Together with an Account of the Civic Celebration of the fourteenth October, 1842, on Occasion of the Completion of the Great Work: preceded by a Preliminary Essay on Ancient and Modern Aqueducts.* New York: printed by Charles King, 1843.

Knight, Sarah Kemble, and Rev. Mr. Buckingham. *The Journals of Madam Knight and Rev. Mr. Buckingham from the Original Manuscripts.* New York: Wilder & Campbell, 1825.

Koke, Richard J. "Milestones Along the Old Highways of New York City: A Record of the Silent Sentinels of the Stagecoach Era." *The New-York Historical Society Quarterly* 34, no. 3 (July 1950).

Koeppel, Gerard. *City on a Grid: How New York Became New York.* New York: Da Capo Press, 2015.

——. *Water for Gotham: A History.* Princeton, NJ: Princeton University Press, 2000.

Kouwenhoven, John A. *The Columbia Historical Portrait of New York: An Essay in Graphic History.* New York: Harper & Row, 1953.

Kowsky, Francis R. *Country, Park and City: The Architecture and Life of Calvert Vaux.* New York: Oxford University Press, 1998.

Kruger, Vivienne. "Born to Run: The Slave Family in Early New York, 1626 to 1827." Ph.D. diss., Columbia University, 1985.

Lamb, Martha J. *The History of the City of New York: Its Origin, Rise, and Progress.* Vol. 3. New York: A. S. Barnes and Company, 1896.

Lepore, Jill. "The Tightening Vise: Slavery and Freedom in British New York." in *Slavery in New York*, ed. Ira Berlin and Leslie M. Harris. New York: New-York Historical Society, 2005.

Levine, Lawrence W. *Highbrow/Lowbrow: The Emergence of Cultural Hierarchy in America.* Cambridge, MA: Harvard University Press, 1988.

Liebman, Bennett. "The Quest for Black Voting Rights in New York State." *Albany Government Law Review* 11 (2018).

Lindfors, Bernth, ed. *Ira Aldridge: The African Roscius.* Rochester, NY: University of Rochester Press, 2010.

——. *Ira Aldridge: The Early Years, 1807–1833.* Rochester Studies in African History and the Diaspora. Rochester, NY: University of Rochester Press, 2011.

Laet, Joannes De, and George Folsom. *Extracts from the New world, or, A description of the West Indies.* New-York, 1841. PDF. https://www.loc.gov/item/11022409/.Lobel, Cindy R. *Urban Appetites: Food and Culture in Nineteenth-Century New York.* Chicago: University of Chicago Press, 2014.

Lofaso, Anthony. *Origins and History of the Village of Yorkville in the City of New York.* New York: Xlibris, 2010.

Loughery, John. *Dagger John: Archbishop John Hughes and the Making of Irish America.* Ithaca, NY: Cornell University Press, 2018.

Lyons, Isaac S. *Recollections of an Old Cartman: Boonton, New Jersey, From the Newark Journal.* Newark, NJ: Daily Journal Office, 1872.

Lyons, Maritcha. "Memories of Yesterday, All of Which I Saw and Part of Which I Was— An Autobiography." Harry Albro Williamson Papers, Reel 1, Schomburg Center, New York Public Library.

Mackenzie, Frederick. *Diary of Frederick Mackenzie: Giving a Daily Narrative of His Military Service as an Officer of the Regiment of Royal Welch Fusiliers During the Years 1775–1781 in Massachusetts, Rhode Island and New York.* Vol. 1. Ed. Allen French. Cambridge, MA: Harvard University Press, 1930.

Manevitz, Alexander. " 'A Great Injustice': Urban Capitalism and the Limits of Freedom in Nineteenth-Century New York City." *Journal of Urban History* (January 23, 2021). https://journals.sagepub.com/doi/10.1177/0096144220976119.

McCadden, Joseph J. "Bishop Hughes versus the Public School Society of New York." *The Catholic Historical Review* 50, no. 2 (1964).

McGrath, Patrick. "Secular Power, Sectarian Politics: The American-Born Irish Elite and Catholic Political Culture in Nineteenth-Century New York." *Journal of American Ethnic History* 38, no. 3 (Spring 2019). www.jstor.org/stable/10.5406/jamerethnhist.38.3.0036.

McKay, Ernest A. *The Civil War in New York*. Syracuse, NY: Syracuse University Press, 1991.

McManus, Edgar J. *A History of Negro Slavery in New York*. 1966; reprint, Syracuse, NY: Syracuse University Press, 1970.

McNeur, Catherine. *Taming Manhattan: Environmental Battles in the Antebellum City*. Cambridge, MA: Harvard University Press, 2014.

Miller, Kerby A. *Emigrants and Exiles: Ireland and the Irish Exodus to North America*. New York: Oxford University Press, 1985.

Miller, Sara Cedar. "A Case of Mistaken Identity: A Historian's Hunt for Buried Treasure." *Site/Lines* (Spring 2019).

——. *Central Park, An American Masterpiece: A Comprehensive History of the Nation's First Urban Park*. New York: Abrams, 2003.

——. "Central Park's Sunken Treasure." *New-York Journal of American History* 65, no. 3 (Spring 2004).

Mines, John Flavel. *A Tour Around Manhattan and My Summer Acre*. New York: Harper & Brothers, 1893.

Minutes of the Common Council of the City of New York, 1784–1831. New York: City of New York, 1930.

Minutes of the National Convention of Colored Citizens; Held at Buffalo; on the 15th, 16th, 17th, 18th, and 19th of August, 1843; for the purpose of considering their moral and political condition as American citizens. https://omeka.coloredconventions.org/items/show/278.

Moore, Clement C. *A Plain Statement Addressed to the Proprietors of Real Estate in the City and County of New-York, by a Landholder*. New York: J. Eastburn and Co., 1818.

Mott, Hopper Striker. *The New York of Yesterday: A Descriptive Narrative of Old Bloomingdale*. New York: G. P. Putnam's Sons, 1908.

Mushkat, Jerome. *Fernando Wood: A Political Biography*. Kent, OH: Kent State University Press, 1990.

Myers, Gustavus. *The History of Tammany Hall*. 2nd ed. New York: Boni & Liveright, 1917.

Narrett, David E. *Inheritance and Family Life in Colonial New York City*. Ithaca, NY: Cornell University Press, 1992.

New York County Jury Census, 1819. Ward 10, Box 8, Vol. 15. New York City Department of Records and Information Services. http://nycma.lunaimaging.com/luna/servlet/detail/NYCMA~10~10~15~1206205?sort=identifier%2Ctitle%2Cdate%2Cvolume_number&qvq=sort:identifier%2Ctitle%2Cdate%2Cvolume_number;lc:NYCMA~10~10&mi=14&trs=21.

New-York As It Is, in 1837: Containing, A General Description Of The City Of New-York, List Of Officers, Public Institutions, And Other Useful Information Including The Public Officers, Accompanied By A Correct Map. New York: J. Bisturnell, 1837.

New-York Historical Society. *The Burghers of New Amsterdam and the Freemen of New York, 1675–1866*. New York: New-York Historical Society, 1885.

New-York Historical Society Education Department. *Seneca Village: A Teacher's Guide to Using Primary Sources in the Classroom*. New York: New-York Historical Society, 2010.

New York State. *The Colonial Laws of New-York From the Year 1664 to the Revolution.* Vol. I. Albany: James B. Lyon, 1894.

——. *Documents of the Assembly of the State of New York.* Vol. 6. 1846.

——. *Journal of the Convention of the State of New-York.* Albany: Cantine & Leake, 1821.

——. *Public Laws of the State of New-York, Passed at the Thirty-Second Session of the Legislature.* Chapter XLIV. Albany: Websters and Skinner, 1809.

——. *Reports of the Proceedings and Debates of the New York Constitutional Convention, 1821.* New York: Da Capo Press, 1970.

[——] Secretary of State. *Instructions for Taking the Census of the State of New-York In the Year 1855.* Albany: Weed, Parsons & Co., 1855.

——. Senate Doc. 83, June 21, 1853. In *Senate Documents*, 76th Session, Vol. 3, No. 71 to No. 86 Inclusive, 16. Albany: C. Van Benthuysen, 1853.

——. *War of 1812, Payroll Abstracts for New York State Militia, 1812–1815.* New York State Archives.

New York State Court of Appeals. *Dunham v. Townshend.* In *Reports of Cases Decided in the Court of Appeals of the State of New York.* Vol. 118. Albany, January 1890.

New York State Supreme Court, J[udge Ira] Harris. "In the Matter of the Application of the Mayor, &c, of the City of New York, Relative to the Opening and Laying Out of A Public Place, Between Fifty-Ninth and One-Hundred and Sixth Streets and the Fifth and Eighth Avenues, in the City of New York." *First Annual Report on the Improvement of the Central Park, New York.* Doc. No. 5, Part I. Appendix H. New York: Chas. W. Baker, 1857.

O'Callaghan, E. [Edmund] B. Bailey. *A Brief and True Narrative of the Hostile Conduct of the Barbarous Natives Towards the Dutch Nation.* Albany, NY: J. Munsell, 1863.

——. *Documents Relative to the Colonial History of the State of New York, Procured in England Holland, and France.* Vol. 1. Albany: Weed, Parsons, and Company, 1856. https://archive.org /details/documentsrelativo1brod/page/n49/mode/2up.

——. *History of New Netherland, or New York Under the Dutch.* New York, D. Appleton, 1848. https://archive.org/details/historyofnewnetho1ocal.

——. *Laws and Ordinances of New Netherland 1638–1674.* Albany: Weed, Parsons and Co., 1868.

Olmsted, Frederick Law. *Civilizing American Cities: Writings on City Landscapes.* Ed. S. B. Sutton. New York: DaCapo Press, 1997.

——. *Forty Years of Landscape Architecture.* Ed. Frederick Law Olmsted Jr. and Theodora Kimball. Cambridge, MA: The MIT Press, 1973.

——. *Walks and Talks of an American Farmer in England.* New York: G. P. Putnam, 1852; reprint, Amherst, MA: Library of American Landscape History, 2002.

Pashman, Howard. "The People's Property Law: A Step Toward Building a New Legal Order in Revolutionary New York." *Law and History Review* 31, no. 3 (2013).

Pessen, Edward. "Did Fortunes Rise and Fall Mercurially in Antebellum America? The Tale of Two Cities: Boston and New York." *Journal of Social History* 4, no. 4 (1971). www.jstor .org/stable/3786475.

Peters, John Punnett. *Annals of St. Michael's: Being the History of St. Michael's Episcopal Protestant Church for One Hundred Years 1807–1907.* New York: G. P. Putnam's Sons, The Knickerbocker Press, 1907.

Peters, Thomas McClure. "Baptisms, Confirmations, Marriages and Burials for the years 1847 to 1865." *All Angels' Church, New York City, Parish Record Book, 1847–1874.* All Angels' Church, Office of the Rector.

——. New York Protestant Episcopal City Mission Society. *The Growth of Charities.* New York: Julius Schlueter Book and Job Printer, 1873.Peterson, Carla L. *Black Gotham: A Family History of African Americans in Nineteenth-Century New York City.* New Haven, CT: Yale University Press, 2012.

Pierce, Carl Horton. *New Harlem Past and Present: The Story of an Amazing Civic Wrong, Now at Last to be Righted.* New York: The Harlem Publishing Company, 1903.

Pirsson, John W. *The Dutch Grants, Harlem Patents and Tidal Creeks.* New York: L.K. Strouse & Co., 1889.

Plunz, Richard. *A History of Housing in New York City.* New York: Columbia University Press, 2016.

Pool, David de Sola. *The Mill Street Synagogue (1730–1817) of the Congregation of Shearith Israel.* New York: [s.n.] 1930.

——. *Portraits Etched in Stone: Early Jewish Settlers 1682–1831.* New York: Columbia University Press, 1952.

Pougher, Richard D. Chapter 9, " 'Averse . . . To Remaining Idle Spectators': The Emergence of Loyalist Privateering During the American Revolution 1775–1778." Vol. II. Ph.D. diss., University of Maine, 2002.

Purcell, Richard J. "The New York Commissioners of Emigration and Irish Immigrants, 1847–1860." *Studies: An Irish Quarterly Review* 37, no. 145 (March 1948): 32. http://www.jstor.org/stable/30100186.

Quarles, Benjamin. *Allies for Freedom and Blacks on John Brown.* Cambridge, MA: Da Capo, 2001.

Ranney, Victoria Post. *The Papers of Frederick Law Olmsted.* Vol. V. Baltimore, MD: Johns Hopkins University Press, 1990.

Rawolle, Charles, and I[gnatz] A. Pilat. *Catalogue of Plants: Gathered in August and September 1857, in the Ground of the Central Park.* New York: M. W. Siebert, 1857.

Ray, Henrietta Cordelia, and Florence Ray. *Sketch of the Life of Rev. Charles B. Ray.* 1887. https://archive.org/details/9342f943-b613-491a-9d22-1f733a906f7c/page/n33/mode/2up.

The Real Estate Record Association. *A History of Real Estate, Building and Architecture in New York City During the Last Quarter of a Century.* New York: Record and Guide, 1898.

Reid, Robert W. *Washington Lodge, No. 21, F. & A.M., and Some of Its Members.* New York: Washington Lodge, 1911.

"Report on The Improvement of Schools for African American Children in New York City." *The Anglo-African Magazine* [New York City] (July 1859).

Rybczynski, Witold. *A Clearing in the Distance: Frederick Law Olmsted and America in the Nineteenth Century*. New York: Scribner, 1999.

Richman, Jeffrey. *Brooklyn's Green-Wood Cemetery: New York's Buried Treasure*. Lunenburg, VT: Stinehour Press, 1998.

Riker, James. *James Riker Papers, 1660–1989*, Series II. Colonial Papers 1660–[1880s], box 3, folder 6. Archives & Manuscripts, New York Public Library.

——. *Revised History of Harlem (City of New York), Its Origin and Early Annals*. New York: New Harlem Publishing Company, 1904.

Roberts, Helene E. "The Exquisite Slave: The Role of Clothes in the Making of the Victorian Woman." *Signs* 2, no. 3 (Spring 1977). https://www.jstor.org/stable/3173265.

Roberts, James A. *New York in the Revolution as Colony and State*. Albany, NY: Press of Brandon Printing Co.,1898.

Rock, Howard B. "The American Revolution and the Mechanics of New York City: One Generation Later." *New York History* 57, no. 3 (July 1976).

Roff, Sandra. "Teaching the Teachers: Black Education in Nineteenth-Century New York City." *New York History* 99, no. 2 (Spring 2018): 183–195. https://www.jstor.org/stable/26905106.

Romer, H. Dorothea, and Helen B. Hartman. *Jan Dyckman of Harlem and His Descendants*. New York: J. A. Thompson, 1981.

Romney, Susanah Shaw. *New Netherland Connections: Intimate Networks and Atlantic Ties in Seventeenth-Century America*. Chapel Hill: University of North Carolina Press, 2017.

Roper, Laura Wood. *FLO: A Biography of Frederick Law Olmsted*. Baltimore, MD: Johns Hopkins University Press, 1973.

Rosen, Deborah A. "Women and Property across Colonial America: A Comparison of Legal Systems in New Mexico and New York." *The William and Mary Quarterly* 60, no. 2 (April 2003).

Rosenberg, Charles. *The Cholera Years: The United States in 1832, 1849, and 1866*. Chicago: University of Chicago Press, 1987.

Rosenwaike, Ira. *Population History of New York City*. Syracuse, NY: Syracuse University Press, 1972.

Rosenzweig, Roy, and Elizabeth Blackmar. *The Park and the People: A History of Central Park*. Ithaca, NY: Cornell University Press, 1992.

Rush, Christopher. *A Short Account of the Rise and Progress of the African Methodist E. Church in America*. New York: self-pub., 1843.

Salwen, Peter. *Upper West Side Story: A History and Guide*. New York: Abbeville Press, 1989.

Sanderson, Eric W. *Manahatta: A Natural History of New York City*, New York: Abrams, 2009.

Santlofer, Joy. *Food City: Four Centuries of Food-Making in New York*. New York: Norton, 2017.

Schecter, Barnet. *The Battle for New York: The City at the Heart of the American Revolution*. New York: Walker & Co., 2002.

Schuyler, David. *Apostle of Taste: Andrew Jackson Downing, 1815–1852*. Baltimore, MD: John Hopkins University Press, 1996.

Schwab, John Christopher. "History of the New York Property Tax." *Publications of the American Economic Association* 5 (1890): 19n2. https://archive.org/metadata/jstor-2485701.

Scobey, David M. "Anatomy of the Promenade: The Politics of Bourgeois Sociability in Nineteenth-Century New York." *Social History* 17, no. 2 (May 1992): 212. www.jstor.org/stable/4286016.

——. *Empire City: The Making and Meaning of the New York City Landscape.* Philadelphia: Temple University Press, 2002.

Scovill, Joseph Alfred. [Walter Barrett, pseud.]. *The Old Merchants of New York.* Vols. 1–5. New York: Thomas R. Knox, 1864–70.

Seaman, [Samuel]. *The Rise of Methodist Society in the City of New York.* New York: 1821.

Selden, Henry R. *Reports of Cases Argued and Determined in the Court of Appeals of the State of New York.* Vol. VI. Albany: Weare C. Little, 1860.

Shorto, Russell. *The Island at the Center of the World.* New York: Vintage, 2005.

Sickles, Daniel E. "The Founder of Central Park, New York." Sickles Papers, Library of Congress, Manuscript Division, undated.

Silber, William B. *A History of the St. James Methodist Episcopal Church at Harlem, New York City, 1830–1880.* New York: Phillips & Hunt, 1882.

Rose-Redwood, Reuben Skye. "Rationalizing the Landscape: Superimposing the Grid Upon the Island of Manhattan." Thesis, Penn State, 2002. http://beyondcentralpark.com/Rationalizing_the_Landscape_FINALCOPY.pdf.

——. "Re-Creating the Historical Topography of Manhattan Island." *Geographical Review* 93, no. 1 (January 2003).

Smith, Gene. "The Haunted Major." *American Heritage* 45, no. 1 (February/March 1994).

Smith, James Reuel. *The Springs and Wells of Manhattan and the Bronx.* New York: New-York Historical Society, 1938.

Sobel, Dava. *Longitude: The True Story of a Lone Genius Who Solved the Greatest Scientific Problem of His Time.* New York: Penguin, 1995.

Spann, E. K. *The New Metropolis: New York City 1840–1857.* New York: Columbia University Press, 1981.

Spellen, Suzanne [Montrose Morris]. "The Gloucester Family of Brooklyn." http://www.brownstoner.com/history/walkabout-the-gloucester-family-of-brooklyn-part-1/ http://www.brownstoner.com/history/walkabout-the-gloucester-family-of-brooklyn-part-2/.

Starna, William. "The Dutch Among the Natives: American Indian-Dutch Relations, 1609–1664." https://www.newnetherlandinstitute.org/history-and-heritage/digital-exhibitions/the-dutch-among-the-natives-american-indian-dutch-relations-1609-1664/the-dutch-among-the-natives-american-indian-dutch-relations-1609-1664.

Steinberg, Ted. *Gotham Unbound: The Ecological History of Greater New York.* New York: Simon & Schuster, 2014.

Stewart, Ian R. "Politics and the Park: The Fight for Central Park." *New-York Historical Society Quarterly* 61, nos. 3, 4 (July/October 1977).

Stokes, I. N. Phelps. *The Iconography of Manhattan Island.* Vol. III. New York: Robert Dodd, 1918.

——. *The Iconography of Manhattan Island.* Vol. IV. New York: Robert Dodd, 1922.

——. *The Iconography of Manhattan Island.* Vol. V. New York: Robert Dodd, 1926.

——. *The Iconography of Manhattan Island.* Vol. VI. New York: Robert Dodd, 1928.

"Subscribers." *For a Review and Increase of Award in the Matter of Extension of Central Park.* New York: Wm C. Bryant & Co., Feb. 21, 1863.

Swan, Robert J. "John Teasman: African-American Educator and the Emergence of Community in Early Black New York City, 1787–1815." *Journal of the Early Republic* 12, no. 3 (Fall 1992).

Swanberg, W. A. *Sickles the Incredible.* New York: Charles Scribner's Sons, 1956.

Swift, Joseph Gardiner. *The Memoirs of General Joseph Gardiner Swift, LL.D, U.S.A.* Worcester, MA: F. S. Blanchard, privately printed, 1890. https://catalog.hathitrust.org/Record/010938918.

Swift, J[oseph] G[ardiner]. *Report on the defence of the City of New York, accompanied with maps, views, and topographical plans, Addressed to the Common Council.* New York, 1814. NYHS, Manuscript Division. https://digitalcollections.nyhistory.org/islandora/object/islandora%3A115181#page/4/mode/2up.

Sylvester Cahill & al. Agst Courtland Palmer and others. New York State Supreme Court General Term, Vol. 83, 1868. https://www.google.com/books/edition/Supreme_Court_General_Term/cDySrWPGbGQC?hl=en&gbpv=1&dq=Sylvester+Cahill&pg=RA1-PA122&printsec=frontcover.

Todd, Charles Burr. *The Story of the City of New York.* New York: G. P. Putnam's Sons, 1888.

Tower, Fayette B. *Illustrations of the Croton Aqueduct.* New York: Wiley and Putnam, 1843.

Tremante III, Louis P. "Agriculture and Farm Life in the New York City Region, 1820–1870." Ph.D. diss., Iowa State University, 2000.

Tuttle, H[enry] Croswell. *Abstracts of Farm Titles in the City of New York, East Side, Between 75th and 120th Streets.* New York: The Spectator Company, 1878.

Ullman, David. "The retreat chronology of the Laurentide Ice Sheet during the last 10,000 years and implications for deglacial sea-level rise." *Vignettes: Key Concepts in Geomorphology.* https://serc.carleton.edu/vignettes/collection/58451.html.

U.S. Congress. Chap. XI An Act providing for the taking of the seventh and subsequent Censuses of the United States, and to fix the Number of the Members of the House of Representatives, and provide for their apportionment among the several States. 31st Cong. (1850).

Van den Hout, Julie. "The Omnipotent Beaver in Van der Donck's *A Description of New Netherland*: A Natural Symbol of Promise in the New World." Thesis, University of California, Spring 2015. https://escholarship.org/content/qt870174nb/qt870174nb_noSplash_506c26-d948-cab2db3fbcdf5c2c01a13f.pdf?t=nqim8z.

Van der Donck, Adrian. *A Description of New Netherland.* 1656. Ed. Charles T. Gehring and William A. Starna. Lincoln: University of Nebraska Press, 2010.

Van Laer, Arnold J. F. *New York Historical Manuscripts: Dutch, Translated.* Vol. I, *Register of the Provincial Secretary, 1638–1642.* Edited with Added Indexes by Kenneth Scott And Kenn Stryker-Rodda. New York: Genealogical Publishing Co., 1974. https://www.newnether-landinstitute.org/files/6514/0151/8811/Volume_I_-_Register_of_the_Provincial_Secretary_1638–1642.pdf.

Van Schaick, Myndert. *Abstract of Corporate Ordinances, And Rules and Regulations adopted by the Croton Aqueduct Board in relation to Water, to which the attention of Consumers, and all others, is earnestly invited.* New York: Collins, Bowne & Co., 1855.

Valentine, David T. *A Compilation of the Laws of the State of New York Relating Particularly to the City of New York.* New York: Edmund Jones & Co., 1862.

Van Alstyne, Lawrence, and Charles Burr Ogden, eds. *The Ogden family in America, Eliz-abethtown branch, and their English Ancestry.* Philadelphia: J. B. Lippincott Company, 1907.

Vaux, Calvert. *Villas and Cottages: A Series of Designs Prepared for Execution in the United States.* New York: Harper and Brothers, 1864. Reprinted in *Villas and Cottages: The Great Architectural Style-Book of the Hudson River School.* New York: Dover, 1970.

Von Krafft, Philip. *Journal of John Charles Phillip von Krafft: Lieutenant in the Hessian Regi-ment Von Bose 1776–1784.* New York: private distribution, 1888. https://archive.org/details/cu31924032740114/mode/2up.

Wall, Diana diZerega, Nan A. Rothschild, and Cynthia Copeland. "Seneca Village and Lit-tle Africa: Two African American Communities in Antebellum New York City." *His-torical Archaeology* 42, no. 1 (2008). https://www.jstor.org/stable/25617485?origin=JSTOR-pdf&seq=1.

Wall, Diana diZerega, Nan A. Rothschild, Meredith B. Linn, and Cynthia R. Copeland, Institute for the Exploration of Seneca Village History, Inc. "Seneca Village, A Forgotten Community: Report on the 2011 Excavations." 2018. http://s-media.nyc.gov/agencies/lpc/arch_reports/1828.pdf.

Walsh, Sister Marie de Lourdes. *The Sisters of Charity of New York 1809–1959.* New York: Fordham University Press, 1960.

White, Shane. *Prince of Darkness: The Untold Story of Jeremiah G. Hamilton, Wall Street's First Black Millionaire.* New York: St. Martin's Press, 2015.

——. *Somewhat More Independent: The End of Slavery in New York City 1770–1810.* Athens: University of Georgia Press, 1991.

Whitfield, Harvey Amani. "The American Background of Loyalist Slaves." *Left History: An Interdisciplinary Journal of Historical Inquiry and Debate* 14, no. 1 (2009).

Wilder, Craig Steven. *In the Company of Black Men: The African Influence on African American Culture in New York City.* New York: New York University Press, 2001.

Wilentz, Sean. *Chants Democratic: New York City and the Rise of the American Working Class, 1788–1850.* New York: Oxford University Press, 1984.

Wilson, James Grant. *Memorial History of the City of New-York, from Its First Settlement to the Year 1892* (New York: New-York History Co., 1892), vol. I.

Wilson, Rufus Rockwell. *Heath's memoirs of the American war, reprinted from the original edition of 1798; with introduction and notes.* New York: A. Wessels Company, 1904.

Woolley, Mary E. "Early History of the Colonial Post Office." *Publications of the Rhode Island Historical Society, 1892–93* [Providence] 1 (1893).

Yoshpe, Harry B. "Record of Slave Manumissions in New York During the Colonial and Early National Periods." *The Journal of Negro History* 26, no. 1 (January 1941).

Zeichner, Oscar. "The Loyalist Problem in New York After the Revolution." *New York History* (July 1940).

Zion Pilgrim Methodist Episcopal Church Site. "Narrative Statement of Significance." National Register of Historic Places. https://www.nps.gov/nr/feature/places/pdfs/14000845.pdf.

MAPS AND PLANS

Bridges, William. *The City of New York As Laid Out by the Commissioners, with the Surrounding Country.* New York: John Randel Jr., 1814.

Bridges, William. *Map of the City of New York and Island of Manhattan as Laid Out by the Commissioners, April 3, 1807.* (Known as the Commissioners' Plan). New York: William Bridges, 1811.

Bridges, William. *Plan of the City of New-York, with the Recent and Intended Improvements.* New York: William Bridges, 1803–07.

British Headquarters Map 1782. Public Records Office, London.

Colton, Joseph H. *Topographical Map of the City and County of New York and the Adjacent Country.* New York: J. H. Colton & Co., 1836.

Dripps, Matthew. *Map of the City of New York Extending Northward to 50th Street.* New York: M. Dripps, 1852.

Grant, W. H. "Map Showing the Original Topography of the Site of the Central Park." In *Second Annual Report of the Commissioners of the Central Park.* New York:, Bryant, 1858.

Graves, Roswell, and and Francis Nicholson. *Topographical Maps &c, In the Matter of Opening Central Park.* New York, July 1855. Commissioners of Estimate and Assessment and R. J. Dillon, counsel to the corporation, Municipal Archives. File No. 83.2, Accession No. 1653. MANY.

Military Topographical Sketch of Haerlem Heights and Plain Exhibiting the Position and forms of Field Works and Block Houses which have been constructed in that Neghbourhood [sic] for the Defence of the City of New York by Genl Swift Chief Engineer copied from a Survey Made by Lieut. Renwick of the 82nd Regt New York Militia by T.E. Craig Lt. Artillery. NYHS.

New York City Farm Maps. City of New York Municipal Archives, 1864–1887.

Olmsted, Frederick Law, and Calvert Vaux. *Greensward*, Entry No. 33. MANY.

Randel Jr., John. *Farm Maps of the City of New York.* 4 vols. manuscript maps. New York: 1820. City of New York, Borough of Manhattan, Office of the President, Topographic Bureau.

——. *A Map of the City of New York by the Commissioners Appointed by an Act of the Legislature Passed April 3rd 1807, known as the "Commissioners' Plan."* New York: John Randel Jr., 1811.

Sackersdorff, Otto. *Maps of Farms Commonly Called the Blue Book, 1815: Drawn from the Original on File in the Street Commissioner's Office in the City of New York, together with Lines of Streets and Avenues, Laid out by John Randel, Jr. City Surveyor, New York.* New York: 1868. NYPL.

Sage, Gardener. *Central Park Condemnation Maps.* MANY.

——. *Map of the area later bounded by 88th and 99th Streets, Central Park near the proposed 7th Avenue, and the Hudson River, Manhattan, New York (N.Y.).* NYHS, Maps (M2.1.24).

——. *Map of the area later bounded by 93rd and 99th Streets, Central Park West and Broadway, Manhattan, New York (N.Y.).* NYHS, Maps (M2.1.24).

Stokes, I. N. Phelps. *The Iconography of Manhattan Island.* Vol. VI. New York: Robert Dodd, 1928.

Serrell, James E. *Maps & Profiles of Ground for New Reservoir Situated Between 86th and 96th Streets and Between 5th and 7th Avenues* (New York, 1853). NYPL, Lionel Pincus and Princess Firyal Map Division.

Stevens, John, Esqr., and T. Pope, del. *Plan of Fortifications for the Defence of the Harbour of New York.* 1807. NYHS.

Viele, Egbert Ludovicus. *Map of the City of New York from the Battery to 80th Street Showing the Original Topography of Manhattan Island.* New York: Egbert L. Viele, 1859. LOC.

——. *Map of Lands Included in The Central Park From a Topographical Survey.* New York: Egbert L. Viele, June 17, 1855. MANY.

——. *Plan for the improvement of the Central Park.* 1857. First Annual Report on the Improvement of the Central Park, New York. Doc. No. 5, Part I. New York: Chas. W. Baker, 1857.

——. *Sanitary and Topographical Map of the City and Island of New York.* New York: Egbert L. Viele, 1865. NYPL.

Index

Page numbers in *italics* refer to images and captions.

abolitionists, 180, 187, 198, 213, 225, 229, 231. *See also* New York Manumission Society; *see by individual names*

Adriance, Isaac, *51*, 57, 198, 431

Adriance, Margaret Eliza (Waldron), *51*, 56–57, 198, 431, 473n, 44

Africa: Ghana, 65; religious traditions, 194; slave trade in, 142, 337, *338*

African Americans. *See* Blacks

African Free School, 113, 187, 208, 214, 215, 219, 227. *See also* New York Manumission Society

African Methodist Episcopal Zion Church (A.M.E. Zion), 172; award to, 363; burial grounds of, 165, 196–197, 312; clergy of, 189, 187–190; founding of, 195–196; in Harlem, 198; "Little Zion," 197–198, 271; nonpayment of assessment, 198. *See also* Aldridge, Daniel; Smith, Leven; Walters, Dr. William A.

African Grove Theater, 187, 210, *211*. *See also* Aldridge, Ira; Hewlett, James

African Union Church, 195, 199, 204, 205, 349; site of, *200–201*. *See also* Colored School No. 3

Albany. *See* Fort Orange

Albany/Boston Post Road. *See* Kingsbridge Road

Aldridge, Daniel, 185–188

Aldridge, Ira, 185–187; *Ira Aldridge as Othello, 186. See also* Aldridge, Daniel

Alexander Hamilton (Conrad), *147*

All Angels' Church, 195, 202–204, *203*, 364, 378

A.M.E. Zion Church. *See* African Methodist Episcopal Zion Church

American Colonization Society, 168, 180, 227

American Party/American Republican Party. *See* Know-Nothing Party

Amory, James: awards to heirs, 355, 358; correspondence with Rufus King, 262–264; description of farm, 259–261; financial problems, 264; last will and testament of, 332; legal problems of heirs, 332–334; location of farm and homestead, 258, *258*, 282, *332*; enslaved persons, runaway, 264; whipmaking of, 261, *262*; yellow fever victims, 263. *See also* Amory, James, Jr., Amory, John; auctions; common lands; trials

Amory, James, Jr., 271

Amory, John, Sr., 261, *262*, 265

Andrew McGown, Jr (1785–1870) (Wright), 60

Angel of the Waters. See Bethesda Fountain

Apthorp, Charles Ward, 141–143; mansion of, *143. See also* Elm Park Hotel

Apthorp (Jauncey) Lane, 61, 81, 142

archeology: discovery of Kingsbridge Road, 44, *45*; of grid markers, 153, *153*; of northern end of Central Park, vii, 461n13, 463n27; McGowan's Pass, 103, *105*, 106; by Reginald Bolton, 15–16, *15, 83*, 84; in Seneca Village, 507–508n2

Arsenal, 116, 120, 121, *121*, 160, 383, 439

Arthur Ross Pinetum, 138, *336*, 337

auctions: of Amory property, 333; of de Forest farm, 31; for common lands, 329–331, 349; for Harlaem Canal Company, 238, 240; for renters of city property, 382; as result of foreclosure or nonpayment of assessments, 185, 192, 232

awards: criteria to determine, 355, 358; decision of New York Supreme Court, 353; to Seneca Village landowners, 361, *362*, 363–364, 383; tabulation of, *356–357. See also* Commissioners of Estimate and Assessment; petitions/petitioners

Barretto, Francis, 145. *See also* Shaw, John

The Battery, 46, 317, 320, 326–327

beach volleyball courts, 75, 263, 334, 355

beavers, 19–22, *21, 22*, 32, 33, 43

Beekman, James W., 112, 327, 329, 340–341

Belmont, August, 398, 402–403, 409–410, 411, 416. *See also* Central Park commissioners; design competition

Belvedere, The, *285. See also* Vista Rock

Bennett, John (Captain), 381, 383–384. *See also* Central Park police

Benson, Adolph, *48*, 50, *51*, 52, 54, 61, 63, 94, 237; as enslaver, 68, 69

Benson, Benjamin, *51*, 52, 54, 68, 87

Benson, Benjamin L., *51*, 52, 129, 165, 237, 239

Benson/McGowan family tree, *51*

Benson, Lanaw (Lane, Len), 8, 69, conveyance to John Rankin, *67*; enslaved

by, 68, 69; family tree, *69*; location of property, 64, *64, 65, 67, 70*; relationship to David Waldron, 69; name of, 65; third party manumissions, 67–68. *See also* Benson, Adolph; Benson, Tanneke; Waldron, Ellenor

Benson, Lawrence, *51*, 61, 87

Benson, Mary (Sickles), 57–59, *58, 51*

Benson, Samson, 50, *51*, 52, 62

Benson, Samson, Jr., *51*, 52, 55, *58*, 59, 63, 87, 88. *See also* enslaved runaway persons, names of

Benson, Sampson Adolphus, *51*, 63, *71*, 71

Benson, Susan, *51*, 64, 71

Benson, Tanneke (Jannike), *51*, 68–70

Benson-Kimmel tavern. *See* taverns

Bethesda Terrace, *249*, 258, *258, 259, 278*, 332, 410; recent improvements by Central Park Conservancy, *447*

Bethesda Fountain (*Angel of the Waters*), 277, *278, 447*

Beth Israel. *See* Jewish burial grounds

Beth Olam. *See* Jewish burial grounds

Billopp family. *See* Conference House

Birkenhead Park (Liverpool), 327, 404

Black Horse Tavern. *See* taverns

Blacks: arrival in New Amsterdam, 29–30; *Book of Negroes*, 486n14; burial grounds of, 197, 203–204, 312, 316; charities of, 205, 208, 229, 364; education of, 205, 216; downtown living conditions of, 180–183; entrepreneurs 6, 7, 208; health threats to, 183–184; labor of during colonial era, 29–30; National Convention of Colored Citizens, 227, 229; private mortgages, 179, political leaders of, 208–231; laws against, 65, 66, 176; religious traditions of, 194, 195; social societies of, 208; voting restrictions, 71, 174–176. *See also* abolitionists; American Colonization Society; Colored School No. 3; enslaved and enslavers, names of; enslaved persons; Gradual Manumission Act; manumission; racism; riots; Seneca Village; slavery; slave trade; War of 1812; *individuals by name*

Bleecker, Anthony J., 422, 423

Blockhouse No. 1: 100, 103, *104*, 117–119, *118*, *120*, 420, *426*. *See also* Nutter, Valentine; War of 1812

Bloemendael. *See* Bloomingdale

Bloomingdale; 16, 17, appeal of living in, 127, 132, 151; division in nineteenth century, 154–162; division in seventeenth and eighteenth centuries, 131–148; location of, 131; map of prepark boundaries, *128*; name of, 132

Bloomingdale Road, 80, 132, 142, 152, 161, 259. *See also* Broadway

B'nai Israel. *See* Jewish burial grounds

B'nai Jeshrun. *See* Jewish burial grounds

Board of Commissioners of the Central Park. *See* Central Park commissioners

Bois de Boulogne (Paris), 403, 409–410

bolt. *See under* grid, markers

Bolton, Reginald, *15, 16, 83*, 84

bone-boiling factories, 294, 307, 308, *308*, 361, 383, 390. *See also* sugar refining

Borrowe, Samuel, Dr., 100, 104, 112, 150, 395

Bow Bridge. *See* bridges and arches in Central Park

Bowne, Robert L., 154–155

Bowne, Walter, 155

Boyle, Elizabeth (Sister), 59, 297, 298

Brace, Charles Loring, 320

breastworks. *See* ramparts

bridges, 54–55, 82

bridges and arches in Central Park: 404; Bow Bridge, 411, *412–413*, 414; Bridge No. 28, *406–407*; in Greensward plan, 404; Inscope Arch, *254*; proposed suspension bridge, 410–411. *See also* transverse roads; Vaux, Calvert

British: attack on Manhattan during Revolutionary War, 75, 79–81, 85, 88;

blockades by, 108; capitulation by Dutch to, 42, 87; encampment, 82, 83, *83, 84*; common law, 222, 223; embargo against, 108; impressment by, 106–107; Mackenzie, Frederick, 81, 85; oppression of Irish, 292–293; parks, 317, 323, 325, 326, 404; war with France, 106, 264. *See also* Conference House; loyalists; prison ships; Vaux, Calvert; War of 1812

Broadway, 46, 79, 123, 132, 161, 216, 262, 320, *320*, 368, 416; historical predecessor, 550–551n2. *See also* Bloomingdale Road

Bronk, Jonas, 37

Brooklyn, 110, 361; Brooklyn Bridge, 431; Brooklyn Heights, 72, 111, 224; Green-Wood Cemetery, 312; Fort Greene Park, 273; Prospect Park, 394; Wallabout Bay, 272, 273; Williamsburg, 219

Bronx, The, 14, 37, 47, 54, 96, 101, 240, 279, 300. *See also* Kingsbridge Road.

Brown, John, 225–226, *225*

Brush, Sylvester, 331, 333

Bryant, William Cullen, 323, *324*, 325, 343, 365, 367

burial grounds: All Angels', 203; Cypress Hills (Queens), 314; grave robbing, 315; laws restricting in Manhattan, 197, 203; Potter's Field, 196; St. Michael's, 203; St. Philip's, 316. *See also* Green-Wood Cemetery, Jewish burial grounds; Rural Cemetery Act; Seneca Village

Burr, Aaron, 161–162, 272

Cahill, Sylvester. See *Cahill v. Palmer*

Cahill v. Palmer (*Sylvester Cahill and Gilliam B. Seeley agst. Courtland Palmer and The Mayor &c*): description of upper park topography in, ix, 98–100; real estate swindle of, 427–433. *See also* Cosse, James A.; Montanye, John; Nutter, Valentine; Palmer, Cortlandt; real estate swindles; Seeley, Gilliam D., Serrell, James E.; trials

Canada: beavers in, 19–21, *21*, 43; *Book of Negroes*, 486n14; strategic importance in Revolutionary War, 74; loyalists in, 96, 131. *See also* Shelburne (Nova Scotia)

canals. *See* Erie Canal; Haerlem Canal; Harlaem Canal Company

cannon, *89, 90*

cartmen, 166 *166*, 167, 185, 191. *See also* Aldridge, Daniel; *Moving Day (In Little Old New York)*; Whitehead, John; Williams, Andrew

Carter, Hannah S., 364

cascade, 423, *424–425*

Catalogue of plants gathered in August and September, 1858 in the terrain of the Central Park (Rawolle and Pilat), 373–374, 375

cemeteries, 197–198, 203, 271, 312–316, 321, 360, *399*. *See also* burial grounds; Jewish burial grounds

Cedar Hill, 267, *268–269*; recent improvements by Central Park Conservancy, *448*. *See also* Wagstaff, David

census takers, 192–193

Central Park, *442–443*; location, 326; management by city commission, 365–367, 380–384; management under state commission, 384–385, 420–427; management under Central Park Conservancy, 440, 445–449; map of, *12, 13*, need for, 317–321; primary purpose of, 410; significance in American history, 451; size of, 5; topography of, 8–16; visitation during draft riots, 524n27. *See also* Central Park Conservancy; Central Park design competition; Central Park events; Jones Wood; *Central Park landmarks and structures by individual names*

Central Park commissioners: against the extension to 110th Street, 423; formation of independent commission

by the state legislature, 384; Olmsted's opinion of, 391. *See also* Central Park design competition; Wood, Fernando, first commission of Central Park; *commissioners by individual names*

Central Park Conservancy, vii, 44, 90, 103, 153, 403, 445–446, *447, 448, 449*

Central Park design competition of 1858: idea by Vaux, *392*, 393–394; illustrations of entries, *370, 403, 404–405, 417*; meeting for, 396–402; objections by commissioners to Greensward plan, 402–411, 414–417. *See also* Central Park commissioners; Greensward plan; Gustin, Samuel

Central Park events, 437–440

Central Park police, 365, 379, 381–384, 400

Central Park West. *See* Eighth Avenue

Central Park Zoo, 116, 121

charities. *See* Blacks, charities of; Irish charities

Charles A. Dana Discovery Center, 99, *449*

Cherry Hill, 259

cholera, 103, 124, 183–184, 274–28, *276*, 291, 293, 315

chronometers, 158–160

churches. *See names of individual churches*

Civil War (U.S.), 119, 176, 212, *217*, 300, 343, *369*

Clapp, Hawley D., 422, 423, 426, 431

Clinton, George (Governor), *76*, 139, 140

Collect, The, 16, 116

Colonial Assembly, 54, 71

Colored Orphans Asylum, 208, 218, 224, 229

Colored School No. 3, 6, 205, 216. *See also* Seneca Village

Combs, John, 68, *69, 70, 70*, 71

Combs, Sarah, 63, *69, 70*, 71

commissioners. *See* Central Park commissioners; Commissioners of Estimate and Assessment (lower

park); Commissioners of Estimate and
Assessment (upper park); Commissioners
Plan of 1811; Croton Commissioners of
Estimate and Assessment
Commissioners of Estimate and
Assessment (lower park): appointed
surveyors, 344; petitions to, 221, 306, 315;
objections to report by landowners, 306–
307, 315, 347–349; process of evaluation,
343–347, 345, 346, 347, 355; approval of
report by, 340, 353, 365
Commissioners of Estimate and
Assessment (upper park): approval of
report, 427; attempt to overturn report,
423, 426; commissioners appointed, 422,
427; objections to report by Central Park
Commissioners, 423
Commissioners' Plan of 1811, 124, 125, 152, 317.
See also grid; Moore, Clement Clark
Committee of Defence, 110, 112, 117, 119
Common Council. See New York City
Common Council
common lands: auctions of, 329–330; awards
to owners of, 358; buyers of, 116, 256–261,
265–267, 272; 330–331; description of, 17,
244–256; location of, 127, 128; given to
city by Dutch, 16, 252; given to city by
British, 16, 127, 252–253; restrictions on
use of, 255, 381; size of, 329; subdivisions
of, 252–253; 255; topography of, 16,
177, 254, 255. See also Yorkville; waste/
wastelands
composting operation in Central Park
(The Mount), 6, 53, 55, 104, 296
Conference House (Billopp estate), 75–76
con men. See real estate swindles
Conservatory Garden, 64, 237, 299, 312, 314, 314
Conservatory Water, 112, 415, 415
constitutional convention. See New York
State, constitutional convention of 1821
and 1846

Cornelis, Metje (Bastiaensen, Jansen,
Kortright), 47, 48, 49–50, 55, 91, 99, 430
Cosse, James A., 428–433. See also Cahill v.
Palmer; real estate swindles
Croton Aqueduct Board, 284–285, 311, 314,
326, 377
Croton Aqueduct System, 279–288, 286
Croton commissioners of Estimate and
Assessment, 312
councils of war (Revolutionary War), 73,
75–79, 77, 87

Dana, Charles A., 367, 411
Danckaerts, Jasper, 134–135
Daniels, Howard, 400–402. See also design
competition
Davis, Epiphany, 172, 174, 176, 191, 196,
336–338, 336, 338, 431
Davy, Tighe, 297, 316
Dean, Nicholas, 326. See also Croton
Aqueduct Board
de Forest, Geertruyt (Bornstra), 24, 30, 31
de Forest, Hendrick, 6, 24–26, 29, 32, 38
de Forest, Isaac, 24–26, 29, 43, 420
de Forest/Montagne homestead and farm,
26–29, 463n27
de Forest/Montagne Homestead and Farm
(Tantillo), 28
deforestation. See environmental
problems; trees
De Laet, Johannes, 22, 23, 25
de la Montagne. See Montagne, de la
Delamontagnie, Abraham and Mary, 261
Delancey, Charlotte, 140–141
Delancey, James, 139
Delancey, Oliver: 138, 139; anti-Semitism of,
139, 140; attack on Bloomingdale home
of, 140–141; in Revolutionary War, 140;
sale of prepark property of, 141
Delancey, Phila (Franks), 139–141
Delancey, Stephen (Étienne de Lancey), 138

Demilt (Benjamin, Samuel, Thomas), 158, *159*, 160, 206

Demilt's Longitude Observatory. *See* Summit Rock

Democratic Party, 164, 351, 385, 389, 397, 401, 422, 426. *See also* Tammany Hall

Dene, 258, 260, 261, 308, 332, 355

design competition. *See* Central Park design competition

de Vries, David, 12, 35–37

Dillon, Gregory, 274, 292, 301–302, 351

Dillon, Robert J.: as candidate for corporation counsel, 349, 351; on Board of Commissioners of the Central Park, 385, 397; objections to Greensward plan, 400, 402–404, 409–411, 414, 416; promotion of Central Park, as corporation counsel, 344, 352–353, 398; plan for Central Park commissioners, 365, 365–367; relation to Benjamin Romaine, 302, 359; relationship to Daniel Sickles, 351. *See also* Belmont, August; Central Park design competition; Dillon, Gregory

distributing reservoir, *279*

Dongan, Thomas (Governor), 16, 253

Douglass, Frederick, *209*, 225–226, 229. See also *Frederick Douglass*

Downing, Andrew Jackson, 325, 326, 392–393

draft riots. *See* riots

Dresser, Horace, 187, 188, 198

drought. *See* environmental problems

Duke Ellington (Graham), *65*

Duke Ellington Circle, 64, *65*

Dutch East India Company, 19, 20

Dutch Reformed Church, 30, 31, 134, 155

Dutch West India Company, 19–22, 25–26, *33*, 36 40–43, 133, 155, 190

Dutch American families: infant betrothals, 56; intermarriage of, 6, 44, 50, 55, 129,

310; naming confusion in, 50; property inheritance, 6, 52; slavery in, 62–71

Dyckman, George, 55

Dyckman, Jacob, 50, *51*, 52–54, *83*, death of, 55, 298

East Green, 258, *258*

East Harlem, *15*, 38, 41, 59, 235, 237, 243, 428

East Meadow, *303*, 304

East River, 10; defense of during Revolution, 81; drainage into, 370; proposed park on, 317; shoreline property on, 266, 323, 326, *371*, 328

Eastern Post Road. *See* Kingsbridge Road

East Road (Park Avenue), 256

education. *See* African Free School; Blacks; Colored School No. 3; Elmwood Hill Boarding School; Hughes, John (Archbishop); Sisters of Charity of Mount Saint Vincent

Eighth Avenue (Central Park West): *13*, 84, 127, 131, 158, 256, 303; awards for property on, 355; and Croton aqueduct, 311; near Seneca Village, *171*, 198, 202, 203, 270, 434

Elgin Botanical Garden. *See* Hosack, David

Ellington, Duke. See *Duke Ellington*; Duke Ellington Circle

Elliott, Charles Wyllys, 393–394, 397, 401, 423. *See also* Central Park commissioners

Elliott, Henry H., 119, 423, 426, 431, 433

Elm Park Hotel, 206, 375

elms. *See* Mall

Elmwood Hill Boarding School, 150–151, 395. *See also* Great Hill

emancipation, 5, 180, 214, 218. *See also* Gradual Manumission Act; manumission; Seneca Village; slavery

embargo, 108

Emigrant Industrial Savings Bank, 274, 351. *See also* Dillon, Gregory; Dillon, Robert J.

eminent domain, 5, 125, 126, 270, 315, 340, 348

English. *See* British

enslaved persons. *See* Blacks; enslaved persons, names of; enslaved runaway persons, names of; Fugitive Slave Act; Gradual Manumission Act; manumission; Underground Railroad

enslaved persons, names of (enslavers): Benson, Lanaw/Len/Lane (Benson, Adolph, Benson Tanneke, Waldron, David and Elizabeth), 65–69, *69*; Betty (McGowan, Andrew), 62; Charlotte (Benson, Sampson Adolphus), 63; Combs, Sarah (Benson Sampson Adolphus), 63; Day (Stilwell), 154; Eliza (McGowan, Andrew), 62, *63*; Harding, Samuel (Glover), 172; Jane (McGowan) 63, *63*; Nancy (Swift, Joseph), 113; Rachel (Stilwell, Samuel), 154; Sam (Nutter, Valentine), 95; Sylvia (Nutter, Valentine), 95; Waldron, Ellenor (Benson, Tanneke), 69, *69*; Waldron, Sam "Free Sam" (Morris, Lewis III), 68

enslaved runaway persons, names of (enslaver): George (Amory, James), 264; Jack (Nutter), 95; Lue (Amory, James), 264; Tom (Benson, Samson, Jr.), 63; unnamed girl, 229. *See also* Douglass, Frederick

environmental problems: deforestation, 85–86; drought, 86, 288; fire, 148, 180–183; illness caused by, 86, 183, 370, 390; poison ivy, 375; poor drainage, 127, 254, *255*, 370, 390; poor sanitation, 124, 263; water pollution, 257; toxic soil, 370; water abuse, 287; water pressure, 242. *See also* Blacks; cholera; Lenape; yellow fever

epidemics. *See* cholera; yellow fever

Erie Canal, 177, 236, 292

extension of Central Park, 306, 420–433. *See also* Commissioners of Estimate and Assessment upper park); real estate swindles

Fairlie, James, 162–165, *163*, 167

farms: 374; Amory Farm, 259–260, de Forest/ Montagne farm (bouwerie), 6, 26, 27, *27*, 28–31, 37; Delancey farm, 141; Idens farm, 135; Nutter farm, 98–101, 239–240; in prepark, 53, *104*, 243, 291, 293–294, *294*, *299*, 304–306, 316, 355, 374, 375, 388; in Seneca Village, *171*, 192, 206–207, 375; Stilwell farm, 151–152; Wagstaff farm, 265–267, *268–269*, 270. *See also* German immigrants; Irish immigrants

Fernando Wood (Elliott), *342*

Fields, Thomas C., 398, 399, 400, 402, 420. *See also* Central Park commissioners; design competition

Fifth Avenue (Middle Road), 116, *248*, 256, 259, 260, 265; awards to owners of property on, 355, *356–357*

fire, 35, 37, 42, 61, 88, 109, *109*, 140, 180, 300, agricultural use of by Lenape, 10; Great Fire of 1835, 148, 180–181, *181*; in Seneca Village, 181–183, *182*, 188–189, 271, 363

First Universalist Church (the Society of United Christian Friends), 168

Fitz, Henry, 168,

Flagg, Azariah, 374, 381

foreclosure. *See* auctions; mortgages

Fort Amsterdam, 20, 36

Fort Fish, 103–*104*, *114*, 119, 401

Fort Clinton, *14*, 82, 89, *90*, 103–106, 110, *111*, *114*, 118, 420

Fort Greene Park, 273

Fort Orange, 20, 41, 52

Forty-Second Street, 80

fortifications: in New Amsterdam, 20, 36; of Revolutionary War, 81, *82*, 82–83, 100; War of 1812, 82, 103–106, *104*, *105*, 106, 108, 110–113, 116, 118–120, *119*, *120*. *See also by individual fortifications*

Franklin, Benjamin. *See* Conference House (Billopp estate)

Franks, Abigail (Levy), 139

Fraunces Tavern. *See* taverns

Frederick Douglass (Koren), *209*

free produce movement, 206–207, 216–217

Fugitive Slave Act, 5, 195, 231. *See also*
Underground Railroad

Geary, John, 205, 284

General Society of Mechanics and
Tradesmen, viii, 160, 265

geology: Manhattan bedrock, 12–13, 245;
glacial erratics, 248–249, *248, 249,
250–251*; glaciers, 245, 248; gneiss, 13,
117, 245; Manhattan schist, 9, 13, 117,
158, 245, 259, 285; marble, 9- 12. *See also*
rock outcrops; topography; waste/
wastelands

George Washington (Peale), *73*

German immigrants: 5–6, 289–291, 302–307,
303, 360. *See also* East Meadow; Forty-
Eighters; Hesser, Jupiter Zeus; North
Meadow; racism; sugar refining

Gibbes, Thomas, 359–360

Gill, *251–252*

glaciers. *See* geology

glacial erratics, 248, *248, 249, 250, 251, 252. See
also* geology

Gloucester, Elizabeth: 6, 208, 221–231,
223, 271, 363. *See also* Brown, John;
Gloucester, James N.; Ray, Charles B.;
Wright, Theodore S.

Gloucester, James N. (Reverend), 208,
221–223, 229

Goerck, Casimir, 152, 158, 256, common
lands map of, *252–253*

Gradual Manumission Act, 62, 66, 171, 196

Gramercy Park, 321, 427

Grand Army Plaza, 75, 310, 355. *See* Kortright,
Nicholas G.; Seaman, Sarah (Billopp)

Graves, Roswell, 248, *249*, 253–254, 344,
346, *347*

Gray, John A.C., 393–394, 397, 401, 403, 421

Great Hill, 395; British cantonment, 82–84,
112, 135; home of Dr. Borrowe, 100, *104*,
149; Elmwood Hill Boarding School,
150–151; Mount Prospect, 371, *371*

Great Lawn, 112, 148, 152, 161, 267, *282, 404.
See also* receiving reservoir

Green, Andrew Haswell, 398, 400–402,
409, 427; bench, 401. *See also*
Central Park commissioners; design
competition

Greene, Nathanael (General), 74, 273

Greensward plan, 400, 402, *404–405*, 411,
416–418, commissioners who voted for
and against, 400–402; objections to, 403,
409–416; transverse roads in, 408–409;
uniqueness of, 417

Greenwich Village (Saponicken), 123, 126,
134–135, 277

Green-Wood Cemetery, 312–313, 321

grid, 245, 256, 317; grid markers, 152–153,
153. See also common lands; Goerck,
Casimir; Moore, Clement Clarke; parks;
real estate speculation

Guignon, Peter, *202*, 208, 212, 219–221, 227, 363

gunpowder, 31, 106, 116, 119–121, *120, 121. See
also* Hazard Powder Company; powder
magazines

Gustin, Samuel, 390, 401, 403, *403*, 410,
415–416. *See also* design competition

Haarlem (Netherlands), 9, *11*, 41

Haarlemmermeer (Netherlands). *See View
of Haarlem and the Haarlemmermeer*

Haff, John P., 190, 206, 375

Half-Way House. *See* taverns

Hall, Thomas, 132, 133, 135

Hamilton, Alexander, 162, *147*, 148, 151, 282

Hamilton, John Church, *147*, 148

Harding family, 174, 364. *See also* Harding,
Samuel; McCollin, Elizabeth (Harding)

Harding, Samuel, 172, 174

Harlaem Canal Company, 236–242, *238*, 427

Harlem: A.M.E. Zion church in, 198; community in War of 1812, 112, Dutch families in, 43, 47, *48*, 50–53, *51*, 54–59; enslaved persons in, 62–71, 134; Lenape settlement in, *15*, 16; map of prepark boundaries, *128*; market in, 304; New Harlem (Nieuw Haarlem), 9, 41, 234; postal service in, 49; property disputes with New York, 234–236; railroad to, 281; road to, 133; suggested name of, 41; topography of, 9–12, 17, 27, *27*, 28, 236, 429. *See also* Harlem Creek; Harlem Commons; Harlaem Canal Company; Muscoota; Pinkney, Mary G.; Sisters of Charity of Mount St. Vincent; Watt, Archibald

Harlem Commons, 135, division with New York, 234; location of, 16, 235; sale and division of, 235–239, 243, 312; topography of, 235

Harlem Creek, 9, *10*; 12, 27, *27*, 28, 41, 55, 66, 86, *104*, 106, 113, 236

Harlem Lane. *See* Kingsbridge Road

Harlem Meer: in prepark: 6, 20, 47, *104*; Harlaem Canal in, 236; in Holland illustration, *113*; Lenape trails, *15*; topography of, 9, 10, *10*, 12, 13, *13. 14*, 20, 27, 86; Nutter property, *91–93*, 99; ramparts to, *105*, real estate swindle, 428, 429; tavern, 61; recent improvements by Central Park Conservancy, *449*

Harlem River, 10, *15*, 27, 90, 279

Harsen's Lane, 259

Harris, Ira (Judge), 352–354, *354*, 365, 368–369, 379. *See also* Sickles, Daniel E.

Havemeyer, William, 310. *See also* sugar refining

Hazard Powder Company, 119–120

Heath, William (General), 76–79, *77*

Hesser, Jupiter Zeus (Victor), 302–306, *305*

Hessians, 74, 80–82, *84*, 88, 95, 100, 103, 112. *See also* von Krafft, John Charles Philipp

Hewlett, James, 187, 210, *211*

Hogg, James, 397. *See also* Central Park commissioners; design competition

Holland, John J., 113; illustrations by, *56, 104, 111, 114*

Hosack, David, 257

Howe, Richard (Admiral Lord), 75, 310

Hudde, Andries, 30, 31

Hudson (North) River, 131, 134–135, 140, 150, *150*, 158, 177, 212, 236, 245

Hughes, John (Archbishop), 296–297. *See also* Sisters of Charity of Mount St. Vincent

Hunt, James and Marcy, 190–191, 199

Hutchins, Waldo, 398, 400, bench, 401. *See also* Central Park commissioners; design competition

Huguenots, 25, 26, 138, 313. *See also* Protestants

ice, 235, 245, *248*, 266, 286–287. *See also* geology: glaciers; receiving reservoir

Idens van Huyse, Theunis, 133–135, *136–137*, 138, 142, 149

immigrants, 5, 6, 139, 191, 206, 288–291. *See also* Dutch; German immigrants; Irish immigrants; Jews; Quakers

indentured servants, 133; Blacks, 6; Irish, 291; Dutch, 26, 29, 30. *See also* Gradual Manumission Act

indigenous peoples. *See* Lenape

Irish charities, 274, 292, 301–302. *See also* Dillon, Gregory; Sisters of Charity of Mount St. Vincent

Irish immigrants, 218, 291–302. *See also* Irish charities; racism; Sisters of Charity of Mount St. Vincent

Irving, Washington, 365, 367, 386

Jansen, Cornelis, 47, *48*, 49

Jauncey Lane. *See* Apthorp Lane

Jay, Peter Augustus, 158, 175. *See also* New
York State, constitutional convention of
1821 and 1846

Jews, 139–140, 164, 313, 315, 398. *See also* Franks,
Abigail (Levy); Jewish burial grounds.

Jewish burial grounds, 6, 312–316, *314*, 360.
See also Conservatory Garden; Reservoir

John Shaw (Stuart), *144. See also* Shaw, John

John Street Methodist Church. *See*
Methodist Church

Jones Wood, 323, 326–329, *328*, 339–343. *See
also* Beekman, James W.

Judah, Naftali, 163–164

Kalch Hoek, 16. *See* Collect, The

Kieft, Willem, 33, *33*, 34

Kieft's War, 34–38; investigation of, 40

Kimmel, John C., 61. *See also* taverns

Kindred Spirits (Durand), 323, *324*

King, Rufus, 261, 262, 264, 384. *See*
Amory, James

King's Bridge, 54, 75, 76

Kingsbridge Road: 14, 44, *45*, 46, *46*, 47, 49,
52, 54, 55, 61, 94, 99, 106, 133, 29, 304, 314,
390; in Revolutionary War, 76, 80, 81, 84,
86, 272; in War of 1812, *104, 114*

Knight, Sarah Kemble, 49

Know-Nothing Party, 290, 343, 385, 398,
400. *See also* Hutchins, Waldo; Morse,
Samuel F.B.

Konaande Kongh, *15*, 16, 47

Kortright, Eve, *48*, 50, *51*, 53, 94

Kortright, Lawrence, Sr., *48*, 50, 135

Kortright (Kortregt), Lawrence, Jr., *48*, 50,
91, 94, 98, 99, 355

Kortright, Nicholas G., 355

Kortright family tree, *48*

Labadists. *See* Danckaerts, Jasper

labor issues: of James Amory, 265; of
receiving reservoir, 282–283

Lake, *294, 329, 391*, 410, 411, *412–413*,
414, 417

land. *See* real estate; topography

Landin, Josiah E., 188–189, 192, 198, 204, 364;
map of former property, *182*

land speculation. *See* real estate speculation

land surveying. *See* surveyors/surveying

Leggett, John, 61. *See also* taverns

Leiden (Netherlands, The), 24–25. *See also*
de Forest, Jessé; Montagne, Johannes
de la in

Lenape: agriculture of, 10; beliefs, 4, 24;
currency of, 32, 34; as hunters, 33, 43;
massacre of, 32–38; on seal of the City
of New York, *22*; settlements, *15*, 16,
47, 462n6; trade with Dutch, *23*, 32–33;
Wickquasgeck trail, 4, 13, 14, *15*, 28, 37, 44.
See also racism

lessees. *See* renters

Lincoln, Abraham (President), 218, 303, 353

Livingston, Ann (Nutter), 95, 102, 240

Loch, 12, 13, *13*, 99, *104*; Montagne's fonteyn,
32, *84*, 151. *See also* Montanye's Rivulet;
Ravine, cascade

Lowery, Archibald, 231, 363

loyalists, 75, 87, 95–98; punishment of, *97. See
also* Apthorp, Charles Ward; Delancey,
Oliver; Ludlow, Gulian; Nutter,
Valentine; Shelburne, Nova Scotia

Ludlow, Gulian, *8*, 202; daughters of, 202

Lyons, Albro/Lyons family, 197, 208,
212–218, *213*, 214, 215, 363. *See also*
Lyons, Maritcha; Lyons, Mary Joseph
(Marshall); riots: draft riots of 1863

Lyons, Maritcha, 178, *178*, 215, *216*, 377

Lyons, Mary Joseph (Marshall), 6–7, 197,
208, 212, 213, *213*

Macomb, William, 115

Madison Avenue, 59, 64, 224, 259, 261, 333, 334

Madison Square Park, 318

Malcolm X Boulevard, 26, 28, 47. *See also*
  Sixth Avenue

Mall, 244, *245*, *246–247*, 253, 258, *258*, 260, 329,
  332, 334, 416, 417

Manhattan: first private landowner on,
  31; Manahate, 16; Manatus map, *27*;
  meaning of name, 245; purchase of by
  Dutch, 24. *See also* geology; topography

Manhattan schist. *See* geology

Manhattanville, 12, 236, 239, 428

manumission, 65–68, 172, 196, 229, 240. *See
  also* Benson, Lanaw; enslaved persons;
  Gradual Manumission Act

marble. *See* geology

markets, 28, 206, 259, 267, 293

Married Women's Property Act, 221, 223

Marshall, Elizabeth (Hewlett), 6, 187, 208,
  210–212. *See also* Lyons, Mary Joseph
  (Marshall); Lyons, Maritcha

Marshall, Joseph, 177–178, 210–212. *See
  also* Lyons, Mary Joseph (Marshall),
  Marshall, Elizabeth (Hewlett)

Martin, David R., 431–432

Mathew, William, 199, 349, 519n122,
  540n15

Mathews, William, 281, 519n122, 540n15

McCollin, Elizabeth (Harding) and
  Obadiah: 172, 174, 271, 525n42; release of,
  362, 363, 364

McDougall, Alexander (General), 76–79
  77, 162. *See also* councils of war; Heath,
  William; Washington, George

McGowan, Andrew, 50, *51*, 54, 57, 59; children
  of, 56; homestead, *56*, 59, 474n49; last will
  and testament of, 57; marriage of, 55–56,
  88; manumission of enslaved person, 62;
  myth of, 88–89; possible disability of, 59,
  87; in Revolutionary War, 79, 87; in War
  of 1812, 112. *See also* enslaved persons,
  named, 62, 63; McGowan, Margaret
  (Benson); Adriance, Margaret Eliza

(Waldron); McGowan's tavern; trials;
  Waldron, John P.

McGowan, Margaret (Benson), *51*, 55, 56, 57,
  58, 59, 88, 198

McGowan, Andrew, Jr., *51*, 56, 59, *60*, 235

McGowan, Catherine (Benson, Shourd), 6,
  51, 54, 55, 68, 87

McGowan, Daniel, *51*, 53–54

McGowan, Margaret (Benson), 51, 55, *58*

McGowan, Samson Benson, *51*, 56, 59, 87, 88,
  99, 235, 431

McGowan family tree, *51*

McGowan's Pass, 13, 45, *46.*, 47, 55, 298,
  405, 414, 429; Gatehouse, *111*, 118; in
  Revolutionary War, 79, 81, 86, 88, 90, 162,
  272; in War of 1812, 99, 103, 104, *104*, *105*,
  106, 110, 111, *111*, 112, *114*, 117

McGowan's tavern. *See* taverns

McGown family. *See* McGowan

McIntosh, Lachlan, 401, 418. *See also*
  Central Park design competition;
  Miller, Michael

Menck, William, 310, 361

Methodist Church, 151–152, 168. *See*
  Methodist Society; A.M.E. Zion
  Church; Stilwell, Samuel

Methodist Society, 189. *See also* Stilwell,
  William (Reverend)

Metropolitan Museum of Art, 148, 265, 282,
  331, 431

milestones, 49, 86

Miller, Michael, 401, 418. *See also* Central
  Park design competition; McIntosh,
  Lachlan

Minturn, Robert Bowne, 325, *325*

Model Boat Pond. *See* Conservatory
  Water

Moller, George H., 308, 310

Montagne, Abraham de la, 261. *See*
  Delamontagnie, Abraham

Montagne, Jan (John) de la, 41, 42, 428

Montagne, Johannes de la: family of, 24, 25, 37, 41, 42; financial problems of, 30, 34, 41–42; provisions of, 31; relationship to Hudde, 31; relationship to Kieft, 34, 36–38; relationship to Stuyvesant, 39–42; role in massacre of Canarsee, 37–38; warning from van der Donck, 40. *See also Cahill v. Palmer*, Cosse, James A.; Kieft's War; Montanye, John; Vredendal

Montagne, Rachel de la (de Forest), 24, 25, 37

Montagne's Flats. *See* Muscoota

Montagne's (Montanye's or Montaigne's) *fonteyn*, 32, 84, *84*, 151. *See also* Loch; run

Montagne's Point, 38, 41. *See also* East Harlem

Montagne's (Montanye's) Rivulet, 84, 86, *104*, 298, 415, 466n45. *See also* Loch

Montanye, John, 428–432. *See also Cahill v. Palmer*; Cosse, James A.; real estate swindles

Moore, Clement Clarke, 125, 235

Morgan, Edwin (Senator), 341

Morningside Heights, 10, 13, 117

Morris family, 96

Morris, Lewis, 68

Morse, Samuel F.B., 290

mortgages, 55, 144, 184–185, 189, 204, 224, 298, 304, 334, 359, 422, 423; foreclosures, 155, 164, 179, 187–188, 189–190, 192, 232, 283, 319; New York law on, 184–185

Mother Zion. *See* African Methodist Episcopal Zion Church

Mount Prospect. *See* Great Hill

Mount, The. *See* composting operation in Central Park (The Mount)

moving day, 191. *See also* renters

Moving Day (In Little Old New York) (artist unknown), *166*

Mrs. Andrew McGown I (Margaret Ann Benson, 1766–1851) (Megary), *58*

Mrs. Samson Benson, Jr. (1745–1835) (unknown artist), *58*

Muscoota, *10*, 11, 44; as cultivated, *104*; location of, 13, 14, *15*, 236; de Forest/ Montagne bouwerie on, 26, 27, *27*, *28*, 29; Haerlem Canal Company, 236; known as Montagne's Flats, 10, 30, 49

Napoleonic wars, 106–108, 264

Natives/Native Americans. *See* Lenape

nativism, 5, 289–290, 398, 400

Netherlands, The, 19, 24, 31, 37, 38, 40, 41, 42, 52, 134, 313, 315. *See also* Dutch East India Company; Dutch West India Company; Leiden; religious persecution of Protestants in Europe

New Amsterdam, 9, 14, 16, 19, 20, *21*, 26, 28, 30, 31, *33*, 38, 40, 41, 42, 48, 49, 52, 57, 61, 123, 133, 155, 252, 313, 428

New Harlem. *See* Harlem

New Netherland, 22, 26, 34, 39, 40, 133

New York City draft riots. *See* riots

New York City landmarks and locations. *See individual names of locations and landmarks*

New York City parks and squares. *See individual names of parks and squares*

New York Harbor, 24, 87, 108, 109, 134, 245

New York Manumission Society, 113, 168, 175, 196, 208, 214. *See also* African Free School

New York Public Library. *See* distributing reservoir

New York State, constitution of 1777, 71, 174

New York State, constitutional convention of 1821 and 1846, 175–176

New-York Harlaem Spring Water Company, 237

Nine Men, 40, 133. *See also* Kieft, Willem

Non-Importation Act of 1806, 107–108

North Meadow, vii, 135, *136–137*, 235, 237, 303, *305*, 306

North River. *See* Hudson River

North Woods, 91, *91*, *92–93*, 99, 100, 117, *426*, 433

Nova Scotia (Canada). *See* Shelburne, Nova Scotia (Canada)

Nutter, Sarah (Gilmore), 91–94, 98

Nutter, Valentine, *241*; in Canada, 95–98; conflict over Kortright property, 91–94, 98; Harlaem Canal Company, *238*, 239–241, *241*; Harlem farm, 98, 99–101; in War of 1812, 102, *104*, 112, 113, 119. *See also Cahill v. Palmer*; enslaved runaway persons, names of; Livingston, Ann (Nutter); loyalists, Nutter, Sarah (Gilmore); Wilkins, Gouverneur Morris; Wilkins, Isaac

Nutter's Battery, 82, *101*, 102, *104*, 106, 114, *114*, 420

Ogden, Samuel, 161–164

Old Harlem Road, 47, 63, *67*, 70, 476n11

Olmsted and Vaux, 11, 245, *252*, 274, 393, 394–395, 398, 439; as codesigners of Greensward plan, *252*, 375, 400–403, 405, *404–405*, 408–409, 411, 414–417

Olmsted, Frederick Law, *388*; early life of, 386–389; marriage, 395–396; relationship with Vaux, 394, 408–409; relationship with Viele, 270, 389–390, 394; as superintendent of Central Park, 294, 389–392. *See also* design competition; Greensward plan; Olmsted and Vaux; Vaux, Calvert; Viele, Egbert L.

Olmsted, John Hull, 395

Olmsted, Mary (Perkins), 395, *396*

ordinaries. *See* taverns

Palmer, Courtlandt, 304, 423, 427, 433. *See also Cahill v. Palmer*

Panic of 1837, 151, 179, 184, 242, 282, 283, 289, 319, 323, 423; causes of, 184

Parade, The. *See* Madison Square Park

Parish, Susan (Delafield), 402

parks before Central Park, *318*. *See also individual names of parks*

Patrick, John. *See* Reckless, Maryann (Patrick); Shedden, William and William Ralston Patrick

Pavonia. *See* Kieft's War

payment to landowners by city. *See* awards

Pearsall, Joseph, 160–161

perimeter of Central Park, *64*, 260, 327

Peters, John Punnett (Reverend), 204, 378

Peters, Thomas McClure (Reverend), 202, 204, 364, 378–379

Peter Stuyvesant (Trumbull), 39

petitions/petitioners objecting to valuation of property, 192, 306, 348–349, 360; responses, 353

Phelan, James, 367

pigs, piggeries, 35, 277, 291, 293–295, 296, 360, 361, 390

Pilat, Ignaz A. See *Catalogue of plants gathered in August and September, 1858 in the terrain of the Central Park* (Rawolle and Pilat), 373

Pinetum. *See* Arthur Ross Pinetum

Pinkney, Mary Goodwin, 7, 119, 129, 241–243, 304–306, 348, 358, 360, 422–423, 427, 433

plants: noted in Dutch documents, 11–12, 28, 31; in prepark reports, 372–375; removal from prepark, 375. See also *Catalogue of plants gathered in August and September, 1858 in the terrain of the Central Park*; free produce movement; tobacco; trees

Plunkitt, George Washington, 232

police. *See* Central Park police

Pond, *290*, 294, 331

Pool, 135, 237, 414, *414*

post office/postal service, 49, 351. *See also* milestones; Sickles, Daniel E.

powder magazine, 116–117, *120*, 121, 383. *See also* Blockhouse No. 1

Price, Francis, 129, 146, 165, 235–241. *See also* Haerlem Canal Company

prison ships, 272

Promenade. *See* Mall

promenading, *319–320*
Prospect Hill. *See* Summit Rock

Quakers (Religious Society of Friends), 141, 154–155, 158, 160, 168, 343

racism: toward Blacks, 168–169, 175, 176, 194, 214, 219, 227, 229, 381; toward Germans, 306; toward Lenape, 22- 24; toward Irish, 296–297, 360, 381. *See also* Know Nothing Party; nativism; riots
Ramble, 155, 310, 394, *355,* 359, 373, *391,* 391, 410; Gill, *251–252. See also* Bowne, Walter; Patrick, John; Reckless, Maryann (Patrick)
ramparts/breastworks, 103, *104, 105,* 106, *111,* 112, 118
Randel, John, 70, 152, 153, *153*
Rankin, John, and heirs of, 66–67, *67,* 68, *70*
Ravine, *13, 84,* 99, 100, *104, 119,* 237, 371, 415, 423; waterfalls in, *424–425*
Rawolle, Charles, 373. See also *Catalogue of plants gathered in August and September, 1858 in the terrain of the Central Park* (Rawolle and Pilat)
Ray, Charles B. (Reverend), 227–231, *230*
real estate: adverse possession, 98; assessments on, 4, 125, 176, 184, 198, 235; assessments for property near Jones Wood or Central Park, 327, 329, 330, 344, 348, 353, 421; Dutch practices, 50, 52; fencing of, 429; investment advice, 433; practices protecting, 435; trumps topography, 123–129. *See also* eminent domain; mortgage law; real estate speculation; real estate swindles; Seneca Village, real estate boom in
Real Estate Record and Builders' Guide, 243, 434
real estate speculation, 4, 125, 148, 184, 235, 243, 330–334, 339, 348, 360, 422, *426,* 427, 430
real estate swindles, 334–336, 337–339, 359, 428–433
receiving reservoir: *282, 287;* construction of 280, 282; labor riots of, 282–283; ice

of, 286–287; remnants in park, 285; keepers, 284; need for, 184, 274, 275–279; topography, 280. *See also* Great Lawn; Seneca Village: York Hill
Rechewanis, *15*
Reckless, Maryann (Patrick), 334–336, 359
religious education. *See* Hughes, John; Sisters of Charity of Mount St. Vincent
religious persecution of Protestants in Europe, 25, 47; of Jews and Quakers in New Amsterdam, 155, 313. *See also* Huguenots; Leiden (Netherlands, The); Walloons
Remond family, 213, 214, 216, 217
renters/lessees 126, 233, 256, 270, 304, 306, 344, 360, 364, 381–382, 427, 432; gardeners, 304, 306, 384, 193, 430; from City of New York, 382–383; turnover of, 344; in Seneca Village, 171, *174,* 181, 191–194, 206, 232, 383–384; verbal leases of, 295, 430. *See also* awards; auctions; Moving Day; Rose, Joseph
Republican Party, 175, 384–385, 389, 397, 426
Reservoir (Jaqueline Kennedy Onassis): *376,* construction of, *372;* design of, *328,* 376–377, *376,* 418; landowners in prepark of, 135, 138, 197, 234, 272, *273,* 312–315, 349, 358; need for, 288, 311, 359, 360; Olmsted's attitude toward, 410. *See also* Jewish burial grounds
Revolutionary War: Benson family in, 79, 87–89; British attack of Manhattan, 74, 79–81, 88; British cantonment on Great Hill, 83, *83;* cannon in Central Park, *89, 90;* conference on Staten Island, 75–76; evacuation of British, 88, 118; evacuation of New York, 75–77, fortifications built in prepark during, *82;* influence of labor, 265; rebel attacks, 140–141; religious views after, 168; voting rights after, 71, 174; Washington's retreat from Brooklyn, 72. *See also* councils of war; loyalists; Delancey, Oliver; Heath, William;

McDougall, Alexander; McGowan's Pass; Washington, George

Rhododendron Mile, 272, *273*, 359

Richmond, William (Reverend), 202, 378, 379, 519n122

Rink, John J., 416, *417*. *See also* design competition

riots: antiabolitionist riots of 1834, 180; Astor Place riot of 1849, 321; draft riots of 1863, *217*, 218

rock outcrops: 13, *14, 46*, 47, 99, 106, *173*, 245, *248*, 258, 285, 294, 346; *347*, 377; awards to lots with, 355; blasting with gunpowder, 106, *113, 130*, 120, 417; homes on, 173, 346; maps showing, *347, 366–367*. *See also* geology; Summit Rock; topography; Umpire Rock; Vista Rock

Romaine, Benjamin, 272–274, 302, 358–359. *See also* Fort Greene Park; prison ships; Tammany Hall

Root, George G., 283–284

Rose, Joseph, 382

Rose-Redwood, Reuben, 126, 153

Ruggles, David, 206

Ruggles, Philo T., 333

Rumsey Playfield, 258 *258*, 260, 332, 355

run, 12, *84*, 99. *See also* Loch; Montagne's *fonteyn*

Rural Cemetery Act, 312, 313, 315

Russell, John, 360

Russell, Charles H., 397, 399, 400, 402. *See also* Central Park commissioners; design competition

Rynders, Isiah, 351

Safari Playground, 6, 145, *145*

St. James's Episcopal Church, 259

St. John's Park, 321

St. Joseph's School for Young Ladies, 297

St. Michael's Cemetery (Astoria), 203, 271

St. Michael's Episcopal Church, 195, 202, 378

St. Philip's Episcopal Church, 180, 197, 212, 214, 221, 224, 316

Sandy Ground (Staten Island), 232

Schagen, Pieter, 24

schools. *See* education

Scudder, Thomas, 383–384. *See also* trials

Seaman, Edmund, 310

Seaman, Sarah (Billopp), 75, 310, 355, 358

Seeley, Gilliam D., 432–433. *See also Cahill v. Seeley*

Selden, Dudley, 235–237

Seneca Village, 8, 71, 169, 170, *346*; assessments of, 171–172, 175, 176, 184, 192, 198; awards to landowners and renters of, 197, 361–364; burial grounds in, 196–198, 202, 312; census data collection in, 192–193; churches in, 194–204; conveyances, 172, 177–179, 184, 337, 339, 510–511n44–46; eviction from, 364, 381, 383; families in, 172, 174, 189, 190, 192, 210, 364, 509n17; financial problems of landowners, 184–191; fires in, 181–183, 270–271; first mention of "Seneca," 378, 519n122); location of, 138, 160, *171*; occupations of residents, 172, 206; police in, 381, 383–384; population estimates, 192, 193, 383, 515n81; proposed origin of name of, 377–379; real estate boom in, 177–179; relationship to receiving reservoir, 184, 281, *282*, 283, 284–285, *286*; renters, 174, 191–194, 206, 285, 382–383; Spring Street/ Stilwell's Lane/Old Lane, 161; structures in, 173, 174, 182, *345*, 564n68; topography of, 161, *171*, 346, *347*; Underground Railroad possibility in, 5, 208, *228*, 229, *230*–231; white landowners in, 179, 231–232; Whiteheads' relationship to, 165, 172. *See also* African Methodist Episcopal Zion Church; African Union Church; All Angels' Church; Blacks; census takers; Colored School No. 3; gardens/farms; receiving reservoir; Whitehead, John; *names of individual landowners*

Serrell, James E., 314, 429

Seventh Avenue: 17, 48, 117, 131, 134, 165, 184, 199, 222, 243, 280, 295, 361, 416; adjacent to Seneca Village, 184, 190, 191, 227, 283, 349; adjacent to common lands, 127, 135, 152, 161, 252, 280, 281, awards along, 355, 361. *See also* receiving reservoir

Shakespeare Garden, *132*

shanty/shanties: 173, description of, 173–174, 360; locations in prepark, 191, 194, 290, 293, 306, 310, 344, 361, 383, 564n68

Shaw, Grizzel (Apthorp), 6, 143–145, *145*

Shaw, Henry, 326

Shaw, John, 144–146, *144*

Shedden, William and William Patrick Ralston, 334–335, 359. *See also* trials

Sheep Meadow, 75, *249*, 258, *258*, 296, 310, 332, 355, 416

Shelburne, Nova Scotia, 96–98

Sickles, Daniel E.: as "Founder of Central Park," 349–353, *350*, 365, 379–380, 431; murder of Philip Scott Key, 351; post office robbery, 349; and Teresa Sickles, 351. *See also* Dillon, Robert J.; Rynders, Isiah; Tammany Hall; Wood, Fernando

Siloam Presbyterian Church, 224–225

Simpson, Caroline W., 205

Sinking Fund of the City of New York, 260, 358, 382

Sisters of Charity of Mount Saint Vincent: chapel, 5, 7, 59, 296–301, *299*, *300*, 316, 375, 381, 438. *See also* composting operation in Central Park (The Mount)

Sixth Avenue (West Road), 47, 99, 127, 224, 256, 259, 272, 280, 295, 303, 304, 306, 313, 329, 331, 333, 405, 416, 430; awards to property on, 355, *356–357*

slavery, 5, 185, 194, 212, 283, 307, 337, *338*; children born under, 62, *63*, 68, 70, 154; under Dutch, 29–30, 62; laws regarding, 62, 65, 66, 71, 113, 195; protests against,

168, 196, 206, 215, 222, 225–227, *225*, 229, 302. *See also* enslaved and enslavers, names of; enslaved runaway persons, names of; Fugitive Save Act; Gradual Manumission Act; manumission; slave trade; Seneca Village; Underground Railroad

slave trade, illustration of slave ship, *336*. *See also* Apthorp, Charles Ward

Smallwood, William (Colonel), 80, 81

Smith, Levin (or Leven) (Reverend), 189, *189*, 196, 198, 260. *See also* Stilwell, William (Reverend)

Smith, James McCune, 185, 214, 215, *215*, 226, 231

Society of United Christian Friends. *See* First Universalist Church

soil, 10, 11, 29, 32, 103, 142, 151, 153, 167, 206, 231, 245, 254, 259; poor conditions, 254, 256–257, 293–294, 370, 390, 391

Somarindyck family, 141, 359

Special Committee on Parks, 327–329, 336, 340, 341

speculation. *See* real estate speculation

springs. *See* Montagne's *fonteyn*; run; topography

Staten Island, 35, 37, 75, 172, 232, 310, 368, 387

States-General (The Hague), 38, 40

Stebbins, Emma. *See* Bethesda Fountain

Stilwell, Samuel, 151–154; conveyances of properties, 154–161; deed to Gulian Ludlow, *8*, 202

Stilwell, William (Reverend), 189–190, 196, 198. *See also* Methodist Society

Strawberry Fields, 112, 230

Stuyvesant Park, 318–319

Stuyvesant, Peter, *39*, 40–43, 133, 155, 313

suffrage. *See* voting

sugar refining, 307–308, 310. *See also* German immigrants

Summit Rock, *150*, 346

surveyors/surveying, 30–31, *80*, 87, 99, 124, 152, *153*, 172, 236, 248, 253, 254, 256, *249*, 270, *345, 346, 347,* 355, 429; by Viele, 368–370, 378, 418. *See also* Commissioners of Estimate and Assessment (lower park); Commissioners of Estimate and Assessment (upper park); Goerck, Casimir; Randel, John; Stilwell, Samuel

Swift, Joseph (General), 113

Swits, Claes Cornelison, 30, 35

Sylvester Cahill and Gilliam D. Seeley v. Courtlandt Palmer, et. al. See *Cahill v. Palmer*

Tammany Hall, 164, 232, 272–273, 351, 398

Tappan, Lewis, 180

taverns, 48; Benson Kimmel tavern, 61, 475n55; Black Horse Tavern (Dyckman), 50, 52, *53*, 54; Black Horse Tavern and McGowan's tavern, 6; 52, 54, 60; Black Horse Tavern (near Ninety-Sixth Street), 60, 61, 81, 85; Cato's, 112; Delamontagnie's tavern, 261; Dyckman's Tavern near Spuyten Duyvil, 54; Half-Way House, *20*, 28, 47, 49–50, 53, 91, 99, 430; Fraunces Tavern, 138; Leggett's Tavern, 61; multiple functions of, 48–49, 61; postrevolutionary growth of, 61; Sunday laws, 61; Tavern on the Green, *309*. *See also* Knight, Sarah Kemble

taxes. *See* assessments

Taylor, Joshua S., 366, 368–369, 381, 384. *See also* Wood, Fernando

Teasman, John, 113

Thompson, Abraham (Reverend), 196

Thompson, Catherine, 6, 205

Tietjen, Christian, 232, 284, 337, 363

Tiffany & Co., 360

Times Square, 80

tobacco, 6, 16, 25, *27*, 28–31, 133

Tomkins, Daniel (Governor), 114

topography: in awards criteria, 355; below Ninety-Sixth Street, 16; grid on Manhattan, 123–126; trumped by real estate, 4, 127–128; unique to Manhattan Island, 9. *See also* common lands; geology; Harlem Commons; Harlem Creek; waste/wastelands

Tories. *See* loyalists

transverse roads, 295–296, 334, *369–370*, 375–376, *408, 411,* 418; similar concepts to, 409; objections to, 409. *See also* design competition; Greensward plan

Treadwell, Charles, 176, 190, 196–198

trees, 25, 53, 59, 117, 151, *171,* 188, 203, 206, 259, in *Catalogue of plants gathered in August and September, 1858 in the terrain of the Central Park*, 373–375; on Cedar Hill, 266; elms on Mall, 244, *246–247,* 417; in Jones Wood, 323, 329; loss in Hurricane Sandy, 103; loss on Nutter property, 119; persimmon grove, 270, 373–374. *See also* Arthur Ross Pinetum; environmental problems, deforestation

trials: *Amory v. Amory*, 334; *John Montanye agt. Patrick Daly*, 431–432; "In re Waldron 1816" (John P. Waldron and Andrew McGowan), 56–57; Reckless, Mary Ann, suit against John Bunting, 336; *Charles Reade Respondent against Anthony Feistel*, 430; of Schermerhorn family, 326, 341; *Scudder vs. John W. Bennett*, 383–384; *William Patrick Shedden, David Oliphant, and Harriett Turner, his wife against Amasa S. Foster, Samuel P. Townsend, Mary Ann Reckless, The Mayor, Aldermen &c*, 359; *Egbert Viele agst. The Mayor, &c.*, 417–418. *See also Cahill v. Palmer*

Tribeca, 196, *228–229*, 321
Trinity Church, 127, 142, 197, 316
Turner, Mary (Whitehead), 165

Umpire Rock, 355
Underground Railroad, 5, 195, 208, 217, *228–231*. *See also* Fugitive Slave Act; slavery
unemployment. *See* Panic of 1837; Seneca Village
Union Square, 422, 427

van der Donck, Adrien, 34, 40
van Brunt, Tunis, 281
Vanden Heuvel family, 143, 146–148, *147*, 359, 360
van Rensselaer, Kilian, 26
Vaux, Calvert, 245, 321, architecture of, 314, 409; design of transverse roads, 405; early career, 392–393; idea for design competition, 392, 394; portrait of, *392*; relationship with Central Park commissioners, 393–394; relationship with Olmsted, *392*, 394, 408–409; opinion of Viele, 393, 418. *See also* Downing, Andrew Jackson; Greensward plan; Olmsted and Vaux; Olmsted, Frederick Law
Viele, Egbert (Lieutenant): design competition, 399, 418; design of Reservoir, 376–377, *376*; early life, 368; landscape theory of, 371; plan for Central Park, 158, 280, 371–372; portrait of, 369; possible name of Seneca Village, 377–379; relationship to Olmsted, 389–390; relationship to first commissioners, 368–370, sanitary engineer, 370; transverse roads, 375, 418; topographic map of Manhattan, 10, *10*; topographic survey of Central Park, *171*, 192, 206, 267, 306, *366–367*; West Point tomb of, 400, *400*. *See also* trials

View of Haarlem and the Haarlemmermeer (van Goyen), *11*
Vista Rock, 280, *285*. *See also* receiving reservoir
von Krafft, John Charles Philip, 85–87
voting: after the Revolutionary War, 71; assessment requirements for Blacks, 174–177. *See also* New York State, constitutional convention of 1821 and 1846
Vredendal: illustration of proposed, *28*, 32, 41, 99, 429

Wagstaff, David: Central Park offices at Wagstaff House, 270, 390; description of farm, 265–267, *268–269*; last will and testament, 267–270; petition about common lands, 267; professions, 265–266; relationship of heirs to Sarah "Sally" Wilson, 270–271; renters, 382; in War of 1812, 112; west side property, 267, 270. *See also* Cedar Hill
Waldron, Catherine Maria (McGowan), *51*, 56
Waldron, David, 64, 65–69
Waldron, Ellenor, 68, *69*, 70, 71
Waldron, John P., *51*, 56–57
Wall Street, 26, 42, 119, 124, 127, 148, 393
Wallabout Bay. *See* prison ships
Wallace, John, 284, 285, 555n45
Walloons, 25–26, 28, 313
Walters, Dr. William A., 198
War of 1812: Blacks in, 113; economic causes leading up to, 107–108; impressment of sailors, 106–107; fortifications, *45*, 82, *82*, 100, *101*, *104*, *111*, *118*, *120*; soldiers in, 114–116, *114*; volunteers in, 110–113. *See also* Blockhouse No. 1; embargo; Fort Clinton; McGowan's Pass, Gatehouse; Nutter's Battery; ramparts (breastworks)
Waring, George, 197, 390, 391, *391*, 416

Washington, George (General), 86, 87, 138, 146, 149, 162–163; councils of war, 75–79, 87; during British attack, 79–81; in McDougall/Heath conflict, 76–79; retreat from Brooklyn, 72; portrait of, *73*, riding crop of, 26, *262*

Washington, D.C.: attack on the Capitol in War of 1812, 109, *109*; Downing and Vaux design, 393

waste/wastelands, 16, 21, 235, 244, 245, 252, *255*, 295, 312, 373. *See also* common lands; Harlem Commons; topography

water. *See* Bethesda Fountain (*Angel of the Waters*); Croton Aqueduct system; East River, environmental problems; Harlem Canal Company; Harlem River; Hudson (North) River; New-York Harlaem Spring Water Company; New York Harbor; topography; *names of individual water bodies in Central Park*

Watt, Archibald, 66, 129, 239–242, 348, 358, 422, 427, 431, 433

West Meadow, 135, *156–157*, 188

West Road, 256, 257, 259. *See also* Sixth Avenue

Whitehead, John, 164, 165–169, 172, 173, 176, 174, 177, 197, 206, 224, 271, 336, 363. *See also* Blacks; cartmen; Seneca Village

Whitehead, Maria (Burtsell, Palmer), 165, 168

Wickquasgeck trail/tribe, 13, 14, 28, 32, 37, 44, 123. *See also* Lenape; Kieft's War

Wilkins, Gouverneur Morris, 100, 101, 241, 348, 427, 431, 484n1. *See also* Nutter, Valentine

Wilkins, Isaac, 96, 97, 102

Wilkins, Sarah (Nutter), 95, 97, 101. *See also* Nutter, Valentine

Williams, Andrew, 172, 176, 194, 363, 364, 377, 529n72

Wilson, Sarah "Sally," property, *182*, 270–271, 363. *See also* Wagstaff, David

Wiswall, Enoch, 129, 165, 236–240. *See also* Harlaem Canal Company; Price, Francis

women, 6, Black, 208; Dutch, 52; education of, 297, examination for conveyances, 223–224; Lenape, 23; as real estate speculators, 243; restrictions of, 69, 71, 176, 222, 525n42; retreat indoors, 321; submission to design competition by, 402; Victorian clothing of, 322; widows, 55, 64, 224. *See also* enslaved and enslavers, names of; Married Women's Property Act; *individuals by name*

Wood, Fernando, 326; altered Dillon plan, 366; first commission of Central Park, 365, 368–369, 380, 381, 382, 384; portrait of, *342*; relationship to board of advisors, 367; veto to diminish size of Central Park, *342–343*

World War I Memorial Grove, *332*

Wright, Theodore S. (Reverend), 208, 214, 227–231, *228*

yellow fever, 146, 149, 152, 183, 196, 263, 277

York Hill, 280, 282, 540n15

Yorkville, *15*, *128*, 129, 266, 271, 277, 283, 299, 378; development of, 237; map of prepark boundaries, *128*; site of receiving reservoir, 281, 282; site of Seneca Village 199, 284, 377

zoo. *See* Central Park Zoo